# Entertainment Industry Economics
*A Guide for Financial Analysis, Seventh Edition*

The entertainment industry is one of the largest sectors of the U.S. economy and is in fact becoming one of the most prominent globally as well. In this newly revised book, Harold L. Vogel examines the business economics of the major entertainment enterprises: movies, music, television programming, advertising, broadcasting, cable, casino gambling and wagering, publishing, performing arts, sports, theme parks, and toys and games. The seventh edition has been further revised and broadened and differs from its predecessors by restructuring and repositioning the previous Internet chapter, including new material on the economics of networks and advertising, adding a new section on policy implications, and further expanding the section on recent theoretical work pertaining to box-office behavior. The result is a comprehensive, up-to-date reference guide on the economics, financing, production, and marketing of entertainment in the United States and overseas. Investors, business executives, accountants, lawyers, arts administrators, and general readers will find that the book offers an invaluable guide to how entertainment industries operate.

Harold L. Vogel is the author of *Travel Industry Economics: A Guide for Financial Analysis* (Cambridge University Press, 2001), a companion volume to this textbook. He was senior entertainment industry analyst at Merrill Lynch & Co. for 17 years and was ranked as top entertainment industry analyst for 10 years by *Institutional Investor* magazine. Mr. Vogel frequently writes and speaks on investment topics related to entertainment and media, leisure, and travel and currently heads an independent investment and consulting firm in New York City.

# Entertainment Industry Economics

*A Guide for Financial Analysis*

SEVENTH EDITION

Harold L. Vogel

CAMBRIDGE
UNIVERSITY PRESS

CAMBRIDGE UNIVERSITY PRESS
Cambridge, New York, Melbourne, Madrid, Cape Town, Singapore, São Paulo

Cambridge University Press
32 Avenue of the Americas, New York, NY 10013-2473, USA

www.cambridge.org
Information on this title: www.cambridge.org/9780521874854

First edition 1986
Second edition 1990
Third edition 1994
Fourth edition 1998
Fifth edition 2001
Sixth edition 2004
Reprinted 2006
Seventh edition 2007

Printed in the United States of America

*A catalog record for this publication is available from the British Library.*

*Library of Congress Cataloging in Publication Data*

Vogel, Harold L., 1946–
Entertainment industry economics : a guide for financial analysis / Harold L. Vogel. – 7th ed.
  p.  cm.
Includes bibliographical references and index.
ISBN-13: 978-0-521-87485-4 (hbk.)
ISBN-10: 0-521-87485-8 (hbk.)
1. Performing arts – Finance.  I. Title.
PN1590.F55V6  2007
338.4'7791–dc22     2006028089

ISBN  978-0-521-87485-4 hardback

TO MY DEAR FATHER

– WHO WOULD HAVE BEEN SO PROUD

# Contents

# Preface

en·ter·tain·ment – the act of diverting, amusing, or causing someone's time to pass agreeably; something that diverts, amuses, or occupies the attention agreeably.

in·dus·try – a department or branch of a craft, art, business, or manufacture: a division of productive or profit-making labor; especially one that employs a large personnel and capital; a group of productive or profit-making enterprises or organizations that have a similar technological structure of production and that produce or supply technically substitutable goods, services, or sources of income.

ec·o·nom·ics – a social science that studies the production, distribution, and consumption of commodities; considerations of cost and return.

*Webster's Third New Unabridged International Dictionary*, G. & C. Merriam Company, Springfield, Massachusetts, 1967.

Each year Americans cumulatively spend at least 140 billion hours and more than $280 billion a year on legal forms of entertainment. And globally, total annual spending is approaching $1 trillion. So we might begin by asking: What is entertainment, why is there so much interest in it, and what do its many forms have in common?

At the most fundamental level, anything that stimulates, encourages, or otherwise generates a condition of pleasurable diversion could be called entertainment. The French word *divertissement* perhaps best captures this essence.

But entertainment can be much more than mere diversion. It is something that is so universally interesting and appealing because, when it does what it is intended to do, it moves you emotionally. As the Latin root verb *tenare* suggests, it grabs you: It touches your soul.

Although life is full of constraints and disciplines, responsibilities and chores, and a host of things disagreeable, entertainment, in contrast, encompasses activities that people enjoy and look forward to doing, hearing, or seeing. This is the basis of the demand for – or the consumption of – entertainment products and services; this is the primary attribute shared by the many distinct topics – from cinema to sports, from theme parks to theater – that are discussed in the pages that follow.

Entertainment – the cause – is thus obversely defined through its effect: a satisfied and happy psychological state. Yet, somehow, it matters not whether the effect is achieved through active or passive means. Playing the piano can be just as pleasurable as playing the stereo.

Entertainment indeed means so many different things to so many people that a manageable analysis requires sharper boundaries to be drawn. Such boundaries are here established by classifying entertainment activities into industry segments, that is, enterprises or organizations of significant size that have similar technological structures of production and that produce or supply goods, services, or sources of income that are substitutable.

Classification along those lines facilitates contiguous discussion of entertainment *software*, as we might more generically label films, records, and video games, and of *hardware* – the physical appurtenances and equipment on which or in which the software's instruction sets are executed. Such classification also allows us to more easily trace the effects of technological developments in this field.

So accustomed are we now to continuous improvements in the performance of entertainment hardware and software that we have trouble remembering that, early in the twentieth century, moving pictures and music recordings were novelties, radio was regarded as a modern-day miracle, and television was a laboratory curiosity. Simple transistors and lasers had yet to be invented, and electronic computers and earth-orbiting communications satellites were still in the realm of science fiction.

These fruits of applied technology have nevertheless spawned new art forms and vistas of human expression and have brought to millions of people around the world, at virtually the flick of a switch, a much more varied and higher-quality mix of entertainment than has ever before been imagined feasible.

Little or none of this, however, has happened because of *ars gratia artis* (art for art's sake) – in itself a noble but ineffectual stimulus for technological development. Rather, it is *economic forces* – profit motives, if you will – that are always behind the scenes, regulating the flows and rates of implementation. Those are the forces that shape the relative popularity and growth patterns of competing, usually interdependent, entertainment activities and products. And those are the forces that ultimately make available to the masses what was previously affordable only by upper-income classes.

It is therefore surprising to find that most serious examinations of the economics of entertainment are desultory and scattered among various pamphlets, trade publications and journals, stockbrokers' reports, and incidental chapters in books on other topics. The widely available popular magazines and newspapers, biographies, histories, and technical manuals do not generally provide in-depth treatments of the subject.

This book, then, is a direct outgrowth of my search for a single comprehensive source. It attempts to present information in a style accessible and interesting to general readers. And, as such, it should prove to be a handy reference for executives, financial analysts and investors, agents and legal advisors, accountants, economists, and journalists. To that end, some supplementary data appear in Appendix C.

Yet *Entertainment Industry Economics* will most likely be used as a text for graduate or advanced undergraduate students in applied media economics and management/administration courses in film, music, communications, publishing, sports, performing arts, and hotel-casino operations. Instructors should find it easy to design one-semester courses focused on one or two areas. A minimum grasp of what entertainment and media economics is all about would require that most students read at least the first halves of Chapters 1 and 2 and, at the end of the course, the first section of Chapter 15. But many different modules can be readily assembled and tailored. Among the most popular would be concentrations on film, television, and music (Chapters 2 through 8); gaming and sports (Chapters 7, 8, 11, and 12); arts and popular culture (Chapters 6, 7, 9, 10, and 13); or entertainment merchandising and marketing (Chapters 2, 7, 9, 10, and 14).

The topics covered in the book have been chosen on the basis of industry size measured in terms of consumer spending and employment, length of time in existence as a distinct subset, and availability of reliable data. In a larger sense, however, topics have been selected with the aim of providing no more and no less than would be required by a "compleat" entertainment and media industry investor. The perspectives are thus inevitably those of an investment analyst, portfolio manager, and economist. Whereas this decision-oriented background leads naturally to an approach that is more practical and factual than highly theoretical, it nevertheless assumes some familiarity, supported by the appended glossary, with the language of economics and finance.

This seventh edition has been further revised and broadened and differs from its predecessors by restructuring and repositioning of the previous Internet chapter, inclusion of new material on the economics of networks and of advertising, a new section on policy implications, and further expansion of the section on recent theoretical work pertaining to box-office behavior.

I am especially grateful to Elizabeth Maguire, former editor at Cambridge University Press, for her early interest and confidence in this project. Thanks are also owed to Cambridge's Rhona Johnson and production editor Michael Gnat, who worked on the first edition, to Matthew N. Hendryx, who worked on the second, and to Scott Parris for the third through seventh.

I am further indebted to those writers who earlier cut a path through the statistical forests and made the task of exposition easier than it would have otherwise been. Particularly noteworthy are the books of John Owen on demand for leisure, Paul Baumgarten and Donald Farber on the contractual aspects of filmmaking (first edition; and second with Mark Fleischer), David Leedy on movie industry accounting, David Baskerville and Sidney Shemel/M. William Krasilovsky and Donald Passman on the music business, John Scarne and Bill Friedman on the gaming field, Gerald W. Scully and Andrew Zimbalist on sports, and William Baumol/William Bowen on the performing arts. Extensive film industry commentaries and data collections by A. D. Murphy of *Variety* (and later, *The Hollywood Reporter* and the University of Southern California) were important additional sources.

My thanks also extend to the following present and former senior industry executives who generously took time from their busy schedules to review and to advise on sections of the first edition draft. They and their company affiliations, as of that time, were Michael L. Bagnall (The Walt Disney Company), Jeffrey Barbakow (Merrill Lynch), J. Garrett Blowers (CBS Inc.), Erroll M. Cook (Arthur Young & Co.), Michael E. Garstin (Orion Pictures Corp.), Kenneth F. Gorman (Viacom), Harold M. Haas (MCA Inc.), Howard J. Klein (Caesars New Jersey), Donald B. Romans (Bally Mfg.), and James R. Wolford (The Walt Disney Company). Greatly appreciated, too, was the comprehensive critique provided by my sister, Gloria. Acknowledgments for data in the second edition are also owed to Arnold W. Messer (Columbia Pictures Entertainment) and Angela B. Gerken (Viacom).

Although every possible precaution against error has been taken, for any mistakes that may inadvertently remain the responsibility is mine alone.

I've been most gratified by the success of the previous editions and, as before, my hopes and expectations are that this work will provide valuable insights and a thoroughly enjoyable adventure.

Now, on with the show.

*Harold L. Vogel*
*New York City*

Entertainment Industry Economics

# Part I
## Introduction

# 1
# Economic perspective

*To everything there is a season, and a time to every purpose under the heaven.* – Ecclesiastes

Extending this famous verse, we can also say that there is a time for work and a time for play. There is a time for leisure.

An important distinction, however, is to be made between the precise concept of a time for leisure and the semantically different and much fuzzier notion of *leisure time*, our initial topic. In the course of exploring this subject, the fundamental economic forces that affect spending on all forms of entertainment will be revealed, and our understanding of what motivates expenditures for such goods and services will be enhanced. Moreover, the perspectives provided by this approach will enable us to see how entertainment is defined and how it fits into the larger economic picture.

## 1.1 Time concepts

Leisure and work

Philosophers and sociologists have long wrestled with the problem of defining *leisure* – the English word derived from the Latin *licere*, which means "to be permitted" or "to be free." In fact, as Kraus (1978, p. 38) and Neulinger

(1981, pp. 17–33) have noted, leisure has usually been described in terms of its sociological and psychological (state-of-mind) characteristics.[1]

The classical attitude was epitomized in the work of Aristotle, for whom the term *leisure* implied both availability of time and absence of the necessity of being occupied (De Grazia 1962, p. 19). According to Aristotle, that very absence is what leads to a life of contemplation and true happiness – yet only for an elite few, who would not have to provide for their daily needs. Veblen (1899) similarly saw leisure as a symbol of social class. To him, however, it was associated not with a life of contemplation, but with the "idle rich," who identified themselves through its possession and its use.

Leisure has more recently been conceptualized either as a form of activity engaged in by people in their free time or, preferably, as time free from any sense of obligation or compulsion.[2] As such, the term *leisure* is now broadly used to characterize time not spent at work (where there is an obligation to perform). Naturally, in so defining leisure by what it is not, metaphysical issues remain largely unresolved. There is, for instance, a question of how to categorize work-related time such as that consumed in preparation for, and in transit to and from, the workplace. And sometimes the distinctions between one person's vocation and another's avocation are difficult to draw: People have been known to "work" pretty hard at their hobbies.

Although such problems of definition appear quite often, they fortunately do not affect analysis of the underlying concepts.

### Recreation and entertainment

In stark contrast to the impressions of Aristotle or Veblen, today we rarely, if ever, think of leisure as contemplation or as something to be enjoyed only by the privileged. Instead, "free" time is used for doing things and going places, and the emphasis on activity more closely corresponds to the notion of recreation – refreshment of strength or spirit after toil – than to the views of the classicists.

The availability of time is, of course, a precondition for recreation, which can be taken literally as meaning re-creation of body and soul. But because such active re-creation can be achieved in many different ways – by playing tennis, or by going fishing, for example – it encompasses aspects of both physical and mental well-being. As such, recreation may or may not contain significant elements of amusement and diversion or occupy the attention agreeably. For instance, amateurs training to run a marathon might arguably be involved in a form of recreation. But if so, the entertainment aspect here would be rather minimal.

As noted in the preface, however, entertainment is defined as that which produces a pleasurable and satisfying experience. The concept of entertainment is thus subordinate to that of recreation: It is more specifically defined through its direct and primarily psychological and emotional effects.

Time

Most people have some hours left over – "free time," so to speak – after subtracting the hours and minutes needed for subsistence (mainly eating and sleeping), for work, and for related activities. But this remaining time has a cost in terms of alternative opportunities forgone.

Because time is needed to use or to consume goods and services as well as to produce them, economists have attempted to develop theories that treat it as a commodity with varying qualitative and quantitative cost features. However, as Sharp (1981) notes in his comprehensive coverage of this subject, economists have been only partially successful in this attempt:

Although time is commonly described as a scarce resource in economic literature, it is still often treated rather differently from the more familiar inputs of labor and materials and outputs of goods and services. The problems of its allocation have not yet been fully or consistently integrated into economic analysis. (p. 210)

Nevertheless, investigations into the economics of time, including those of Becker (1965) and DeSerpa (1971), have suggested that the demand for leisure is affected in a complicated way by the cost of time to both produce and consume. For instance, according to Becker (see also Ghez and Becker 1975):

The two determinants of the importance of forgone earnings are the amount of time used per dollar of goods and the cost per unit of time. Reading a book, getting a haircut, or commuting use more time per dollar of goods than eating dinner, frequenting a nightclub, or sending children to private summer camps. Other things being equal, forgone earnings would be more important for the former set of commodities than the latter.

The importance of forgone earnings would be determined solely by time intensity only if the cost of time were the same for all commodities. Presumably, however, it varies considerably among commodities and at different periods. For example, the cost of time is often less on weekends and in the evenings. (Becker 1965, p. 503)

From this it can be seen that the cost of time and the consumption-time intensity of goods and services (e.g., intensity, or commitment, is usually higher for reading a book than reading a newspaper) are significant factors when selecting from among entertainment alternatives.

Expansion of leisure time

Most of us do not normally experience sharp changes in our availability of leisure time (except on retirement or loss of job). Nevertheless, there is a fairly widespread impression that leisure time has been trending steadily higher ever since the Industrial Revolution of more than a century ago. Yet the evidence on this is mixed. Figure 1.1 shows that in the United States the largest increases in leisure time – workweek reductions – for agricultural and nonagricultural industries were achieved prior to 1940. But more recently, the lengths of average workweeks, as adjusted for increases in holidays and vacations, have scarcely changed for the manufacturing sector and have also stopped declining in the services sector (Table 1.1 and Figure 1.2). By

Table 1.1. *Average weekly hours at work,
1948–2004[a], and median weekly hours at work for
selected years[b]*

| Average hours at work | | | Median hours at work | |
|---|---|---|---|---|
| Year | Unadjusted | Adjusted[c] | Year | Hours |
| 1948 | 42.7 | 41.6 | 1975 | 43.1 |
| 1956 | 43.0 | 41.8 | 1980 | 46.9 |
| 1962 | 43.1 | 41.7 | 1984 | 47.3 |
| 1969 | 43.5 | 42.0 | 1987 | 46.8 |
| 1975 | 42.2 | 40.9 | 1995 | 50.6 |
| 1986 | 42.8 | | 2004 | 50.0 |

[a] Nonstudent men in nonagricultural industries. *Source*: Owen
   (1976, 1988).
[b] *Source*: Harris (1995), www.Harrisinteractive.com.
[c] Adjusted for growth in vacations and holidays.

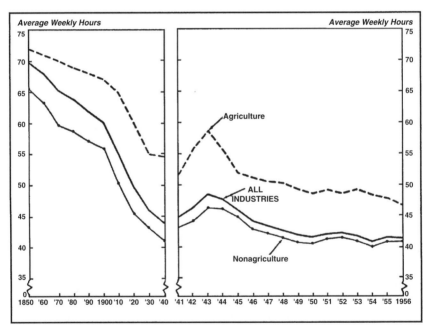

Figure 1.1. Estimated average weekly hours for all persons employed in agricultural and
nonagricultural industries, 1850–1940 (ten-year intervals) and 1941–1956 (annual
averages for all employed persons, including the self-employed and unpaid family
workers). *Source*: Zeisel (1958).

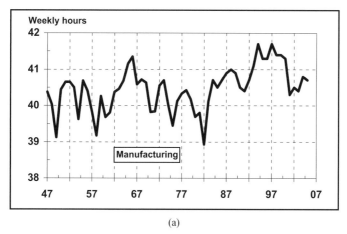

(a)

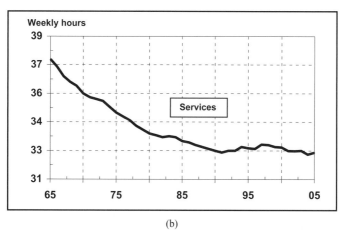

(b)

Figure 1.2. Average weekly hours worked by production workers in (a) manufacturing industries, 1947–2005, and (b) service industries, 1965–2005. *Source*: U.S. Department of Commerce.

comparison, average hours worked in other major countries, as illustrated in Figure 1.3, have declined markedly since 1970.

Although this suggests that there has been little, if any, expansion of leisure time in the United States, what has apparently happened instead is that work schedules now provide greater diversity. As noted by Smith (1986), "A larger percentage of people worked under 35 hours or over 49 hours a week in 1985 than in 1973, yet the mean and median hours (38.4 and 40.4, respectively, in 1985) remained virtually unchanged."[3]

If findings from public-opinion surveys of Americans and the arts are to be believed, the number of hours available for leisure may at best be holding

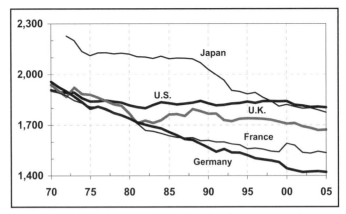

Figure 1.3. Average annual hours worked in the United States versus other countries, 1970–2005. *Source*: *OECD Employment Outlook.*

steady.[4] Schor (1991, p. 29), however, says that between 1969 and 1987, "the average employed person is now on the job an additional 163 hours, or the equivalent of an extra month a year . . . and that hours have risen across a wide spectrum of Americans and in all income categories."[5] Aguiar and Hurst (2006) argue the opposite.

And Robinson (1989, p. 34), who has measured free time by age categories, found that "most gains in free time have occurred between 1965 and 1975 [but] since then, the amount of free time people have has remained fairly stable." By adjusting for age categories, the case for an increase in total leisure hours available becomes much more persuasive.[6] In addition, Roberts and Rupert (1995) found that total hours of annual work have not changed by much but that the *composition* of labor has shifted from home work to market work, with nearly all the difference attributable to changes in the total hours worked by women. A similar conclusion as to average annual hours worked was also reached by Rones, Ilg, and Gardner (1997).[7] Yet, as Jacobs and Gerson (1998, p. 457) note, "even though the average work week has not changed dramatically in the U.S. over the last several decades, a growing group of Americans are clearly and strongly pressed for time."

In all, it seems safe to say that for most middle-aged and middle-income Americans – and recently for Europeans too – leisure time is not expanding.[8] However, no matter what the actual rate of expansion or contraction may be, there has been a natural evolution toward repackaging the time set aside for leisure into more long holiday weekends and extra vacation days rather than in reducing the minutes worked each and every week.[9] Particularly for those in the higher-income categories – conspicuous consumers, as Veblen would say – the result is that personal-consumption expenditures (PCEs) for leisure activities are likely to be intense, frenzied, and compressed instead of evenly metered throughout the year. Moreover, with some adjustment for cultural

Table 1.2. *Time spent by adults on selected leisure activities, 1970 and 2005 estimates*

| Leisure activity | Hours per person per year[a] | | % of total time accounted for by each activity | |
|---|---|---|---|---|
| | 1970 | 2005 | 1970 | 2005 |
| Television | 1,226 | 1,730 | 46.5 | 50.1 |
| Network affiliates | | 754 | | 21.8 |
| Independent stations[c] | | 104 | | 3.0 |
| Basic cable programs | | 792 | | 22.9 |
| Pay cable programs | | 80 | | 2.3 |
| Radio | 872 | 1,053 | 33.1 | 30.5 |
| Home | | 380 | | 11.0 |
| Out of home | | 673 | | 19.5 |
| Newspapers | 218 | 135 | 8.3 | 3.9 |
| Recorded music | 68 | 199 | 2.6 | 5.8 |
| Magazines | 170 | 74 | 6.5 | 2.1 |
| Leisure books | 65 | 87 | 2.5 | 2.5 |
| Movies: theaters | 10 | 11 | 0.4 | 0.3 |
| home video | | 46 | | 1.3 |
| Spectator sports | 3 | 16 | 0.1 | 0.5 |
| Video games: home | | 99 | | 2.9 |
| Cultural events | 3 | 6 | 0.1 | 0.2 |
| Total | 2,635 | 3,456 | 100.0[b] | 100.0[b] |
| Hours per adult per week | 50.7 | 66.5 | | |
| Hours per adult per day | 7.2 | 9.5 | | |

[a] Averaged over participants and nonparticipants.
[b] Totals not exact because of rounding. Also excludes 60 hours of Internet usage in 2005.
[c] Includes Spanish-language stations and PAX.
*Sources*: CBS Office of Economic Analysis and Wilkofsky Gruen Associates, Inc.

differences, the same pattern is likely to be seen wherever large middle-class populations emerge.

Estimated apportionment of leisure hours among various activities, and the changes in such apportionment between 1970 and 2000, are indicated in Table 1.2.[10]

## 1.2 Supply and demand factors

Productivity

Ultimately, though, more leisure time availability is not a function of government decree, labor union activism, or factory-owner altruism. It is a function of the rising trend in output per person-hour – in brief, rising productivity of

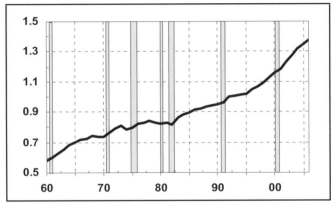

Figure 1.4. Nonfarm business productivity in the United States, 1960–2006, shown by output per hour. Index 1992 = 100. Bars indicate periods of recession. *Source*: U.S. Department of Labor.

the economy. Quite simply, technological advances embodied in new capital equipment, in the training of a more skilled labor pool, and in the development of economies of scale allow for more goods and services to be produced in less time or by fewer workers. Thus, long-term growth in leisure-time-related industries depends on the rate of technological development throughout the economy.

Information concerning trends in productivity and other aspects of economic activity is provided by the National Income and Product Accounting (NIPA) figures of the U.S. Department of Commerce. According to those figures, overall productivity between 1973 and 1990 rose at an average annual rate of approximately 1.2% as compared with a rate averaging 2.8% between 1960 and 1973 (Figure 1.4). But productivity growth in the 1990s rebounded to an average annual rate of 2.0%, thereby implying that the *potential* for leisure-time expansion remained fairly steady in the last third of the twentieth century.[11] And after 2000, productivity has again accelerated.

Demand for leisure

All of us can choose to either fully utilize our free time for recreational purposes (defined here and in NIPA data as being inclusive of entertainment activities) or use some of this time to generate additional income. How we allocate free time between the conflicting desires for more leisure and for additional income then becomes a subject that economists investigate with standard analytical tools.[12] In effect, economists can treat demand for leisure as if it were, say, demand for gold, or for wheat, or for housing. And they often estimate and depict the schedules for supply and demand with curves of the type shown in Figure 1.5. Here, in simplified form, it can be seen that, as the price of a unit rises, the supply of it will normally increase and

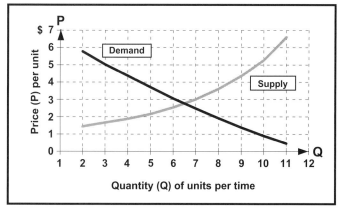

Figure 1.5. Supply and demand schedules.

the demand for it decrease so that, over time, price and quantity equilibrium in an openly competitive market will presumably be achieved at the intersection of the curves.[13]

It is also important to note that consumers typically tend to substitute less expensive goods and services for more expensive ones and that the total amounts they can spend – their budgets – are limited or constrained by income. Owen (1970) extensively studied the effects of such substitutions and changes in income as related to demand for leisure and observed:

An increase in property income will, if we assume leisure is a superior good, reduce hours of work. A higher wage rate also brings higher income which, in itself, may incline the individual to increase his leisure. But at the same time the higher wage rate makes leisure time more expensive in terms of forgone goods and services, so that the individual may decide instead to purchase less leisure. The net effect will depend then on the relative strengths of the income and price elasticities. . . . It would seem that for the average worker the income effect of a rise in the wage rate is in fact stronger than the substitution effect. (p. 18)

In other words, as wage rates continue rising, up to point A in Figure 1.6, people will choose to work more hours to increase their income (income

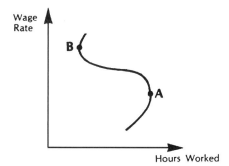

Figure 1.6. Backward-bending labor-supply curve.

effect). But they eventually begin to favor more leisure over more income (substitution effect, between points A and B), resulting in a backward-bending labor-supply curve.[14] Although renowned economists, including Adam Smith, Alfred Marshall, Frank Knight, A. C. Pigou, and Lionel Robbins, have substantially differed in their assessments of the net effect of wage-rate changes on the demand for leisure, it is clear that "leisure does have a price, and changes in its price will affect the demand for it" (Owen 1970, p. 19). Indeed, results from a Bureau of Labor Statistics survey of some 60,000 households in 1986 suggest that about two-thirds of those surveyed do not want to work fewer hours if it means earning less money.[15]

As Owen (1970) has demonstrated, estimation of the demand for leisure requires consideration of many complex issues, including the nature of "working conditions," the effects of increasing worker fatigue on production rates as work hours lengthen, the greater availability of educational opportunities that affect the desirability of certain kinds of work, government taxation and spending policies, market unemployment rates, and several other variables.[16]

### Expected utility comparisons

Individuals differ in terms of the sense of psychic gratification experienced from consumption of different goods and services. Consequently, it is difficult to measure and compare the degrees of satisfaction derived from, say, eating dinner as opposed to buying a new car. To facilitate comparability, economists have adapted an old philosophical concept known as utility (which is essentially pleasure).[17] As Barrett (1974, p. 79) has noted, utility "is not a measure of usefulness or need but a measure of the desirability of a commodity from the psychological viewpoint of the consumer."[18]

Of course, rational individuals try to maximize utility – in other words, make decisions that provide them with the most satisfaction. But they are hampered in this regard because decisions are normally made under conditions of uncertainty, with incomplete information, and therefore with risk of an undesired outcome. People thus tend to implicitly include a probabilistic component in their decision-making processes – and they end up maximizing *expected utility* rather than utility itself.

The notion of expected utility is especially well applied in thinking about demand for entertainment goods and services. It explains, for example, why people may be attracted to gambling, or why they are sometimes willing to pay scalpers enormous premiums for theater tickets. Its application also sheds light on how various entertainment activities compete for the limited time and funds of consumers.

To illustrate, assume for a moment that the cost of an activity per unit of time is somewhat representative of its expected utility. If the admission price to a two-hour movie is $6, and if the purchase of video-game software for $25 provides six hours of play before the onset of boredom, then the cost per minute for the movie is 5 cents whereas that for the game is 6.9 cents. Now, obviously, no one decides to see a movie or buy a game based on explicit comparisons of cost per minute. Indeed, for an individual, many qualitative (nonmonetary) factors, especially fashions and fads, may affect the perception of an item's expected utility. However, in the aggregate and over time, such implicit comparisons do have a significant cumulative influence on relative demand for entertainment (and other) products and services.

### Demographics and debts

Over the longer term, the demand for leisure goods and services can also be significantly affected by changes in the relative growth of different age cohorts. For instance, teenagers tend to be important purchasers of recorded music; people under the age of 30 are the most avid moviegoers. Accordingly, a large increase in births following World War II created, in the 1960s and 1970s, a market highly receptive to movie and music products. As this postwar generation matures past its years of family formation and into years of peak earnings power and then retirement, spending may be naturally expected to collectively shift to areas such as casinos, cultural events, and tourism and travel, and away from areas that are usually of the greatest interest to people in their teens or early twenties.

The expansive demographic shifts most important to entertainment industry prospects in the United States include (1) a projected increase of the numbers of 18- to 34-year-olds in the early 2000s (4.8 million more in 2010 than in 2000), (2) a projected rapid growth in the large group of 35- to 64-year-olds (up from 105 million in 1990 to 118 million in 2010), and (3) a significant expansion of the population over age 65 (Table 1.3).

That the number of people in the 45 to 64 age group will be gaining rapidly in proportion to the number of people in the 18 to 34 age group is of particular importance given that those in the younger category are generally apt to spend much of their income when they enter the labor force and form households. Those in the older category, however, are already established and are thus more likely to be in a savings mode, perhaps to finance college education for their children or to prepare for retirement, when earnings are lower. A ratio of people in the younger group to those in the older group – in effect, the spenders versus the savers – is illustrated in Figure 1.7a.

Although it depends on the specific industry component to be analyzed, proper interpretation of long-term changes in population characteristics may also require that consideration be given to several additional factors that include dependency ratios (Figure 1.7a), fertility rates, number of first births, number of families with two earners, and trends in labor-force participation rates for women (Figure 1.7b).[19]

Indeed, two paychecks have become an absolute necessity for many families as they have attempted to service relatively high (in proportion to income) installment and mortgage debt obligations that have been incurred in the household-formative years. As such, elements of consumer debt (Figure 1.7c), weighted by the aforementioned demographic factors,

Table 1.3. *U.S. population by age bracket, components of change, and trends by life stage, 1970–2010*

**Components of population change**

| | Percentage distribution | | | | | Change (millions) | | |
|---|---|---|---|---|---|---|---|---|
| Age | 1970 | 1980 | 1990 | 2000 | 2010 | 1980–1990 | 1990–2000 | 2000–2010[a] |
| Under 5 | 8.4 | 7.2 | 7.6 | 6.9 | 6.6 | 2.4 | 0.0 | 0.8 |
| 5–17 | 29.3 | 24.6 | 18.2 | 18.8 | 17.6 | −1.9 | 6.5 | 0.5 |
| 18–34 | 15.1 | 18.2 | 28.1 | 23.1 | 23.0 | 2.0 | −6.4 | 4.8 |
| 35–65 | 33.2 | 34.3 | 33.6 | 38.5 | 39.5 | 13.7 | 21.7 | 12.3 |
| 65 and over | 14.0 | 15.7 | 12.5 | 12.7 | 13.3 | 5.5 | 3.7 | 4.8 |
| Total | 100.0 | 100.0 | 100.0 | 100.0 | 100.00 | 21.7 | 25.5 | 23.2 |

**Population trends by life stage (millions)**

| Life stage | 1970 | 1980 | 1990 | 2000[a] | 2010[a] |
|---|---|---|---|---|---|
| 0–13 Children | 53.8 | 47.6 | 50.9 | 55.0 | 55.2 |
| 14–24 Young adults | 40.6 | 46.5 | 40.1 | 41.9 | 46.9 |
| 25–34 Peak family formation | 25.3 | 37.6 | 43.1 | 37.4 | 38.4 |
| 35–44 Family maturation | 23.1 | 25.9 | 37.8 | 44.7 | 38.9 |
| 45–54 Peak earning power | 23.3 | 22.8 | 46.3 | 37.1 | 43.7 |
| 55–64 Childless parents | 18.7 | 21.8 | 21.1 | 24.0 | 35.4 |
| 65 and retirement | 20.1 | 25.7 | 31.2 | 34.9 | 39.7 |
| Total | 204.9 | 227.9 | 249.4 | 275.0 | 298.1 |

[a] Forecast.
*Source*: U.S. Department of Commerce, series P25.

probably explain why, according to the Louis Harris surveys previously cited, leisure hours per week seem to have declined noticeably since the early 1970s. As the median age rises, however, these very same elements may combine to abate pressures on time availability.

As can be seen from Figure 1.8, aggregate spending on entertainment is concentrated in the middle-age groups, which are the ages when income usually peaks even though free time may be relatively scarce.

Barriers to entry

The supply of entertainment products and services offered would also depend on how readily prospective new businesses can overcome barriers to entry and thereby *contest* the market. Barriers to entry restrict supply and fit largely into the following categories listed in order of importance to entertainment industries:

Capital
Know-how
Regulations[20]
Price competition

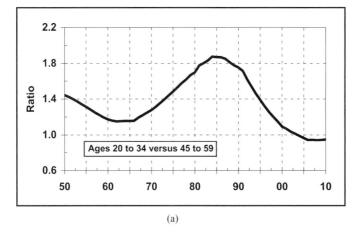

(a)

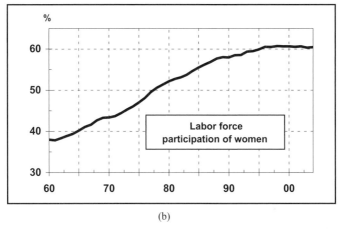

(b)

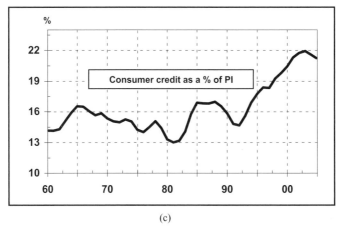

(c)

Figure 1.7. (a) Ratio of spenders to savers, 1950–2010. (b) Labor force participation rate for women (20+), 1960–2005. (c) Consumer credit as a percentage of personal income, 1960–2005.

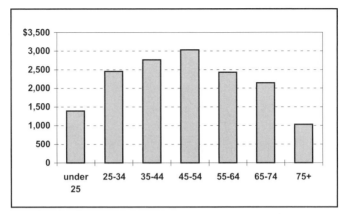

Figure 1.8. Spending on entertainment classified by age groups, 2005. *Source*: U.S. Department of Commerce survey.

To compete effectively, large corporations must of necessity invest considerable time and capital to acquire technical knowledge and experience. But the same goes for individual artists seeking to develop commercially desirable products in the form of plays, books, films, or songs. Government regulations such as those applying to the broadcasting, cable, and casino businesses often present additional hurdles for potential new entrants to surmount. Furthermore, in most industries, established firms would ordinarily have some ability to protect their positions through price competition.

## 1.3 Primary principles

Marginal matters

Microeconomics provides a descriptive framework in which to analyze the effects of incremental changes in the quantities of goods and services supplied or demanded over time. A standard diagram of this type, Figure 1.9, shows an idealized version of a firm that maximizes its profits by pricing its products at the point where marginal revenue (MR) – the extra revenue gained by selling an additional unit – equals marginal cost (MC), the cost of supplying an extra unit. Here, the average cost (AC), which includes both fixed and variable components, first declines and is then pulled up by rising marginal cost. Profit for the firm is represented by the shaded rectangle (price [$p$] times quantity [$q$] minus cost [$c$] times quantity [$q$]).

Given that popular entertainment products feature one-of-a-kind talent (e.g., Elvis or Sinatra recordings) or brand-name services (e.g., MTV, Disney theme parks), the so-called competitive-monopolistic model of Figure 1.9a, in which many firms produce slightly differentiated products, is not farfetched. The objectives for such profit-maximizing firms are to both rightward-shift and also steepen the demand schedule idealized by line D. A shift to the

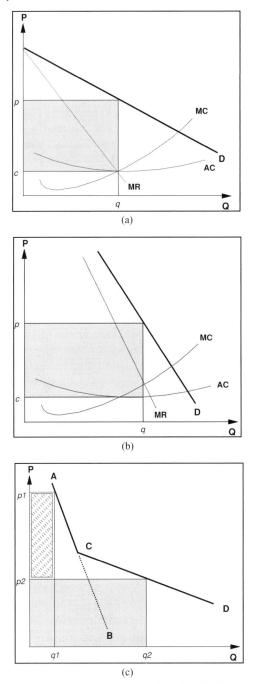

Figure 1.9. (a) Marginal costs and revenues, normal setting, (b) demand becomes more inelastic and right-shifted, and (c) consumers' surplus under price discrimination.

right represents an increase in demand at each given price. And a schedule of demand that becomes more vertical – that is, quantity demanded becomes less responsive to change in price (i.e., becomes more price-inelastic) through promotional and advertising efforts – enables a firm to reap a potentially large proportionate increase in profits as long as marginal costs are held relatively flat (Figure 1.9b). In all, the more substitutes that are available, the greater is the price elasticity of demand.

Look, for example, at what happens when a movie is made. The initial capital investment in production and marketing is risked without knowing how many units (including theater tickets, home video sales and rentals, television viewings, and the like) will ultimately be demanded. The possibilities range from practically zero to practically infinite.

Whatever the ultimate demand turns out to be, however, the costs of production and marketing, which are large compared with other, later costs, are mostly borne upfront. Come what may, the costs here are *sunk* (i.e., the bulk of the money is already spent and should be presumed as being unrecoverable) whereas in many other manufacturing processes, the costs of raw materials and labor embedded in each unit produced (variable and marginal) may be relatively high and continuous over time.

In entertainment, the cost of producing an incremental unit (e.g., an extra movie print) is normally quite small as compared with the sunk costs, which should by this stage be considered as irrelevant for purposes of making ongoing strategic decisions. It may thus, accordingly, be sensible for a distributor to take a chance on spending a little more on marketing and promotion in an attempt to shift the demand schedule into a more price-inelastic and rightward position. Such inelastic demand is characteristic of products and services that

Are considered to be necessities
Have few substitutes
Comprise a small part of the budget
Are consumed over a relatively brief time
Are not used often

Economists use estimates of elasticity (i.e., responsiveness) to indicate the expected percentage change in demand if there is a 1% change – up or down – in prices or incomes (or some other factor). In the case of price, this can be stated as

$$\text{price elasticity} = \varepsilon_p = \frac{\% \text{ change in quantity demanded}}{\% \text{ change in unit price}}.$$

All other things being equal, demand would be normally expected to rise with an increase in income and decline with an increase in price.[21] For example, if demand declines 8% when price rises 4%, the price elasticity of demand would be –2.0. In theory, cross-elasticities of demand between goods and services that are close substitutes for each other (a new *Star Trek* film versus a new *Star Wars* film), or complements to each other (movie admissions and sales of popcorn), might also be estimated.

Similarly, elasticity with respect to *income* can be estimated for goods and services classifiable as luxuries, necessities, or inferiors. With luxuries, demand grows faster as income rises, and the income elasticity is greater than 1.0. For necessities, demand increases as income rises but more slowly than income (elasticity 0.0 to 1.0). And for inferior goods, income elasticity is negative, with demand falling as income rises. By these measures, most entertainment products and services are either necessities or luxuries for most people most of the time (but with classification subject to change over the course of an economic or individual's life cycle).

Price discrimination

If, moreover, a market for, say, airline or theater seats (see Chapter 13) can be segmented into first and economy classes, profits can be further enhanced by capturing what is known in economics as the *consumers' surplus* – the price difference between what consumers actually pay and what they would be willing to pay. Such a price discrimination model extracts, without adding much to costs, the additional revenues shown in the cross-hatched rectangular area of Figure 1.9c. The conditions that enable discrimination include

Existence of monopoly power to regulate prices
Ability to segregate consumers with different elasticities of demand
Inability of original buyers to resell the goods or services

Public good characteristics

Public goods are those that can be enjoyed by more than one person without reducing the amount available to any other person; providing the good to everyone else is costless. In addition, once the good exists, it is generally impossible to exclude anyone from enjoying the benefits, even if a person refuses to pay for the privilege. Such nonpayers are, therefore, "free riders." Spending on national defense or on programs to reduce air pollution would be of this type. And in entertainment it is not unusual to find near public good characteristics: The marginal cost of adding one viewer to a television network program or of allowing an extra visitor to a theme park is not measurable.

## 1.4 Personal-consumption expenditure relationships

Recreational goods and services are those used or consumed during leisure time. As a result, there is a close relationship between demand for leisure and demand for recreational products and services.

Table 1.4. *PCEs for recreation in real (2000) dollars, 1990–2005[a]*

| Type of product or service | 1990 | 2000 | 2005* |
|---|---|---|---|
| **Total recreation expenditures** | **290.2** | **585.7** | **756.3** |
| **Percentage of total personal consumption** | **7.6** | **8.7** | **8.7** |
| Books and maps | 16.2 | 33.7 | 42.2 |
| Magazines, newspapers, sheet music | 21.6 | 35.0 | 43.8 |
| Nondurable toys and sport supplies | 32.8 | 56.6 | 67.2 |
| Wheel goods, sports, and photographic equipment[b] | 29.7 | 57.6 | 81.5 |
| Video and audio goods, including musical instruments, computers, etc. | 53.0 | 116.6 | 141.2 |
| Radio and television repair | 3.2 | 4.2 | 4.8 |
| Flowers, seeds, and potted plants | 10.9 | 18.0 | 19.7 |
| Admissions to specified spectator amusements | 15.1 | 30.4 | 38.3 |
| Motion picture theaters | 5.1 | 8.6 | 9.7 |
| Legitimate theaters and opera, and entertainments of nonprofit institutions[c] | 5.2 | 10.3 | 12.7 |
| Spectator sports[d] | 4.8 | 11.5 | 15.9 |
| Clubs and fraternal organizations[e] | 13.5 | 19.0 | 23.5 |
| Commercial participant amusements[f] | 25.2 | 75.8 | 107.3 |
| Pari-mutuel net receipts | 3.5 | 5.0 | 6.2 |
| Other[g] | 65.4 | 133.9 | 180.0 |

* In 2000 dollars.

[a] In millions of dollars, except percentages. Represents market value of purchases of goods and services by individuals and nonprofit institutions. See *Historical Statistics, Colonial Times to 1970*, series H 878–893, for figures issued prior to 1981 revisions.

[b] Includes photo equipment, boats, and pleasure aircraft.

[c] Except athletic.

[d] Includes professional and amateur events and racetracks.

[e] Consists of dues and fees excluding insurance premiums.

[f] Consists of billiard parlors; bowling alleys, dancing, riding, shooting, skating, and swimming places; amusement devices and parks; golf courses; sightseeing buses and guides; private flying operations; and other commercial participant amusements.

[g] Consists of net receipts of lotteries and expenditures for purchase of pets and pet care services, cable TV, film processing, photographic studios, sporting and recreation camps, and recreational services, not elsewhere classified.

*Sources*: U.S. Bureau of Economic Analysis, *The National Income and Product Accounts of the United States, 1929–1976*; and *Survey of Current Business*, July issues.

As may be inferred from Table 1.4, NIPA data classify spending on recreation as a subset of total personal-consumption expenditures (PCEs). This table is particularly important because it allows comparison of the amount of leisure-related spending to the amount of spending for shelter, transportation, food, clothing, national defense, and other items.[22] For example, percentages of all PCEs allocated to selected major categories in 2005 were as follows:

| Medical care | 17.1% |
|---|---|
| Housing | 14.9 |
| Food (ex. alcohol bev.) | 13.7 |
| Transportation (total) | 12.0 |
| *All* recreation | 8.7 |
| Clothing | 3.9 |

Also, as may be seen in Figure 1.10, spending on entertainment services has trended gradually higher as a percentage of all PCEs, whereas the percentage spent on clothing and food has declined.

That spending on total recreational goods and services responds to prevalent economic forces with a degree of predictability can be seen in Figure 1.11 and in Supplementary Table S1.1.[23] Figure 1.11 illustrates that PCEs for recreation as a percentage of total disposable personal income (DPI) had held in a band of roughly 4.0% to 6.5% for most of the 60 years beginning in 1929. It is only since the late 1980s that new heights have been achieved as a result of a relatively lengthy business cycle expansion, increased consumer borrowing ratios, demographic and household formation influences, and the proliferation of leisure-related goods and services utilizing new technologies.

Measurement of real (adjusted for inflation) per capita spending on total recreation and on recreation *services* provides yet another long-term view of how Americans have allocated their leisure-related dollars. Although the services subsegment excludes spending on durable products such as television sets, it includes movies, cable TV, sports, theater, commercial participant amusements, lotteries, and pari-mutuel betting – areas in which most of the largest growth has been recently seen. The percentage of recreation services

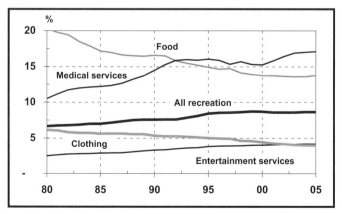

Figure 1.10. Trends in percent of total personal consumption expenditures in selected categories, 1980–2005.

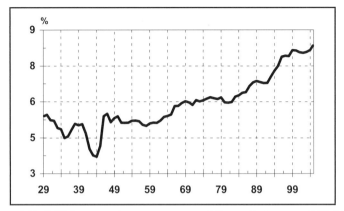

Figure 1.11. PCE for recreation as percentage of disposable income, 1929–2005.

spending is now above 40% of the total spent for all recreation (Figure 1.12), and a steeper uptrend in real per capita PCEs on total recreation and on recreation services beginning around 1960 is suggested by Figure 1.13.[24]

This apparent shift toward services, which is also being experienced in other economically advanced nations, is a reflection of relative market saturation for durables, relative price-change patterns, and changes in consumer preferences that follow from the development of new goods and services. As such, even small percentage shifts of spending may represent billions of dollars flowing into or out of entertainment businesses. And for many firms, the direction of these flows may make the difference between prosperous growth or struggle and decay.

Because various entertainment sectors have such different responses to changing conditions, the degree of recession resistance, or cyclicity of the

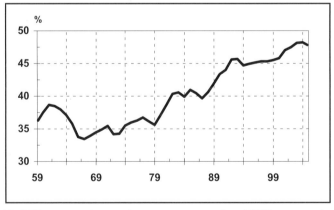

Figure 1.12. PCE on recreation *services* as percentage of total PCE on recreation, 1959–2005.

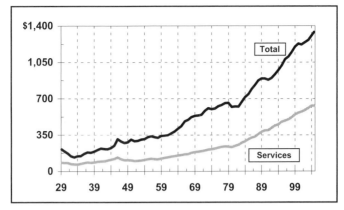

Figure 1.13. Real per capita spending on total recreation and on recreation services, 1929–2005.

entertainment industry relative to that of the economy at large, is unfortunately not well depicted by such time series. For example, broadcasting revenue trends are dependent on advertising expenditures, which are, in turn, related to total corporate profits. However, the movie and theater segments often exhibit contracyclical tendencies and, to effectively study these business cycle relationships, data at a less aggregated level must therefore be used. In other words, measures of what is known as the gross national product (GNP), or of the more recent standard of gross domestic product (GDP), can provide only a starting point for further investigations.[25]

## 1.5 Industry structures and segments

Structures

Microeconomic theory suggests that industries can be categorized according to how firms make price and output decisions in response to prevailing market conditions. In the model assuming *perfect competition*, firms all make identical products, and each firm is so small in relation to total industry output that its operations have a negligible effect on price or on quantity supplied. At the other idealized extreme is a *monopoly* structure, in which there are no close substitutes for the single firm's output, the firm sets prices, and there are barriers that prevent potential competitors from entry.

In the real world, the structure of most industries cannot be characterized as being perfectly competitive or as monopolistic but as somewhere in between. One of those in-between structures is known as *monopolistic competition*, in which there are many sellers of somewhat differentiated products and in which some control of pricing and competition through advertising is seen. An *oligopoly* structure is similar, except that in oligopolies, there are only a few sellers of products that are close substitutes and pricing decisions may affect the pricing and output decisions of other firms in the industry. Although the distinction between monopolistic competition and oligopoly is often blurred, it is clear that when firms must take a rival's reaction to changes of price into account, the structure is oligopolistic. In media and entertainment, industry segments fall generally into the following somewhat overlapping structural categories:

| Monopoly | Oligopoly | Monopolistic Competition |
|---|---|---|
| Cable TV | Movies | Books |
| Newspapers | Recorded music | Magazines |
| Professional sports teams | Network TV | Radio stations |
| | Casinos | Toys and games |
| | Theme parks | Performing arts |

These categories can then be further analyzed in terms of the degree to which there is a concentration of power among rival firms. A measure that is sensitive to both differences in the number of firms in an industry and differences in relative market shares – the *Herfindahl–Hirschman* Index – is then frequently used by economists to measure the concentration of markets.[26]

Segments

The relative economic importance of various industry segments is illustrated in Figure 1.14, the trendlines of which provide long-range macroeconomic perspectives of entertainment industry growth patterns. These patterns then translate into short-run financial operating performance, which is revealed by Table 1.5, where revenues, pretax operating incomes, assets, and cash flows (essentially EBITDAs) for a selected sample of major public companies are presented. This sample includes an estimated 80% of the transactions volume in entertainment-related industries and provides a means of comparing efficiencies in various segments.

Cash flow is particularly important because it can be used to service debt, acquire assets, or pay dividends. Representing the difference between cash receipts from the sale of goods or services and cash outlays required in production of the same, operating cash flow is usually understood to be operating income before deductions for interest, taxes, depreciation, and amortization (EBITDA) and more recently and alternatively, operating income before depreciation and amortization (OIBDA).[27] Although it has lost analytical favor in recent years, cash flow (EBITDA), so defined, has customarily been used as the basis for valuing all kinds of media and entertainment properties because the distortionary effects of differing tax and financial structure considerations are stripped away: A business property can thus be more easily evaluated from the standpoint of what it might be worth to potential buyers.[28]

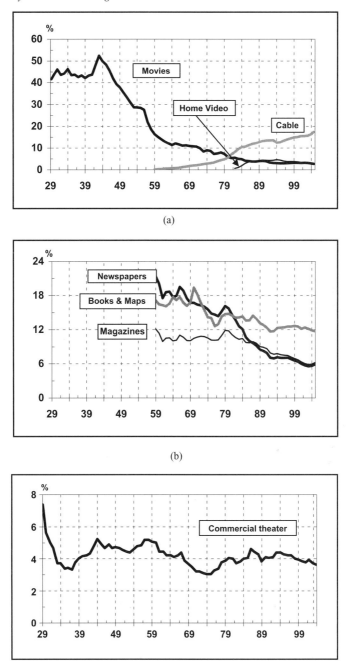

Figure 1.14. PCEs of selected entertainment categories as percentages of total PCE on recreation, 1929–2005.

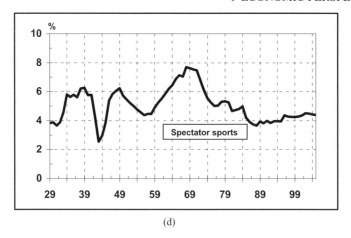

(d)

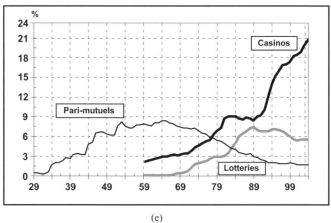

(e)

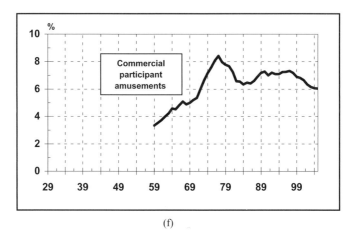

(f)

Figure 1.14. (*cont.*)

Table 1.5. *Entertainment industry composite, selected sample, 2001–2005*

**Compound annual growth rates (%): 2001–2005**

| Industry segment | No. companies in sample | Revenues | Operating income | Assets | Operating cash flow |
|---|---|---|---|---|---|
| Broadcasting (TV & radio) | 24 | 3 | 39 | 5 | −6 |
| Cable (video subs.) | 24 | 18 | NM[b] | 3 | 34 |
| Filmed entertainment | 6 | 8 | 24 | −1 | 6 |
| Gaming (casinos) | 22 | 3 | 7 | 11 | 5 |
| Publishing (books, cons. mag., newsp.) | 25 | 5 | 11 | 5 | −3 |
| Recorded music | 4 | −3 | 71 | −17 | 4 |
| Theatrical exhibition | 5 | 1 | 117 | 8 | 17 |
| Theme parks | 7 | 6 | −2 | 4 | 0 |
| Toys | 8 | 6 | 10 | 3 | 10 |
| Total | 125 | | | | |

**Total composite**

| | Pretax return (%) on | | Revenues | Operating income ($ billions) | Assets | Operating cash flow |
|---|---|---|---|---|---|---|
| | Revenues | Assets | | | | |
| 2005 | 16.4 | 6.6 | 291.4 | 47.8 | 718.9 | 67.3 |
| 2004 | 15.6 | 6.0 | 275.2 | 42.8 | 716.9 | 63.1 |
| 2003 | 13.8 | 5.3 | 258.5 | 35.8 | 677.8 | 56.4 |
| 2002 | 7.5 | 2.4 | 234.9 | 17.7 | 724.9 | 46.4 |
| 2001 | 6.1 | 1.8 | 220.5 | 13.3 | 732.5 | 41.3 |
| CAGR[a] | | | 7.2 | 37.5 | −0.5 | 13.0 |

[a] Compound annual growth rate (%).
[b] Not meaningful.
*Source*: Company reports.

More immediately, we can further see that entertainment industries generated revenues (on the wholesale level) of about $290 billion in 2005 and that annual growth between 2001 and 2005 averaged approximately 7.2%. Over the same span, operating income rose from recession lows at a compound rate of 37.5%, whereas assets have remained largely unchanged. Clearly then, operating cash flows, rising at a rate of 13.0%, have more than kept pace with the growth of revenues. Additions to assets have been financed by borrowings and/or by sales of equity (i.e., shares of stock) but also out of cash flows.

A thorough analysis of the composites shown in Table 1.5 would nevertheless further require consideration of many business-environmental features, including interest rates, antitrust policy attitudes, the trend of dollar exchange

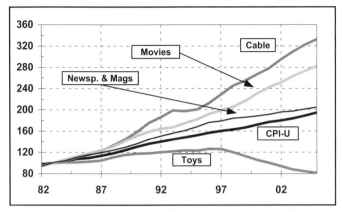

Figure 1.15. Inflation-rate comparisons for Consumer Price Index (CPI-U) and selected industry segments, 1982–2005. *Source*: Bureau of Labor Statistics.

rates, and relative pricing power. This last factor is suggested by Figure 1.15, which compares the rise of the Consumer Price Index for a few important entertainment segments against the average of all items for all urban consumers (CPI-U). From this, we can see that cable television service prices have been rising at well above average rates, while toys have been below the average.

Although economists also examine various segments through the use of what are known as input–output (I/O) tables, such tables are more robustly employed in the analysis of industrial products and commodities and in travel and tourism than they are in entertainment and media services. A typical I/O table in entertainment (see Table 2.2) would, for example, indicate how much the advertising industry depends on spending by entertainment companies.[29]

Finally, an indexed comparison of the percent of personal consumption expenditures going to different segments reveals the effects of changes in technology and in spending preferences. Three such trends are reflected in Figure 1.16, which illustrates the indexed percentages of total PCEs going to movie admissions, spectator sports, and live entertainment (including legitimate theater, opera, and entertainments of nonprofit institutions, i.e., "performing arts"). Interestingly, since around 1980, live entertainment, with a boost from relatively rapidly rising prices, had until recently gained in comparison with the spending percentage on spectator sports. Meanwhile, though, the percentage of PCE spending for movie tickets has fallen sharply now that technology has provided many other diversions and/or alternative means of seeing films (e.g., on videocassettes, DVDs, satellite or cable television hookups, or the Internet).

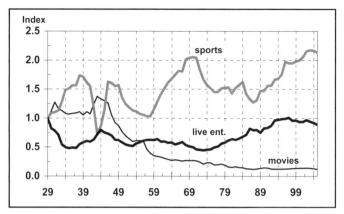

Figure 1.16. Indexed personal consumption expenditures on spectator sports, live entertainment, and movie theater admissions as a percent of total PCEs (1929 = 1.0), 1929–2005.

## 1.6 Valuation variables

Important as it is to understand the economic perspectives, it is ultimately the role of the financial analyst to condense this information into an asset valuation estimate. The key question for investors is whether the market is correctly pricing the assets of an industry or of a company. In attempting to arrive at an answer, we find that valuation of assets often involves as much art as science.

Valuation methods fall into three main categories of approach, using discounted cash flows, comparison methods, and option pricing models. Sometimes all three approaches are suitable and the results of each are compared. At other times the characteristics of the asset to be valued are such that it makes sense for only one approach to be used. In most cases, however, discounted cash flow is the central concept that takes account of both the time value of money and risk.

### Discounted cash flows

Given that the primary assets of media and entertainment companies are most often intangible and are embodied in the form of intellectual property rights, it makes sense to base valuations on the expected future profits that the control of such rights might be reasonably expected to convey over time. Although it is not a flawless measure, estimated cash flow (or perhaps EBITDA) discounted back to a present value will usually provide a good reflection of such profit potential as long as the proper discount rate is ascribed: Cash flow to *equity* must use a cost of equity capital discount rate (i.e., after interest expenses and principal payments), whereas cash flow to the *firm* (i.e., prior to interest expenses and principal payments) would use a weighted average cost of capital (WACC) discount rate.

Essentially, the discounted cash flow approach takes the value of any asset as the net present value (NPV) of the sum of expected future cash flows as represented by the following formula:

$$NPV = \sum_{t=1}^{n} CF_t/(1+r)^t,$$

where $r$ is the risk-adjusted required rate of return (tied to current interest rates), $CF_t$ is the projected cash flow in period $t$, and $n$ is the number of future periods over which the cash stream is to be received.

To illustrate this most simply, assume that the required rate of return is 9%, that the projected cash flows of a television program in each of the next three years are $3 million, $2 million, and $1 million, and that the program has no value beyond the third year. The *NPV* of the program would then be $3(1.0 + 0.09) + 2/(1.0 + 0.09)^2 + 1/(1.0 + 0.09)^3 = 2.75 + 1.683 + 0.7722 = \$5.205$ million.

## Comparison methods

Valuations can also be made by comparing various financial ratios and characteristics of one company or industry to another. These comparisons will frequently include current price-multiples of cash flows and estimates of earnings, shareholders' equity, and revenue growth relative to those of similar properties. For instance, often one of the best yardsticks for comparing global companies that report with different accounting standards is a ratio of Enterprise Value (EV) to EBITDA. Enterprise Value, subject to adjustment for preferred shares and other off-balance sheet items, equals total common shares outstanding times share price (i.e., equity capitalization) plus debt minus cash.

A ratio of price to cash flow, earnings, revenues, or some other financial feature should of course already reflect inherently the estimated discounted cash flow and/or salvage (terminal) values of an asset or class of assets. If cable systems are thus being traded at prices that suggest multiples of ten times next year's projected cash flow, it is likely that most other systems with similar characteristics will also be priced at a multiple near ten.

In valuations of entertainment and media assets, this comparative-multiple approach is the one most often used even though it is not particularly good in capturing what economists call *externalities* – those factors that would make a media property especially valuable to a specific buyer. Prestige, potential for political or moral influence, or access to certain markets are externalities that ordinarily affect media transaction prices.

Options

For assets that have option-like characteristics or that are not traded frequently, neither the discounted cash flow nor the price and ratio comparison approaches can be readily applied. Instead, option-pricing models (e.g., the Black–Scholes model) that use contingent claim valuation estimates (of assets that pay off only under certain contingencies and assumed probability distributions) are usually employed.

With the possible exception of start-up Internet shares in the late 1990s, however, this approach has not normally been used in entertainment industry practice unless the asset to be valued is an option contract (e.g., a warrant, call, or put) or is a contract for marketing or distribution rights or for some form of intellectual property right, such as for a patent.[30]

## 1.7 Concluding remarks

This chapter has sketched the economic landscape in which all entertainment industries operate. It has indicated how hours at work, productivity trends, expected utility functions, demographics, and other factors can affect the amounts of time and money we spend on leisure-related goods and services. It has also provided benchmarks against which the relative growth rates and sizes of different industry segments or composites can be measured. We can see, for example, that as a percentage of disposable income, U.S. PCEs for recreation – encompassing spending on entertainment as well as other leisure-time pursuits – first rose to well over 6% in the 1980s. And we can see that entertainment is big business: At the wholesale level, it is now generating annual revenues exceeding $300 billion. Moreover, as measured in dollar value terms, entertainment has consistently been one of the largest net export categories (estimated to be at least $9 billion in 2006) for the United States.[31]

Technological development has obviously played an important role, too. It underlies the very growth of productivity and thus of the relative supply of leisure time. But just as significantly, technological advancement, tracked in Figure 1.17, has changed the way in which we think of entertainment products. Such products – whether movies, music, TV shows, video games, or words – must now be regarded as composite bits of "information" that can be produced and processed and distributed as a series of digits – coded bursts of zeros and ones that can represent sounds and pictures and texts. Already, this has greatly altered the entertainment industry's economic landscape.

The past, then, is clearly not a prologue – especially in a field where creative people are constantly finding new ways to turn a profit. The wide-ranging economic perspectives discussed in this chapter, however, provide a common background for all that follows.

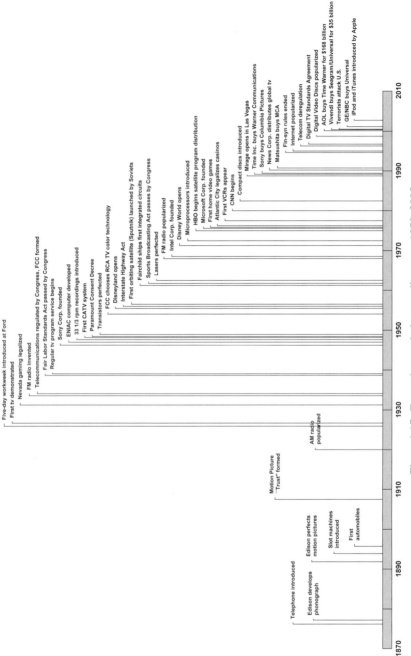

Figure 1.17. Entertainment industry milestones, 1870–2005.

32

# Notes

**1.**  Similarly, the concept of *play* has been studied under the disciplines of sociology and psychology. The Dutch anthropologist Johan Huizinga in his book *Homo Ludens* (Man the Player, 1938, 1955) advanced the notion that play might be its own end. Huizinga (1955, p. 8) notes that the first main characteristic of play is "that it is free, it is freedom. A second characteristic . . . is that play is not 'ordinary' or 'real' life." It also demands order, casts a spell over us, and contains elements of tension and solution, such as in gambling.

Torkildsen (1999, p. 93) makes further distinctions between play, recreation, and leisure. *Play* activity is "freely chosen and indulged in for its own sake and for the satisfaction it brings in the doing: it exhibits childlike characteristics of spontaneity, self-expression and a creation of its own special meaning . . . *Recreation*, unlike play, appears to need to be justified . . . It carries greater social responsibilities than leisure . . . *Re-creation* is another meaning. In its purest sense, it is characterized by an inner-consuming experience of oneness that leads to revival . . . *Leisure* is perceived in different ways – time, activity, experience, state of being, a way of life, and so on . . . It can encompass play and recreation activity." Here, recreation, play, and leisure concepts form partially overlapping circles centered on pleasure. See also Roberts (1995).

**2.**  As De Grazia (1962, p. 13) notes, it is obvious that "time on one's hands is not enough to make leisure," and free time accompanied by fear and anxiety is not leisure.

**3.**  As Smith (1986, p. 8) has further noted, such surveys indicate that for full-time, day-shift plant workers, the average workweek decreased by 0.8 hour between 1973 and 1985 but that, over the same period, "the schedule of full-time office workers in the private sector rose by 0.2 hour, with the result that the workweek of these two large groups converged markedly."

Also, Hedges and Taylor (1980) show that hours for full-time service workers declined faster than for white-collar and blue-collar employees between 1968 and 1979. And the Bureau of Labor Statistics estimated that the percentage of nonagricultural salaried jobs in which the workweek exceeded 49 hours rose to 18.5% in 1993 as compared with 14.2% in 1973. Through World War I Americans regularly worked six days a week, and it was not until after passage of the Fair Labor Standards Act in 1938 that overtime pay and a 40-hour workweek became the norm. See also Supplementary Table S1.2.

**4.**  A Louis Harris nationwide survey found that the estimated hours available for leisure had been steadily decreasing from 26.2 hours per week in 1973 to 16.6 hours per week in 1987. Since 1989 this has stabilized at around 20 hours. Harris argues that an apparent combination of economic necessities and choices by women who want to work has increased the number of families in which both husbands and wives hold jobs. Also see Gibbs (1989).

**5.**  These estimated changes in hours worked appear strikingly high. It seems that, although the analysis could have been correct in catching the direction of change, it might have mistakenly estimated its magnitude. Schor's book is so politically imbued with an anticapitalist theme that the methodology and the objectivity of its findings are accordingly suspect. See also Robinson and Godbey (1997) and *The Economist*, December 23, 1995, p. 12.

**6.**  Robinson (1989, p. 35) found, for example, that "people aged 51 to 64 have gained the most free time since 1965, mainly because they are working less. Among people in this age group, the proportion of men opting for early retirement increased considerably between 1965 and 1985." Also, Robinson and Godbey (1997) suggest that Americans, in the aggregate, have more time for leisure because of broad trends toward younger retirements and smaller families. Except for parents of very young children, or those with more than four children under 18, everyone else, they say, has gained at least one hour per week since 1965.

**7.** Roberts and Rupert (1995) state that the presumption of declining leisure is a fallacy. "Previous studies purporting to have uncovered such a fact have not adequately disentangled time spent in home production-activities . . . from time spent enjoying leisure activities. [W]hile hours of market work and home work have remained fairly constant for men since the mid-1970s, market hours have been rising and home production hours have been declining for women . . . Possible reasons include an increase in market versus nonmarket productivity or labor-saving technological advancements in the home."

Rones, Ilg, and Gardner (1997) concluded that, between 1976 and 1993, "after removing the effect of the shifting age distribution, average weekly hours for men showed virtually no change (edging up from 41.0 to 41.2 hours), and the average workweek for women increased by only a single hour [but] . . . a growing proportion of workers are putting in very long workweeks . . . This increase is pervasive across occupations, and the long workweek itself seems to be associated with high earnings and certain types of occupations." See also Kirkland (2000). Also note that the U.S. Federal Government approved funding in December 2000 for an *American Time Use Survey of Activity*. See Shelley (2005).

**8.** Divergence of results in studying hours of work may be caused by differences in how government data are used. For example, such data generally are based on hours paid rather than hours worked. This means that a worker on paid vacation would be counted as working, even though he or she is not. Also, hours per job, rather than hours per worker are used. The shift in work-hour trends in Europe is a function of competition from low-wage countries and is discussed in Landler (2004).

**9.** Rybczynski (1991) provides a detailed history of the evolution of the weekend. And Spring (1993) provides a study of the popularity of spare-time activities classified by day of the week. Television viewing, consuming one-third of free time on weekdays and one-fourth on weekends, leads the list by far on every day of the week.

**10.** Also, studies comparing time allocation in different countries can be found in Juster and Stafford (1991), where, for example, it can be seen that both men and women allocate more time for leisure in the United States than in Japan or Sweden. As Bell and Freeman (2000) note, however, the differences in hours worked in different countries are related less to cultural values than to a greater diversity of wages, the effects of number of hours worked on future compensation, and less job security in the United States than elsewhere. They find that an American working 2,000 hours per year who increases that by 10%, to 2,200 hours, can generally expect a "1 percent increase in future wages."

**11.** The apparently reduced rate of improvement between 1973 and 1990 may have been caused by unexpected sharp cost increases for energy and capital (interest rates), by high corporate debt levels, or perhaps by the burgeoning "underground" (off-the-books) economy not directly captured in (and therefore distorting) the NIPA numbers. As McTague (2005) suggests, growth of the underground economy still creates important distortions, especially in the measurement of productivity.

**12.** There are many fine texts providing full description of these tools; see, for example, Henderson and Quandt (1971).

**13.** In most mathematical presentations, the independent variable or "cause" of change is presented along the horizontal $x$-axis and the dependent variable on the vertical $y$-axis. Economists, however, have generally found it more convenient to depict prices (the independent variable) and quantities by switching the axes. Thus, prices are usually seen on the vertical axis and quantities on the horizontal one. Werner (2005, p. 326) notes that "The variable that produces the equilibrium in this model is price. However, to achieve this outcome, perfect information is required. If there is imperfect information, there is no guarantee that equilibrium will ever be obtained. It would be pure chance if demand equaled supply."

**14.** In Linder (1970), standard indifference-curve/budget-line analysis is used to show how the supply of labor is a function of income and substitution effects. The standard consumers' utility function is $V = f(Q, T_c)$, where $Q$ is the number of units of consumption goods and $T_c$ is the number of hours devoted to consumption purposes. Two constraints are $Q = pT_w$ and $T = T_w + T_c$, where $p$ is a productivity index measuring the number of consumption goods earned per hour of work $(T_w)$ and $T$ is the total number of hours available per time period.

To maximize utility, $V$ now takes the Lagrange multiplier function

$$L = f(Q, T_c) + \lambda[Q - p(T - T_c),$$

which is then differentiated with respect to $Q$, $T_c$, and multiplier $\lambda$.

**15.** See Trost (1986) and *Monthly Labor Review*, U.S. Department of Commerce, Bureau of Labor Statistics, November 1986, No. 11.

**16.** Owen's (1970) exhaustive study of these issues leads to a model supporting the hypothesis of a backward-bending labor-supply curve and suggesting that demand for leisure activity has positive income and negative price elasticities consistent with economic theory. More recent work by Deidda and Cerina (2002) explores the elasticity of wages per unit of labor relative to the fraction of labor income saved.

**17.** Utility can often be visualized in the form of a mathematical curve or function. For instance, the utility a person derives from purchase of good $x$ might vary with the square root of the amount of $x$ (i.e., $U(x) =$ square root of $x$). Also see Section 11.5 and Levy and Sarnat (1972).

**18.** Taking this a step further, one finds that a marginal rate of substitution (MRS) between good $x$ and good $y$ can then be presented in the form of *indifference curves* that are a ratio of the marginal utility (MU) of $x$ to the marginal utility of $y$, and along which utility is constant. The underlying assumption is that of diminishing marginal utility, which means that the curves never intersect and are negatively sloped and generally convex to the origin.

**19.** A dependency ratio is the number of people who are net consumers (children and senior citizens) divided by the number of net producers; see, for example, Burton and Toth (1974), and Gladwell (2006).

**20.** Regulation is often deemed politically necessary to offset alleged imperfections in the market economy. At times, for example, there have thus been movements to contain monopoly power, to control excessive competition, to provide public goods, and to regulate externalities.

**21.** Price or other elasticities are also often taken at a point and expressed in the calculus as $\varepsilon_p = -(p/q) \times (dq/dp)$, where $q$ is a measure of quantity of units demanded and $p$ is price per unit.

**22.** The table, however, does not do justice to the cable television and lottery spending categories, which have been among the largest and fastest growing segments but are unfortunately lumped into the "other" section.

**23.** Both Figure 1.10 and Supplemetary Table S1.1 are based on NIPA data series.

**24.** However, the entertainment services series as a percentage of total recreation spending has demonstrated considerable volatility since 1929. This series hit a peak of nearly 50% in the early 1940s, when there were relatively few consumer durables available. Then, for a dozen or so years ending in the late 1970s, the percentage had been confined to a fairly narrow band of 33% to 36%.

**25.**   GNP measures output belonging to U.S. citizens and corporations wherever that output is created, whereas GDP measures the value of all goods and services produced in a country no matter whether that output belongs to natives or foreigners. In actuality, in the United States, the differences between the values of the two series have been slight.

However, critics of National Income Accounting, for example, Cobb, Halstead, and Rowe (1995), argue that GDP measurements allow activities in the household and volunteer sectors to go entirely unreckoned. As a result, GDP measurements mask the breakdown of the social structure and are grossly misleading. "GDP does not distinguish between costs and benefits, between productive and destructive activities, or between sustainable and unsustainable ones. The nation's central measure of well-being works like a calculating machine that adds but cannot subtract. . . . The GDP treats leisure time and time with family the way it treats air and water: as having no value at all" (pp. 64–67). See also Uichitelle (2006).

**26.**   The Herfindahl–Hirschman Index (HHI) – used by the Department of Justice in determining whether proposed mergers ought to be permitted – is calculated as the sum of the squared market shares of each competitor in the relevant product and geographic markets:

$$\mathrm{HHI} = \sum_{i=1}^{n} S_i^2,$$

where $S$ is the market share of the $i$th firm in the industry and $n$ equals the number of firms in the industry. Generally, near monopolies would have an *HHI* approaching 10,000, modest concentration would fall between 1,000 and 1,800, and low concentration would be under 1,000.

**27.**   OIBDA eliminates the uneven effect across company business segments of noncash depreciation of tangible assets and amortization of certain intangible assets that are recognized in business combinations. The limitation of this measure, however, is that it does not reflect periodic costs of certain capitalized tangible and intangible assets used in generating revenues. OIBDA also does not reflect the diminution in value of goodwill and intangible assets or gains and losses on asset sales. In contrast, free cash flow (FCF) is defined as cash from operations less cash provided by discontinued operations, capital expenditures and product development costs, principal payments on capital leases, dividends paid, and partnership distributions, if any.

**28.**   Enthusiasm for use of EBITDA as an important metric of comparison has waned in light of the accounting scandals of the early 2000s. Increasingly, investors appear to favor measures of free cash flow and net earnings, especially now that the rules for writing down goodwill have been changed (see Chapter 5) and given that EBITDA does not indicate the detrimental effects of high and rising debt obligations on balance sheets and rising interest expenses on net earnings.

**29.**   The input–output (I/O) accounts show how industries interact; specifically, they show how industries provide input to, and use output from, each other to produce gross domestic product (GDP). These accounts provide detailed information on the flows of the goods and services that make up the production process of industries. I/O accounts are presented in a set of tables: Use, Make, Direct Requirements, and Total Requirements. The Use table shows the inputs to industry production and the commodities that are consumed by final users. The Make table shows the commodities that are produced by each industry.

**30.**   See also Lev (2001) for discussion of measurement and valuation of intangibles.

**31.** Official data on entertainment industry exports are sketchy, but as noted by the U.S. Department of Commerce (1993, p. 20), net exports (using country-based rather than firm-based measurements) of motion picture and television programming amounted to $2.122 billion in 1991. For the same year, net exports of records, tapes, and other media amounted to $283 million. Other areas may have generated the following amounts: theme parks, $0.5 billion; casinos, $0.5 billion. Also, according to the OECD Services, *Statistics on International Transactions* Table A-21, net U.S. film and television exports in 1994 were $2.48 billion as compared with $195 million in 1980. See also Bernstein (1990), who discusses the implications of global acceptance of American entertainment products and services, and *Variety*, January 9, 1991.

More recent estimates based on different data and *not* netted against imports appear in *Copyright Industries in the U.S. Economy* (2002) prepared by Stephen E. Siwek Economists Incorporated (Washington, DC) for the International Intellectual Property Alliance (www.iipa.com). In that report, foreign sales and exports for broadly defined copyright industries, the largest of any other grouping, including aerospace and chemicals, are estimated to have been $89 billion in 2001. The core copyright industries are here defined to include newspapers and periodicals, music publishing, radio and television broadcasting, cable television, records and tapes, motion pictures, theatrical productions, advertising, and computer software and data processing. Within this core, for 2001, motion pictures, television, and video are estimated to have accounted for $14.69 billion, music, $9.51 billion, and publications, $4.03 billion.

## Selected additional reading

Albarran, A. (1996). *Media Economics: Understanding Markets, Industries and Concepts.* Ames, IO: Iowa State University Press.

Alexander, A., Owers, J., Carveth, R., *et al.*, eds. (2004). *Media Economics: Theory and Practice*, 3rd ed. Mahwah, NJ, and London: Lawrence Erlbaum Associates.

Aron, C. S. (1999). *Working at Play: A History of Vacations in the United States.* New York: Oxford University Press.

"Crossroads for Planet Earth," *Scientific American*, September, 2005.

Cutler, B. (1990). "Where Does the Free Time Go?," *American Demographics*, 12(11)(November).

"The Determinants of Working Hours," *OECD Employment Outlook*, September 1983.

"The Entertainment Economy," *BusinessWeek*, No. 3362 (March 14, 1994).

Epstein, G. (1995). "Myth: Americans Are Working More. Fact: More Women Are Working," *Barron's,* April 3.

Filer, R. K., Hamermesh, D. S., and Rees, A. E. (1996). *The Economics of Work and Play*, 6th ed. New York: HarperCollins.

Fuchsberg, G. (1994). "Four-Day Workweek Has Become a Stretch for Some Employees," *Wall Street Journal*, August 3.

Gabriel, T. (1995). "A Generation's Heritage: After the Boom, a Boomlet," *New York Times*, February 12.

Gray, M. B. (1992). "Consumer Spending on Durables and Services in the 1980s," *Monthly Labor Review*, 115(5)(May).

Hedges, J. N. (1980). "The Workweek in 1979: Fewer but Longer Workdays," *Monthly Labor Review*, 103(8)(August).

(1973). "New Patterns for Working Time," *Monthly Labor Review*, 96(2)(February).

Hunnicutt, B. K. (1988). *Work without End: Abandoning Shorter Hours for the Right to Work*. Philadelphia: Temple University Press.

Jablonski, M., Kunze, K., and Otto, P. (1990). "Hours at Work: A New Base for BLS Productivity Statistics," *Monthly Labor Review*, 113(2)(February).

Kilborn, P. T. (1996). "Factories That Never Close Are Scrapping 5-Day Week," *New York Times*, June 4.

Malabre, A. L., Jr., and Clark, L. H., Jr. (1992). "Productivity Statistics for the Service Sector May Understate Gains," *Wall Street Journal*, August 12.

Marano, H. E. (1999). "The Power of Play," *Psychology Today*, 32(4)(August).

Meyersohn, R., and Larrabee, E. (1958). "A Comprehensive Bibliography on Leisure, 1900–1958," in *Mass Leisure*. Glencoe, IL: The Free Press. Also in *American Journal of Sociology*, 62(6)(May 1957): 602–615.

Moore, G. H., and Hedges, J. N. (1971). "Trends in Labor and Leisure," *Monthly Labor Review*, 94(2)(February).

Oi, W. (1971). "A Disneyland Dilemma: Two-Part Tariffs for a Mickey Mouse Monopoly," *Quarterly Journal of Economics*, 85(February).

Owen, J. D. (1971). "The Demand for Leisure," *Journal of Political Economy*, 79(1)(January/February): 56–75.

Pollak, R. A., and Wachter, M. L. (1975). "The Relevance of the Household Production Function and Its Implications for the Allocation of Time," *Journal of Political Economy*, 83(2).

"The Productivity Paradox," *BusinessWeek*, No. 3055 (June 6, 1988).

"The Revival of Productivity," *BusinessWeek*, No. 2828 (February 13, 1984).

Rhoads, C. (2002). "Short Work Hours Undercut Europe in Economic Drive," *Wall Street Journal*, August 8.

"Riding High: The Productivity Bonanza," *BusinessWeek*, No. 3445 (October 9, 1995).

Rifkin, J. (1995). *The End of Work*. New York: Putnam.

Robbins, L. (1930). "On the Elasticity of Income in Terms of Effort," *Economica*, 10 (June).

Robinson, J. P., and Godbey, G. (1996). "The Great American Slowdown," *American Demographics*, June.

Rosen, S., and Rosenfield, A. (1997). "Ticket Pricing," *Journal of Law & Economics*, XL(2)(October).

Scott, J. (1999). "Working Hard, More or Less," *New York Times*, July 10.

Staines, G. L., and O'Connor, P. (1980). "Conflicts among Work, Leisure, and Family Roles," *Monthly Labor Review*, 103(8)(August).

"Wheel of Fortune: A Survey of Technology and Entertainment," *The Economist*, November 21, 1998.

Yoon, L. (2006). "More Play, Less Toil Is a Stressful Shift for Some Koreans," *Wall Street Journal*, August 10.

# 2
# Basic elements

*Listen to the technology and find out what it is telling you.*
– Carver Mead, chip design pioneer

Entertainment and media industries all operate within a framework of commonly shared elements. All sectors are conditioned by the same underlying rules, are affected by changes in distribution technologies at approximately the same time, and, because of the nature of the products and services offered, are often both buyers and sellers of advertising services. The relevance of these basic and usually invisible aspects common to every entertainment and media business sector is explained in this chapter.

## 2.1 Rules of the road

Laws of the media

Media pioneer Marshall McLuhan (1964, p. 305) early on noted that "the content of any medium is always another medium." In other words, each medium, whether it be books, music, film, games, or theater, borrows from the others and is interdependent: The content of the movie may be based on the novel, or the novel may inspire the movie or the song. *The Lion King* animated movie, for example, led to the introduction of a children's game, while the video games *Mortal Kombat* and *Tomb Raider* ended up being made into movies. *Chicago* went from a play to a Broadway musical to an award-winning film.

This notion, however, forms the basis of only one of McLuhan's four immutable "laws" of media (McLuhan and McLuhan 1988, p. viii), which may be directly verified by observation and applied to every product of human effort.

1. *Extension*: *Every technology extends or amplifies some organ or faculty of the user*. For example, the wheel (e.g., in the form of a bicycle or a car) is an extension of the foot. Media amplify or enhance aspects of social culture.

2. *Closure*: Equilibrium requires that, when one area of experience is heightened or intensified, another is diminished or numbed. For instance, it's possible to read a book and listen to music at the same time, but neither the reading nor the listening experience can then be of maximum intensity. Or, in another meaning, in watching a film or television show, the viewer's attention to dialog and sound or vice versa will be overpowered by extremely bright colors or graphic images. In the same way, *new media create obsolescence or push older media out of prominence*.

3. *Reversal*: *Every form, pushed to the limits of its potential, reverses its characteristics* – for example, the network (Internet) is a computer and the computer has become part of the network.[1]

4. *Retrieval*: *The content of any medium is retrieved from an older medium or previous medium* (e.g., the book spawns the movie, which begets the play, the record album, the video game, or vice versa).[2]

In addition to these, however, there appears to be a fifth "law" of media that McLuhan might have missed (or that could arguably be taken as a corollary of retrieval). It is also derived by observation and can be stated as:

5. *Entropy/Fragmentation*: *Every successful form, immediately after introduction, rapidly fragments* into many slightly different subsidiary niches. We can readily see this, for example, in the proliferation of magazine titles, cable channels, books, television shows, video games, popular music, and movie genres.[3]

Fragmentation and proliferation are seen in all media and every time a new form is successfully developed. This process is akin to biological cell division and proceeds until the economic energy of the sector is exhausted and risks of financial failures rise to intolerable levels.[4] And the comparably described concept in the physical sciences, commonly called entropy, also applies. *Media entropy*, as in physics and communications theory, increases as we go, via the process of fragmentation, from a state of order to disorder.[5]

Fragmentation also leads us to further observe that the success of media and entertainment products and services (like many others) can be ranked (scaled) according to an exponential, or power law that has mathematical characteristics similar to those that are used to rank the strength of earthquakes, the sizes of cities, or percentage changes in stock prices. The essence here can be distilled into the notion that for movies, books, recordings, television shows, toys and games, cable channel viewers, Internet site visitations, actors' salaries, and virtually anything else in the field, at least 80% of the total income is generally derived from sometimes much less than 20% of the product or service categories. Such power law relationships (discussed in greater detail in Chapter 4 and illustrated in Figure 4.9) are the basis for the sixth and seventh "laws" of media.

6. *Exponentiality*: Income is scaled exponentially, with relatively few items or categories accounting for most of the results while a much larger number of items or categories adds little or nothing to the total. Many different industries will operate with an 80:20 rule of this type – that is, 80% of revenues or profit come from 20% of the items. But especially in entertainment, the realities are often much harsher; in music, for example, the ratio is probably closer to 98:2.

7. *Spread*: Like water flowing downhill into a basin, media content will always try to be spread as widely as possible, with content seeking maximum distribution and distribution seeking maximum content.[6]

## Network features

In entertainment and media, content is often said to be king. What this means is that companies with recent popular content in the form of films, books, records, television shows, or game software, for example, obtain competitive marketing and equity valuation advantages. Content is certainly where most consumer and investor attention is typically focused.

Yet, were it not for the presence of vast distribution networks that quietly operate behind the scenes and that constantly evolve from new technologies, most content alone would not have inherently great financial value and impact on society and culture. It is in this sense, then, that distribution power trumps control of content: The best content in the world is not worth anything if it cannot be made readily available to audiences.[7] This is then the imperative for spread, the aforementioned notion that content seeks maximum distribution and distribution seeks maximum content. Networks are thus a basic element embedded in the operating context of all entertainment and media businesses.

Although media networks adhere to McLuhan's laws, their most important feature is perhaps better described by Metcalfe's *Law of Connectivity*, which applies to all networks, whether composed of computers, telephones, or roads, or of people who express their opinions to their families and friends about things like movies, music, television programs, or toys or books.[8]

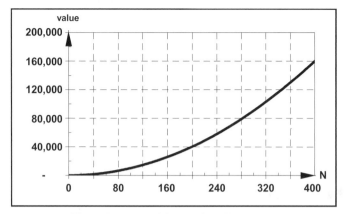

Figure 2.1. Law of Connectivity illustrated.

If a network has sufficient capacity to remain unclogged even while carrying lots of traffic, its utility (or value) rises by at least the number of users (or nodes) squared. More formally,

$$V = aN^2 + bN + c,$$

where $V$ is the value, $N$ is the number of users, and the other terms are constants. Figure 2.1 illustrates the concept.

The only difference in the case of the Internet is that nodes are able to connect simultaneously with more than one other node, which means that unlike most (single point-to-point) telephone connections, the value rises faster than $N$ squared. Such networks therefore show exponential, not linear, growth and increasing, not decreasing, returns to scale.[9]

As Shy (2001, p. 5) further explains, in network industries, including those of software development, banking, broadcasting, cable, and airlines, the huge upfront sunk cost (i.e., cost that cannot be recovered) of developing the first unit of a product or service "together with almost negligible marginal cost implies that the average cost function declines sharply" as the number of product or service units sold increases. "This means that a competitive equilibrium does not exist and that markets of this type will often be characterized by dominant leaders that capture most of the market."[10]

## 2.2 Internet

The Internet is not only a major new medium for the transmission of information and entertainment – a network of all networks, if you will – but also by now an integral part of every modern business operation. It has rudely upended the long-standing business models of virtually every industry, especially those pertaining to media and entertainment. Figure 2.2 illustrates

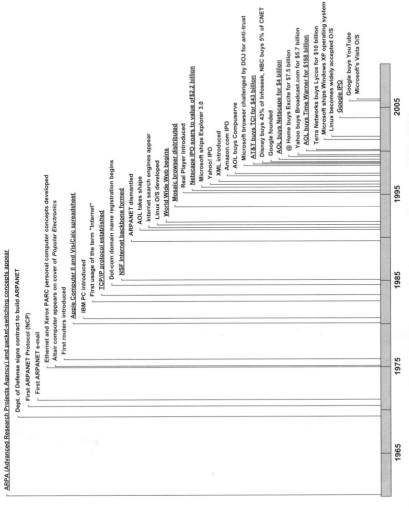

Figure 2.2. Internet development milestones, 1960–2006.

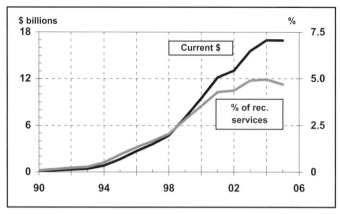

Figure 2.3. Personal-consumption expenditures for Internet service providers (left scale) and as a percent of total PCEs for recreation services, 1990–2005.

the historical milestones in the evolution of the Internet, while Figure 2.3 indicates that personal-consumption expenditures for Internet services have grown rapidly as a percent of total spending for recreation services.[11]

## Agent of change

It is the unregulated aspect of the Internet that, in particular, makes it a powerful agent of change that allows alternative forms of service distribution to readily circumvent traditionally structured segments. The Net is a constantly evolving organism, and anyone on it can be a global publisher or a broadcaster of self-produced content with no need to obtain a government agency license or to navigate a labyrinth of corporate gatekeepers. All entertainment industry segments are being constantly transformed because, in each industry segment, the Internet fundamentally

- Redefines and rearranges (but does not necessarily wholly eliminate) the functions of the middleman or wholesaler/distributor
- Changes the nature of customer relationships by altering the proportion of total revenues derived from advertising, subscriptions, and sales
- Increases the amount, variety, and accessibility of entertainment program content and related products and services (through what is known as a long-tail effect)[12]
- Opens the way for new forms of entertainment products and services to be developed[13]
- Challenges the entire technological and geographical *rights-based* business structures that have evolved

Of these, the last will likely prove to be the most disruptive of them all over the longer term. For instance, movie theater distribution contracts are based on geographically defined exhibition rights. Broadcast television signal distributions (and to a lesser extent radio) are technologically limited by distance from the transmission source and to time of transmission. Programming as played on DVDs and iPods is device dependent. And cable and satellite program reception rights are tied directly to the location of the receiving household's location. With the Internet, geography, device type, and household location are no longer relevant: Traditional rights-defined "fences" are no longer restrictive because the Internet enables all content to be distributed and played on numerous devices at any time and anywhere.

Within this context are generally two major business-model types that describe Internet-related companies:

- As in broadcast television, information (content) is bundled with advertising and provided at no or minimal cost to users.[14]
- As in pay cable, content can be paid for through subscription, license, and other fees – including percentages of transaction prices – that compensate service providers and intellectual property owners.[15]

Revenue streams that are based on a combination of both advertising and fees are preferred because cyclical risk is reduced through such diversification.

*– can't measure, still growing*

## Accounting and valuation

*Accounting*  At least in the early years of the Internet, traditional yardsticks – multiples of cash flow or of earnings or sales as well as balance sheet ratios of leverage and debt – had not served well in the valuation of Internet company shares and their assets. In part, this is because Internet businesses had been growing so rapidly and with so much potential presumed to be still ahead. Also, established accounting methods have not been able to fully explain the growth in value of companies that are mostly composed of intangible assets built through intensive early-stage spending on advertising, marketing, and research and development. Traditional accounting is based on measurements taken when transactions occur, whereas with knowledge assets, value can be created or destroyed without making any transactions at all.[16] Accounting controversies in this area extend to problems of revenue recognition, discounts, and even routine issues of when to recognize expenses.[17]

*Valuation*  As Internet and other early-stage media companies mature, conventional valuation metrics ultimately become more relevant. But, in the meantime, the assets clearly have option-like characteristics, which suggest that the application of option pricing models (e.g., Black–Scholes) is appropriate. Such models explicitly take into account the volatility of returns and the enormous operating leverage potential of most early-stage companies.[18] The fundamental presumption here is that new firms will be able to generate much higher returns on invested capital (ROIC) than older ones.[19]

Many new companies also do not, at least initially, have any earnings
at all. In such instances, analysts will usually first seek to compare market
valuations against recent takeover prices for similar assets or to compare
ratios of market price to revenue (or, perhaps, price to cash flow) for similar
companies. Ratios such as market capitalization to advertising views or to
unique users, average revenues per subscriber, revenues per viewer-hours,
and other such indicators are often then also calculated. All such metrics
will over time fall into and out of favor and depend on investors' needs
and interests of the moment.[20] But value investors will not pay much for
growth alone unless a firm has some kind of special franchise or protected
position.[21]

### 2.3 Advertising

Advertising is the key common ingredient in the tactics and strategies of all
entertainment and media company business models. Indeed, it might further be said that advertising has substantively subsidized the production and
delivery of news and entertainment throughout the last century. As Figure 2.4
shows, advertising moves pretty much in tandem with personal-consumption
expenditures.[22] Some companies, depending on the sector, are more apt to
be buyers than sellers, or vice versa. Toy companies, casinos, and theme
parks are typical of the first category, and broadcasters, newspapers, and
magazines are typical of the second.[23] Relatively high advertising-to-sales
(A/S) ratios are typical of heavily branded products and services, many of
which are offered by media and entertainment firms.

The top ten advertising categories in the United States in 2004 appear in
Table 2.1, with movies and media near the top of the list. These category
rankings do not normally change much over time and would also appear
largely in the same order in other developed countries.

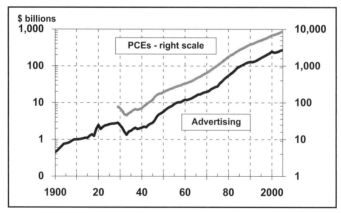

Figure 2.4. Advertising expenditure and PCE trends, log scale, 1900–2005.

*Products have a time period*

*Price - inelastic*

*Does not increase sales*

Table 2.1. *Top ten ad spending categories in the United States, 2004*

| Category | $ millions | Print | Broadcast | Internet | Outdoor |
|---|---|---|---|---|---|
| Automobiles | 20,518 | 9,199 | 10,582 | 375 | 362 |
| Retail | 17,285 | 8,820 | 7,039 | 1,108 | 318 |
| **Movies & media** | 9,059 | 2,975 | 4,554 | 1,362 | 168 |
| Drugs | 8,168 | 2,234 | 5,528 | 388 | 18 |
| Food & beverages | 7,343 | 2,783 | 3,425 | 915 | 220 |
| Financial services | 6,840 | 1,794 | 4,889 | 79 | 78 |
| Home furnishings | 6,270 | 2,896 | 2,405 | 520 | 449 |
| Telecommunications | 5,528 | 2,048 | 3,411 | 53 | 16 |
| Personal care | 5,339 | 1,667 | 3,450 | 116 | 106 |
| Airlines & travel | 5,246 | 2,506 | 2,606 | 128 | 6 |

*Source*: *Advertising Age*.

However, another way to see the uses and sources of advertising in the economy as a whole is through analysis of what are known as input–output (I/O) tables. Excerpts of I/O tables relating to advertising and selected other media sectors are illustrated in Table 2.2. Such grids indicate what individual industries buy from and sell to each other.[24]

Functionality

Advertising is especially important to media and entertainment industries because the products normally have unique, time-perishable characteristics in which, as shown in Chapter 1, there is a substantial financial gain to be derived by shifting a demand curve to the right and making it more price-inelastic. In fact, once the relatively large investment in the project's original development has been assimilated, each additional unit of a product or service then normally entails little extra marginal cost to make or to provide. At that point, advertising often becomes the primary marketing tool and the dominant component of unit cost.[25]

Table 2.2. *Input/output direct industry requirements, selected sample, 1992*

| Direct requirements per dollar of industry output at producers' prices, inputs to industry in columns | Radio & TV broadcasting | Advertising | Newspapers and periodicals | Amusements |
|---|---|---|---|---|
| Advertising | .02830 | .00606 | .00020 | .03896 |
| Radio & TV broadcasting | .02064 | .00496 | – | – |
| Newspapers and periodicals | .00024 | .00023 | .02026 | .00052 |
| Amusements | .37883 | .02056 | .00062 | .16209 |

Advertising is similarly important to the sellers of advertising spaces and time slots. Broadcasters, cable networks, and newspapers, for example, provide the content and thus the context in which advertising is placed. The large upfront investments required for advancement of these information delivery formats have already long been made, and fixed costs hardly change over the near to medium term. Thus, even small positive or negative changes in demand for advertising, as reflected in pricing of the inventory of spaces and slots, have immediate and significant effects on profits.

From all this we can see that, especially for entertainment and media industries, advertising plays a central role for both buyers and sellers. And advertising has also become fully integrated – through merchandising, licensing, event sponsorships, tie-ins, and placements – with the distribution and propagation of many entertainment products and services. It is another basic element.

Economic aspects

In an exhaustive survey of the literature, Bagwell (2001, 2005) shows that the economic aspects of advertising – its effectiveness and its role in product branding, for example – have by now been extensively explored but that much remains to be done. From this work there has emerged three somewhat conflicting conceptual views that characterize advertising as being persuasive, informative, or complementary (i.e., advertising complements a consumer's stable preferences for prestige, brand affiliation, and so on). The theoretical base for all of these views evolved out of theories of monopolistic competition that were formalized by economists of the 1930s.

According to the *persuasive view*, advertising not only makes the demand for a firm's products and services more inelastic – thereby enabling higher average prices to be obtained – but it also presents a barrier to entry that is especially important when economies of scale come into play. The persuasive view appears to best describe the situation for most entertainment products and services. In part this is because many such products are sold at relatively fixed prices (e.g., movie tickets) and in quasi-monopolistic temporal situations (e.g., "must-see" events or "must-have" toys). Targeted advertising then allows a firm to segment consumers and to command a higher return by implementing price discrimination strategies (as described in Chapter 1).

The *informative view*, in contrast, suggests that advertising information enables consumers to find low prices. Advertising of this kind thus promotes competition among established firms and has the potential to facilitate entry of new firms.[26]

The largely *complementary view* discussed in Becker and Murphy (1993, p. 943) is, however, also pertinent. As they note, "advertising tends to raise elasticities of demand for goods advertised by lifting the demands of marginal

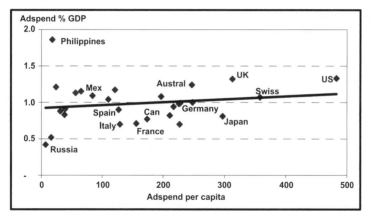

Figure 2.5. Advertising and GDP per capita, selected countries, 2000.

consumers . . . Firms do not advertise when they cannot differentiate their products from many competing products." In entertainment and media, such differentiation is considered to be essential by both buyers and sellers even though the effectiveness of the advertising in terms of costs incurred versus benefits attained is not always clear.

Although the same basic principles apply everywhere, different countries and cultures have developed their media industries differently, which means that the intensity of advertising on a per capita basis is not the same everywhere. A comparison of GDP per capita as measured against per capita spending on advertising is shown in Figure 2.5, and representative advertising-to-sales ratios for selected items appear in Figure 2.6. As per Motion Picture Association of America (MPAA) data, movies here have the high

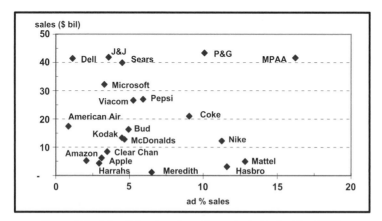

Figure 2.6. Advertising-to-sales ratios, selected industries, 2004.

*A/S* ratio that characterizes star-branded and time-perishable products and services.

Advertising is generally seen as a barrier to market entry by new competitors, who must devote a relatively high proportion of sales to advertising merely to gain name recognition and attention to new products. The optimal proportion of sales that should be spent on advertising, however, is a central question for all firms, whether old or new. Yet it is difficult to implement in practice the formal theoretical approach to finding the optimal monopoly *A/S* ratio that was first developed by Dorfman and Steiner (1954).[27] The model shows that the ratio of advertising expenditures to revenues, known as the advertising intensity, must equal the ratio of elasticities of demand with respect to advertising and price. Symbolically,

$$kA/S = \varepsilon_a/\varepsilon_p,$$

where $k$ is a constant, $\varepsilon_a$ is elasticity of demand with respect to advertising, and $\varepsilon_p$ is elasticity with respect to price.

## 2.4 Concluding remarks

Media and entertainment industry segment operations are all guided by the simple but usually unstated rules initially formulated by Marshall McLuhan; by the imperatives of a network economy now amplified in its effect on profits, culture, and society through growth of the Internet; and by a common need to buy and/or sell advertising. As such, distribution is at least as important as content, though content is what receives the most attention.

We have already seen enough of the Internet to recognize that it is, in many ways, often as disruptive as it is supportive and expansive. The benefits extend primarily from the ability of the Internet to transmit existing libraries of films, television programs, games, written materials, and music into new markets and to change them into new forms. Yet, the more bandwidth availability expands, the more the Net has the ability to upend traditional business models, changing customer relationships in terms of distribution structure, pricing, convenience, advertising, and fees.

The Internet is also still evolving in ways that are not entirely understood or predictable. A not fully comparable but similar situation involved the development of television in the 1920s and 1930s. In those early days, television could be described only as a radio service with pictures. After all these years, we now know that the influence and reach of television and its impact on society and on our collective psyche has been much greater than what a mere radio-with-pictures description would suggest. The impact of the Internet has already been at least as profound.

# Notes

**1.** An example of *reversal* given by McLuhan and McLuhan (1988, pp. 107–109) includes the change of the country, which used to be the center of all work, into a place of leisure and recreation, and vice versa for cities. More recently, cable companies are turning into telephone companies, while telephone companies are providing cable services. Perhaps the best example is that telephone service used to be exclusively by wire and broadcasting over the air. These days telephony is increasingly provided by wireless means and broadcasting delivery is increasingly by wire (cable). As noted, the network (Internet) has become a computer, and computers have become the network. Kelly (1998, p. 76) notes that a "car becomes not wheels with chips, but a chip with wheels."

**2.** For example, Marks (2002) and also Isenberg (2005) note that Broadway producers now turn increasingly to movies for familiar source material and Nussenbaum (2003) describes how toy product brands are the basis for movies.

**3.** Each fragment appeals to ever-smaller slivers; for example, horror films become horror films for teens, or in magazines, there might be titles targeted at gardening for people over 50 and some for people under 50. In cable, there are now more than 300 special-interest networks. And in books, there might be hundreds of variations on different diet segments. Once fragmentation is no longer seen to be a profitable strategy, a reversal occurs as survival then requires again appealing to a larger audience. Martin (2004) writes that, to remain profitable, many niche cable channels have begun to program for more general-interest audience preferences.

**4.** The first *Star Trek* film or television show is, for instance, new, fresh, and exciting. But by the time the $n$th version in the series or the $m$th imitation or clone appears, the energy of the original concept has been fully dissipated: Instead of a tight, unifying concept, we are left with an indistinguishable disordered mass (and mess).

**5.** Entropy also is a sometimes confusingly used term in communications theory as developed by Shannon and Weaver (1949) and described in Pierce (1980, p. 80). In communications theory, the entropy measure is described by the equation $H = -k\Sigma_i p_i \log p_i$, in which $k$ is a constant (equal to 1) and $p_i$ may represent ordinary, joint, or conditional (marginal) probabilities of selecting one item out of a large sample of similar items.

**6.** This rule was first noted in the Manager's column of the *Wall Street Journal* of March 30, 2004 by D. Tapscott.

**7.** The value of self-produced programming can be enhanced if there is also ready access to distribution. The relevance of content to distribution and vice versa was underscored by the March 2004 dispute between EchoStar and Viacom. EchoStar resisted demands by Viacom for price increases and bundling of additional carriage of new, unproven channels. For part of a week, EchoStar did not show Viacom's CBS station and cable (e.g., MTV, Nickelodeon) programs. The circumstances and results were similar to those played out in May 2000, when Time Warner dropped Disney's ABC signals from its cable systems and bore the brunt of public and political wrath. Disney had pressed Time Warner for carriage of new cable networks in return for what are called retransmission rights. In each situation, the distributor was trying to keep prices down and retain channel space for carriage of smaller independent programming producers but was largely blamed for the problem. See *Wall Street Journal*, March 10, 2004, and *New York Times*, May 2, 2000.

**8.** The law is named after Robert Metcalfe, one of the Internet and Ethernet engineering pioneers.

**9.** The only cautionary aspect is that for small $N$, the cost of maintaining a network usually exceeds its value and a critical mass must be reached if the network is to succeed in the long run. Network effects are most visible in the establishment of services such as those enabling e-mail, auctions, instant messaging, and chat rooms. Also, as Huberman (2001, p. 25) notes, "distributions describing patterns observed on the Web have a particular form, called a power law . . . The probability of finding a Web site with a given number of pages, $n$, is proportional to $1/n_B$, where $B$ is a number greater than or equal to 1." Kelly (1998, p. 32 and p. 115) has, in addition, noted that in a network economy, knowledge is substituted for materials, the prosperity of a firm depends on the prosperity of its network, and the more plentiful things become, the more valuable they become.

**10.** Using concepts of game theory, Shy (2001, pp. 136–159) further describes how and why broadcast and cable industries and viewers respond to various aspects of deregulation and competition.

**11.** The underlying software linkages of the Internet began to develop in the 1960s, when scientists at the Pentagon's Defense Advanced Research Projects Agency (DARPA), now ARPA, sought to build a communications network that would enable different kinds of computers running different software systems to exchange information with each other. The first "node" in the network was installed at UCLA in 1969 by Bolt, Beranek, & Newman (now BBN Corp.), and by 1975, about 100 such nodes linking research centers and government facilities had been established around the world. Meanwhile, significant advances in signal compression algorithms (mathematical formulas for manipulating data) were being incorporated into the software of signal-transmission systems.

The pace of development, though, has always been ultimately tied to progress in the design and production of hardware in the form of microprocessor chips and memory storage devices. And throughout the 1980s and 1990s, hardware speed and efficiency rose rapidly even as unit prices fell dramatically; the functionality of a 1970s-era room-sized computer that cost $1 million could be replicated a decade later in a desktop unit costing only a few thousand dollars. In all, the underlying technological concepts driving the Internet's growth might be summarized as (a) the network is the computer; (b) computing power doubles every 18 months (Moore's law); (c) bandwidth, a measure of how many bits per second can be transmitted, is doubling every year; and (d) the bandwidth capacity of fiber approaches infinity. By 1985, these developments in both software and hardware had enabled the National Science Foundation to create a high-speed, long-distance artery – the network's "backbone" – and to supplant the original military network. However, by 1995, the NSF backbone was replaced by services operated primarily by seven companies. The World Wide Web, developed by British scientist Tim Berners-Lee in 1991, then allowed researchers to readily swap images instead of just messages. Images were the key to unlocking the power of the Internet. See also Ziegler (1996). Despite an early ban on them, commercial Internet services quickly emerged. The catalyst for commercial use was the development of effective "browser" software exemplified by the Mosaic program that was nurtured and distributed for free by the University of Illinois. And by the late 1990s, the Internet had already evolved into a low-cost mass communications medium that empowered anyone to instantly relay – anywhere around the world – words, moving pictures, music, computer software, and anything else that can be digitized. As noted by Anderson (2004), this opens the way for older, archived art, films, music, books, and so on to be remixed and changed into new products. Thus instead of the usual brief shelf life of even the most highly visible and successful productions, a longer tail of usage and economic value develops.

**12.** The long-tail concept was popularized by Anderson (2004, 2006) and implies that in movies, books, music, and other such items, the pre-Internet concept that 80% of the sales are generated by 20% of the items is no longer valid. On the Web it is just as profitable to download any movie or book or piece of music as any other because there is no physical inventory required beyond the one copy. That is not the case, say, at the local cinema or at Wal-Mart, where the titles displayed are only those likely to be selected by a mass audience. This thus makes for a long tail of demand in which even old and obscure titles can now be made readily available without penalizing profitability. See also Gomes (2006).

**13.** The downloading of films via the Internet to digital projectors in theaters eliminates the costs of handling reels of film. Progress in this direction as of 2005 is reviewed in McBride (2005a) and financing in Verrier (2006a). Traditional video stores are being rendered obsolete as true video-on-demand distribution of any film, anytime, anywhere becomes ever less expensive and more technologically feasible.

The first Internet-based video-on-demand services supported by the major studios began to be made available in late 2002 with the introduction of Movielink, owned by Sony, Warner, Paramount, Universal, and MGM. The service allows features to be downloaded for a cost to the viewer ranging between $1.99 and $4.99 for 24-hour availability, but had not gained wide support in its first years. Starz Entertainment Group introduced Vongo, a service that for $9.99 a month allows subscribers to view around 850 films as many times as wanted until the subscription expires or the available titles are rotated out of the roster. This was the first service making recent (one-year delayed) mainstream films available on a flat-rate subscription plan over the Internet. In 2006 Movielink began to allow downloads that enable consumers to own copies of the films, whereas before it was rental only. CinemaNow, a competitor, has done the same with films from Sony and Lionsgate. Newer releases on Movielink are priced at between $20 and $30, with older catalog titles, $10 to $16. A 2006 agreement between BitTorrent and Warner Bros. that makes 200 digitally encrypted films available online the same day the DVD is released may also be significant. See also McBride (2006), Hansell (2004), Colker (2006), and Fritz and Snyder (2006).

Internet program distribution is covered in Grant (2006) with a focus on Brightcove, whose technology enables producers of any size to distribute videos through any number of Web sites. The basic business model is that Brightcove, the producers, and the sites share revenues from advertising and/or sales. The commercials appear before the videos are played. If the video content is to be sold without advertising, Brightcove shares the revenues thus generated.

Harmon (2003) discusses the digital distribution restrictions being technologically placed on movies and television shows. And Grant and Orwall (2003) discuss the growth of broadband availability. It should be noted, too, that the Internet seems to reduce time spent in watching movies or television programming through traditional means. A Stanford University survey suggested that 60% of regular Internet users reduced television viewing, and 33% said they spent less time reading newspapers. See Markoff (2000, 2004).

In cable, the Internet has become the catalyst for growth and consolidation and widespread installation of digital signal delivery devices (in set-top boxes and cable modems). Meanwhile, it is not at all clear that television viewing – the original raison d'être of the cable business – will be sustained near previous levels. Traditional broadcast industry reliance on the placement of television and radio programs into specifically designated time slots and dayparts will also have to be modified as audiences obtain greater flexibility in electing where and through which medium they watch or listen. Audience viewing and listening patterns thus are not as easily controlled or measured as in the past.

Music has been in even more turmoil given that it is the easiest to download with currently available technology. The major distribution companies are just beginning to develop standards and procedures on how best to charge for music sold over the Internet and on how to protect against "piracy" of intellectual property rights (which in noncommercial instances often is more accurately described as free-ridership). The Net also effectively allows artists to function as labels, which means that artists can bypass the major record distribution companies and the onerous contracts that artists are often forced to accept in return for distribution services.

The changes are just as great in all corners of the publishing businesses. In books, authors, like musicians, may now have an option to bypass the large publishing distributors. On the newspaper and magazine fronts, highly profitable classified advertising is meanwhile being supplanted by online classifieds even as Internet companies are creating a large new category of demand for advertising in these traditional media. See also *BusinessWeek*, May 2, 2005.

And in games it is now not unusual to play with a cyberspace partner halfway across the world. While the local arcade can benefit from downloads of new games into existing video cabinet circuits, the video arcade industry's growth may be slowed as the ability of the Internet to deliver high-quality games to the at-home market increases. The Internet has also shifted the preferences of toy and game buyers toward computer-related items.

Although wagering over the Internet is still ambiguously illegal in the United States, many fully operational, internationally based Internet gaming and wagering sites already exist. Such sites may ultimately call into question the need for construction of more local casino properties even while the sites expand the total worldwide amount spent on gaming and wagering activities. In the closely related hotel and airline businesses that feed casino-hotel traffic, the flow of bookings and control of prices has already, to an extent, been unwillingly surrendered to new online distribution wholesalers like InterActiveCorp. See Mullaney and Grover (2003).

**14.** Measures of effectiveness of Internet ads similar to those used in traditional broadcast and print media (e.g., reach, frequency, gross ratings points, circulation, demographic spread, and cost per thousand) have only recently begun to be established. Meanwhile, evolution of legal and technological standards continues for Internet distribution rights and for webcasting, which uses software to automatically organize advertiser-supported content into channels selected by viewers. See Gaither (2006).

Unlike the situation in broadcasting, Internet advertising space is theoretically unlimited. However, inventory on the most popular branded Web entry points, the so-called portals, nonetheless commands premium pricing for the traffic attracted. Advertisers would pay more for an ad on a World Wide Web (i.e., graphical/multimedia) site that must be "clicked through" than for one that only appears as a banner on a page that is merely "hit."

Advertising on the Net, as noted in *BusinessWeek* of March 27, 2006, is divided into two general categories: search term related, such as in the Google model, and banner ads, as might be found on a portal such as Yahoo or MSN. As of 2006, a banner on a leading portal might cost around $500,000 for a day, which is comparable to the cost of a 30-second spot on a popular network television series. On search advertising, of the average of 35 cents a click that advertisers might for example pay, Yahoo might retain at least 21 cents. Audits by third-party firms such as Nielsen's NetRatings or comScore Networks enable advertisers to analyze reach, Web site visits per month, visit length, visits by day, week, or time of day, number of unique visitors, etc. Such information is essential to building advertising activity. For ads that appear each time a search engine like Google finds key words, the price in 2004 might have averaged around 40 cents per click-through. See also Wingfield (1999), Delaney (2004), and *BusinessWeek* of March 24, 2003.

**15.** Subscription (or membership), transaction, and other fees are significant sources of revenue for many Internet companies. While transaction fees normally amount to at most 2% to 5% of the price of an item sold, other fees, such as those for links to other sites or for listing, would usually be scaled to the perceived value of the services provided. The mix of fee versus advertising income will vary not only with the type of Internet services a company provides but also with the company's stage of development (i.e., maturity) and strength of brand identity.

In all, the Internet's ability to generate revenues from a mix of advertising, service subscription fees, and potential participations in online sales has turned it into an important direct-marketing and program distribution medium with companies specializing in categories that include business services, e-services, marketplaces, portals, and retailers. As such, the Web has become an integral and unexceptional part of most business-to-business transactions.

**16.** This is noted in Lev (2000a, 2000b). Accounting controversies for most Internet companies begin at the top line where, as Kahn (2000) notes, firms report "the entire sales price a customer pays at their site when in fact the company keeps only a small percentage of that amount." In fact, such reported figures are more akin to gross bookings by travel agents or to the total amount bet at a casino's table games (handle) than to actual revenues generated through exchange of goods and services for hard currency. See also Porter (2001) and Thurm and Delaney (2004).

**17.** Revenue-recognition problems often involve barter, which for old-media companies might typically amount to 5% of total sales but for new-media companies might be as much as 50%. Although barter helps build brand awareness and conserves cash, by its nature it cannot directly contribute to coverage of everyday out-of-pocket cash expenses such as employee salaries, rent, insurance, and so forth. The Financial Accounting Standards Board's Emerging Issues Task Force (EITF) has proposed that advertising should be counted as revenue only when a company has an established history of earning cash for the same space that is being bartered.

Internet company offerings of coupons and discounts may, moreover, cause classifications of revenues and costs to be confused, much in the same way that this often occurs in movie industry accounting. For instance, it is possible to book a full, undiscounted price as revenues and to then take a charge for discounts as marketing expenses. A more conservative approach would be simply to book the discounted price as revenues (with no charge for marketing expenses), but that would, of course, make revenues appear to be smaller.

The timing of recognition for various expenses is more routine, yet also an issue. Should, for example, product shipment fulfillment costs (involving warehousing, packaging, and shipping) be considered as part of a company's long-run cost structure (which would reduce reported gross margins) or as a mere period marketing expense? Should customer acquisition costs be amortized over several years or be expensed immediately?

**18.** As noted in Ip (1999), Internet stocks appear to adhere to a downward-sloping trendline if size of capitalization in dollars (*y*-axis) and rank of size (*x*-axis) are both placed on logarithmic scales. This suggests option-like characteristics. If the company begins to lose financial backing and fails, the option is worthless, but if the company begins to succeed on a financial basis, the value of the option accelerates upward. With valuations largely dependent on perceived growth potential, one relatively simple way to estimate the option values attributable to new companies is to derive a ratio of total invested capital (TIC) – that is, market value of equity (shares outstanding times price per share) plus debt – to sales. Then apply this ratio to a current sales estimate for the new media company.

For example, assume that the total invested capital-to-sales ratio of a traditional retailer is 3:1. If there were no growth expectations above those of the traditional retailer, the estimated value of an early-stage company with no debt and annual sales of $10 million would be $30 million. However, the market may price the equity at $100 million, thereby suggesting that the option value of the young company's growth opportunities is worth $70 million more. The reality of growth assumptions can be assessed by comparing company revenues estimated a few years into the future against the projected size of the related industry at that time.

**19.** For instance, two companies begin with $1 million in earnings and want to grow by 20%. The one with an ROIC of 10% would have to invest an additional $2 million, while the one with an ROIC of 40% would require only $500,000. Investors will naturally pay a premium valuation for such relatively cheap growth (i.e., efficient use of capital), and it is then the analyst's function to make a determination, on the basis of competitive conditions, rates of technological change, and other elements, as to how large this premium ought to be. The market usually gets it right over the long run but not necessarily so in the short run.

Another approach that has intuitive appeal is to take the overall market's estimated price-to-earnings (P/E) ratio as a base from which projected P/E ratios for faster-than-average growth companies may be calculated. For instance, using standard finance models, the P/E ratio for the Standard & Poor's 500 index might be estimated as

$$\text{S\&P market}\, P/E = \frac{\text{dividend payout ratio}}{(\text{equity discount rate} - \text{earnings growth rate})}.$$

For the market as a whole, the dividend payout for the S&P 500 companies is approximately 40%, and the earnings growth rate might be 6% while the discount rate is 8%. The estimated market P/E ratio would then be $0.4/(0.08 - 0.06) = 20$. The next step is to calculate an earnings payback period over which $1 of current earnings will *sum* to $20. At a growth rate of 6%, that requires approximately 13 years. However, should the growth rate of the company in question be 20% instead of 6%, in 13 years, the sum of $1 of original investment will be $54. This suggests that the appropriate estimated P/E multiple for the faster-growing company ought to be 54. But then further adjustments for volatility would have to be made: Those companies with greater than average volatility of returns (i.e., riskiness) should normally have a lower P/E, and vice versa.

Another comparison is enterprise value (EV is stock market capitalization, i.e., share price times number of shares outstanding, plus net debt) divided by total revenues (TR). Usually, high EV/TR ratios relative to other similar companies (and to the same ratio for the whole market as measured by the S&P 500) would suggest that the shares in question might be too high in price.

A more informal approach that is also often used in many industries involves dividing the P/E ratio by the projected long-term growth rate of earnings (G). Such so-called PEG ratios may then be used to derive a sense of relative valuations within an industry group. For example, shares of a company sporting, say, a P/E ratio of 30 but growing by more than 30% (i.e., a PEG ratio below 1.0) might be attractively priced for purchase as compared with a similar company with a PEG ratio significantly above 1.0.

**20.** Still, all of these methodologies are just roundabout ways to define future cash flows and to attach a probability that such estimated cash flows will be realized at some point in the future. The cash flows that will be discounted back to determine present value, the discounted cash flows (DCFs), are simply probability weighted and are what statisticians call an *expected value*. If, for instance, in five years there is a 20% probability that the cash flow of an enterprise will be $2 million, a 30% probability that it will be $10 million, and a 50% probability that it will be $7 million, the expected value of the future cash flow that is to be discounted is $0.2 \times 2 + 0.3 \times 10 + 0.5 \times 7 = \$6.9$ million. As such, even small changes in probability estimates and discount rates (which are relatively high because of the inherently higher risks incurred with investments in new, untested companies) lead to large and rapid changes (volatility) in present-value estimates and thus in the share prices of publicly traded companies.

**21.** This approach is more fully developed in Greenwald *et al.* (2001).

**22.** The advertising time series is cointegrated with the PCE time series. However, which causes which is an open question. That is, does advertising cause PCEs to rise or is it that rising PCEs lead to higher corporate profits and thus more advertising? See also Gertner (2005).

**23.** Advertising goes back a long time in human history. Merchants in ancient Rome, for example, had street signs advertising their wares. The main advances, however, came with the invention of the printing press, which enabled handbills and circulars and later newspapers to be readily printed, and with the rise of broadcast technologies in the early twentieth century. N. W. Ayer & Son, founded in Philadelphia in 1869, was one of the first agencies to define precise financial terms between advertisers and publishers and to establish set percentage fees for the agency's services. At around the same time, J. Walter Thompson began to use advertisements in magazines. Nevertheless, it was the rise of broadcast media, especially radio in the 1920s that carried the advertising industry into its heyday and made it central to the operations of so many different industries, including everything from cereals and soaps, to cars, clothing, and beer, and to the whole gamut of entertainment products and services. By the late 1930s, radio advertising accounted for more than one-third of top agency billings. And starting in the 1950s, television advertising began its rise to prominence, surpassing newspaper advertising dollar volume by 1994. Internet advertising then began to take significant share away from more traditional media beginning around the year 2000. As shown in Chapter 7 (Figure 7.2), advertising expenditure on a global basis now amounts to nearly $500 billion, with spending in the United States accounting for some 45% of the total.

There are currently more than 21,000 advertising establishments in the United States, with some 6 out of 10 writing, copying, or preparing artwork, graphics, and other creative works.

**24.** As Wassily Leontief said at a 1973 press conference after the announcement of his Nobel Laureate for development of I/O concepts, "When you make bread, you need eggs, flour, and milk. And if you want more bread, you must use more eggs. There are cooking recipes for all the industries in the economy" (Harvard University *Gazette*, February 11, 1999).

**25.** Think, for example, in terms of a movie or theme park attraction that costs $100 million to make or build. Each additional unit sold in the form of a theater or park admission ticket has virtually *zero* incremental cost except for the advertising needed to bring another person through the turnstile. This would hardly describe the situation for manufactured products like cars, which though relying heavily on advertising, also incur high costs of incremental materials and labor for each unit made.

**26.** As Bagwell (2001) summarizes, studies of the 1970s generally concluded that (a) advertising is associated with an increase in sales, but the effect is short-lived; (b) advertising is combative in nature; and (c) the effect on demand is difficult to assess and differs across industries. Also, while the evidence suggests that retail advertising leads to lower retail prices, the evidence concerning the association between advertising and ease of entry is mixed. The informative view of advertising appears to be relevant for sets of frequently purchased consumer goods (e.g., gas, milk, sodas, and tissues), especially those for which experience is an important determinant of purchase behavior.

**27.** This advertising intensity model is described in Bagwell (2005). Elasticity estimates, as first presented in Chapter 1, are the first step in applying the theory. An advertising elasticity measure, $\varepsilon_a$, estimates the percent change of sales to the percent change in advertising expenditures. A second measure, price elasticity of demand, $\varepsilon_p$, represents the percent change in sales to the percent change in price. This model shows that it makes sense to increase spending on advertising as long as the sales gain from doing this is greater than the sales to be gained if such spending were to instead be used for price reductions.

## Selected additional reading

Abbate, J. (1999). *Inventing the Internet*. Cambridge, MA: MIT Press.

Altman, D. (2002). "Is the P/E Ratio Becoming Irrelevant?," *New York Times*, July 21.

Anders, G. (1999a). "Eager to Boost Traffic, More Internet Firms Give Away Services," *Wall Street Journal*, July 28.

(1999b). "The Race for 'Sticky' Web Sites," *Wall Street Journal*, February 11.

Anderson, C. (2003). "Wi-Fi Revolution," *Wired*, Special Report.

Baker, S. (2004). "The Online Ad Surge," *BusinessWeek*, November 22.

Baker, S., and Green, H. (2005). "Blogs Will Change Your Business," *BusinessWeek*, May 2.

Bane, P. W., and Bradley, S. P. (1999). "The Light at the End of the Pipe," *Scientific American*, October.

Bank, D. (1996). "How Net Is Becoming More Like Television to Draw Advertisers," *Wall Street Journal*, December 13.

Barfield, C. E., Heiduk, G., and Welfens, P. J. J., eds. (2003). *Internet, Economic Growth and Glatization: Perspectives on the New Economy in Europe, Japan, and the USA*. Berlin: Springer-Verlag.

Berners-Lee, T., and Fischetti, M. (1999). *Weaving the Web*. New York: HarperCollins.

Bianco, A. (2004). "The Vanishing Mass Market," *BusinessWeek*, July 12.

"Business and the Internet Survey," *The Economist*, June 26, 1999.

Cassidy, J. (2002). *Dot.Con: The Greatest Story Ever Sold*. New York: HarperCollins.

Cauley, L. (2000). "Heavy Traffic Is Overloading Cable Companies' New Internet Lines," *Wall Street Journal*, March 16.

Clark, D. (1997). "Facing Early Losses, Some Web Publishers Begin to Pull the Plug," *Wall Street Journal*, January 14.

Copeland, T., Koller, T., Murrin, J., and McKinsey & Co. (2000). *Valuation: Measuring and Valuing the Value of Companies*, 3rd ed. New York: John Wiley & Sons.

Cortese, A. (1997). "A Way Out of the Web Maze," *BusinessWeek*, no. 3515, February 24.

Cukier, K. N. (2000). "The Big Gamble," *Red Herring*, April.

Dejesus, E. X. (1996). "How the Internet Will Replace Broadcasting," *Byte*, February.

Delaney, K. J. (2006a). "Once-Wary Industry Giants Embrace Internet Advertising," *Wall Street Journal*, April 17.

(2006b). "In Latest Deal, Google Steps Further into World of Old Media," *Wall Street Journal*, January 18.

(2005a). "In 'Click Fraud,' Web Outfits Have a Costly Problem," *Wall Street Journal*, April 6.

(2005b). "In Hunt for Online Advertising, Yahoo Makes Big Bet on Media," *Wall Street Journal*, March 1.

(2004). "Ads in Videogames Pose a New Threat to Media Industry," *Wall Street Journal*, July 28.

Delaney, K. J., and Barnes, B. (2005). "For Soaring Google, Next Act Won't Be as Easy as the First," *Wall Street Journal*, June 30.

Downes, L., and Mui, C. (1998). *Unleashing the Killer App*. Boston: Harvard Business School Press.

"E-Commerce Takes Off," *The Economist*, May 15, 2004.

Flynn, L. J. (1999). "Battle Begun on Internet Ad Blocking," *New York Times*, June 7.

Grover, R., and Green, H. (2003). "Hollywood Heist: Will Tinseltown Let Techies Steal the Show?," *BusinessWeek*, no. 3841, July 14.

Grow, B., and Elgin, E. (2006). "Click Fraud: The Dark Side of Online Advertising," *BusinessWeek*, October 2.

Gunther, M. (2001). "The Cheering Fades for Yahoo," *Fortune*, 144(9) (November 12).

(1999). "The Trouble with Web Advertising," *Fortune*, 139(7) (April 12).

(1998). "The Internet Is Mr. Case's Neighborhood," *Fortune*, 137(6)(March 30).

Hafner, K., and Lyon, M. (1996). *Where Wizards Stay Up Late: The Origins of the Internet*. New York: Simon & Schuster.

Hagerty, J. R., and Berman, D. K. (2003). "New Battleground over Web Privacy: Ads That Snoop," *Wall Street Journal*, August 27.

Hansell, S. (2006). "As Internet TV Aims at Niche Audiences, the Slivercast Is Born," *New York Times*, March 12.

(2005). "It's Not TV, It's Yahoo," *New York Times*, September 24.

(1999). "Now, AOL Everywhere," *New York Times*, July 4.

Hansell, S., and Harmon, A. (1999). "Caveat Emptor on the Web: Ad and Editorial Lines Blur," *New York Times*, February 26.

Hardy, Q. (2003). "All Eyes on Google," *Forbes*, 171(11) (May 26).

Hoskins, C., McFadyen, S., and Finn, A. (2004). *Media Economics*. Thousand Oaks, CA: Sage.

Hwang, S., and Mangalindan, M. (2000). "Yahoo's Grand Vision for Web Advertising Takes Some Hard Hits," *Wall Street Journal*, September 1.

"Keep It Simple: Survey of Information Technology," *The Economist*, October 30, 2004.

Kenner, R. (1999). "MyHollywood!," *Wired*, October.

Knecht, G. B. (1996a). "Microsoft Puts Newspapers in Highanxiety.com," *Wall Street Journal*, July 15.

(1996b). "How Wall Street Whiz Found a Niche Selling Books on the Internet," *Wall Street Journal*, May 16.

La Franco, R. (2000). "Faces of a New Hollywood?," *Red Herring*, April.

LaPlante, A., and Seidner, R. (1999). *Playing for Profit: How Digital Entertainment Is Making Big Business out of Child's Play*. New York: Wiley/Upside.

Lohr, S. (2005). "Just Googling It Is Striking Fear into Companies," *New York Times*, November 6.

Lyons, D. (1999). "Desperate.com," *Forbes*, 163(6) (March 22).

Mahar, M. (1995). "Caught in the 'Net,'" *Barron's*, December 25.

Mangalindan, M., Wingfield, N., and Guth, R. A. (2003). "Rising Clout of Google Prompts Rush by Internet Rivals to Adapt," *Wall Street Journal*, July 16.

Manly, L. (2005). "The Future of the 30-Second Spot," *New York Times*, March 27.

Markoff, J. (2000). "The Soul of the Ultimate Machine," *New York Times*, December 10.

Markoff, J., and Zachary, G. P. (2003). "In Searching the Web, Google Finds Riches," *New York Times*, April 13.

McKnight, L. W., and Bailey, J. P., eds. (1997). *Internet Economics*. Cambridge, MA: MIT Press.

McLuhan, E., and Zingrone, F., eds. (1995). *Essential McLuhan*. New York: Basic Books (HarperCollins).

McLuhan, M., and Powers, B. R. (1989). *The Global Village*. New York: Oxford University Press.

Mehta, S. N. (2005). "How the Web Will Save the Commercial," *Fortune*, 152(3)(August 8).

Motavalli, J. (2002). *Bamboozled at the Revolution: How Big Media Lost Billions in the Battle for the Internet*. New York: Viking.

Mullaney, T. J. (2003). "The E-Biz Surprise," *BusinessWeek*, May 12.

Noam, E., Groebel, J., and Gerbarg, D., eds. (2004). *Internet Television*. Mahwah, NJ: Lawrence Erlbaum Associates.

Nocera, J. (1999). "Do You Believe?: How Yahoo! Became a Blue Chip," *Fortune*, 139(11)(June 7).

Nocera, J., and Elkind, P. (1998). "The Buzz Factory," *Fortune*, 138(2)(July 20).

Orwall, B., and Swisher, K. (1999). "As Web Riches Beckon, Disney Ranks Become a Poacher's Paradise," *Wall Street Journal*, June 9.

Owen, B. (1999). *The Internet Challenge to Television*. Cambridge, MA: Harvard University Press.

Perkins, M. C., and Perkins, A. B. (1999). *The Internet Bubble*. New York: HarperCollins.

Port, O. (2002). "The Next Web," *BusinessWeek*, March 4.

Reid, R. H. (1997). *Architects of the Web*. New York: Wiley.

Roth, D. (2005). "Torrential Reign," *Fortune*, 152(9)(October 31).

Savitz, E. J. (2005). "Gone Digital," *Barron's*, March 7.

Schwartz, E. S., and Moon, M. (2000). "Rational Pricing of Internet Companies," *Financial Analysts Journal*, 53(3) (May/June).

Searcey, D., and Schatz, A. (2006). "Phone Companies Set Off a Battle over Internet Fees," *Wall Street Journal*, January 6.

Segaller, S. (1999). *Nerds 2.0.1: A Brief History of the Internet*. New York: TV Books.

"Shopping around the Web: A Survey of e-Commerce," *The Economist*, February 26, 2000.

Stille, A. (2000). "Marshall McLuhan Is Back from the Dustbin of History," *New York Times*, October 14.

Stross, R. E. (2006). "Hey, Baby Bells: Information Still Wants to Be Free," *New York Times*, January 15.

    (1998). "How Yahoo! Won the Search Wars," *Fortune*, 137(4)(March 2).

"Thrills and Spills: A Survey of e-Entertainment," *The Economist*, October 7, 2000.

Totty, M., and Mangalindan, M. (2003). "As Google Becomes Web's Gatekeeper, Sites Fight to Get In," *Wall Street Journal*, February 26.

Vogelstein, F. (2005a). "Yahoo's Brilliant Solution," *Fortune*, 152(3) (August 8).

    (2005b). "Search and Destroy," *Fortune*, 151(9) (May 2).

    (2004). "Google @ $165: Are These Guys for Real?," *Fortune*, 150(12) (December 13).

    (2003a). "Can Google Grow Up?," *Fortune*, 148(12) (December 8).

    (2003b). "Mighty Amazon," *Fortune*, 147(10) (May 26).

Wiggins, R. (1996). "How the Internet Works," *Internet World* (October).

Wingfield, N. (2005). "Web's Addictive Neopets Are Ready for Big Career Leap," *Wall Street Journal*, February 21.

Wiseman, A. E. (2000). *The Internet Economy: Access, Taxes, and Market Structure*. Washington, DC: Brookings Institution.

Woolley, S. (2006). "Video Fixation," *Forbes*, 178(8) (October 16).

# Part II
## Media-dependent entertainment

# 3
# Movie macroeconomics

*You oughta be in pictures!*

A more appealing pitch to investors would be hard to find. Many people imagine that nothing could be more fun and potentially more lucrative than making movies. After all, in its first four years, *Star Wars* returned profits of over $150 million on an initial investment of $11 million (and many millions more on re-release 20 years later). Nonetheless, ego gratification rather than money may often be the only return on an investment in film. As in other endeavors, what you see is not always what you get. In fact, of any ten major theatrical films produced, on the average, six or seven may be broadly characterized as unprofitable and one might break even. Still, as we shall soon discover, there are many reasons why such characterizations must be applied with care and why the success ratio for studio/distributors is considerably better than for individual participants.

Be that as it may, moviemaking is still truly entrepreneurial: It is often a triumph of hope over reality, where defeat can easily be snatched from the jaws of victory. But its magical, mystical elements notwithstanding, it is also a business, affected as any other by basic economic principles.

This chapter is concerned with macroeconomic trends and movie asset valuations; the next two chapters deal with issues of operational structure, accounting, and television-related microeconomics.

## 3.1 Flickering images

Snuggled comfortably in the seat of your local theater or, as is increasingly likely, in front of the screen attached to your home video exhibition device, you are transported far away by your imagination as you watch – a movie. Of course, not all movies have the substance and style to accomplish this incredible feat of emotional transportation, but a surprising number of them do. In any case, what is seen on the screen is there because of a remarkable history of tumultuous development that is still largely in progress.

Putting pictures on a strip of film that moved was not a unique or new idea among photographers of the late nineteenth century. As noted by Margolies and Gwathmey (1991, p. 9), it was by then already known that the way we see film move is an optical illusion based upon the eye's persistence of vision; an image is retained for a fraction of a second longer than it actually appears. But the man who synthesized it all into a workable invention was Thomas Edison. By the early 1890s, Edison and his main assistant, William Dickson, had succeeded in perfecting a camera ("Kinetograph") that was capable of photographing objects in motion. Soon thereafter, the first motion picture studio was formed to manufacture "Kinetoscopes" at Edison's laboratory in West Orange, New Jersey. These first primitive movies – continually looping filmstrips viewed through a peephole machine – were then shown at a "Kinetoscope Parlor" on lower Broadway in New York, where crowds formed to see this most amazing novelty.

The technological evolution of cameras, films, and projection equipment accelerated considerably at this stage. In Europe, for instance, full-time cinemas proliferated in London after 1906 and France reigned powerfully in the initial growth of all global film industry segments.[1] And everywhere entrepreneurs were quick to grasp the money-making potential in showing films to the public.

The early years in the United States, though, were marked by a series of patent infringement suits and attempts at monopolization that were to characterize the industry's internal relations for a long time. As Stanley (1978, p. 10) notes:

Movies were being shown in thousands of theaters around the country . . . After years of patent disputes, the major movie companies realized it was to their mutual advantage to cooperate . . . A complex natural monopoly over almost all phases of the nascent motion picture industry was organized in December 1908. It was called the Motion Picture Patents Company.

This company held pooled patents for films, cameras, and projectors, and apportioned royalties on the patents. It also attempted to control the industry by buying up most of the major film exchanges (distributors) then in existence, with the goal of organizing them into a massive rental exchange, the General Film Company.[2]

The Patents Company and its distribution subsidiary (together known as the "Trust") often engaged in crude and oppressive business practices that fostered great resentment and discontent. However, eventually the Trust was overwhelmed by the growing numbers, and by the increasing market power, of the independents that sprang up in all areas of production, distribution, and exhibition (i.e., theaters). The Trust's control of the industry, for example, was undermined by the many "independent" producers who would use the Patent Company's machines, without authorization, on film stock that was imported. Yet more significantly, it was from within the ranks of these very independents that there emerged the founders of companies that were later to become Hollywood's giants: Carl Laemmle, credited with starting the star system and founder of Universal; William Fox, founder of the Fox Film Company, which was combined in 1935 with Twentieth Century Pictures; Adolph Zukor, who came to dominate Paramount Pictures; and Marcus Loew, who in the early 1920s assembled two failing companies (Metro Pictures and Goldwyn Pictures) to form the core of MGM.

At around the same time, there began a distinct movement of production activity to the West Coast. Southern California was not only far for the Trust enforcers to reach, but it could also provide low-cost nonunion labor and an advantageous climate and geography for filming. By the mid-1920s, most production in these film "factories" had thus shifted to the West, although New York retained its importance as the industry's financial seat.

Hollywood had also by this time begun to dominate the world cinema, competing effectively against filmmakers in Europe, especially those in England and France. As Trumpbour (2002, pp. 18–19) has noted, the U.S. industry exploited several advantages over its rivals: Even then it already had the world's largest domestic market composed of diversified immigrant cultures; it had a well-developed industrial organization as compared with the largely artisanal production and distribution systems in other countries; and it had an ideology of optimism and happy endings as compared with the often morose fade-outs of films made abroad.

By the late 1920s, though, the industry was shaken by the introduction of motion pictures with sound and, soon thereafter, by the Great Depression. In that time of economic collapse, the large amounts of capital required to convert to sound equipment could only be provided by the Eastern banking firms, which refinanced and reorganized the major companies. Ultimately, it was those companies with the most vertical integration (controlling production, distribution, and exhibition) that survived this period intact. Those companies were Warner Brothers, RKO, Twentieth Century Fox, Paramount, and MGM. On a lesser scale were Universal and Columbia, which were only producer-distributors, and United Artists, which was essentially a distributor. The Depression, moreover, also led to the formation of powerful unions of skilled craftsmen, talent guilds, and other institutions that now play an important role in the economics of filmmaking.

Except for their sometimes strained relations with the unions, the eight major companies came out of this period of restructuring with a degree of control over the business that the early Patents Company founders could envy, and the complaints of those harmed in such an environment began to be heard by the U.S. Department of Justice. After five years of intensive investigation, the government filed suit in 1938 against the eight companies and charged them with illegally conspiring to restrain trade by, among other things, causing an exhibitor who wanted any of a distributor's pictures to take all of them (i.e., block booking them). By agreeing to a few relatively minor restrictions in a consent decree signed in 1940, the majors were, however, able to settle the case without having to sever the link between distribution and exhibition. Because of this, five majors retained dominance in about 70% of the first-run theaters in the country.[3]

Not surprisingly, complaints persisted, and the Justice Department found it necessary to reactivate its suit against Paramount in 1944. After several more years of legal wrangling, the defendants finally agreed in 1948 to sign a decree that separated production and distribution from exhibition. It was this decree – combined with the contemporaneous emergence of television – that ushered the movie business into the modern era (Table 3.1 and Figure 3.1).

### 3.2 May the forces be with you

Evolutionary elements

The major forces shaping the structure of the movie industry have historically included (1) technological advances in the filmmaking process itself, in marketing and audience sampling methods, and in the development of distribution and data storage capabilities using television signals, cable, satellites, video recorders, computers, and laser discs; (2) the need for ever-larger pools of capital to launch motion-picture projects; (3) the 1948 consent decree separating distribution from exhibition; (4) the emergence of large multiplex theater chains in new suburban locations; and (5) the constant evolution and growth of independent production and service organizations. Each of these items will be discussed in the context of a gradually unfolding larger story.

*Technology* Unquestionably the most potent impetus for change over the long term has been, and will continue to be, the development of technology. As Fielding has observed:

If the artistic and historical development of film and television are to be understood, then so must the peculiar marriage of art and technology which prevails in their operation. It is the involvement of twentieth-century technology which renders these media so unlike the other, older arts. (Fielding 1967, p. iv)

In the filmmaking process itself, for instance, the impact of technological improvements has been phenomenal. To see how far we have come, we need only remember that "talkies" were the special-effects movies of the

Table 3.1. *Chronology of antitrust actions in the motion-picture industry,*
*1900–1999*

| | |
|---|---|
| 1908 | Motion Picture Patents Co. established; horizontal combination of ten major companies that held most of the patents in the industry; cross-licensing arrangement |
| 1910 | General Film Co. purchased 68 film exchanges (local distribution companies) (vertical integration) |
| 1914 | Five film exchanges combined as Paramount to distribute films (vertical integration) |
| 1916 | Famous Players merged with Lasky to form major studio (horizontal integration) |
| 1917 | Famous Players-Lasky acquired 12 small producers and Paramount (vertical and horizontal integration) |
| 1917 | Motion Picture Patents Co. and General Film Co. dissolved as a result of judicial decisions and innovations by independents |
| 1917 | 3,500 exhibitors became part of First National Exhibitors Circuit; financed independents, built studios (vertical and horizontal integration) |
| 1918 | Exhibitor combination formed in 1912 partially enjoined |
| 1925 | Series of federal suits brought against large chains of exhibitors for coercing distributors |
| 1927 | Paramount ordered to cease and desist anticompetitive practices |
| 1929 | Standard exhibition contract struck down as restraint of trade |
| 1929 | Exhibitor suit resulted in injunction against restrictive practices of sound manufacturers (talkies) |
| 1930 | Full vertical integration established as norm (production/distribution/ exhibition); major exhibitor circuits given special treatment such as formula deals, advantageous clearances; studios owned supply of natural resources (stars) |
| 1932 | Uniform zoning protection plan for the Omaha distributing territory enjoined |
| 1938 | Start of a series of Justice Department antitrust actions against the industry (Paramount case I) |
| 1940 | Major studios entered into a series of consent decrees |
| 1944 | Justice Department brought Paramount case II, asked for divestiture of exhibition segment of major studios; District Court stopped short of divestiture but ordered other practices to cease; both parties appealed |
| 1948–49 | Supreme Court (in effect) ordered divestiture; under jurisdiction of District Court, major studios divested themselves of their theaters and entered into consent decrees in other areas |
| 1950–99 | Series of antitrust actions (private and federal) against various segments of the industry for past practices, violations of the consent decree, price fixing, block booking, product splitting, and other anticompetitive activities |

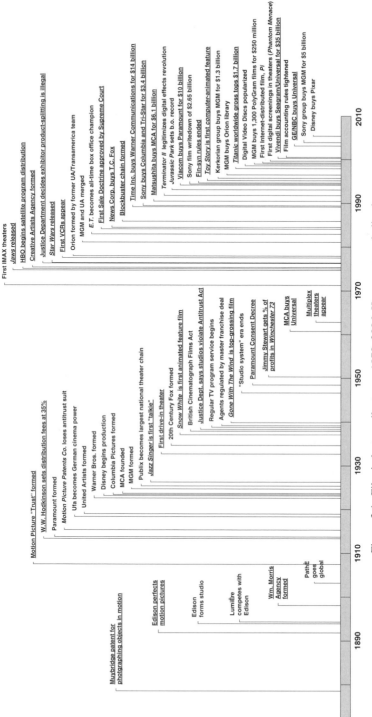

Figure 3.1. Film industry milestones, 1870–2006. Key events underlined.

First IMAX theaters
Jaws released
HBO begins satellite program distribution
Creative Artists Agency formed
Justice Department decides exhibitor product-splitting is illegal
Star Wars released
First VCRs appear
Orion formed by former UA/Transamerica team
MGM and UA merged
E.T. becomes all-time box office champion
First Sale Doctrine approved by Supreme Court
News Corp. buys T.C. Fox
Blockbuster chain formed
Time Inc. buys Warner Communications for $14 billion
Sony buys Columbia and Tri-Star for $3.4 billion
Matsushita buys MCA for $6.1 billion
Terminator II legitimizes digital effects revolution
Jurassic Park sets b.o. record
Viacom buys Paramount for $10 billion
Sony film writedown of $2.65 billion
Fin-syn rules ended
Toy Story is first computer-animated feature
Kerkorian group buys MGM for $1.3 billion
MGM buys Orion library
Titanic worldwide gross tops $1.7 billion
Digital Video Discs popularized
MGM buys 1,300 PolyGram films for $250 million
First Internet-distributed film, Pi
First digital screenings in theaters (Phantom Menace)
Vivendi buys Seagram/Universal for $35 billion
Film accounting rules tightened
GE/NBC buys Universal
Sony group buys MGM for $5 billion
Disney buys Pixar

Motion Picture "Trust" formed
W.W. Hodkinson sets distribution fees at 35%
Paramount formed
Motion Picture Patents Co. loses antitrust suit
Ufa becomes German cinema power
United Artists formed
Warner Bros. formed
Disney begins production
Columbia Pictures formed
MCA founded
MGM formed
Publix becomes largest national theater chain
Jazz Singer is first "talkie"
First drive-in theater
20th Century Fox formed
British Cinematograph Films Act
Snow White is first animated feature film
Justice Dept. says studios violate Antitrust Act
Regular TV program service begins
Agents regulated by master franchise deal
Gone With The Wind is top-grossing film
"Studio system" era ends
Paramount Consent Decree
Jimmy Stewart gets % of
profits in Winchester 73
MCA buys
Universal
Multiplex
theaters
appear

Muybridge patent for
photographing objects in motion
Edison perfects
motion pictures
Edison
forms studio
Lumière
competes with
Edison
Wm. Morris
Agency
formed
Pathé
goes
global

1870    1890    1910    1930    1950    1970    1990    2010

late 1920s; indeed, it was not until the 1970s that special effects began to be created with the help of advanced computer-aided designs and electronic editing and composition devices. *Titanic*, *Terminator 2*, *The Matrix*, and *Spider-Man* are examples of films that would not and could not have been made without the new machines and methods.

In addition, new technologies have enabled distributors to launch international marketing campaigns with much more speed and complexity than could have been imagined in the early years of the industry. And distributors and exhibitors now have the ability – using sophisticated sampling techniques and forecasting models – to closely estimate audience size and demographic responsiveness to a picture within a day or two of its release, and therefore to make quick adjustments.

The ready availability of television, cable, and other home video displays has also been important in changing the movie industry's economic and physical structure; film presentations on any of these media are competitive as well as supplementary to theatrical exhibitions, which historically constitute the core business. And advancements in program distribution and storage capabilities have made it possible to see a wide variety of films in the comfort of our homes and at our own discretion. Such unprecedented access to filmed entertainment – enabling viewers to control the time and place of viewing – has redirected the economic power of studios and distributors and opened the way for new enterprises to flourish. As the rate of change in signal distribution technology (Internet bandwidth, for example) begins to outpace the rate of change in production technology, filmed-entertainment products and services are sure to become ever more personalized and adaptable.[4]

*Capital* After technology, the second most important long-term force for change has been the packaging and application of relatively large amounts of capital to the total process of production, distribution, and marketing. In this regard, financing innovations (as discussed in the next chapter) have played a leading role. Without the development of sophisticated financing methods and access to a broad and deep capital market, it is doubtful that the movie industry could have arrived at the position it occupies today.

From an economist's standpoint, it is also interesting to observe further that the feature-film business does not easily fit the usual molds. Industries requiring sizable capital investments can normally be expected to evolve into purely oligopolistic forms: steel and automobile manufacturing are examples. But because movies – each uniquely designed and packaged – are not stamped out on cookie-cutter assembly lines, the economic structure is somewhat different. Here, instead, we find a combination of large oligopolistic production/distribution/financing organizations regularly interfacing with and being highly dependent on a fragmented assortment of small, specialized service and production firms.

At least in Hollywood, energetic little fish often can swim with great agility and success among the giant whales, assorted sharks, and hungry piranha.

Hollywood is always in flux, a prototype of the emerging network economy, assembling and disassembling itself from one deal and one picture and one technology to the next.

Pecking orders

*Exhibition* Back in the 1920s, a 65-cent movie ticket would buy a few hours in a comfortable seat in the grandeur of a marbled and gilded theater palace in which complimentary coffee was graciously served while a string quartet played softly in the background. But those were the good old days.

The 1948 antitrust consent decree had considerable impact on movie industry structure because it disallowed control of the retail exhibition side of the business (local movie theaters) by the major production/distribution entities of that time. Disgruntled independent theater owners had initiated the action leading to issuance of the decree because they felt that studios were discriminating against them: Studios would book pictures into their captive outlets without public bidding.

However, the divestitures – ordered in the name of preserving competition – turned out to be a hollow victory for those independents. Soon after the distribution–exhibition split had been effected, studios realized that it was no longer necessary to supply a new picture every week, and they proceeded to substantially reduce production schedules. Competition for the best pictures out of a diminished supply then raised prices beyond what many owners of small theaters could afford. And by that time, television had begun to wean audiences away from big-screen entertainment; the number of movie admissions had begun a steep downward slide. The 1948 decree thus triggered and also hastened the arrival of a major structural change that would have eventually happened anyway.[5]

In the United States, exhibition is dominated by several major theater chains, including Regal Entertainment Group (United Artists, Edwards Theaters, Hoyts, and Regal Cinemas), AMC Entertainment (American Multi-Cinema, Loews Cineplex including Sony, Plitt, Walter Reade, and RKO), Carmike Cinemas, Redstone (National Amusements, Inc.), Cinemark USA, and Marcus Corp. In aggregate, these companies operate approximately 20,000 of the best-located and most modern urban and suburban (e.g., shopping mall) movie screens, with most of the other 15,000 or so older theaters still owned by individuals and small private companies. As such, the chains control about 65% of the screens, but they probably account for at least 80% of the total exhibition revenues generated.

In Canada, however, Cineplex (controlled through Onex) is estimated to control about 65% of total annual theatrical revenues (with about 1,300 screens in 132 theaters as of 2005). The Canadian market is roughly 10% that of the United States.

In both the United States and Canada, construction of conveniently located multiple-screen (i.e., multiplexed) theaters in suburban areas by these large

Table 3.2. *Exhibition industry composite, five companies, 2001–2005*

|  |  | Revenues | Operating income | Operating[a] margin (%) | Assets | Operating cash flow |
|---|---|---|---|---|---|---|
| CAGR(%)[b] | 2001–2005 | 1.3 | 117.3 | NM[c] | 8.0 | 17.0 |

[a] Average margin, 2001–2005 = 7.4%.
[b] Compound annual growth rate.
[c] Not meaningful.

chains has more than offset the decline of older drive-in and inner-city locations and has accordingly helped to stave off competition from other forms
of entertainment, including home video. The chains, moreover, have brought
economies of scale to a business that used to be notoriously inefficient in
its operating practices and procedures. As a result, control of exhibition has
been consolidated into fewer and financially stronger hands, and the five
companies aggregated in Table 3.2 together account for more than 70% of
total industry dollar volume.[6]

*Production and distribution* Theatrical film production and distribution have
evolved into a multifaceted business, with many different sizes and types of
organizations participating in some or all parts of the project development and
marketing processes. However, companies with important and long-standing
presence in both production and distribution, with substantial library assets,
and with some studio production facilities (although nowadays this is not a
necessity) have been collectively and historically known as the "majors."

As of the early 2000s, subsequent to many mergers and restructurings,
there were six major theatrical-film distributors (studios): The Walt Disney
Company (Buena Vista, Touchstone, Hollywood Pictures, and Pixar), Sony
Pictures (owned by Sony and distributor of Columbia/TriStar and MGM/UA
films), Paramount (Viacom Inc. and DreamWorks), Twentieth Century Fox
(News Corp.), Warner Bros. (Time Warner Inc.), and Universal (formerly
MCA, Inc. and now part of GE/NBC Universal).[7] These companies produce,
finance, and distribute their own films, but they also finance and distribute pictures initiated by so-called independent filmmakers who either work directly
for them or have projects "picked up" after progress toward completion has
already been made.[8]

Of somewhat lesser size and scope in production and distribution activities are so-called minimajors such as New Line Cinema (Time Warner),
Lionsgate, and The Weinstein Company. (The now-defunct Orion Pictures,
whose library was bought by MGM, fit into this category, too, as did Mira-
max and DreamWorks when those were run by the founders.) Many smaller
production companies also often have significant distribution capabilities
in specialized market segments. Generally, such smaller companies would

not handle theatrical product lines that are as broad as those of the majors, nor would they have the considerable access to capital that a major would have. Nevertheless, these smaller companies can occasionally produce and nationally distribute pictures that generate box-office revenues that are large enough to attract media attention.[9]

Several smaller, "independent" producers also either feed their production into the established distribution pipelines of the larger companies or have minidistribution organizations of their own. Many of these newer independents largely finance their productions away from the majors and then, in effect, merely make distribution agreements with the larger studios (i.e., they "rent" the studio's distribution apparatus). They thus retain much more control over a film's rights and can build a library of such rights. In addition, many executive project development firms do not produce films but instead option existing literary properties and/or develop new properties for others to produce.

Small independent firms, sometimes called "states-righters," will also still occasionally handle distributions in local and regional markets not well covered by the majors or submajors.[10] And Lionsgate, IFC, and Picturehouse (HBO/Newmarket) are examples of relatively new significant independent distribution companies in the United States, with counterparts in overseas markets, where distributors of various sizes operate.

Although at first it may be a bit startling to learn of the existence of so many different production and service organizations, their enduring presence underscores the entrepreneurial qualities of this business. The many "independents" have been a structural fact of life since the industry began, and they add considerable variety and verve to the filmmaking process.

## 3.3 Ups and downs

### Admission cycles

There has long been a notion, derived from the Depression-resistant performance of motion-picture ticket sales, that the movie business has somewhat contracyclical characteristics (Figure 3.2). Indeed, it may be theorized that as the economy enters a recessionary phase, the leisure-time spending preferences of consumers shift more toward lower-cost, closer-to-home entertainment activities than when the economy is robust and expansionary. If so, this would explain why ticket sales often remain steady or rise during early to middle stages of a recession, faltering only near the recession's end. By that stage, many people's budgets are apt to be severely stretched and long-postponed purchases of essential goods (e.g., new cars) and services (e.g., fixing leaky ceilings) will naturally take priority over spending on entertainment. The performance of movie-ticket sales vis-à-vis the economy during recessionary episodes since 1929 is illustrated in Figure 3.3.

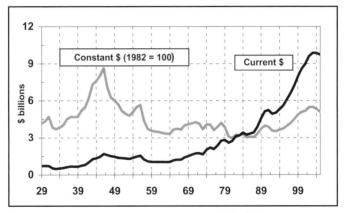

Figure 3.2. PCEs on movies, 1929–2005.

In fact, an important study of cycles in ticket demand (Nardone 1982) has indicated that the motion-picture industry acts contracyclically to the economy 87.5% of the time in peaks and 69.3% of the time in troughs. Also, there are suggestions that both a four-year and a ten-year cycle in movie admissions may be present, but the statistical evidence in this regard is inconclusive.[11] Ticket sales peaked in 1946 and troughed in 1971 – a time when the economic survival of several major distributors was seriously in question.

Although seasonal demand patterns are not as sharply defined as they used to be (largely because there are now so many multiscreen theaters around the country), it is still much easier to discern and to interpret such seasonal rather than long-wave cycles. Families find it most convenient to see films during vacation periods such as Thanksgiving, Christmas, and Easter, and children out of school during the summer months have time to frequent the

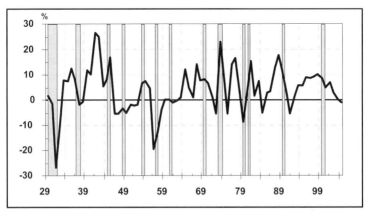

Figure 3.3. Motion-picture receipts: percentage change over previous year's receipts, 1929–2005. Bars indicate periods of recession.

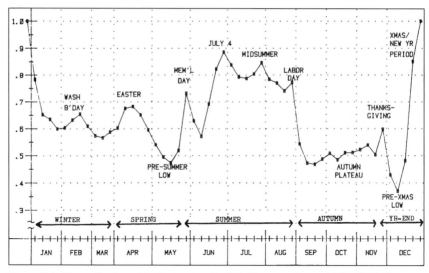

Figure 3.4. Normalized weekly fluctuations in U.S. film attendance, 1969–1984. *Source*: *Variety*, copyright 1984 by A. D. Murphy.

box office.[12] In the fall, however, school begins again, new television pro-grams are introduced, and elections are held; people are busy with activities other than moviegoing. And in the period just prior to Christmas, shop-ping takes precedence. Thus, the industry tends to concentrate most of its important film releases within just a few weeks of the year. This makes the competition for moviegoers' attention and time more expensive than it would be if audience attendance patterns were not as seasonally skewed (see Sec-tion 4.4 on marketing costs). Normalized seasonal patterns are illustrated in Figure 3.4.

Prices and elasticities

Ticket sales for new film releases are typically insensitive to changes in box-office prices per se, but sales may be more responsive to the total cost of moviegoing, which can include fees for complementary goods and services, such as those for babysitters, restaurant meals, and parking. Although demand for major-event movies, backed by strong word-of-mouth advertising and reviewer support, is essentially price inelastic, exhibitors are sometimes able to stimulate admissions by showing somewhat older features at very low prices during off-peak times (e.g., Tuesday noon screenings when schools are in session). Many retired and unemployed people, and probably bored housewives and truants, like to take advantage of such bargains. There is, moreover, a widespread impression that ticket prices have risen inordinately. Yet, as Figure 3.5 indicates, movie-ticket prices, as deflated by the consumer price index, remain below the peak of the early 1970s.

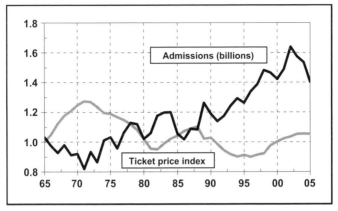

Figure 3.5. Motion-picture admissions in billions and average real ticket-price index, 1965–2005.

In addition to price, many other factors – from story type, stars, and director to promotional budgets, demographics, ratings, awards, and critical reviews – will usually enter into the moviegoing (or home video purchase/rental) decision. Viewed collectively, the economic studies that have been done in this area seem most of all to suggest that movie-audience tastes and responses to such different variables shift fairly often.[13]

Production starts and capital

In at least one respect, the movie industry is no different from the housing construction industry. The crucial initial ingredient is capital. Without access to it, no project can get off the ground. It should thus come as no surprise to find that the number of movies started in any year may be sensitive to changes in interest rates and in the availability of credit. To illustrate this relationship, a statistical experiment was conducted using the *Daily Variety* end-of-quarter production-start figures from 1969 to 1980, the quarterly average bank prime interest rate adjusted by the implicit gross national product (GNP) deflator for the same period, and the banking system's borrowed reserves (also deflated) as a proxy for the availability of capital. The results were as follows:

1. There may be a moderate, statistically significant inverse correlation, with at least a one-quarter lag, between real interest rates and the number of production starts.
2. There probably exists, with a six-quarter lag, an inverse relationship between production starts and borrowed reserves (credit availability) (Figure 3.6).

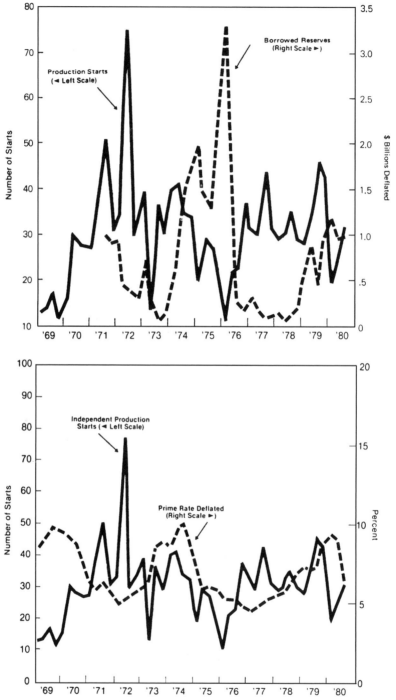

Figure 3.6. Production starts, interest rates, and borrowed reserves lagged six quarters, 1969–1980.

That production starts should lag behind changes in the availability of capital by as much as six quarters should not be unexpected in view of the long lead time usually needed to assemble the many diverse components required for motion-picture productions. Beginning with a rudimentary outline or treatment of a story idea, it can often take over a year to arrange financing, final scripts, cast, and crew. In total, it normally requires at least 18 months to bring a movie project from conception to the answer-print stage – the point at which all editing, mixing, and dubbing work has been completed.

Moreover, because the industry ordinarily depends on a continuous flow of cash, when credit is restricted by the Federal Reserve Bank, sources of funding for movie projects rapidly dry up: Everyone in the long chain of revenue disbursement slows payments on bills, and it becomes more difficult to effectively attract relatively scarce capital flows away from alternative uses that promise higher returns for less risk. Thus, especially for independent filmmakers, the cost and availability of credit with which to finance a project are often the most important variables affecting the amount of time that elapses from start to finish.

No matter what the monetary environment, however, in theory (but not always in practice) only the worthiest of projects are supported, with the best concepts presumably first being offered to, and sometimes erroneously rejected by, the large studios/financiers/distributors. In this respect, it is significant that the number of potential film projects on Hollywood's drawing boards always far exceeds the number that can actually be financed. Parkinson's law applies here: The number of projects will always expand to fully absorb the capital available, regardless of quality, and without regard to the quantity of other films scheduled for completion and release at around the same time.

Releases and inventories

Variations in production starts are eventually reflected in the number of films released (supplied) to theaters. In turn, the number of releases and the rate of theater admissions influence industry operating profits. But it is difficult to estimate (using regression models) how large this effect may be; variations in the numbers of releases and admissions are not independent of each other, and aggregate profits are also influenced by the demand for filmed entertainment products in television, cable, and other markets.[14]

Sometimes, a more practical way to view the effects of changes in supply is through comparison of total dollar investments in film inventories against sales (i.e., film rentals). As in other industries, such comparisons often lead to the discovery of important economic relationships. For instance, a falling ratio of inventory to sales may be a manifestation of improving demand and/or of declining investments in production; either way, inventories become less financially burdensome to carry as cash is being recycled relatively rapidly.

Table 3.3. *Filmed entertainment industry operating performance, major theatrical distributors, 1975–2005*

|  | Revenues ($ millions) | Oper. income ($ millions) | Margin (%) | Film inventory ($ millions) | Invent./revenue ($ millions) |
|---|---|---|---|---|---|
| 2005 | 44,300 | 3,782 | 8.5 | 19,176 | 0.43 |
| 2004 | 44,799 | 4,544 | 10.1 | 18,881 | 0.42 |
| 2003 | 42,036 | 4,072 | 9.7 | 18,194 | 0.43 |
| 2002 | 37,808 | 3,064 | 8.1 | 18,771 | 0.51 |
| 2001 | 31,547 | 1,590 | 5.0 | 18,846 | 0.60 |
| 2000 | 29,416 | 900 | 3.1 | 22,959 | 0.78 |
| 1999 | 29,651 | 1,062 | 3.6 | 21,033 | 0.71 |
| 1998 | 29,468 | 2,153 | 7.3 | 20,412 | 0.69 |
| 1997 | 28,758 | 2,143 | 7.5 | 18,371 | 0.64 |
| 1996 | 25,644 | 1,884 | 7.3 | 16,404 | 0.64 |
| 1995 | 22,073 | 1,831 | 8.3 | 12,361 | 0.56 |
| 1994 | 19,850 | 927 | 4.7 | 12,288 | 0.62 |
| 1993 | 17,583 | 733 | 4.2 | 11,597 | 0.66 |
| 1992 | 16,147 | 1,302 | 8.1 | 10,374 | 0.64 |
| 1991 | 14,128 | 941 | 6.7 | 9,663 | 0.68 |
| 1990 | 12,676 | 1,103 | 8.7 | 8,127 | 0.64 |
| 1989 | 11,571 | 1,130 | 9.8 | 7,242 | 0.63 |
| 1988 | 9,121 | 1,151 | 12.6 | 5,089 | 0.56 |
| 1987 | 8,251 | 928 | 11.2 | 4,710 | 0.57 |
| 1986 | 6,839 | 799 | 11.7 | 4,458 | 0.65 |
| 1985 | 6,359 | 465 | 7.3 | 4,216 | 0.66 |
| 1984 | 5,839 | 516 | 8.8 | 3,370 | 0.58 |
| 1983 | 5,324 | 590 | 11.1 | 2,980 | 0.56 |
| 1982 | 4,548 | 565 | 12.4 | 2,729 | 0.60 |
| 1981 | 3,749 | 301 | 8.0 | 2,267 | 0.60 |
| 1980 | 3,997 | 489 | 12.2 | 1,423 | 0.36 |
| 1979 | 4,009 | 661 | 16.5 | 1,538 | 0.38 |
| 1978 | 3,498 | 606 | 17.3 | 1,212 | 0.35 |
| 1977 | 2,739 | 406 | 14.8 | 973 | 0.36 |
| 1976 | 2,336 | 336 | 14.4 | 936 | 0.40 |
| 1975 | 2,078 | 353 | 17.0 | 822 | 0.40 |
| Five- and ten-year compound annual growth rates | | | | | |
| 2000–2005 | 8.5 | 33.3 | | −3.5 | |
| 1995–2005 | 7.2 | 7.5 | | 4.5 | |

Estimated inventory-to-sales figures for the major studios are shown in Table 3.3, where proper interpretation requires recognition that *many independently produced projects are carried off-balance-sheet* until release impends. The visible ratios – generally around 0.6 or higher since the early 1980s – are consequently somewhat akin to the tip of an iceberg, the size of which is often more easily gauged from the number of films rated each year by the Motion Picture Association of America (MPAA).[15] Additional industry data are shown in Table 3.4.

### Market-share factors

Many consumer-product industries rely on market-share information to evaluate the relative positions of major participants. However, because consumers have little, if any, brand identification with movie distributors (or most producers), and because market share tends to fluctuate considerably from year to year for any one distributor, such data generally have limited applicability and relevance. In the picture business, the approach is of necessity far different than in market-share research for soaps, or cigarettes, or beverages.

This kind of information therefore seems best suited for contrasting the effectiveness of major distributor organizations over the long term or for comparing a film's short-term rental performance in one region against that for another film in the same region. In long-term analysis, for example, averaging of Disney's share and those of other distributors over the years beginning in 1970 quantifies that company's significant erosion of market presence in the 1970s and subsequent rebound into the 1990s (see Supplementary Data Table S3.4).

### Collateral factors

*Exchange-rate effects* Between 30% and 45% of gross rentals earned by the majors usually are generated outside the so-called domestic market, which includes both the United States and Canada (about 10% of the U.S. total). Swings in foreign-currency exchange rates may therefore substantially affect the profitability of U.S. studio/distribution organizations.

For instance, during most of the 1970s and after 1985, with the U.S. dollar relatively weak against major export-market currencies (Japanese yen, British pound sterling, Deutsche mark, French franc, and Swiss franc), studio profitability was significantly enhanced as movie tickets purchased in those currencies translated into more dollars. Contrariwise, in the late 1970s and early 1980s, a strengthening dollar probably reduced the industry's operating profits by some 10% to 15% ($100 million or so) under what would otherwise have been generated. In other words, although there is some countervailing effect from the higher costs of shooting pictures in strong-currency countries and from maintaining foreign-territory distribution and sales facilities in such locations, a weakening dollar exchange rate will, on balance, noticeably improve movie industry profitability.

Estimates of the importance of foreign-currency translation rates on industry profits are shown in Figure 3.7, from which it can be seen that a weakening dollar results in significant net benefit. Aggregate theatrical admissions

Table 3.4. *Motion picture theater industry statistics, 1965–2005[a]*

| | Total U.S. BO[b] revs ($ millions) | MPAA U.S. rentals[c] ($ million) | MPAA Canadian rentals ($ millions) | MPAA U.S. rentals % of BO[d] | U.S. + Canadian rentals % of BO | Worldwide (U.S. + foreign rentals) ($ millions) | Foreign rentals ($ millions) | Foreign as a % of total (%) |
|---|---|---|---|---|---|---|---|---|
| 2005 | 8,891.2 | 3,486.0 | 289.3 | 38.8 | 42.0 | 6,683.0 | 3,197.0 | 47.8 |
| 2004 | 9,539.2 | 3,600.0 | 279.7 | 37.7 | 40.7 | 7,480.0 | 3,837.0 | 51.3 |
| 2003 | 9,488.5 | 3,980.3 | 261.0 | 41.9 | 44.7 | 7,510.0 | 3,529.7 | 47.0 |
| 2002 | 9,519.6 | 3,575.0 | 242.0 | 37.6 | 40.1 | 6,715.0 | 3,140.0 | 46.8 |
| 2001 | 8,412.5 | 3,270.0 | 221.7 | 38.9 | 41.5 | 5,710.0 | 2,440.0 | 42.7 |
| 2000 | 7,661.0 | 2,850.0 | 189.3 | 37.2 | 39.7 | 5,480.0 | 2,630.0 | 46.8 |
| 1999 | 7,448.0 | 3,120.0 | 207.8 | 41.9 | 44.7 | 5,970.0 | 2,854.0 | 47.8 |
| 1998 | 6,949.0 | 2,787.0 | 174.1 | 40.1 | 42.6 | 5,695.0 | 2,908.0 | 51.1 |
| 1997 | 6,365.9 | 2,640.0 | 175.5 | 41.5 | 44.2 | 5,320.0 | 2,680.0 | 50.4 |
| 1996 | 5,911.5 | 2,417.5 | 146.7 | 40.9 | 43.4 | 4,921.5 | 2,504.0 | 50.9 |
| 1995 | 5,493.5 | 2,393.7 | 110.2 | 43.6 | 45.6 | 4,609.6 | 2,215.9 | 48.1 |
| 1994 | 5,396.2 | 2,040.3 | 126.8 | 37.8 | 40.2 | 4,089.1 | 2,048.8 | 50.1 |
| 1993 | 5,154.2 | 1,997.6 | 131.9 | 38.8 | 41.3 | 4,017.6 | 2,020.0 | 50.3 |
| 1992 | 4,871.0 | 2,005.0 | 130.4 | 41.2 | 43.8 | 3,444.1 | 1,439.1 | 41.8 |
| 1991 | 4,803.2 | 1,847.5 | 133.9 | 38.5 | 41.3 | 3,273.2 | 1,425.7 | 43.6 |
| 1990 | 5,021.8 | 1,829.0 | 148.3 | 36.4 | 39.4 | 3,478.4 | 1,649.5 | 47.4 |
| 1989 | 5,033.4 | 1,780.0 | 152.5 | 35.4 | 38.4 | 3,126.9 | 1,346.9 | 43.1 |
| 1988 | 4,458.4 | 1,413.6 | 125.2 | 31.7 | 34.5 | 2,433.9 | 1,020.3 | 41.9 |
| 1987 | 4,252.9 | 1,244.5 | 96.7 | 29.3 | 31.5 | 2,179.6 | 935.1 | 42.9 |
| 1986 | 3,778.0 | 1,165.1 | 86.8 | 30.8 | 33.1 | 1,963.4 | 798.3 | 40.7 |
| 1985 | 3,749.4 | 1,109.1 | 76.8 | 29.6 | 31.6 | 1,729.0 | 619.9 | 35.9 |

| | | | | | | | |
|---|---|---|---|---|---|---|---|
| 1984 | 4,030.6 | 111.0 | 32.6 | 1,313.2 | 35.3 | 1,967.2 | 654.0 | 33.2 |
| 1983 | 3,766.0 | 94.2 | 34.5 | 1,297.4 | 37.0 | 2,136.2 | 838.8 | 39.3 |
| 1982 | 3,452.7 | 99.8 | 38.9 | 1,342.7 | 41.8 | 2,061.3 | 718.6 | 34.9 |
| 1981 | 2,965.6 | 88.7 | 39.2 | 1,163.6 | 42.2 | 2,015.0 | 851.4 | 42.3 |
| 1980 | 2,748.5 | 91.5 | 43.0 | 1,182.6 | 46.4 | 2,093.7 | 911.2 | 43.5 |
| 1979 | 2,821.0 | 75.0 | 37.8 | 1,067.7 | 40.5 | 1,966.6 | 911.4 | 46.3 |
| 1978 | 2,643.0 | 77.6 | 42.4 | 1,119.9 | 45.3 | 1,949.4 | 829.5 | 42.6 |
| 1977 | 2,372.0 | 66.8 | 36.6 | 868.0 | 39.4 | 1,466.8 | 597.6 | 40.7 |
| 1976 | 2,036.0 | 60.8 | 28.3 | 576.6 | 31.3 | 1,147.5 | 570.9 | 49.8 |
| 1975 | 2,115.0 | 63.2 | 29.7 | 628.0 | 32.7 | 1,232.2 | 604.2 | 49.0 |
| 1974 | 1,909.0 | 54.4 | 28.6 | 545.9 | 31.4 | 1,040.7 | 494.8 | 47.5 |
| 1973 | 1,524.0 | 39.9 | 25.6 | 390.5 | 28.2 | 819.3 | 428.8 | 52.3 |
| 1972 | 1,583.0 | 38.7 | 26.9 | 426.4 | 29.4 | 827.7 | 401.3 | 48.5 |
| 1971 | 1,350.0 | 29.4 | 24.9 | 336.7 | 27.1 | 684.7 | 348.0 | 50.8 |
| 1970 | 1,429.0 | 27.4 | 26.7 | 381.3 | 28.6 | 741.7 | 360.4 | 48.6 |
| 1969 | 1,294.0 | 27.7 | 24.5 | 317.4 | 26.7 | 665.8 | 348.4 | 52.3 |
| 1968 | 1,282.0 | 30.0 | 29.0 | 372.3 | 31.4 | 711.3 | 339.0 | 47.7 |
| 1967 | 1,110.0 | 28.1 | 32.1 | 355.9 | 34.6 | 713.7 | 357.8 | 50.1 |
| 1966 | 1,067.0 | 26.4 | 29.9 | 319.5 | 32.4 | 680.9 | 361.4 | 53.1 |
| 1965 | 1,042.0 | 23.2 | 27.6 | 287.2 | 29.8 | 630.7 | 343.5 | 54.5 |
| CAGR:[e] | 5.5% | 6.5% | | 6.4% | | 6.1% | 5.7% | |

[a] Totals may be affected by rounding.

[b] Box office.

[c] Motion Picture Association of America (MPAA) rentals are assumed to be about 95% of total U.S. rentals. Remainder is from non-MPAA member companies.

[d] Rentals percentage for United States is understated by 1%–2% because state admissions taxes are not deducted from box-office figures.

[e] Compound annual growth rate, 1965–2005 (%).

Table 3.4. (cont.)

| | U.S. number of admissions (billions) | Avg. ticket price ($) | Total number of MPAA releases | Number of domestic$^f$ screens | | | Average per screen | | Screens per MPAA release |
|---|---|---|---|---|---|---|---|---|---|
| | | | | Total | Indoor | Drive-in | Dom. BO ($) | Admissions | |
| 2005 | 1.403 | 6.41 | 198 | 37,740 | 37,092 | 648 | 238,241 | 37,162 | 190.6 |
| 2004 | 1.536 | 6.21 | 199 | 36,652 | 36,012 | 640 | 260,264 | 41,910 | 184.2 |
| 2003 | 1.574 | 6.03 | 198 | 35,995 | 35,361 | 634 | 263,606 | 43,728 | 181.8 |
| 2002 | 1.639 | 5.81 | 225 | 35,836 | 35,170 | 666 | 265,643 | 45,745 | 159.3 |
| 2001 | 1.487 | 5.66 | 196 | 35,173 | 34,490 | 683 | 239,175 | 42,285 | 179.5 |
| 2000 | 1.421 | 5.39 | 197 | 36,280 | 35,567 | 683 | 211,163 | 39,162 | 184.2 |
| 1999 | 1.465 | 5.08 | 218 | 37,131 | 36,448 | 683 | 200,587 | 39,460 | 170.3 |
| 1998 | 1.481 | 4.69 | 235 | 34,168 | 33,418 | 750 | 203,377 | 43,336 | 145.4 |
| 1997 | 1.388 | 4.59 | 253 | 31,865 | 31,050 | 815 | 199,777 | 43,549 | 125.9 |
| 1996 | 1.339 | 4.42 | 240 | 29,731 | 28,905 | 826 | 198,833 | 45,024 | 123.9 |
| 1995 | 1.263 | 4.35 | 234 | 27,843 | 26,995 | 848 | 197,303 | 45,347 | 119.0 |
| 1994 | 1.292 | 4.18 | 183 | 26,689 | 25,830 | 859 | 202,188 | 48,398 | 145.8 |
| 1993 | 1.244 | 4.14 | 161 | 25,626 | 24,789 | 837 | 201,132 | 48,544 | 159.2 |
| 1992 | 1.173 | 4.15 | 150 | 25,214 | 24,344 | 870 | 193,186 | 46,530 | 168.1 |
| 1991 | 1.141 | 4.21 | 164 | 24,639 | 23,740 | 899 | 194,943 | 46,292 | 150.2 |
| 1990 | 1.189 | 4.23 | 169 | 23,814 | 22,904 | 910 | 210,876 | 49,912 | 140.9 |
| 1989 | 1.263 | 3.99 | 169 | 22,921 | 21,907 | 1,014 | 219,598 | 55,094 | 135.6 |
| 1988 | 1.085 | 4.11 | 160 | 23,129 | 21,632 | 1,497 | 192,762 | 46,902 | 144.6 |
| 1987 | 1.089 | 3.91 | 129 | 22,679 | 20,595 | 2,084 | 187,526 | 47,996 | 175.8 |
| 1986 | 1.017 | 3.71 | 139 | 22,765 | 19,947 | 2,818 | 165,957 | 44,683 | 163.8 |
| 1985 | 1.056 | 3.55 | 153 | 21,147 | 18,327 | 2,820 | 177,302 | 49,941 | 138.2 |
| 1984 | 1.199 | 3.36 | 167 | 20,200 | 17,368 | 2,832 | 199,535 | 59,361 | 121.0 |

| Year | | | | | | | | | |
|---|---|---|---|---|---|---|---|---|---|
| 1983 | 1.197 | 3.15 | 190 | 18,884 | 16,032 | 2,852 | 199,428 | 63,382 | 99.4 |
| 1982 | 1.175 | 2.94 | 173 | 18,020 | 14,977 | 3,043 | 191,604 | 65,228 | 104.2 |
| 1981 | 1.060 | 2.78 | 173 | 18,040 | 14,732 | 3,308 | 164,390 | 58,758 | 104.3 |
| 1980 | 1.022 | 2.69 | 161 | 17,590 | 14,029 | 3,561 | 156,254 | 58,073 | 109.3 |
| 1979 | 1.121 | 2.52 | 138 | 16,901 | 13,331 | 3,570 | 166,913 | 66,327 | 122.5 |
| 1978 | 1.128 | 2.34 | 114 | 16,251 | 12,671 | 3,580 | 162,636 | 69,411 | 142.6 |
| 1977 | 1.063 | 2.23 | 110 | 16,041 | 12,434 | 3,607 | 147,871 | 66,268 | 145.8 |
| 1976 | 0.957 | 2.13 | 133 | 15,832 | 12,197 | 3,635 | 128,600 | 60,447 | 119.0 |
| 1975 | 1.033 | 2.05 | 138 | 15,030 | 11,402 | 3,628 | 140,719 | 68,729 | 108.9 |
| 1974 | 1.011 | 1.89 | 155 | 14,417 | 10,839 | 3,578 | 132,413 | 70,126 | 93.0 |
| 1973 | 0.865 | 1.76 | 163 | 14,420 | 10,765 | 3,655 | 105,687 | 59,986 | 88.5 |
| 1972 | 0.934 | 1.70 | 193 | 14,428 | 10,694 | 3,734 | 109,717 | 64,735 | 74.8 |
| 1971 | 0.820 | 1.65 | 183 | 14,055 | 10,335 | 3,720 | 96,051 | 58,342 | 76.8 |
| 1970 | 0.921 | 1.55 | 185 | 13,750 | 10,000 | 3,750 | 103,927 | 66,982 | 74.3 |
| 1969 | 0.912 | 1.42 | 183 | 13,480 | 9,750 | 3,730 | 95,994 | 67,656 | 73.7 |
| 1968 | 0.979 | 1.31 | 196 | 13,190 | 9,500 | 3,690 | 97,195 | 74,223 | 67.3 |
| 1967 | 0.927 | 1.20 | 199 | 13,000 | 9,330 | 3,670 | 85,385 | 71,308 | 65.3 |
| 1966 | 0.975 | 1.09 | 181 | 12,930 | 9,290 | 3,640 | 82,521 | 75,406 | 71.4 |
| 1965 | 1.032 | 1.01 | 210 | 12,825 | 9,240 | 3,585 | 81,248 | 80,468 | 61.1 |
| **CAGR:** | | | | | | | | | |
| 1965–2005 | 0.8% | 4.7% | 2.7 | 3.5 | -4.2 | 2.7 | -1.9 | | |
| 1980–2005 | 1.3 | 3.5 | 3.1 | 4.0 | -6.6 | 1.7 | -1.8 | | |

$^f$ In traditional industry parlance, the term *domestic* includes U.S. and Canadian rentals. In this table, *foreign* includes Canada.

Sources: *Variety* and *Daily Variety* as based on MPAA-MPEAA data.

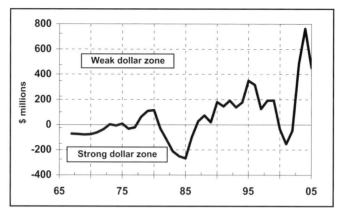

Figure 3.7. Film industry foreign theatrical rentals, estimated differentials for dollar exchange rate effects, 1965–2005.

in five developed countries are shown in Figure 3.8a, with theatrical admissions on a per capita basis and screen availability comparisons shown in Figures 3.8b and 3.8c.[16] As of 2005, there were approximately 149,000 screens in the world generating a global box-office total of around $24 billion from estimated unit ticket sales (admissions) of 8 billion. Total feature film production was approximately 4,600 titles, of which 1,100 were made in India. China, too, now produces a large number of titles.[17]

*Trade effects* Although every region of the world produces and distributes film and television programming, the United States has long been the dominant exporter, with a net trade balance for these products of at least $4 billion a year. This dominance can be explained as a function of historical happenstance, technological development, availability of capital, application of marketing prowess, and culture. But from an economist's standpoint, the essential elements are that

- Movies and television programs have public-good/joint-consumption attributes wherein the viewing by one consumer does not use up the product or detract from the enjoyment of other viewers.
- The home market in the United States is relatively large in terms of population and per capita or per household penetration of cinema screens, television sets, cable connections, and video playback devices – all of which provide relatively greater opportunity for cost amortization in the home market.
- The base language is English, the second most-used after Mandarin Chinese, with the majority of the speakers residing in the wealthiest countries. This means that the "cultural discount" – the diminished value of an imported film or program due to differences of style, cultural references and preferences, and relevance – on shipping U.S. programming to other English-speaking countries is relatively small.[18]

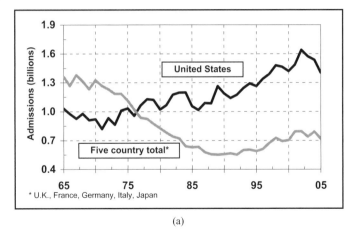

(a)

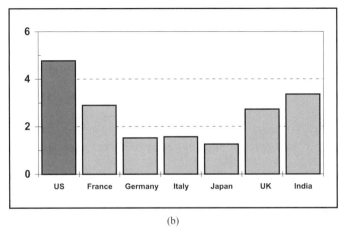

(b)

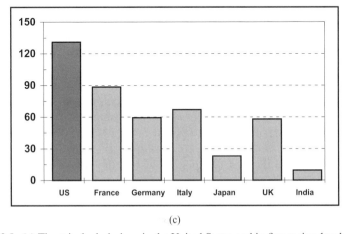

(c)

Figure 3.8. (a) Theatrical admissions in the United States and in five major developed countries, 1965–2005. *Sources*: Country statistical abstracts and MPAA data. (b) Admissions per capita, selected countries, 2005. (c) Screens per 1 million population, selected countries, 2005.

Given all these advantages it seems unlikely that the export dominance of the U.S. feature film business will be greatly eroded anytime soon. In television, however, application of new technologies and the development of regional production skills suggest that the U.S. share will probably continue to be gradually reduced.[19]

Financial aggregates

As we have already seen, for all its purported sophistication and glamor, the movie industry remains fragmented in its organizational structure: Especially on the creative ends it remains a cottage industry, and there are good economic reasons to believe that it will remain so, if only because many small service firms and production units are efficiently scaled.

The majors, though, still consistently generate the bulk of industry revenues (an estimated 90% of gross domestic film rentals), and when they have problems, so does everyone else in the business. The financial statements of these large companies accordingly provide, in the aggregate, a useful overall representation of the industry's financial performance trends (Table 3.3). But because entertainment companies often find it difficult to systematically match overhead and financing costs against revenues from specific sources, these data do not normally allow us to analyze whether profit potential is greater in theatrical, television, or ancillary-market sales. Such issues are best addressed through an understanding of the microeconomic aspects of the business, which are discussed in the chapters that follow.[20]

### 3.4 Markets – primary and secondary

Theaters have historically been the primary retail outlet for movies and the place where most of the revenues had been collected and where most of the viewing had occurred. But since the mid-1980s, the total fees from the licensing of films for use in ancillary markets (network and syndicated television, pay cable, and home video) have collectively far overshadowed revenues derived from theatrical release. Table 3.5 illustrates what an "average" feature film released through a major distributor might receive from each of the ancillary markets as of the early 2000s.

Technological development, the driving force behind the transition to dominance by so-called ancillary markets, has led to sharp decreases in the costs of distributing and storing the bits of information that are contained in entertainment software. Yet it is still an open question as to whether such unit-cost decreases are in themselves sufficient to sustain the industry's profitability.

An individual seeing a newly released feature film in a theater would, for example, ordinarily generate revenue (rental or gross) to the distributor of anywhere between $2.00 and $4.50. However, viewing on pay television, or from a rented prerecorded disc or cassette, sometimes results in revenue per person-view of as little as 20 to 30 cents (Table 3.6). That happens when

Table 3.5. *Estimated ancillary revenues for an*
*"average" MPAA-member film[a] in 2005*
*($ millions)*

| Typical license fees or revenues per film[b] | |
| --- | --- |
| Pay cable | 9.5 |
| Home video (cassettes and DVDs) | 13.0 |
| Network TV licenses | 2.5 |
| Syndication | 1.5 |
| Foreign TV | 3.0 |
| Total | 29.5 |

[a] Per-film figures for ancillary markets represent the approximate going rate for representative pictures. However, they are not derived by dividing total ancillary-market revenues by an exact number of releases. Averages would, of course, be much lower if non-MPAA member films were to be included.

[b] Also see Section 3.5 where it is explained why averages such as those used here require careful interpretation. Examples of wide positive and negative deviations from these approximate averages are shown in Table 5.8.

several people in a household watch a film at the same time, or when one watches several times without incurring additional charges.

It may, of course, be argued that in recent years declining average unit costs at home have had no discernible effect on theater admissions and that, indeed, markets for filmed entertainment products have been broadened by attracting, at the margin, viewers who would anyhow not pay the price of a ticket. In addition, it seems that, no matter how low the price at home, people still enjoy going out to the movies.

As sensible as this line of reasoning appears to be (it is platitudinous within the industry), there are several problems in accepting it without challenge.

Table 3.6. *Approximate cost of movie viewing*
*per person-hour, 2005[a]*

| | |
| --- | --- |
| Theater (first-run big cities) | $4.50 |
| Pay cable channel | 0.50 |
| Home video | 0.60 |
| "Free" commercial television[b] | 0.06 |

[a] Assumes two-hour movie and two-person household.

[b] Calculated by assuming $30 billion in TV advertising, divided by 2,555 (7 hours a day average viewing time × 365 days) × 100 million households.

One of the most noticeable tendencies, for instance, has been the virtual dichotomization of the theatrical market into a relative handful of "hits" and a mass of also-rans. This can be seen from several recent peak-season box-office experiences, in which four out of perhaps a dozen major releases have generated as much as 80% of total revenues.

Although "must-see" media-event films are as much in demand as ever – and are now able to generate the bulk of their ultimate box-office take within the first three weeks of release – such dichotomization suggests that ticket sales for pictures that are of less immediate interest to audiences are probably being replaced by home screenings that on average generate much less revenue per view. The new home-video options obviously allow people to become much more discriminating as to when and where they spend an evening out. And recent surveys strongly suggest that young people no longer necessarily regard theaters as the preferred medium for viewing films. [21]

In other words, what is gained in one market may be at least partially lost in another: In the aggregate, ancillary-market cash flow is often largely substitutional. For example, extensive exposures on pay cable prior to showings on network television have sharply reduced network ratings garnered by feature film broadcasts, and the networks now accordingly bid much less than they used to for most feature-film exhibition rights.

The progression of ancillary markets has also frequently been heralded as a boon to movie industry profitability. However, contributions from new revenue sources, especially those from pay cable and home video, have not been sufficient to offset rapidly rising costs of theatrical production and release. Between 1980 and 2005, for example, the cost of the average picture made by a major studio rose from $9.4 million to $60.0 million and average marketing costs soared from $4.3 million to $36.2 million. Returns on revenues (operating margins) have meanwhile fallen by at least one-third and have remained well below the peaks of the late 1970s (see Table 3.3). Table 3.7 shows recent aggregate industry financial performance.

Just as significantly, though, the existence of ancillary markets has enabled many independent producers to finance their films through *presales* of rights. As Goodell (1998, p. xvii) notes, an independently produced film may be

Table 3.7. *Filmed entertainment industry operating performance: composite of six companies, 2001–2005*

| | Revenues | Operating income | Operating margin[a] (%) | Assets | Operating cash flow |
|---|---|---|---|---|---|
| CAGR(%)[b] | 8.5 | 24.1 | 8.3[c] | −0.8 | 5.9 |

[a] Average margin = 8.3%.
[b] Compound annual growth rate.
[c] Not meaningful.

defined as one "that is *developed* without ties to a major studio, regardless of where subsequent production and/or distribution financing comes from." Or it is a project in which the producer bears some financial risk.

Such presales, often in the form of funds, guarantees, or commitments that may be used to obtain funds, will at times support projects that perhaps could not and should not have otherwise been made. Indeed, projects financed in this manner, routinely through sale of foreign rights, are often unable to generate cash flows in excess of the amounts required to cover the costs of both production and release (marketing and prints).[22]

Companies generally relying on presale strategies manage to cushion, but not eliminate, their downside risks while giving away much of the substantial upside profit and cash flow potential from hits. Such companies will also inevitably have a relatively high cost of capital as compared with that of a major studio if only because presale cash commitments (from downstream distributors) are generally relayed to the producer in installments. The producer will still usually need interim (and relatively costly) loans to cover cash outlays during the period of production and perhaps up until well after theatrical release. And, over the longer run, the relatively few hits firms of this kind might produce are often insufficient in number or in degree of success to cover their many losing or breakeven projects.[23]

As we can see from the data, ancillary-market expansion has not as yet been (and may never be) fully translated into enhanced industry profitability. In essence, weak cost constraints, fragmentation of markets and audiences, and increased competition for talent resources have capped profit margins, incremental new-media revenue contributions notwithstanding.[24] Still, there can be no doubt that the new media have forever changed the income structure of the film business at large. As Table 3.8 illustrates, as recently as 1980,

Table 3.8. *Film industry sources of revenue: worldwide studio receipts, in U.S.\$ billions (2004 dollars), 1948–2004*

| Year | Theater | Video/DVD | TV, Pay[a] | TV, Free[b] | Total | Theater share (%) |
|------|---------|-----------|---------|----------|-------|-------------------|
| 1948 | 7.80 | – 0 – | – 0 – | – 0 – | 7.80 | **100.0** |
| 1980 | 4.50 | 0.20 | 0.39 | 3.35 | 8.44 | **53.3** |
| 1985 | 3.04 | 2.40 | 1.07 | 5.74 | 12.25 | **24.8** |
| 1990 | 5.28 | 6.02 | 1.66 | 7.60 | 20.56 | **25.7** |
| 1995 | 5.72 | 10.90 | 2.40 | 8.13 | 27.15 | **21.1** |
| 2000 | 6.02 | 11.97 | 3.20 | 11.03 | 32.22 | **18.7** |
| 2004 | 7.40 | 20.90 | 4.00 | 12.60 | 44.90 | **16.5** |

[a] Includes both PPV and subscription pay TV.
[b] Includes network TV, cable TV, and local stations.
*Sources*: Epstein (2005), Slate.com, and MPAA.

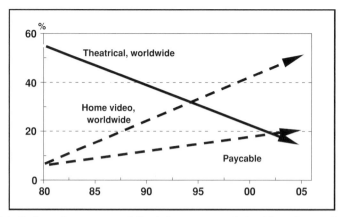

Figure 3.9. Estimated percentage of film industy revenue derived from feature film exploitation in theatrical, home video, and pay cable markets, 1980 and 2005.

theatrical sources accounted for over half of all industry revenues. Twenty-five years later (Figure 3.9), theatrical accounted for less than a fifth of all such revenues, and TV licensing is the most profitable source.

Although a distinct shift of preference away from "free" advertiser-supported programming and toward the direct purchase of entertainment in the form of movie tickets, pay cable services, and home video units (through either sales or rentals) would, with all other things being held equal, lead to a significant improvement in profitability, such a shift appears to be happening only gradually.[25] For the most part, the inherent uncertainties have instead created a constantly shifting jumble of corporate cross-ownership and joint-venture arrangements (Figure 3.10) that, in a scramble for control of content, distribution supremacy, and access to audiences, more often resemble hedged bets than bold and insightful strategic maneuvers.[26]

Internet-based technology already provides viewers with unprecedented control over when and where entertainment may be enjoyed. Such technology has already appreciably lowered the price per view and further diffuses the economic power of the more traditional suppliers of programming. However, because new viewings invariably displace older ones, marketing costs remain inordinately high as both the old and the new compete for the attention of wide-ranging, yet fickle, audiences.

### 3.5 Assets

Film libraries

More guesswork and ambiguity appear in the valuation of film library assets than in perhaps any other area relating to the financial economics of the movie business. Yet this topic is, nonetheless, of prime concern to investors who, over the years, have staked billions of dollars on actual and rumored studio

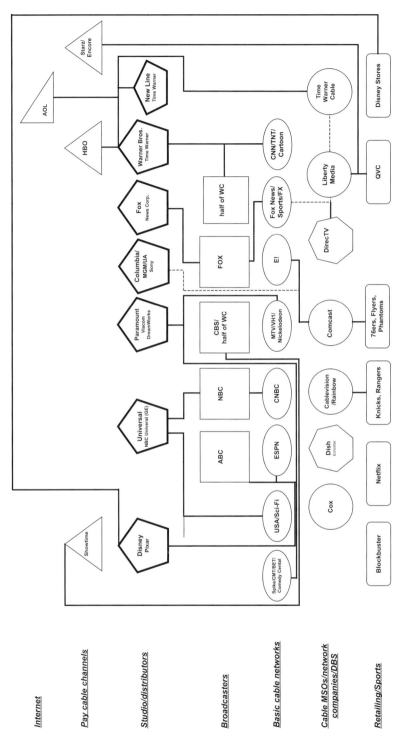

Figure 3.10. Significant entertainment company interrelationships, 2007. Dashed lines indicate indirect relationships.

takeovers. Twentieth Century Fox, United Artists, Columbia Pictures, and
MCA Inc. (now Universal) have been among the many major acquisitions
in an industry long rife with buy-out attempts. Factors that might not at first
glance be considered significant – technological advances, interest rates,
legislative developments, recent utilization (depletion) rates, and prevailing
social temper – all affect a library's perceived value.

*Technology* Of all these factors, technological advances have been by far
the most important and have generated the most controversy. Certainly the
flourishing new electronic media have increased the demand for programming, effectively providing opportunities to sell a lot of old wine in a wide
variety of new bottles. Yet new entertainment delivery and storage technologies have made it possible for practically anyone to record programming
conveniently, inexpensively, and often illegally. This capability has, to some
unknown extent, adversely affected library values as consumers now control
or have ready access to millions of copies of once-scarce programming.[27]

*Utilization rates* The prior degree of public exposure (i.e., the utilization
rate) of major features is a key element in valuation. Utilization-rate considerations, in particular, involve some interesting economic (and philosophical)
trade-offs: For a library to be worth a lot, it cannot be exposed (i.e., exhibited) too frequently. However, to generate cash, and to thereby reflect its
latent or inherent worth, it either must be licensed for exhibition or must be
sold outright.

Moreover, because the most recent pictures generally arouse the greatest audience interest, and thus at the margin amass the greatest amount of
revenue, there is usually (except for those rare features deemed classics) a
time-decay (perishability) element involved. In this regard, changes in social
temperament may be important. A vault full of war epics, for instance, might
be very popular with the public during certain periods but very unpopular
during others. Some humor in films is timeless; some is so terribly topical
that within a few years audiences may not understand it. In addition, because
everything from hair and clothing styles to cars and moral attitudes changes
gradually over time, the cumulative effects of these changes can make movies
from only two decades ago seem rather quaint.

Of the more than 19,000 features in the vaults of Hollywood's majors
(Table 3.9), it is therefore difficult to imagine (after considering the cost of
prints and advertising) that more than fifty or so per annum could be profitably
reissued to theaters. Demand for older movies is not much greater on pay
cable channels, which generally thrive on new materials (but demand can
be substantial on long-tailed advertiser-supported channels, DVDs, and the
Internet). And although home video has also become an important avenue
for exploitation of libraries, the major studios would normally find it difficult
to promote effectively an average of much more than one new title per week.

Table 3.9. *Approximate number of majors' feature titles as of 2004*[a]

| Studio | Approximate no. of titles |
|---|---|
| Sony (Columbia/TriStar) | 2,500 |
| Disney | 700 |
| Paramount | 1,100 |
| Twentieth Century Fox | 2,100 |
| MGM (including Orion) | 4,500 |
| Universal | 4,100 |
| Warner Bros. (including New Line, pre-1987 MGM) | 4,500 |
| Total | 19,500 |

[a] Universal owns 1,000 pre-1948 Paramount features, and UA owns 745 pre-1950 Warner Bros. films. UA also owns free-TV rights to 700 pre-1950 RKO pictures. Also see chapter note 28.

Moreover, syndicated television, long the main market for older features, also relies heavily on the relative handful of titles that have consistently proved strong enough to attract audiences.

In all, then, the structural constraints are such that the industry probably cannot in the aggregate regularly deploy in the domestic and foreign markets more than about 1,000 or so items (5%) a year from its full catalog of features (out of an estimated worldwide total of 500,000 movies and 3 million television shows and video clips).

*Interest and inflation rates* The effect of interest rates, the single most important external variable in valuation, can be best understood by visualizing a portfolio of film-licensing contracts (lasting for, say, the typical three to five years) as entitling the holder to an income stream similar to that derived from an intermediate-maturity bond or annuity. As in the bond market, rising interest rates diminish a portfolio's value, and vice versa. In other words, the net present value (*NPV*) of a library is the sum of all discounted cash flows, risk-adjusted for uncertainties, that are estimated to be derived from the future licensing of rights or from outright sales of films in the group. A discounted cash flow concept of this kind may be mathematically presented in its most elementary form as

$$NPV_a = \sum_{t=0}^{n} A_t/(1 + r)^t,$$

where $r$ is the risk-adjusted required rate of return (which is linked to interest rates), $A$ is the estimated cash to be received in period $t$ for film $a$, and $n$ is

Table 3.10. *Selected film library transfers, 1957–2006*[a]

| Year | Assets transferred | Sold by | Bought by | Approximate price |
|---|---|---|---|---|
| 1957 | 700 Warner Bros. features, shorts, cartoons | Associated Artists | United Artists | $30 million |
| 1958 | 750 pre-1948 features | Paramount | MCA | $50 million |
| 1979 | 500 features | American International Pictures | Filmways | $25 million |
| 1981 | 2,200 features, shorts, studio, and distribution system | Transamerica | MGM | $380 million |
| 1981 | 1,400 features, Aspen Skiing, Coke Bottling, Deluxe Film Labs, 5 TV stations, Intl Theater Chain, studio real estate | Twentieth Century Fox | Marvin Davis, private investor | $722 million |
| 1982 | 1,800 features, studio property, TV stations, arcade games manufacturing | Columbia Pictures | Coca-Cola | $750 million |
| 1982 | 500 features | Filmways | Orion Pictures | $26 million |
| 1985 | 4,600 features, 800 cartoons, shorts, Metrocolor Lab, studio property | MGM/UA Entertainment (K. Kerkorian) | Turner Broadcasting (T. Turner) | $1.5 billion |
| 1985 | 950 features, distribution system, and other rights to MGM library | Turner Broadcasting | United Artists (K. Kerkorian) | $480 million |
| 1989 | 2,400 features and 20,000 TV episodes plus distribution system, 800 screens, and other rights | Columbia Pictures Entertainment and Coca-Cola | Sony Corp | $4.8 billion[b] |

| Year | Assets | Seller | Buyer | Amount |
|---|---|---|---|---|
| 1990 | 3,100, features, 14,000 TV episodes | MCA Inc. | Matsushita Electric | $6.1 billion[c] |
| 1993 | 200 features | New Line | Turner Broadcasting | $500 million |
| 1994 | 900 features, 4,000 TV episodes, 1/2 USA network, teams, TV stations, publishing | Paramount | Viacom Inc. | $9.6 billion |
| 1995 | 3,200 features, 14,000 TV episodes | Matsushita[d] | Seagram Co., Ltd. | $5.7 billion |
| 1996 | 1,500 features and 4,100 TV episodes | Credit Lyonnais | K. Kerkorian/ Seven Network | $1.3 billion |
| 1997 | 2,000 features | Orion/Samuel Goldwyn | Metro-Goldwyn-Mayer | $573 million |
| 2003 | 7,000 features | Artisan | Lions Gate | $210 million |
| 2006 | 59 features | DreamWorks | Paramount (Viacom) | $1.5 billion |

[a] Several other transactions or proposed transactions reflect library values. In 1985, a half interest in Twentieth Century Fox was obtained by Rupert Murdoch for $162 million in cash and an $88 million loan, equivalent to about $180,000 a title if real estate, studio assets, and distribution are assumed to comprise half of the asset valuation.

In 1982, the pre-1948 Warner Bros. library, including 745 features, 327 cartoons, all the outstanding syndication rights, and the MGM/UA music publishing business was almost sold to Warner Communications for around $100 million. Adjusting for the nonfilm assets in the proposed sale would indicate a per title average of somewhat under $100,000 a title.

[b] Includes assumption of debt of $1.4 billion. In addition, subsequent buy-out of Guber–Peters Entertainment assets required several hundred million dollars more.

[c] Includes recorded music, theme parks, and publishing.

[d] Matsushita retained 20% equity interest.

the number of future periods over which the cash stream is to be received. Because it is often procedurally difficult to make precise estimates of revenues and net residuals and other participant costs more than a few years into the future, relatively large adjustments for risk must normally be assumed either directly in the formula (by raising the assumed $r$) or by further trimming of the calculated $NPV$s.

Inflation is, of course, one of many possible reasons for license fees to rise over time. But to the extent that license fees reflect general inflationary pressures, there is merely an illusion of enhanced worth. Another inflation illusion appears when people speak of "priceless" assets that are often priceless primarily in an artistic sense. Many animated Disney classics, for example, could not be made today at less than astronomical cost, and these pictures are widely considered to be "priceless." However, that does not necessarily mean that these films can consistently generate high license fees or box-office grosses every year. Most of them, in fact, cannot.

*Collections and contracts*  Other factors entering into an evaluation process include questions of rights ownership and completeness. As in philately or numismatics, a complete collection of a series (e.g., all *Rocky* or James Bond or Marx Brothers films) is obviously more valuable than an incomplete set. Control over a complete series of related films (and their elements, such as original negatives and soundtracks, stills, one-sheets, and TV commercials) makes full marketing exploitation much more efficient.

Rights-ownership splits can, in addition, present especially nettlesome problems. To fully assess a library, many hundreds of detailed contracts signed over the span of many years must be reviewed to determine the sizes of participations and residual payments, the licensability of rights (including copyright protections), and also any potential restrictions as to transferability. But because such contract stipulations are often not well documented (or, for that matter, made available to outsiders), most evaluations must be made at a distance from extrapolations of what is known about available rights to a few key properties. The total number of films in a library may thus provide only a rough measure of its potential value.

*Library transfers*  From the outside, the most obvious method of determining what a library might be worth is to study previous asset transfer prices for comparable film portfolios. This approach, though, may be difficult to implement because library sales are fairly infrequent and because the conditions under which such trades take place may differ significantly. The motives for transfer and the prevailing market sentiment for entertainment products at the time of transfer often carry great weight in establishing a transfer price. Consequently, even for two libraries of substantially the same size and quality, the prices may be greatly dissimilar.[28]

From the information in Table 3.10, we can see that the going rate for a major feature film title has varied widely. We can also say that the

Table 3.11. *Major studio real estate assets, 2005*

| Studio | Assets |
|--------|--------|
| Columbia Pictures (Sony Corp.) | 44 acres in Culver City, near Los Angeles (formerly MGM) |
| Walt Disney Company | 27,500 acres, Disney World, Florida |
| | 160 acres, Disneyland, California |
| | 44 acres, Burbank, California headquarters |
| | 691-acre ranch outside Los Angeles |
| Fox (News Corp.) | 63 acres, studio and headquarters, Los Angeles |
| NBC Universal (MCA) | 420 acres, Los Angeles headquarters and studio-tour |
| | 875 acres, Orlando, Florida, studio-tour |
| Paramount (Viacom, Inc.) | 50 acres, studio, Los Angeles |
| Warner Bros. (Time Warner, Inc.) | 140 acres, Burbank studios |

film-asset evaluation process is neither simple nor precise. As with assessments of beauty, value is often only a function of the beholder's imagination.

Real estate

For a long time, the Hollywood majors neglected and underutilized their real estate assets which, prior to the 1948 consent decree and in the form of exhibition sites, provided important collateral to banks supporting production loans. However, such neglect is no longer in evidence.[29] By the early 1980s, studio real estate assets were in the middle of a steep valuation uptrend as proximity to major urban growth areas and the numbers of made-for-television movies, theatrical features, and cable productions rose to new heights.[30]

Compared with the downsizing of a generation ago, it is clear that movie-company real estate assets are now being actively managed and are becoming more impressive all the time. The scope of those assets is revealed in Table 3.11.

As always, real estate values in Hollywood or elsewhere will be sensitive to changes in interest rates and to the growth rates of the economy as a whole. Nevertheless, anticipated rising demand for new entertainment software-production facilities and completion of ambitious property-development plans suggest that these assets have become significant in the financial analysis of film companies and their corporate parents.

## 3.6 Concluding remarks

This chapter has taken a macroeconomic view of the movie industry. As we have seen, many of the things that affect other industries – economic cycles, foreign exchange rates, antitrust actions, technological advances, and interest rates – also affect profits and valuations here. From this angle, moviemaking is a business like any other. How the film business differs from other businesses will more easily be seen from the microeconomic and accounting perspectives that are presented in the next two chapters.

## Notes

**1.** As Putnam (1997) notes, in Europe development was spearheaded by the Lumière family and by the "industrialization" of the business by Charles Pathé. It was the Europeans who early began to regard cinema as a cultural art form. As Roud (1983, p. 7) notes and probably exaggerates, by 1914 the French had captured 90% of the world's film market, but by 1919, this share had dropped to 15%. Still, in London Kinetosope peepshow machines, including a venue on Oxford Street, had been operating commercially as early as 1895 – that is, before the 1896 premiere of the Lumière brothers' Cinématographe and Robert Paul's Theatrograph systems. See also Chapter 9 in Trumpbour (2002).

**2.** Emergence of film exchanges moved the industry away from the purchasing to the leasing of films. This increased the turnover of titles and also the pool of available films for nickelodeons.

**3.** At around the same time, consolidation of production, distribution, and exhibition in England was being spearheaded by J. Arthur Rank, who, as Trumpbour (2002, p. 179) notes, indirectly benefited from provisions in the British 1938 Cinematograph Films Act (i.e., quota legislation). More detailed accounts of the economic history of film are also given in Sedgwick and Pokorny (2005).

**4.** This argument has especially been advanced by Gilder (2000), who makes the case that because bandwidth (or signal-carrying capacity) of fiber optic cable is tremendously larger than that of ordinary electronic computers and switches, fiber optic networks will quickly supplant the current electronics-based communications infrastructure.

**5.** This and other aspects of the industry's long and colorful history are recounted in books such as those by Stanley (1978), Knight (1978), and Balio (1976).

**6.** The exhibition industry continues to consolidate, with values in this business calculated in terms of EBITDA multiples. At the height of the bidding in the 1980s, multiples for properties in large cities reached to the range of ten to fourteen times projected cash flows. But many properties in smaller cities have been typically priced at only five or six times. Also, although many big-city purchase prices averaged well over $1 million per screen, transfer prices per screen averaged just below $500,000 during the 1980s. However, by 2000, overbuilding of expensive theaters with stadium seating had caused most of the major chains to declare bankruptcy.

**7.** Tri-Star Pictures was a new studio formed in 1982 by Columbia (Coca-Cola), CBS, and Home Box Office (see Sansweet 1983), with equal initial capital contributions totaling $50 million. Prior to a public stock and debt offering in 1985, the principal shareholders contributed another $50 million. CBS soon thereafter, however, sold its interest, while Coca-Cola increased its share of ownership. Nonetheless, in late 1987, Coca-Cola merged the former Embassy Pictures and Merv Griffin Enterprises television properties into Tri-Star and renamed the whole package Columbia Pictures, while retaining a 49% interest in the total entity. All of Columbia was then bought by Sony, the Japanese electronics giant, in November 1989. Universal, originally MCA Inc., went through several hands, from

Seagram in 1995 to Vivendi in 2000 and then finally to GE/NBC in 2003. MGM was sold as a film library play in 2004 to a group led by Sony in a buy-out partially financed by Comcast.

**8.** Although distributors such as Disney and Warner Bros. are capable of handling between 40 and 60 titles a year, they are normally not interested in handling that many films.

**9.** Two large companies that made feature films, CBS and ABC, reentered production (but not distribution) in the early 1980s after a hiatus of about ten years. Both companies had produced movies in the late 1960s and early 1970s, but after sustaining substantial losses, they had withdrawn from the field. CBS originally distributed its Cinema Center Films (e.g., *My Fair Lady*) through National General Corp., and American Broadcasting's ABC Pictures used a now-defunct subsidiary of Cinerama (Cinerama Releasing). By 1984, however, both companies had again withdrawn from theatrical production.

**10.** The term *states-righters* was appropriately applied at a time prior to when national distribution networks had become fully operational.

**11.** Contracyclicity of ticket demand was studied by Albert Kapusinski (see Nardone 1982), who matched 42 economic measures of the motion-picture industry for the 1928– 1975 span against similar variables used to assess the performance of the whole economy. The variables were then subjected to five tests of cyclical movement and led to the results cited.

Preliminary experiments using spectral-analysis techniques hint at the possibility of a four-year cycle and a ten-year cycle in movie admissions, but, as noted, the statistical evidence in this regard is inconclusive. A more heuristic approach based on unit ticket sales and general operating conditions also seems to suggest the possible existence of a 25-year cycle. Spectral analysis is a statistical technique often used in signal-processing applications (in this case, economic time series) to determine whether or not cyclical patterns exist. References include Hamilton (1994), Koopmans (1974), and Gottman (1981).

**12.** Such seasonal relationships remain consistent over long periods. For instance, between 1983 and 1992, the summer box office as a percent of the year's total ranged between 35% and 41% and averaged 37.8%.

**13.** Determinants of theater attendance and video rental demand were studied by De Silva (1998), who found that a movie's director, advertising, and reviews and the viewer's age and marital status were significantly related to attendance. Other similar studies are in Litman (1998) and Sochay (1994).

**14.** Regression models attempt to explain, via statistical testing based on probabilistic assumptions, the extent to which some variables affect others. For example, a mathematical relationship might be in the form of an equation indicating that aggregate industry profit (the dependent variable) is a function of the number of admissions and the number of releases (the independent variables).

**15.** The number of films rated by MPAA is published each year in *Variety*.

**16.** These comparisons would suggest that significant marketing opportunities may be available in foreign markets. However, it is not enough for a country to have a large population base. For example, even with the large population bases in Russia and China, theater ticket prices are relatively low so that a large number of admissions would hardly generate an important amount of income for the major studios or exhibitors.

**17.** See B. Wallace (2005).

**18.** Putnam (1997) discusses the trade issues, but from an anti-American point of view. Hoskins, McFadyen, and Finn (1997) extensively discuss trade and the cultural discount.

They cite (p. 33) the Hoskins and Mirus (1988) definition of cultural discount attached to a given imported program or film as

(Value of domestic equivalent – value of import) / (value of domestic equivalent).

See also Jayakar and Waterman (2000), who concluded that a "home market effect" prevails in theatrical film trade and Moran (1996), Wildman and Siwek (1988), and Oh (2001). The issue of cultural diversity and protection of home markets against U.S. audiovisual dominance – that is, a U.S. trade surplus with Europe estimated at $8.1 billion in 2000 (half television and half film) – is covered in Riding (2003). Cowen (2002) discusses the reasons for Hollywood's dominance and contrasts the situation in several countries. Scott (2004) and Hirschberg (2004), respectively, explore the meaning of foreign and American films. See also Acheson and Maule (2005).

**19.**   As noted in Kapner (2003), the U.S. television industry share of a growing international market has continued to diminish, with 71% of the top ten programs in 60 countries being locally produced in 2001.

**20.**   However, the former United Artists subsidiary of Transamerica, which did not engage in series production activities, reported operating income on sales to both theatrical and television markets. Supplementary Table S2.2 illustrates the performance of United Artists in each of those markets during the 1970s.

**21.**   It was not until 1983 and 1984 that many large urban cable systems began to be constructed or to be activated. And it was not until 1985 that video recording or playback-only machines were present in over 20% of U.S. television households. When videocassette recorders (VCRs) reached into more than 20% of households in Germany and Australia, theatrical admissions in those countries declined noticeably, and pretty much the same effect was seen in the United States by 1986.

**22.**   Also, presales impair industry profitability because projects financed in this way (about one of every six involves presales of foreign rights) increase the supply of films and heighten the demand for, and thus the cost of, various input factors (screenplays, actors, sound stages, etc.). Country-by-country sales of distribution rights are used by independent producers to secure bank loans to fund production.

**23.**   Case histories from the mid-1980s include Cannon Group and De Laurentiis Entertainment as examples of presales-strategy companies that ultimately ran into such fatal financing problems.

**24.**   For example, in pay cable, Time Warner's cable program wholesaler, Home Box Office (HBO), emerged in the 1970s as a powerful, almost monopsonistic (a market with one buyer and many sellers) intermediary for Hollywood's products. In its position as dominant gatekeeper to the nation's wired homes, HBO was able to bargain effectively for retention of an important part of the revenue stream derived from sale of pay cable services (also see Chapter 8). By 1981, HBO had already surpassed the large theater chains to become Hollywood's single largest customer, licensing in excess of $130 million in that year (and around $500 million by the early 1990s). But it was not until the alternative The Movie Channel (TMC) and Showtime pay cable services merged, and until videocassette recorder (VCR) penetration rates reached over 20% of television households (in 1984), that HBO experienced significant competition. Prior to merging, Showtime was owned by Viacom and TMC was jointly owned by Warner Communications and American Express. Ownership of Showtime/TMC was split 50% Viacom, 40.5% Warner, and 9.5% American Express until 1985, when Viacom bought it all. In 1989, half of Showtime was then sold to Tele-Communications Inc.

The preceding history is that, around 1980, the major studios finally recognized that they had lost control of unit pricing and distribution in the important new medium of pay cable, and they accordingly attempted to reassert themselves by launching their own pay channel called Premiere. The studio consortium participants, however, encountered great difficulty in arriving at consensus decisions – especially under threat of antitrust litigation aimed at preventing films from being shown exclusively on Premiere. Showtime was meanwhile able to formulate exclusive five-year license agreements with Paramount. This $500 million agreement, signed in 1983, has subsequently been followed by other exclusive arrangements between cable wholesalers and film producers. See also Mair (1988).

**25.** To see this, note that consumers' out-of-pocket costs per hour of entertainment generally range from approximately 50 cents to $2, with pay-per-view events occasionally at $3 or more. On average, a typical household may buy about 100 hours of such entertainment in a year.

Still, that same average household spends about 2,500 hours per year (almost seven hours per day) with free advertiser-supported television. Sponsors reach this audience at a cost of around 12 cents per hour per household ($30 billion divided by 2,500 hours divided by 100 million households). If it were possible to sell another 100 hours or so per household per year at 50 cents rather than at 10 cents, all other things being equal (and they never are), entertainment industry revenues would be enhanced by about $4 billion. However, this is easier said than done in view of the time and income constraints discussed in Chapter 1.

As of 2006, U.S. consumers spent approximately $89 billion on such direct purchases ($9 billion in tickets, $55 billion on cable, and $25 billion for home video), whereas advertisers spent about $55 billion to sponsor programming.

**26.** The motivation for this type of activity is most often based on a desire to achieve *economies of scope*, which Hoskins, McFadyen, and Finn (2004, p. 100) define as when "the total cost of producing two (or more) products within the same firm is less than producing them separately in two (or more) nonrelated firms." If products are produced jointly, one product may be a by-product of the other, and the factors of production are shared. Movies and television shows, for example, often share processes of production, utilize many of the same windows of exhibition, are distributed through DVDs and cable networks, and generate by-products that may include merchandise. See also Peers (2005), Orwall and Peers (2002), and Brown (1984).

**27.** Ready availability of older materials on the Internet has made them more competitive with newer programs. Also, advances in technology have made it easier to slow or prevent chemical and physical decay of important film masters. Many libraries literally fade in the vault as color dyes decompose over time. Although chronically inadequate funding of preservation efforts permits a part of the industry's heritage to fade into oblivion every year, the costs of restoration or of colorization have declined along with the cost of computing power. Filmmakers concerned about detracting from the artistic integrity of the originals have often denounced such colorizations (of materials largely in the public domain from a copyright standpoint). As Linfield (1987) notes, colorization does not destroy the original black and white negatives or prints, which remain available for viewing by future generations. See *Variety*, March 11, 1996.

**28.** The most important transfer of the early 1980s was MGM's 1981 purchase of the United Artists subsidiary of Transamerica for $380 million (including UA's worldwide distribution organization and library of over 900 titles, many of Academy Award–winning best-picture stature). A subsequent (1985) transaction then again split MGM/UA Entertainment into separate pieces. The whole company, including MGM/UA's distribution arm and a combined total of about 4,600 features, was sold to Turner Broadcasting for $1.5 billion, which was only the first of numerous transactions of great complexity. Turner, later part of Time Warner, ended up owning MGM films made before 1986. In 1989, United Artists' 1,000-feature library, distribution arm, and television business again came up for sale. But by 1992, the MGM remnants were acquired by the French bank Credit Lyonnais after Giancarlo Parretti had defaulted on paying $1.7 billion (including debt) for MGM. The French bank then sold MGM back to Kirk Kirkorian's group in 1996 at a price of $1.3 billion. See Marr and Peers (2004).

In 1981 and 1982, there were two other notable transfers involving more than just film libraries and distributing organizations. The 1981 takeover of Twentieth Century Fox for $722 million included extensive real estate properties and several profitable divisions (a soft-drink-bottling franchise, an international theater chain, Aspen Ski Corporation, five television stations, and Deluxe Film Laboratories). Likewise, the 1982 purchase of Columbia Pictures (for about $750 million) by the Coca-Cola Company included some broadcasting properties, part of the Burbank Studios real estate, and an arcade-game manufacturing subsidiary. And, in 2003, Lionsgate acquired the Artisan library of 7,000 films for approximately $210 million.

Also of historical interest, Warner Bros. sold 850 features and 1,500 shorts to PRM, an investment firm, and Associated Artists Productions, a television distributor, in March 1956. Through its purchase of Associated Artists Productions in late 1957, United Artists, for about $30 million, then gained control of some 700 pre-1948 Warner films and several hundred other features, short subjects, and cartoons. In addition, as Stanley (1978, p. 152) notes, in 1958 MCA paid approximately $50 million ($10 million cash) to acquire Paramount's pre-1948 library of 750 features.

**29.**   Significant changes in studio real estate included the early 1970s combination of the Columbia Pictures and Warner Bros. lots (at a time when Columbia was in great financial distress) and MGM's decision in 1973 to reduce production and to thus sell 130 out of 175 acres in Culver City. Eighteen acres of the Columbia studio were sold in 1977 for $6.1 million, while MGM's early 1970s sale of the Culver City assets brought $12 million. The former MGM Culver City property was subsequently bought by Lorimar, which was soon thereafter merged into Warner Communications (now Time Warner). In 1989, Columbia (Sony) then swapped its Burbank holdings for the Culver City property held by Warner. Lorimar's 1987 purchase from Turner Broadcasting of the remaining Culver City property was for over $50 million, but it is impossible to attribute an exact price because other assets were included in the transaction.

**30.**   Demand for production space had become so strong that other parts of the country were able to compete effectively against Hollywood with so-called runaway studios by promising more accommodating shooting schedules or lower overall costs. See Bagamery (1984) and also Harris (1981). Benefiting from lower costs, fewer union restrictions, and a weak currency versus the U.S. dollar, Canada had by the early 2000s taken a significant share of Hollywood's filmed entertainment production work. But this began to change when Canadian tax shelters, as McNary (2003) notes, were removed. As of 2002, Canada and Australia, respectively, attracted projects with film-production tax credits equal to 11% and 12.5% of labor costs. See DiOrio and McNary (2002) and Boucher (2005) concerning filming of *Superman Returns* in Australia.

## Selected additional reading

Altman, D. (1992). *Hollywood East: Louis B. Mayer and the Origins of the Studio System.* New York: Carol Publishing (Birch Lane).

Balio, T. (1987). *United Artists: The Company That Changed the Film Industry.* Madison, WI: University of Wisconsin Press.

Baughman, J. L. (1992). *The Republic of Mass Culture: Journalism, Filmmaking and Broadcasting in America since 1941.* Baltimore: Johns Hopkins University Press.

Berg, A. S. (1989). *Goldwyn: A Biography.* New York: Knopf (and Berkley Publishing Group paperback, 1998).

Brownstein, R. (1990). *The Power and the Glitter: The Hollywood–Washington Connection.* New York: Pantheon Books and 1992 Vintage paperback.

Cieply, M. (1984). "Movie Classics Transformed to Color Films," *Wall Street Journal,* September 11.

Cieply, M., and Barnes, P. W. (1986). "Movie and TV Mergers Point to Concentration of Power to Entertain," *Wall Street Journal,* August 21.

Egan, J. (1983). "HBO Takes on Hollywood," *New York,* 17(24)(June 13).

Fowler, G. A., and Mazurkewich, K. (2005). "How Mr. Kong Helped Turn China into a Film Power," *Wall Street Journal,* September 14.

Friedrich, O. (1986). *City of Nets: A Portrait of Hollywood in the 1940s.* New York: Harper & Row.

Goldstein, P. (2005). "In a Losing Race with the Zeitgeist," *Los Angeles Times,* November 22.

Izod, J. (1988). *Hollywood and the Box Office, 1895–1986.* New York: Columbia University Press.

Kafka, P., and Newcomb, P. (2003). "Cash Me Out If You Can," *Forbes,* 171(5)(March 3).

Klein, E. (1991). "A Yen for Hollywood: Hollywood vs. Japan," *Vanity Fair,* 54(6)(September).

Landro, L. (1995). "Ego and Inexperience among Studio Buyers Add Up to Big Losses, *Wall Street Journal,* April 10.

Leonard, D. (2001). "Mr. Messier Is Ready for His Close-up," *Fortune,* 144(4)(September 3).

Rose, F. (1998). "There's No Business Like Show Business," *Fortune,* 137(12)(June 22).

Sherman, S. P. (1986a). "Ted Turner: Back from the Brink," *Fortune,* 114(1)(July 7).
    (1986b). "Movie Theaters Head Back to the Future," *Fortune,* 113(2)(January 20).
    (1984). "Coming Soon: Hollywood's Epic Shakeout," *Fortune,* 109(9)(April 30).

Steinberg, C. (1980). *Reel Facts.* New York: Vintage Books (Random House).

Thompson, K. (1986). *Exporting Entertainment: America in the World Film Market, 1907–1934.* London: British Film Institute.

Turner, R., and King, T. R. (1993). "Disney Stands Aside as Rivals Stampede to Digital Alliances," *Wall Street Journal,* September 24.

Twitchell, J. B. (1992). *Carnival Culture: The Trashing of Taste in America.* New York: Columbia University Press.

Waterman, D. (2005). *Hollywood's Road to Riches.* Cambridge, MA: Harvard University Press.

# 4
# Making and marketing movies

*Dough makes bread and dough makes deals.*

Some people would argue that deals, not movies, are Hollywood's major product. "Contract-driven" is a handy way to describe the business.

Although we frequently think of studios as monolithic enterprises, in actuality, they have become intellectual property clearinghouses simultaneously engaged in four distinct business functions: financing, producing, distributing, and marketing and advertising movies.[1] Each function requires the application of highly specialized skills that include raising and investing money, assessing and insuring production costs and risks, and planning and executing marketing and advertising campaigns. Indeed, every motion picture and television project must inevitably confront and then cope with three main risks, first in financing, then in completion, and then in performance. This chapter describes the framework in which these functions are performed.

## 4.1 Properties – physical and mental

A movie screenplay begins with a story concept based on a literary property already in existence, a new idea, or a true event. It then normally proceeds in stages from outline to treatment, to draft, and finally to polished form.[2]

Prior to the outline, however, enters the literary agent, who is familiar with the latest novels and writers and always primed to make a deal on the client's behalf. Normally, unsolicited manuscripts make little or no progress when submitted directly to studio editorial departments. But with an introduction from an experienced agent – who must have a refined sense of the possibility of success for the client's work and of the changing moods of potential producers – a property can be submitted for review by independent and/or studio-affiliated producers. Expenditures to this stage usually involve only telephone calls and some travel, reading, and writing time.

However, should the property attract the interest of a potential producer (or perhaps someone capable of influencing a potential producer), an option agreement will ordinarily be signed. Just as in the stock or real estate markets, such options provide, for a small fraction of the total underlying value, the right to purchase the property in full. Options have fixed expiration dates and negotiated prices, and depending on the fine print, they can sometimes be resold. Literary agents, moreover, usually begin to collect at least 10% of the proceeds at this point.

Now in the unlikely event that a film producer decides to adapt one of the many properties offered, the real fund-raising effort begins. This effort is legalistically based on what is known as a literary property agreement (LPA), a contract describing the conveyance of various rights by the author and/or other rights-owners to the producer. To a great extent, the depth and complexity of the LPA will be shaped by the type of financing available to the producer of this project.

For example, if the producer is affiliated with a major studio, the studio will normally (in the LPA) insist on retaining a broad array of rights so that a project can be fully exploited in terms of its potential for sequels, television series spin-offs, merchandising, and other opportunities. Such an affiliation will often significantly diminish, if not totally relieve, the producers' financing problems because a studio distribution contract can be used to secure bank loans. Better yet, a studio may also invest its own capital. But more commonly, "independent" producers will have to obtain the initial financing from other sources – which means that they are thus not fully independent. In the pursuit of such start-up capital, many innovative, if not truly ingenious, financing structures have been devised.

Even so, funding decisions are normally highly subjective, and mistakes are often made: Promising projects are rejected or aborted, and whimsical ones accepted (i.e., "green-lighted" in industry jargon). The highly successful features *Star Wars* and *Raiders of the Lost Ark*, for instance, were shopped around to several studios before Twentieth Century Fox and Paramount, respectively, agreed to finance and distribute them. *Jaws* was, moreover, nearly canceled midway in production because of heavy cost overruns, *Home Alone* was placed in turnaround well after its preparation had started, and the script for *Back to the Future* was initially rejected by every studio.[3]

Of course, for funding to be obtained, a project must already be outlined in terms of story line, director, producer, location, cast, and estimated budget. To reach this point, enter the talent agents, or pejoratively, the "flesh peddlers." Agents play an important role in obtaining work for their clients, sometimes by assembling into "packages" the diverse but hopefully compatible human elements (and more recently, the financings) that go into the making of good feature films or television programs.[4]

The largest multidivision talent agencies are The Creative Artists Agency (CAA), which became a Hollywood powerhouse in the 1980s, The William Morris Agency, United Talent Agency, International Creative Management (ICM), United Talent Agency, and Endeavor.[5] In addition, there are also smaller and highly specialized firms, among which are "discount" agencies that place talent for fees of less than the standard 10% of income.

Agents, in the aggregate, perform a vital function by generally lowering the cost of searching for key components of a film project and by relaying and replenishing that constant and necessary industry data base known as gossip. As such, gossip is a natural offshoot of an agent's primary purpose, which is to advance the careers of clients at whatever price the talent market will bear. The use of agents also permits talent employers to confine their work relations to artistic matters and to delegate business topics to expert handling by the artists' representatives.

## 4.2 Financial foundations

Some of the most creative work in the entire movie industry is reflected not on the screen, but in the financial offering prospectuses that are circulated in attempts to fund film projects. As we shall see, financing for films can be arranged in many different ways, including the formation of limited partnerships and the direct sale of common stock to the public. However, financing sources fall generally into three distinct classes:

1. *Industry sources*, which include studio development and in-house production deals and financings by independent distributors, talent agencies, laboratories, completion funds, and other end-users such as television networks, pay cable, and home video distributors
2. *Lenders*, including banks, insurance companies, and distributors
3. *Investors*, including public and private funding pools arranged in a variety of organizational patterns

The most common financing variations available from investors and lenders are discussed in the following section. Industry sources are discussed in Chapter 5.

Common-stock offerings

Common-stock offerings are structurally the simplest of all to understand. A producer hopes to raise large amounts of capital by selling a relatively small percentage of equity interest in potential profits. But as historical experience has shown, common-stock–based offerings do not, on the average, stand out as a particularly easy method of raising production money for movies. Unless speculative fervor in the stock market is running high, movie-company start-ups usually encounter a long, torturous, and expensive obstacle course.

The main difficulty is that a return on investment from pictures produced with seed money may take years to materialize, if it ever does, and underlying assets initially have little or no worth. Hope that substantial values will be created in the not-too-distant future is usually the principal ingredient in these offerings. In contrast to boring but safe investments in Treasury bills and money-market funds, new movie-company issues promise excitement, glamor, and risk.[6]

Straight common-stock offerings of unknown new companies are thus generally difficult to launch except in all but the frothiest of speculative market environments.[7] Strictly from the stock market investor's viewpoint, experience has shown that most of the small initial common-stock movie offerings have provided at least as many investment nightmares as tangible returns.

More recently, though, large private equity and hedge fund investors have begun to funnel money into portfolios of films through special arrangements with both major studios and established independents.[8] These pools of funds now contribute some of the financing that had been previously done through tax shelters and partnerships (see below).

Combination deals

Common stock is often sold in combination with other securities so as to appeal to a wider investor spectrum or to more closely fit the financing requirements of the issuing company. This is illustrated by the Telepictures equity offering of the early 1980s. At that time, Telepictures was primarily a syndicator of television series and feature films and a packager and marketer of made-for-television movies and news.

As of its initial 1980 offering by a small New York firm, Telepictures had distribution rights to over 30 feature films and to about 200 hours of television programming in Latin America. The underwriting was in the form of 7,000 units, each composed of 350,000 common shares, warrants to purchase 350,000 common shares, and $7 million in 20-year 13% convertible subordinated debentures. In total, Telepictures raised $6.4 million in equity capital.

Another illustration of a combination offering was that of De Laurentiis Entertainment Group Inc., which in 1986 separately but simultaneously sold 1.85 million shares of common stock and $65 million in 12.5% senior subordinated 15-year notes through a large New York underwriting firm. In this instance, the well-known producer Dino De Laurentiis contributed his previously acquired rights in the 245-title Embassy Films library and in an operational film studio in North Carolina to provide an asset base for the new public entity. Among the several major films in the library were *The Graduate*, *Carnal Knowledge*, and *Romeo and Juliet*.

The underlying concept for this company, as well as for many other similar issues brought public at around the same time, was that presales of rights to pay cable, home video, and foreign theatrical distributors could be used to cover, or perhaps more than cover, direct production expenses on low-budget pictures. The subsequent difficulties experienced by this company and several others applying the same strategy, however, proved that the concept most often works better in theory than in practice. The reason is that companies in the production start-up phase of development normally encounter severe cash flow pressures unless they are fortunate enough to have a big box-office hit early on.[9]

### Limited partnerships and tax shelters

Limited partnerships have in the past generally provided the opportunity to invest in movies, but with the government sharing some of the risk. In fact, before extensive tax-law adjustments in 1976, movie investments were among the most interesting tax-shelter vehicles ever devised. Prior to that revision, limited partners holding limited recourse or nonrecourse loans (i.e., in the event of default, the lender cannot seize all of the borrower's assets, thus making these loans without personal liability exposure) could write down losses against income several times the original amount invested; they could experience the fun and ego gratification of sponsoring movies and receive a tax benefit to boot.

Such agreements were in the form of either purchases or service partnerships. In a purchase, the investor would buy the picture (usually at an inflated price) with, say, a $1 down payment and promise to pay another $3 with a nonrecourse loan secured by anticipated receipts from the movie. Although the risk was only $1, there was a $4 base to depreciate and on which to charge investment tax credits.

In the service arrangement, an investor would become a partner in owning the physical production entity rather than the movie itself. Using a promissory note, deductions in the year of expenditure would again be a multiple of the actual amount invested – an attractive situation to individuals in federal tax brackets of over 50%.

Tax-code changes applicable between 1976 and 1986 permitted only the amount at risk to be written off against income by film "owners" (within a strict definition). The code also specified that investment tax credits (equivalent to 6 2/3% of the total investment in the negative if more than 80% of the picture had been produced in the United States) were to be accrued from the date of initial release.[10] Revised tax treatment also required investments to be capitalized – a stipulation that disallowed the service-partnership form.

Beginning with the Tax Reform Act of 1986, however, the investment tax credit that many entertainment companies had found so beneficial because it had helped them to conserve cash was repealed. And significantly, so-called passive losses from tax shelters could no longer be used to offset income from wages, salaries, interest, and dividends. Such passive losses became deductible only against other passive activity income. Since 1986, notably fewer and differently structured movie partnerships have accordingly been offered to the public: Most of the more recent ones have appeared outside the United States.[11]

More prototypical of the partnership structures of the 1980s, though, was the first (1983) offering of Silver Screen Partners. Strictly speaking, it was not a tax-sheltered deal. Here, Home Box Office (HBO, the Time Inc. wholesale distributor of pay cable programs) guaranteed – no matter what the degree of box-office success, if any – return of full production costs on each of at least ten films included in the financing package.

However, because only 50% of a film's budget was due on completion, with five years to meet the remaining obligations, HBO in effect received a sizable interest-free loan, while benefiting from a steady flow of fresh product.[12] For its 50% investment, HBO also retained exclusive pay television and television syndication rights and 25% of network TV sales. This meant that partners were largely relying on strong theatrical results, which, if they occurred, would entitle them to "performance bonuses."[13] Subsequent Silver Screen offerings of substantially the same structure, but of larger size (up to $400 million), had also been used to finance Disney's films (see Table 4.1).[14]

Such partnership units, though, are not the only types available. Quasi-public offerings that fall under the Securities and Exchange Commission's Regulation D may still, for example, be used by independent filmmakers in structuring so-called Regulation D financings for small corporations or limited partnerships. Regulation D offerings allow up to 35 private investors to buy units in a corporation or a partnership without registration under the Securities Act of 1933.[15]

Limited-partnership financing appeals to studios because the attracted incremental capital permits greater diversification of film-production portfolios: Cash resources are stretched, and there are then more films with which to feed ever-hungry distribution pipelines.[16] Also, a feature may not provide any return to investors owning an equity percentage of the film yet, as determined by the partnership structure, it may contribute to coverage of studio fixed costs (overhead) via earn-out of distribution fees that are taken as a percentage of the film's rental revenues.[17]

From the standpoint of the individual investor, most movie partnerships cannot be expected to provide especially high returns on invested capital. Few of them have historically returned better than 10% to 15% annually. But

Table 4.1. *Movie partnership financing: a selected sample, 1981–1987*

| Partnership | Total amount sought ($ millions) | Minimum investment ($ thousands) | Management fee as % of funds raised | Limited partners' share of profits |
|---|---|---|---|---|
| Delphi III (January 1984) | 60 | 5 | 1.16% for 1985–89, then 0.67% for 1990–94 | 99% to limited partners, 1% to general partners until 100% capital return; then general partners entitled to 20% of all further cash distribution |
| SLM Entertain- ment Ltd. (October 1981) | 40 | 10 | 2.5% of capitalization in 1982, 3% in 1983–87, and 1% in 1988–94 | 99% until 100% returned, then 80% until 200% returned, and 70% afterward |
| Silver Screen Partners (April 1983) | 75 | 15 | 4% of budgeted film costs + 10% per year to the extent payment is deferred | 99% until limited partners have received 100% plus 10% per annum on adjusted capital contribution; then 85% |
| Silver Screen Partners III (October 1986) | 200 | 5 | 4% of budgeted film cost + 10% per year on overhead paid to partnership | 99% to investors until they have received an amount equal to their modified capital contribution plus 8% priority return |

*Source*: Partnership prospectus materials.

such partnerships occasionally generate significant profits, and they have provided small investors with opportunities to participate in major studio-packaged financings of pictures such as *Annie*, *Poltergeist*, *Rocky III*, *Flashdance*, and *Who Framed Roger Rabbit*. More often than not, however, when the pictures in such packages succeed at the box office, most investors would probably find that they could have done at least as well by investing directly in the common stocks of the production and/or distribution companies (if for no other reason than considerations of liquidity) than in the related partnerships.

Bank loans

Established studios will normally be able to raise capital for general corporate purposes through debt or equity financings, or through commercial bank loans. In these situations, there is a considerable amount of flexibility as to the terms and types of financings that may be structured; a wide variety of corporate assets may be used as collateral.

For example, studios have recently been more willing to consider *loan securitization* structures similar to those used to create intermediate-term securities backed by packages of assets such as car and home equity loans. In the movie industry, investors contribute relatively small amounts of equity capital to form specially created "paper companies," and banks then arrange for loans and for the sale of commercial paper and medium-term notes to fund production costs – with the contributed equity and the projected value of the films to be produced over a three-year period serving as collateral. In this way, production costs are kept off studio balance sheets, earnings can be smoothed, borrowing costs may be reduced, and some of the risks can be shifted to equity investors even though ownership rights eventually revert back to the studio.[18]

Production loans to an independent producer are, however, quite another story: An independent producer may have little or no collateral backing except for presale contracts and other rights agreements relating directly to the production that is to be financed. As a practical matter, then, the bank, which views a film as a bundle of potentially valuable rights, must actually look to the creditworthiness of the various licensees for repayment of not only the loan itself but also of the interest on the loan. This accordingly makes a production loan more akin to an accounts receivable financing than to a standard term loan on the corporate assets of an ongoing business.[19]

From the producer's standpoint, such bank loan financing may be attractive because it can provide a means of circumventing the high costs and the rigidities, both financial and artistic, that normally come with a studio's distribution and financing deal. However, the fractionalization of distribution rights across many borders and across many different media absorbs time and effort that the producer might better apply to a project's creative aspects.

### Private equity and hedge funds

In recent years private equity and hedge funds have become much more active in providing large pools of production capital, particularly to the major studios. Such pools are collectively funded by pension plans and wealthy individuals and often seek to diversify into areas that are alternatives to stocks, bonds, and real estate.

These funds, with their ability to commit several hundred million dollars to a slate of perhaps ten or twenty pictures at a time, provide a welcome source of capital that allows studios to retain territorial rights as well as a large amount of control over creative issues. Studios, in effect, transfer some of the risks – including those relating to financing, completion, and marketplace performance – to the funds. And the funds, for their part, expect to receive above-average returns while at the same time lowering their overall risk through diversification into (what is presumed to be relatively low covariance) film asset investments.

The typical deal here is for an even split of carefully defined profits after a studio deducts a 12% to 15% distribution fee. The studio often also puts up money for prints and advertising that is recouped before profits are split. In structuring a deal, large investment banks will normally provide senior debt instruments that are paid back first and that will be priced to reflect their relatively low-risk position (expected rates of return in 2006 in the range of 6% to 8%). Private equity or hedge funds then take on the progressively riskier positions. For "mezzanine" investors, the expected return is for at least 15% (annually), while equity players will expect the return to be at least 20%. The guiding principle is that diversification over a large portfolio of film projects will considerably reduce risk exposure for all participants.[20]

## 4.3 Production preliminaries

The big picture

Data from the Motion Picture Association of America (Table 4.2) indicate that between 1980 and 2005, the *negative cost*, which is the average cost of production (including studio overhead and capitalized interest) for features produced by the majors, rose at a far-above-inflation compound annual rate of more than 7.5%. And by 2005, the average cost of producing an MPAA-member film had risen to approximately $60 million.[21]

Costs in this industry always tend to rise faster than in many other sectors of the economy because moviemaking procedures, although largely standardized, must be uniquely applied to each project and because efficiencies of scale are not easily attained. But other factors also pertain.

For example, during the 1970s, fiscal sloppiness pervaded the industry as soon as it became relatively easy to obtain financing using other people's tax-sheltered money. Indulgence of "auteurs," who demanded unrestricted funding in the name of creative genius, further contributed to budget bloating. And "bankable" actors and directors (popular personalities expected to draw an audience by virtue of their mere presence) came to command millions of dollars for relatively little expenditure of time and effort. It was only a short while before everyone else involved in a production also demanded more.[22]

By the early 1980s, the burgeoning of new media revenue sources, primarily in cable and home video, also naturally attracted (until the 1986 tax code changes) relatively large and eager capital funding commitments for investments in movie and television projects. But none of this could have gone quite so far without the ready availability of funds from so-called junk-bond financings, an upward-trending domestic stock market, and the spillover of wealth and easy credit from Japan's "bubble" economy.[23] In fact, it was not until the early 1990s, when more stringent limitations on access to bank financing were imposed, and when movie stock takeover speculation

Table 4.2. *Marketing and negative cost expenditures for major film releases, 1980–2005*

| Year | MPAA releases (Total) | Average cost per film ($ millions) | | | Total releasing |
|---|---|---|---|---|---|
| | | Negatives[b] | Ads | Prints | |
| 2005 | 198 | 60.0 | 32.4 | 3.8 | 96.15 |
| 2004 | 199 | 62.4 | 30.6 | 3.7 | 96.73 |
| 2003 | 198 | 63.8 | 34.8 | 4.2 | 102.87 |
| 2002 | 225 | 58.8 | 27.3 | 3.3 | 89.4 |
| 2001 | 196 | 47.7 | 27.3 | 3.7 | 78.7 |
| 2000 | 197 | 54.8 | 24.0 | 3.3 | 82.1 |
| 1999 | 218 | 51.5 | 21.4 | 3.1 | 76.0 |
| 1998 | 235 | 52.7 | 22.1 | 3.3 | 78.0 |
| 1997 | 253 | 53.4 | 19.2 | 3.0 | 75.7 |
| 1996 | 240 | 39.8 | 17.2 | 2.6 | 59.7 |
| 1995 | 234 | 36.4 | 15.4 | 2.4 | 54.1 |
| 1994 | 183 | 34.3 | 13.9 | 2.2 | 50.3 |
| 1993 | 161 | 29.9 | 12.1 | 1.9 | 44.0 |
| 1992 | 150 | 28.9 | 11.5 | 2.0 | 42.3 |
| 1991 | 164 | 26.1 | 10.4 | 1.7 | 38.2 |
| 1990 | 169 | 26.8 | 10.2 | 1.7 | 38.8 |
| 1989 | 169 | 23.5 | 7.8 | 1.4 | 32.7 |
| 1988 | 160 | 18.1 | 7.1 | 1.4 | 26.6 |
| 1987 | 129 | 20.1 | 6.9 | 1.4 | 28.3 |
| 1986 | 139 | 17.5 | 5.4 | 1.2 | 24.1 |
| 1985 | 153 | 16.8 | 5.2 | 1.2 | 23.2 |
| 1984 | 167 | 14.4 | 5.4 | 1.3 | 21.1 |
| 1983 | 190 | 11.9 | 4.2 | 1.0 | 17.1 |
| 1982 | 173 | 11.8 | 4.1 | 0.9 | 16.8 |
| 1981 | 173 | 11.3 | 3.5 | 0.9 | 15.7 |
| 1980 | 161 | 9.4 | 3.5 | 0.8 | 13.7 |
| CAGR[a] (%): 1980–2005 | | 7.7 | 9.3 | 6.6 | 8.1 |

[a] Compound annual growth rate.
[b] Negative costs for the years 1975 to 1979 were $3.1, $4.2, $5.6, $5.7, and $8.9, respectively. Costs include studio overhead and capitalized interest.
*Source*: MPAA.

was cooled by the onset of an economic recession, that cost pressures were somewhat abated.

Even under the best of circumstances, though, production budgets, in which there are thousands of expense items to be tracked, are not easy to control.[24] The basic cost components that go into the making of a film negative are, for example, illustrated in Figure 4.1.

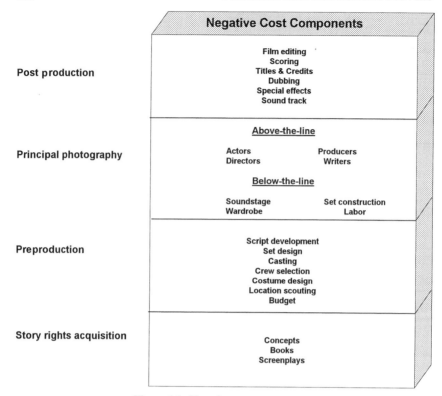

Figure 4.1. Negative cost components.

In the category of *above-the-line costs* – that is, the costs of a film's creative elements including cast and literary property acquisition (but not deferments) – contracts are signed and benefits and payments administered for sometimes hundreds of people.

Good coordination is also required when budgeting *below-the-line costs* – the costs of crews and vehicles, transportation, shelter, and props.[25] For each film, wardrobes and props must be made or otherwise acquired, locations must be scouted and leases arranged, and scene production and travel schedules must be meticulously planned. Should any one of those elements fall significantly out of step (as happens when the weather on location is unexpectedly bad, or when a major actor takes ill or is injured), expenses skyrocket. At such points of distress, a film's completion bond insurance arrangements become significant because completion guarantors have the option to loan money to the producer to finish the film, to take full control of the film and finish it, or to altogether abandon the film and repay the financiers.[26] Also, additional below-the-line costs would be incurred in postproduction activities.[27]

In general, the lower the budget, the higher will be the percentage of the budget spent on below-the-line costs and vice versa. But, interestingly, the higher the budget, the more a distributor would likely be willing to pay for rights because – regardless of cast, script, or anything else – financing requirements are usually calculated as a percent of the budget.

Labor unions

Unions have an important influence on the economics of filmmaking, beginning with the very first phase of production. Indeed, union guidelines for compensation at each defined level of trade skill allow preliminary below-the-line production cost estimates to be determined with a fair degree of accuracy. Major unions in Hollywood include

American Federation of Television and Radio Artists (AFTRA)
Directors Guild of America
International Alliance of Theatrical and Stage Employees (IATSE)
Producers Guild of America
Screen Actors Guild (SAG)
Writers Guild of America

Individuals belonging to these unions will normally be employed in the production of all significant motion pictures. The unions, in turn, will negotiate for contract terms with the studios' bargaining organization, the Alliance of Motion Picture and Television Producers (AMPTP).[28] Generally, these guilds and their members receive so-called residual payments (evolved out of old practices in vaudeville and on Broadway) that, for theatrical films, are calculated on gross revenues obtained from video, television, and other nontheatrical sources whether or not the production is profitable.

Still, it is possible to produce a film with no noticeable qualitative differences for up to 40% less in nonunion or flexible-union territories outside of Hollywood, and independent producers may sometimes attempt to reduce below-the-line costs by filming in such territories.[29] Studios may sometimes also make use of an IATSE contract provision (Article 20) that allows the financing of low-budget nonunion movies and television shows if the studio claims to have no creative control.[30]

## 4.4 Marketing matters

Distributors and exhibitors

*Sequencing* After the principal production phase has been completed, thousands of details still remain to be monitored and administered. Scoring, editing, mixing sound and color, and making prints at the film laboratory are but a few of the essential steps. Once the film is in the postproduction stages, however, perhaps the most critical preparations are those for distribution and marketing.

Sequential distribution patterns are determined by the principle of the second-best alternative – a corollary of the price-discriminating market-segmentation strategies discussed in Chapter 1. That is, films are normally first distributed to the market that generates the highest marginal revenue over the least amount of time. They then "cascade" in order of marginal-revenue contribution down to markets that return the lowest revenues per unit time. This has historically meant theatrical release, followed by licensing to pay cable program distributors, home video, television networks, and finally local television syndicators.

However, because the amounts of capital invested in features have become so large, and the pressures for faster recoupment so great, there appears to be a trend toward earlier opening of all windows (Figure 4.2 ). This already applies especially to the window for DVDs, which is now often capable of generating higher revenues than theatrical ticket sales in even less time. It is not yet clear how increasing availability of high-speed broadband Internet technology and the trend toward viewing mobility (on small-screen devices such as cellphones) will ultimately rearrange the historical window sequences.[31]

Sequencing is always a marketing decision that attempts to maximize income, and it is generally sensible for profit-maximizing distributors to price-discriminate in different markets or "windows" by selling the same product at different prices to different buyers.[32] Thus, it should not be

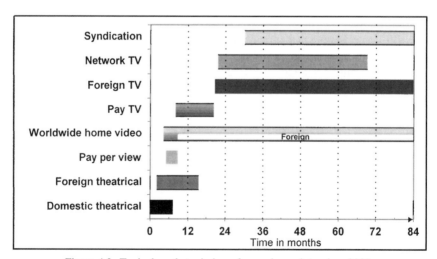

Figure 4.2. Typical market windows from release date, circa 2005.

surprising to find that, as new distribution technologies take hold and as older ones fade in relative importance, shifts in sequencing strategies will occur.[33] For example, the Internet's ability to make films instantly available anywhere now requires simultaneous worldwide day-and-date release for major projects. Such "windowing" is also a way in which the public-good characteristics of movies used as television programs can be fully exploited.[34]

All this threatens exhibitors, who – if they were to lose first-play rights on important films – would find it difficult, if not impossible, to survive on just leftovers. The resulting shrinkage of the theatrical-distribution pipeline would then potentially make it more difficult to nurture lightly marketed but nonetheless promising releases to the point at which such releases could attract enough attention to be profitable.

*Distributor–exhibitor contracts* Distributors normally design their marketing campaigns with certain target audiences in mind, and marketing considerations are prominent in a studio's decision to make (i.e., "green-light") or otherwise acquire a film for distribution. Indeed, at the earliest stages, marketing people will attempt to forecast the prospects for a film in terms of its potential appeal to different audience demographic segments, with male/female, young (under 25)/old (known as "four quadrant"), and sometimes also ethnic/cultural being the main categorizations.[35]

Distributors will then typically attempt to align their releases with the most demographically suitable theaters, subject to availability of screens and to previously established relationships with the exhibition chains. They accomplish this by analyzing how similar films have previously performed in each potential location and then by developing a releasing strategy that provides the best possible marketing mix, or platform, for the picture. Sometimes the plan may involve a slow buildup through limited local or regional release; at other times it may involve a broad national release on literally thousands of screens simultaneously.

Although no amount of marketing savvy can make a really bad picture play well, an intelligent strategy can almost certainly help to make the box-office (and ultimately the home video and cable) performance of a mediocre picture better. It has thus now become characteristic of distributors to negotiate arrangements with exhibitors for specific theater sites.

Nevertheless, instead of negotiating, distributors may also sometimes elect, several months in advance of release, to send so-called bid letters to theaters located in regions in which they expect (because of demographic or income characteristics) to find audiences most responsive to a specific film's theme and genre.[36] This would normally be the preferred method of maximizing distributor revenues at times when the relative supply of pictures (to screens) is limited, as had happened in the late 1970s (Figure 4.3a). Theaters that express interest in showing a picture then usually accept the *terms* (i.e., the implied cost of film rental and the

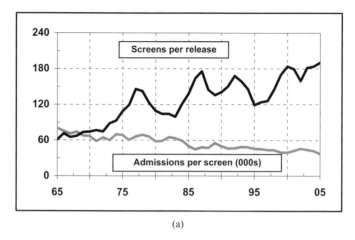

(a)

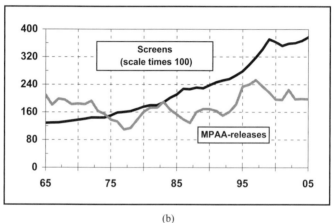

(b)

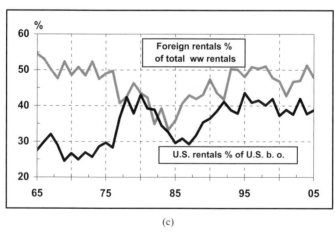

(c)

Figure 4.3. Exhibition industry trends, 1965–2005: (a) screens per release and admissions per screen, (b) number of screens and number of MPAA-member releases, and (c) rentals percentages: foreign versus total, and as a percentage of U.S. box-office receipts.

playing times) suggested by the distributor's regional branch exchange (sales office).

Such contracts between distributors and exhibitors are usually of the boilerplate variety (fairly standard from picture to picture) and are arranged for large theater chains by experienced film bookers who bid for simultaneous runs in several theaters in a territory. Smaller chains or individual theaters might also use a professional agency for this purpose. They key phrases used in all contracts are *screens*, which refers to the number of auditoriums, and *playdates* (sometimes called *engagements*), which refers to the theater booked (even if the theater shows the film on several screens at the same location).

Still, there can be variations. For example, in the early 1970s the film *Billy Jack* received wide publicity for its distribution through "four-wall" contracts. Here the distributor in effect rents the theater (four walls) for a fixed weekly fee, pays all operating expenses, and then mounts an advertising blitz on local television to attract the maximum audience in a minimum of time. Yet another simple occasional arrangement is flat rental: The exhibitor (usually in a small, late-run situation) pays a fixed fee to the distributor for the right to show the film during a specified period. And, more recently, there has been a trend toward simple aggregate booking contracts in which all box-office revenue is divided by a negotiated percentage formula that does not include provision for the theater's expenses (i.e., the house "nut" as explained below).

Conventional contracts between distributors and exhibitors would, however, almost always call for a sliding percentage of the box-office gross after allowance for the exhibitor's nut (house expenses, which include location rents and telephone, electricity, insurance, and mortgage payments). This house allowance is now largely a function of the quality of the theater location, number of screens, and number of seats and is also often supplemented by payments for placements of trailers, which are ads for coming attractions. Whether assumed or negotiated, however, it is generally conceded that the allowance will normally provide exhibitors with an additional cushion of profit.

For a major release, sliding-scale agreements may stipulate that 70% or (sometimes) more of the first week or two of box-office receipts after subtraction of the nut are to be remitted to the distributor, with the exhibitor retaining 30% or less. Every two weeks thereafter, the split (and also the floor) may then be adjusted by 10% as 60/40, then 50/50, and so forth in the exhibitor's favor.[37]

If it is assumed that the house nut is $10,000 a week, and that the first week agreement on a picture that sells $50,000 in tickets is 90/10 with a 70% floor, the distributor would receive (see also Table 3.7) the larger of

90/10 split: 90% × ($50,000 − $10,000) = $36,000 or
70% floor: 70% × $50,000 = $35,000.

But by the fifth week, with the film taking $30,000, the arithmetic might be

70/30 split: 70% × ($30,000 − $10,000) = $14,000 or
50% floor:   50% × $30,000 = $15,000.

Thus, the distributor's gross (otherwise known as "rentals") is in effect received for a carefully defined conditional lease of a film over a specified period. Lease terms may include bid or negotiated "clearances," which provide time and territorial exclusivity for a theater.[38] No exhibitor would want to meet high terms for a film that would soon (or, even worse, simultaneously) be playing at a competitor's theater down the block. In addition, such contracts would usually include a "holdover" clause that requires theaters to extend exhibition of the film another week (and also perhaps revert to payment of a higher percentage) if the previous week's revenue exceeds a predetermined amount.

Should a picture not perform up to expectations, the distributor also usually has the right to a certain minimum or "floor" payment. These minimums are direct percentages (often more than half) of box-office receipts prior to subtraction of house expenses, but any previously advanced (or guaranteed) exhibitor monies can be used to cover floor payments owed. And for many films (especially for those that flop) the distributor may reduce (in a nonbid situation) the exhibitor's burden through a quietly arranged settlement.[39] The upshot is that, on the average, exhibitors normally retain around 50% of box-office receipts in the United States (but closer to 70% in the United Kingdom).

Consequently, the largest profit source (and about one-third of revenues) for many exhibitors is often not the box office, but the candy, popcorn, and soda counter – where the operating margin may readily exceed 50% (and 90% on purposely salty popcorn). Theater owners have full control of proceeds from such sales; they can either operate food and beverage stands (and, increasingly, video games) themselves or lease to outside concessionaires. The importance of these concession profits to an exhibitor can be seen in the numerical example in Table 5.7. On-screen advertising has also become, since the early 1980s, a third significant source of profit for theater operators.

Given the high percentage normally taken by the distributor, it is in the distributor's interest to maintain firm ticket pricing, whereas it may be in the exhibitor's interest to set low ticket prices to attract high-margin candy-stand patronage. In most instances, exhibitors set ticket prices and the potential for a conflict of interest does not present any difficulty to either party. But there have been situations (e.g., the releases of *Superman*, *Annie*, and a few Disney films) in which the distributor has suggested minimum per capita admission prices to protect against children's prices that are too low. What distributors fear is that low admissions prices will divert spending from ticket sales (where they get a significant cut) to the exhibitor's concessions sales.

Although most theater operators will also attempt to enhance profitability through sales of advertising spots, some distributors (e.g., Disney since the early 1990s) may limit or bar exhibitors from showing advertisements before the film is run.[40]

*Release strategies, bidding, and other related practices* Large production budgets, high interest rates, and the need to spend substantial sums on marketing provide strong incentives for distributors to release pictures as broadly and as soon as possible (while also, incidentally, reducing the exhibitor's risk). A film's topicality and anticipated breadth of audience appeal will then influence the choice of marketing strategies that might be employed to bring the largest return to the distributor over the shortest time.[41] Of greatest interest to the market research departments are a film's *marketability* – how easily the film's concept can be conveyed through advertising and promotion – and its *playability*, which refers to how well an audience reacts to the film after having seen it.

Many alternatives are available to distributors. Some films are supported with national network-television campaigns arranged months in advance, whereas others use only a few carefully selected local spots, from which it is hoped that strong word-of-mouth advertising will build. Sometimes a picture will be opened (limited release) in one or two theaters in New York or Los Angeles the last week of the year to qualify for that year's Academy Award nominations and then be broken wide the following spring. Or there may be massive simultaneous (saturation) release on more than 3,000 screens around the country at the beginning of summer. Regional or highly specialized release is appropriate if a picture does not appear to contain elements of interest to a broad national audience. And simultaneous global release is now often used to thwart unauthorized copying.

In any case, different anti–blind-bidding laws (laws that prohibit completion of contracts before exhibitors have had an opportunity to view the movies on which they are bidding) are effective in at least 23 states. These statutes were passed by state legislatures in response to exhibitor complaints that distributors were forcing them to bid on and pledge (guarantee) substantial sums for pictures they had not been given an opportunity to evaluate in a screening; in other words, buying the picture sight unseen. Distributors now generally screen their products well in advance of release, but large pledges from exhibitors may still sometimes be required for theaters to secure important pictures in the most desirable playing times, such as the week of Christmas through New Year's. For these seasonal high periods, theaters might sometimes have to offer a substantial advance in nonrefundable cash against future rentals owed (i.e., guarantees).

Whereas in theory movie releases from all studios can be expected to play in different houses depending only on the previously mentioned factors, some theaters, mostly in major cities, more often than not end up consistently showing the products of only a few distributors. Industry jargon denotes these as theater "tracks" or "circuits." Tracks can evolve from long-standing personal relationships (many going back to before the Paramount consent decree) that are reflected in negotiated rather than bid licenses, or they may indicate de facto *product-splitting* or *block-booking* practices.[42]

Product splitting occurs when several theaters in a territory tacitly agree not to bid aggressively against each other for certain films, with the intention of reducing average distributor terms. Each theater in the territory then has the opportunity, on a regular rotating basis, to obtain major new films for relatively low rentals percentages. Block booking, in contrast, occurs when a distributor accepts a theater's bid on desirable films contingent on the theater's commitment that it will also run the distributor's less popular pictures.[43]

As may be readily inferred, symbiosis between the exhibitor and distributor segments of the industry has not led to mutual affection. The growth of pay-per-view cable and the possibility of simultaneous releases (known as day and date in the industry) in home video and Internet-related formats may further strain relations. And as De Vany and Walls (1997, p. 796) have noted, the legal constraints stemming from the Paramount decree have prevented multiple-picture licensing so that

[N]o contracts can be made for the whole season of a distributor's releases, nor for any portion of them. Nor is it possible to license a series of films to theaters as a means of financing their production. The inability to contract for portfolios of motion pictures restricts the means by which distributors, producers and theaters manage risk and uncertainty.

*Exhibition industry characteristics: (a) Capacity and competition*  The long-run success of an exhibition organization is highly dependent on its skill in evaluating and arranging real estate transactions. Competition for good locations (which raises lease payment costs) and the presence of too many screens relative to the size of a territory will generally reduce overall returns.

To achieve economies of scale, since the 1960s exhibitors have tended to consolidate into large chains operating multiple screens located near or in shopping-center malls. Meanwhile, older movie houses in decaying center-city locations have encountered financial hardships as the relatively affluent consumers born after World War II have grown to maturity in the suburbs, and as rising crime rates and scarcity of parking spaces had become deterrents to regular moviegoing by city residents. (Ironically, the very same social pressures contributed to the disappearance of many drive-in theaters situated on real estate too valuable to be used only for evening movies.[44])

In 2005 there were approximately 37,740 screens, a diminishing proportion of which were drive-ins. The total has been increasing since 1980 at

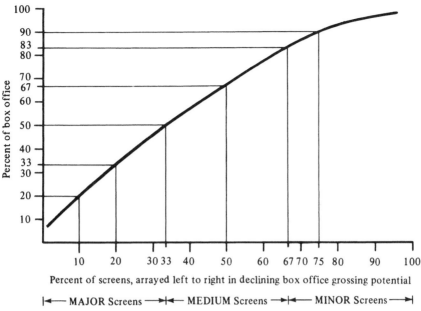

Figure 4.4. Domination of box-office performance by key U.S. movie theaters. *Source*:
*Variety*, July 7, 1982. Copyright 1982 by A. D. Murphy.

an average rate of 3.1%, with box-office gross per screen rising an average 1.7% per year (see Table 4.2). During this time, operating incomes and
market shares for large, publicly owned theater chains (especially regional)
have obviously gained rapidly at the expense of single-theater operators.
For example, as of 1982, the top-grossing third of screens generated half of
the box office, with the bottom third generating about one-sixth of the box
office (Murphy 1983 and Figure 4.4). Currently, the top one-third of screens
probably account for 75% of all theater grosses.

Although the number of screens in North America has been increased
substantially (Figure 4.3b), the number of separate theater locations has not
grown by nearly as much: Many locations have simply been "multiplexed."
It is now therefore more difficult to "platform" a film because there are
essentially only two types of theaters: first-run multiple-screen houses and
all others. Previously, there had been at least three tiers of theater quality
ranging from first-run fancy to last-run, small, neighborhood "dumps."

Whether or not a film has "legs" (i.e., strong popular appeal so that it
runs a long time), the maximum theoretical revenue $R$ is a function of the
average length of playing time $T$, the number of showings per day $N$, the
average number of seats per screen $A$, the number of screens $S$, the average
ticket price $P$, and audience suitability ratings (G, PG, PG-13, R, NC-17/X).

Exclusive of the ratings factor, which also influences the potential size of the audience,[45]

$$R = P \times N \times A \times S,$$

where $N = f(T)$.

For example, if the average ticket price is \$6, the average number of showings per day is four, the average number of seats per theater is 300, and the number of screens is 500, the picture can theoretically gross no more than \$3.6 million ($6 \times 4 \times 300 \times 500$) per day, or \$25.2 million per week. This type of analysis is of interest to distributors as comparisons are made to the potential of pay-per-view cable release, from which there is the possibility to earn, on a \$4-per-view charge, at least \$20 million overnight.[46]

Because the preceding figures used in calculating a theoretical weekly total gross for a single picture are about average for the whole industry, they can also be used to estimate an aggregate for all exhibitors. Following this line, we can determine that in 2005, the maximum theoretical annual gross, based on 37,740 screens, was about \$272 million per day or about \$99 billion per year. The industry obviously operates well below its theoretical capacity because there are many parts of the week and many weeks of the year during which people do not have the time or inclination to fill empty theater seats: In 2005, the industry's average occupancy rate per seat per week was roughly 2.4 times, and box-office receipts of around \$9.0 billion in 2005 were thus only around 9% of theoretical capacity.

For the major film releases most likely to be opened during peak seasons, calculations of this kind do not actually have much relevance because there are no more than about 12,000 quality first-run screens, of which perhaps only 4,000 can normally be simultaneously booked. By far, the most important effect of severe competition for quality playdates in peak seasons is that marketing budgets must be raised to levels much above where they would otherwise be (and for economic reasons explained in Section 1.3). In such an environment, modestly promoted films, even those of high artistic merit, may have little time to build audience favor before they are "pulled" from circulation.[47]

In comparing the popularity of different films in different years, most newspaper accounts merely show the box-office grosses: Film $A$ did \$10, and film $B$ did \$11; therefore $B$ did better than $A$. In addition, a deeper, but still often misleading, comparison is sometimes derived by calculating an average gross per screen. However, close analysis and comparison of box-office data require that variables such as ticket-price inflation, film running time, season, weather conditions, number and quality of theaters, average seats per theater, and types of competing releases be considered.[48]

*(b) Rentals percentages* All other things being equal, when the supply of films is small compared with exhibitor capacity, the percentage of box office reverting to distributors (the rentals percentage) rises.[49] Faced with a

relatively limited selection of potentially popular pictures, theater owners tend to bid more aggressively and to accede to stiffer terms than they otherwise would. Especially in the late 1970s, for example, there were loud complaints by exhibitors of "product shortage" as the total number of new releases and reissues declined by 43% to 110 in 1978 from the preceding 1972 peak of 193. As might be expected, distributor rental percentages (and thus profit margins) were high in the late 1970s (Table 3.4 and Figure 4.3c).

To some extent, however, the rentals percentage also depends on ticket prices and on how moviegoers respond to a year's crop of releases. A poorly received crop tends to reduce the average distributor rentals percentage as "floor" (minimum) clauses on contracts with exhibitors are activated, as advances and guarantees are reduced in size and number, and as "settlements" are more often required. Even important releases now tend to have only one or two weeks of box-office presence before quickly fading and thereby denying theaters of the higher percentages that would be earned if pictures were to play more strongly over more weeks, as they had often done prior to the late 1990s.

Although theatrical exhibition is inherently volatile over the short run, over the longer run there is nevertheless a remarkable consistency in the way the domestic business behaves. Since the 1960s, for instance, in a typical week approximately 8% to 10% of the U.S. population buys admission to a movie. And as can be seen in Figure 4.5a, the top 20 grossing films of any year will normally account for an average of around 40% of that year's box-office total, with a giant hit every so often temporarily boosting the percentage. Figure 4.5b meanwhile suggests that the variance of results for the top 20 is not large and that growth in constant dollars has been modest. The long-term per capita admissions trend is depicted in Figure 4.5c, and Figure 4.5d shows that the top 100 films of any year have been consistent in drawing approximately half of their total box-office income in foreign markets.

Home video and merchandising

*Home video* Until the 1980s, moviemakers both large and small were primarily concerned with marketing their pictures in theaters. But starting in 1986, distributors generated more in domestic wholesale gross revenues from home video (about $2 billion) than from theatrical ($1.6 billion) sources. Home video has thus forever altered the fundamental structure of the business and changed the ways in which marketing strategies are pursued.[50]

Digital video disc players (DVDs) as well as the older videocassette recorders (VCRs) are by now familiar items in households around the world. Indeed, in most developed nations, including the United States, Japan, Britain, France, Germany, Italy, The Netherlands, and Scandinavia, DVDs (and VCRs) are already found in over two-thirds of the television households. This enormous installed base has become an incredibly powerful funds-flow engine for filmmakers.[51]

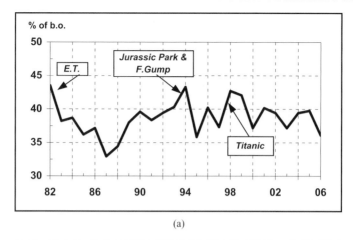

(a)

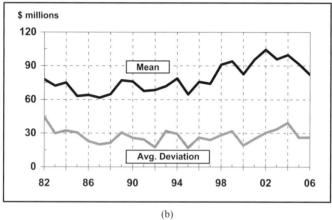

(b)

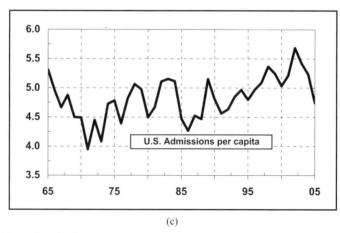

(c)

Figure 4.5. (a) Top 20 films, domestic box-office gross, 1982–2006. (b) Top 20 films, domestic box-office gross, constant dollar mean and variance, 1982–2006. (c) U.S. per capita theater admissions, 1965–2005. (d) Top 100 films, domestic and foreign gross comparisons, 1993–2006.

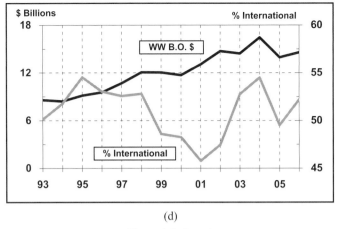

(d)

Figure 4.5. (*cont.*)

As a result, prerecorded home video software sales (Figure 4.6) have grown into a business that now generates more than $16 billion in domestic retail revenues. The bulk of those revenues (two-thirds or so) are consistently derived from sales or rentals (to the consumer) of feature films.[52] Also, given, that some 45% to 60% of Hollywood's aggregate releasing costs are covered by domestic home video receipts, it is easy to see why filmmakers and distributors cannot afford to treat video marketing-campaign strategies lightly.

Perhaps the most important decision for the home video divisions of the major studios concerns pricing. Up until the late 1990s, when steep discounting became available to high-volume retailers not participating in revenue-sharing plans (as described below), the choice had been either to price high for the video store *rental* market or to price low for what is known as the *sell-through* (consumer) market. Since the cost of manufacturing and

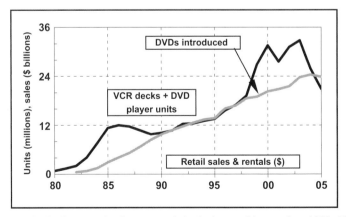

Figure 4.6. Hardware and software trends in the home video market, 1978–2005.

marketing a cassette or DVD is about the same (under $4 a unit) for all regular feature films, the decision has always come down to whether the distributor can earn more from rentals or from sell-through to individuals.[53] In recent years, more than 50% of total U.S. consumer spending on video has been for sell-through products, with more than half of this total generated by feature films.[54]

Introduction of the DVD format in 1997 has had great impact. With the profit per unit on a DVD – which often costs less than $5 per unit to manufacture, market, and distribute and sells at $15 wholesale – around twice as high as on a tape, studios now have an incentive to return to the simple consumer purchase model that has long been used in the recorded music business.[55] DVDs have, in effect, greatly undermined the rental tape-pricing model (as well as the revenue-sharing model) that had carried the home video industry through its first 20 years. And DVDs have caused a shift of profitability structure toward a model that is more favorable to studios now that they are able to retain a larger portion of a film's total revenues (as compared with exhibitors and retailers) than previously.

In the late 1990s, though, a "revenue-sharing" variation of the traditional rental arrangement (that is applied much more to tapes than to DVDs) had been widely adopted by studios and major retailers. Such revenue-sharing models originally had been promoted to studios with the promise of guaranteed minimum revenues (with the retailer taking all the studios' offerings). The system works as follows: A large video chain-store operator like Blockbuster buys a tape from a studio for perhaps $7, or one-tenth of the rental market price. The studio then initially shares between 30% and 40% of the rental revenues of the stores – with the percentage shared sliding to zero over a six-month period. At that point, the chain can recoup its capital outlay by selling the used tape. But it will also, on the average, end up retaining 50% to 60% of total transaction revenues.[56]

For "evergreen" titles, such as many of the Disney animations, the decision is normally to go for sell-through because the arithmetic can be so compelling. Nevertheless, the much likelier alternative (prior to revenue-sharing) had been to set the suggested retail price of the cassette much higher so that it would become primarily a rental item. Most such "A"-title releases, as films with the potentially widest appeal are known, would list for $89.95 or above, and of this price the distributor would probably retain around $56.57 (i.e., 63%) from the initial sale.[57] In this situation, a distributor would *not* participate further in the cash flow that is derived from retailers' rentals of the cassette.[58]

All other things being equal, then, the studio-distributor (in effect, the home video's publisher) would select the larger of the following options:

Expected number of rental units times 63% of rental unit retail price or

Expected number of sell-through units times wholesale unit price[59]

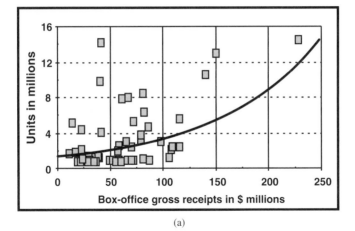

(a)

(b)

Figure 4.7. An example of box-office gross receipts (*x*-axis) versus (a) video unit sales, and (b) rental dollars, circa 1990.

Yet because marketing costs figure prominently in the success of sell-through titles, the distributor generally must be able to project sales of at least seven to eight times as many copies of a sell-through than a rental title to justify the decision. Such projections would be made, for example, on a typical fitted curve (Figure 4.7), off which the number of home video units demanded might be estimated as a function of the domestic box-office performance of recent titles.[60]

Independent filmmakers would, of course, face a different set of problems. To finance production, "indies" will typically be most interested in preselling (or fractionalizing) rights to their pictures. For this purpose, they can approach one of the majors or submajors, or go to an independent home video distributor.[61] Rights fractionalization proposals are not, however, normally welcomed by large distributors.[62]

So-called direct-to-video features, which are designed to skip a theatrical release phase entirely and go directly to the home video market, have also become more important, especially in the family film genre. Elimination of relatively high theatrical releasing costs here enhances the profit potential of such titles.[63]

Moreover, all film distributors must of necessity now take the projected rapid growth of pay-per-view/video-on-demand (PPV/VOD) cable and Internet distribution into consideration. At a minimum, the rise of PPV technology appears likely to dampen the growth of home video unit demand, to reduce the importance of video chain retailers, and also to alter the sequential release patterns for certain types of films.[64]

*Merchandising*  Product merchandising opportunities relating to film characters and concepts began in earnest in the 1970s with *Jaws* and *Star Wars* and have increased noticeably since then. "Franchise" pictures able to sustain a long series of sequels using the same major characters (e.g., James Bond, *Star Wars*, *Jurassic Park*, Batman, Spider-Man, Superman) are the main vehicles. Indeed, studios have become highly sophisticated in marketing tied directly to the action and children's film genres, where licensing potential in music, books, comics, multimedia and other interactive formats (DVDs, CD-ROMs, etc.), fast food restaurants, and toys abounds.[65] An important product license to a major toy manufacturing company might, for instance, return at least 6% to 7% of wholesale merchandise revenues to the studio. For releases such as Disney's animated features *Beauty and the Beast*, *Aladdin*, and *The Lion King* and Universal's (MCA) *Jurassic Park*, merchandise license profits can easily exceed $100 million.[66]

## Marketing costs

In theory, studios have much greater cost-control potential in a film's marketing phase than in its production and financing phases. But distributors have no choice but to spend aggressively on marketing if only to defend against and offset the efforts of many other films and entertainment pursuits vying to be noticed at the same time. In effect, the distributor must shape and create an audience with advertising and promotional campaigns (i.e., "drives") that have only one quick shot to succeed immediately upon theatrical release.

As a result, expenditures on the marketing of films have long tended to rise considerably faster than the overall rate of inflation, and restraint in such expenditures is rarely seen. In fact, studios will often readily add 50% to a picture's production budget just for advertising and publicity as they attempt to maximize capital turnover when quality, peak-season exhibitor playdates are at a premium and unavoidable seasonal, cyclical, and other factors routinely contribute to the bunching of important releases.[67]

In practice, marketing decisions in filmmaking and distribution have an important effect on how a movie is initially perceived and on how it might play out in ancillary-market exposures. As De Vany and Walls (1996) note, "the opening performance is statistically a dominant factor in revenue generation."[68] But it is also clear that audiences sift the good from the bad pretty quickly and that no amount of spending or targeted promotion can save a poorly made, ill-conceived, or boring film once the information about its true quality is in circulation.

## 4.5 Economic aspects

Profitability synopsis

That a person can drown in a river of an average depth of six inches underscores the difficulty in analyzing data by means of averages alone. Many, if not most, films do not earn any return, even after taking account of new-media revenue sources; it is the few big winners that pay for the many losers. Outside investors, who, in terms of the funds-flow sequence are often the first to pay in and the last to be paid out, thus often incur the greatest risks.

Because pictures are financed largely with other people's money, there is an almost unavoidable bias for costs to rise (Parkinson's law again) at least as fast as anticipated revenues. This implies that much of the incremental income expected from growth of the new-media sources is likely to be absorbed, dissipated, and diverted as cost. And it is an especially daunting consideration if, as is now common for a film released by a major studio, only a much-diminished share of such costs is recovered directly from domestic theatrical rentals (Figure 4.8a). Figure 4.8b illustrates that costs have often grown faster than revenues while industry operating margins have been erratic and have generally trended lower (Figure 4.8c).[69]

If we use data on the number of releases, the effects of ancillary-market revenue growth (Sections 3.4 and 4.4), average negative and marketing costs, and aggregate rentals (Section 3.3), there emerges a profile suggesting that, in a statistical sense, most major-distributed films do no better than to financially break even, with deviations from this mean extreme in both directions (Table 5.8).[70]

In fact, the "average" movie does not really exist and average industry revenue and profit are primarily determined by only a few runaway hits. This pattern, a Pareto law that is illustrated in Figure 4.9, is not only true for movies in general but also for films with small or large budgets from different genres, and with or without stars.[71] The financial performance of a movie is unpredictable because each one is unique and enters competition for audiences in a constantly shifting marketing environment. Moreover, the situation is unlike that in most other industries: Although ticket prices are relatively inflexible, the supply is elastic because it can quickly respond to

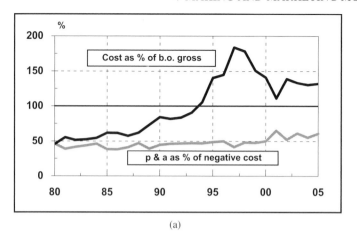

(a)

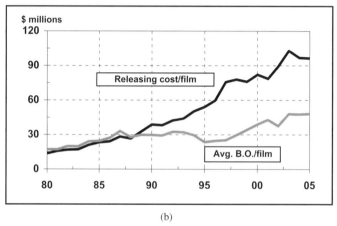

(b)

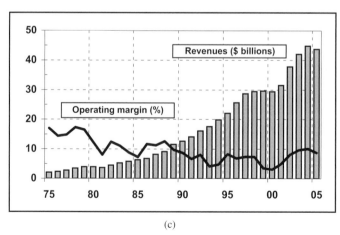

(c)

Figure 4.8. Film industry revenue and cost trends. (a) MPAA-member production
(negative) costs as a percentage of domestic box-office gross receipts and prints and
advertising (p & a) as a percent of production costs, 1980–2005 MPAA films. (b) Average
per MPAA-film: releasing cost (including negative plus p & a) and domestic box-office
revenue, 1980–2005. (c) Revenues and operating margins for major studios, 1975–2005.

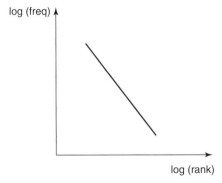

Figure 4.9. An idealized Pareto (power) law.
*Note*: Many films have box-office grosses of under $50 million, and only a few take in more than $300 million. *Titanic*, with the highest domestic gross as of 2005, would have the highest rank as scaled in terms of receipts and would be at the far lower right.

unexpected demand through dynamic expansion of the length of run and the number of screens on which the film is shown.

The remarkable aspect of all this is that, despite the potential for loss, most major studios, bolstered by distribution revenues related to library titles and television programs, have long been successfully engaged in this business.[72] The existence of profitable studio enterprises in the face of apparent losses for the "average" picture can be reconciled only when it is realized that the heart of a studio's business is distribution and financing and that, therefore, the brunt of marketing and production-cost risk is often deflected and/or transferred to (sometimes tax-sheltered) outside investors and producers. Indeed, it is worldwide distribution (licensing) to television in all forms (network TV, cable and local syndication, foreign, etc.) that truly carries the load.[73] While the front-end production and release attracts all of the attention, studio profits are thus actually focused and highly dependent on the much more prosaic functions of collecting distribution and other fee income.

### Theoretical foundation

That the movie industry is complex and that it often operates near the edge of chaos in the midst of uncertainty is almost an inescapable inference for anyone who has been even a casual observer of, or participant in, the process of financing, making, and marketing films. Seemingly sure-bet, big-budget films with "bankable" stars flop; low-budget titles with no stars sometimes inexplicably catapult to fame, and some releases perform at the box office inversely to what the most experienced professional critics prognosticate.

In recent years, though, economists have begun to build a framework that explains why these things happen and why the industry is structured in the way that it is. The theoretical foundation that is emerging is based significantly on the combined works of De Vany and Walls (1996, 1997), Caves (2000), and, to a more limited extent, modern portfolio theory. Caves found that a only a few basic features (described in Section 13.4) typify the organizational structure of all creative industries, be they movies, art, music, books, or live performances. Prominent among the features is the large sunk-cost nature of these activities and the resulting need to use option contracts among the many coordinating parties involved in the financing, production, and distribution of creative goods and services.[74] Modern portfolio theory further suggests that studios inherently adjust and mitigate their risk exposure to the uncertain performance of any single film by balancing the mix of high-, medium-, and low-budget films in their yearly crops of releases.[75]

These cornerstone concepts connect well with the studies of De Vany and Walls, who found that movie viewers, randomly exchanging information about their preferences, end up generating box-office revenues that are not normally distributed (i.e., bell-shaped, clustered around a mean in the center, and tailing off sharply at the tails). Box-office returns instead follow power laws that differ from normal distributions in that variation is not symmetrical: A few "blockbuster" outliers in the upper tail influence the mean. (The departure from a normal distribution is not as severe, however, if revenues from home video and international markets are included.)

Movies, in other words, have a low probability of earning high revenues and a high probability of earning low revenues. And this leads to an estimate that perhaps 5% of movies earn about 80% of the industry's total profits and that exhibition on a large number of screens can as easily lead to rapid failure as to quick and great success.

Such power law–distributed behavior makes it futile to attempt partition of movies into genre or budget categories because, no matter how detailed the categorization, the same distribution appears (i.e., the behavior is fractal).[76] According to this body of work – which explains the movie business as a complex system (i.e., with nonlinear feedback in the information cascade and sensitivity to initial conditions) – just about the only thing that can be predicted with some degree of confidence is a film's revenue next week based on last week's. As De Vany (2004, p. 2) notes, "There is no typical movie and averages signify nothing. . . . The movie business is completely and utterly non-Gaussian because it is a business of the extraordinary."

Moreover, this work has also shown that movie box-office performance can be modeled as a weekly contest for survival in which a film's likelihood of being held over another week is a function of the time that it has been in theatrical release. A hazard function, $h(t)$, of this type may be estimated as the proportion of films surviving in an interval per unit time given that the film has already survived to the beginning of the interval.[77]

As we shall see, this analytical methodology – this approach to thinking about films in terms of power laws, fractals, and hazard rates – is readily applicable and relevant to the study of all entertainment and information-based products, services, and attractions. For, no matter what the entertainment industry segment, when it comes to new product introductions, we are always positioned somewhere between risk, where the odds are known, and uncertainty, where the mean-wandering, infinite variance of a returns distribution process implies that anything from a huge hit to a total flop might occur.[78] In statistical terms, there is thus great behavioral similarity in movies, television series, books, music recordings, stage plays, video games, and toys. Fads come and go. And fewer than 20% of the items often produce more than 80% of the revenues or profits (the "long-tail" effect of Internet distribution notwithstanding).

## 4.6 Concluding remarks

Since the mid-1970s, the movie industry has been in a transition phase characterized by a shift to electronic/optic distribution and storage methods and by declining control of distribution and product pricing through traditional organizational arrangements. Although this transition has already provided consumers with an increasingly varied selection of easily accessed, low-cost entertainment, it has not been beneficial to all industry segments. In fact, technology has made it possible for more content to be created by more people, and to be distributed more widely and at lower cost (e.g., via the Internet), than ever before.

Despite these changes, the movie business remains as fascinating as it is unique. That feeling has been summarized by veteran movie writer A. D. Murphy (1982), who has made the following observations:

Even after a history of over 100 years, the business remains entrepreneurial and capitalistic.

Films are by nature research-and-development products; they are perishable and cannot be test marketed in the usual sense.

The film industry manufactures an art form for the masses.

Despite long-standing trade restrictions, a strong export market reinforces a fairly stable domestic market.

From acquisitions of literary properties to final theater bookings, every phase of the industry's operations is negotiated and this, contrary to widespread opinion, implies that personal trust and high standards of professional integrity largely prevail.

As Squire (1992, p. 23; 2004, p. 4) further said:

In no other business is a single example of product fully created at an investment of millions of dollars with no real assurance that the public will buy it. In no other business does the public "use" the product and then take away with them [as Marx (1975) observed] merely the memory of it.

## Notes

**1.**   The clearinghouse concept, which aptly sees the modern studio as an intellectual property rights service organization that collects and then disburses fee income as would a bank's clearinghouse, originated in Epstein (2005, p. 107). Risk issues are discussed in Eliashberg, Elberse, and Leenders (2006).

**2.**   See, for example, Root (1979) and Nash and Oakey (1974).

**3.**   Other box office hits, such as *Driving Miss Daisy, Gandhi, Teenage Mutant Ninja Turtles, Gosford Park, Black Hawk Down,* and *My Big Fat Greek Wedding,* also encountered difficulties in finding distributors, and *On the Waterfront* was rejected by every studio (see *LA Times,* June 5, 2005). The *Turtles* story is described in Brown (1991) and the *Gandhi* experience in Eberts and Ilott (1990). *Daisy*'s situation is mentioned in Landro (1990), *Gosford Park*'s problem in finding $6 million for North American rights is covered in King (2002), and the *Greek Wedding* story is reported in Eller (2002). Moreover, *Independence Day* was rejected by Sony; Fox lost faith in *The English Patient,* which Miramax (Disney) distributed; TriStar put *Pulp Fiction* into turnaround; and Universal passed on the opportunity to co-finance *Titanic.* Warner Bros. also passed *Forrest Gump* to Paramount. As described by Shone (2004, pp. 46–52), even *Star Wars* had an uncertain start. And Leipzig (2005) shows how improbable it is that even a completed project is ever accepted for distribution. Goldstein (2005) further recounts how best-picture Oscar nominees *Ray, Finding Neverland, Sideways, Million Dollar Baby,* and *The Aviator* were initially unable to find major studio financing but were instead jump-started by entrepreneurial outside sources such as Graham King (*Aviator*) and Phil Anschutz (*Ray*). The rejections occurred even with legendary Clint Eastwood already attached to *Million Dollar Baby* and with Martin Scorsese and Leonardo DiCaprio already attached to *Aviator.* See also Mlodinow (2006). McNamara (2006) indicates that pictures that have already been approved for production are, because of budget concerns, sometimes canceled.

**4.**   To preclude excessive charges ("double-dipping") on the talent packages put together for television, agencies have devised alternative compensation approaches for themselves. The alternative, in its simplest form, and as described by Davis (1989), is to receive "the equivalent of 5 percent of the money paid the show's production company by the network, 5 percent of half the profit, if any, the production company gets from the network, and 15 percent of the adjusted gross – basically, syndication sales less the costs not picked up by the network.... An agency like [William] Morris can expect to make anywhere from $21,000 to $100,000 from every episode of a network show, and the eventual take from the syndication of a hit can be staggering. The Cosby show, a Morris package, is expected to give the agency an income of $50 million from reruns alone." In consideration for negotiating and structuring television deals, many powerful agencies will charge 5% of revenues (including those derived from syndication). Others may charge a 3% packaging fee plus 10% of the "backend" revenues.

A so-called 3%-3%-10% package had been the most common in the late 1980s, but more aggressive agents have extracted 5%-5%-10% formulas. The first figure is a percentage of the per episode license fee that is paid to the agent, which the agent receives for the life of the show. The second figure, also based on the license fee, is tied to the profitability of the series and is deferred until net profit is achieved. The third figure, however, is the one that is most lucrative to the agencies and is tied to the backend or syndication revenues.

In the movie business, package deals essentially turn studios into banks that finance film ideas generated outside the studio. More recently, talent agencies have become active in arranging financing packages from private equity and hedge fund operators in return for consulting fees and perhaps an economic interest in projects. However, as noted in Hoffman (2006a), it is not clear whether such economic interests are antagonistic to a previous Screen Actor Guild agreement expired in 2002 that barred agencies from involvement in the production business. See Akst and Landro (1988), Gubernick (1989b), and especially Davis (1989). Such package deals effectively offset the condition that agents are not allowed to own a piece of television and movie productions. See also *Variety*, March 25, 1991, and *Broadcasting*, September 23, 1991.

**5.** ICM was a subsidiary of Josephson International, which had been publicly traded. With the exception of the years in which Josephson was public, financial statements are not available. However, estimated revenues (in $ millions) and the number of agents in 2002 were approximately as follows:

|  | Revenues | Agents |
|---|---|---|
| Creative Artists | 250+ | 184 |
| William Morris | 250 | 215 |
| International Creative Management | 150 | 165 |
| United Talent Agency | 100 | 80 |

*Source*: *Wall Street Journal*, February 22, 2002.

The number of clients represented by each agency ranges from 1,200 at CAA to 2,200 at ICM. See Lippman (1995). But note that in 1999 the agency business experienced major upheaval, with many veteran agents and clients shifting their positions. As noted in Horn (2005a), CAA is considered to be the most powerful agency, with William Morris, United Talent, Endeavor, and ICM the other majors. See also Kelly (2005), Kelly (2006a), and Fleming (2006).

CAA was formed by former William Morris agents in 1975 and over the next 20 years went on to become the most powerful movie packager in Hollywood as well as the most broadly influential agency across all entertainment industry segments.

By the late 1990s, however, talent managers had also come into prominence. Managers, unlike agents, are not licensed by the state and are not allowed to solicit employment or negotiate deals for their clients. But they have the right to produce and own a piece of television and movie productions. As Masters (1999) suggests, the line between agents and managers has blurred. As of 2002, a revision of Screen Actors Guild rules (dating from 1939) had been negotiated with the Association of Talent Agents. The new rules would have permitted the purchase of talent agencies by advertising agencies and/or allowed them to be more economically linked to production companies (but not to the large media conglomerates like Disney, Viacom, and others). Also, talent agencies would have been allowed to invest up to 20% in an independent production company. However, in April 2002, SAG members rejected the proposed changes, in part reflecting fear among actors that agents would be biased toward producers of TV shows in which the agents have an interest. See Whitaker (2002), Lippman (2002b), and Hoffman (2006b).

**6.** The following example of a common-stock offering in the 1980s is illustrative. In the case of a Kings Road Productions offering in the early summer of 1981, rapidly deteriorating market conditions caused withdrawal of the proposed sale of 1.8 million shares at prices between $10 and $12 per share through a large managing underwriter. Experienced producer Stephen Friedman contributed as a core of assets his previously released theatrical features – *Slapshot*, *Blood Brothers*, *Fast Break*, *Hero at Large*, and *Little Darlings* – several of which had already been profitable. United Artists, moreover, was at that time about to distribute Friedman's *Eye of the Needle*, a $15 million picture based on the best-selling novel of the same title. Options on several promising literary properties were also among the Kings Road assets.

It was not until 1985, however, that Kings Road Entertainment finally raised capital from the public in an offering, led by two small underwriters, of 1.5 million shares at $10 a share. The assets included profit participations in the aforementioned pictures and in five others, the most prominent of which was *All of Me* (domestic rentals as of 1987 were $6.7 million). At the time of the offering, MCA Universal had been granted domestic theatrical and most other distribution rights (except for home video) in most of the company's upcoming productions. MCA, in turn, had agreed to provide material cash advances for the production of those films.

In the 1980s, many other new companies raised or attempted to raise public capital through common-stock offerings at low prices. Although most of these small companies began with an intention to eventually produce films on their own, some of them were organized solely for the purpose of developing and arranging financing, production, and distribution for others; that is, they functioned as executive production outfits.

**7.** Arguably, an exception in 1993 was the flotation of the Australian *Lightning Jack* Film Trust of 36 million units to solely finance the $26 million Paul Hogan production. Still, nearly $3 million and three months were spent putting the deal together. Also, Australian tax laws had helped by allowing investors to deduct 90% of their investment over two years. See *The Hollywood Reporter*, 1993 Independent Producers Issue.

**8.** As discussed in *Variety* of August 8, 2005, two such large pools include Legendary Pictures and Melrose Investors. The typical deal is for the studio and investors to each fund half of the budget and sometimes half the cost of prints and advertising (p & a). The studio then takes a fee of 10% to 20% of revenues. After the studio recoups p & a and sets aside other money to pay for participant points and incidentals, the remainder is split 50/50. The investors here put up as much as half of a film's budget, with the studios retaining creative control and distribution rights. See also Kelly (2006b), *Variety*, November 21, 2005, and *Los Angeles Times*, January 20, 2006. Active private equity firms as of 2006 also include Qualia Capital, Dune Capital Management, and Relativity Media (Gun Hill Road), which had raised $700 million to co-finance 19 films at Sony and Universal. Along the same lines, Mehta (2006) also discusses such deals, including a J. P. Morgan Hemisphere Film Partners fund that is designed to invest only in pictures budgeted at more than $100 million. That is because the fund's analysis showed a historic cash-on-cash return of 32% for such films, as compared with a 2% return for films in the $75 million to $100 million range, and 5% for those in the $50 million to $75 million range.

Horn (2006b), however, discusses how *Poseidon*, with a $160 million budget, may have resulted in a $50 million loss to the private equity fund (Virtual) that participated in financing the picture. Virtual covered around half of the $250 million that it cost to produce and market *Poseidon*. In the deal, Warner Bros. and Virtual split production and marketing costs, but Warner recoups p & a, collects interest, and also a distribution fee of 12.5% before sharing any revenue with Virtual. An offsetting example of a private equity financed (by Legendary) picture that succeeded (with a domestic box office of more than $200 million) was *Batman Begins*, distributed by Warner in 2005.

The main problem generally faced by funds is that the pool of pictures made available for their potential investment often excludes the major studio franchise titles. Moreover, returns for funds come after studios have deducted distribution fees. Melrose 2, however, is an example in which Paramount cannot withhold the best prospects for itself.

The funds often assume that film *slates*, as opposed to individual films, generate portfolio returns that are close to being normally distributed. Professor Art De Vany, as quoted in an article by John Gapper in the October 9, 2006 *Finanical Times*, notes, though, that benefits from the portfolio effect are likely to be more than offset by greater variability in returns. Investors, he says, "do not know what probability distribution they are up against." See also Holson (2006a), which describes how hedge and private equity funds are making deals directly with veteran producers, who can thus potentially share in 100% of DVD sales instead of the normal 20% studio deal.

**9.**   This occurs despite the fact that presales for domestic home video may be payable 25% upon commencement of principal photography, 25% upon delivery of an answer print, 25% three months after initial theatrical release, and the remainder on availability in home video markets.

**10.**   Until the Tax Reform Act of 1986, which caused the gradual withdrawal of invest-ment tax credits (ITCs) for the entertainment industry, such credits had been one of the most important sources of cash for movie and television-series producers. Feature films – recognized in the tax code as capital assets having useful lives of over three years – had been eligible for ITC treatment. Such qualification had resulted from the industry's lobby-ing efforts directed at Congress and from precedents set in tax litigation involving Disney and MCA. In the 1970s, both companies won ITC benefits in appeals-court rulings. Dekom (1984, p. 194) discussed the ITC options available to filmmakers under Section 48K of the pre-1986 IRS code.

Good examples of widely distributed pre-1986 U.S. limited partnerships are to be found in the 1981 SLM Entertainment Ltd. offerings of participations in a package of MGM's films and in the 1982, 1983, and 1984 Delphi-series packages of Columbia Pictures films that Merrill Lynch originated.

The SLM limited partnership was sold in units valued at $5,000, with a general partners' contribution of 1%. Investors shared up to 50% ownership with MGM of some 15 films (five films were initially specified) and were entitled to 99% of capital-contribution recoupment and a sliding percentage of profits generated by those productions.

Similarly, in Delphi II (1983), the partnership retained all distribution rights, and until the limited partners received cash equal to their investment, they were entitled to 99% of all cash distributions and equal allocation of all income, loss, or credits. After cash payments to limited partners equaled the proceeds of the offering (less selling commissions and mar-keting and sales management fees), the general partners were to receive 20% of all cash distributions. Any partnership losses were thus compensated out of distribution fees due the studio.

Delphi III (1984), also offered in units of $5,000 (for a total of $60 million), was even more favorable to investors because all distribution fees were to be deferred until the part-nership recouped 100% of its share of a film's negative (production) costs. Only after that condition had been satisfied was the distributor entitled to recoup its deferred distribution fee of 17.5% of gross receipts from the film. In addition, Delphi III partners were entitled to 25% of net proceeds earned by a film (after deducting a 17.5% distribution fee), or 8% of gross receipts, whichever was greater. This ensured some payment to the partnership even if the film was unsuccessful.

**11.**   For example, a more recent variation on tax-sheltered film financing appeared in Germany in the late 1990s. Under German tax law, investors in films deducted 100% of their investment up front and then reported license receipts as ordinary income. The structural core of such deals was a sale-leaseback arrangement in which the film studio effectively charged from 6% to 8% of the production budget to a pool of capital funded by German investors.

That is, the partnership bought the film from the studio and then leased back worldwide distribution rights, with the studio retaining the option to repurchase the copyright from the investment partnership at the end of perhaps as few as seven years. By leveraging the amount invested through nonrecourse loans, with additional write-downs of up to three times the original investment, potential tax-sheltered returns from successful films could then be greatly magnified. By the end of 2002, however, proposed changes to Germany's tax laws and collapse of the Neuer Markt caused many German investors to reduce capital commitments to films, with the amount shrinking by at least 60% from an annual average that had been €5 billion. As Moore (2002, pp. 22–23) notes, the funds are of two types: defeased and equity. An example: *Alexander*, an epic costing more than $150 million was financed with a package assembled by IM Internationalmedia AG. See also "Hollywood's Big Loss," November 21, 2005, and "How to Finance a Hollywood Blockbuster: Start with a German Tax Shelter," April 25, 2005, both by E. J. Epstein at www.slate.com. Additional references include Bardeen and Shaw (2004) and Desai *et al.* (2002a, 2002b).

Film industry development incentives differ by country or region and can be in the form of direct subsidies, grants, levies on box-office receipts, and tax credits or deductions. Incentives for filming in Hungary and other Eastern European countries are discussed in Barrionuevo (2004). Hungary, for example, provides 20% tax breaks on film productions. In France, the film industry is subsidized by a box-office tax on American films. In Britain, filmmakers receive some proceeds from the national lottery. See also Gorham (2002), Brown (2002), Tunick (2002), Gerse (2004), and Meza (2005).

**12.** From the investors' perspective, the interest-free loan contains a not-so-obvious cost of inflation (i.e., the guaranteed return of capital is in absolute dollars, not inflation-adjusted dollars). Moreover, because HBO retains pay TV and syndication rights, major theatrical distributors would normally be reluctant to distribute Silver Screen features – perhaps unless offered a juicier-than-average distribution fee.

**13.** As may be inferred, this type of partnership arrangement, and HBO's other participations (e.g., in TriStar Productions and in Orion Pictures), have made HBO a major force in feature-film production, as well as in distribution on pay cable systems. HBO's interest in filmmaking stems from a simple economic fact: Given its large subscriber base, it often costs less ($10 million on average as of the early 2000s and as little as $4 million) to produce an original feature directly for cable than to buy rights on a per subscriber basis from the other studios. Also see Mair (1988).

**14.** According to Securities Exchange Commission 10-K filings, as reported in *Variety* of May 10, 1989, Silver Screen Partners (SSP) I through IV were all profitable in 1988. SSP IV ended 1988 with net income of $16.15 per unit. Each unit was sold for $500 in June 1988. In the same year, SSP III, which raised $300 million and invested in 19 pictures – including *Good Morning Vietnam*, *Three Men and a Baby*, and *Who Framed Roger Rabbit* – netted $61.63 per unit. Roughly, that would suggest that the return for the year, including these three extraordinarily popular films, was 12.3% on the base of $500 a unit. A discussion of film partnership financial performance through the 1980s appears in *Variety*, November 5, 1990.

**15.** Under Regulation D, accredited individual investors (as of 1986) are those with at least $1 million of liquid net worth and $200,000 of annual income in each of the two most recent years. Rules for a Regulation D offering are differentiated for issues of over and under $5 million. As Cones (1998, pp. 143–155) notes, Reg D exemptions from securities registration are governed under specific rules 504, 505, and 506. Rule 506 does not impose a ceiling on the amount of money that can be raised, whereas rules 504 and 505 do impose ceilings. Perhaps the most noteworthy of such Reg D partnerships was FilmDallas, originally established in 1984 as a private limited partnership with an initial capital contribution of $2.4 million. This company subsequently produced the well-regarded low-budget pictures *Kiss of the Spider Woman* and *The Trip to Bountiful*. Note, however, that a filing under the SEC's Regulation A is actually a small registered public offering limited to $5 million during a given one-year period. See also Muller (1991).

**16.** As in modern portfolio theory applied to stocks and bonds, diversification over many projects reduces overall risk. However, systemic risk (i.e., risk inherent to investment in the movie industry as a whole) cannot be diversified away. See, for example, Elton *et al.* (2003).

**17.** In the mid-1990s, new financing structures, not all fully tested against tax and accounting challenges, began to emerge. The goal is to finance with off–balance sheet debt through, say, a bank joint venture that can defer and smooth some of the risks through pooling (cross-collateralization) of potential profits while still allowing the distribution company to earn its fees. See *Daily Variety*, February 21, 1997.

**18.** As of the late 1990s, Fox, Universal, DreamWorks, and PolyGram had all made use of securitization structures, with loans provided by Citigroup, Chase, and others that allow the studios to tap into commercial paper and note markets. See Hazelton (1998). Co-financing deals and fractionalization of rights (see Chapter 5) is another aspect of this. Co-financing as a means of reducing risk was shown to be questionable in Goettler and Leslie (2003), and is covered in Amdur (2003). As described in greater detail in Eisbruck (2005), deals are generally of three types: future film ("slate") portfolio financings, in which investors are entitled to share in future "first-cycle" revenues after distribution fee and p & a deductions; film revenue advance deals, in which funds are invested *after* films have been released; and library sales, in which first-cycle performance is already known so that risk is relatively low and predictability is high. An example of this is the sale of Viacom's DreamWorks 59-feature library (including Oscar-winning titles such as *Gadiator* and *American Beauty*) in 2006 for $900 million to George Soros and Dune Capital. Viacom has the right to repurchase the asset after five years, retains a small interest, and collects an 8% distribution fee, while Soros bought the rights to sell DVDs and rebroadcast the films. See *Wall Street Journal*, March 17, 2006.

**19.** Receivables formed by aggregation of presale contracts for major territories may nonetheless be sometimes used to draw financially subsidized production cost loan guarantees from the foreign government agencies, primarily European, that have been established for this purpose. In the U.K., Article 48, which expired in 2005 and was replaced by a tax credit scheme (16% above £20 million, 20% under), was representative. Lenders would be exposed to loss if, for whatever reason, a licensee failed to accept delivery of a completed picture in foreign jurisdictions, where remedies may be difficult to obtain. Also, a motion picture loan will often be made for a term of more than three years because it will usually require more than three years for full syndication, network television, and other downstream revenues to be realized. The longer the term, the greater the risk that the underlying credit conditions will become substantially changed. For all these reasons and more, a bank will advance less than the total value (usually less than 75%) of the presales advances.

**20.** See Snyder (2006) and also note 11 above.

**21.** This could arguably be compared with the average production cost of a major feature of $300,000 in 1940 and of $100,000 during the depths of the Depression in 1932. Marr and Kelly (2006) also show that newer special-effects technology for major "tentpole" releases by the major studios has also contributed to rising costs of production.

**22.** Wealthy people from outside the Hollywood establishment also decided to apply their fortunes earned in other diverse endeavors to the movie business. Their infusive and intrusive effect on the industry's financing rhythms and processes added visibly to the aggressive bidding for scarce talent resources. As summarized by Kiger (2004), outside investors usually do not fare well in Hollywood. In the 1970s and early 1980s, these out-siders were probably led astray by extrapolating the then record-breaking box-office per-formances of *Jaws* and *Star Wars* and by enthusiasm for the "new media" revolution. More recently, however, such outsiders, guided by experienced agents, have been much more successful. As Goldstein (2006b) notes, many of the 2006 Oscar-nominated films were made for under $14 million and were financed at least in part by outsiders such as Mark Cuban (Dallas Mavericks owner) and Todd Wagner (*Good Night, and Good Luck*); Bill Pohlad, owner of the Minnesota Twins (*Brokeback Mountain*); and real estate entrepreneur Bob Yari (*Crash*).

**23.** Easy credit conditions in Japan during the late 1980s enabled Japanese companies to borrow at tax-adjusted rates of as low as 1% and boosted Japanese real estate and equity values to incredible heights. As a result, Japanese industrial companies such as Sony and Matsushita could bid for American movie studios (Matsushita bought MCA in 1990) at prices that no one else could come close to matching.

**24.** There are still a few instances in which small studios produce feature films for modest sums. For example, Troma Inc., based in New York City, specializes in the production and theatrical distribution of raunchy comedies that are also of interest to pay cable networks. In addition, several other independent filmmakers had specialized in the production of low-budget features. EO Corporation (Earl Owensby) was one such company (in North Carolina) that, in the early 1980s, specialized in films that appealed primarily to working-class and rural audiences.

Troma was featured in Schumer (1982) and Trachtenberg (1984). See also Cox (1989b). EO Corporation was described in *Variety*, July 23, 1980, in *Esquire*, November 1980, and on the CBS *60 Minutes* program of August 8, 1982. Rosen and Hamilton (1987) also describe low-budget independent feature marketing and financing in more detail.

**25.** It is estimated that labor fringe benefits add 20% to 30% to above-the-line costs and 30% to 40% to below-the-line costs. Such costs had, on average, approximately doubled to $200,000 a day (for an "A" title) in the early 1990s as compared with the cost ten years prior, while average shooting schedules had expanded from around 40 days to 60 days over the same time. Goodell (1998, p. 111) notes that the cost of below-the-line personnel ranges generally between 11% and 15% of the total budget regardless of its size. As Moore (2002, p. 46) also explains, "deferments and participations are not included in the budget," even though self-charged "producer's fees" paid to the producer are included.

**26.** Therefore, to avoid major financial losses in case of natural or other catastrophe, and to secure the positions of major lenders on a picture (be they studios or banks), completion-bond guarantees must normally be obtained from specialty insurers. Such contracts were historically priced at about 6% of a film's budget, and with a 50% rebate in the event there were no claims. A part of this fee goes to insurance companies. However, there is some variation depending on the riskiness of the location, on the previous experience of the director and producer, and on the size of the production budget. As a practical matter, lending institutions do not provide interim financing for projects whose completion is not assured. To activate loan agreements, independent producers must thus always obtain completion bonds in conjunction with signed distribution contracts from creditworthy organizations. The completion guaranty protects financiers, assuring either repayment or completion of the film. If a film is going substantially over budget or encounters other completion problems, the guarantor is required to provide funding but also would have the right to invade producer and director contingent and/or cash compensation arrangements. A standby investment commitment to cover over-budget costs differs in that it allows the investor to reach into the profit participations of other earlier equity investors. See Moore (2002, pp. 71–80) and Rudman and Ephraim (2004).

The worldwide completion-bond business is about $700 million in size and, as Angeli (1991) notes, two companies, Film Finances and The Completion Bond Company (a part of Transamerica Insurance since 1990), dominated the business in the early 1990s. Each of these companies had been guaranteeing over 100 pictures a year. By 1993, however, price competition, with rates often as low as 1% of budget, forced The Completion Bond Company to discontinue operations. As a result, a third company, International Film Guarantors (IFG), owned by Fireman's Fund Insurance, has become more important. *The Hollywood Reporter* of June 29, 1998, updates the history, noting several new entrants. Also see Scholl (1992), *Variety*, April 12, 1993 and June 7, 1993, and *The Hollywood Reporter*, May 9, 2000, in which Film Finances is described. As of 2002, IFG and Film Finances were the industry leaders in writing new business, with Cinema Completions (a CNA and AON joint venture) and Motion Picture Bond Co. (St. Paul Insurance) dropping back. As of 2005, active companies also included Near National Group.

**27.** The accounting classifications for below-the-line costs are thus normally broken into three components: production, postproduction, and other.

**28.** It may be argued that the unions' featherbedding and work-restriction rules have also contributed to unemployment. Hollywood unemployment rates, as estimated from industry pension-plan contributions that depend on person-hours worked, are chronically high; they vary cyclically with changes in production starts and, to a lesser extent, secularly with growth of new entertainment media. Perhaps as a result, negotiations between the AMPTP and the guilds have not normally been cordial. Indeed, with regard to DVDs, one reason production has run away to Canada is that the unions there allow producers to buy out residual royalties. From the standpoint of producers, as Lubove (2004) notes, "In what other business do you get paid handsomely for a day's work – and then keep getting paid over and over again for years to come."

Relations became especially bitter during bargaining sessions in 1980 and 1981, when SAG and the Writers Guild demanded significant participation rights in license fees from new media sources such as pay cable, discs, and cassettes. Then again, in 1988, the Writers Guild and the AMPTP sustained a lengthy strike centered on the issue of television residual payments. A settlement was ultimately reached on a formula with elements similar to those used for television-license residuals originally negotiated in the early days of television by SAG's then-president, Ronald Reagan. See also McDougal (1998, pp. 183–186).

In outline, the writers agreed to 2% of producers' revenues after the producer had recouped $1 million per hour of taped programming and $1.2 million per hour of filmed programming from any combination of sales to pay television systems, videodiscs, and cassettes. Actors received residuals for original programming made for pay television and received 4.5% of a distributor's gross after a program had played for ten days within a year on each pay television system.

In the SAG-AFTRA settlement in 1983 with the AMPTP, there was an increase from 4.5% to 6% of distributors' gross (4.95% to 6.66% counting pension and welfare contributions) and no change in the terms requiring sales of 100,000 videocassettes before compensation begins. Terms of the SAG settlement of 2001, as discussed in the *Los Angeles Times*, July 4, 2001, include a 3% raise in minimum payments for TV work the first two years of the contract and 3.5% the final year. However, actors received no increase in payments for video and DVD sales. Studios held the line on changing the current system, under which they can claim 80 cents of every $1 of video or DVD sales as a manufacturing and marketing cost and then allocate 5.4% of the remaining money to actors. As noted in Marr (2004), studios try to limit the share of overall revenues from all sources that goes to talent at 25% of a film's total and have been particularly protective of margins on DVDs, which can be as high as 50% to 60%. Also, *Variety*, February 23, 2004 notes that only a few actors and directors can command 35% to 40% of home video/DVD revenues to be a base for royalties. The practice of paying residuals began innocently enough in 1941 in radio broadcasts that were taped in the East and then repeated on the West Coast.

In 1984, the Directors Guild won an increase in the share of residuals from films distributed on videocassettes. Directors had been entitled to 1.2% of producers' revenues on cassette sales, but under the 1984 contract this rose to 1.5% of the first $1 million and 1.8% thereafter. The directors had initially sought to link home video royalties to the much larger base of distributors' revenues. Also, under the previous agreement, directors are entitled to receive a fraction of a cent for each subscriber to pay television systems until a production has recouped $2 million per hour of programming. They are then entitled to 2% of gross receipts.

A 2006 agreement by the SAG and the studios covers use of television programs on cellphones and serves as a blueprint concerning residual payments on other new distribution platforms. The agreement, as described in Verrier (2006b), calls for writers and actors to receive minimums per two-minute episode, and after the episodes are run for 13 weeks, writers and directors are to receive residual payments that equal 1.2% of ABC's license fee (on the show *Lost*), while actors are to receive 3.6%.

Major strikes in the industry involved SAG in 1980 for three months, writers in 1988 for 22 weeks, and actors in 2000 for six months.

**29.**  Seligman (1982) supports the notion that, in the absence of union featherbedding and other work-restriction rules, the available capital resources for production could be spread over more film starts, capital costs would be lower, and moviemakers would not be as eager to shift production to foreign locations, where wages are lower. Labor inefficiencies also raise the cost of capital by inordinately increasing investors' risk of loss. Over the long run, such higher capital costs would tend to reduce employment growth opportunities by decreasing the number of film starts.

**30.**  Article 20 is controversial because studios can cut costs by developing a film concept, farming it out to a nonunion independent, and then taking it back for distribution as a negative pickup while claiming to have no creative control. See Cones (1998, p. 56) and *Variety*, September 14, 1992.

**31.**  By 2005, the DVD window after theatrical had been abbreviated to a little more than 4 months, as compared with 6 months a few years earlier. And unauthorized copying of movies on the Internet had by 2003 already reached such proportions that many films were commonly available on the Net even before theatrical release. The film industry has thus far been unable to respond effectively to the involuntary rearrangement of release sequencing. See Grover and Green (2003) and also Holson (2005b) about disruptive effects of new technologies. See also Healey and Phillips (2005) for a description of the film piracy process, and McBride and Fowler (2006) and Fowler (2006) about estimated losses. As of 2006, the television windows follow approximately after theatrical release in the following sequence: pay-per-view to satellite and cable, 180 days after; subscription TV (HBO, Showtime, etc.), one year after; network television (usually three runs), two years after; cable, one year after network television or just after subscription TV if no network showings (usually seven years' duration); local television stations, just after cable (duration up to 30 years).

**32.**  With widespread availability of pay-per-view cable, for instance, studios will have the potential to generate millions of dollars by one-night showings of their most important films. This would, in effect, raise viewing prices per person well beyond those traditionally received from subscription-television channels (see Chapter 8).

However, total revenues might be adversely affected by diminishing contributions from markets pushed farther downstream in the distribution sequence: For example, now that films are first widely exposed to large pay cable audiences, broadcast networks are, with only a few exceptions, no longer as interested in bidding aggressively for licenses to run theatrical features. Networks seem more interested in first-run made-for-television productions, which are less expensive and often more effective in generating high ratings.

Windowing strategies, as Owen and Wildman (1992, p. 30) have noted, must therefore account for many factors, among which they list

(a) differences in per-viewer prices earned in different channels of distribution;
(b) incremental differences in each channel's contribution to a program's total audience;
(c) interest rates as a measure of opportunity costs of money;
(d) the extent to which viewers of one channel are eliminated as viewers of another;
(e) the vulnerability of each channel to unauthorized copying; and
(f) the rate at which viewing interest declines after initial release.

**33.** Conceivably, major pay-per-view film events might occasionally be scheduled just ahead of theatrical release. In 1995, Carolco and Tele-Communications Inc. planned to make the first attempts at this, but with no follow-through. However, an old (and odd) example of rearranged sequencing occurred in 1980, when Twentieth Century Fox showed *Breaking Away* on network television before showing it on pay cable. Fox even contemplated simultaneous release in theaters and on videocassettes. Unsuccessful contemporaneous release in several distribution windows was also attempted by a small distributor in 2004 for the film *Noel*. Exhibitors were also upset in 2005 when *Ray* was released to DVD in February, while the film was still playing in theaters. As described by Carr (2005), a more ambitious approach also began in 2005, when 2929 Entertainment set up a venture to make films simultaneously available in theaters, on DVD, and on high-definition broadcast and cable networks. The first feature to be released in this way was the low-budget *Bubble*, which did not perform impressively at the box office. For most pictures, the greatest marginal revenue per unit time remains to be derived from theatrical issue, and most pictures require theatrical release in order to generate interest from sources farther down the line. For the foreseeable future, theatrical release will thus come first for the great majority of films. Also see Section 3.4 and also Weinberg (2005) and Holson (2005a).

**34.** A pure public good is defined by economists as one for which the cost of production is independent of the number of people who consume it. This would apply, for example, to television programs or to other performances as discussed in Section 13.4. See also the glossary.

**35.** Marich (2005, pp. 26–27) notes that the two quads of most importance are those for under age 25. Several different types of research, including concept testing, positioning studies, focus groups, test screenings, tracking surveys, advertising testing, and exit surveys, are discussed. The three major research companies are National Research Group, the oldest and owned by VNU; MarketCast, owned by Reed Elsevier; and OTX Research.

**36.** Such bid letters would always include a schedule of admission prices, the number of showings on weekends and weekdays, the number of seats in the auditorium in which the film is expected to play, and other conditions that the distributor might find desirable. Some studios prefer to bid their pictures and some don't, or they will bid their pictures only in some cities or under special circumstances. The process itself, however, is often in the nature of a public auction. As already noted, the majority of exhibition licenses are negotiated.

Whether bid or negotiated, under a gross-receipts formula, first-run film rental usually begins at 70% of box-office admissions receipts and gradually declines to as low as 30% over a period of four to seven weeks. Second-run rentals begin at 35% of box-office admissions and often decline to 30% after the first week. For instance, in the 1995 release of *Batman Forever*, the admissions revenue sharing formula terms were 90/10 (after house expenses) for the first three weeks and 80/20 for the next three weeks; or, under the gross receipts formula, theaters paid 65% of the aggregate box office for the run, whichever formula was higher.

Although there has been little formal economic analysis of bidding behavior in the movie business, game theory provides many economic bidding models that could be readily adapted; for example, see Davis (1973).

**37.** Given the increasingly common first-week saturation booking strategies and consolidation of exhibition chains in the early 2000s, the industry has begun some movement toward simply leaving exhibitors with 40% of box office averaged over all the weeks that a picture plays. See, for example, *Variety*, March 25, 2002. However, as Goldsmith (2004) reports, by 2004 the industry began to move to an even 50/50, so-called "aggregate settlement," split taken over the life of the film. Although this change appears on the surface to favor exhibitors over distributors as compared with the traditional sliding scales from the first week onward, in practice, it is much simpler to implement and, for each of the parties, usually generates approximately the same income as under the prior method. For the majors, foreign settlements averaged around 43% or 44% in 2005. This suggests that even if a film's foreign box-office receipts are above those in the U.S. market, the distributor will see approximately the same income from each market.

**38.** Use of "clearance" rights became an issue with Sony's June 1996 release of *Cable Guy*, in which Sony attempted to open the picture as wide as possible in metropolitan areas by asking national theater owners for a waiver on clearances. Some theater owners agreed to honor Sony's request. See *The Hollywood Reporter*, June 13, 1996. Also, it seems probable that film rental and clearance agreements are basically evolving into being negotiated on an annual aggregate basis instead of picture by picture and theater by theater as has been the tradition. This was the norm in Canada, where the duopoly of Cineplex Odeon and Famous Players provided near-national coverage and bookings did not need to be done on the basis of American-style geographic zones. However, for distribution purposes, Canadian box office is combined with that of the United States into what is called the domestic market.

**39.** Doman (2001) notes that in the early 2000s distributors began to negotiate "firm terms" on film rentals *before* release. And so-called aggregate deals, wherein a percentage is applied to a film's entire run, are also an alternative to the usual 90/10 weekly box-office computations. As noted in the 2003 AMC Entertainment Inc. Form 10-K, "under a firm terms formula, we pay the distributor a specified percentage of box office receipts, with the percentages declining over the term of the run. Firm term film rental fees are generally the greater of (i) 70% of box office admissions, gradually declining to as low as 30% over a period of four to seven weeks versus (ii) a specified percentage (i.e., 90%) of the excess of box office receipts over a negotiated allowance for theater expenses (commonly known as a 90–10 clause). The settlement process allows for negotiation based upon how a film actually performs. A firm term agreement could result in lower than anticipated film rent if the film outperforms expectations, especially in regards to length of run, and, conversely, there is a downside risk when the film under performs." More details on this and on the issue of settlements can be found in Section 5.3, where a sample calculation illustrating split percentages and minimum conditions can be found. The historical backdrop for settlements is in Hanssen (2005). It is worthwhile noting, too, that the subjective nature of settlement adjustments affects profit participations.

**40.** As of the late 1990s, advertisers paid theaters an average of $1.25 million for 60 seconds of time in screenings during a film's four-week run. See Gubernick (1999).

**41.** To this end, the marketing tail may sometimes wag the production dog: Studios will now often attempt to build already well-accepted titles into long-lived strings of brand-name sequels, among the best examples of which have been the James Bond, Batman, Harry Potter, and Lord of the Rings lines. Whereas sequels had, on the average, usually been able to generate 65% of the original's box-office gross, they are now often able to far surpass the performance of the original release as, for instance, *Austin Powers* and *Rush Hour* have done. See also Lyman (2002) and Waxman (2003).

**42.** Tracks have historically been more prominent in Canada, where according to Marich (2005, p. 200), "before AMC's entry, Famous Players booked on a national basis movies from Disney, MGM, Paramount, and Warner Bros. (and more recently DreamWorks). Cineplex Odeon was the circuit for Columbia/Sony, Twentieth Century Fox, and Universal Pictures."

**43.** In mid-1983, a U.S. district court ruled that splits are a form of price fixing and an illegal market allocation in violation of the Sherman Antitrust Act. According to the court's ruling, split agreements entered into by Milwaukee exhibitors caused the amounts paid to distributors to be reduced by 92% from $1.8 million in 1977 to $140,000 in 1981. The ruling had been appealed by the defendant exhibitors (see *The Hollywood Reporter*, June 22, 1983, *Variety*, March 23, 1988, and other legal transcriptions regarding the Kerasotes Theater cases). The practice of product splitting was brought to the attention of the Department of Justice by distributors, who responded to exhibitors' charges that distributors had been illegally engaged in the practice of block booking. See also Stigler (1963) and note 3 of Chapter 8 on cable channel bundling.

**44.** Real estate value is the key determinant as to whether or not existing theater sites can be used more profitability for office buildings, parking lots, or other purposes. And standard discounted–cash flow and internal-rate-of-return modeling methods, as in Damodaran (1996), can be applied.

As an illustration, consider a theater generating an average annual net income of $100,000 over its expected ten-year life. The internal rate of return on an original $500,000 investment will be just over 15%. However, if the required rate of return is 18%, then, using the net present value (NPV) method, the net present value of this theater is about $450,000. Typical operating profit margins for a theater range between 15% and 45% and are closer to the lower end if the theater is leased as opposed to owned by the operator.

**45.** Ratings are now set by the Classification and Ratings Administration (CARA), an autonomous unit associated with the MPAA. The ratings are: *G*: General Audience – all ages admitted; *PG*: Parental guidance suggested – some material may not be suitable for children; *PG-13*: Parents strongly cautioned – some material may be inappropriate for children under age 13; *R*: Restricted – under age 17 requires accompanying parent or adult guardian; *NC- 17*: No one 17 and under admitted.

**46.** If each household pays $4, if one-third of that is remitted as rental to the distributor (the remainder to cable operators and program wholesalers), and if there are 15 million households, then $20 million will be generated. There is an additional benefit to the distributor because of the much faster cash return than from theaters.

**47.** Pressure to do well on opening weekends has been significantly intensified in recent years. It all began with *Jaws* in 1975, which was the first major film nationally advertised and widely released, day and date, on over 700 screens. Nowadays, pictures that do less than $10 million in domestic box office on an opening weekend are likely to be pulled rather quickly. Conversely, a film that declines by 20% or less on its *second* weekend is considered to be a potentially large winner. As of 2004, it was no longer unusual for films to drop 50% by the second weekend as compared with half that percentage ten years earlier. As Lippman (2002a) notes, first weekends used to account for an average of 20% to 25% of a film's total receipts, but that percentage has risen toward 33%. Since the early 1990s, seasonality has begun to blur at the edges, and it is thus less of an issue given the large number of screens in modern theaters and the sophisticated marketing campaigns that studios now launch year round. Such campaigns are significantly influenced by prerelease audience research provided by the dominant NRG, a division of Dutch media company VNU (and owner of *The Hollywood Reporter*), or by MarketCast, which also conducts movie-tracking reports and is owned by *Daily Variety* publisher Reed Elsevier.

Also, one strong film will occasionally block another. Such a situation arose when the long-running *Star Wars* blocked the timely exhibition of a previously booked run of *Close Encounters of the Third Kind*, thereby starting a round of lawsuits involving distributors and an exhibitor. Details on this particular situation can be found in *Variety*, December 21, 1977. But note also that, to get around this problem, exhibitors occasionally "piggyback" one film with another in violation of their contracts.

**48.**    An even better measure of how one film has performed as compared with another can, in theory, be derived by calculating the percentages of potential total weekly exhibitor capacity that the films have utilized. It would, for instance, be interesting to see how opening-week receipts from *Indiana Jones* compared with opening-week receipts from *Superman* by deriving for each picture a capacity-utilization percentage – profiled first across the whole industry's capacity and then across the capacity of theaters that played both pictures in their initial weeks of release. Unfortunately, data of this kind are rarely available.

Opening weekend gross receipts for important releases are, however, carefully analyzed and compared with those of previous important releases. *Pirates of the Caribbean: Dead Man's Chest* in 2006 had the highest opening weekend at $132 million. *X-Men: The Last Stand* also generated $120.1 million over the four-day Memorial Day weekend in 2006. *The Lost World: Jurassic Park* had previously (in May 1997) generated the largest three-day opening weekend up to that time, with receipts of $72.4 million and a four-day total of $92.7 million. *Lost World* also held the record for the highest single-day grosses for Friday ($22 million), Saturday ($24.8 million), and Sunday ($25.6 million) up until the releases of *Harry Potter and the Sorcerer's Stone* ($90.3 million) in November 2001, and of *Spider-Man* in May 2002 ($114.8 million). *Mission Impossible* set the prior four-day record, with a total of $56.8 million in May 1996. In 1995, *Batman Forever* generated a three-day opening weekend with receipts of $52.8 million. And in 1993, *Jurassic Park* generated $50.2 million in three days. *Star Wars Episode III – Revenge of the Sith* took the highest single-day ticket sales of $50 million in 3,661 theaters until it was surpassed by *Pirates of the Caribbean: Dead Man's Chest* with a one-day total of $55.5 million in 4, 133 theaters. The film crossed the $100 million mark in a record two days. The second largest *worldwide* opening weekend after *Star Wars III* was *Da Vinci Code*, which garnered $224 million in May 2006. *Shrek 2* in May 2004 opened in a record 4,163 theaters nationwide with single-day ticket sales of $44.8 million. It had the highest five-day opening with $125.3 million. This was around the same as *The Lord of the Rings: The Return of the King* ($124.1 million) in December 2003. But *Spider-Man2* in July 2004 pulled in $180.1 million in its first six days and took the third highest opening-day receipts of $40.5 million. *Shrek 2* was the first picture for which the initial release was played in more than 4,000 theaters. Opening weeks for an average picture now typically account for at least 33% of a film's total theatrical gross versus 24% in 1990. See also Lyman (2001).

An additional new complication is that variable pricing strategies such as those used by airlines for "yield management" are only now being considered by theater owners who, in response to challenges from DVDs and the Internet, are beginning to charge premium prices for more comfortable reserved seating. See Leonhardt (2006b).

**49.** The correlation between number of releases and rentals percentage is about −0.4. Eliashberg *et al.* (2006) also notes that the industry rule of thumb is that with per capita moviegoing frequency of 5.5 films a year, one screen for every 10,000 people is needed.

**50.** At first, of course, it was not at all clear how the home video market would evolve. As with subsequent new media including DVDs and the Internet, the only sure thing was that the pornographic entertainment segment would be an early adopter. The subject is covered in Rich (2001), Lane (2001), and "Porn in the U.S.A.," broadcast on the CBS news show *60 Minutes*, September 5, 2004, and originally November 21, 2003.

Lardner (1987) notes that it was not at all evident that the videocassette recorder (VCR), introduced by the Sony Corporation in 1975, would prevail. The machine was not perceived as something for which plentiful software in the form of movies would be available: At the time, there was no prerecorded software. Also, the machine, known as the Betamax, could only record on one-hour magnetic tape cassettes. Worse still, it soon faced competition from a noncompatible but similar two-hour videocassette format, the VHS system (Video Home System) that was quickly introduced by Sony's manufacturing rival, Matsushita. This battle of the formats caused great confusion and hampered the initial growth of the market for VCRs, following as it did close on the heels of earlier home video technologies that had notoriously failed. Those technologies included the so-called Electronic Video Recording (EVR) system developed by Dr. Peter Goldmark at CBS Laboratories in the late 1960s, and Cartrivision. See Lessing (1971) for a description of Cartrivision, Donnelly (1986) for a quick overview of the development of EVR, Wasser (2002) and Sweeting (2004) for a history of the VCR's impact on the movie industry, and Epstein (2005, Chapter 17) for a concise history of the DVD's development and impact.

After a prolonged battle, the computer and movie industries finally agreed on a DVD standard that enabled introduction of DVDs in late 1997. These first-generation DVDs hold 4.7 gigabytes (GB) of information, or about seven times the 650 megabytes of a CD. With a dual layer (one opaque, one shiny), storage can be almost doubled again to 8.56 GB. And a second side can be further added. Using MPEG-2 compression, the ordinary DVD can thus store, on one side, a 133-minute movie along with Dolby AC-3 audio tracks. As of 2005, the Blu-ray DVD format backed by Sony has a data capacity of 25 GB, and the HD DVD backed by Toshiba has a capacity of 15 GB as compared with the first DVDs with only 4.7 GB and a much lower image resolution. The older DVD format does not have capacity sufficient for the 8 GB required for a two-hour high-definition movie. See also Lake (2002), Brinkley (1999), Rothman (2003), and Belson (2003, 2006b).

The early evolution of DVD also had been confused by introduction of a controversial variant of DVD called DIVX, which was a DVD disc with a lower initial price to the consumer of around $4 but with a built-in 48-hour viewing time limit after the disc was activated. Promotion of DIVX was discontinued in 1999. A similar concept, the ED-D, in which inexpensive ($5 to $7) DVDs chemically self-destruct a fixed number of hours after the purchaser opens the package, was introduced in 2003 by Disney but has not caught on. Netflix Inc. took advantage of the DVD's size and convenience by offering $20 monthly subscriptions that allow consumers to rent as many DVDs as they want for as long as they want but keeping no more than three at any time. See also Lippman (1999), Ramstad (1999), and Taub (2003).

Going back even further, in the late 1970s, consumers were being introduced to so-called videodisc players that did not have a recording capability and were therefore useless for "time-shifting" (i.e., the recording of a program for delayed viewing). These videodisc machines were developed in two versions: a laser/optical system (closely related to the now standardized system in compact disc players), which used a laser beam to read encoded video and audio signals, and a capacitance system, which used a stylus to skim a recording and measure changes in electrical capacitance. Both versions fared poorly and were eventually withdrawn by their respective corporate sponsors. The optical videodisc was at the time promoted by MCA and Pioneer, while RCA spent hundreds of millions of dollars before scrapping the capacitance system in 1984. See Graham (1986) for details on RCA's system.

**51.**    This was despite the fact that the studios initially fought hard against the introduction of VCRs into the home. See Chapter 6 for discussion of the First Sale Doctrine. The related Supreme Court ruling in 1984 was *Sony v Universal City Studios*. A 2005 Supreme Court case, *Metro-Goldwyn-Mayer v Grokster*, pitted Hollywood studios against computer hardware and software companies on issues of file sharing and threatened to significantly revise the earlier decision. The court ruled generally against Grokster. See *New York Times* and *Wall Street Journal*, June 28, 2005.

**52.**    It seems likely that the proportion of feature films to other home video software categories (e.g., exercise, instructional) will likely remain fairly close to the two-to-one ratio that has thus far prevailed.

**53.**    As described by Blumenthal and Goodenough (2006, p. 23), for example, the typical cost breakdown for a DVD is as follows: $30 retail price, retailer's markup (cut) $15, mastering and authoring $2, packaging $2, warehousing and inventory $1, and marketing perhaps another $2. All of this leaves between $8 and $10 as profit.

**54.**    Estimates for 1990–2004 by New York video consulting firm Alexander & Associates (www.alexassoc.com) and for 2005 from *Video Business* are as follows:

| | Total rentals (millions of units) | | Total rental spending ($ millions) | | Total purchases (millions of units) | | Total purchase spending ($ millions) | |
|---|---|---|---|---|---|---|---|---|
| | DVD | VHS | DVD | VHS | DVD | VHS | DVD | VHS |
| 2005* | N/A | N/A | 6,700 | 1,090 | N/A | N/A | 15,730 | 320 |
| 2004 | 2,134.4 | 1,052.1 | 8,175 | 3,346 | 1001.4 | 283.0 | 16,052 | 3,501 |
| 2003 | 1,695.3 | 2,028.1 | 6,171 | 6,338 | 688.4 | 440.2 | 12,276 | 6,239 |
| 2002 | 1,155.2 | 2,616.1 | 4,286 | 8,792 | 492.8 | 582.6 | 8,418 | 6,997 |
| 2001 | 616.1 | 3,308.5 | 2,156 | 10,819 | 220.4 | 600.7 | 4,150 | 7,611 |
| 2000 | 245.8 | 3,717.3 | 781 | 11,621 | 97.0 | 576.4 | 1,834 | 7,620 |
| 1995 | 4,194.8 | | 10,948 | | 682.9 | | 9,738 | |
| 1990 | 4,132.5 | | 10,331 | | 231.0 | | — | |

*\*Video Business* data

*Video Store* data of Figure 4.5 are believed to include mostly larger retailers and may thus understate the industry's size. Also, from the retailer's perspective, at an average per rental price of $3 and an average cost per tape of $66, it takes at least 22 turns over a period of four to six weeks to reach breakeven. The early weeks usually generate 40% of the total expected for the first six months after release.

**55.** For example, a studio's revenue from sell-through of a tape unit might average $9 and from revenue-sharing, $25 to $30. The cost of manufacturing the tape is perhaps $1.75 a unit. However, for a DVD sale, the average revenue per unit to the studio is closer to $16 with the manufacturing cost around one-third lower than for a tape. A good example of the potential profitability of DVD sales is *Spider-Man*, in which the DVD generated around $190 million in its first weekend of sales and an estimated $160 million of that reverted to the studio (*Los Angeles Times* of November 19, 2002). While studios receive about half of a $10 theater ticket and almost nothing for a home video rental, the studio usually takes a little more than 50% of the DVD's price. As noted in Kirkpatrick (2003), high DVD unit sales for action films have also begun to influence the types of films that are made. Johnson (2005b) similarly notes that DVDs sold abroad have added significantly to studio profits and indeed affected how the movie business is run. Marr (2005) shows how DVD sales projections (*Shrek 2*) can go awry. And Belson (2006a) discusses implications of the slowing of DVD sales relative to growth of movie downloads, which might generate profit per unit of no more than $2.40 for the studios (approximately one-fourth the profit from a DVD unit sale).

**56.** Revenue-sharing was a concept promoted in the late 1990s by Viacom and its Block-buster stores as a way of increasing A-title availability, and thus customer satisfaction. The offset, however, is that with more A-titles available, the demand for nonhit titles would normally be diminished. See also *Variety*, July 20, 1998, and Mortimer (2000), who notes that retailers choose revenue-sharing for about half of all movie titles for which both fixed-fee and sharing terms are offered (excluding direct-to-video releases). With sharing, stores must adhere to both minimum and maximum inventory restrictions to participate in the pro-grams. This study found that, with sharing, both distributor and retailer profits are increased modestly and that consumers benefit substantially.

Inventory restrictions also appear to increase distributors' profits and decrease profits for retailers as compared with sharing agreements without such restrictions. Gross margins for retailers renting DVDs are generally above 70% as compared with around 60% for revenue-sharing on tapes. It is significant that Blockbuster does not share DVD rental revenues with most studios though it does share on tapes. As noted in *BusinessWeek* of September 16, 2002, "Blockbuster buys most disks outright from the studio, for an average $17 each – end of deal." On rental tapes under revenue-share agreements, the cost per tape ranges between $22 and $25. And as explained in Peers (2003), Blockbuster in 2002 enjoyed a profit margin on its rental business of 65% as compared with 15% in its retailing activities. How-ever, late fees, which were discontinued in 2005, are estimated to have contributed at least $250 million or around 15% of annual revenues when they had been in effect.

**57.** Film company distributors, in effect, the "publishers" of home video titles, generally sell units designated for the rental market at a 37% discount to the suggested retail price. As noted by R. Childs in Squire (1992), this figure is derived from a "30 plus 10" formula in which the retailer buys at 30% discount, and 10% of the balance (7%) goes to wholesalers. This then leaves the film distribution company (the publisher) with 63% of the suggested retail price.

**58.** This is because of the First Sale Doctrine. However, if special arrangements known as pay-per-transaction were agreed upon in advance, there is no theoretical reason for the distributor not to participate in subsequent rental income. Several companies have, with varying degrees of success, established such pay-per-transaction operations.

**59.** As of the mid-1990s, the indicated crossover point was around 1.6 million sell-through units, or about four times what could be expected from the rental market. But in consideration of higher marketing costs, most distributors would want to be assured of a ratio of six to ten times the number of rental units before deciding on a sell-through strategy.

As of 1992, for example, the priced-for-rental best-seller of all time was *Ghost*, which shipped about 645,000 units. This, in effect, implied that a realistic ceiling in the rental unit market was on average around one-half million units. If so, the marketing decision becomes relatively easy since the for-rental revenues under these conditions peak at roughly $32 million ($100 a unit times 0.63 times 500,000). If a $13.50 wholesale sell-through price is assumed, for-rental market revenues would be exceeded with sell-through shipments of 2.4 million units – which, as the following commentary indicates, has been readily exceeded by many "A" titles.

On *Top Gun*, for example, Paramount decided to promote a sell-through by going with a suggested retail price of around $25 (but with the tape including a brief Pepsi-Cola advertisement). Paramount ended up selling almost 3 million units, thereby generating over $40 million in revenues. Given that the cost of manufacturing the physical product was (and is still) so low, Paramount probably netted over $30 million in profits from this one home video release. In this situation, Paramount almost surely generated more profit in targeting the sell-through rather than rental market. One of the largest sell-throughs on tape was Disney's *Snow White* (27 million units, 1994). But this was exceeded with record DVD sell-through of around 30 million units of the 2003 Disney/Pixar release of *Finding Nemo*.

**60.** Though video revenues are now increasingly less correlated to box-office performance than in the past, video revenues still often turn out to be the same percentage of production costs as are the costs of p & a. It is convenient to thus assume that video revenues approximate p & a.

**61.** "Fractured-rights" deals – in which producers could package a film idea, presell domestic and international video rights, and then arrange for a major studio to distribute the film (for a fee) in domestic theatrical markets – flourished during the first days of the home video business in the early to mid-1980s. Such presales typically covered all of the production and most, if not all, of the domestic releasing costs – leaving the producer's share of theatrical revenues and television rights as potential sources of profit. Such deals worked until the studios developed strong video distribution facilities of their own and as long as banks were willing to fund such production costs. Once the value of home video and international rights failed to keep pace with the rise of production and releasing costs, the viability of such deals fell apart. By the early 1990s, so-called split-rights deals in which a studio took *all* domestic rights, while a producer retained international rights, came into greater use. Studios today will rarely split domestic rights.

Separated rights are another variation that is derived from Writers Guild contracts stipulating that the creator of a TV show retains the show's movie rights. Studios or independent producers can acquire those rights that allow the property to be made into a movie separately, but only following narrow guidelines. As a result, lawsuits involving separated rights have become more frequent in recent years as Hollywood has come to rely more on previous television-show concepts. See Lippman (2005).

**62.** As a result, even if an independently made film is fortunate enough to obtain domestic theatrical distribution, it will likely not benefit proportionately from ancillary markets, especially in licensing to broadcast television and cable outlets. Note also that, in return for making a commitment to finance (or partially finance) a picture, an independent home video distributor would normally insist that the picture receive a predetermined amount of support in initial theatrical release through spending on prints and advertising, or p & a as it is known. Such p & a commitments are important because they, in effect, "legitimize" the picture by bringing name recognition to what is hoped will be a broad audience for the home video product. Home video distribution rights contracts with independent filmmakers will typically extend over seven years. And the producer might normally receive an advance against a royalty base of between 20% and 40% (i.e., the producer of a $20 million picture could expect an advance of between $4 million and $8 million for domestic home video rights).

Perhaps the best-known home video independent of the mid-1980s was Vestron, which went public in 1985 in the hopes of becoming an important video alternative to the releasing arms of the majors. However, the company ultimately failed once the majors took full control of their video rights and after Vestron attempted to develop its own library of feature films.

**63.** Interest in this area was heightened with Disney's 1994 direct-to-video release of the *Aladdin* sequel, *Return of Jafar*, which at a production cost of $5 million generated estimated wholesale revenues of $120 million on unit sales of 11 million. See Hofmeister (1994). Since then the business has moved to direct-to-DVD, with Disney's *Lion King* $1\frac{1}{2}$, released in 2004, being the most successful, with $160 million in sales. See *Variety*, September 13, 2004.

**64.** For example, there was evidence that the frequency of home video rental – which had averaged almost one tape a week for the typical VCR-owning household of the late 1980s – had declined in the 1990s even though the cost of an overnight rental (averaging around $2.50 per night in 1997) had remained low. And newer home video distribution methods via Internet downloads provided by services such as Movielink or through online ordering and prepaid DVD postal delivery as provided by Netflix already undermine the video store business model, which benefits greatly from late-return fees (estimated to be $1 billion in 2003). Digital VOD services offered by cable systems for $5 to $10 a month on top of normal cable bills plus $3.95 for recent titles and $2 or $3 for older titles are also quickly gaining importance. See Orwall, Peers, and Zimmerman (2002) and also Orwall (2003), in which Disney's initially unsuccessful MovieBeam VOD service is described. MovieBeam competes with the other studio-sponsored VOD services, Movielink and CinemaNow, and also Netflix, and cable and satellite services. Disney sold off a partial interest in MovieBeam to Cisco and Intel and then in 2006 attempted to relaunch the service. See also *Los Angeles Times*, February 14, 2006, and Pogue (2006).

Still, large video superstores such as Blockbuster Entertainment, and more recently giant retailer Wal-Mart Stores, have long been Hollywood's major customers. Indeed, Wal-Mart in 2006 accounted for 40% of home video and DVD sales (more than $3 billion at wholesale) and 20% of all music sold in the United States. And Target accounted for 15%. Such giant stores compete on service by carrying many thousands of titles and by having great depth-of-copy (i.e., lots of copies) of the most popular films. Horn (2005c) indicates that as of 2005, Wal-Mart, Target, and BestBuy accounted for half of a new DVD title's sales, with 60% of that coming in the first six days of release.

Video rental store profits are derived from fast turnover of a title in the first six months after release. With overhead and other costs included, the normal retailer would probably require at least 30 turns to break even. As of the early 1990s, the typical cassette was rented an average of some 50 times. Video stores are able to measure gross profits by multiplying the number of times a copy is rented by the average rental price, adding salvage-value revenues, and then subtracting the cost of the tape. For each title, the average weekly turn per copy thus becomes the critical variable.

**65.** In 1998, sales of comics were $500 million, down 50% from five years earlier. But many published products are designed for purposes of entertainment. Although comic and children's books are among the most obvious categories, most, if not all, fiction and some nonfiction also qualify. Moreover, newspapers and magazines often have entertainment motives in mind when they publish about personalities or develop "lighter" subjects or "style" or "leisure" sections. Indeed, as Table 1.4 illustrates, sales of newspapers, books, and magazines are included in National Income Accounting data as a part of recreation expenditures. Marvel Enterprises, which owns rights to Spider-Man, Hulk, and many other such characters, produces 60 comic book titles a month, but comic publishing contributes only 15% of the company's operating income, with licensing revenues from films and related merchandise contributing almost 85%. Marvel often receives 2% to 3% of a film's worldwide sales, including those from DVD and cable. See Warner (2004).

The publishing industry has also become involved in what is generally called multimedia: products and services blending digitalized images, sounds, and text that can be used with personal computers and distributed over cable, telephone, or wireless networks. See also Chapter 9.

**66.**   The first movie merchandising license was, according to Marich (2005, p. 128), probably issued in 1929 for a Mickey Mouse image placed on a children's writing tablet. U.S. and Canadian retail sales of entertainment-based licensed merchandise were estimated by the *Licensing Letter*, a trade publication, to have been $13.4 billion in 2004. The total for toys and games was $2.8 billion.

Most royalties would be in the area of 5% to 6% of the value of wholesale shipments, but the percentages can reach higher, and terms might also include advances and guarantees against royalties. Food and confectionary license percentages generally range lower than others, at between 3% and 7%. Of such revenues, producers might, depending on contractual details, be entitled to perhaps a 25% to 50% share. And, on products using an actor's visage, the percentage can range from 2.5% to 8.0% of the studio's net.

An example of how lucrative merchandising can be is provided by the 1989 release of *Batman*, in which Warner Bros. received licensing fees ranging from $2,000 to $50,000 plus royalties of 8% to 10% on revenues estimated to be $250 million in the first year of release. And Mattel reportedly agreed in the year 2000 to pay Warner Bros. a $35 million advance and a 15% royalty for toy rights to the Harry Potter book series. For a licensing deal overview, see Ovadia (2004), and also Lipman (1990), Lane (1994), and Bannon and Lippman (2000).

**67.**   Marketing cost is also seasonally influenced by Oscar nomination concerns, which tend to concentrate releases of those films thought to have the strongest creative elements into the fourth calendar quarter of the year. This is done to essentially use the same advertising expenditures to simultaneously attract general audiences and Oscar voters. See Goldstein (2006a).

An empirical study by Prag and Cassavant (1994), for example, suggests the importance of marketing expenditures to a film's success. Also note that independent producers in particular also incur additional costs in attempting to market their pictures directly at various international marketing conventions, the most important of which are the American Film Market (AFM) based in Santa Monica in early November, the Cannes Film Festival held in Cannes, France, in early May, and MIFED (*Mercato Internazionale del Cinema e della Televisione*), a somewhat similar event held in Milan, Italy, each October. Negotiations between foreign sales agents and foreign distributors' representatives form the core of these conventions. Sales agents' fees are often 15% to 20% of defined rental revenues. The sales agents' trade group, American Film Marketing Association (AFMA), provides credit reports on foreign distributors.

Television producers and distributors also have several marketing conventions, including the midwinter National Association of Television Program Executives (NATPE), held in the United States, and the *March Internationale des Programmes de Télèvision* (MIP), held each spring in France.

**68.**   The study by De Vany and Walls (1996) delves deeply into the dynamics of demand for movies, suggesting that the industry's structure is well suited to adapt sequentially to changes in supply and to provide reliable signals of demand given relatively fixed admissions prices and real-time reporting of box-office revenues. This study, also found in De Vany (2004a), indicates that (a) weekly revenues are autocorrelated; (b) audiences select or ignore films largely through an informational cascade in which individuals follow the behavior of preceding individuals or "opinion-makers" without regard to their own information; (c) widely released films show more variance in revenues and, on average, shorter run lives; (d) distribution of box-office revenue is not log normal; and (e) revenues in the industry follow a Bose-Einstein distribution in which outcomes differing "in the extreme are equally likely and similar outcomes are extremely unlikely" – "the quintessential characteristic of the movie business." Informational cascades are analyzed in Bikhchandani *et al.* (1992). See also Dellarocas *et al.* (2004), De Vany (2004b), Rusco and Walls (2004), Ravid (2004), and the informal overview by Mlodinow (2006).

Another study of interest is by Ravid (1999), who found from a random sampling of nearly 200 films that

- Lower-budget movies tended to be more profitable than those with big budgets.
- Movies with lesser-known actors tended to be more profitable than star-driven films.
- There was no correlation between the strength of reviews and profitability, but there was a relationship between the number of reviews, no matter how positive, and profitability.
- The strongest correlation for profitability was a G or PG rating.
- Sequels tend to be more profitable than the average film.
- Stars may bring in higher revenues, but the profitability is smaller. (This means that stars tend to capture their "economic rent.")

Although the aforementioned studies ascribe relatively little importance to presence of stars for purposes of predicting film results – even with big stars films sometimes do poorly – Albert (1998) found that stars have value as markers that help a film to be made and also provide information about the probability of a film's potential success.

**69.**   But generally, as Kagan (1995) illustrates, the following relationships derived over a large sample of major studio releases between the years 1989 and 1993 would seem to apply:

- To reach cash-on-cash breakeven, *domestic box-office receipts should approximate the negative cost* (or, comparably, half the negative cost should be recovered from domestic theatrical rentals).
- Worldwide rentals (including all theatrical, home video, cable, TV receipts, etc.) tend to be twice the domestic box-office receipts.

**70.**   Although it is not usually practicable to calculate precisely the return on investment (ROI) for a specific production, such a figure could be approximated by taking the total profit (if any) of all participants (including the distributor), adding the cost of capital, and then dividing by the total amount invested.

To be placed in proper perspective, this rate should always be annualized and compared with the risk-free rate of return available on government securities during the period the film project went through its life cycle (from production start to ancillary-market release).

**71.**   The financial characteristics of movies are thus fractal in nature. The discussion here follows Postrel (2000), who cites the De Vany and Walls (1996) work that can be found at www.socsci.uci.edu/mbs/personnel/devany/devany.html. As Postrel notes, "stars have their main effect not so much by helping movies open as by extending their runs. But most stars do not really make a difference." See also Ravid (1999) and Elberse (2006) about the influence of stars and Eliashberg and Shugan (1997) about the influence of critics. The ability of online reviews to be used as a box-office forecasting tool is presented in Dellarocas *et al.* (2004), found at http:// ccs.mit.edu/dell/papers/movieratings.pdf.

**72.** Even with the aforementioned advantages, however, it is not always easy for a studio to be profitable. Assuming, for example, a full production slate of 20 pictures per year made at an average cost of $25 million (which includes negative costs and operating expenses), and prints and advertising at an average of $10 million per movie, the total investment to be amortized over the releasing cycle is $700 million. If 40% of this cost is to be amortized against theatrical revenues (see Chapter 5), the minimum theatrical distributors' gross to reach breakeven would have to be $280 million. Using an approximate industry rentals percentage of 42%, we find that this is equivalent to $667 million (in retail terms) at the box office. With total domestic box-office figures in 1993 having been around $5 billion, such a studio would require a minimum market share of over 13% to break even. Yet, as of the early 1990s, with the equivalent of some eight major studios in operation, a share of that size had become much more difficult to regularly attain. As shown in Supplementary Table S3.4, there have been many years when various studios have achieved much less than 10% share.

**73.** MPAA worldwide gross profit data for the six major studios and subsidiaries in 2004 (revealed in "Hollywood's Profits, Demystified: The Real El Dorado Is TV" by E. J. Epstein in Slate.com, August 8, 2005) indicates that theatrical release generated an estimated loss of $2.2 billion, while video (DVD and VHS) generated gross profit of $14 billion, and television licensing in all forms brought gross profits of $15.9 billion.

**74.** Game theory and what is known as the "winner's curse" may in addition be applied to bidding situations of all types, be they for scripts, acting talent, books, etc. As indicated by Thaler (1992, p. 51), the winner of an auction is likely to be a loser and, somewhat counterintuitively, the more bidders there are in competition, the less aggressive the bidder ought to be.

**75.** The Capital Asset Pricing Model (CAPM) is widely applied in finance and suggests that the risk of holding a portfolio of securities, or in this case, films, can be reduced through diversification. Pokorny (2005) attempts to relate this to the release portfolios of the major studios in the 1990s.

**76.** Pareto power laws were originally used to describe the distribution of incomes in the form $P(\mu) \sim C\mu^{-\alpha}$, where $\alpha > 0$. Such laws are also sometimes known as a Zipf's law. If we were to rank box-office revenue totals by frequency of occurrence within a specific interval of time, we would find that the vast majority of releases generate under $100 million worldwide and that very few generate more than $1 billion: *Titanic* has thus far been the only film to approach $2 billion, but there are many films that make $40 million.

**77.** A Weibull probability function that allows for constant, increasing, or decreasing hazard-rate functions of time is well suited for and is thus most often used in such analyses.

**78.** This follows observations in De Vany (2004a, p. 68).

## Selected additional reading

Akst, D. (1987). "Directors and Producers Face Showdown over Residuals," *Wall Street Journal*, June 11.

Attanasio, P. (1983). "The Heady Heyday of a Hollywood Lawyer," *Esquire*, 99(4)(April).

Bach, S. (1985). *Final Cut: Dreams and Disaster in the Making of "Heaven's Gate."* New York: William Morrow.

Barboza, B. (2005). "Hollywood Movie Studios See the Chinese Film Market as Their Next Rising Star," *New York Times*, July 4.

Bart, P. (1999). *The Gross: The Hits, The Flops – The Summer That Ate Hollywood.* New York: St. Martin's Press.

(1990). *Fade Out: The Calamitous Final Days of MGM.* New York: William Morrow.

Bonnell, R. (1989). *La Vingt-Cinquième Image: Une Économie de l'Audiovisuel.* Paris: Gallimard FEMIS.

Brown, E. (2005). "Coming Soon to a Tiny Screen Near You," *Forbes*, 175(11)(May 23).

Brown, G. (1995). *Movie Time: A Chronology of Hollywood and the Movie Industry.* New York: Macmillan.

Bunn, A. (2004). "Welcome to Planet Pixar," *Wired*, June.

Canby, V. (1990). "A Revolution Reshapes Movies," *New York Times*, January 7.

Carr, D. (2003). "Major Stars Not So Crucial as Concept Trumps Celebrity," *New York Times*, June 23.

Carvell, T. (2000). "The Talented Messrs. Weinstein," *Fortune*, 141(5)(March 6).

(1998). "How Sony Created a Monster," *Fortune*, 137(11)(June 8).

Cassidy, J. (1997). "Chaos in Hollywood," *The New Yorker*, March 31.

Cieply, M. (1987). "MCA Is in Front Line of Hollywood's Fight to Rein in TV Costs," *Wall Street Journal*, March 6.

(1986). "An Agent Dominates Film and TV Studios with Package Deals," *Wall Street Journal*, December 19.

Clark, J. (2005). "The Soul of Sundance's Machine," *New York Times*, December 4.

Cooper, M. (1987). "Concession Stand: Can the Hollywood Unions Survive?," *American Film*, XIII(3)(December).

Cox, M. (1984). "A First Feature Film Is Made on the Cheap, Not Hollywood's Way," *Wall Street Journal*, May 14.

Daly, M. (1984). "The Making of *The Cotton Club*: A True Tale of Hollywood," *New York*, 17(19)(May 7).

DeGeorge, G. (1996). *The Making of a Blockbuster: How Wayne Huizenga Built a Sports and Entertainment Empire.* New York: Wiley.

Denby, D. (2007). "Hollywood Looks for a Future," *The New Yorker*, January 8.

(1986). "Can the Movies Be Saved?," *New York*, 19(28)(July 21).

De Vany, A., and Walls, W. D. (2000). "Does Hollywood Make Too Many R-Rated Movies? Risk, Stochastic Dominance, and the Illusion of Expectation," Irvine, CA: University of California, Department of Economics, asdevany@uci.edu.

(1999). "Uncertainty in the Movie Industry: Does Star Power Reduce the Terror of the Box Office?" *Journal of Cultural Economics*, 23(4).

Eller, C. (2003). "Movie Studios Learn Sharing Burden Can Be Risky Business," *Los Angeles Times*, April 16.

(2002). "Marketing Costs Scale the Heights," *Los Angeles Times*, October 21.

Eller, C., and Bates, J. (2000). "Talent Agents about to Demand Bigger Piece of Pie," *Los Angeles Times*, October 31.

Eller, C., and Hofmeister, S. (2005). "DreamWorks Sale Sounds Wake-Up Call for Indies," *Los Angeles Times*, December 17.

"The Entertainment Glut," *BusinessWeek*, No. 3565 (February 16, 1998).

Epstein, E. J. (2005). "Hollywood, the Remake," *Wall Street Journal*, December 29.

Evans, D. A. (1984). "Reel Risk: Movie Tax Shelters Aren't Box-Office Boffo," *Barron's*, January 9.

Fabrikant, G. (1999). "Plenty of Seats Available," *New York Times*, July 12.

Finler, J. W. (1988). *The Hollywood Story*. New York: Crown Publishers.

Fleming, C. (1995). "$200 Million under the Sea: The Inside Story of Kevin Costner's Disaster-Prone *WaterWorld*," *Vanity Fair*, August.

Frank, B. (1994). "Optimal Timing of Movie Releases in Ancillary Markets: The Case of Video Releases," *Journal of Cultural Economics*, 18.

Gabler, N. (1997). "The End of the Middle," *New York Times Magazine*, November 16.

Garcia, B. (1989). "Who Ya Gonna Call If a Ghostbuster's Proton Pack Breaks?: Insurance Helps Hollywood Survive Almost Anything," *Wall Street Journal*, August 24.

Gimbel, B. (2006). "The Last of the Indies," *Fortune*, 154(2)(July 24).

Goldman, W. (1983). *Adventures in the Screentrade: A Personal View of Hollywood and Screenwriting*. New York: Warner Books.

Goldsmith, J. (2007). "Wall Street Wise to Summer B.O. Ways," *Variety*, January 22.

Gregory, M. (1979). *Making Films Your Business*. New York: Schocken Books.

Griffin, N. (1993). "How They Built the Bomb: Inside the Last Seven Weeks of 'Last Action Hero'," *Premiere*, September.

Gubernick, L. (1988). "Miss Jones, Get Me Film Finances," *Forbes*, 142(14)(December 26).

Gubernick, L., and Lane, R. (1993). "I Can Get It for You Retail," *Forbes*, 151(12)(June 7).

Gunther, M. (2006). "Fox the Day after Tomorrow," *Fortune*, 153(10)(May 29).

Hand, C. (2002). "The Distribution and Predictability of Cinema Admissions," *Journal of Cultural Economics*, 26(1)(February).

Hanssen, F. A. (2000). "The Block-Booking of Films: A Reexamination," *Journal of Law and Economics*, October.

Harmetz, A. (1993). "Five Writers + One Star (A Hit?)," *New York Times*, May 30.

    (1987). "Hollywood Battles Killer Budgets," *New York Times*, May 31.

Hayes, D., and Bing, J. (2004). *Open Wide: How Hollywood Box Office Became a National Obsession*. New York: Hyperion.

Hirschberg, L. (1995). "Winning the TV Season," *New York*, 28(27)(July 10).

Hirschhorn, C. (1979). *The Warner Bros. Story*. New York: Crown Publishers.

Holson, L. M., and Lyman, R. (2002). "In Warner Brothers' Strategy a Movie Is Now a Product Line," *New York Times*, February 11.

Horn, J. (2004). "HBO Emerges as a Mecca for Maverick Filmmakers," *Los Angeles Times*, September 19.

Hughes, K. (1990). "Hunt for Blockbusters Has Big Movie Studios in a Spending Frenzy," *Wall Street Journal*, May 3.

Jayakar, K. P., and Waterman, D. (2000). "The Economics of American Theatrical Movie Exports: An Empirical Analysis," *Journal of Media Economics*, 13(3)(July).

Kehr, D. (2004). "A Face That Launched a Thousand Chips," *New York Times*, October 24.

Kenney, R. W., and Klein, B. (1983). "The Economics of Block Booking," *Journal of Law and Economics*, 26.

Kindem, G., ed. (2000). *The International Movie Industry*. Carbondale, IL: Southern Illinois University Press.

King, T. R. (1995). "Why *Waterworld*, with Costner in Fins, Is Costliest Film Ever," *Wall Street Journal*, January 31.

    (1993). "*Jurassic Park* Offers a High-Stakes Test of Hollywood Synergy," *Wall Street Journal*, February 10.

King, T. R., and Bannon, L. (1995). "No Longer Bit Players, Animators Draw Fame as Hollywood Stars," *Wall Street Journal*, October 6.

Knowlton, C. (1988). "Lessons from Hollywood Hit Men," *Fortune*, 118(5)(August 29).

Koch, N. (1992). "She Lives! She Dies! Let the Audience Decide," *New York Times*, April 19.

Landro, L. (1990a). "Hollywood in Action: Making a Star," *Wall Street Journal*, February 16.

(1990b). " 'Godfather III' Filming Begins after 15 Years and 3 Studio Regimes," *Wall Street Journal*, February 9.

(1989). "Sequels and Stars Help Top Movie Studios Avoid Major Risks," *Wall Street Journal*, June 6.

(1986). "The Movie 'Top Gun' and Deft Management Revive Paramount," *Wall Street Journal*, July 14.

(1985). "Movie Partnerships Offer a Little Glitz, Some Risk – and Maybe a Decent Return," *Wall Street Journal*, May 20.

(1984). "Frank Mancuso's Marketing Savvy Paves Ways for Paramount Hits," *Wall Street Journal*, June 27.

(1983). "If You Have Always Wanted to Be in Pictures, Partnerships Offer the Chance, but With Risks," *Wall Street Journal*, May 23.

Landro, L., and Akst, D. (1987). "Upstart Movie Makers Are Fast Fading Out after a Year's Showing," *Wall Street Journal*, November 3.

Lees, D., and Berkowitz, S. (1981). *The Movie Business*. New York: Vintage Books (Random House).

Leonard, D. (2002). "This Is War," *Fortune*, 145(11)(May 27).

Lippman, J. (2002). "In Sequel-Crazy Hollywood, Studios Couldn't Resist 'T3'," *Wall Street Journal*, March 8.

(1995). "How a Red-Hot Script That Made a Fortune Never Became a Movie," *Wall Street Journal*," June 13.

Lyman, R. (2001a). "Hollywood, an Eye on Piracy, Plans Movies for a Fee," *New York Times*, August 17.

(2001b). "Movie Marketing Wizardry," *New York Times*, January 11.

(1999a). "Hollywood's Holiday Bets," *New York Times*, December 6.

(1999b). "New Digital Cameras Poised to Jolt World of Filmmaking," *New York Times*, November 19.

Lyman, R., and Holson, L. M. (2002). "Holidays Now Hottest Season in Hollywood," *New York Times*, November 24.

Magnet, M. (1983). "Coke Tries Selling Movies Like Soda Pop," *Fortune*, 108(13)(December 26) and also counterpoint by Murphy, A. D. (1983). "In Defining 'Hit Film' Economics, 'Fortune' Looks in Wrong Eyes," *Variety*, December 14.

Mayer, M. F. (1978). *The Film Industries: Practical Business/Legal Problems in Production, Distribution, and Exhibition*, 2nd ed. New York: Hastings House.

McClintick, D. (1982). *Indecent Exposure: A True Story of Hollywood and Wall Street*. New York: William Morrow.

Moldea, D. (1986). *Dark Victory*. New York: Viking.

Noglows, P. (1990). "Newcomers Turn Completion Game into Risky Business," *Variety*, August 8.

O'Neill, K. (1995). "Gumption," *Premiere*, 8(8)(April).

Orwall, B. (2002). "At Disney, String of Weak Cartoons Leads to Cost Cuts," *Wall Street Journal*, June 18.

(1998). "Here Is How Disney Tries to Put the 'Event' into the Event Film," *Wall Street Journal*, June 30.

Orwall, B., and Lippman, J. (1999). "Hollywood, Chastened by High Costs, Finds a New Theme: Cheap," *Wall Street Journal*, April 12.

Orwall, B., and Ramstad, E. (2000). "Web's Reach Forces Hollywood to Rethink America-First Policy," *Wall Street Journal*, June 12.

Orwall, B., and Zuckerman, G. (2000). "Regal Cinemas Joined Megaplex Frenzy, Ended Up in Back Row," *Wall Street Journal*, September 27.

Peers, M. (2002). "Blockbuster Breaks Away," *Wall Street Journal*, April 22.

Porter, E., and Fabricant, G. (2006). "A Big Star May Not a Profitable Movie Make," *New York Times*, August 28.

Racanelli, V. J. (2001). "Blockbusters?," *Barron's*, August 27.

Rensin, D. (2003). *The Mailroom: Hollywood History from the Bottom Up*. New York: Random House/Ballantine.

Rose, F. (1999). "A Strategy with a Twist," *Fortune*, 139(4)(March 1).

    (1996). "This Is Only a Test," *Premiere*, August.

Rosen, D., and Hamilton, P. (1987). *Off-Hollywood: The Making and Marketing of American Specialty Films*. New York and Colorado: The Independent Feature Project and The Sundance Institute; New York: Grove Weidenfeld (1990).

Rudell, M. I. (1984). *Behind the Scenes: Practical Entertainment Law*. New York: Harcourt Brace Jovanovich.

Salamon, J. (1991). *The Devil's Candy: The Bonfire of the Vanities Goes to Hollywood*. Boston: Houghton Mifflin.

Salmans, S. (1984). "A Nose for Talent – and for Tradition," *New York Times*, May 20.

Sansweet, S. J. (1982). "Who Does What Film? It Depends on Who Talks to What Agent," *Wall Street Journal*, June 23.

Sansweet, S. J., and Landro, L. (1983). "As the Money Rolls in, Movie Makers Discover It Is a Mixed Blessing," *Wall Street Journal*, September 1.

Schlender, B. (1995). "Steve Jobs' Amazing Movie Adventure," *Fortune*, 132(6)(September 18).

Schmidt, R. (2000). *Feature Filmmaking at Used-Car Prices*, 3rd ed. New York: Putnam Penguin.

Serwer, A. (2006). "Extreme Makeover," *Fortune*, 153(10)(May 29).

Sharpe, A. (1995). "Small-Town Audience Is Ticket to Success of Movie-House Chain," *Wall Street Journal*, July 12.

Sherman, S. P. (1986). "A TV Titan Wagers a Wad on Movies," *Fortune*, 113(10)(May 12).

Sing, A., and Mohideen, N. (2006). "Bollywood's New Vibe," *Bloomberg Markets*, 15(10)(October).

Singular, S. (1996). *Power to Burn: Michael Ovitz and the New Business of Show Business*. Secaucus, NJ: Birch Lane (Carol Publishing).

Slater, R. (1997). *Ovitz: The Inside Story of Hollywood's Most Controversial Power Broker*. New York: McGraw-Hill.

Sochay, S. (1994). "Predicting the Performance of Motion Pictures," *Journal of Media Economics*, 7(4).

Spragins, E. (1983). "Son of Delphi," *Forbes*, 132(2)(July 18).

Sterngold, J. (1997). "The Return of the Merchandiser," *New York Times*, January 30.

Taub, E. (2003). "Digital Projection of Films Is Coming. Now Who Pays?," *New York Times*, October 13.

Tromberg, S. (1980). *Making Money Making Movies: The Independent Moviemaker's Handbook*. New York: New Viewpoints/Vision Books (Division of Franklin Watts).

Turner, R. (1994). "Disney, Using Cash and Claw, Stays King of Animated Movies," *Wall Street Journal*, May 16.

(1989a). "A Showdown for Discount Movie Houses," *Wall Street Journal*, July 18.

(1989b). "A Hot Movie Studio Gobbles Up the Cash but Produces No Hits," *Wall Street Journal*, June 14.

Weinraub, B. (2000). "Tentative Pact Set to Expand Agents' Power in Hollywood," *New York Times*, February 21.

Welkos, R. W. (1996). "Starring in the Biggest Deals in Hollywood: Top Lawyers Rival Agents as Power Brokers," *Los Angeles Times*, January 12.

Wiese, M. (1986). *Home Video: Producing for the Home Market*. Stoneham, MA: Butterworth.

Wolf, J. (1998). "The Blockbuster Script Factory," *New York Times Magazine*, August 23.

Zweig, P. L. (1987). "Lights! Camera! Pinstripes!," *Institutional Investor*, XXI(9) (September).

# 5
# Financial accounting in movies and television

*Happy trails to you, until we meet again.* – Dale Evans.[1]

This song is perhaps more appropriately sung by Hollywood accountants than by cowboys. But, as this chapter indicates, the problems that arise in accounting for motion-picture and ancillary-market income are more often due to differing viewpoints and interpretations than to intended deceits.

## 5.1 Dollars and sense

Contract clout

No major actor, director, writer, or other participant in an entertainment project makes a deal without beforehand receiving some kind of high-powered help, be it from an agent, personal manager, lawyer, accountant, or tax expert. In some cases, platoons of advisors are consulted; in others, only one person or a few individuals may perform all functions. Thus, an image of naive, impressionable artists negotiating out of their league with large, powerful, and knowledgeable producer or distributor organizations is most often not accurate.

As in all loosely structured private-market negotiations, bargaining power (in the industry's jargon, "clout") is the only thing that matters. A new, unknown talent who happens on the scene will have little if any clout with anyone. Top stars, by definition, have enough clout to command the attention of just about everyone. In Hollywood as in other businesses, it has been observed, "you don't get what's fair; you get what you're able to negotiate."[2]

By hiring people whose ability to attract large audiences has already been proved, a producer can gain considerable financial leverage. It may be less risky to pay a star $2 million than to pay an unknown $100,000; the presence of the star may easily increase the value of the property by several times that $2 million salary through increased sales in theatrical and other markets, whereas the unknown may contribute nothing from the standpoint of return on investment. Clout, it seems, is best measured on a logarithmic scale.[3]

Contracts are usually initially agreed on in outline (i.e., a *deal memo*, *letter of intent*, or *term sheet*), with the innumerable details presumably left for later structuring by professionals representing both sides. However, final contracts normally are complex documents and, if imprecisely drawn, are open to different interpretations that can lead to disputes. It is, of course, in the nature of this industry to attract a disproportionate amount of publicity when such disputes arise.

Orchestrating the numbers

Accounting principles provide a framework in which the financial operating performance of a business can be observed and compared with the performance of other businesses. But it was not until 1973 that the American Institute of Certified Public Accountants (AICPA) published a guide, *Accounting for Motion Picture Films*, that pragmatically resolved many (but far from all) controversial issues. Publication of that guide significantly diminished the number of interpretations used in describing film industry transactions and thus made comparisons of one company's statements with those of another considerably easier and more meaningful than before.

The AICPA guide, however, has not prevented accountants from tailoring financial reports, starting with a set of base figures, to suit the needs and purposes of the users and providers of funds. Just as there are different angles from which to photograph an object to illustrate different facets, there are different perspectives from which to examine the data derived from the same base. In fact, given the complexity of many contracts, it is an absolute necessity to view financial performance from the angle that suits the needs of the viewer.

For example, outside shareholders generally need to know only the aggregate financial position of the company, not the intricate details of each participant's contract. Those participants, by the same token, usually will care only about their own share statements, from which the aggregates are constructed. In the sections that follow, the two different accounting perspectives are more fully described.

## 5.2 Corporate overview

Because this is not strictly an accounting text, no attempt will be made to describe the full terminology used by CPAs. It will be useful, however, to note instances in which movie business definitions are different from those used in other industries.

Revenue-recognition factors

Industry practice with regard to recognition of revenues from theatrical exhibition is fairly straightforward. With either percentage or flat-rent contracts, revenues from exhibitors are accrued and recognized by distributors when receivable, which, because of cash intake at the box office, is almost immediately. Contrariwise, ancillary-market revenue recognition is potentially much more complex. Prior to the issuance of the aforementioned accounting guide, four methods existed:

1. Contract method: All revenue is recognized on contract execution.
2. Billing method: Revenue is recognized as installment payments become due.
3. Delivery method: Revenue is recognized on delivery to the licensee.
4. Deferral or apportionment method: Revenue is recognized evenly over the whole license period.

To place the entire industry on a uniform basis, the AICPA guide indicated that television license revenues for feature films should not be recognized until all the following conditions are met.

1. The license fee (sales price) for each film is known.
2. The cost of each film is known or reasonably determinable.
3. Collectibility of the full license fee is reasonably assured.
4. The licensee accepts the film in accordance with the conditions of the license agreement.
5. The film is available; that is, the right is deliverable by the licensor and exercisable by the licensee.

Although there are many further complicating elements – discounting for the time value of money on long-term receivables or the possibly different methods used for tax-reporting purposes as compared with those used for shareholder reports – for most analytical purposes only a few points need be noted.

Availability (item 5) is most important with regard to television or other ancillary-market licenses. Even when contract-specified sequencing to downstream markets restricts a distributor from making films available at certain times, the distributor often retains great discretion as to when product is to be made available. For example, television networks interested in obtaining a movie may be totally indifferent as to whether the picture is available on September 30 or on October 1. But to a distributor company trying to smooth its reported quarterly earnings results, the difference of one day could be substantial.

Another sensitive and potentially litigious area concerns fees allocated to films in a package of features that might be sold to a network.[4] Packages usually contain a dozen or so films, with, of course, some titles much stronger than others. Theoretically, each film is individually negotiated, but in practice the package is offered as whole. The problem is then to allocate the total-package revenues among all the films according to a proportion formula based on relative theatrical grosses, genre, and other criteria. It has been estimated that the strongest film in a package might be worth 2.5 times the value of the weakest, with strength being defined by box-office performance (and price per film typically equaling 12% to 15% of domestic box-office totals). Allocation procedures are further discussed in Section 5.4.

Of further significance are "backlogs" – the accumulation of contracts from which future license fees will be derived. Important contracts for ancillary-market exhibition are often written far in advance, sometimes even before the film is produced or released in theaters. Such backlogs generally do not appear directly anywhere on the balance sheet as contra to inventories, except when there are amounts received prior to revenue recognition. In those cases, the amounts are carried as advance payments and are included in current liabilities.

It has with some justification thus been argued that film company financial statements only partially reflect true corporate assets. However, companies ordinarily will indicate in balance sheet footnotes or other reports, such as annuals and 10-K filings with the Securities and Exchange Commission, the extent to which backlogs have changed during the reporting period.


Inventories

Perhaps the greatest conceptual difference between the movie industry and other industries has been in the definition of inventory, which is normally taken to be a current asset (i.e., an asset that is used for production of goods or services in a single accounting period). Because the life cycles of filmed entertainment products (from beginning idea or property to final distribution) are measured in years, entertainment company inventories had until recently been categorized, in balance sheets that are classified, into current-period and noncurrent-period components. Included in such assets are the costs of options, screenplays, and projects in the preproduction, current-production, and postproduction phases awaiting release.

More formally, according to the early accounting guide, inventories classified as current assets included the following:

1. For films in release, unamortized film costs allocated to the primary market
2. Film costs applicable to completed films not released, net of the portion allocable to secondary markets
3. Television films in production that are under contract of sale

Under the early AICPA guide, costs allocated to secondary markets and that are not expected to be realized within 12 months, and all other costs related to film production, are classified as noncurrent. Typically, a film company included the following captions:

Film productions:

> Released, less amortization
> Completed, not released
> In process
> Story rights and scenarios

Amortization of inventory

Inventories are matched in a "cost-of-goods-sold" sense against a *forecasted* schedule of receipt of income. Although forecasts of film receipts are mostly best guesses, in the aggregate it is fairly certain that, on the average, perhaps 85% of all theater-exhibition revenues will be generated in the first nine months of release and almost all the remainder by the end of the second year.

Rather than using a cost-recovery theory, in which no gross profit is recognized until all costs and expenses have been recovered, the film industry's theoretical approach is based on a system in which costs are amortized in a pattern that parallels income flows. With this flow-of-income approach, gross profit is recognized as a standard portion of every dollar of gross revenue recorded.

Prior to implementation in 1981 of Statement 53 of the Financial Accounting Standards Board (FASB), which essentially formalized the aforementioned AICPA guidelines, two amortization approaches were generally applied. A company could use separate estimates of gross revenue for each film or it could use average tables (as in Supplementary Table S5.1 in Appendix C) based on the combined experience for many films. The use of such tables is, however, no longer practicable or permitted.[5]

With costs in the industry now reported at the lower of unamortized cost or net realizable value on a film-by-film basis (i.e., on an individual rather than group average), accountants' procedures require that estimates be reviewed periodically (at least quarterly and at the end of each year) to be sure that the best available data are being used (Table 5.1). In the absence of any changes in the revenue estimates for an individual film, costs are amortized

Table 5.1. *Individual-film-forecast-computation method of amortization: an example*

| *Assumptions* | |
| --- | --- |
| Film cost | $10,000,000 |
| Actual gross revenues: | |
| First year | 12,000,000 |
| Second year | 3,000,000 |
| Third year | 1,000,000 |
| Anticipated total gross revenues: | |
| At end of first year | 24,000,000 |
| At end of second and third years | 20,000,000 |

*Amount of amortization*

*Amortization*

First-year amortization

$$\frac{\$12,000,000}{\$24,000,000} \times \$10,000,000 = \$5,000,000$$

Second-year amortization (anticipated total gross revenues reduced from $24,000,000 to $20,000,000)[a]

$$\frac{\$3,000,000}{\$8,000,000^{b}} \times \$5,000,000^{c} = \$1,875,000$$

Third-year amortization

$$\frac{\$1,000,000}{\$8,000,000^{d}} \times \$5,000,000^{d} = \$625,000$$

---

[a] If there were no change in anticipated gross revenues, the second-year amortization would be as follows:

$$\frac{\$3,000,000}{\$24,000,000} \times \$10,000,000 = \$1,250,000.$$

[b] $20,000,000 minus $12,000,000 or anticipated total gross revenues from beginning of period.

[c] $10,000,000 minus $5,000,000 or cost less accumulated amortization at beginning of period.

[d] The $8,000,000 and $5,000,000 need not be reduced by the second-year gross revenue ($3,000,000) and second-year amortization ($1,875,000), respectively, because anticipated gross revenues did not change from the second to the third year. If such reduction were made, the amount of amortization would be as follows:

$$\frac{\$1,000,000}{\$5,000,000} \times \$3,125,000 = \$625,000.$$

*Source*: Appendix to FASB Statement 53. © Financial Accounting Standards Board, High Ridge Park, Stamford, CT 06905, USA. Reprinted with permission. Copies of the complete document are available from the FASB.

and participation costs are accrued (expensed) in a manner that thus yields a constant rate of profit over the estimation period.

If there are material revisions in gross-revenue estimates, however, amortization schedules must be recomputed. For this reason, films performing poorly in early release are quickly written down. Moreover, a write-down before release will be required in the rare situations in which the cost of a production obviously exceeds expected gross revenues.[6]

This methodology also presumes that properties are to be reviewed periodically and that, if story rights have been held for three years and the property has not been set for production, or if it is determined that the property will not be adapted for film projects, those story costs will be charged to production overhead in the current period.

Unamortized residuals

Before the days of pay cable, home video, and the Internet, most of a film's income was derived from movie theaters (and also to a much lesser extent from free television broadcasts).[7] That was indeed the situation in 1981, when FASB Statement No. 53 was adopted. However, although FASB 53 has been recently rescinded and replaced by SOP 00–2 (with differences discussed below), the basic architecture of FASB Statement 53 remains in place and still provides a useful framework for discussion of film accounting concepts and controversies. Among the most important of these are unamortized residuals.

By the early 1980s, an ever-larger stream of film revenues was being derived from nontheatrical sources of distribution, and it became increasingly important to more closely match revenue and cost. A portion of a production's cost known as an *unamortized residual* was therefore set aside to be written down against expected future income from television.[8] For a major feature in the 1970s, an unamortized residual of $750,000 or so was typical.

As income "ultimates" (revenues ultimately receivable from pay cable, DVDs, syndication, etc.) have grown proportionally more significant in comparison with those derived from theatrical exhibition, unamortized residuals have also been set aside, pro rata, to be relatively matched against these additional estimated ancillary-market revenues. Such residuals have, on the average, accordingly become much larger than in the past, and it now would not be unusual for the bulk of a picture's cost to be written down against future revenues from nontheatrical sources.[9]

Interest expense and other costs

As interest rates and average production budgets have soared, interest expense has also become a more noticeable component of feature filmmaking. Until 1980, when FASB Statement 34 concerning treatment (capitalization) of interest was issued, such costs had been written off as incurred. Under this new standard, interest costs are capitalized and then charged as part of the negative cost.

Although studio period outlays, including those for rents and salaries, fall into a normal-expense category, studios also incur other costs of distribution (exploitation) that are capitalized. These may include, but are not limited to, prints and advertising and payments of subdistribution fees. For example, prior to the use of digital projectors and satellite feeds, prints would typically cost over $2,000 each (for five reels), and because simultaneous saturation booking is now common and often requires that well over 1,000 copies be made, this had amounted to a substantial investment. Such print costs were, under FASB Statement 53, usually amortized according to a formula similar to that used for amortization of the negative.

According to FASB Statement 53, all exploitation costs (for prints, advertising, rents, salaries, and other distribution expenses) that are clearly to benefit future periods should be capitalized as film-cost inventory and amortized over a period in which the major portion of gross revenue from the picture is recorded. This method especially pertains to national advertising, in which expenses before release can be considerable. Local and cooperative advertising expenditures, however, are generally closely related to local grosses and are normally expensed as incurred because they usually do not provide any benefits in future periods.

Calculation controversies

FASB Statement 53 certainly contributed to a much-improved basis for comparison of film and television company financial data versus the relatively amorphous conditions that had prevailed prior to its issuance. Yet the statement had nevertheless drawn criticism for allowing considerable discretionary variation in the treatment of marketing and inventory cost amortizations in particular. With marketing costs often amounting to more than 35% of inventory, and overhead for another 10%, the recoupment of such costs is proportionally far more important to earnings reports in films and television programming than in other, say, manufactured-products industries. In most other industries, such cost amortizations constitute a relatively smaller percentage of total expenses and are much more closely related to the projected useful lives of assets based on prior experiences with other similar assets.

According to the rules for movies and television productions, the rate of amortization instead depends on *management's* projections (market-by-market and media-by-media) of often-uncertain *revenue* streams that are expected sometime in the possibly distant future. Moreover, because income recognition is generally unrelated to cash collections, it is entirely possible to report earnings and yet to be insolvent at the same time. It was thus often argued that the accounting picture rendered by application of FASB Statement 53 did not accurately reflect the true earnings power, cash flow potential, or asset value of a company.

Using FASB Statement 53, for example, some companies might have assumed that all advertising costs incurred during theatrical release create values in the ancillary markets. As such, they would have capitalized some of the costs despite the fact that local advertising in Tampa will ordinarily have no effect on video market sales in Toronto or Tanzania. In addition, some companies would have amortized prints over estimated revenues from all markets rather than against revenues generated in specific markets, for instance, domestic versus foreign.

Other companies might have assumed long lives for their films and television series and thus included second- or third-cycle syndication sales even though such syndication sale events may not have been known in terms of precise timing or pricing. And still others might have differed on how long, or through what means, development-project costs from in-house independent producers were to be capitalized and then written off as studio overhead. In general, the costs of abandoned properties should be amortized as soon as it is clear that the properties will not be produced, but it is not unusual for many projects to be lost in creative limbo for relatively long periods.[10]

Under FASB Statement 53, even receivables presented problems: Receivables, according to these rules, were shown on the balance sheet as *discounted* to present value, whereas estimates of far more uncertain revenue ultimates, made largely on the basis of a film's genre and the star power of its actors at the time of initial release, were not. The effect of this was to lower the amount of cost to be amortized in the current year (which boosts reported earnings) and to raise (via capitalization of costs) the asset values carried on the balance sheet.[11]

Under FASB Statement 53 there was thus ample room for substantial variations in earnings reporting practices to appear.[12] In many instances, analysts could only compare specific company results against industry standards for financial statement ratios such as those presented in Table 5.2.

Statement of Position 00–2

The variations and controversies that appeared in the applications of FASB Statement 53 finally led to a request by the FASB in 1995 for the AICPA to develop new guidelines in the form of a Statement of Position (SOP) that would tighten the reporting requirements for producers or distributors of films, television specials, television series, or similar products that are sold, licensed, or exhibited. SOP 00–2 took effect as of the year 2000, and a new FASB Statement 139 rescinded the previous FASB Statement 53.

In all, the tighter rules require, among other things, that

- Exploitation costs are to follow SOP 93–7 (*Reporting on Advertising Costs*), which requires that all marketing and exploitation costs should, for the most part, be expensed as incurred (or the first time that the advertising takes place), with the cost of film prints charged to expense over the period benefited. Previously, such costs had often been capitalized and then amortized over a film's full distribution lifetime.

Table 5.2. *Accounting ratio benchmarks for major film studio/distributors, 1985–2005*

| | Film cost amortization as % of | | | Unamortized film costs of released films as a % of inventories | Additions to film costs as a % of film cost amortization[a] |
|------|----------|-------------|---------------------|-------------|-------------|
| | Revenues | Inventories | Operating cash flow | | |
| 2005 | 39.6 | 89.7 | 69.0 | 49.4 | 118.6 |
| 2004 | 34.3 | 83.2 | 84.9 | 46.0 | 110.4 |
| 2003 | 27.8 | 78.2 | 83.9 | 46.6 | 115.2 |
| 2002 | 29.1 | 74.2 | 87.7 | 59.4 | 66.2 |
| 2001 | 28.5 | 51.2 | 84.3 | 57.3 | 67.3 |
| 2000 | 27.2 | 32.4 | 57.4 | 57.5 | 60.4 |
| 1999 | 49.2 | 66.7 | 89.6 | 59.1 | 51.6 |
| 1998 | 40.1 | 60.7 | NA[b] | 52.2 | 48.7 |
| 1997 | 38.9 | 59.8 | 92.3 | 54.9 | 98.6 |
| 1996 | 43.2 | 68.4 | 100.4 | 58.4 | 89.1 |
| 1995 | 51.9 | 80.9 | 92.3 | 61.7 | 63.2 |
| 1994 | 46.0 | 74.1 | 100.5 | 59.9 | 66.9 |
| 1993 | 60.5 | 71.8 | 109.0 | 53.5 | 95.6 |
| 1992 | 50.6 | 74.4 | 84.4 | 52.4 | 84.2 |
| 1991 | 43.8 | 75.4 | 77.4 | 58.0 | 83.7 |
| 1990 | 41.8 | 69.0 | 70.0 | 50.0 | 104.9 |
| 1989 | 38.4 | 69.2 | 66.0 | 54.4 | 104.0 |
| 1988 | 46.2 | 91.4 | 76.0 | 56.3 | 112.9 |
| 1987 | 46.1 | 95.3 | 80.6 | 61.9 | 113.3 |
| 1986 | 47.8 | 69.7 | 85.1 | 51.5 | 112.2 |
| 1985 | 52.6 | 80.9 | 88.8 | 65.4 | 128.3 |
| Mean | 44.2 | 72.2 | 101.2 | 55.5 | 90.3 |

[a] Based on a smaller sample since 1996.
[b] Not available.
*Source*: Company reports.

- Total film revenue estimates against which production costs are amortized are based on estimates over a period not to exceed ten years following the date of the film's initial release, with some limited exceptions. Previously, this period might have been as long as 20 years.
- For episodic television series, ultimate revenue should include estimates of revenue over a period not to exceed ten years from the date of delivery of the first episode or, if still in production, five years from the date of delivery of the most recent episode. Ultimate revenues should include estimates of secondary market revenue for produced episodes only if an entity can demonstrate that *firm* commitments exist and that the episodes can be successfully licensed in the secondary market. Previously, the episodic revenue assumptions had been largely open-ended.

- Syndication revenues for television series episodes are to be recognized over the life of the contract rather than at the first available playdate if certain revenue recognition criteria are not met. Those criteria include the completion, delivery, and immediate availability of the series for exploitation by the licensee and the establishment of a fixed or determinable fee that is reasonably assured of being collectable. For some syndicated series, the effect is to spread the one-period earnings bump previously seen under FASB Statement 53 over more earnings periods.
- Ultimate revenue should include estimates of the portion of the wholesale or retail revenue from an entity's sale of items such as toys and apparel and other merchandise only if the entity can demonstrate a history of earning such revenue from that form of exploitation in similar kinds of films.
- Abandoned-project development costs and certain indirect overhead costs are to be charged directly to the income statement and are thus no longer part of total negative costs – that is, included in a studio's overhead pool.[13]
- Films are to be defined as long-term assets (i.e., as film cost assets), not inventories. This means that their worth is to be based on future cash flow estimates discounted to present or fair value as compared with the previous condition in which revenue estimates were not discounted. Interest income would be earned as the films play off.
- If the percentage of unamortized film costs for released films (excluding acquired film libraries) expected to be amortized within three years from the date of the balance sheet is less than 80%, additional information regarding the period required to reach an amortization level of 80% must be provided.

Although SOP 00–2 does not fully resolve all controversies, it goes a long way toward standardizing applications of the individual film-forecast method, which has long served as the conceptual foundation of movie industry accounting.

Beyond this core, however, there remain many thorny issues that arise from the differing assumptions made by studio corporations as compared with those made by individuals. Among the most important of these differences concerns the timing of receipts and the subsequent disbursements to participants. For example, distributors would normally use accrual accounting methods (booking income when *billed*) for their own financial-statement reporting purposes and they would use cash accounting methods (based on revenues when *collected* and out-of-pocket expenses when incurred) for tracking disbursements to producers and others.[14]

Indeed, all levels of the industry are extremely sensitive to cash flow considerations, and delays of payments tend to compound rapidly on the way to downstream recipients. Although the financial performance of a film company can sometimes be disguised by accounting treatments, the true condition becomes evident once the flow of new investment stops.

Neither can mergers forever hide true conditions. Until 2001, merger and acquisition accounting had followed either a "pooling of interest" or a "purchase" methodology.[15] While use of either purchase or pooling has not been unique to the media industries (and is of historical interest), it is important to remember that film and television program assets are, by nature, intangibles, that valuations are often highly subjective, and that all accounting methods contain elements of both art and science.[16] This aspect will be further amplified as we next explore specific financial relationships between studios and creative participants.

## 5.3 Big-picture accounting

Financial overview

Preceding sections have described how financial statements appear from the corporate angle. But accounting statements for individual participants are properly viewed from a different perspective. This section illustrates the results for typical production, distribution, and exhibition contracts in terms of profit-and-loss statements for individual projects.

For the producer, the legal heart of most such projects is the production-financing-distribution (PFD) agreement, which may broadly contain one or more of the following four sometimes overlapping financial attributes or elements:

1. *Step deals*, in which the financing proceeds in steps that allow the financing entity to advance additional funds or to terminate involvement depending upon whether various predetermined conditions (e.g., approvals of screenplay drafts and casting choices) are met.
2. *Packages/negative pickups*, in which a producer, or an agent, assembles the key elements of a project and then attempts to interest a studio in financing that project. A bank will lend against such a studio promise as long as the producer has obtained a completion guarantee bond. The studio will then "pick up" the negative upon its completion.
3. *Presales*, in which the producer has financed all or part of a picture by selling off various exhibition or distribution rights to the completed picture prior to its being produced. Such sales of what are, in effect, licenses to distribute, normally involve home video and foreign distribution entities that provide promissory notes discountable at banks. However, no more than 60% of the negative cost can usually be financed in this way.
4. *Private fundings*, in which the producer, usually of only a low-budget picture, taps into private sources of funds through arrangement of a limited partnership.

Each of these financing options provides the producer with different trade-offs in terms of creative controls and profits. In step deals, for instance, a relatively large degree of creative control and of potential share of producer profit may be relinquished in favor of speed and efficiency. At the opposite end of the spectrum, private financings may allow for unrestricted creative control, but they may also severely limit the time and money available for actual production.

More generally, however, the production section of a PFD concerns the development process of making a feature (and, as such, does not normally apply to small-budget productions). It specifies the essential ingredients of a feature project: screenplay, director, producer, principal cast, and budget. It then further spells out who will be responsible for which steps in bringing the film to completion, who gets paid when, and under what conditions the studio-financier can place the project in "turnaround," that is, abandon the project and attempt to establish it elsewhere.

Also, of course, the financial section of a PFD provides financing arrangement descriptions and stipulates completion-guarantee details and costs (which would normally average about 6% of total budget before rebates).[17]

Ultimately, though, it is the distribution-agreement section that is of greatest importance in the allocation of revenue streams. Included here are definitions of distribution fees (in effect, sales commissions or service charges for soliciting playdates, booking films, collecting rentals, and negotiating with other distribution outlets) and specifications concerning audit and ownership rights, accounting-statement preparations (frequency, details included, and time allowed), and advertising and marketing commitments.

The matrix of Table 5.3 illustrates the various ways in which the five basic financing, production, and distribution options described by Cones (1997, p. 29) can be combined. These options are as follows:

1.  *In-house production/distribution*, wherein the studio/distributor funds development and distribution of the project. Here, an independent producer attached to a project is considered an employee of the studio

Table 5.3. *Basic film financing matrix*

|  | In-house production/ distribution | Production financing/ distribution | Negative pickup arrangement | Acquisition deal | Rent-a-distributor |
|---|---|---|---|---|---|
| **Source of production funds** | Studio/ distributor | Studio/ distributor | Lender | Third party | Third party |
| **Source of p & a funds** | Distributor | Distributor | Distributor | Distributor | Nondistributor |
| **Time of agreement** | Prior to production | Prior to production | Before film completed | After film completed | After film completed |

*Source*: Cones (1997, p. 30). Reproduced by permission.

(which broadly funds the affiliated producer's overhead in the development period).

2. *Production-financing and distribution* (*PFD*) *agreements,* in which a project is brought to the studio/distributor by an independent producer as a fairly complete package and the studio provides production and distribution funding.

3. *Negative pickup arrangements,* in which the distributor commits to distribution and to payment of production costs (i.e., to *buying* the original negative along with the rights to distribute) pending suitable delivery of the completed project.[18]

4. *Acquisition deals,* in which the distributor funds distribution but the film's production cost is already financed by other parties.

5. *Rent-a-distributor* deals, in which virtually all the funding for production and distribution has already been provided by others and the completed film is ready for distribution. (Because of the low fees and limited upside potential, studios are not likely to place a priority on the marketing of rent-a-system films.)

An overview of revenue flows for a typical theatrical release would then follow as in Table 5.4. In looking at this, however, it helps to keep in mind that the exhibitor's objective is to minimize rentals while the distributor's

Table 5.4. *Flowchart for theatrical motion-picture revenue: box-office receipts*

Distributor's gross receipts less
   1. Distribution fees
   2. Distribution costs
   3. Third-party gross participations
     ↓
Producer's gross proceeds less
   1. Negative cost
     (a) Direct cost
     (b) Overhead
     (c) Interest on loans
   2. Contingent deferments
First net profits
    ↓
Break-even
    ↓
Third-party net-profit participations (100% of net profits of picture)
    ↓
Producer's share of net profits of picture

*Source*: Breglio and Schwartz (1980). © John F. Breglio.

objective is to maximize them. Also, what participants see as their gross is the distributor's rental, not box-office gross as usually reported in the trade papers. For reasons previously discussed, the box-office gross can be much larger than the distributor's gross (i.e., rentals).

A convenient illustration of PFD concepts has been provided by Leedy (1980, p. 1), from which the following descriptions are drawn. Leedy's illustration (Table 5.5) for a major successful picture is particularly useful because it well illustrates the typical deferred payments to the writer and director, profit participations by the leading actors, and contingent compensations to the financier and producer. It further shows how a $14 million (negative cost) picture earning $100 million in distributor's rentals might generate $16 million of profit for financier and producer before participations and $8.1 million after adjustment for participations and deferments.

Although this model does not provide detailed revenue specifications for all new media sources, it nevertheless properly portrays typical domestic theatrical-distribution fees (i.e., U.S. and Canadian) at about 30%, foreign distribution and television syndication fees at 40%, and other distribution fees at 15%.[19] Such distribution charges are, by long-standing industry practice, largely nonnegotiable. But because the charges are unrelated to actual costs, they will, on relatively rare occasions, be adjusted to retain the services of important producers. In those cases, use is made of a sliding-fee scale down to a predetermined minimum, with perhaps a 5% reduction for every $20 million of theatrical rentals generated.

Table 5.5 can also provide an indication of how sensitive profits are to changes in the cost of capital. For example, an assumption of interest rates of 20% for this type of project brings interest cost on the production closer to $3 million than to the $2 million that is shown. If so, $1 million additional interest cost would reduce investors' profits by about 12% from $8.1 million to $7.1 million.[20]

Table 5.6 summarizes how other participants might have fared in Leedy's example of a picture bringing rentals of $100 million. Here it is important to remember that, in contrast to the financiers and distributors, the potential profit participants, including the director and lead actors, are at no risk of loss. They generally do not have equity capital invested in a project, and their profit participations, if any, should thus be appropriately characterized as contractually defined salary bonuses.

Participation deals

From a major studio's standpoint, risk is reduced if a production schedule contains a balanced mix of project-source financings. For instance, a studio might plan to release 24 films a year, of which perhaps four might be fully financed and produced in-house, another 14 might be financed using PFD arrangements with affiliated production entities, and the remainder financed with pickups and acquisitions.

Table 5.5. *Revenues and costs for a major theatrical release, circa 1992*

| | |
|---|---:|
| *Gross revenue* | |
| Subject to a 30% distribution fee | |
|    Theatrical film rental (U.S. and Canada) | $50,000,000 |
|    Nontheatrical film rental | 1,000,000 |
|    Royalty on home video | 5,000,000 |
|    U.S. network television | 4,000,000 |
|      Total | 60,000,000 |
| Subject to a 40% distribution fee | |
|    Foreign film rental | 20,000,000 |
|    Foreign television license fees | 5,000,000 |
|    Royalty on foreign home video | 5,000,000 |
|    Television, pay & syndication | 9,000,000 |
|      Total | 39,000,000 |
| Subject to a 15% distribution fee | |
|    Merchandise royalties | 950,000 |
|    Advertising sales | 50,000 |
|      Total | 1,000,000 |
|        Total gross revenue | $100,000,000 |
| *Distribution fee* | |
| 30% × $60,000,000 | $18,000,000 |
| 40% × $39,000,000 | 15,600,000 |
| 15% × $1,000,000 | 150,000 |
|      Total distribution fee | $33,750,000 |
|    Balance | $66,250,000 |
| *Distribution expenses* | |
| Cooperative advertising | $20,000,000 |
| Other advertising and publicity | 5,000,000 |
| Release prints, etc. | 3,000,000 |
| Taxes | 2,000,000 |
| Trade-association fees and other | 1,500,000 |
| Bad debts | 1,000,000 |
| All other expenses | 1,750,000 |
|      Total distribution expenses | $34,250,000 |
|    Balance | $32,000,000 |
| Production cost    $14,000,000 | |
| Interest thereon    2,000,000 | $16,000,000 |
| Net profit before participations | $16,000,000 |
| Deferments paid | 125,000 |
|    Participations in gross and net | 7,775,000 |
|    Total | 7,900,000 |
| Net profit to be split 50:50 | $8,100,000 |

*Source*: Leedy (1980, pp. 1–3 and unpublished updates).

Table 5.6. *Fee splits, deferments, and participations for a major motion-picture release: an example based on the results of Table 5.5*

| | | |
|---|---|---|
| Writer | | |
| Fee | $250,000 | |
| Deferment | 50,000 | $300,000 |
| Director | | |
| Fee | 525,000 | |
| Deferment | 75,000 | 600,000 |
| Major lead actor | | |
| Fee | 2,000,000 | |
| Participation[a] | 6,875,000 | 8,875,000 |
| Major lead actress | | |
| Fee | 500,000 | |
| Participation[b] | 900,000 | 1,400,000 |
| Producer | | |
| Fee | 500,000 | |
| Contingency comp. | 4,050,000 | 4,550,000 |
| Financier | | |
| Interest income | 1,000,000 | |
| Contingency comp. | 4,050,000 | 5,050,000 |
| Distributor | | |
| Fee | | 33,750,000 |

[a] Actor participation based on $2 million against a participation of 10% of gross revenue, less cooperative advertising and taxes before breakeven, and an additional 2.5% participation rate on this basis after breakeven.

[b] Actress participation based on 10% of net profits contractually defined as after the deferments and after the participation in gross:

| | |
|---|---|
| Net profit before participations | $16,000,000 |
| Deferments paid | 125,000 |
| Participation in gross | 6,875,000 |
| Total | 7,000,000 |
| Net profit after participations | $9,000,000 |
| Participation rate | 10% |
| Participation | $900,000 |

*Source*: Leedy (1980, p. 3 and unpublished updates).

No matter what the financing sources, however, revenue and profit participations are always the central issues. Participation arrangements are limited only by the imagination and bargaining abilities of the individuals who negotiate them. But only talents in great demand can command significant participations in addition to fees or salaries. In most situations, the filmmaker's trade-off for major studio funding includes ceding ownership of the film and control of the project to the studio, which then also shares substantially in the film's financial returns (if any).

*Pickups* Of the several major variants of participation agreements, perhaps the simplest is a "pickup" – a completed or partially completed project presented to studio-financiers or distributors for further funding and support.[21] From the distributor's point of view, pickups are somewhat less risky than are other early-stage projects in which it may be especially difficult to evaluate how all in-process artistic elements may fit together. For this reason, independent filmmakers often find that their best opportunity to distribute through a major is via such pickup agreements.[22] Yet deals with independents may also vary widely.[23]

Indeed, if it is assumed that the producer is able to fully fund prints and advertising (p & a) for the film through other sources – such as through private funds specializing in this type of financing – and deliver a completed (or nearly completed) film, a "rent-a-studio" deal can often be made in which access to a major's domestic theatrical distribution organization and collection system can be obtained for relatively low fees (usually ranging between 12.5% and 17.5%).[24] Distribution arrangements for the second cluster of George Lucas–financed *Star Wars* films that began to be released in 1999 provided a prominent example of this type of deal (wherein the distribution fee earned by Fox was 6%).

*Coproduction-distribution* Distributor-financiers often make coproduction deals with one or more parties for one or more territories so as to share risks. For instance, domestic and foreign distributors, in a "split-rights" arrangement, might each contribute half of a picture's production cost and each be entitled to distribution fees earned in their respective territories. Because distribution costs and box-office appeal often vary significantly in different markets, however, a picture might be profitable for one distributor and unprofitable for another. Also, the results for all distributors may be aggregated, with profits or losses split according to aggregate performance rather than territorial performance.

*Talent participations and breakeven* Participations in net profits or in gross receipts (often described in so-called "Exhibit A" contract definitions) are contingent on a film's making enough money to break even. Participations are thus a form of *contingent* compensation and, as such, may never be payable. Moreover, so-called *at-source* provisions require that royalties and participations tied to gross receipts be calculated at contractually defined links in the distribution chain; for example, film rentals in theatrical release and wholesale prices charged to retailers in video release.

Writers, directors, or actors may become financial participants if their agents have been able to negotiate for gross "points," which can be defined on a number of different grosses. Distributors' grosses are what have been called rentals, and participation points defined on this basis are obviously valuable because a picture does not have to be profitable for such points to be earned. Participations of this kind are thus rare and are assigned to only the very strongest box-office draws.

Nevertheless, as studios have attempted to contain the costs of production, they have in recent years begun to more frequently offer gross participation deals that can generally be categorized and ranked from rarest to most common into three basic types: first-dollar, adjusted gross, and gross after breakeven.[25] These are defined as follows:

- *First-dollar gross*: First-dollar ("dollar-one") gross participations after certain limited expenses (trade dues and other "off-the-tops" totaling perhaps 3% of revenues) have been deducted. Cash compensation goes *against* a percentage of defined first-dollar receipts.[26]
- *Adjusted gross*: Gross after cash breakeven, in which a participant receives a share of gross receipts after the studio has recouped its negative and print and ad (and perhaps some other imputed) costs and taken a somewhat reduced distribution fee ranging between 12% and 25%. Compensation is not against receipts, but is an addition (bonus) contingent on reaching cash breakeven.
- *Gross after breakeven*: Gross after actual breakeven, in which a participant receives a share of gross receipts after the studio has recouped all its costs and taken standard (i.e., full) distribution fees (of as much as 40%), or, alternatively, gross after rolling breakeven (described below), in which the studio continues to deduct distribution expenses in relation to a distribution fee even after the picture has achieved net profits.

In practice, the most routine participation would be based on a designated actual or artificially set breakeven level. For example, some talent participants might receive a percentage of distributor's gross after the first $40 million has been generated. In other instances, participations might begin after breakeven – defined as distributor's gross minus distribution fees and distribution costs that might include collection and currency conversion costs, duties, trade dues, licenses, taxes, and other charges known as *off-the-tops*. Additional points might then be earned after, say, rentals reach 3.5 times the production cost. As may be imagined, the variations on these concepts are infinite.

The more gross players attached to a project, however, the less the likelihood that a project will go into a net profit position.[27] This means that often the greater potential for conflict may not be with the participant against the studio but instead with the participant against all the *other* participants! Also, net profit is itself not a static concept because additional distribution fees and expenses will be routinely incurred even after reaching breakeven.

With multiple-talent participations, the accounting complexities are merely compounded: What usually begins as a simple agreement between an agent and a studio attorney or business-affairs representative often ends as a complicated financial-accounting document replete with the potential for widely divergent interpretations.

Is star *A*'s participation deducted before that of star *B*? Is participation based on only domestic rentals or on both foreign and domestic? Which distribution costs are subtracted before artificial breakeven? Are both television advertising and national-magazine advertising included or excluded? And perhaps, more fundamentally, under what method are subdistributor and home video revenues represented in "gross receipts"? Those are some of the subjects on which opinions may differ, especially within the context of the tens of thousands of transaction entries that are typically generated in the course of bringing a major feature to the screen. No wonder, then, that even in the best of circumstances, in which contract terms are sharply defined, it is time consuming and expensive to follow an audit trail.

Moreover, with the concept of a *rolling breakeven* – defined as the point at which revenues are equal to production costs plus distribution fees and expenses on a continuing (cumulative) basis – still further complications would be introduced. For instance, once gross participations kick in, they become deferred production costs that are retroactively added to the film's budget. Equity financing partners may also be able to carve out geographic market entitlements or "corridors" that siphon revenues from a specific territory before others are allowed to participate. And with a picture approaching profitability, a distributor's decision to spend more on advertising will delay or defer breaking even, thereby adversely affecting talent participants entitled to receive points in the picture's "net" profits. Yet some participants higher up the food chain could hardly object to their careers and compensations so being enhanced from the increased exposures and grosses that additional advertising usually brings.

As shown in the following formula, the amount of rentals required for a new breakeven ("rolling break" in industry jargon) is found by dividing total expenses exclusive of the distribution fee (i.e., prints and ads plus negative costs) by 1 minus the distribution-fee percentage. Let $a$ = required rentals, $b$ = total expenses, and $r$ = distribution-fee percentage. Then

$$a = b/(1-r).$$

For instance, if $r = 30\%$ and $b = \$7$ million, then $a = \$10$ million. But if another \$1 million is spent on advertising, then $b = \$8$ million and $a = \$11.43$ million. In this situation, every \$1 million of additional expenditure requires an additional \$1.43 million of rentals to be generated to remain at breakeven.

Because the studio views the cost of financing a film as a loan, breakeven is also greatly affected by studio deductions for interest that are charged (normally at 125% of the bank prime rate) on the unrecouped production cost of the picture. In such calculations, studio overhead and surcharges for use of facilities and equipment (usually in the range of 12.5% to 17.5% of the cost of the picture) are often included. But as Goodell (1998, p. 14) notes, the studio is paying *itself* with so-called soft dollar budget items. These charges are paid back to the studio before any money is shared with participants, and with interest being charged on overhead – and sometimes, alternatively, even with overhead being charged on interest (which is chargeable on unrecouped production costs).

Similarly, for downstream participants, the decision as to whether an expense item is to be categorized as belonging to production cost or to distribution expenses may be important. In a PFD arrangement, the distributor will generally prefer to characterize as much expense as possible as production cost because, as such, the studio will derive more income from interest and overhead charges if the production cost base is larger. But for pickups or acquisitions, the studios' preference may often be to instead bulk up distribution expenses: In pickup, acquisition, or rent-a-studio deals, the use of production facilities on which overhead can be charged and profit earned may be minimal.

Some of the quirkiest contractual ambiguities often also hinge on how various tax credits and remittances, advertising and film lab rebates, guild fees, licensing costs, and blocked currency effects are treated in the film's accounting. Rebates or tax credits might, for instance, be counted in the distributor's definition of gross receipts. If so, the inference is that the studio's 30% distribution fee is applicable, thereby leaving that much less available for participants to share.

As a result of such complications and the aforementioned sequencing of deductions for fees and costs, potential profit participants often find that the "net" profits of a picture are elusive and subject to widely varying accounting definitions and interpretations (especially in relation to earlier upstream claims made by participants in the "adjusted-gross" receipts). Profit calculations are not, moreover, even fixed in time, being instead continually subject to recalculations in each accounting period as film revenues and costs accrue.

As Daniels *et al.* (1998, 2006) suggest, revenues do not necessarily represent *all* dollars generated by the picture, production cost is not necessarily what it costs to shoot the film but rather what the participant contract says are the costs that may be reported as production cost, and breakeven comes in many flavors (e.g., cash, actual, rolling, and artificial – i.e., a negotiated multiple of certain receipts). When it comes to profit participation agreements, it is thus crucial to understand that *all contract terms and accountings are specifically defined for each film* (and also for each participant). As Baumgarten *et al.* (1992, p. 3) have noted, terms such as *gross receipts* and *net profits* have no intrinsic meaning. "The words mean whatever the participants decide they mean."[28]

*Producers' participations and cross-collateralizations* Producers are responsible for a film's production costs, and they often have contractual incentives to keep project expenses down. When costs exceed approved budgets by certain percentages, producers' shares may be penalized by several times the percentage overage. However, the share of profit, if any, that the producer will receive (in addition to earned production-services fees) can be structured so as to provide a floor or minimum payment (i.e., a *hard floor*) that has priority over other (third-party) participations, which are borne by the distributor. Were it not for this hard floor (as opposed to a *soft floor*), the presence of several third-party participations – each at perhaps 10% of 100% of net profit (equal to a 20% slice out of the producer's half of total net profit) – would severely diminish the producer's potential income (from a project that the producer may have long nurtured and promoted well before any other participants had been signed).

Producers are also affected if the financial fate of one picture is tied to that of another, or if the box-office performance of a single picture in one territory is linked to its performance in another. Such *cross-collateralizations* of producers' shares, done on either or both the production and distribution ends, may imply that the profits of one picture must exceed the losses of another for there to be anything to share. It is especially frustrating for potential profit participants when profitable picture *A* is cross-collateralized with picture *B* that has perhaps yet to be produced, to be distributed, or to show a profit. In these situations, none of the profit on picture *A* will be credited to participants until picture *B* recovers most of its costs.

*Home video participations* Because the system for distribution of DVDs (and earlier, tapes) has been developed from hybrid roots in the distribution of recorded music (see Chapter 6) and book products, a different – and controversial – basis for participation accounting has evolved. Rather than subtracting distribution fees and expenses directly from defined gross receipts, as has already been described, home video participants are instead entitled to royalties that are normally set (but subject to bargaining power) at 20% of the unit's wholesale price for units to be marketed as rentals and 10% for those as sell-throughs. As a result, studios will usually at most include only 20% of total home video unit sales royalties in participants' gross receipt calculations and retain, except for residuals, the remaining 80% to cover the relatively modest costs of manufacturing, advertising, and duplication. The studio then still subjects the participant's home video gross receipts to distribution and other fees, which reduce the participant's net royalty to perhaps only 10% to 12%.[29]

With the bulk of home video, now primarily DVD, revenue thus accordingly shunted aside (to the studio's wholly owned manufacturing/wholesaling subsidiary) and taken out of the participants' calculation of a particular film's gross receipts performance, the arithmetic for a studio's profitability on home video distribution is compelling. It is therefore easy to see why home video

Table 5.7. *Film rentals calculations: examples contrasting floor minimums versus percentages of net box-office receipts*

|                                              | Case 1   | Case 2  |
|----------------------------------------------|----------|---------|
| Box-office receipts                          | $10,000  | $8,000  |
| Less deductions for second feature           | 2,500    | 2,000   |
| Net box-office receipts                      | 7,500    | 6,000   |
| Minimum film rental at 70% of net            | 5,250    | 4,200   |
| Contractual theater overhead (nut)           | 1,500    | 1,500   |
| Net box-office receipts after nut            | 6,000    | 4,500   |
| Maximum film rental at 90% of net after nut  | 5,400    | 4,050   |

has become such a boon for the filmed entertainment industry and such an acute issue for the participants to negotiate. Indeed, from a corporate standpoint, it might reasonably be argued that home video (i.e., DVDs) has now become the primary source of profits.[30]

Distributor–exhibitor computations

As already indicated, rentals are that portion of box-office receipts owed the distributor. Table 5.7 shows an example in which the exhibitor's nut for fixed overhead is negotiated or set at $1,500 and there is a 90:10 split (90% for distributor, 10% for exhibitor) of box-office receipts after the nut (but not less than the previously agreed 70% of total box-office receipts to the distributor).

In case 1, the distributor will be owed $5,400, whereas in case 2 the distributor will be entitled to $4,200. In neither case will the distributor share in the theater's concession income from candy, beverages, popcorn, and video games (see Section 4.4). As can be inferred from Table 5.8, such concession sales are a significant profit-swing factor for exhibitors.[31]

Rentals usually are accounted for on a cash basis when collected by the distributor, and expenses are recorded as incurred. In fact, this reporting method – reflecting the normally slow collection of cash and the delayed billing of period expenses such as co-op advertising – is reasonably equitable from the viewpoints of all participants.

Co-op advertising is normally calculated on gross receipts and allocated according to the distributor-exhibitor percentage revenue split in effect at the time the advertising appears. The following example indicates the true net percentage:

| Box-office gross     | $20,000  |
|----------------------|----------|
| less house expenses  | 4,000    |
| Net                  | $16,000  |

Table 5.8. *Exhibitor operating revenues and expenses: an example*

| | |
|---|---|
| Box-office (BO) weekly gross | $3,000 |
| Concession sales (at 15%) | 450 |
| Total weekly gross | 3,450 |
| Deduct: | |
| Distributor's share at 50% of BO | 1,500 |
| Advertising (10% of BO) | 300 |
| Payroll (10% of BO) | 300 |
| Food cost (23% of sales) | 104 |
| Rent and real estate taxes at 15% of BO | 450 |
| Utilities at $150/week | 150 |
| Management fee at 10% of total weekly gross | 345 |
| Insurance and employee benefits | 100 |
| Repairs and maintenance | 100 |
| Miscellaneous (tickets, etc.) | 100 |
| Total average weekly expenses | 3,449 |

*Source*: Lowe (1983, p. 346). From the book *The Movie Business Book* by Jason E. Squire,© 1983 by Jason E. Squire. New York: Simon & Schuster/Fireside.

Ninety percent goes to the distributor: $14,400 (90:10 split); the true distributor co-op percentage here is 72% (14.4:20.0), not 90%.

In analyzing the corporate accounting statements of exhibition companies, it should also be noted that the mix of owned versus leased real estate and the methods of accounting for real-estate transactions and leasehold improvements can vary significantly from one company to another, thereby limiting financial comparability.[32] In all, it might be said that exhibitors are actually engaged in four distinct business operations: movie exhibition, concession stands, on-screen advertising, and real estate.

Distributor deals and expenses

The previous hypothetical example of a film generating $100 million in rentals (Table 5.5) showed a distributor fee, or service charge for the sales organization, of $33.75 million. Although much of the fee may here be regarded as profit, it is this very distribution profit on a hit that would be expected to more than offset losses sustained on other releases; 10% of the films released generate 50% of the total box-office receipts (Figure 5.1).

Simplistically, then, it is distribution profit (perhaps for a major distributor averaging over time a third or more of total distribution fees) that would normally provide the positive cash flow for investment in new films. And it is this very profit, derived by subtracting from distribution fees all office overhead costs, compensation for sales personnel, and various other publicity and promotion expenses *not* recouped through other charges that keeps the

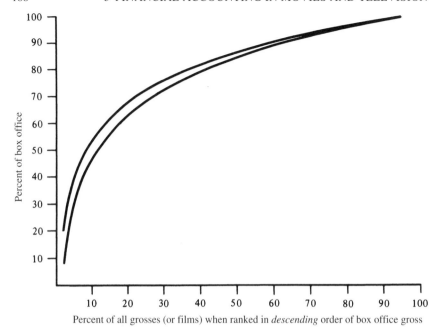

Figure 5.1. Ten percent of films generate 50% of the box office. When film box-office figures are ranked (either by individual weekly grosses or by individual films in order of their box-office grosses), the results fall in the range shown by the plotted curves. *Source*: *Daily Variety*, July 31, 1984. Copyright 1984 by A. D. Murphy.

distributor in business despite the high probability that many pictures will *in toto* lose money when *all* input factor costs and expenses are tallied. Still, even with all the contractual advantages that studios typically hold, this remains a relatively risky business; there have been many instances and many years when studios have not earned enough to cover their weighted average costs of debt and equity capital (WACC). Modern finance teaches that, for companies in any industry to survive, the cost of capital must be earned.

The distribution fee itself is a prior claim on a film's cash flows. But it is perhaps best conceptualized as being an access charge or a toll paid to a distribution organization for use of the established turnpikes and bridges that allow direct access to large audiences. As with all such major access routes or pipelines, there can only be a few, and the upfront capital investment required to establish them is sizable.[33] The tolls or rents charged by distributors for such access are thus not especially sensitive to bargaining pressures and are, by nature, quasi-monopolistic and unrelated to direct costs.

Within this structure, many, if not most, pictures operate under a "net deal," in which the distributor charges a fixed or graduated percentage of rentals (e.g., 30% in domestic theatrical markets) as a distribution fee and then advances the funds for other distribution costs, including those for prints, trailers, and national advertising. In addition, there may be charges related to publicity and personal-appearance tours, co-op advertising with exhibitors, taxes (based on rentals) by countries and localities, trade-association and guild fees in the form of residuals (for exhibitions in ancillary markets), and bad debts. The distributor normally recovers these expenses before making any payments to the producer and, as shown in Table 5.4, would normally, before arriving at a definition of "net profit," prioritize recoupment by taking distribution fees and expenses (prints, ads, publicity, etc.) first, then interest on negative costs, then negative costs (here including all gross participations), and finally deferments and various other participations.

Although the aforementioned net deal predominates, there is also a so-called gross deal wherein the distributor (usually of low-budget independently made and independently distributed films) is not separately reimbursed for distribution expenses but instead retains a distribution fee (e.g., 50% to 70%) that is considerably higher than normal. Distribution expenses are then recouped out of this higher fee, while the producer receives the remaining unencumbered portion of the gross rentals.[34]

For a picture performing poorly at the box office, the producer with a gross deal will have an advantage because overall distribution costs (which can be quite high on a percentage-of-revenue basis) are not chargeable. Contrarily, for a picture doing well at the box office, a producer might prefer a net deal because marketing costs as a percentage of revenues then diminish rapidly and specific marketing charges become more bearable. A structure in which gross-deal and net-deal characteristics are combined as certain performance criteria are met may also be arranged.

In negotiating such formulations the potential advantages to be derived from the control of ancillary-market revenues have inspired many independent producers to attempt to strip from domestic theatrical-distribution contracts, and to thus retain for themselves, the rights to exploit cable, home video, and other sources of income. Studios are, however, ordinarily reluctant to allow these rights to be taken away ("fractionalized") through so-called split-rights deals unless there is compensation through participations or through some other means. Clearly, the larger the total upfront studio fee, the less there is available for recoupment of production costs – and, ultimately, for profit of the independent filmmaker.

As we have seen, studio profits are centered on distribution activities, where fees range to over 30% of gross receipts, while out-of-pocket expenses might be covered by 15% to 25% of gross receipts. This cushion of profit is earned, in part, for taking the risk that a picture will not earn its releasing costs. As opposed to licensing to home video, pay cable, syndication, and network markets, *theatrical release is the only area where there is the possibility of a negative cash flow* (i.e., where releasing costs can exceed income). But the cushion also, in effect, pays for maintenance and extension of the distribution pipeline; when a picture is doing well at the box office, distribution profits soar. Meanwhile, the initial performance in theaters still largely determines, through direct arithmetical links, the prices that the film will be able to command in all the markets that follow the theatrical.[35]

As broadband distribution of films via the Internet takes hold, Internet distribution fee formulas will most likely evolve along the lines of the pay-per-view cable or the home video 20% royalty models in which gross receipts defined for purposes of participations are bounded. Yet prices for Internet viewings will likely be below those for DVDs or videos since manufacturing and distribution costs are nominal as compared with those of more traditional distribution methods. The prominent issues here involve ownership of Internet distribution rights, sequencing of exhibition, and territoriality – all of which will eventually be standardized across the industry.

### Studio overhead and other production costs

The inclusion of talent participations as a part of production costs and not as distribution expenses allows interest and overhead fees to be charged on the participations. From the participants' view, large proportions of production costs are thus often seen as studio overhead charges, which are calculated by applying a contract-stipulated rate to all direct production costs. Such overhead charges may or may not, however, have any close relationship to the actual costs of, for example, renting sound stages or buying props and signs outside the studio's shops and mills.

Because it would almost always be less expensive to buy or lease items on a direct-cost basis, participants may question what services and materials are actually covered by the studio rate. If agreements are not clearly written, and are thus open to different interpretations, disputes may arise with regard to contractual overhead charges for everything from cameras and sound equipment to secretarial services. Probably the most important question, however, is whether or not full rates are applicable to location shooting. How these matters are resolved – before, during, or (hopefully not) after production – depends on relative bargaining positions.

Producers are motivated to obtain independent financing to avoid or reduce the effects of these charges, which can add between 15% and 25% to a picture's budget (plus 10% applied to direct ad and publicity costs) and thereby significantly raise the breakeven point required to activate net-profit participants' share payments.[36] Sometimes it is worthwhile and feasible for an independent producer with outside financing to minimize studio overhead charges by offering the film for pickup in an advanced stage of production.[37] In other instances it is less time consuming and, in the long run, less expensive to go with the studio.

In brief, although overhead rates generally are not negotiable, the things to which those rates apply (offices, vehicles, etc.) may be, and hence it is important for producers to have a clear understanding of what their contracts specify. If a studio wants a project badly enough, the items excluded from the standard rule will be more numerous.

Once production begins, cost accounting follows a job-order cost procedure wherein time and materials are "charged against" a job or charge number. This is where careful control by the producer, who has final responsibility during the production phase, is essential. Costs can easily get out of hand because everyone from painters and electricians to cameramen and editors may have at least some authority to charge against the picture's number for materials and services. Detailed budgets for a major feature film shoot lasting ten weeks can easily run to 80 pages and cover several hundred item expense categories.

Truth and consequences[38]

A synopsis of what usually happens to a dollar that flows from the box office will help clarify the processing thus far described. If we assume that house expenses are 10%, there remains 90 cents of every dollar to which (for an important release by a major) a 90:10 split for the first two weeks in favor of the distributor may be applied. That, in turn, leaves a distributor's gross ("rentals") of around 81 cents.

In the United States and Canada, a 30% distribution fee totaling 24 cents is then subtracted, leaving 57 cents. Advertising and publicity costs, which are generally at least 20% to 25% of rentals, require deduction of another, say, 20 cents. The remainder is now 37 cents, out of which about 6 cents more is required for miscellaneous distribution expenses, including prints, taxes, MPAA seal, and transportation.

Before the usually substantial negative cost of the picture is even considered, there is thus a residual pool of only 31 cents of the original dollar.

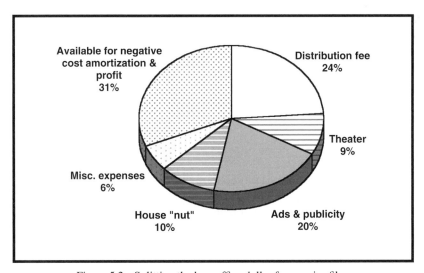

Figure 5.2. Splitting the box-office dollar for a major film.

Table 5.9. *Selected theatrical winners and losers*

| Title | Distributor | Year of first release | Est. neg. cost ($ millions) | Est. domestic rentals ($ millions) |
|---|---|---|---|---|
| **Winners (high and low budget)** | | | | |
| *Jaws* | Universal | 1975 | 8 | 130 |
| *Star Wars* | Lucasfilm/Fox | 1977 | 11 | 225 |
| *Kramer vs. Kramer* | Columbia | 1979 | 7 | 60 |
| *Airplane* | Paramount | 1980 | 3 | 41 |
| *Raiders of the Lost Ark* | Lucasfilm/Fox | 1981 | 22 | 116 |
| *E.T. The Extraterrestrial* | Universal | 1982 | 12 | 228 |
| *Return of the Jedi* | Lucasfilm/Fox | 1983 | 33 | 168 |
| *Beverly Hills Cop* | Paramount | 1984 | 14 | 80 |
| *Batman* | Warner | 1989 | 41 | 151 |
| *Home Alone* | Fox | 1990 | 18 | 140 |
| *Jurassic Park* | Universal | 1993 | 70 | 212 |
| *The Lion King* | Disney | 1994 | 65 | 173 |
| *Four Weddings & . . .* | PolyGram | 1994 | 7 | 25 |
| *Independence Day* | Fox | 1996 | 65 | 171 |
| *Titanic* | Fox/Paramount | 1997 | 200 | 1,214 |
| *Blair Witch Proj.* | Artisan | 1999 | <1 | 141 |
| *Spider-Man* | Sony | 2002 | 175 | 406 |
| *My Big Fat Greek . . .* | IFL Films | 2002 | 5 | 241 |
| *Diary of a Mad . . .* | Lionsgate | 2005 | 6 | 51 |
| **Losers (high budget)** | | | | |
| *Heaven's Gate* | UA | 1980 | 44 | 2 |
| *Reds* | Paramount | 1981 | 52 | 21 |
| *Howard the Duck* | Universal | 1986 | 37 | 10 |
| *Ishtar* | Columbia | 1987 | 45 | 8 |
| *Hudson Hawk* | TriStar | 1991 | 55 | 6 |
| *Last Action Hero* | Columbia | 1993 | 75 | 28 |
| *Town & Country* | New Line | 2001 | 105 | 7 |
| *Adventures of Pluto Nash* | Warner | 2002 | 100 | 4 |
| *Treasure Planet* | Disney | 2002 | 140 | 38 |

*Source*: *Variety*, Anniversary and Cannes issues.

Should there also be gross participations, say 10% (of rentals) to a major actor, there would then be 8 cents less with which to recoup the negative cost. And if the picture is studio financed, half of any profit after recoupment would ordinarily be owed the studio, with the other half split among other participants (Figure 5.2).[39] Including the cost of the negative, the whole box-office dollar (and usually more) has by this stage been already spent and the picture is in financial deficit, a loss. Indeed, full cost recovery now generally

Table 5.10. *Real reel numbers, selected examples, big and small*[a]

| Title | **Who Framed Roger Rabbit** | **Commando** |
|---|---|---|
| Domestic release date | June 1988 | October 1985 |
| Distributor | Walt Disney Co. | 20th Century Fox |
| Period end | 12/31/90 | 2/29/92 |
| **Gross receipts** | | |
| Domestic theatrical | $80,763 | $17,941 |
| Foreign theatrical | 80,102 | 24,022 |
| Pay television | 9,680 | 8,005 |
| Home video | 26,573 | 6,045 |
| Nontheatrical | 2,316 | |
| Television | | 8,507 |
| Consumer products & other | 5,686 | 725 |
| Total | $205,119 | $65,245 |
| *minus* | | |
| **Distribution fees and costs** | | |
| Distribution fees | 68,259 | 22,122 |
| Advertising and publicity | 48,333 | 11,529 |
| Checking, collections, conversion, etc. | 655 | 194 |
| Other version | 1,076 | 156 |
| Residuals | 3,415 | 3,135 |
| Trade dues | 843 | 371 |
| Taxes, insurance | 2,949 | 1,608 |
| Prints | 5,746 | 3,387 |
| Transportation | 951 | 431 |
| Miscellaneous | 166 | 140 |
| Total | $132,394 | $43,073 |
| *minus* | | |
| **Negative costs** | | |
| Production cost | 50,579 | 15,946 |
| Production overhead | 7,587 | |
| Interest | 17,105 | 3,129 |
| Gross participations deferments | 17,054 | 396 |
| Total | $92,325 | $19,471 |
| **Net profit (loss)** | **($19,600)** | **$2,701** |

[a] Data in $000s.

*Source*: Adapted from *The Hollywood Reporter*, with permission, August 17 and September 14, 1992.

requires more than theater exhibition alone; for any further recoupment of costs and for profitability to be reached, a picture relies on ancillary-market revenues (DVDs, cable and network TV sales, etc.) that, incidentally, also happen to be circularly tied to box-office performance. So, normally, the worse your picture initially does, the worse it does, and vice versa. It is no wonder then that so many firms have found production to be more difficult and less profitable than they had at first thought.[40]

The partial list of high-budget theatrical flops shown in Table 5.9 illustrates that box-office failure is usually congenital: No matter how large ancillary markets grow, they cannot a golden goose of a turkey make. And, there truly is little, if any, correlation between the cost of a picture and the returns it might generate (Table 5.10).

Still, despite the odds against profitability, many people find filmmaking financially attractive and worth taking a risk on. With a proper combination of luck and pluck, independent producers are sometimes able to arrange financing sufficient to own much or all of a possibly valuable negative at little or no direct cost to themselves.

## 5.4 Television-programming accounting

Television was initially thought to threaten the very survival of movies. The tube's mesmerizing influence and its nearly ubiquitous presence had indeed contributed to the reduction of annual theater admissions from the all-time peak of about 4 billion in 1946 to about 1 billion in the early 1960s. Yet television eventually became the film industry's first major ancillary market and, in the process, probably its savior. It was a long time before the value of the television market was fully understood by moviemakers.

Studios today engage in three distinct television-related activities: licensing of features to networks; syndication of features, series, and other programs to local stations; and production of made-for-television movies, series, and programs. Many small firms are also active in these areas. But easy this business is not. In comparison with the situation in feature films, the full earnings potential of a program or series is normally quite limited, while the uncertainty of sale or of eventual price in aftermarkets is at least as great.[41] Moreover, potential participant accounting problems (delay and minimization of income recognition and applications of numerous deductions) are often similar to those found in feature film accountings.

### Feature licensing

The peak demand for network feature-film licenses appears to have been reached in the late 1970s, when pay cable was still in its infancy and when the American Broadcasting Corporation, flush with ratings victories and cash, had the wherewithal to bid aggressively for rights to exhibit recent theatrical hits. Many of the major licenses at the time permitted up to five runs for fees that (with escalator clauses based on box-office performance) frequently were in the neighborhood of $20 million.

Bidding fervor cooled, however, when it became apparent that pay cable was siphoning off the potential for high network ratings with early showings of uncut movies without commercial interruptions. The ratings of all but the biggest box-office hits also diminished relative to those of made-for-television movies. But, in spite of this, films making their first network appearance in the early 1980s could command an average of perhaps $5 million for two runs. That price reflected expected ratings for the film, the number of weekly hours allotted by the networks for feature-movie programming, and the cost of producing comparable programming in terms of running time and content.

Out of any television-license fees, residual payments to participants have to of course be made, and other distribution costs (including high-priced legal talent and, on a rainy day, taxi fare up New York's Sixth Avenue) must be deducted. A feature film licensed to network television might thus generate for the studio-distributor a profit margin in the range of 40% to 65%.

An important accounting dilemma, nevertheless, appears in the situation in which a package of several features is licensed by a single vendor to one purchaser. According to trade-paper reports, for example, United Artists had followed an allocation formula that

- divided the package price by the number of pictures in the package to determine average price per picture,
- assigned a value of 1.5 times the average price to the feature with the highest theatrical rentals,
- assigned a value of 0.5 times the average price to the feature with the lowest theatrical rentals, and
- ranked the remaining features by rentals earned and assigned a value in between the range of 1.5 and 0.5 times the average price.[42]

Similar formulas had been used by other distributors with the rationale that, over the years "it has been determined that the ratings of the most successful pictures on television, in both domestic and foreign markets, receive no more than three times the rating of the least successful pictures."[43]

However, such formulas were legally challenged because they seemed to produce unfair results for some participants. Thus, under current practices, prices for features in a package are supposed to be negotiated separately for each title even though questions concerning the basis for arriving at a specific price may still arise.

For outside participants, probably the easiest way to account for income from television-license fees is on a cash basis as of telecast date. Nevertheless, there can be many variations that are to some extent configured by relative negotiating power. As already noted, for purposes of financial reporting, the studio-distributor will recognize revenues at the time the pictures are made available for exhibition. However, actual contract terms might stipulate cash payments of 20% on signing, 50% on availability, and 30% on subsequent runs, and with down payments on older features being even smaller.

Problems as to the timing of cash receipts, allocations, and different reporting requirements also frequently arise in situations involving licensing of syndication, pay cable, and other ancillary-market rights (novelizations, games and toys, character merchandise, and music).

### Program production and distribution

*Development and financing processes* Production of original programming for network television is generally in the form of made-for-television movies ("made-fors") or regularly scheduled series and miniseries such as *War and Remembrance* or *Roots*.[44] Each of these program forms may receive somewhat specialized cost-accounting treatment, with the procedures and methods applied to made-fors being similar to those used in making feature films.

Financing for made-fors and series, however, is provided by the networks on a piecemeal basis. About a year ahead of anticipated playdates, networks and program producers, including the television arms of the major film studios and many large television production independents, sift through hundreds of concepts to select those with the potential to become two-hour movies, miniseries (usually eight to twelve hours in length), or one-hour or half-hour series. No more than two or three dozen of these concepts will then be provided with funding, and each will be developed into a "pilot" production that will introduce the major themes and characters.

Pilots allow network advertisers to sense how well the elements in a proposed program will work together on the screen. However, in an attempt to stimulate the buyers, who make their judgments based largely on first impressions, pilots are often loaded with costly production values.[45]

Of the 30 or so pilots ordered for the start of the television season, no more than half are likely to be accepted for regularly scheduled series programming by the four major networks combined. Acceptance by a network is usually accompanied by a funding commitment to produce thirteen episodes initially and by an option contract for additional episodes (usually nine to eleven more) if the program attracts relatively large audiences. For each episode, the network may pay one-third on commencement of filming or taping, another third on completion, and the last third on delivery and clearance (by network censors and others). The percentages at the various steps of a deal occasionally vary, however, and there may be an additional payment of 10% or so on rerun of an episode (even though, since the late 1990s, the ratings performance of reruns, and thus their economic value, has fallen sharply).

There are two reasons that producers do not generally profit immediately or directly from series or made-fors developed by the process just described. First, network funding via license fees (normally for two runs) does not typically cover all out-of-pocket cash expenditures incurred by the program producer. In fact, on the average, such production costs may be only 80% to 85% recouped from the network license fee, with the remainder expected to be eventually covered by revenues generated through licensing in foreign markets.[46] Under these circumstances, even a relatively efficient producer would have difficulty coming out ahead on a cash basis of accounting.[47]

But a financial deficit is also virtually assured using the accrual method of accounting, wherein noncash accruals for studio overhead expenses (at 10% or more of the budget) are included. It is thus common for program producers to "deficit finance" their series and made-fors while trusting that the network ratings will be strong enough to carry the show into the potentially more lucrative off-network syndication aftermarket at some future time.[48]

Network option clauses, however, are another reason that producers might not immediately profit from a successful series introduction. Option clauses for series usually allow the network to order (i.e., "pick up") programs for four or more (six is now not unusual) additional broadcast seasons, with episode fees increasing at least 3% to 5% and more likely 7% to 8% each year. The contracts also provide for first right of refusal for extensions beyond the initial period. This means that even if another network or perhaps cable channels were to offer the production company more money for a program, the offer could not be immediately accepted. Option clauses thus enable a network to retain a show at a cost below the current market rate in compensation for taking the original risk of placing the show in a crowded schedule before the willingness of an audience to watch it has been demonstrated.

Nevertheless, with a network contract in hand, a studio or, more likely, an independent producer can obtain additional financial support by borrowing from a bank, another lending institution, or investors' groups. Cash can also be obtained by selling in advance a program's anticipated syndication rights to distributors, who are generally in need of programs to fill their already established pipelines. Distributors will often obtain rights from a producer by guaranteeing a certain level of program sales, and they may also include cash advances as part of the guarantee. Such advances are then recouped by the distributor from the producer's initial share of program sales, with the distributor taking the risk that program sales will be sufficient to cover the outlay.

After the initial run (and, presumably, rerun), the production company ends up owning the program and can do with it whatever it pleases. The real payoff, if any, however, comes if the series can sustain competitive network ratings for at least three full seasons (and probably four seasons) so that more than 60 episodes (typically 22 per season, or as many as 88) can be completed. Yet the probability of this occurring is relatively low; at best, about one in five new series survives the ratings wars that long.[49] Consolidation of station ownership has, moreover, resulted in only five station group owners, Fox and

Tribune predominantly but also ABC, NBC, and CBS, becoming the major decision makers in the scheduling and buying of blocks of off-network and also off-cable fare (e.g. *Sex and the City* and *The Sopranos*) for the lucrative slots in access and late-fringe times.

As for movies-of-the-week, first-run syndicated productions (i.e., programming designed for a non-network initial run), prime-time-access shows, and made-for-cable programs, financing is available from well-heeled television-program distribution companies (including the television divisions of all major movie studios). For exclusive rights to such productions, a distributor will typically contribute part of the funding in return for profit participations and the opportunity to earn distribution fees.

*Syndication agreements* As already noted, should a series last three seasons on a network, it begins to have significant value for the syndication (used-film) market: Local television stations and cable systems can then obtain enough episodes to "strip" the program into scheduled daily runs over a period of at least several months.[50] Syndication-market licenses, which go to the highest local station or cable network bidder, are conventionally for six consecutive runs of a series in a period of not more than five years and are now commonly for no longer than three years.[51] For long-running series, DVD sales directed to consumers have also evolved into an important new source of additional revenues.[52]

A typical broadcast syndication agreement will provide that, out of the gross revenues collected, the syndication company will first deduct syndication fees, then deduct out-of-pocket expenses (including costs for shipping, advertising, and prints), and then recoup advances made to producers. Fees for syndication services (i.e., distribution fees) as a proportion of gross income are generally 15% to 20% for net stripping sales, 30% to 35% for domestic syndication, and 40% to 50% for foreign syndication.

Syndication examples typical of a major movie studio appear in Table 5.11, where the profit potential for a distributor and the similarity in structure to the aforementioned gross deal used in theatrical distribution of features can be seen. Operating margins for distributors of shows produced by others would normally average 30%, and for long-running, self-produced programs around 40%.[53]

Television networks have historically relied on feature films and series to fill most of their prime-time hours. But since the early 1980s, *first-run* syndication has developed into an important means for obtaining programming for independent (i.e., non–network-affiliated) local television stations as well as network affiliates seeking to fill their prime-time access hours (i.e., the hours just before the network's evening schedule begins). First-run syndication, primarily of game, talk, or tabloid news shows, provides television stations with a relatively low-cost, disposable form of programming that is immediately topical and does not depend on, or require, a lengthy network

Table 5.11. *Network television program production and syndication:*
*a structural example of successful program series, circa 2000*

**Production**

Network license fee covers 80%–85% of cash outlay.

Foreign sales may recoup remainder of cash outlay on 1-hour shows,
  but only half of remaining cash deficit on 1/2-hour shows.

Status on accrual basis including overhead and interest

| | | |
|---|---|---|
| 1-hour shows: | 22 episodes/season | |
| | Cost per episode, $1.2 million | |
| | Accrued deficit per episode $= \$250,000$ | |
| 1/2-hour shows: | 22 episodes/season | |
| | Cost per episode, $600,000 | |
| | Accrued deficit per episode $= \$150,000$ | |

**Syndication**

Distribution fees: domestic 35%, foreign 50%

Assuming 100 episodes are available for syndication

| | | |
|---|---|---:|
| 1-hour shows: | Revenues per episode | |
| | Domestic | $325,000 |
| | Foreign | 250,000 |
| | | $575,000 |
| | Minus: | |
| | Residuals, six runs | |
| | Domestic | 65,000 |
| | Foreign | 25,000 |
| | Production deficit | 250,000 |
| | Distribution costs[a] | 65,000 |
| | Studio profit[b] | $170,000 |
| 1/2-hour shows: | Revenues per episode | $1,000,000 |
| | Minus: | |
| | Residuals, six runs | 40,000 |
| | Production deficit | 150,000 |
| | Distribution costs[a] | 50,000 |
| | Talent profit participations | 200,000 |
| | Studio profit[b] | $560,000 |

[a] Primarily promotion and distribution "bicycling."

[b] Profit would be split if show is independently produced and does not take account of losses
on shows that fail.

run: The programming skips the network entirely and is syndicated to local
stations onward from its first broadcast appearance.

Although an infinite number of variations can be devised to finance and
distribute first-run programming, the primary requirement in launching a
first-run program series is to have commitments from enough stations so
that at least 65% to 70% of the national viewing audience can see the

Table 5.12. *Barter-syndication revenue estimate: an example*

| Assume: | • 100 million TV households<br>• average ratings of 5.0, i.e., 5 million homes viewing<br>• percent of viewers in target demographic of 60%<br>• a cost per thousand, or CPM, of $9.00 for a 30-second spot |
|---|---|
| Then: | The estimated number of targeted viewers = 3 million<br>    (i.e., 5 million times 0.60)<br>the revenues per spot = $27,000<br>    (i.e., 3,000 times $9.00)<br>net revenues after deducting a 15% agency commission = $22,950<br>barter revenue for 10 spots a week = $229,500<br>cash license fee per week = $100,000<br>total revenue per week = $329,500<br>total syndicator revenues for 52 weeks = $17.65 million[a] |
| Costs: | Production of 39 weeks at $125,000 a week = $4.9 million<br>local marketing = $2.5 million<br>distribution fees = 30% of revenues = $5.3 million |
| Profits: | $7.45 million[a] |

[a] Available to be shared with producers and any other "backend" participants.

show. These commitments, though, are normally made on the basis of pilots that are much less elaborately produced than are those for network series proposals. Also, unless a production is a proven ratings winner, it is unlikely that a station would make a syndication agreement that spans more than one year.[54]

Producers and distributors will generally prefer that stations pay cash for the rights to air the programs. But more often than not, the stations instead prefer to swap, or to barter, some of their advertising time slots in return for broadcast rights. Such *barter syndication* arrangements, as discussed in more detail in Chapter 7, have grown rapidly since the late 1970s into a $4.2 billion-a-year business that, on the margin, reduces revenues available to the networks.[55] Table 5.12 provides an example of how barter-syndication revenue for a particular program might be estimated. The sensitivity of the syndicator's profits to relatively small changes in ratings (Tables 5.13 and 5.14) – and the degree of risk thus assumed by the syndicator – is notable.

The key accounting issue in barter syndication concerns the time at which barter revenues ought to be recognized. According to rulings by an FASB task force, such revenues should be recognized to the extent they are covered by noncancelable contracts (less an estimated value for "make-good" spots, i.e., adjustments for less-than-expected ratings) and at the point when a program is available for first telecast.[56]

*Costs of production* Networks attempt to keep their costs under control through tough negotiations on production contracts. The producer's

Table 5.13. *Program syndication expenditure estimates, 1985–2005*

| Year | Total station[a] syndication expenditures[a,c] ($ millions) | Barter-syndication[b] revenues ($ millions) |
|------|------|------|
| 1985 | 1,168 | 550 |
| 1990 | 1,864 | 1,200 |
| 1995 | 2,120 | 1,800 |
| 2000 | 2,600 | 2,650 |
| 2005 | 4,300 | 4,200 |

[a] *Source*: Association of Independent Television Stations (INTV), *Estimated TV Syndication Expenditures*, 1975–1990. December 1985, Wilkofsky Gruen Associates.
[b] Advertiser Syndicated Television Association, Nielsen Monitor-plus.
[c] Affiliates normally account for one-third, and independents two-thirds, of the total.

problem is to then live within the budget constraints imposed by those contracts. That is often difficult, given the limited production time and the sharp union-mandated pay escalations for overtime work related to frequent rewriting and rehearsal.

As of the early 2000s, a prime-time one-hour network show required, on the average, up to eight days to shoot (several more to edit) and around $2 million to produce, although less popular shows with lower-paid performers might be made for perhaps 70% to 80% of that amount (and half-hour sitcoms for $1.6 million).[57]

For a long-running series, however, the fixed costs for sets, props, and general story concept decrease on a unit basis as more episodes are produced. Everything else then being equal, a series will, over time, become more

Table 5.14. *Summary profit accounting for the television series participant: an example*

| *Studio's self-produced series (over five years)* | |
|------|------|
| Revenues ($ millions) | |
| Network payments for production | 50.0 |
| 10% selling fee (program to network) | 5.0 |
| 40% syndication distribution fee (125 episodes at $200,000 each) | 10.0 |
| 40% foreign-sales distribution fee | 5.0 |
| Interest and other | 3.0 |
| Total | 73.0 |
| Expenses ($ millions) | |
| Production costs (including overhead) | 65.0 |
| Direct distribution costs | 2.0 |
| Residuals and other | 6.0 |
| Total | 73.0 |
| Studio profit before taxes | 0.0 |

profitable to make. But the way in which this is reflected in cost accounting depends on several additional factors.

First and foremost is the inclination of performers on a highly rated series to begin demanding much higher compensation per episode under threat of resignation. Per episode compensation for stars can easily exceed $125,000 (e.g., up to $1 million in *Seinfeld*, $1.6 million in *Frasier*, and $40 million a season for Ray Romano in *Everybody Loves Raymond*). And although most of the extra production cost can be passed on to the network through a higher license fee, there have been instances (e.g., *Three's Company*) in which performers' demands have been rejected.[58] Original cable series can generally be produced for around 15% less per hour and in seven instead of the usual eight days per episode.

Another important determinant of reported profitability is the rate at which production costs are amortized. This, to an extent, depends on the number of exhibition windows through which a program can be exploited.[59] Generally, as Owen and Wildman (1992, p. 48) have noted, the more windows there are, the higher the production budget that can be afforded.

Indeed, the theory plays out in practice whenever a producer-distributor begins to see series-syndication potential. At that point, the rate of cost amortization is reduced (i.e., amortization is stretched out over time) so that a portion of expenses can be charged against anticipated future syndication revenues. This treatment of amortization is consistent with that used in accounting for unamortized feature-film residuals, as discussed in Section 5.2.

In contrast, however, first-run production and syndication are relatively attractive to show producers and syndicators because the production costs of such shows are normally much below those of network series and because the returns from syndication of a successful first-run series materialize much sooner than with syndicated off-network programs. Whereas it might cost well over half a million dollars to produce a typical half-hour network comedy series, a first-run half hour might cost two-thirds as much. And a week's worth of half-hour game shows (five) can be produced for not much more than a quarter-million dollars.[60]

As for what are known as made-for-television movies ("made-fors"), or equivalently, movies-of-the-week (MOWs), the production cost considerations more resemble those of a standard filmed television series episode than those of a full-blown theatrical feature. As of 2005, for instance, most two-hour MOWs were being produced at a cost of approximately $4.5 million. With network license fees for two runs perhaps covering up to 85% of the cost, and with foreign sales and syndication bringing additional revenues, MOW productions can often turn an immediate though modest profit for the producer.[61] (The network will cover its outlay by selling 45 or more 30-second spots for each run at a price to advertisers of at least $60,000 a spot.)

*Costs and problems of distribution* Distribution costs for television programming include sales-office overhead, travel, and the important variables of participant residual payments. Indeed, differences in residual payment schedules for broadcast as compared with cable network syndication often dictate syndication marketing decisions.[62] But, in addition, there may also be expenses for retitling episodes, for possible dubbing into other languages, and for printmaking, which taken together can become significant.[63]

As can be seen from Table 5.13, syndication expenditures have grown substantially as both independent and network-affiliated stations have come to depend on programming provided by syndication companies through combinations of cash and time-barter arrangements. Inevitably, the same types of arrangements will also become quite common as European, Asian, and Latin American commercial television markets develop.

Nevertheless, in the 1990s, the greatest changes in program distribution relationships in the United States stemmed from elimination of the government's so-called financial interest and syndication ("fin-syn") rules. These rules had barred television networks from owning any syndication interests in shows that they had broadcast and had placed limits on the number of program hours that a network might self-produce.[64] Indeed, the expiration of fin-syn restrictions in 1995 opened the way for networks to obtain a significant second source of income through sales of self-produced entertainment programming.[65] More importantly, however, the end of fin-syn made it possible for studios and broadcast networks to be merged.[66]

Although the former dominance of the networks has, in the meantime, been eroded by collectively severe competition (from cable, independent television stations, and other home-viewing options), television program development, production, and distribution have become largely consolidated into the hands of the major movie studios and other media companies with deep pockets. Small independent companies have not been able to thrive given the sizable risks and capital investments now required to launch, market, and distribute prime-time television series.

*Timing troubles* Whenever a distributor owns a program series, revenues and earnings are recognized when the series is made available to stations – a practice identical with that established for feature-film licenses.[67] But for series in which only distribution services are being rendered, distribution fees would normally be recognized as being earned period by period as the episodes are played out and as cash payments are accordingly received.[68]

Producers, distributor-syndicators, and individual profit participants all have different claims on the television-license income stream, and individuals or corporations may simultaneously function in one or in several of these roles. Also, much as on the theatrical side, differences in perspective may often lead to great controversies and to audits. Disputes may occur because the timing of the disbursements and the profits recognized by one participant in a series project may be vastly different from the timing and profits received by another.

Illustrative cases, as discussed in a segment of the CBS show *60 Minutes* (December 7, 1980) and in a *TV Guide* story (Swertlow 1982), have involved actors Fess Parker of the *Daniel Boone* series, produced by Twentieth Century Fox, and James Garner of the Universal series *Rockford Files*. These stars, who had contracted for deferred profit-participation points in addition to, or in lieu of, greater immediate salary, asserted that the distributors had earned substantial profits totaling many millions of dollars, whereas they had yet to receive any profit on participants' shares.

Parker sued Fox for $48 million claiming that the one-hour series that ran in prime time for six years on NBC moved into successful syndication and grossed $40 million. Garner claimed that his long-running network series grossed over $52 million from both domestic and foreign sales. How, they asked, is it possible for these series to be reported as unprofitable?

The answer lies in the definition of "profits" used in the contracts. Just as in feature-film participations, a few rare talents may bargain for and be powerful enough to command high fees plus a percentage of gross revenues. Some others may bargain for a high salary and be entitled to only a small (or no) percentage of narrowly defined "profits." And most others are not participants at all; they are fortunate simply to get a job at minimum scale.

Take, for example, a hypothetical situation described by Robert Leeper, a former executive at Universal and Fox, in the *TV Guide* story:

A studio claims a production cost of $10 million for the first year of a one-hour series . . . 70 percent of those are hard, or actual costs for such items as sets, lights and film – but the remaining 30 percent includes studio charges for overhead such as the studio's parking lots and offices.

If the network carrying the $10 million show pays $8 million for the series the first year, then the series has lost $2 million for the year. If the series is a hit and runs for five years on that basis, it means that on the book, technically, the hit series has lost $10 million in production costs alone. There are other charges too. The studio also gives itself 10 percent as a commission for "selling" the series to the network. That's $800,000 a year – an additional $4 million in costs over five years, plunging the series $14 million in the hole on the books. The studio then charges the show interest on these losses. Say that, over the five years, with a fluctuating prime rate, the interest has amounted to $2.2 million. The series is now $16.2 million in the red.

. . .[N]ow, the 125 episodes produced over the five years are sold for a total of $100,000 per episode – a grand total of $12.5 million. The profit participant may think that the series' deficit has now been reduced to $3.7 million, and that he is on the verge of turning a profit. Wrong. Forty percent of the syndication revenue is lost to the distribution fee – the money the studio gives itself for selling the show to stations buying the reruns. In this case, that's $5 million. The remaining $7.5 million is then deducted, leaving the series $8.7 million in the red. The studio then charges the series what are called "actual costs" for distributing the series to syndication. They include costs for editing, making prints and negatives, costs for shipping the series to stations buying the reruns. These "actual costs" may amount to another $1.3 million. So our one-hour series is still $10 million in the red. (Reprinted with permission from *TV Guide* magazine, copyright 1982 by Triangle Publications, Inc., Radnor, Pennsylvania.)

Despite the deficit reported to participants, does the studio make a profit? The answer, in the case of a long-running series, is a qualified yes if it is indeed assumed that "soft" costs (which help to absorb the general overhead costs of running a studio) are embedded in the total production cost figure, if it is understood that the studio is in business to make a profit out of renting its distribution capability (and thus make a profit on the distribution fees charged), and if it is recognized that the studio tends to receive its cash payments a lot faster than do the participants, who might see only a summary accounting such as that shown in Table 5.14.[69]

Studios do not deny that production and distribution of series can be profitable for them even while the statements of individual participants indicate losses. But again, as in feature films, the difference is that the studio places some operating capital at risk with its investments in plant and equipment, sales offices, and other assets required to run the business over the long term. In contrast, participants are normally paid handsome salaries for their services, and they do not incur such risks.

## 5.5 Weakest links

Well-publicized financial-accounting disputes in movies and television support an impression that dishonesty and cheating are rampant in entertainment industries. Keen news-media coverage catering to the high level of public interest in industry affairs tends to also magnify whatever problems exist. But just as in other segments of the economy, the great majority of individuals and companies in entertainment conduct their businesses ethically. Indeed, because creation of entertainment products is such a people-intensive, collaborative process, success may depend as much on esteem and trust as on ability.

To guard against improper conduct, however, it is necessary to know where "leakages" in the revenue stream are most likely to occur. In this section we shall consider how and where people might cheat.[70]

Exhibitors: the beginning and the end

Customers' cash payments at the box office represent both the beginning of a chain of remittances and the end of a long creative manufacturing process – with a single, simple idea for a movie eventually generating hundreds of pounds of legal paperwork and hundreds of thousands of feet of processed film (and/or computer hard drives filled with trillions of digits).

Because the precise terms of distributor–exhibitor contracts are seldom made known to anyone not party to the agreements, both exhibitors and distributors can, for publicity purposes, sometimes distort the true size of the box-office gross.[71] In this way, a small picture can, for a brief while, be made to look like a modest hit and a modest hit may be proclaimed practically a blockbuster.

On the next level of the cash stream's cascade, the exhibitor's house expense (nut) is a negotiated item that can be inflated to ensure a profit to the exhibitor. In fact, a given theater may simultaneously have different house-expense understandings with different distributors. The degree of this inflation can be the result of long-standing tacit agreements, or it may be subject to momentary relative bargaining strength. Either way, though, the size of the nut ultimately affects the grosses (rentals) received by the distributor and thus the incomes of other parties downstream. The incomes of those parties would, of course, also be reduced if theater owners pay their bills slowly or if there are significant "adjustments" to the allowances for co-op advertising or for "settlements."[72] As Cones (1997, p. 44) notes, a distributor's relationship with exhibitors is usually more important than that with gross or net participants.

Ticket-pricing policies, however, may generally have the greatest effect on what the downstream participants might ultimately receive. Pricing is subject to local competitive conditions, moviegoer-demand schedules, and the exhibitor's interest in making as much as possible from concession sales. Exhibitors who attempt to promote concession sales by setting low admissions prices are in effect diverting and thereby diminishing monies available for downstream disbursements. To prevent abuses in this area, distributors occasionally write contracts specifying minimum per capita ticket prices (see Section 4.4).

Playing the " float " (i.e., the time value of money) is another endemic industry problem. This is somewhat surprising because box-office income is almost always in cash, and, in theory, exhibitors should have absolutely no difficulty in paying rentals immediately due. Moreover, because theater owners normally have an interest in playing a distributor's next film, large distributors have important leverage to encourage prompt remittances. Nevertheless, in practice, playing the float appears at all levels of the industry, and at high interest rates it has a significant cumulative adverse effect on profit participants.[73]

Outright fraud occurs if exhibitors and distributors cooperate to falsely claim national advertising when the advertising is characteristically local. In such situations, national advertising is charged to the producer's share, leaving the exhibitor and distributor a larger profit. It is also sometimes possible for an unscrupulous exhibitor to obtain false invoices for more local advertising (paid on a co-op basis by the distributor) than is actually placed in local papers. Exhibitors might also conveniently forget to inform distributors that, after a certain amount of newspaper lineage is placed, a quantity rebate is obtained.

In addition, distributor–exhibitor *settlements*, which are renegotiations of terms for pictures that do not perform according to expectations or that reflect shifting bargaining leverage, might be abused.[74] In this case, distributors join with exhibitors in actions that deprive producers and other participants of income that would otherwise be theirs.

Other unscrupulous practices that can be used to skim rentals properly belonging to the distributor include the following:

- Bicycling (i.e., using a single print, without authorization by the exhibition contract, to generate "free" revenues by showing it at more than one location owned by the same management). In multiscreen theaters, for example, a picture that is not playing to capacity might, in violation of day and date (simultaneity) contract terms, be replaced in some showings by another feature that is unauthorized but more popular.
- Running the film for an extra showing unauthorized by contract.
- Palming tickets (i.e., leaving the ticket untorn and recycling it to the box office, where it can be resold without disturbing the number sequence of the ticket roll).
- Changing the ticket roll after a few hundred tickets have been sold. Ticket sales on the substituted roll then go unreported.
- Unauthorized reprinting of the negative. Nowadays this includes felonious reproductions of DVDs, tapes, and Internet site downloads, the distribution of which results in significant diminishment of revenues.
- "Product-splitting" practices (discussed in Section 4.4) that reduce bidding competitiveness and, in turn, the percentage of box office received by distributors.

### Distributor–producer problems

As we have seen, the income of profit participants is affected by charges for studio overhead, by publicity and other marketing fees charged for in-house departments, and by deductibles from the producer's share that may include dubbing, editing, checking distributor receipts, copyrighting, screenings, censorship clearances, trailer preparation, insurance, tariffs, trade-association dues, print examinations, and print junking costs. If participant contracts are not carefully negotiated, the extent to which these charges are applied in any project is sometimes a source of dispute.

Major profit participants, such as leading performers, can also adversely affect the interests of other participants. For instance, this occurs when special antique furnishings, wardrobes, houses, or cars originally bought for a film are given to performers for personal use after production is completed.

Another version of this occurs when films are being shot in countries (e.g., Hungary and India) that have blocked currency remittances because of foreign-exchange controls. In these instances, it is not unusual for family and friends of important actors to receive free trips to exotic film locales. Blocked currency earned within a country must be spent within the country of origin.[75]

As already indicated, there is inordinate potential for controversy in allocations of television-license fees, cross-collateralization deals, and studios' accounting for foreign taxes, which may be charged to a picture even though the parent company later receives a credit against U.S. taxes. Also, accounting for remittances from foreign-based sources may be especially difficult because auditing privileges may be contractually restricted to books based in the United States, foreign-exchange rates may be rounded off in favor of the distributor, and foreign collections may be unusually slow.

Producers may attempt to avoid entanglement in these issues by making their own arrangements for independent foreign distribution. This is often done most efficiently by contracting with experienced overseas foreign sales companies, whose service fees are generally in the range of 10% to 15% of revenues collected and are subject to the right of recoupment of direct-sales costs if the film's gross is insufficient.[76]

## 5.6 Concluding remarks

The essential strength of the major film studios has been derived from their ability to control distribution from the early financing stages to the timing of theatrical release. However, developments in technology are always presenting new challenges and growth opportunities for industry participants, with the Internet being the latest and perhaps the greatest.

Such opportunities will allow many smaller companies to carve out profitable niches for themselves. Yet the enormous amount of capital required to operate film and television program production and distribution facilities on a global basis ultimately presents a significant barrier to entry and reinforces the trend toward vertical integration of the industry. Because the costs of production are what financial economists call *sunk costs* (i.e., most of the expenditure to create a product is invested up front, and incremental expenditures are thereafter relatively modest), it makes sense for a production to be exposed in as many windows of exhibition as possible. Indeed, for products like films, in which variable and marginal costs are relatively small as compared with large fixed and sunk costs, market size is the key to viability.[77]

That is not necessarily to imply, however, that the emergence of new media markets has eliminated downside risk, or that a flood of eager new entrants will not drive down investment returns for the industry as a whole, or that product-appeal cycles have disappeared. These elements are a part of this business, just as they are for any other.

Although industry consolidation appears to be largely completed, the financial-economic structure of the movie and television production and distribution industry is becoming ever more complex and, as such, is providing a more interesting and occasionally more profitable arena for investors.

## Notes

**1.** Copyright 1951 and 1952 by Paramount–Roy Rogers Music Co., Inc. Copyright renewed 1979 and 1980 and assigned to Paramount–Roy Rogers Music Co., Inc.

**2.** Bart and Guber (2002, p. 155).

**3.** Rosen (1981) was the first to apply rigorous economic analysis to the "superstar" phenomenon. Subsequent papers on the same subject include those by Adler (1985), MacDonald (1988), and Hamlen (1991). See also Frank and Cook (1995).

**4.** Litigation concerning *Bad News Bears*, which was licensed to ABC by Paramount for $6.75 million as part of an $18.5 million package, helped set legal precedent in a 1979 lawsuit. Details are in *Variety*, January 21, 1981, and July 2, 1980.

**5.** Companies using amortization tables periodically tested their continuing validity based on actual experience, with most tables amortizing total production costs allocated to theatrical exhibition over a 104-week period by charges to income equal to about 65% of such costs in the first 26 weeks of release and 90% in 52 weeks. MCA Inc., for example, had amortized according to tables prior to FASB Statement 53 but found that such estimates were not consistent with those on an individual-picture basis. To restore consistency, in 1981 the company adjusted its inventories on films already released by taking a "write-down" of about $50 million against previous years' retained earnings.

**6.** A write-down before release is a relatively rare event because, if the correct low-performance box-office estimates were available early in the production process, the film wouldn't ever be financed, made, or distributed. An example of SOP 00–2 rules requiring restatement of a previously announced quarter was seen in December 2002, when Disney adjusted downward by 2 cents per share ($74 million pretax and $47 million after tax) its already announced fourth-quarter 2002 earnings per share results immediately after the disappointing first (five-day Thanksgiving) weekend box-office take ($16.6 million) of the animated *Treasure Planet*, which had an estimated cost of $140 million.

**7.** There were also some 16-mm screenings at educational and penal institutions.

**8.** Growth in television revenues is illustrated by the following: In 1956, MGM received about $250,000 for a network showing of *Gone with the Wind*; in 1979, based on a $35 million face-value 20-year contract with CBS, the average per run was over $1 million. More recently, networks have been paying record amounts for top films. For example, in a 1994 agreement, NBC paid MCA $50 million for pre-cable rights (four runs) of *Jurassic Park*. And, in 1996, ABC acquired the rights to two runs (after pay-per-view and pay cable) to *Mission: Impossible* for $18 million to $22 million, depending on box-office performance. Other important deals include the Fox network agreement in 1997 to pay $80 million for early broadcast rights to *Lost World*, Fox's $80 million television rights deal for *Star Wars Episode I: The Phantom Menace*, and Disney's acquisition of the broadcast and basic cable television rights to *Harry Potter and the Sorcerer's Stone* in 2001 for about $70 million (plus rights to the sequel for an additional $60 million). Most pictures would likely receive 20% to 25% of theatrical box-office gross for two prime-time network runs.

**9.** In the late 1970s and early 1980s, unanticipated rapid growth of revenues from the new media sources did in fact upwardly bias reported industry profits. At the time, amortization was primarily against income derived from initial theatrical release, and thus there was little if any cost left over to match against windfall receipts from pay cable and home video markets.

To remedy the situation, the AICPA appointed a task force to recommend disclosures that would better explain cost-recoverability methods without unduly burdening the industry. The result is that companies now disclose information about their assumed revenue cycles, the composition of their film costs, and the expected timing of future amortization of the unamortized costs of released films. According to SOP 00–2, if the percentage of costs expected to be amortized within three years from the date of the balance sheet is less than 80%, additional information is required.

**10.**  In 2004, the IRS provided guidance as to how abandoned projects ought to be treated for tax purposes. Revenue Ruling 2004–58 indicated that unless taxpayers (studios) had formally established an intention to abandon the creative property, they cannot claim a loss deduction for the capitalized costs of acquiring and developing the property. Also, should the property become worthless, the taxpayer can only take the related deduction if there is a closed and completed transaction fixed by an identifiable event establishing the worthlessness of the property. See also Revenue Procedure 2004–36 and www.irs.gov/newsroom.

**11.**  The current year's amortization equals unamortized costs times current year's gross income divided by remaining estimated gross income (including the current year's), which means that any increase in the denominator decreases the amount currently expensed; hence, higher earnings are reported.

**12.**  For instance, when Lorimar-Telepictures was acquired by Warner Communications in early 1989, over $450 million of its equity was eliminated through adoption of Warner's more conservative accounting practices. Another example of accounting distortion occurred when Viacom, parent of Paramount, booked $1 billion of revenue for a ten-year pay TV output deal with German television mogul Leo Kirch (Kirch Group). About halfway through the ten years, Kirch was unable to pay license fees.

The sensitivity of reported earnings to relatively small changes in early period revenue estimates is also substantial. For instance, a 10% increase in total estimated revenues could normally be expected to at least double profit margins in such early periods. Companies with high inventory-to-sales ratios will generally correlate with optimistic projections of income ultimates, and vice versa.

**13.**  This is the reason for the downward adjustment in Table 4.2 of average negative costs for MPAA companies beginning with the year 2000.

**14.**  Leedy (1980, p. 9) expresses the view that accrual accounting would be to the detriment of outside participants. Daniels *et al.* (2006, pp. 45–48) notes that the industry is unique in using a mix of both accrual and cash accounting methods primarily because the cash flow patterns coming from various exhibition license windows are much different and better suited to accrual than those for participants, where it makes sense for studios to use cash methods and thus not have to possibly later bill participants for refunds.

**15.**  As described by Accounting Principles Board Opinion 16, the "purchase" method accounts for business combinations such as the acquisition of one company by another, with the acquiring corporation recording as its cost the assets less liabilities assumed. Under this method, goodwill is the difference between the cost of an acquired company and the sum of the fair values of tangible and identifiable intangible assets less liabilities. Prior to 2001, when purchase accounting had been conditionally allowed, goodwill had been amortized over a period not exceeding 40 years.

According to new FASB Statement No. 142, effective 2001, however, in business combinations companies no longer have to amortize the value of intangible assets for which they can identify cash flows and show that the assets have indefinite lives. Under the new rules, goodwill need not be amortized unless the related asset values are impaired. If impaired, the assets must be written down to their estimated fair value. See the *New York Times* and *Wall Street Journal*, December 7, 2000.

In contrast, a business combination using "pooling of interests" is viewed as "the uniting of the ownership interests of two or more companies by exchange of equity securities. No acquisition is recognized because the combination is accomplished without disbursing resources of the constituents. Ownership interests continue and the former bases of accounting are retained."

**16.** The quasi-reorganization of Filmways Corporation in 1982 illustrates this point well. A spate of expensive box-office failures had led Filmways into financial difficulties. It was only through injection of fresh capital and reorganization that the company was saved from probable bankruptcy.

As applied here, the "quasi" is a form of purchase accounting in which the film library is assessed on a picture-by-picture basis, with some written up and some written down. New amortization rates are then established for recent releases and in-process productions, and a fair market valuation of the company's distribution system is made. In the case of Filmways, immediate cash infusion of $26 million (in exchange for issuance of debt and equity securities) combined with sale of assets and various accounting adjustments gave the company a new lease on life under the name Orion Pictures. Although tax credits previously accumulated from the Filmways net operating losses had to be abandoned, the film library (composed of over 600 theatrical and television motion pictures) was written up by $18.2 million. In addition, the distribution system, which had not been on the balance sheet as such, was assigned an estimated fair-market value of $14 million (out of the eliminated $22.2 million in goodwill carried on the prior company's books).

Welles (1983) discusses Orion's quasi-reorganization and overhead-amortization accounting policies in a generally critical vein. Note, however, that the reorganization was done in consultation with various regulatory agencies and under the guidance of auditors from Arthur Young & Co. Filmways' auditor had been Arthur Andersen & Co.

MGM's acquisition in 1981 of United Artists Corporation from Transamerica Corporation provides another example of applied purchase-method accounting. The $380 million purchase price was allocated to the assets and liabilities of United Artists based on independent appraisals of such assets and liabilities. That portion of the acquisition cost not allocated to specific assets – in other words, goodwill – and the appraised value of the worldwide distribution organization acquired in the purchase of United Artists were to be amortized on a straight-line basis over a 40-year period. But MGM's assigned distribution-system value of $190 million is being amortized over 40 years, whereas Orion's distribution system is being amortized on a straight-line basis over only 25 years. A faster amortization rate places a greater burden on current reported income.

**17.** If a picture is completed on time, and is within 10% of budget, as much as half the premium may be refunded. See also Chapter 4, note 26.

**18.** A pickup arrangement should not be confused with the rare situation in which a distributor would actually agree to guarantee a bank loan instead of just promising distribution. In directly guaranteeing a bank loan, a contingent liability must be immediately recorded on the studio's balance sheet. In contrast, distribution guarantees and pickups do not appear on the balance sheet until the picture is delivered.

**19.** A notable exception to the standard 30% theatrical rate existed in the 1970s when United Artists distributed MGM's products for 22.5% of gross. In addition, limited financing partnerships such as those discussed in Chapter 4, have more recently been able to obtain agreements for below-average rates.

**20.** Return on investment in this example is, simplistically, 54% (i.e., $8.1 million/ $15 million). However, many other factors, including length of time needed to make the movie, taxes, and so forth, would need to be known to make useful comparisons.

**21.** However, as Cones (1998, p. 46) notes, "when a film is independently financed and presented to a distributor for pick-up, that transaction is more accurately referred to as an *acquisition*." The term *negative pickup* should be more properly reserved to describe lender-financed transactions.

**22.** After seeing what is in most cases the equivalent of a rough draft of the movie, an interested distributor will attempt to forecast a minimum rentals expectation and then offer an advance toward further production and postproduction costs based on the forecast. Knowing, for example, that distribution expenses for release in, say, the 450 theaters sought by the producer will be $6 million, and taking a standard distribution fee of 30%, the distributor will break even on film rentals of $20 million.

Minimum distribution expense/fee = distributor's breakeven point.
$6,000,000/30% = $20,000,000.

Given these circumstances, the distributor could extend a maximum advance of $14 million to the producer or promoter.

However, the amount of advance actually offered by the distributor may be only half of that indicated because (a) the distributor requires a cushion against the risk that the rentals forecast may turn out to be too optimistic; (b) the distributor is in business to do better than break even; (c) not all distribution expenses are included in the minimum figure; (d) this variable-cost example does not reflect the large fixed costs of maintaining a major distribution organization, nor does it reflect studio operating expenses; and (e) studio distribution slot availabilities are time perishable. See also Curran (1986), Baumgarten *et al.* (1992), and Bluem and Squire (1972).

**23.** Deals with independent producers, as noted in Berney (2004, p. 382), range from a fairly standard distribution advanced in return for distribution rights and fees to "rent-a-system" deals in which producers hire distributors for specific tasks (i.e., finding theaters, planning marketing, etc. as, for instance, in *My Big Fat Greek Wedding*), and on to " costs off-the-top" deals in which the distributor first recoups advances for prints and advertising (p & a) from first dollar of rental and thereafter splits 50/50 with the producer. Studio development deals, as discussed in McNary (2006), have also been notably scaled back. A typical deal might now pay between $500,000 and $1 million annually for overhead plus a "draw" on fees, but producers with successful track records are sometimes able to command deals several times as large.

**24.** Private funds specializing in p & a financing are relatively safe investments because the funds are repaid before or immediately after the distributor is paid and repayments are collateralized by income from video and other ancillary-market sales. In this situation, the distributor is less at risk and is therefore willing to accept a lower fee. Revolution Studios, founded in 2000 by former Disney head Joe Roth, for example, is structured on a similar concept; Sony owns equity in Revolution and pays 40% of each film's cost plus all marketing expenses. Sony gets theatrical and video rights (except for Germany and Japan) and charges only 12.5% as a distribution fee. See *BusinessWeek*, March 5, 2001. The second Disney/Pixar deal that covered *Finding Nemo*, for another example, called for an even sharing of profits and a 12.5% distribution fee. Pixar was acquired by Disney in 2006.

**25.** The effect on studio profits of gross participations is discussed in Holson (2002). For instance, the film cost for producing and marketing *Men in Black II* was estimated to be

$200 million, and at least 40% of the gross was earmarked for actors Will Smith and Tommy Lee Jones, director Barry Sonnenfeld, and others. The actors were paid a salary in advance but agreed to stop collecting their share of the film's revenue when the box-office gross reached $200 million, thereby allowing the studio to recoup its investment. Once that is achieved, what is known as the hiatus period ends and the stars again begin to collect their checks. As noted in *Variety* of November 25, 2002, however, studios had by late 2002 begun to limit first-dollar gross deals to even major stars to no more than 25% (instead of 30% or higher). To compensate for the higher percentage deals, studios had used a distorted economic model in which as much cost as possible was packed into negative costs. Gross participations of the lesser kind began to be offered more frequently in the late 1990s. In 1999, Columbia Pictures offered the first gross participation to writers. A writer with sole credit for a movie will receive 2%, and a coauthor 1%, of gross profits, defined as any sums left after the studio recoups the costs of producing, distributing, and marketing the film but before the studio pays itself a distribution fee. This means that if a film cost $50 million to make and another $30 million to market and the studio received $120 million in revenues from theatrical, television, and home video distribution, a sole credit writer would receive an additional $800,000 over and above the minimum Writers Guild minimum. See also *Variety*, February 8, 1999. The modern era of "profit" participations for talent began in the 1950s with Jimmy Stewart's deal for *Winchester '73*, which was negotiated by Universal studio head Lew Wasserman at a time when the studio was short of funds. Earlier participations, however, go back to the days of Irving Thalberg at MGM in the 1930s.

**26.** First-dollar deals finally began to be trimmed or eliminated in 2006, when studios faced slower growth of box-office and DVD sales. Under the reworked deals – which are called cash breakeven – studios keep 100% of revenues until recoupment of production, marketing, and distribution costs. Some such deals may also require that studios count all of a film's video revenue toward its recoupment instead of the typical 20%. Among the films first affected were *Da Vinci Code, Mission: Impossible III, Holiday*, and two *Pirates of the Caribbean* sequels. See also Kelly and Marr (2006) and Holson (2006a). An example based on Horn (2006c):

| | |
|---|---|
| **Cash breakeven method** | |
| Gross revenue to studio | $200.0 million |
| Studio payback for cost of making the movie | −$160.0 million |
| Net revenue for filmmakers, cast, and studio | +$40.0 million |
| Payments to filmmakers and cast at 50% of net revenue | −$20.0 million |
| Studio bottom line | +$20.0 million |
| **First-dollar gross method** | |
| Gross revenue to studio | $200.0 million |
| Profit shared with filmmakers and cast at 25% of that revenue | −$50.0 million |
| Studio gross revenue | +$150.0 million |
| Total cost of making the movie | −$160.0 million |
| Studio bottom line | −$10.0 million |

Epstein (2006) further explains how first-dollar gross is modified. Top gross players receive both fixed and contingent compensation. "The fixed part is the upfront money that gross players are paid whatever happens to the movie. The contingent part is the percentage of a pool called the 'distributor's adjusted gross' . . . The pool is 'filled' with the money that the studio's distribution arm collects or, in the case of DVDs, gets credited with . . . . The standard DVD royalty is 20 percent of the wholesale price." For TV licensing, the contribution to the pool is license fees minus residuals paid to actors, directors, and others. (So-called 100% accounting, usually only for corporate partners such as Pixar, credits the pool with DVD proceeds less manufacturing and packaging costs.) Gross players are entitled to a share of the pool only after certain conditions are met. Those conditions normally include the film earning back the fixed compensation and reaching contractually defined cash breakeven. Epstein shows that the Schwarzenegger contract for *Terminator-3* included a DVD royalty contribution to the pool of an unusually high 35%, which meant that the star was entitled to 7% (20% of 35%) of the studio's DVD sales receipts.

**27.** The bigger the budget is, the more costly is the advertising campaign, and the more gross players that are involved, the less the likelihood is that the net profits point will be reached. Gross participants' payments, for example, are cycled back into the negative cost. As a rough approximation, net profits are achieved when the studio's revenues are about 1.5 times the studio's costs of production and promotion, including the salaries of the stars. According to Robb (1992), net profits of $155 million were paid to 94 participants on Paramount releases between the years 1974 and 1987.

**28.** Philip Hacker, one of the leading forensic movie accountants, said (in Hennessee 1978), "The Warner Brothers definitions of net runs on for five single-spaced pages; of gross receipts, four pages. One makes or loses money by the definitions. Participants don't have either net or gross. All they really have is an arrangement to receive a contingent sum of money that is based on an arithmetic calculation spelled out in the agreement." Contingent compensation is discussed in Nochimson and Brachman (2003) and in Weinstein (1998, 2005), where it is shown that the court's findings in this case were misguided. Now that DVD sales from new movies, television shows, and classic films have come to represent an estimated 60% of studio profits, the most important accounting disputes are now with regard to DVDs. See also Horn (2005b) and Vogel (2005).

Note that current studio agreements tend to use phrases such as "defined proceeds" instead of "net profits." This comes in the wake of a well-publicized dispute over the definition of "profits" developed in a 1990 case in which writer Art Buchwald won credit in a state court for developing the concept behind Paramount's *Coming to America*, one of the highest-grossing films of 1988. The issue then fought in Los Angeles Superior Court concerned the definition of such profits. Studios would generally argue that they deserve to take a large part of their profits up front to compensate for the risk of investing their money in flops that never show any return on investment. Buchwald, however, argued that such upfront studio profits should not come at the expense of net profit participants and that the studios unfairly manipulate such net profit contracts. Overviews of this case are presented in Stevenson (1990), Weinstein (1998), Appleton and Yankelevits (2002), and in Robb (1990a, 1990b), with the Buchwald side fully described in O'Donnell and McDougal (1992). The accountings for this picture (in $ millions) by Paramount and by Buchwald's attorney were as follows:

**Paramount**

| | |
|---|---:|
| Gross receipts | 125 |
|   minus distribution fee | 42 |
| | 83 |
|   minus distribution expenses | 36 |
| | 47 |
|   minus Murphy, Landis gross participations | 11 |
| | 36 |
|   minus interest | 5 to 6 |
| | 30 to 31 |
|   minus negative costs including | |
|     direct production costs and studio overhead | 48 |
|     net deficit | 17 to 18 |

**Buchwald's Interpretation**

| | |
|---|---:|
| Income | 151 |
|   minus distribution fee | 53 |
| | 98 |
|   minus distribution expenses | 40 |
| | 58 |
|   minus negative costs including | |
|     direct production costs, | |
|     studio overhead, and | |
|     gross participations | 63 |
|   deficit | 5 |
|   minus interest | 6.2 |
| net deficit | 11.2 |

The accounting for one of Warner's largest box-office hits, *Batman*, has also been revealed, and it suggests that net-profit participants will probably not be compensated. McDougal (1991) shows that, as of 1991, the film had grossed $253.4 million from all sources, but from that amount the distribution fee of 32% or $80 million was first, as usual, taken out. Then, expenses (in $ millions) included the following:

| | |
|---|---:|
| Advertising and publicity | 62.4 |
| Prints | 9.0 |
| Editing and dubbing | 1.1 |
| Taxes, duties, and customs | 4.7 |
| Trade association fees | 2.1 |
| Freight, handling, and insurance | 1.4 |
| Checking, collection, etc. | 1.6 |
| Guild and union residuals | 1.6 |

These expenses, however, do not include the film's actual production cost, at $53.5 million, interest charges, and gross-profit participations. Through September 1990, interest on the entire production cost was $10.8 million. Yet it was gross participations, especially that of star actor Jack Nicholson (who played The Joker), that truly rolled the breakeven point upward. In addition to an "upfront" fee advance of $6 million, the actor also reportedly negotiated to receive 15% of the gross, with an escalator clause that ultimately brought his total percentage of the gross close to 20%. Other participants had similar advances-against-gross embedded in the film's production cost but at much smaller "adjusted gross" levels. In all, the gross-profit participants took about $60 million of the film's income and left net-profit participants with nothing.

Several other examples of profit participation statements, for example, *Who Framed Roger Rabbit, Three Men and a Baby,* and *Beverly Hills Cop,* are shown in Robb (1992). The effect of gross participations can also be seen in the case of *Last Action Hero,* wherein production, overhead, and p & a costs of $150 million were almost fully recouped from all markets until gross participation talent and interest costs ate up another $15 million. See *Variety,* September 13, 1993, and also *Daily Variety,* November 20, 1995. A suit concerning net profits contracts for the film *JFK* also moved through the courts in the late 1990s. And in 2003 there was an accounting lawsuit concerning *My Big Fat Greek Wedding* filed at Los Angeles Superior Court.

**29.** Breimer (1995, p. 76) notes that studios also receive benefit from any nonreturnable advances for sale of cable or home video rights and that such advances are not included in calculation of participants' grosses until they are *earned.* Here, again, there is a different definition for the studio and for the participant. However, as noted in *Variety* of April 1, 2002, major star participants have begun to command a larger percentage of the home video royalties. The important deal point in figuring residuals and payments to gross players with regard to DVD revenues is what is known as the *video-to-gross* (VTG) ratio. Most participants would only share in 20% of home video revenues, with 80% allocated for the studio. Yet even those few who are major participants will not ever see a VTG ratio greater than 50%.

See also Lubove (2004), Horn (2005b), and Snyder (2005). A brief history of the 20% royalty arrangement is in Daniels *et al.* (2006, pp. 59–64).

**30.** Cones (1997, p. 58) notes that there are four problems in the majors' treatment of home video revenues: (a) royalties are taken on a royalty rather than on a subdistribution fee basis; (b) the royalty paid to the distributor is only 20% of the wholesale price; (c) since studios own the home video distribution arm, they participate twice in the video revenue stream by also taking a distribution fee on the royalties; and (d) expenses for marketing the videos are deducted by the distributor in figuring profit participations.

A simple example makes the point. If, for instance, half a million cassettes are sold at $50 a unit ($25 million in total), $5 million might be credited to gross receipts of the participant, out of which a distribution fee is taken. The studio then retains $20 million out of total revenues. And after deduction of expenses of perhaps $6 a unit for manufacturing, sales, and advertising, and perhaps another $2 a unit to cover overhead, the studio-distributor still has a gross profit of $16 million ($20 million minus $8 times 500,000) before adding back the distribution fee earned out of the participant's gross receipts.

From the industry's viewpoint, a fix on the order of magnitude can be obtained by assuming, say, that each studio on average releases about 20 titles a year (less than two a month), that each title sells a domestic average of 200,000 units, and that the gross profit per unit, blending both sell-through and rental titles, is $10. Then, with the equivalent of seven studios, total gross profits from domestic shipments would be $280 million. Further assuming that foreign home video profits are at least as much would imply that aggregate studio profits from home video might be in the area of $600 million, or about half what total industry profits had been in the early 1990s.

**31.** A study sponsored by the National Association of Concessionaires and Coca-Cola indicated that, in dollar terms, about 40% of refreshment-stand sales come from popcorn, 40% from soft drinks, and 20% from food items and candy. A 1990 study further indicated that, at some theaters, concession sales might account for 90% of profits. The reason: A soft drink priced at $2.50 may cost the owner less than 25 cents. As of 1990, the national average spent on snack bar items was $1.20, with urban area averages around $1.60.

**32.** For instance, in its 1988 annual report, Cineplex Odeon shows a significant operating income figure; however, if profits from real estate transactions are excluded, it can be seen that the company's basic theater business operated at a loss. See also Wechsler (1989).

**33.** The cost of operating a major domestic-distribution organization is estimated to be $50 million annually circa 2005. If an average fee of 33% is assumed, this $50 million nut, which covers sales expenses, is earned after the first $150 million of theatrical rentals. But as A. D. Murphy notes in Squire (1992, p. 286), earnings in excess of that figure should not be called profits "in the sense of free-and-clear money available for dividends and such." The excess is instead first largely used to recover other out-of-pocket unrecouped marketing and production costs and is also recycled into new film productions. See also Wechsler (1990).

**34.** Donahue (1987, p. 183) provides a good example: " . . . a picture earns $10 million in film rental while the marketing costs amount to $5 million. In the distribution fee deal, the distributor takes $3 million and costs are recouped out of the $7 million, with $2 million left for the producer. In the gross percentage deal, the independent producer receives $3 million, costs are recouped out of the $7 million, leaving $2 million for the distributor."

**35.** For instance, pay television license fees are often benchmarked at $7 million for films that generate $50 million in domestic box office and at $10 million if the box office exceeds $75 million. A scaled agreement might also state that films grossing under $5 million at the domestic box office (dbo) are to have a pay TV license fee of 50% of the dbo, those in the $60 million to $100 million range a base fee of $11 million plus 5% of the revenue over $60 million, and those over $200 million dbo capped at a fee of $15 million. In the future, as the proportion of total revenues derived from theatrical diminishes, it is likely that such arithmetic links to box-office performance will also be weakened.

**36.** Major studios, however, no longer include overhead in the budgets of their own productions. They instead budget actual cash costs, but will still generally charge a 15% overhead fee on the negative cost for the purpose of figuring participant payouts.

**37.** In the 1990s, completion bond companies began to provide "gap financing" to independent producers. The "gap" refers to the funding that producers need to make the film and what they have already arranged for by using expected revenues from unsold territories as collateral. At the peak of popularity, the gap had often been as high as 50% to 60% of production costs, but lenders have become more cautious in recent years as the risk of nonrecoupment has risen.

**38.** This example follows Garey (1983, p. 104).

**39.** The traditional estimate is that the box-office gross must be two or three times the negative cost to reach breakeven. However, for major-event pictures, this ratio might actually be nearer to two times.

**40.** The following is a partial list of companies that, since the early 1970s, have attempted to enter production and either have failed totally or have substantially withdrawn from the field: ABC Pictures (ABC's first venture distributed by Cinerama in the early 1970s), Associated Communications, Avco-Embassy, Cannon Group, Cinema Center Films (CBS's first venture distributed by National General in the early 1970s), De Laurentiis Entertainment Group, Filmways (reconstituted as Orion), General Cinema Corp., and Time-Life Films. Some of these production entities had considerable financial backing and experience and yet (the new-media revolution notwithstanding) couldn't buck the odds. As one industry CEO said, "You put $200 million in and make a movie no one likes and everyone has been paid off except the people who financed it" (*Daily Variety*, November 25, 2002).

**41.** A good real-world example of this is discussed in Eberts and Ilott (1990, p. 109).

**42.** See *Daily Variety*, October 24, 1979.

**43.** Quoted from *Daily Variety*, October 24, 1979. Litman, in Kindem (1982), discusses pricing of series and movies from the perspective of the 1970s. As of the late 1990s, it has been common in the industry that, for an "A" title, studios get $1.5 million for each $10 million of domestic box-office gross of up to $150 million.

**44.** *War and Remembrance* was noted not only for its high-quality production values but also for its huge cost and the over $20 million in losses that the ABC network sustained on its original broadcast of the 32-episode, $110 million miniseries that was shown in the fall of 1988 and the spring of 1989. See Kneale (1988). In 2001, HBO produced a similar epic at a cost of $125 million for ten episodes of *Band of Brothers*. See also Carter (2001a).

**45.** The high costs and generally unrepresentative nature of pilots, and the great probability that most will not be extended into full series, have led many in the television industry to question the wisdom of using this massive and wasteful spending system for program-development purposes. Unfortunately, satisfactory alternatives have yet to be discovered. Bunn (2002) states that in 2002, an hour-long pilot cost $2.5 million or more and $1.8 million for a 26-minute "presentation" (minipilot). Barnes (2004b) notes that pilots are not too reliable in predicting success. *Seinfeld* and *The A-Team* tested poorly yet became hits, while other programs tested well but failed to perform on the air.

**46.** Prior to the phasing out of investment tax credits in 1986, 6 2/3% of production costs had qualified as tax credits – a factor that had considerably eased the production deficit problem.

**47.** Indeed, because it is so difficult to generate positive cash flows in the start-up phase of production, many production companies have encountered financial difficulties and have been forced to co-venture or to merge with larger organizations or studios.

**48.** The issue of deficit financing is at the heart of the financial interest and syndication rule debate that had raged since the early 1980s. In return for paying higher license fees for original programming, the networks have long felt entitled to participation in some of the so-called backend syndication profits, which, at least through 1990, they had been barred from sharing. Deficits had risen from an average of around $64,000 a half-hour show in 1982–83 to over $170,000 by 1986–87. For hour-long shows, the deficits are estimated to have risen from $198,000 to over $370,000 in the same period. And in the 1989–90 season, the Alliance of Motion Picture & Television Producers indicated that deficits averaged $300,000 for one-hour series and $258,000 for half-hour series. As Steinberg (2006) illustrates with the Fox show *24* as an example, DVDs are now an important swing factor in offsetting such deficits. Previously, international sales alone filled the profit gap. The 120 episodes of the series *24* cost just under $2.5 million each or $300 million to make. Network license fees covered $1.3 million an episode, and another $1 million came from international sales – thus contributing $276 million toward covering the cost but still leaving a deficit of $24 million. Total DVD sales of more than $200 million turned the production profitable. As noted by Munoz (2006), Lionsgate has been able to avoid deficits in making series for cable. The company does this by assembling money from license fees, income from international sales, and from state and local tax rebates and subsidies.

**49.** As indicated in Owen and Wildman (1992, p. 184), the probability of renewal increases markedly for series that have been renewed at least once. The longest-running TV series through the 1992–93 season were *Gunsmoke* with 402 episodes, *Dallas* with 356, *Knots*

*Landing* with 344, *Bonanza* with 318, and *The Love Boat* with 255. Through 2003, the longest-running prime-time series have been *60 Minutes* (35 years beginning in 1968), *The Ed Sullivan Show* (24 years, 1948–71), *20/20* (24 years), *Gunsmoke* (21 years, 1955–75), and *The Red Skelton Show* (21 years, 1951–71). Though not in primetime, *Saturday Night Live* has been running on NBC since October 1975. And as of 2005, *The Simpsons*, with 16 seasons completed, surpassed *Ozzie & Harriet* as the longest-running sitcom.

**50.** In the late 1960s and early 1970s, the probability of making a syndicatable, highly profitable series was greater than in the late 1970s and early 1980s. By the 1980s, viewers had become increasingly discriminating in their choices. Because of disruptions by strikes and other factors, the start of the TV season had become irregular, and cable, videocassette, and movie-of-the-week viewing alternatives had become more numerous.

**51.** The increasing competitive influence of pay TV implies that producers now may be less willing to tie up their best properties for long periods, whereas networks will seek longer option periods. The relative values of syndicated half-hour and hour series episodes, as well as typical contract terms, are thus in a state of flux. Furthermore, networks may have a strategic interest in "warehousing" best-drawing feature films in order to delay appearance on competing pay cable networks.

As noted in *Variety* of January 13, 1997, the Katz TV Group has formulated three criteria for predicting the syndication success of an off-network sitcom: (a) at least 18% of viewers of a comedy during its prime-time network run should be men 18 to 49 years old; (b) if a show substantially benefits from a network hit-comedy lead-in, its syndication performance will probably be disappointing; and (c) throughout its four-year network prime-time run, a comedy series should have a Nielsen rating 20% above the average sitcom rating for adults 25 to 54 years old.

**52.** As recounted by Sporich (2003), in 1999 Paramount was the first studio to put a television series (*Star Trek*) on DVD, and Fox was the first to have a huge hit (*The Simpsons*). Fox then followed up with several other popular series (e.g., *X-Files, Buffy the Vampire Slayer, 24*) and by 2003 had captured 42% share of the TV-to-DVD market. HBO Home Video (along with sister company Warner Home Video) also did well with high DVD sales of *Friends, The Sopranos,* and *Sex and the City*. TV-to-DVD sales were around $3 billion in 2005. In that year, the top-selling *Seinfeld* (seasons I & II) generated $90 million. See also Barnes (2005b) and Collins (2005). Steinberg (2006) indicates that DVD sales of $200 million between 2002 and 2006 for the Fox series *24* made the show profitable for the producers. See also note 48 above.

**53.** For a show with the potential to last at least three years on a network, program-distribution companies may be willing to guarantee, in installments, say, at least $50,000 per episode against a percentage of anticipated syndication profits. Here producers may sacrifice some percentage of ownership in return for immediate cash, and distributors may obtain long-term project commitments on which they can rely to keep pipelines filled. The risk to the distributor is that the program will be canceled or that the show will lose its audience appeal. According to a Warner Bros. study cited in Flint (2004), for example, of 436 comedies launched between 1990 and 2002, only 54 lasted at least four years, and of those, only nine, or 2% became big rerun hits. Should the producer enter into such an agreement, an important issue for negotiation is which party will pay what percentage of talent residuals and royalties.

As in features, however, residuals would normally be expected to come out of the producers' side. For top producers, the percentage of the back end can be quite high. Witt Thomas Harris, producers of *The Golden Girls*, which is distributed by Disney and is estimated to have earned about $1.5 million for each of its 150 episodes, might have received as much as a 25% cut out of the backend profits. The milestone Carsey-Werner deal for *The Cosby Show* is believed to have been for a 33% cut.

**54.** An important exception has been the distributor King World (now owned by CBS Corporation), which had signed stations to three-year contracts on the basis of the ratings strength of its shows *Wheel of Fortune*, *The Oprah Winfrey Show*, and *Jeopardy!*. Among the longest-running shows in syndication are *Soul Train* (33 years) and *Entertainment Tonight* (23 years) as of 2004.

**55.** Barter prices naturally ride on the back of network cost per thousand (CPM) prices and are usually 80% of what a network might charge. Barter, however, clearly shifts the financial burden from the station to the syndicator, who must arrange to aggregate and sell the time to national advertisers.

**56.** Because barter contracts are not negotiated until fairly close to actual time of telecast, the carrying value of such bartered shows cannot be accurately assessed and therefore be subsumed as a part of a production/distribution company's long-term license-fee "backlog." The effect is that barter-program licenses tend to generate earnings that, for the distributor, are much more dispersed over time and that are of smaller relative magnitude than is the case with cash-licensed, off-network program syndication fees (which are recognized in large clusters at the time of first availability). See also Accounting for Advertising Barter Transactions (EITF 99–17).

**57.** The costs of network prime-time productions are estimated to have risen at a 14.4% compound annual rate during the 1970s. Although comparable data are not available for the 1980s, it seems fair to assume that the cost of production probably continued to rise by an average of 10% a year between 1980 and 1990, and by at least 5% a year beginning in the late 1990s.

**58.** The squeeze from higher star salaries comes mostly out of network profits. For instance, in *Seinfeld* (one of the most expensive regular series in television history and costing $4 million per ninth-season episode), NBC sold nine 30-second spots for about $500,000 each, or $4.5 million. With a rerun, the gross is $9 million, and less agency commissions, the total for the year might approach $8 million per episode. If 25 episodes per season were assumed, NBC would take in $200 million in revenues. But with the series stars receiving as much as $1 million each under proposed new contracts, the cost of the show might rise to $5 million an episode, up from perhaps $2 million in the early years of the program. The $3 million difference would thus reduce NBC profits from $150 million to $75 million. In addition, as of 1998, NBC agreed to pay a record $13 million per episode for *E.R.* – equivalent to $850 million over three years. Of the total, Warner would retain an estimated $330 million, with the remainder going to producers, creators, and agency fees. See also *BusinessWeek*, June 2, 1997, and the *Los Angeles Times*, January 16, 1998.

The NBC deal for renewal of the *Friends* series, in which each of the six stars was to receive $750,000 per episode plus a percentage of the backend profits ($40 million over two years), is described in the *New York Times*, May 15, 2000. Also see Carter (2002b), in which the contract extension for *Friends* was based on NBC's paying $7 million per half-hour episode, with each of the six stars being paid $1 million per episode. A second extension of *Friends* into a tenth season (see *New York Times*, December 21, 2002, and Nelson and Flint 2002) was made possible by a December 2002 agreement to pay Warner Bros. around $10 million (up from $7 million) for each half-hour episode, a record for a 30-minute series. A similar situation concerning NBC's potential renewal of *Frasier* is discussed in the *New York Times* and *Los Angeles Times* of December 7, 2000, while *Dharma & Greg* is discussed in Carter (2001b). Flint (2001) covers the resolution (three years and a bit more than $5 million per episode) of the NBC and *Frasier* negotiations. Note also that in 2001, *Frasier* star Kelsey Grammer was able to negotiate for the upcoming tenth and eleventh seasons (48 shows) a record $1.6 million per episode.

In effect, networks now extract ownership in shows from outside suppliers in return for airtime. In reaction to such price increases, as Weinraub and Carter (2002) note, networks make increasing use of shows that they own and develop themselves through multipurpose exposures on their other secondary and cable outlets.

**59.** In the case of a popular series coming off-network, such syndication window revenues can be substantial. For instance, a record total of $200 million ($1.5 million per episode) was initially received in the mid-1980s by MCA for the one-hour series *Magnum, P. I.* And syndication of the half-hour *Seinfeld* in 1998 brought a record $6 million an episode for a total $1.6 billion, which compares against the previous record of $600 million for half hours of the *Cosby* series in 1988. *Seinfeld* is the only major series besides *MASH* to take more money in its second-cycle syndication than in the first. The *Friends* second cycle of around $1 billion total was about equal to the first cycle, which means that through two cycles and the license fees for the 236 episodes, the show generated $3 billion, a total only exceeded by *Seinfeld* in its third cycle. *Seinfeld, Frasier, Friends,* and *Everybody Loves Raymond* each had enough episodes and high first-cycle per episode prices to be billion-dollar properties. First-cycle cash-license values (in $ millions) per episode for those shows were, respectively, $3.3, $3.1, $3.0, and $2.5. See *Variety,* March 23, 1998, and Flint (2004). The first syndicated show was *The Lone Ranger.*

Many series, especially hour-longs, have not until recently even come close to the positive results shown in Table 5.11. *Walker, Texas Ranger* was sold in 1996 for $750,000 per episode to the USA Network and for about the same from weekend runs on broadcast stations. As of 2005, the leading cable syndication prices per episode were $2.5 million for *Sopranos* (A&E), $1.9 million for *Law and Order: Criminal Intent* (Bravo and USA), $1.6 million for *CSI,* and $1.2 million for *West Wing.* See *New York Times,* February 1, 2005. Lifetime also pays $1.35 million an episode for *Medium* and TNT $1.4 million for *Cold Case* (in 2005). The possible adverse affect from VOD on such prices is discussed in Lieberman (2005).

Soon after the record price for *Magnum* (which ultimately averaged $1.7 million per episode) was obtained, television industry demand for hour-long series plummeted and, through the second half of the 1980s, most off-network hour-long series could not command more than $300,000 to $400,000 per episode – scarcely enough to cover the costs of marketing and of residual payments. For example, eight of the top ten programs in the 1983–84 season were one-hour dramas, but the number had fallen to nearly zero by the end of the decade before a revival, led by the Fox network, ensued in the early 1990s. Licensing to cable networks has thus developed as an attractive alternative to syndicating to local TV stations, especially in that Hollywood guilds take 10% of the cash license fees in cable sales, which is half the cost of broadcast-deal residuals. Hour-long series sold to such networks for prices up to $250,000 an episode include *Murder She Wrote, Cagney and Lacey,* and *Miami Vice.* And hour-long dramas such as *E.R.* have later been sold to cable for $1.2 million an episode. Lifetime, owned jointly by Disney and Hearst, bought rights in 1996 to 112 episodes of the sitcom *Ellen* for more than $600,000 per episode, a record for a cable network purchase. See also Goldman (1992).

**60.** As of the early 2000s, most magazine-style shows had weekly production budgets upwards of $450,000 a week (double the cost of the early 1990s), whereas most new game and talk shows cost in the range of $150,000 to $250,000 a week to produce. Most such shows would need to attract at least $90,000 a week in national barter advertising in order to reach breakeven. The theme and content of a program like *Entertainment Tonight,* however, brings production costs up to more than $500,000 a week. Such magazine shows would have to maintain a minimum household rating of 4.5 to be profitable.

But not all first-run series are necessarily low-budget productions: *Star-Trek . . . The Next Generation*, with an initial per episode budget of $1.3 million plus $75,000 for special effects, had been among the costliest first-run series produced in the early 1990s. Nor are all network productions high budget; for example, as of 1997 it had cost about $400,000 an hour (one-third as much as drama) to produce network newsmagazine programs such as *60 Minutes* (CBS), *20/20* (ABC), *PrimeTime Live* (ABC), and *Dateline* (NBC). Similarly, *Who Wants to Be a Millionaire* (ABC) is estimated to have averaged $750,000 because the top prizes were not usually won in most episodes. With ad unit prices averaging $300,000 and with exposure in four prime-time hours a week (200 episodes a year), it is estimated that *Millionaire* generated more than $1 billion of revenues and perhaps $800 million of EBITDA for ABC in the year beginning with the fall 2000 season.

**61.** As of the mid-1990s, U.S. distributors took in an estimated $225 million in foreign sales of two-hour movies. Titles generally gross between $400,000 and $1.4 million overseas, with producers of major telefilms able to get a $400,000 to $900,000 advance from a distributor for foreign sales rights. This often amounts to one-third of the financing of a network TV movie. In all, some 250 such films are made each year.

**62.** For example, in syndicated television, talent unions have negotiated a sliding scale of residuals that calls for 75% of original pay for the first and second replay, 50% for the third through fifth, 10% for the sixth, and 5% for every run beyond that. However, for cable network syndication, there is only a one-time flat 10% of the gross that is divided among writers, actors, and directors. Thus, syndication of an off-network series to one of the national cable networks for, say, $150,000 an episode would cost the distributor only $15,000, whereas broadcast syndication of six runs of the same series to broadcast stations could cost anywhere from $120,000 to $150,000 an episode in residuals (because the charge per episode is fixed no matter what the license fee). In addition, selling into broadcast syndication incurs more expense because the series must be sold market-by-market instead of to just one buyer. This means that, for the distributor to profit from a broadcast syndication of an off-network series, gross revenues generally must well exceed $300,000 an episode – which is nowadays difficult to amass.

**63.** The number of prints needed for national syndication can be reduced by "bicycling," the swapping of episodes from one station to the next, only when the sequencing of episodes does not matter. In theory, however, increased use of low-cost distribution by satellite technology promises that ultimately only one print will be required.

Prior to the advent of "superstations" – local television stations that send their signals via satellite to cable systems around the country – syndicated programs in a local market had been protected from competition through contract exclusivity clauses. Such protection was restored only in 1990, when the Federal Communications Commission (FCC) reinstated such exclusivity with so-called syndex rules.

**64.** Constraints on self-production were the result of a 1980 consent decree that limited each network to in-house production of two and one-half hours on average per week until the fall of 1985, when the cap began to rise gradually toward five hours per week in 1988. In actuality, however, networks have to date not proven to be particularly efficient in production. An episode of the once-popular one-hour ABC network–produced series *Moonlighting* reportedly set a 1980s record at a cost of $3 million. NBC's *Studio 60*, introduced for the fall 2006 season, reportedly cost (*Wall Street Journal*, May 15, 2006) at least $2.5 million an episode. The pilot cost $6 million and the initial marketing budget was set at $10 million.

The end of fin-syn rules has made it more likely for a network to own a stake in new series productions, but as Flint (2002b) suggests, such arrangements do not necessarily lead to successful program schedules or to smoother relations between producers and distributors. As an example, in 1992, ABC made an agreement with Wind Dancer Productions to fund the entire cost of producing a new series rather than paying a flat license fee, which typically compensates the producer for only 80% to 85% of the full cost of production. By owning such a stake, ABC would participate in potential syndication revenues should the shows succeed in the ratings comparisons. Disney, for instance, also decided not to incur deficits on the show *CSI: Crime Scene Investigation* when it was picked up by CBS, the network rival to Disney's ABC. The show went on to garner huge ratings, and Disney thus gave up not only the large advertising income that would have accrued if the show had been kept by ABC but also the enormous later profits from syndication sales. Manly (2005a) notes that after an upsurge favoring sister production companies, networks have become more open to buying from outside producers.

Moreover, with broadcast networks now owned by studio-distributors, there have been instances in which producers and other profit participants have sued the distributors for self-dealing (i.e., selling a show into syndication to a distributor's sibling branches at less than market prices). In 1999, in addition to the Wind Dancer/*Home Improvement* dispute alleging that Disney sold the show at a discount to its own ABC network, there were similarly based suits against Fox involving the *X-Files* and *NYPD Blue* series. See Lubove (1999) and *Los Angeles Times* of April 9, 2001, on settlement of *NYPD Blue* issues.

A similar suit, discussed in Johnson (2005a), was brought against New Line Cinema by *Lord of the Rings* director Peter Jackson, claiming that self-dealing among different parts of the New Line–Time Warner conglomerate underpaid him as much as $100 million.

Incongruous arrangements have also developed, as in the case of *Scrubs*, in which NBC derives revenues only from broadcast advertising sales because it doesn't own the show. ABC is the developer and producer of *Scrubs* and will receive the DVD and syndication fees that will be generated in the future. Were NBC to drop the hit show from its prime time schedule, ABC would likely place it on its own network. See Rhodes (2006).

**65.** Both the Syndication and Financial Interest and the Prime Time Access Rules were adopted by the FCC in 1970 in response to conditions that had existed in the 1960s, when the networks had been at the peak of their relative competitive strength. These rules had originally been proposed as a means by which independent producers could flourish and to prevent program domination by the three major networks. Up to that time, the networks owned and produced many of the shows they aired. The disallowance of network financial interest went into effect on August 1, 1972, and of network syndication on June 1, 1973.

In 1980, the three national networks also entered into consent decrees in connection with antitrust suits brought against each of them by the Department of Justice in the early 1970s. These consent decrees contain provisions that parallel but are not identical to the original Syndication and Financial Interest Rules.

In 1983, movement toward deregulation encouraged networks to challenge some of the restrictions, and a bitter political battle ensued between the networks on one side and independent producers, independent television stations, and movie studios on the other. The independents feared that the networks would stifle their creative and financial well-being, while the networks contrarily argued that they were no longer oligopolistic because of the inroads made by strongly competitive cable and home video industries. See Section 7.1 and also Crandall (1972), Landro and Saddler (1983), Colvin (1983), Kneale and Carnevale (1991), Owen and Wildman (1992), and *Variety*, August 10, 1983.

Relaxation of the restrictions on network participation in foreign syndication and ownership of financial interests was first approved by the FCC in April 1991. As of 1992, rule modifications had allowed a network to distribute or to have an interest in the proceeds from distributing its own product. And in prime time the networks were allowed to produce or coproduce up to 40% of their schedules. But by early 1993, almost all restrictions on financial interest were dropped, and all restrictions expired in late 1995. Networks can now negotiate for equity, syndication rights, longer license terms, and more network replays. Or they can produce shows themselves. The Prime Time Access Rules, restricting affiliates in the top 50 markets from running syndicated off-network series in the hour before prime time, were allowed to expire in 1996. Subsequent developments are described in *Entertainment Media*, January 29, 2001. Impact on producers of the FCC media ownership rule changes of 2003 is explained in Carter and Rutenberg (2003).

**66.**    The Fox network evolved in the late 1980s. Because it did not program a full week's schedule and because it thus did not fall under the FCC's definition of a network, it was free to own syndication interests in its self-developed shows. Under the modified fin-syn rules of 1991, Fox was allowed to broadcast no more than an average of 15 hours of programming per week in prime time during any six-month period (and an unlimited number of hours of non–prime time programming). News Corp., the parent company, thus owned a movie studio, a quasi-network, and a television syndication arm prior to the 1993 relaxation of the rules. By 1994, however, other network-studio combinations had begun to form, with United/Paramount (UPN) and Warner Bros. (WB) becoming the fifth and sixth networks. And, in 1995, Disney bought ABC. After more than a decade in which cumulative losses mounted into the billions of dollars, UPN and WB were merged in 2006 to form the CW network. Here stations bid to become affiliates through "reverse compensation" to the network. See also Barnes (2006b).

**67.**    However, the cash flow sequence may begin with up to a 10% down payment on signing or on first availability date and be followed by three annual installments of 30% of total revenues due. Following standard accounting procedures, the future cash receivables are then discounted, using an appropriate interest rate, to a present-value receivable that appears on the balance sheet.

**68.**    Foreign receipts would also normally be booked on an episode-by-episode cash basis, but unlike the domestic situation, without regard as to whether a show is self-produced and/or owned.

**69.**    Mr. Garner's *Rockford Files* (NBC, 1974–1980) agreement with Universal had entitled him to 37.5% of the net profits of the show in return for taking a smaller upfront fee. By 1988, receipts from the show had reached $119.3 million according to Universal's own accounting. Nevertheless, Universal claimed that the show would have to earn another $1.6 million before it would realize net profits as described in Garner's contract.

According to the accounting statement, as described by Scholl (1989b), subtracted from the $119.3 million was $32.6 million for distribution fees. Then another $14.6 million was deducted for distribution expenses, including the cost of prints and storage. Then another $57.8 million was taken off for production costs, which left only $14.2 million. That $14.2 million, however, by Universal's accounting, was insufficient to cover the $15.8 million in interest expenses that the company (and most other studios) charges on the theory that the money spent on production could have been invested at risk-free rates.

However, according to Garner's auditors, Universal overstated costs and/or underestimated receipts by at least $10.9 million. For example, the auditors claimed that Universal failed to pass along quantity discounts (of $443,000) received on development of extra print copies.

Another issue involved whether to count print and dubbing costs as gross receipts or as expense reimbursements. If counted as the former, Universal would take a 50% fee off the top, whereas in the latter case, it is a direct expense reduction that leads to faster profitability for the participant. An even larger amount ($7.9 million), and one that is at the crux of the interest payments charges issue, involved Universal's alleged practice of immediately recording expenses while deferring the recording of revenues and profits until cash was in hand. As Scholl (1989a) indicates, the Garner suit, initiated in 1983, was settled in 1989 for approximately $10 million.

**70.** See also Salemson and Zolotow (1978).

**71.** This is especially seen in preliminary distributor weekend box-office estimates, which are made by (sometimes aggressively) extrapolating Entertainment Data Inc. (EDI) and Rentrak Friday and Saturday tallies through Sunday and by estimating uncounted results from small and rural theaters to gain position in early weekend rankings. Lippman (2004), however, notes that data on actual number of tickets sold are not sent by theaters until their contracts obligate payment to studios, about six weeks after a film opens. Per screen box-office averages may also be misleading as a film that plays on three screens in the same multiplex is still counted as playing on one screen. This may mean that the audience is smaller than the reported per screen averages might suggest.

**72.** Settlements may further involve backdoor payments or other rewards for placement of trailers, picking up costs of newspaper ads, paying the cost of broken reels, and sharing a larger slice of the box office with the exhibitor. See Munoz (2004). Bart and Guber (2002, p. 231) have likened contracts between exhibitors and distributors to prenuptial agreements in that the contracts are an invitation to endless negotiations.

**73.** During periods of high interest rates and economic duress, playing the float is obviously not unique to entertainment businesses.

**74.** The practice of settlements, also known as selling subject to review, is sometimes pushed to the ethical borderline and, interestingly, does not seem to apply in reverse. That is, if a picture performs better than expected, distributors do not ordinarily extract stiffer terms from exhibitors. Settlements are much less likely to be found in exhibitor contracts that are bid rather than negotiated. Universal, Fox, Sony, and DreamWorks apparently negotiate on the basis of "firm terms," which are terms supposedly not reviewable after a movie closes. But many studios and exhibitors favor "settling" terms 60 to 90 days after a picture opens, and even those studios with firm terms may compensate exhibitors for box-office losers with better terms on future releases. See *Variety*, March 17, 1997, and Cones (1997).

**75.** Blocked currency funds have occasionally served as a source of new film production financing. Normally, different companies or industries operating in a country accumulate such funds and, as long as the funds are used within that country, it does not matter that the funds were generated in selling automobiles or textiles. See also *Variety*, August 20, 1986.

**76.** There are several foreign sales organizations, but most are relatively small. The most famous of these, mentioned in Paris (1984) and Salamon (1984), was Producers Sales Organization, which eventually went out of business.

**77.** Bakker (2005, p. 37) makes this point in discussing how Hollywood came to dominate world cinema.

## Selected additional reading

Abelson, R. (1996). "The Shell Game of Hollywood 'Net Profits'," *New York Times*, March 4.

Abrams, B. (1984). "Why TV Producers Flock to New York to Just Sit and Fret," *Wall Street Journal*, May 7.

Barnes, P. W. (1987). "How King World Reaps Riches, Fame as a TV Syndicator," *Wall Street Journal*, June 9.

Briloff, A. J. (1998). "Disney's Real Magic: Is the Entertainment Giant's Accounting Pure Mickey Mouse?," *Barron's*, March 23.

Carvell, T. (1999a). "Lights! Camera! Lawsuit!," *Fortune*, 140(7)(October 11).

   (1999b) "Hello, Mr. Chips (Goodbye, Mr. Film)," *Fortune*, 140(4)(August 16).

Chambers, E. (1986). *Producing TV Movies*. New York: Prentice–Hall.

De Vany, A., and Walls, W. D. (1999). *Uncertainty in the Movie Industry: Does Star Power Reduce the Terror of the Box Office?* Irvine, CA: University of California, Department of Economics, asdevany@uci.edu.

Gottschalk, E. C., Jr. (1978). "Feud in Filmdom: Movie Studios' System of Splitting Profits Divides Hollywood," *Wall Street Journal*, October 16.

   (1972). "Film Makers Struggle with Major Studios for 'Creative' Control," *Wall Street Journal*, December 29.

Harmetz, A. (1987). "Now Lawyers Are Hollywood Superstars," *New York Times*, January 11.

Harwood, J. (1985). "Hollywood Exposing More of Its Ledgers," *Variety*, March 13.

Kopelson, A. (1985). "Presales of Independently Produced Motion Pictures," *The Hollywood Reporter*, March 5.

Landro, L. (1985). "Overseas Distributor Takes on Big Studios by Doing Own Films," *Wall Street Journal*, April 16.

Lippman, J. (2001). "Battle over Residuals Could Set the Stage for a Hollywood Strike," *Wall Street Journal*, March 28.

Litwak, M. (1994). *Dealmaking in the Film & Television Industries*. Los Angeles: Silman-James.

Mariet, F. (1990). *La Télévision Américaine: Médias, Marketing et Publicité*. Paris: Economica.

Mayer, J. (1991). "Hollywood Mystery: Woes at Orion Stayed Invisible for Years," *Wall Street Journal*, October 16.

McGrath, C. (2003). "Law & Order & Law & Order . . .," *New York Times*, September 21.

Meyer, M., and Viera, J. D., eds. (1984). *1984 Entertainment, Publishing and the Arts Handbook*. New York: Clark Boardman.

Morgenstern, S., ed. (1979). *Inside the TV Business*. New York: Sterling.

Pope, K. (1999). "A Profligate Producer Helps Hallmark Corner TV-Miniseries Market," *Wall Street Journal*, May 21.

Price Waterhouse & Co. (1974). *Accounting for the Motion Picture Industry*. New York: Price Waterhouse.

Rose, F. (1995). *The Agency: The William Morris Agency and the Hidden History of Show Business*. New York: HarperBusiness.

   (1991). "The Case of the Ankling Agents," *Premiere*, 4(12)(August).

Sabin, R. (2000). "The Movies' Digital Future Is in Sight and It Works," *New York Times*, November 26.

Sansweet, S. J. (1983). "Even with a Hit Film, a Share of the Profits May Be Nothing at All," *Wall Street Journal*, July 21.

Scholl, J. (1986). "Bad Show: Picture Dims for Syndicators of TV Programs," *Barron's*, December 15.

Schuyten, P. (1976). "How MCA Rediscovered Movieland's Golden Lode," *Fortune*, XCIV (5)(November).

Sherman, S. P. (1985). "Hollywood's Foxiest Financier," *Fortune*, 111(1)(January 7).

Sterngold, J. (1999). "A Preview of Coming Attractions: Digital Projectors Could Bring Drastic Changes to Movie Industry," *New York Times*, February 22.

Stevens, A. (1993). "Court Allows Movie Industry Big Tax Benefit," *Wall Street Journal*, July 20.

Turner, R. (1989). "For TV Comedy Writers, the Money Grows Serious," *Wall Street Journal*, August 2.

Turner, R., and King, T. R. (1994). "Movie Makers Find That Rights to Films Overseas Often Pay Off," *Wall Street Journal*, November 22.

# 6
# Music

*Life in the fast lane's no fun if you're running out of gas.*

That is exactly what people in the music business discovered toward the end of the 1970s, when after three uninterrupted decades of expansion, recorded-music sales stopped growing. A new spurt of growth starting in the mid-1980s then carried through to the late 1990s, when the industry peaked with aggregate worldwide revenues of some $40 billion per year.[1] Since then, problems have abounded.

Still, however, music is the most easily personalized and accessible form of entertainment and it readily pervades virtually every culture and every level of society. As such, it may be considered as the most fundamental of all the entertainment businesses.

## 6.1 Feeling groovy

Experimentation with reproduction of moving images can be traced back to the early 1800s. But there was apparently little interest in the mechanical reproduction of sound until the venerable Thomas Edison in 1877 developed yet another of his novelty items – a tinfoil-wrapped cylinder that was rotated with a handle. While he cranked the handle and recited the nursery rhyme

"Mary Had a Little Lamb" into a recording horn, Edison's voice vibrated a diaphragm to which a metal stylus was attached. The stylus then cut grooves on the surface of the tinfoil and – voilà! When the procedure was reversed, the stylus caused the diaphragm to vibrate and the amplified recorded sounds to emanate.

Although early investors indeed tried to popularize the invention through demonstrations in concert halls, country fairs, and vaudeville theaters, the scratchy sound and limited number of times the foil could be used before it deteriorated discouraged enthusiasm for Edison's "phonograph." So it was not until other inventors (including Alexander Graham Bell) got into the act and improved the original phonograph by using a wax-coated cardboard tube over the cylinder, and until electric power was added, that the popularly called "talking machine" (and also forerunner of the jukebox) finally caught on.

At that stage, people would actually go to a parlor and pay a nickel to listen to these wax cylinders reproduce songs and comic monologues. And ludicrous as it now seems, "a brass band recording a two-minute march had to play that march over and over again, perfectly, to turn out hundreds of recordings."[2]

Already by the 1890s, though, home phonographs had begun to appear. By then, a German immigrant, Emile Berliner, had developed a prototype that cut recording grooves onto discs – a modification that within ten years led to the introduction of the gramophone or the "Victrola" by the Victor Talking Machine Company.

Technological development, this time of radio and of an electrical recording process, then led to further sound reproduction improvements and also to conflicts among competing interest groups. Composers encountered tremendous resistance when they tried to collect royalties for performances of their music. Radio station owners meanwhile insisted that once they had bought a recording, it was theirs to use without any further financial obligation to composers.[3] Indeed, throughout the 1920s, but especially in the early half of that decade, it was radio, not phonograph equipment, that experienced the greatest rise in demand.

The Great Depression triggered a collapse of record sales – from $75 million in 1929 to only $5 million in 1933 – and it was not until the late 1930s that recovery became evident. Recovery was, however, hindered by World War II and by a protracted musicians' union strike that prevented the manufacture of new records for over a year.[4] By 1945, industry sales were thus still only $109 million.

Postwar development of tape recordings, which replaced inefficient wax-blank masters, and introduction of the 12-inch long-playing (LP) vinyl record by Columbia Records in 1948 then initiated a tremendous wave of growth. But the new LPs, played at 33 1/3 revolutions per minute (rpm), could hold only 23 minutes of music per side and did not clearly win out over older 45 rpm and 78 rpm configurations until the late 1950s – when industry sales first exceeded $500 million. The 1950s were also a time of innovation. New low-cost recording equipment made it possible for many small independent companies to spring up in competition with RCA, Columbia, and Decca – the long-established majors of the time.[5] The independents were the catalysts in bringing traditional jazz, southern rhythm and blues, and gospel-based music styles into the American mainstream.

It was not until the mid- to late 1960s, however, that the business soared. Universal introduction of truer-to-life hi-fi stereo sound recordings came at a time when the postwar baby boomers, then teenagers with lots of money to spend, were becoming ever more attracted to the expanding rock 'n' roll genre. The sixties were also a time in which the record business, paralleling the development of the film business some 30 years earlier, consolidated distribution (and the ownership of "independent" labels) into the hands of a few corporate giants that included RCA, CBS, Warner Communications, and PolyGram. This high-growth phase lasted through the 1970s and was given a powerful boost by the introduction of the standardized portable cassette configuration. By the late 1970s, industry sales at retail list prices hovered at the $4 billion level.

Yet not all was well with the industry as it entered the 1980s in the fast lane and then promptly ran out of gas. A somewhat older population base with a diminished interest in the new recordings of the time, coupled with poor quality control of vinyl pressings, contributed to a noticeable decline in demand that was not to be reversed until the arrival of the compact (4.7-inch) disc (CD) configuration in 1983. Such digitally (computer) encoded and optically (laser beam) decoded discs provided consumers with distortion-free sound reproduction and with good reasons to again buy music. By the early 1990s, CDs had become predominant and vinyl nearly extinct, while U.S. industry sales soared to $7 billion.

An important peak in both domestic and worldwide sales was, however, reached in the late 1990s as access to low-cost computers, widely available access to Internet connections, and introduction of file-swapping software enabled music to be readily copied at little or no cost to the consumer. The resulting global "piracy" problem was then only worsened by the stubborn state of denial and delusion that, at the time, characterized the industry's response and eventually led to the alienation of the most avid music fans as well as many of the most prominent recording artists. In the five years ending in 2004, industry sales (both domestic and global) had plunged by about one-third.

Although CDs, in standardized versions for use in audio, video, and personal computer applications, continue to be the primary physical configuration, they are being gradually supplanted by more advanced DVD (digital video disc) formats and by portable digital storage devices, most importantly iPods and cellphones (that have become important outlets for music videos and ringtones).[6] Key events in the history of the music business, of which recordings are only a part, are displayed in Figure 6.1.

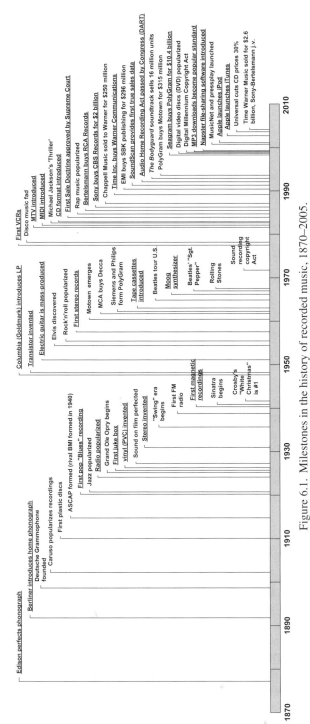

Figure 6.1. Milestones in the history of recorded music, 1870–2005.

From this it may be inferred that the industry has gone through three broad and somewhat overlapping business-model phase transitions that are characterized by the ways in which music is performed, stored, and distributed. In the wax cylinder days, the business model was that of a *performance* service. The model then changed into a *product* service in which the sound-carrier formats ranged from singles and album compilations on vinyl to cassette tapes and then CDs. This product service phase required extensive physical and marketing presence through retail stores and distribution centers (including mail order). Now, in the age of wireless Internet and cellphones and everything digital, we are well into the *service* distribution phase in which music is totally portable and available everywhere at any time via ubiquitous music service providers.

Of the industry's four major revenue streams, proceeds from physical recordings, historically the largest category, are thus beginning to be overshadowed by those generated from provision of services such as ringtones and monthly download subscriptions. Publishing meanwhile remains the most consistently stable and live performances the smallest of the main revenue sources.

## 6.2 Size and structure

Economic interplay

*The American scene*  The United States has long accounted for a major portion of the world's recorded music business, both as a place of origination of new music trends and as a consumer of music products. Furthermore, despite rapid growth of consumption in the rest of the world, and in developing countries in particular, the United States still absorbs (in dollar terms) about 30% of all the recorded music produced. Moreover, the structure of the business everywhere largely follows that which has been developed in North America and which is illustrated in Figure 6.2. This historical structure and now rapidly changing business model approach has evolved as a result of the need to efficiently compensate authors, composers, publishers, and performing artists for their work in creating the final product – be it a jingle, song, album, or opera.

If we first look at the market in the United States, we see from Figure 6.3 that the demand for recorded music has tended to fluctuate cyclically and with some sensitivity to general economic trends. Although annual growth in unit terms has averaged about 0.4% (and in dollar terms 4.3%) over the 25 years beginning in 1980, growth in recessionary periods has been notably below trend. And consumer spending on music typically appears to peak at or just after a peak of economic activity and to trough a few months after the overall economy does. Also, the secular influence of new sound-carrier format introductions such as cassettes in 1973 and compact discs in 1983 can be clearly seen.

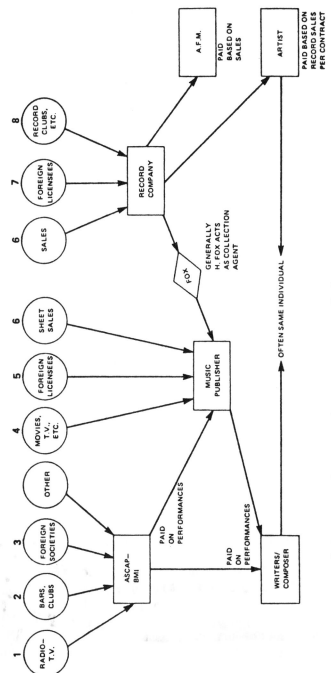

Figure 6.2. Music income flow in the entertainment field. *Source:* Arthur Young & Co. (prepared by E. Cook).

1. Paid on contractual amount based on percentages.
2. Paid on contractual amount based on usage, etc.
3. Paid on usage of songs.
4. Paid on negotiated amount per use.
5. Paid on contractual amount per use.
6. Based on sales of actual units.
7. Based on percentage of sales of product.
8. Based on percentage of sales of product.

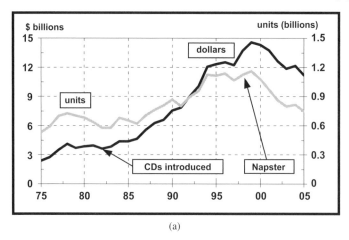

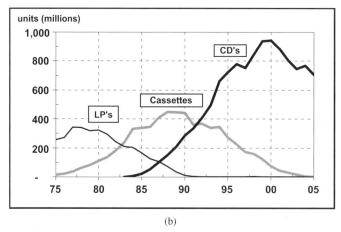

Figure 6.3. Trends in the American recorded music market, 1975–2005. (a) Recorded music physical shipments in dollars and units (billions). (b) Unit sales by configuration. *Source*: Recording Industry Association of America (RIAA).

The experience in the United States and Canada since World War II suggests that development of a strong and rapidly growing market for recorded music requires the conjunction of several elements. First and foremost is an expanding teenage/young adult population within a thriving middle class. Then it is essential that there be national advertising media in which large and cost-efficient marketing campaigns can be placed. Retail outlets ought to be plentiful and well stocked. And it also helps to have steady price and performance improvements in audio hardware and recording technologies.

All these elements were present in the postwar period in North America and, not surprisingly, the recorded music business grew from $100 million to almost $6 billion in domestic (U.S.) retail sales in the span of 40 years. Because many of the same factors were present in other developed countries, sales of recorded music outside the United States have grown similarly.[7]

But changes in the system of distributing music products also had an important effect on the industry's sales. Until the late 1970s, records were essentially distributed on consignment: Unsold units were returnable for full (or nearly full) credit against new albums. This meant that many stores could be opened on shoestring capitalizations and could pay their bills with "plastic" (i.e., returned records) instead of cash. Ultimately, however, as unit demand growth slowed and the major distributors sharply curtailed their returns policies, retailers were for the first time faced with a significant inventory risk. Retailers accordingly became much more cautious and selective in their purchases. And that, in turn, made manufacturers and distributors less willing to risk large sums on unproven new artists.

In addition, success up to the mid-1970s led to excess, as budgets and costs spiraled out of control, mostly in the areas of artists' royalty guarantees and marketing. Even the largest companies subsequently found that their stars could not consistently assure the ever-increasing "megaton" record shipments needed to underwrite large royalty advances.

Fortunately, by 1983, the advance of technology once again – as it had so often before – bailed the industry out of its funk. The catalyst this time was the development of low-cost, high-speed microprocessor and memory devices: In brief, the era of cheap computing power had arrived. And with this power came the ability to digitize sound, that is, to reduce sound to equivalent numerical data through frequent sampling and processing. As a result, undesired noises could be eliminated and a marked improvement in sound fidelity could be brought to the mass market in the form of inexpensively manufactured compact discs. Introduction of music synthesizers, computers capable of producing and mixing sounds in a manner not possible with traditional instruments, also followed quickly.[8]

The emergence of MTV, the new rock-music cable channel started in 1981, was significant as well in reversing the early 1980s downturn in demand for recorded music. By 1984, MTV had gained wide distribution and influence as both a promotional platform for record labels and as a distinctive programming service.[9]

*The global scene* As nations emerge from under repressive or dysfunctional economic structures and then see discretionary incomes rise rapidly, one of the first areas to benefit is music – which is relatively low in cost to enjoy, yet highly personalizable. But although demand for music products is everywhere affected by the demographic, economic, and technological factors already discussed, development of local repertoire is now another important part of the international sales and marketing mix: Recordings of artists with a global following may account for only half to two-thirds of the total.

From Figure 6.4a it can also be seen that global sales, as represented in dollar list prices at the retail level, have, since the mid-1980s, grown much

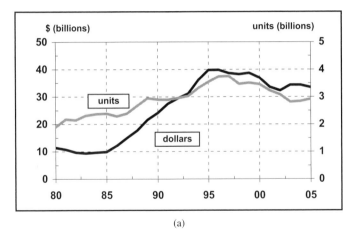

(a)

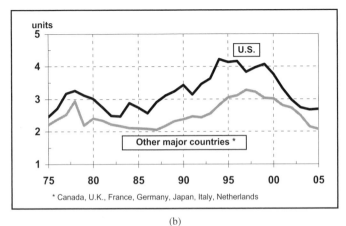

(b)

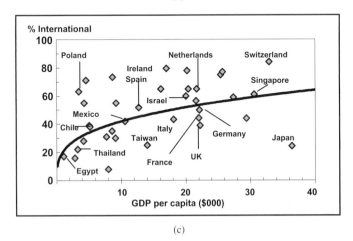

(c)

Figure 6.4. The global music market. (a) Worldwide recorded music sales in units and in retail dollars, 1980–2005 (data beginning in 2004 include digital single downloads). (b) Per capita physical unit sales in the eight largest markets, 1975–2005. (c) GDP per capita in thousands of U.S. dollars and percent of international (nonregional) sales by country. *Source data*: IFPI, MBI World Report, 1999.

faster than *unit* sales over the same span.[10] It would thus seem that price increases related to the migration of consumers toward higher-priced (but better-quality) sound-carrier formats were what actually boosted total sales growth.

However, per capita unit demand in the seven largest markets outside the United States (Figure 6.4b) has not changed much, probably as a consequence of the relatively older population skews in those countries. Figure 6.4c also suggests that, although rising Gross Domestic Product (GDP) per capita is positively correlated to a country's percentage of international music purchases, factors such as language and culture, median age of population, and relative creative strength of the local industry also play a role. Japan, for example, has a high GDP per capita but a relatively low percentage of international music purchases as a percent of the total.

Composing, publishing, and managing

The process of creating a musical property and of then exploiting it is in many ways similar to property development and exploitation in movies. In both areas, relative bargaining power is a key element. An important difference, however, is that in music an enterprise can be launched with fewer people and with far smaller commitments of capital.

A new composer has several avenues through which work may begin to generate revenues, but the first step is usually publication. The composer can attempt to interest an existing publisher or can establish a new publishing firm. In any case, the normal arrangement is for publisher and composer to share evenly any income from their joint venture.

The publisher's role is to monitor, promote, and generate revenues from use of music in everything from sheet-music sales ("paper" houses specialize in this) to live performances and recordings to digital downloads and ringtones. At each step, royalty income, which may have to be further shared by subpublishers and coauthors, is derived. For a new artist or composer, contract terms are fairly well standardized, but for a recognized talent, many complex variations depending on tax, managerial, and other considerations are negotiated. There are tens of thousands of publishers and self-publishers in the United States, but the business is dominated by the publishing affiliates (Warner/Chappell, EMI, Universal, and BMG) of the major worldwide record distributors.

The services of lawyers and accountants are required in most stages of a composer's career, but if the composer is also a performing artist, as is increasingly common, any degree of success will entail the hiring of a manager and an agent to book concerts, television appearances, and recording schedules. Managers will, in aggregate, generally take between 15% and 30% of a performer's income (with personal managers taking 15% of gross artists' earnings before deducting expenses) while talent agents extract another 10%. For a new artist or composer, the functions of manager, legal advisor, and talent agent may be handled by a single individual.[11]

Royalty streams

*Performances* If a "demo" (demonstration) record or tape has attracted a publisher's interest, the next step is to work on a full-fledged recorded performance by the composer or to attract the interest of other performers in cutting a so-called cover record of the material. Publishers and performers are always on the lookout for good, fresh material, but only a small fraction of what is offered is accepted, and only a small fraction of what is accepted for publication succeeds in the marketplace. Of hundreds of new works introduced each week, on average not more than five to ten seem to have any chance of receiving widespread recognition.

Whether the music is performed by orchestras, by college bands at football games, by radio stations, by nightclub singers, or by Muzak® speakers in elevators, it is entitled to performance royalties that are collected by two major agencies (and one smaller agency) in the United States. Of the two majors, the oldest and by far the largest in terms of billings is the American Society of Composers, Authors, and Publishers (ASCAP), but the larger as measured by number of "affiliates" is Broadcast Music Incorporated (BMI). These two agencies combined collect over 95% of all U.S. performance royalties, with the Society of European Stage Authors and Composers (SESAC) receiving the remainder. All three organizations are protectors of composers' rights.[12] Similar licensing and rights fee collection societies are GEMA in Germany and JASRAC in Japan. In satellite and Internet radio, however, royalties are collected and distributed to performer and copyright holders by SoundExchange.[13]

Because about 60% of performance royalties are derived from use in television, radio, and films, the major agencies have accordingly developed extensive computerized logging and sampling procedures to assure that composers receive proper remuneration for performances of their works anywhere in the world. To accomplish this, agencies in other countries cooperate with ASCAP, BMI, and SESAC.

The formulas used to determine royalty rates depend on the frequency of use and length of time the music is used, the estimated size of the audience, and other factors. For example, classical compositions are accorded more weight than popular jingles. Greater weighting compensates for the relatively greater expenditure of effort in classical composition and for the probable smaller size of audience and lesser frequency of play.

However, the sizes of royalties and the ways in which licenses should be granted to television and radio stations (i.e., blanket versus specific performances) have often been subject to proposed legislative changes.[14]

*Mechanical royalties* Under so-called compulsory licenses, mechanical royalties (named for sounds that were mechanically reproduced at the time of the 1909 copyright law and up until the early 1940s) are derived from sales of recordings and from publication in sheet-music form (normally at a rate between 3% and 10% of retail price per copy in the United States). Of the two sources, recordings are far more important and, as of 2007, the statutory rate (i.e., the rate set by the Copyright Statute) for each recorded copy of a song was raised to the larger of 9.1 cents or 1.75 cents per minute of playing time or fraction thereof, whichever is greater. Outside the United States, however, royalties are instead taken as a percentage of an album's wholesale published price to dealers (PPD), which means that the rate has no relationship to the length of composition or to the number of songs per album.

Mechanicals were introduced early as statutory royalties on piano player rolls that "mechanically" reproduced music. To keep pace with changing marketplace conditions, however, they are now subject to upward revision over time and are either negotiated by the interested parties or go to arbitration by the Copyright Arbitration Royalty Panel (CARP).[15] Publishers generally split such royalties 50:50 with new writers and 25:75 (or 20:80) with more established composers. These royalties, which typically account for around 45% to 55% of all publishing revenues, are taken after deduction of a 4 1/2% collection charge (on gross amounts collected) by the Harry Fox Agency in the United States or a 5% charge by the Canadian Mechanical Rights Reproduction Agency (CMRRA) in Canada.

*Synchronization fees* In addition to paying a performance fee, anyone using music in films requires a synchronization license, which is a license to use music that is timed to the display of visual images. The various parties individually negotiate these royalties, which are normally based on established standards for music length, potential audience, and frequency of use. In radio commercials, similar user fees are gathered from the granting of transcription licenses.

Publishers' synchronization and mechanical fees usually are collected from film and record companies by the Harry Fox Agency, a wholly owned subsidiary of the National Music Publishers Association, or one of its smaller competitors, such as AMRA, the American Mechanical Rights Agency. These agencies license copyrights for commercial recordings, music used in television and movie productions and commercials, and background music used in public places. These agencies also audit the books of record companies. The commission charged to affiliated publishers and writers is 4.5% of the royalty money collected.

*Copyright* The aforementioned royalty streams, including license fees from jukebox and other uses (e.g., wired music services such as Muzak®), were adjusted by Congress in a 1976 revision of the original, but technologically outdated, 1909 copyright law. The 1976 law grants copyright owners of a musical composition the exclusive right to be the first to record and distribute (or to assign to someone else) recordings embodying that composition.[16]

The Copyright Arbitration Royalty Panel meets to arbitrate disputes and to make adjustments for the effects of technological developments. Predictably, many such changes will, over time, alter allocation formulas for the industry's income.[17]

Another issue of particular importance in the rental of videocassettes involves the doctrine of "first-sale" rights; rights that allow the person or company initially purchasing a product to resell or rent that product to other parties without further obligation or compensation to the original seller.[18] Because of first-sale rights, producers do not receive compensation each time a videocassette is rented; they are compensated only on the first sale to the rental stores.[19]

In all, copyrights, and the protection of intellectual properties from counterfeiting and piracy, have played an important role in the growth of the music and home video businesses. But royalty income losses from piracy remain substantial and widespread.

### Guilds and unions

The effects of labor-union contracts, primarily those of the American Federation of Television and Radio Artists (AFTRA) and the American Federation of Musicians (AFM), extend to every area of the music-making business. Singers, soloists, and choral ensembles are generally represented by AFTRA, whereas other musicians, including conductors, arrangers, copyists, and instrumentalists, are members of the AFM. The American Guild of Musical Artists (AGMA) may cover opera, ballet, and classical concert and recital performances, while other representations may be made through the Actors Equity Association or the Screen Actors Guild. The New York Dramatists Guild is a trade association representing lyricists, composers, and writers for the Broadway musical theater (see also Chapter 13).

As in any other industry, labor unions help their employed membership by bargaining for higher wages and pension benefits. But it can also be argued that, if it were not for the high production costs inherent in using union performers, there might be many more productions in which musicians could find work, albeit at lower average wages. It is not unusual for new artists and new record companies to attempt to circumvent the use of union labor, or for background-music recordings to be made in Europe, where labor costs are lower.

Both AFTRA and AFM have tried to maintain strict union shops, but right-to-work laws in various states have reduced union influence, especially in the rock, country, and rhythm and blues (R&B) segments. However, if a record master copy is transferred from a nonunion independent producer to a record company that is party to AFM agreements (which most record companies of any significance are), then union control over wages is reasserted. This control also appears in areas such as voice overdubbing, a situation in which a union contractor will charge a producer for an additional voice even though it is only electronically mixed.

Royalty artists, who are entitled to AFTRA scale plus royalties based on the number of records sold, must also conform to union-negotiated rules. For musicians who participate in making broadcast commercial spots, there are, of course, extended repetitive payments. Whenever an AFTRA member performs on tape for one medium and that tape is used in another medium, the performer receives additional payments.

Concerts and theaters

Concerts by popular performers (in which an advance against a percentage of anticipated gate receipts may be obtained) may be profitable for their organizers if they are skillfully budgeted and planned. Most of the time, however, the purpose of a concert tour (that is typically arranged for by an agent) is to provide artists' exposure that can leverage sales of records and other licensed merchandise.[20]

Even less likely to turn a profit are theater presentations on Broadway, summer musical theater, classical music concerts, and opera. In fact, it has been estimated that, on average, performing-arts organizations, including symphonies, operas, and ballet companies, earn less than 40% of their costs of operation (Baumol and Bowen 1968). Moreover, an increase in the number of performances, or in ticket and subscription prices, will not ordinarily reduce operating deficits (see Chapter 13). Instead, financial support from municipal and private sources is normally required to sustain these activities. Through creation in 1965 of the National Endowment for the Arts (NEA), Congress has also provided support by allocating federal funds to match local contributions. Some 1,500 orchestras and 600 opera companies, plus individual artists, are eligible for grants. (The NEA's legislative mandate is limited to support for individuals and organizations that are tax exempt.)

## 6.3 Making and marketing records

Deal maker's delight

*Production agreements* As seen in previous chapters, creativity is not limited to finished products; it also appears in financial and manufacturing arrangements. In fact, the scope for deal making in records as compared with movies is potentially even greater because of the relatively smaller capital commitments and fewer people involved in making a recorded-music product. Still, most record companies are highly selective in signing talent, and fancy deal making is a privilege mostly reserved for already established artists.

Whereas in the early days of the business the record companies simply signed an artist and had an in-house producer known as an artist-and-repertoire (A&R) man guide the project, today there is a tendency for artists to work with independent producers. Like record-company A&R people, these independents will help the artist select material and a music style, decide where and how the recording is to be made, and generally watch over budgets for studio recording and rehearsal times, mixing, and editing. Sometimes they also become involved with the design and artwork for CD-album liner notes.

Variations in financial arrangements usually develop as independent producers and independent "labels" (companies) work with the artist as subcontractors for the major record companies.[21] As noted by Baskerville (1982, p. 300) and Passman (2000, p. 203), deals are typically structured in one of the following ways:

1.  The label signs the artist and an in-house producer, compensated through salary plus perhaps some royalties, to handle the project.
2.  Talent is already under contract with a label and the label retains an independent producer or company to deliver a master tape. The outside producer will initially receive a production fee and also negotiate a royalty of 1% to 5% based on retail sales. The record company will normally set the budget to which the independent will adhere.
3.  Independent artists and producers make a master tape and then try to sell the master to a label. If the master is accepted, the label compensates the artist-producer team through royalties perhaps earned against an advance.
4.  A label may form a joint venture with an independent producer or artist. Royalties will then be shared in proportion to the size of financial commitments.
5.  An artist may form a production company to make and deliver a master tape to a label. A freelance producer may then be hired by the artist's production company.
6.  An artist may be employed by a corporation (his/her own) that then sells (i.e., loans out) the artist's services (through a "loan-out" corporation) to a label in return for royalty considerations.
7.  An artist may have a self-owned recording and producing company that makes a pressing and distribution agreement (P&D deal) wherein a large record company handles manufacturing and wholesale distribution (for a fee of around 20%). This is analogous to the "rent-a-studio" distribution deals seen in films.

Within the context of these variations, many "independent" labels emerge. But few are truly independent because the initial financing, manufacturing, and distribution of the final product are much more efficiently handled by large record companies that are able to diversify their risks over many different labels while enjoying many other economies of scale.[22]

Independent labels and producers may also negotiate adjustments when, as is often the case, a given individual functions in several different capacities. The producer may be trained in both music and audio engineering; the performing artist may be a coproducer and fund-raiser. In the end, however, whether the producer or artist receives the most compensation depends on relative bargaining strengths. Important producers may receive several percentage "points" from the label in addition to production fees often between $25,000 and $150,000 (half paid on signing) that are nonrecoupable against royalties. In total, this may be more than what the artist receives.

*Talent deals* Talent royalty rates depend on the degree to which the artist is in demand. Major artists often can command over 15% of retail price, which would amount to well over $1 per album, but minor players will be signed at a rate of 10% or less of retail. A sliding scale may be used whereby the first 100,000 units sold are at 9% and for every 100,000 units thereafter, the royalty rate is scaled upward by one or two percentage points. In most cases, record companies will estimate the artist's annual royalties and then advance about one-half that amount. For *all-in* deals, the artist is also responsible for paying the producer (perhaps 3% of retail) out of the artist's share of royalties. An artist entitled to a royalty of 15% of the suggested retail list price "all-in" might thus have to share at least one-fifth of such income with the producer, who is the functional equivalent of a director and producer in the movie industry. Moreover, unlike artists, producers are paid for all records sold, and recording costs are not against producer royalties.

An important reason for the decline in record-industry profitability during the late 1970s was excessive royalty bidding by major companies for popular artists whose contracts were up for renegotiation. Significant losses ensued when large royalty advances were not covered by subsequent album sales. Hence, to partially protect themselves from such potential losses, companies may sign an artist to deliver several albums over a certain period of time and then, as in films, partially cross-collateralize royalty advances over those albums.

Production costs

Once the deal-making phase is completed, musicians and producers begin a long process that leads to delivery of a completed master. Decisions concerning the time and place of recording and the numbers of backup singers and musicians must be made. Rehearsals must be scheduled.

Production costs for popular albums are generally budgeted for at least $200,000, and, if much studio time is used, costs can soar well past $350,000. As production costs rise, it naturally becomes progressively more difficult for the record company to make a profit from the album (no matter what the sound-carrier medium).

Having delivered a master tape mixed down to two-channel stereo and formatted for an album, the producer will then typically be paid the remaining half of the production fee or an advance on royalties. But for the record company, other expenses are just beginning: A marketing campaign must be planned, album cover artwork must be commissioned, and a timetable for production and distribution – be it either downloaded or shipped physical product – must be established.[23]

Marketing costs

Marketing campaigns for albums may frequently involve concert tours, cooperative advertising with local retailers, in-store merchandising aids (e.g., displays, posters, and T-shirts), radio and television commercials, and "promo" press kits. Also, free records may be sent to hundreds of radio stations. But none of this comes cheap: Marketing costs can often reach $100,000 for a fairly standard release and in excess of $500,000 for one by a major artist.

Promotional efforts are generally aimed at the most influential reporting stations, that is, some 200 to 300 stations monitored by tip sheets and trade papers such as *Billboard* and *Radio & Records*. And indirect spending for promotional purposes also used to include significant sums for bribery of station managers and program directors until such "payola" was publicized and then outlawed in the 1960s. Nowadays, any station of importance is careful to set policies limiting the size and frequency of gifts or favors that employees are allowed to accept. Nevertheless, as documented by Dannen (1990), in the 1980s, payola again tainted the industry – this time through the hiring of independent promoters, who remain important middlemen in the selection of music for radio airplay through legal payments to stations.[24]

Record companies will also have their own staffs of "trackers," whose job it is to aid in promotional efforts by knowing which songs and albums radio stations around the country are adding to or deleting from their play lists. With popular-music stations able to add at most three or four new cuts per week to their lists, competition for airplay is intense: Every year an estimated 11,000 (nonclassical) major-label albums averaging some ten cuts per album are released, but it is now unusual for more than around 120 of these to sell more than 500,000 units in physical (i.e., CD) format.

Consequently, perhaps as little as 10% of new material must make a profit large enough to offset losses on the majority of releases – a situation that is even worse than in films, where, on average, 70% of projects are losers. Labels will encourage production of much more material than can possibly succeed, in essence diversifying their portfolio of bets on new releases. This is done because upfront investments are at this stage relatively small as compared with later costs of promotion and distribution, a hit can come unexpectedly, and the most popular recordings – especially those by newly trendy artists starting at relatively low royalty bases – are immensely profitable. Again, as in other entertainment industry segments, a small part of the product line will generate a large part of the profits.[25]

Distribution and pricing

*Distribution* With the rate of project failure so high, and with all but the most successful recorded music products having a relatively short life cycle, lasting at most a few months, there is no room for distribution inefficiency: It is essential that retailers located over a wide geographic swath have their inventories of hits quickly replenished. Most records are thus distributed by large organizations with sufficient capital to stock and ship hundreds of thousands of units on a moment's notice. In the United States (and globally), the industry has consolidated into four major companies: Universal Music Group (UMG), Sony/BMG, Warner Music Group (WMG), and EMI.

Two major record distributors in the United States have long been Warner Music Group, the former distribution arm for the Time Warner Inc. labels (including Warner Bros., Elektra, Atlantic, Asylum, Nonesuch, Reprise, Giant, Sire), and Sony (including the Columbia, Epic, and Masterworks labels, which were bought from CBS by the Sony Corporation of Japan in 1987).[26] These companies have together often handled up to half the albums sold in North America and about 35% of the total elsewhere.

Subsequent to the combination of BMG with Sony through a 50/50 joint venture in 2004, however, the total share for Sony-BMG has now grown to approximately the same size (around 28%) as that of Universal Music Group, which was acquired by French-owned Vivendi (via takeover of Seagram) in 2000. UMG labels include, from the PolyGram side (acquired by Seagram in 1998), Deutsche Grammophone, Mercury/Island, Polydor, London, A&M, Def Jam, and Motown, and also, from the predecessor companies, MCA and Geffen. The other major distributor is the British EMI Group (CEMA), whose labels include Capitol, Angel, EMI, Chrysalis, Virgin, Manhattan, and Blue Note. For the most part, the market shares of these major distributors tend to be fairly stable over long periods.[27]

Success in distribution depends on the size of capital commitment and on the ability to quickly sense where and how well new music is selling. To this end, distributors employ large staffs of sales and promotion people and rely extensively on outside intelligence-gathering sources. Although this structure works well in large regions, it is not nearly as efficient in servicing smaller stores and out-of-the-way territories. Thus, there exists a second tier of smaller independent distributors, known as *one-stops*, who handle all labels, including those of the majors. One-stops evolved in the 1940s to accommodate the needs of jukebox operators; today they also work with orders from small stores and from Internet-based promotional and marketing sites.

Another formerly significant distribution channel for records and CDs had been through clubs and *rack jobbers*. Columbia House, originally part of CBS Records and the largest club in the United States, was combined in 2005 with BMG, the second largest. Clubs now account for under 5% of total dollar volume but had been above 10% as recently as 1997. However, unlike retailers, such clubs do not buy product directly from labels but instead license it.[28]

Rack jobbers have also substantially contributed to the growth of the music business since 1950 and, more recently, to the growth of the home video industry.[29] "Racks" may operate record departments in space leased from department stores. Or, for maintaining inventories and promotion displays in record departments owned and operated by other parties, they may earn fees based on a percentage of sales. Agreements with rack jobbers can take many different forms and may include such diverse retailing environments as drugstores and supermarkets. But the main attraction is always that the jobber can obtain quantity discounts and provide expertise in the rapid selection, display, and maintenance of inventories (i.e., warehousing) of products that have a relatively short life cycle.

Rack jobbers, in effect, thus absorb the nonspecialized retailer's risk of purchasing too much of the wrong product or too little of the right product. In return, jobbers operate on the spread between large-quantity discount prices of major distributors and their own higher quasi-wholesale prices. Generally, the jobber's risk of guessing wrong on the order size for a particular item is reduced through diversification over many titles and also through some return privileges. The margin for error, though, is not large, especially when changes in musical tastes become unusually volatile.

Last in the distribution chain is the cutout wholesaler, who buys, for prices at or below cost, records that have been returned to the distributor. *Cutouts* – which appear as secondary merchandise in discount stores – are the industry's errors in judgment as to production quantity and/or quality, and they often provide real bargains for patient and knowledgeable consumers.

But because contracts are normally written in terms of royalties on the number of recordings *sold*, not the number manufactured, cutouts and over-stocks have long been an area of dispute and litigation between artists and record companies. Such excess recordings may be used in barter for other goods and services or to raise cash for the record company. Yet only major artists have the bargaining power to negotiate that excess inventory be destroyed rather than disposed as cutouts.

*Pricing* As might be expected, major-distributor pricing policies have an important effect on firms farther downstream in the distribution chain. There is, nevertheless, no easy method by which to analyze such policies because all major companies now have different scales for quantity discounts and return-privilege limits; the sizes of discounts are normally proportioned according to order quantities, which means that jobbers and one-stops operate in whole-saler price niches. From the artists' standpoint, top-line pricing is defined by contract to be of limited duration, and after the product goes into the company's catalog classification (i.e., it no longer qualifies for specific pro-motional efforts), it will then likely be sold at midline and then later still as a budget-priced album – with royalty rates also accordingly diminished.

Although wholesale pricing is relatively straightforward, in retail pricing, there is also often an interesting economic anomaly in that, to attract impulse buyers, the newest products in strongest demand may be priced lower than older items that are in lesser demand.[30]

*Internet effects* All of these traditional distribution and pricing elements are, however, in some way or another being greatly affected by the Internet, which is an ideal medium for the distribution of music. In ordering albums directly through Internet storefronts, at least one stage of product shipping and handling is eliminated and costs are accordingly lowered. But the downloading of music files from Internet sites to home computers (most likely using the MP3, i.e., MPEG-1, Layer 3 format), or the sharing of such files are further steps that eliminate the package altogether and also make it easier to obtain music without compensation to artists or labels.[31] In theory, the technology also makes it possible for an artist to circumvent a distributor, maintain control of the master recording, and capture a significant part of the distributor's margin – perhaps up to 50% of the retail price.

As these newer forms of distribution develop, the older physically packaged products will become less important, and expertise in marketing that can distinguish content and break through the clutter will become more important. Alternate pricing and releasing strategies have begun to evolve: For instance, music on such cyberlabels may be given away for free to build fan loyalty and make a profit selling related merchandise and concert tour tickets. Apple Computer's iTunes Music Store, introduced in 2003, effectively started a new sound-carrier format. Via the Net, almost all music will ultimately be available on demand anywhere and at any time.[32]

## 6.4 Financial accounting and valuation

As might be expected, the corporate financial-accounting perspective is different from that of the artist. From the corporate view, enough profit simultaneously must be generated to compensate shareholders with a competitive return on investment and also to underwrite development of as many new talents as possible. Individual artists, of course, are concerned primarily with their own financial statements.

### Artists' perspective

Among the basic issues that need to be negotiated between artists and record companies are the date of contract expiration, the number of albums committed, exclusivity, foreign-release intentions, and royalties and advances. For example, a contract may require that three master tapes be delivered within three years of signing and may further stipulate penalties to be paid if the albums are not released. Throughout, however, it is important for the artist to recognize that record companies do not actually give money to their artists:

In effect, the companies instead *loan* (i.e., advance) the money and expect that artists will pay the loans back out of royalties earned.[33]

With the possible exception of contracts in the jazz field, labels generally require their artists to provide exclusive services, which may extend to music-video performances on cassettes and discs. And artist contracts may also delineate the foreign countries or territories for which album release is planned. This can be significant in that a major portion of sales may occur outside the United States (sometimes at royalty rates 75% of the domestic rate).

Greatest attention, however, is usually focused on negotiations for performing artist royalties and advances.[34] Ten percent of suggested retail price (SRP) has historically been a normal starting point, and percentages are often scaled upward from this level in proportion to the artist's sales potential.[35] Rates for new artists signed to independent companies might range from 9% to 13% of SRP, while rates for new artists signing with a major label might be 13% to 14% and rates for superstars 18% to 20%. In classical music, though, where typical expected unit sales are much lower, royalty rates, at perhaps 7.5% to 10% of SRP, and advances are much lower than in pop music.[36]

Royalties and advances may, however, also be based on a published dealer (wholesale) price, which is actually a better benchmark given that record companies cannot set retail prices and that such "retail" (SRP) prices are largely fictional. In fact, outside the United States, the wholesale price is called Published Price to Dealers (PPD) or the Base Price to Dealers (BPD). Either way, though, using SRP or an imputed ("uplifted") multiple of PPD, payout increments are frequently contingent on attainment of a Recording Industry Association of America (RIAA)-certified sales level of gold (500,000 unit sales for albums and singles), platinum (1 million albums and singles), or diamond (10 million albums).[37] The International Federation of the Phonographic Industry (IFPI) has a similar award program in many other countries, excluding the United States.

Contract discussions may furthermore involve issues of creative control, ownership of masters, publishing-rights ownership, production-budget minimums, conditions under which a contract can be assigned to another person or company, the artist's right to audit the firm's books, and the label's minimum commitment to spend on promotion, tour support, and music videos. Charge-back items such as production expenses that the record company has the right to recoup before paying royalties beyond the negotiated advance will always have significant financial effects on the artist's compensation. Also, default and arbitration-procedure clauses are included in many contracts in case of unforeseen disagreements or problems.

Such situations will readily arise if the label and artist do not have a clear understanding of the numerous deductions that are taken after the royalty rate has been established. For example, the record company will usually specify a discounting of the sales base on which royalties are to be applied by up to 15% for free goods (i.e., for promotional copies that are given away to radio stations or that represent a quantity discount to retailers). Other discounts to royalties might include 20% for packaging (a "container" charge) on cassettes and 25% for CDs (but only 10% in vinyl), or 50% for record-club sales.[38] And clauses involving merchandising, production costs for music videos, and cross-collateralizations of one album's financial performance against another's (see Section 5.3) may further affect the royalties paid to artists. Only recently have companies, in response to criticism, begun to change contract stipulations by basing royalties on wholesale prices actually received from retailers and by eliminating archaic packaging and new media deductions.[39]

Recording agreements generally take all such factors into account by structuring themselves as funds in which a fixed amount is set aside to accommodate the estimated costs of recording and of the artist's advance (the "recoupment fund," which is also sometimes called "the aggregate sum"). Advances may, in turn, be further governed by formulas that include floor and ceiling payments contingent on performance. Funds can range from as little as a few thousand dollars for beginners to well into the millions for superstars.

Royalties are paid only on the number of units that are sold, not the total units shipped. In addition, however, as noted earlier, pop-music artist royalty rates are usually calculated as "all-in," which means that the artist is responsible for paying the record producer out of the artist's share of royalties. A typical payment out of the artist's share to a producer would be 3% or 4% of the SRP. Therefore, even if an artist were to recoup record company advances for marketing and production, he or she might still end up owing money to the producer and chasing a moving recoupment target. Unless it is specifically written into the contract, it is also possible for an album to be produced but not released (or not to even be produced). These situations usually fall under "pay or play" clauses that are similar to those used in the film business.

To recoup an advance against royalties fully and to begin to earn on incremental unit sales, artists will thus normally have to sell one album for every dollar spent on production and marketing and generate 1 million unit sales. As Dannen (1990, p. 143) suggests, recoupment terms in standard industry contracts, in fact, imply that "most of the costs of making a record are to be repaid out of the artist's royalties rather than gross receipts."[40] Given that probably fewer than 10% of artists recoup their royalty advances, a recording contract is thus essentially a loan from the label to the artist, who is expected to pay the loan back out of the royalties that are earned.[41]

How a relatively new artist with a first gold album might fare financially can be seen from the hypothetical example of Table 6.1, in which the significant leverage for sales above 500,000 units is apparent. The artist makes more on the incremental 300,000 units than on the first 500,000 units. Even so, the artist may initially receive only partial payment because the record company will hold back some funds in reserves for returns, perhaps as much as 50%, until it knows how many records have actually been sold through to

Table 6.1. *Artist's financial perspective, first cassette gold album*

| | |
|---|---|
| Cassette's SRP | $10.98 |
| Less: Packaging (20%) | 2.00 |
| | $8.98 |
| Net royalty rate to artist 16% "all-in" less 4% to producer | 12% |
| Gross royalty per unit | $1.08 |
| Number of albums | 500,000 |
| Subtotal | $538,800 |
| Royalty-bearing percentage after "free goods" deduction | 85% |
| Gross royalty | $457,980 |
| Less recording costs and advances | $250,000 |
| *Total artist's royalty with 500,000 units*[a] | $207,980 |
| Additional units | |
| Additional royalty/unit of 18% on next 300,000 units | $1.26 |
| Number of units | 300,000 |
| Royalty-bearing percentage | 85% |
| Total artist's royalty on additional 300,000 units | $321,300 |
| *Total artist's royalties with 800,000 units*[a] | $529,280 |

[a] From these amounts, half of independent promotion and of video costs would be further deducted.

consumers. The size of this holdback is determined in part by how well the artist's previous works have fared because records that do not sell-through (and thus become non–royalty earning "cutouts") are shipped back to the distributor at a charge to the artist. Once sales to the retailer are deemed to be final, the held-back monies are paid to the artist (within two years of shipments); that is, the return reserve is "liquidated." Additional deductions may further include those for independent promotions and for half of video costs.

In this example, note too that the packaging fee of 20% applies to cassettes but that the industry standard is 25% for CDs and other new technologies (even when there isn't any packaging, as in Internet downloads!). Moreover, with CDs, the royalty rate would most likely be 85% of the rate for analog cassettes. On a cents per unit basis, as Table 6.2 illustrates, the artist nevertheless comes out about the same or perhaps better because the SRP is normally three or four dollars higher for a CD than for a cassette.

In addition to artist royalties shown in Table 6.1, the income of an artist may also be greatly affected by the terms of what is known as the controlled composition clause, which governs songwriting/publishing payments to the artist. A *controlled composition* is a song that is owned, written, or otherwise controlled by the artist (and sometimes the producer, too). The clause applies a schedule for payment of mechanical royalties out of which no recoupment and no recording cost deduction is taken, but it generally places limits on the amounts that the artist will receive for each album. These limits normally

Table 6.2. *Royalties on cassettes versus CDs*

| | Cassette | | CD | |
|---|---|---|---|---|
| | % rate | $/unit | % rate | $/unit |
| SRP | | $11.98 | | $15.98 |
| – Packaging fee | 20% | 2.40 | 25% | 4.00 |
| Royalty base | | 9.58 | | 11.98 |
| Royalty | 10% | 0.96 | 8.5% | 1.02 |

begin at ten times the single song rate, which itself might begin at 75% (the "three-quarter rate") of whatever statutory rate is in effect, according to the Copyright Statute, at the time the song is recorded, mastered, or released. For example, if an album contains ten controlled songs and the statutory rate is 8 cents taken at 75%, the royalty per album would be 60 cents.

Unlike the artists' often fruitless and futile recoupment situation in regard to recording contracts, publishing deals can provide artists with significant monetary advances relatively early on. However, this is in exchange for the right of the publishing company to control 50% of the song's copyright (i.e., money that it earns). Publishers charge around 10% for administrative costs, which are also deducted before the 75% rate is applied to recoupment of the songwriter's advance.

From the preceding we can see that recording contracts are unusually complex and reflect artifacts of previous technologies that are of diminishing importance or that have already become totally irrelevant. In recognition of this, contracts are slowly beginning to change to a more artist-friendly format.[42]

## Company perspective

Major record companies, in the aggregate, maintain a sophisticated, difficult-to-replicate infrastructure that provides relatively efficient financing, marketing, artist development, and distribution services. In return for providing such services, the companies benefit from pockets of potential profit at many different levels, including markups in the form of production fees, recoupment of recording costs (and some portion of video production costs) out of royalties, charges for equipment rental and packaging, and interest on royalty payment holdbacks.

Given the nature of the business, the companies also face a substantial risk of capital loss because, after all, the degree and longevity of success for the artists they sign are highly uncertain and the distribution company customarily pays for an album's nonrecoupable manufacturing, promotion, marketing, and shipping costs and also finances (carries) the artist's unrecouped (and nonreturnable) advance (i.e., deficit). As previously indicated,

Table 6.3. *Unit costs to labels for direct distribution on a major-label record, circa 2004*

| | |
|---|---|
| Retailers pay distributors | $12.00 |
| Minus | |
| Distributor's (record company) fee[a] | 2.40 |
| Musicians' union (AFM) fee (approx.) | 0.08 |
| Mechanical license to songwriters | 0.60 (3/4 rate) |
| Artist's royalty | 0.83 |
| Producer's royalty | 0.27 |
| Free goods | 1.80 |
| Duplication/packaging cost | 1.00 |
| ***Gross profit to label before overhead*** | ***5.02*** |

[a] Added back to distributor revenue.
*Source*: Based on Avalon (2002, p. 90).

large profits from a few winners (usually fewer than 10% of all releases) must more than offset losses on the many others.[43]

The corporate financial-accounting perspective thus differs considerably from that of the artist. Table 6.3 illustrates how the numerous participants on the corporate side would divide revenues from a typical CD priced to retail in the United States for at least $16. In the example given, the major record company's distribution arm sells new releases of mainstream artists for around $12, a markup of $2.40 or 25% from the price paid to the label. But since the label is normally also wholly or partially owned by the major, this distribution markup should usually be added to the gross profit of the company when estimating the total gross profit per unit (i.e., *before* deduction of its overhead, salaries, and financing costs).

From study of publicly owned recorded-music company reports, we can see that pretax operating profits and margins for distributors of major labels have historically fluctuated unpredictably and that steady growth for even the largest organizations is far from assured. Although the basic financial operating structures are similar for all the major distributors, there are, nevertheless, differences in how interest and overhead expenses are charged to music divisions and also differences in "return reserves." Such reserves are set aside as a fixed percentage of domestic sales (with much less need for them outside the United States and Canada) and are closely related to recent experiences with records returned by retailers.

The following excerpt from the 1982 Warner Communications annual report illustrates return-reserves accounting policies:

In accordance with industry practice, certain products are sold to customers with the right to return unsold items. Revenues from these sales represent gross sales less a provision for future returns. It is general policy to value returned goods included in inventory at estimated realizable value but not in excess of cost.

As a cushion against potential product returns from retailers, it is therefore not unusual for companies to retain 30% to 50% of artists' royalties (and 50% to 75% of mechanicals) for up to two years after initial shipment to retailers. These retentions provide an important source of working capital liquidity to the companies (but are, of course, a source of friction with the artists).[44]

Industry practices in this area are delineated by Financial Accounting Standards Board (FASB) Statement 48, which specifies how an enterprise should account for sales of its products when the buyer has a right to return the (nondefective) product. The key condition that must be met for applicability of this statement is that the amount of future returns must be reasonably estimable. In the case of music products, there is generally enough volume and historical experience with which to make such estimates.

Other corporate accounting issues are largely governed by FASB Statement 50. In particular, under this statement, royalties earned by artists, as adjusted for anticipated returns, are charged to the expense of the period in which sale of the record occurs. But advance royalties paid to an artist are to be reported as assets (i.e., are capitalized) if the past performance and current popularity of that artist provide a sound basis for forecasting recoupment of the advance. Amortization of the asset would then, as in films, be related to the amount of net revenue expected to be realized over the estimated life of the recorded performance. Royalties and advances for new artists with unknown potential would thus normally be expensed in the period of payment.

In accounting for license agreements, minimum guarantees, and advance royalties, FASB Statement 50 also specifies that licensors should initially report minimum guarantees as a liability and then recognize the guarantees as revenue as the license fee is earned under the agreement.

Valuation aspects

Valuation of music company assets must always begin with an assessment of the breadth and depth of the company's catalog of past releases: A catalog in recorded music – whether it be in the form of publishing rights or of ownership of master recordings – plays a role in valuation that is analogous to that of a film library in the motion picture business. The catalog, which is often nothing more than a bundle of rights, is usually the starting point for assessment; it can often account for half of revenues and three-fourths of profits at a major label.

As in other areas, music-related assets will generally be evaluated on their ability to generate cash in future periods. A multiple of such projected cash flows (defined as operating income before amortization, interest, and taxes) is always a function of interest rate levels and the economic, political, and technological background at the time of assessment. But, of these factors, the interest rate is usually the most significant because it inversely affects the discounted present value of the future expected cash flows and also the ability of the purchaser of the asset to obtain or to service financing obligations.

This suggests that the value of music company assets can generally be found by taking the going multiple of projected cash flow as determined from recent sales of similar properties and then subtracting net debt – a formula that is identical to the one shown in Section 7.4 for evaluating broadcast properties.[45] A variation on this is found, however, in the evaluation of music publishers. Here, the key figure to which the multiple is applied is called the *net publisher's share* (NPS), which is equal to all the royalties the company takes in minus everything it must pay out to writers and artists.[46] NPS thus would be broadly defined as gross income minus deductions for administration fees (usually 10% to 20% of gross income), songwriter royalties, and other expenses, including those for preparation of lead sheets, demos, collection costs and subpublisher fees, and copyright registrations. Publishing margins are typically twice those in recording activities, and with about half of gross revenues being royalties payable to artists, some 80% of publisher costs can be classified as variable.

Other assets of value might include record masters. Yet masters having a useful commercial life of more than a year from date of indicated release are uncommon.[47]

## 6.5 Concluding remarks

The music business never stops changing. And never has this been more evident than over the last half-century. The takeovers of CBS and RCA by foreign interests have given the industry a truly global dimension, and systems of distribution and finance have essentially been consolidated into four giant companies.

But just as significantly, we have recently witnessed a time of major technological advances in the way music is produced, reproduced, packaged, and distributed. Until the computers of the 1980s, for example, sound was recorded and replayed using only embellishments of the processes discovered by Thomas Edison 100 years earlier. Now, thanks to new technology, most recently embodied in the Internet, we can be assured that the potential for creation, for enjoyment, and for use of music has never been greater.[48]

## Notes

**1.** According to the International Federation of the Phonogram Industry (IFPI), an international industry trade organization, direct world sales of CDs, records, and cassettes were approximately $33 billion in 2005. See Figure 6.4.
**2.** As noted by Eliot (1989, p. 15). For a detailed history of recorded sound, also see Gelatt (1977), Read and Welch (1976), Welch and Burt (1994), and White (1988).

**3.** It was not until 1941 that the originally formed ASCAP (American Society of Composers, Authors and Publishers) settled on the same royalty formula (based on 2 3/4% of radio stations' annual advertising revenues) as had been standardized by BMI (Broadcast Music Inc.), the organization that had been formed in 1939 to compete with ASCAP.

**4.** The musicians' union (American Federation of Musicians) sought compensation from the record companies for income lost as demand for live performances declined as a result of the increasing use of recorded performances.

**5.** New majors of the latter half of the 1950s included Capitol, MGM, and Mercury, for a total of six dominant companies in all.

**6.** Crockett (2005) reviews how the mobile phone, through ringtone sales and instant downloads, has begun to supplant and/or compete with Apple Computer's iPod, which ushered in the modern portable music era. Since its introduction in 2001 (October 23) and through 2006, more than 45 million units have been sold, and in the first three years since the introduction of the iTunes online Music Store in 2003 (April 28), more than 1 billion songs have been downloaded. The iPod video was launched in October 2005, and within six months, 15 million videos had been downloaded.

In 1999, DVD for audio purposes was introduced in two versions – Super Audio (SACD) and DVD audio. These were then followed a few years later by DualDisc and DVD album formats, of which none ever became widely used. See also Brinkley (1999), Rothman (2003), Belson (2003), and Smith (2006).

**7.** In the United States, unit shipments of albums increased at a compound annual rate of 3.9% between 1971 and 1980 (Table S6.1). But the combination of economic recession, higher prices, more off-the-air taping, and other factors caused shipments in the 1980s to decline. Over this period, however, the prerecorded-cassette format gained steadily against the vinyl disc and eight-track and open-reel tape configurations, and by 1984, cassettes accounted for over half of total album units. Moreover, according to surveys, the largest groups of record buyers in the 1980s were not teenagers but young adults. Teens of the 1950s and 1960s thus apparently carried an interest in music well into their twenties and thirties, thereby broadening the market's demographic boundaries. In addition, there was a substantial increase in the number of new households as the relatively large post–World War II population cohorts matured. And major improvements in semiconductor technology had, by this time, also brought down the prices of stereo components for home and car. Accordingly, the emergence of FM stereo radio as the popular music medium of choice was of considerable importance.

Note, too, that because of the much higher costs of petroleum-based products such as vinyl, record prices in the late 1970s were sharply increased, while the quality of vinyl pressings decreased. Indeed, for a while it was not uncommon for consumers with top-of-the-line stereo receivers located in strong-signal areas to make off-the-air recordings whose quality matched or surpassed that of some store-bought records.

**8.** After the 1982 introduction of a so-called musical-instrument digital interface (MIDI) that converts musical control information into a uniform computer code, the productivity of recording studios, musicians, and composers increased substantially. MIDI standardization was introduced through the efforts of Yamaha Corp., Kawai Instrument Manufacturing Co., Roland Corp., and Sequential Circuits Inc.

**9.** Music Television (MTV) is a 24-hour network that bases its programming on a mixture of music videos, music news, and specials. Owned by Viacom Inc., MTV now attracts a global audience measured in the hundreds of millions. MTV's development was also accompanied in the early 1980s by introduction of low-cost videocassette machines, which enabled a whole subindustry of music video recordings to spring up. MTV also ignited

interest in cable subscriptions, changed the way in which records are promoted, and practically defined a generation of young people. MTV's history is discussed in Banks (1996).
**10.**   Better reporting of data, as well as more stringent policies against bootleggers, may
also account for the apparently higher growth rates of demand reported in the less-developed
countries.
**11.**   The role of managers is comprehensively covered in Frascogna and Hetherington
(1978) and in Passman (2000, pp. 49–50). The personal manager's role will usually be
to decide which record companies to sign, to select producers, to coordinate publicity,
and to assemble lawyers and business managers. The length of the manager's contract is
now generally geared to the term of an album cycle (production through touring), and
compensation relates to number of albums sold rather than dollars of gross generated.
**12.**   In Spain and Latin America, the Sociedad General de Autores y Editores (SGAE)
handles rights collections and payments.
**13.**   SoundExchange, founded in 2000 as part of the Recording Industry Association of
America (RIAA), is a nonprofit agency in Washington that is authorized by the United
States Copyright Office to collect royalties from digital broadcasters (e.g., XM and Sirius
in radio) and pay them directly to performing artists and copyright holders of the recording,
usually a record label. As noted in Sisario (2004), this is a new category of payment in that
artists in the United States, unlike those in Europe and elsewhere, have never before received
performing rights royalties. Royalties from terrestrial radio have normally paid royalties
only to song publishers and composers, not performers or owners of the recording. The
Digital Performance Right in Sound Recordings Act of 1995 and the Digital Millennium
Copyright Act of 1998 established this special royalty apart from those paid to publishers
and songwriters. The Library of Congress sets the rate (7 cents per 100 listeners as of 2005),
with 50% of the royalty going to the recording's copyright holder, 45% to the "featured"
performer(s), and 5% to backups.
**14.**   Disputes in this area have mostly concerned music rights in syndicated television
programming and commercials. Stations generally do not receive music rights along with
the other rights conveyed in consideration of their broadcast license fees. Instead, they
normally operate under blanket music licenses – by definition nonspecific as to the music
used in the show – for which they are charged by ASCAP and BMI about 2% of adjusted
station gross receipts, and which entitle stations to use any of the more than 5 million titles
in the ASCAP and BMI catalogs. For example, BMI has indicated (in *Broadcasting &
Cable*, October 25, 1999) that a radio station blanket license was 1.4% of revenues after
deductions. For 2005, revenues for BMI were $779 million, and for ASCAP, $749 million.
    A *blanket license*, however, is only one of four ways in which to license music for a
show: A blanket license can cover any music used in the composers' rights catalogs through
licenses issued to each composer, on a per program basis, and through the producer, who
has already obtained a license. See Boucher (1986); *Broadcasting*, February 1, 1988, p. 44;
and especially Flick (1988), who provides a cogent description of the situation, and Zollo
(1989). As described in *Broadcasting & Cable*, May 17, 1993, SESAC is now also offering
Hispanic broadcasters a niche blanket license or per program license.
    Note also that performing rights royalties are negotiated with Internet site owners. A
music robot ("bot") goes into Internet sites all over the world and brings back information
about music files on those sites. Moreover, great controversy was seen in the early 2000s
as the business of Internet radio broadcasting (i.e., "webcasting") began to grow rapidly.
The Copyright Arbitration Royalty Panel (CARP) initially proposed to set royalty rates of
0.14 cent per streamed song per listener for webcasts that aren't retransmissions of radio
broadcasts, and 0.07 cent per streamed song per listener for webcasts that are retransmissions

of radio broadcasts. Radio stations argued that they shouldn't have to pay royalties when they put their regular programming online. The ruling, as of June 20, 2002, was for the royalty rate to be set at 0.07 cent per song per listener (about $92 per listener per year) for both types of transmissions. Although radio stations already pay royalties to songwriters, as of that time no fees had been paid to labels and recording artists. However, in 1998, Congress ordered online stations to pay royalties to labels and artists for songs transmitted digitally, See Holland (2002), Angwin (2002), and the *Wall Street Journal* and *Los Angeles Times* of June 21, 2002.

**15.** The Copyright Royalty Tribunal, created by the 1976 Copyright Act, was abolished in December 1993, when its functions were transferred to the Library of Congress and the Copyright Office. After January 1988, this rate had been adjusted every two years in proportion to changes in the Consumer Price Index. See *Billboard*, October 1, 1994.

**16.** This compulsory license system, in which the copyright owners have the opportunity to be the first to record and distribute their works, is intended to provide such owners with fair remuneration while preventing the owners from retaining a monopoly over all future uses of a particular musical composition. According to the 1976 copyright law, which largely parallels those in other countries, an author retains a copyright for life plus 50 years.

A license to use a song *must* be granted by the copyright (i.e., limited duration monopoly) owner if the song is a nondramatic musical composition and has been previously recorded and distributed publicly in phonorecords with the copyright owner's permission and the requested license is for use in phonorecordings only. There is no compulsory license for songs used in home videos and movies.

**17.** The Copyright Royalty Tribunal, established in 1978 and disbanded in 1993, had also collected and distributed license fees from cable television operators. Of the pool of $161 million in 1990, 60% went to the MPAA and 24% to sports. See Carlson (1984).

**18.** As Lardner (1987) describes, legal and marketing battles fought over the introduction of home videocassette recorders were intense until the U.S. Supreme Court ruled in January 1984 that off-the-air taping of movies for noncommercial purposes is legal.

Yet the issue of home taping and the degree to which such taping harms the video and music industries is one of great importance and complexity. Of the many studies that have been conducted to determine the net effects, the most comprehensive has been the 1989 Survey of Home Taping and Copying conducted by the Office of Technology Assessment, an advisory agency to the U.S. Congress. According to the study (U.S. Congress 1989), the net effects on the entertainment industries may not be as severe as had originally been feared. Economic models that explain why some consumers copy are discussed in Johnson (1985).

Also, passage of the Audio Home Recording Act of 1992 by the U.S. Congress provided compensatory royalties to record companies, publishers, and songwriters by imposing a 2% surcharge on digital audio tape recorders (with a $1 minimum fee and an $8 cap for single recorders) and a 3% surcharge on blank digital tapes. However, no royalties will be paid for analog hardware or blank analog tapes. Royalties are paid by manufacturing companies to the Copyright Office. In the United States, unlike in other countries such as Germany, there had not until 1992 been any tax placed on blank tape or on taping machines to compensate composers and authors for purported royalty losses from home duplication of audio-visual materials created by others.

**19.** However, several pay-per-transaction schemes have been developed that would allow producers and distributors to participate directly in the revenues from each and every rental transaction. For example, Rentrak Corporation offers pay-per-transaction services. Video suppliers such as movie studios receive a cut of every rental transaction and, in return, participating stores buy tapes at very low prices, which allows them to stock more hit titles. In 1999, Rentrak's standard arrangement for new accounts was for retailers to keep 55%; vendors, 40%; and Rentrak, 5%. See also Section 4.4 and *Billboard*, July 10, 1999.

**20.** The financial dynamics of a concert tour are discussed by Kronholz (1984), Newcomb (1989), and Kafka (2003). See also *Variety*, March 22, 2004.

**21.** It is estimated that there are 1,200 record companies and over 2,600 labels in the United States. However, most of the recording activity is concentrated with the largest dozen firms.

**22.** The Alternative Distribution Alliance (ADA), owned by Warner Music, is an important one-stop distribution arm for independent labels that was formed in the mid-1990s. It charges distribution fees of as much as 25% of an album's wholesale price for the service. Other majors have similar independent label distribution arms. See Duhigg (2005).

**23.** Unlike the period of the late 1970s, the costs of raw materials for cassettes and compact disc composites, album covers, and liners and outer plastic shrink-wrapping have been relatively well contained in recent years. And with the costs of manufacturing a typical CD (or DVD) well under $1 a unit, the profitability of the CD configuration was most impressive (and is further enhanced by an artist's royalty rate, often 80% to 85% of that paid on cassettes).

Release strategies have occasionally been hampered by production or distribution bottlenecks. At CBS and Capitol Records, the major domestic pressing companies of the late 1970s, short-run demand outstripped production capacity when release of the until-then all-time best-selling (20 million plus) *Saturday Night Fever* album and the deaths of Elvis Presley and Bing Crosby occurred within an 18-month span. The industry has since experienced no significant problems in servicing demand, as can be seen when Bertelsmann's Arista label soundtrack album to the film *The Bodyguard* sold over 20 million units (and made an estimated $60 million in worldwide profits) in 1993. Michael Jackson's 45 million worldwide sales of *Thriller*, issued in 1982, is generally considered to be the global all-time top-selling album. Official selected RIAA domestic unit-sale certifications (in millions) as of 2006 from RIAA.com are as follows:

| | |
|---|---|
| Eagles, *Greatest Hits, 1971–75* (Elektra/Asylum, 1976) | 29 |
| Michael Jackson, *Thriller* (Epic, 1982) | 27 |
| Pink Floyd, *The Wall* (Capitol, 1979) | 23 |
| Led Zeppelin, *Led Zeppelin IV* (Atlantic, 1971) | 23 |
| Billy Joel, *Greatest Hits*, vol. I & vol. II (Columbia, 1985) | 21 |
| Fleetwood Mac, *Rumours* (Warner Bros., 1977) | 19 |
| The Beatles, *The Beatles* (Capitol, 1968) | 19 |
| *Bodyguard* soundtrack (Arista, 1992) | 17 |
| Boston, *Boston* (Epic, 1976) | 17 |
| Eagles, *Hotel California* (Elektra/Asylum, 1976) | 16 |

Hootie & the Blowfish's *Cracked Rear View* (Atlantic, 1994) and Alanis Morissette's *Jagged Little Pill* (Maverick/Reprise/Warner, 1995) are tied at 16 million units, with Bruce Springsteen's *Born in the U.S.A.* (Columbia, 1984) at 15 million. Until Elton John's 1997 version of *Candle in the Wind*, with sales of 33 million units, Bing Crosby's *White Christmas* of 1942 had been the best-selling single, with 30 million units sold. However, as of 2004, Elvis Presley was the best-selling solo artist in U.S. history. And the *Titanic*'s film soundtrack of 1997 was the second-largest movie-based album.

**24.** The laxity of enforcement of laws against payola and the tremendous pressures on artists and their managers to obtain broadcast exposure of their songs led the largest record distribution companies to come to depend on the services of independent promoters, some of whom had alleged ties to organized crime families. As Dannen (1990, p. 9) said, "promotion, the art and science of getting songs on the air, drove the record business. Not marketing, because no amount of advertising or even good reviews and publicity were enough to sell millions of albums. Not sales, because record stores only reacted to demand and did not create it. Even the best A & R – artist and repertoire – staff in the world couldn't save you if radio gave you the cold shoulder."

As Dannen (1990, p. 15) further notes, "For all its power, the network (of independent promoters) could not make a hit record. No one could do that except the marketplace. You could saturate the airwaves with an uncommercial song and have some moderate success, but in the end you could not force people to buy a record they did not like." This "new payola" as it has come to be known, and which involves large fees paid to promoters for getting songs added to station play lists, is also described by Goldberg (1988). Knoedelseder (1993, p. 305) indeed notes that the "payola law was poorly written, taking into account primarily money . . . [B]ut record promotion practices had become increasingly sophisticated in the years since the law was passed." ABC's *20/20* program "Pay for Play?" (May 24, 2002) showed that the independents legally pay radio stations for access, and record companies appear to have little choice except to pay these "indies." Leeds (2002), however, suggests that both record companies and stations seem to be reducing the role of independent promotion. Further reductions were forced in 2005 by the $10 million fine paid by Sony/BMG Music to settle with the New York attorney general, who alleged improper practices (i.e., bribes including cash, vacations, and gifts) to influence radio programmers. See *New York Times* and *Los Angeles Times* articles, July 26, 2005, and *Wall Street Journal*, July 25, 2005. In all, record companies follow the letter of the law, as they no longer pay stations *directly* or for specific adds. See also Blumenthal (2002) and Mathews and Ordonez (2002).

Another form of payola may also occur when stations (and sometimes also record stores) overstate a song's popularity to the chart services in return for record-company advertising. Because such overstatements are not based on actual sales but just on inflated figures put down on paper, they had been known in the industry as "paper adds" (Hull 1984). Today's computer-scanned retail sales reports make this more difficult but, as Philips (2001) notes, not impossible to do. See also Sorkin (1997).

**25.** As shown in Ordonez (2002), on the basis of Soundscan data, in 2001 major-label distributors released 6,455 new albums. Of these, 60 sold more than 1 million units, 52 sold between 500,000 and 999,000 units, 95 sold between 250,000 and 499,000 units, and 208 sold between 100,000 and 249,000 units.

**26.** The transaction is described by Boyer (1988). As with most other entertainment company assets, including film libraries and broadcast stations, music-related assets are generally evaluated on the basis of projected pretax, preinterest cash flow multiples.

Although there have been several significant corporate asset transfers in recent years, which include the sale of CBS Records to Sony, of RCA Records to Bertelsmann, and of Chappell Music Publishing to Warner Communications, financial data as to the precise cash flow multiples used in these transactions have been difficult to obtain. A rough estimate of the Sony/CBS deal is that the transfer price was probably at around nine times projected cash flow. Measuring transfer prices as a multiple of revenues provides another valuation angle. In 1992, for example, Thorn EMI paid approximately $960 million to acquire Virgin Music. This was 1.6 times Virgin's 1991 sales. By comparison, PolyGram paid about 2.1 times sales for A&M Records in 1989, and 2.3 times Motown's (prior year) sales in

1993, while MCA paid about 2.6 times sales when it bought Geffen Records in 1990. The aforementioned sale of CBS Records to Sony in 1987 was at 1.3 times sales. PolyGram was itself bought by Seagram in 1998 for $10.4 billion. See also Leeds (2005) for a review of the Warner Music IPO.

**27.** The German-owned BMG or the Bertelsmann Group (RCA, Ariola, Arista), had long been an important distributor outside the United States, hence the merger with Sony, which has a strong American presence. Kronemyer and Sidak (1986) analyzed the industry for the years 1970 to 1984 and provided the most comprehensive market share data available for that span.

As for PolyGram, it was almost merged with Warner Communications in 1984, but the Federal Trade Commission blocked the merger. At the time, PolyGram had sales of around $700 million. PolyGram, with 1989 sales of over $1.5 billion, sold 20% of its shares to the public in December 1989 and was acquired by Seagram for $10.6 billion (plus $400 million in debt) in 1998.

**28.** Clubs typically give away one album for every one sold, with the manufacturing cost in 1999 for two CDs of around $2.50. The clubs then pay (on a title priced at $16.98 retail and a 25% deductible assumed for packaging) a 9% master-use royalty, or $1.15 (split evenly with the artist) for each unit sold and nothing on the CDs given away. Mechanical royalty costs are paid on all albums, but normally at a 75% rate or about 80 cents for the sold and given-away units combined. Clubs also pay labels a trademark royalty of 35% of the master-unit royalty of $1.15, which amounts to about 40 cents only on units sold. The total product cost per unit is thus $4.85 ($2.50 + $1.15 + $0.80 + $0.40). This compares with the $10.70 unit price that retailers pay. The reduced royalty rates adversely affect compensation for artists, and some record companies no longer license their catalogs to clubs. See *Billboard*, January 30, 1999. In 2002, Columbia House was acquired for around $400 million by The Blackstone Group, a private equity firm.

**29.** In the 1970s, Pickwick International was the largest rack jobber in the United States. It was acquired by American Can Co., which in 1984 sold most of the Pickwick assets to Handleman. Handleman, long the dominant rack jobber, acquired the second-largest jobber, Lieberman Enterprises, in 1991.

**30.** Although suggested retail list prices are used to compile industry sales figures, these numbers are misleading because record stores normally do not charge suggested list. Universal Music's uneven attempt to lower wholesale prices in 2003 in response to Internet downloading is discussed in Smith (2004b).

**31.** In attempts to thwart piracy, the major distributors launched the Secure Digital Music Initiative (SDMI) in 1999. Under this plan, those who try to copy a music file must first get permission from a clearinghouse of central server computers run by the record labels or their technical affiliates. However, with such authorization, a listener might not be able to send a downloaded song from one home computer to another, even though taping for personal use is legal in the United States. Because MP3 is unrestricted and the majors appeared to have lost control over much of their catalog, there was doubt that SDMI could succeed. Indeed, as Harmon (2002c) has noted, such copy-protected discs do not play well on MP3 and portable or computer CD devices.

Napster was a software system developed in 1999 that enabled interconnected computers to search for songs on a peer-to-peer basis. Because it posed serious intellectual property rights threats to the industry, Napster subsequently faced severe legal challenges. Nevertheless, other free-music sites, such as the Fast Track network based outside the United States and programs called Morpheus, Kazaa, and Grokster, sprung up and allowed users to exchange music freely online as well as to download or transfer it to portable players. See Goodell (1999), Harmon (2000), Varian (2000), the *Wall Street Journal*, July 28, 2000, *The New York Times*, November 29, 2001, and especially Kelly (2002), who places free music in an historical and technological context. The threat is similar for movies in that so-called DeCSS (de–Content Scrambling System) software, which allows the copying of digitally encoded full-length features, is available on the Internet. However, as described in Richtel (2003), a U.S District Court eventually ruled that Grokster and Morpheus, offered by StreamCast Networks, are not guilty of copyright infringement. Economic analyses of free downloading effects are in early stages and discussed in Gross (2004).

**32.** MusicNet was formed by AOL Time Warner, Bertelsmann, and EMI and Pressplay by Universal Music Group and Sony. Both were launched in late 2001 partially in response to the threat posed by Napster. However, these systems were strongly opposed by artists because the systems provided minuscule compensation. As Strauss (2002) notes, "when their music is used in movies, in commercials and on Internet sites, artists are paid a licensing fee, which, after payments to the producer and the publisher, is split 50-50 between artist and label. Although Pressplay and MusicNet license the music, the bands are not paid a licensing fee. The labels instead pay their artists a standard royalty for each song accessed, as they would for a CD sold. This means that the artist gets on average less than 15 percent instead of 50 percent. Out of that, 35 to 45 percent is deducted for standard CD expenses like packaging and promotional copies — expenses that obviously don't exist in the online world." As reported by Mathews, Peers, and Wingfield (2002), the systems were also initially not much liked by consumers. Pressplay was acquired in 2003 by Roxio and renamed Napster after the predecessor had gone bankrupt.

By mid-2002, distributors had begun to offer songs for 99 cents (the same profit per track as on a CD) on Listen.com (later acquired by RealNetworks). Some observers suggested that the actual price might end up being 25 cents, and at that price many more songs (around 50) would have to be downloaded to reach the average profit of $5 per CD. See also Harmon (2002a and 2002b). As for Apple's iTunes, discussed in Leonard (2003), the initial price per song for largely unrestricted use was set at 99 cents, with record companies receiving around 65 cents. Wingfield and Smith (2003) doubt profitability at 99 cents given that providers pay 65 cents to 79 cents wholesale to music companies and also incur many other costs.

Hansell (2003) noted that, by 2003, the emerging economic model seemed to be settling into streaming services that rent access to large libraries for around $10 a month and download services that charge 99 cents for a downloaded song. Streaming services then pay between two-tenths of a cent and a penny to the label every time a user listens to a song. But with additional monthly guarantees to the labels, the minimum monthly cost for music licenses to offer an unlimited streaming service ends up at around $5. By comparison, Internet radio is far cheaper for the online services to offer, costing stations seven one-hundredths of a penny a song for each listener, a royalty arrangement that conforms to federal government guidelines set in 2002.

By late 2004, the music industry began experimenting with digital-only releases in which the company does not pay artists an advance or cover the cost of producing an album, which is financed by the musicians. The artists, however, retain ownership of their master recordings and are paid around 25 percent royalty on the retail price of downloads, without standard deductions for CD packaging and promotional giveaways. The license is for a limited time, with the company having the option to pick up distribution of the CD if certain unit sales targets are exceeded. The industry appears to be moving toward a model in which artists will, instead of signing long-term contracts, license individual projects to labels. With online subscription-services, consumers already lease rather than buy access to company libraries. See also Leeds (2004).

**33.** As Avalon (2002, p. 55) notes, such loans/advances are forgiven debts if a record flops. However, in return for this privilege, record companies "have the right to ask for a disproportionate split of the proceeds. For a new artist, typically the split is 12% artist, 88% record company," with the artist repaying the advance out of the 12%, which is really usually 9% after the record producer is paid (from the first record sold, and without needing to wait for recoupment).

**34.** However, songwriters have different issues from those of performing artists. Performing artist royalties may be greatly diminished if outside songwriters are used because the outsiders are not subject to what are known as *controlled composition* contract clauses. A controlled composition clause is a song written, owned, or controlled by the artist. The companies usually ask the artist to license the songs they control for 75% of the minimum statutory mechanical rate. As Naggar and Brandstetter (1997, p. 52) note, the money performers earn for *writing* songs that appear on a record is reduced if the artist performs on the record. See also Biederman and Phillips (1980).

**35.** The highest royalty rate ever paid by the industry to a single artist was apparently established by Sony in 1991, when Michael Jackson reportedly commanded 22% of retail, or $1.90 an album, on 100% of units sold. Other top acts have only been able to receive royalty rates approaching this level on a standard 85% of unit sales. See *Rolling Stone*, May 4, 1991. However, the largest advance was reportedly the $10 million per album for six albums (*if* the albums sell over 5 million units each) on the deal that Prince signed with Warner Bros. Records in 1992. By comparison, Michael Jackson and Madonna are believed to have unconditionally gotten about $5 million per album, and the Rolling Stones $8 million. Also, in 2001, Mariah Carey reportedly signed a five-album deal with Virgin Records at $23.5 million per album, and Whitney Houston signed with Arista for $100 million. Carey's new $7 million per album contract in 2002 with Universal is discussed in the *Wall Street Journal* of May 9, 2002. See also *The Hollywood Reporter*, September 4, 1992. Note that such mega-deals also often include establishment of star-affiliated labels and aspects related to movie and television production activities.

**36.** However, in contrast to pop music contracts, recording costs are not recouped against an advance, and the artist is paid on every record sold.

**37.** As the importance of singles has diminished, the RIAA has reduced the unit sales requirements for gold and platinum certification of singles by half since 1990. Also, in recognition of the importance of electronic downloads, *Billboard* and the RIAA now report digital tracks bought. The *Billboard* data include track-equivalent album (TEA) sales, using 10-track downloads as equivalent to one physical album sale. A Digital Gold award represents 100,000 downloads, and a Digital Platinum, 200,000 downloads.

**38.** Fortunately, one other complicating item, the allowance for breakage, which used to be used as a 10% of reduction of the sales base on which royalties are calculated, has mostly disappeared. This deduction was originally related to the breakage of fragile shellac records in the industry's early days.

**39.** See, for example, *Los Angeles Times*, March 20, 2003.

**40.** Similarly, Wadhams (1990, p. 109) says, "The record industry is the only one, even among the entertainment industries, in which the creative artist is ultimately charged for the entire cost of producing the work." In theory, artists should be able to trade off a lower advance for a higher royalty rate but, in practice, industry custom will normally favor higher advances and lower royalty rates.

**41.** Record companies will, in addition, typically profit from a hefty markup on actual touring and other such expenses, thereby making it difficult for artists' advances to be fully recouped and also making it advisable for artists to pay for some of these items directly: On concert tours, performers can often take home 35% of gate receipts and 50% of merchandise revenues without sharing any of it with the labels, but as noted by Leeds (2006), this may be changing. Amphitheaters normally take 65% of the gross receipts, but major acts can command much more, leaving promoters only with profits from parking and concessions. Promoters profit from the difference between production and administrative costs and the gross, taking at least the first 10%. See also Kafka (2003).

**42.** See also Philips (2002) and Holloway (2002), which describe BMG's intent to eliminate typical deductions off retail price for packaging, new technology, and free goods; increase royalty rates for digital downloads; and cut the duration of contracts in exchange for a share of artist commercial sponsorship and film-deal revenues. Companies now also appear to be more inclined to alter royalty formulas for online music by eliminating certain fees that had been fixed regardless of actual costs. Other experiments with new business models include EMI's taking a stake in almost every dollar that the band *Korn* earns worldwide over at least five years. As reported in the *Los Angeles Times* of September 12, 2005, EMI would pay the band an estimated $15 million up front in return for more than 25% of the band's publishing, merchandising, and touring revenues as well as album profits.

**43.** It would, in fact, be usual for a major-label company to do more than break even on a "gold" album selling 500,000 units (though a large cost-conscious "independent" label might be profitable after selling only 100,000 copies).

**44.** During the late 1970s, when return privileges were still almost unlimited and the rate of returns accelerated, some distributor companies found their reserves inadequate; losses, instead of profits, began to appear.

**45.** Multiples of sales over the last 20 years have averaged around 1.75 times, and multiples of EBITDA around 17.1 times, but it isn't unusual to see transactions done at multiples far above or below these means.

**46.** From the mid-1980s, the multiple of NPS rose from the area of five or six times to around ten times in the 1989 SBK/EMI deal. More recently, however, Rondor was acquired in 2000 by Vivendi Universal for approximately 20 times NPS, which was believed at the time to be at the high end of the estimated going range of 12 to 20 times. In cases in which a song still generates earnings, the amortization period for the copyright might be up to 20 years, but regular impairment reviews might require that the speed of amortization be substantially accelerated.

In many situations, song publisher catalogs seem to have been transferred at a going rate of around $1,000 per title. For example, Thorn EMI bought the rights to 90,000 titles held by independent British music publisher Filmtrax Copyright Holdings for $115 million in August 1990. Filmtrax, formed in 1984 to acquire the music assets of Columbia Pictures Entertainment, owned rights to songs such as "Stormy Weather" and "Ain't Misbehavin'." And in July 1999, EMI Group bought 40,000 song copyrights from a unit of Japan's Fuji-pacific Music Inc. for $200 million ($5,000 a title). See also Gubernick (1989a); *Variety*, August 15, 1990; and Krasilovsky and Shemel (1994, Chapter 12).

More recently, an important royalty battle between record companies and publishers has developed with regard to cellphone ringtones. As Smith (2004a) notes, on ringtones publishers typically earn 10% of the sale price or 10 cents, whichever is higher. However, recording companies want a larger royalty share by paying the same as on CDs (8.5 cents in 2004).

**47.** Shemel and Krasilovsky (1985, p. 362) note that, in terms of tax treatment, "the costs incurred in preparing master recordings, used for substantially more than one year to produce records for sale, are required to be depreciated over the period that the master recordings are utilized for that purpose."

Also, prior to the 1976 tax-code revisions, recording costs could be treated as totally current expenses deductible from current income, or they could be capitalized and subject to regular depreciation deductions. As of the 1976 revisions, however, for noncorporate producers, the costs attributable to the production of a sound recording, film, or book are deductible (on a "flow-of-income" basis) pro rata over the period in which the property generates income. This "flow of income" method of cost amortization for noncorporate producers also applies to record master costs and uses the same approach as in the film business, where estimates as to the total amount of income to be received over the economic life of the asset must also be made. But corporate producers may have the option to treat recording costs as current expenses deductible in the year incurred.

In other words, producers must capitalize costs incurred in the production of record masters and then deduct the costs over time using the income-forecast method of depreciation. However, costs incurred to produce demo records are not capitalized or recovered through depreciation deductions. Producers may instead elect to treat such demo costs as research and developmental expenses to be amortized over a period of 60 or more months. See also *Billboard*, April 9, 1994.

**48.** Although an estimated 40 million Americans play musical instruments, aggregate industry sales have not grown in real terms since the early 1970s – when unfavorable demographic, economic, and social trends first appeared. Indeed, the percentage of personal-consumption expenditures going to this segment appears to have diminished as interest in learning to play and availability of equipment and instruction in schools has declined.

According to *The Music Trades* annual survey of April 2003, musical instrument retail sales rose to $6.97 billion in 2002 as compared with $4.2 billion in 1992 and $2.2 billion in 1980. Aggregate figures, however, mask the variation in popularity of different instruments. For instance, in the 1960s and 1970s, unit shipments of guitars gained rapidly, while shipments of pianos leveled off.

Shrinking school enrollments and municipal and state funding problems had the greatest effects in retarding sales growth beginning in the 1980s. But young people's fascination with video games and computers has also diverted spending that might otherwise have been directed to this area.

## Selected additional reading

Baig, E. (1984). "The Can-Do Promotor of the Jacksons Tour," *Fortune*, 110(4) (August 20).

Brabec, J., and Brabec, T. (1994). *Music, Money, and Success*. New York: Macmillan (Schirmer).

Brinkley, J. (1997). "After 15 Years, the Music CD Faces an Upscale Competitor," *New York Times*, July 28.

Brownstein, S. (1986). "Music Videos Hit a Sour Note," *New York Times*, July 6.

Burnett, R. (1996). *The Global Jukebox: The International Music Industry*. New York and London: Routledge.

Caramanica, J. (2005). "I Screen, You Screen: The New Age of the Music Video," *New York Times*, July 31.

Cieply, M. (1986). "A Few Promotors Dominate Record Business," *Wall Street Journal*, April 18.

Clark, D., and Peers, M. (2000). "Can the Record Industry Beat Free Web Music?," *Wall Street Journal*, June 20.

Clarke, D. (1995). *The Rise and Fall of Popular Music*. New York: St. Martin's Press (London: Viking).

Cox, M. (1992). "Rock Is Slowly Fading as Tastes in Music Go Off in Many Directions," *Wall Street Journal*, August 26.

Dannen, F. (1994). "Showdown at the Hit Factory," *The New Yorker*, November 21.

Farr, J. (1991). "Turning Rock into Gold," *New York Times Magazine*, December 8.

Gottlieb, A. (1991). "The Music Business," *The Economist*, December 21.

Hamlen, W. A., Jr. (1991). "Superstardom in Popular Music: Empirical Evidence," *Review of Economics and Statistics*, 73(4) (November).

Harmon, A. (2003). "What Price Music?," *New York Times*, October 12.

Harrison, A. (2000). *Music: The Business*. London: Virgin.

Healy, J., and Leeds, J. (2004). "Online Music Alters Industry Sales Tempo," *Los Angeles Times*, April 28.

Hirschberg, L. (2002). "Building the Post-Britney," *New York Times*, August 4.

Kerr, P. (1984). "Music Video's Uncertain Payoff," *New York Times*, July 29.

Knoedelseder, W., Jr. (1985). "Cut Rate Albums Hit Sour Note," *Los Angeles Times*, May 18.

Kozinn, A. (2000). "Classical Concerts and Recordings Seek an Audience on the Web," *New York Times*, June 13.

Kupfer, A. (1991). "The Next Wave in Cassette Tapes," *Fortune*, 123(11) (June 3).

Landro, L. (1985). "Producers, Artists Push Music-Video Sales as Market for VCRs Expands and Changes," *Wall Street Journal*, March 20.

(1984). "Merger of Warner Unit, Polygram Angers Troubled Record Industry," *Wall Street Journal*, April 12.

Leland, J. (2001). "For Rock Bands, Selling Out Isn't What It Used to Be," *New York Times*, March 11.

Leonard, D. (2003). "Facing the Music," *Fortune* 147(6) (March 31).

Mann, C. A. (2003). "The Year the Music Dies," *Wired*, 11.02 (February).

Mardesich, J. (1999). "How the Internet Hits Big Music," *Fortune*, 139(9) (May 10).

Mathews, A. W. (2001). "Royalty Fight Threatens Record Industry's Plans to Deliver Songs Online," *Wall Street Journal*, May 1.

Mathews, A. W., and Ordonez, J. (2003). "Clear Channel Revamps Its Concert Strategy," *Wall Street Journal*, June 2.

Millard, A. (1995). *America on Record: A History of Recorded Sound*. New York: Cambridge University Press.

Miller, M. W. (1987). "High-Tech Alteration of Sights and Sounds Divides the Arts World," *Wall Street Journal*, September 1.

"Music Reborn," *Wired*, 14.09, September, 2006.

Newcomb, P., and Palmeri, C. (1991). "What's Not to Love?," *Forbes*, 148(7) (September 30).

O'Connor, A. (2001). "Record Labels Shed Big Name Sales Risks," *Financial Times*, December 23.

Ordonez, J. (2002). "Courting the Aging Rocker," *Wall Street Journal*, April 23.

Orwall, B. (2001). "Colombian Pop Star Taps American Taste in Repackaged Imports," *Wall Street Journal*, February 13.

Palmer, J. (1999). "Swan Song," *Barron's*, August 30.

Pareles, J. (1999). "Trying to Get in Tune with the Digital Age," *New York Times*, February 1.

Pulley, B., and Tanzer, A. (2000). "Sumner's Gemstone," *Forbes*, 165(4) (February 21).

Richtel, M. (2002). "Napster Wins One Round in Music Case," *New York Times*, February 23.

Rose, F. (1999). "Help! They Need Somebody," *Fortune*, 139(10) (May 24).

Sancton, T. (1990). "Horns of Plenty," *Time*, 136(17) (October 22).

Sanjek, R., and Sanjek, D. (1991). *American Popular Music Business in the 20th Century*. New York: Oxford University Press.

Serwer, A. (2002). "Inside the Rolling Stones Inc.," *Fortune*, 146(6) (September 30).

Sharpe, A. (1994). "Country Music Finds New Fans, and a Firm in Nashville Prospers," *Wall Street Journal*, January 19.

Starr, L., and Waterman, C. A., (2002). *From Minstrelsy to MTV*. New York: Oxford University Press.

Strauss, N. (1999). "A Chance to Break the Pop Stranglehold," *New York Times*, May 9.

Tommasini, A. (2003). "Companies in U.S. Sing Blues as Europe Reprises 50's Hits," *New York Times*, January 3.

Trachtenberg, J. A. (1995). "Clive Davis, Once Hit by Controversy, Is Back at Top of the Charts," *Wall Street Journal*, March 13.

Turner, R. (1991). "How MCA's Relations with Motown Records Went Sour So Fast," *Wall Street Journal*, September 25.

U.S. Congress, Office of Technology Assessment. (1989). *Copyright and Home Copying: Technology Challenges the Law, OTA-CIT-422*. Washington, DC: U.S. Government Printing Office.

Wade, D., and Picardie, J. (1990). *Music Man: Ahmet Ertegun, Atlantic Records, and the Triumph of Rock'n'Roll*. New York: W. W. Norton.

Weisbard, E. (2000). "Pop in the 90s: Everything for Everyone," *New York Times*, April 30.

Zaslow, J. (1985). "New Rock Economics Make It Harder to Sing Your Way to Wealth," *Wall Street Journal*, May 21.

# 7
# Broadcasting

*Programs are scheduled interruptions of marketing bulletins.*

Marketing bulletins, in fact, are the essence of commercial broadcasting in the United States.

This chapter is concerned with the economics of radio and television broadcasting, a topic closely tied to developments in the movie, recorded music, sports, and other entertainment-distribution businesses. By its end, it should be evident that maybe Marshall McLuhan (McLuhan 1964) was onto something when he said, "the medium is the message."[1]

## 7.1 Going on the air

Technology and history

Broadcasting began the twentieth century as a laboratory curiosity; it ended the century as a business generating over $50 billion per year. But monolithic the industry is not. In fact, many subsegments compete vigorously with each other.

Strictly speaking, commercial broadcasters sell time that is used for dissemination of advertising messages. In actuality, though, what is sold is access to the thoughts and emotions of people in the audience. Companies selling beer prefer to buy time on sports-events programs, whereas toy and cereal manufacturers prefer time on children's shows.

To distribute commercial messages to audiences, or conversely, to deliver audiences to advertisers, four basic broadcasting media have evolved over the past 80 years: AM (amplitude-modulation) and FM (frequency-modulation) radio and VHF (very high frequency) and UHF (ultra-high frequency) television. All these technologically defined media operate under identical macroeconomic conditions but different microeconomic conditions.

AM radio was the first broadcast medium to gain widespread popularity, attracting, in the 1920s, a national mass audience. Also, as described by Barnouw (1990), television (VHF) was well into development at that time. In fact, by the early 1930s the National Broadcasting Company (NBC) had begun transmitting experimental telecasts from the Empire State Building. However, it was not until the 1939 World's Fair that NBC began regular program service to those few receivers then in existence. And, despite great consumer interest in this new medium, receivers did not begin to appear in significant numbers of households until the early 1950s: Economic restraints and contingencies related to World War and to the Korean War, and the high initial prices of receiving equipment, bridled the industry's progress.

Neither FM radio, with its high-fidelity stereo-signal capability, nor UHF television became financially viable until the late 1960s and early 1970s. FM radio achieved this through a shift to album-oriented popular music appealing to a rapidly expanding population of teens and young adults. UHF television was helped along by the emergence of a third major network (American Broadcasting), more powerful UHF transmitters, and a congressional mandate for the manufacture of equipment with tuners able to receive UHF. Meanwhile, AM radio had by the 1970s become more a local than a national service, with local advertising aimed at narrowly defined audience segments accounting for 75% of a typical station's revenues.

Indeed, throughout the history of broadcasting, portrayed by Figure 7.1, the economic values of television and radio properties have been closely related to the technological characteristics of the means of transmission.

Consider AM radio stations. AM signals bounce off the ionosphere at nighttime and can thereby cause interference with other stations operating on the same frequency hundreds or thousands of miles away. To prevent such interference, the Federal Communications Commission (FCC) does not permit many small stations to transmit, or to transmit at full power, once the sun sets. That obviously limits audience size and reduces a station's value. However, so-called clear-channel stations are permitted to transmit at a maximum of 50,000 watts (W) and can be heard at all times of the day and night over broad regions of North America.

FM radio is, in contrast, essentially a local medium from a transmission perspective (yet is national to the extent of its reliance on syndicated programming) because signals can rarely be well received beyond a 60-mile

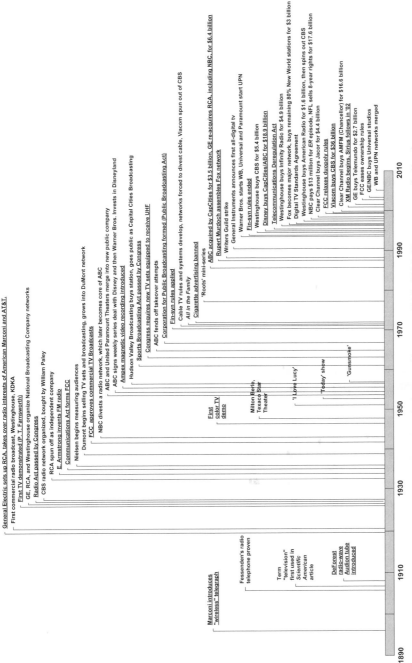

Figure 7.1.  Broadcast industry milestones, 1910–2006. Key events underlined.

radius from the transmitter. But beginning in the late 1990s, Web radio, available everywhere on the Internet, became a new radio-format medium that now enables local content to be distributed globally. The pairing of analog radio transmissions with digital signals (producing CD-quality sound while remaining within the FCC's strict power limits) as well as the development of pay radio satellite services (XM Satellite Radio and Sirius Satellite Radio) has helped radio remain a viable medium, though one of somewhat diminished interest to advertisers now that alternative distribution and listening devices (e.g., Apple's iPod and Internet stations) have emerged.[2]

VHF television signals, which have the same travel characteristics as FM, must be boosted by relay stations to reach beyond about 100 miles.[3] And, all other things being equal, UHF signals travel even less distance than VHF signals while requiring significantly greater electric power for transmission, often more than 1 megawatt (MW). Not surprisingly, then, UHFs were last to be commercially developed.[4]

As of 2006 there were 4,760 authorized AM radio stations, 6,250 commercial FM stations, and 1,375 commercial VHF and UHF television stations in the United States. In addition, there are hundreds more educational installations and television-signal translators (relay stations).

Basic operations

The success of a television or radio station in attracting an audience is measured by *ratings points:* the percentage of all TV- or radio-owning households tuned to a show. If, for example, 100,000 households in a defined area own radios and 12,000 of these households are listening to a particular station, then that station's *rating* is 12.0.

A station's *share*, however, is measured as the percentage of all *switched-on* sets tuned to a show. Assume that a signal area contains 100,000 households with televisions, that 60,000 of those sets are switched on, and that 20,000 are watching channel 2. Then channel 2's share is 33.3.

In other words, the combined ratings of all stations or networks during a particular "daypart" provide an estimate of the number of homes using television (HUT) or persons using radio (PUR). Thus, arithmetically,

share $= 100 \times$ Rating/HUT.

Regular measurements of ratings and shares have historically been offered by two major services: Nielsen (A. C. Nielsen Co.) and Arbitron (American Research Bureau). Arbitron (which discontinued its television services in 1993) took its measurements over a signal's *area of dominant influence* (ADI), regions essentially coinciding with the U.S. Census Bureau's standard metropolitan statistical areas (SMSAs). Nielsen's equivalent is a *designated market area* (DMA).

In the so-called sweeps months (each November, February, May, and July), local-station advertising rates for upcoming periods are established with the assistance of the ratings measured by the ratings services. Although the May sweeps period is considered by stations and networks to be the most important of the year, programming battles remain particularly intense in the months of November and February, during which there is a strong seasonal tendency toward stay-at-home viewing and listening. Many appealing "specials" are aired in those months in attempts to boost audience levels.[5]

The methods used by ratings services to sample homes using television – or in radio, persons using radio – vary to a degree and are sometimes subject to dispute. But the methods will generally provide consistent trend results over time.

Nielsen measurements for national network prime-time television shows, that is, programs broadcast in the period 8 to 11 p.m. for the East and West coasts (one hour earlier for central and mountain time zones), are made through devices called people meters that are connected to the sets, VCRs, cable boxes, and satellite dishes in a scientifically selected sample of around 10,000 homes. The Nielsen television index (NTI) that is so derived then provides advertisers with significant data on the audiences for various programs and thus forms the basis for how much a network can charge for the commercial time breaks within those programs. The Nielsen station index (NSI), derived from a combination of people meters and viewers' diaries, provides similar information for local program and station evaluations.[6]

Advertisers will always want their messages to be delivered to the audiences most likely to be interested in purchasing their products or services. Advertising agencies accordingly attempt to find programs or stations attracting the best target audience, defined by demographic, income, and ethnic mix: Razor-blade commercials appear regularly on sports/action programs; ads for laundry products appear on the eponymic daytime soap operas. And Nielsen now also measures how many people actually watch TV commercials.

Further distinctions are made among national (network) ads, national spot ads, and local ads. Large brand-name companies with national distribution often find that purchases of national-network time through agencies (which typically receive fees of 15% of their gross billings) are the most efficient (least expensive on a cost-per-viewer basis) means of communicating with potential customers.

For some nationally distributed products, however, a particular local audience can often be reached more effectively through so-called national spot purchases on local outlets and as arranged with station representatives (reps). Rep firms function as extensions of a station's sales staff and are familiar with various rate cards (prices) and program research demographics. In return for such services, the firms charge commissions that range to an average of about 7% to 8%.[7]

On a local level, though, smaller businesses buy time directly from local stations. Many of these transactions are at unpublished prices.

Broadcasters sell time to advertisers using the concepts of gross rating points (GRP), reach, and frequency. Because a rating point is the estimated

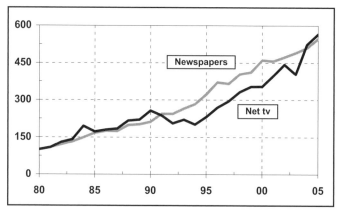

Figure 7.2. Cost per thousand (CPM) index trends (1970 = 100) for network television (prime time) and newspapers, 1970–2005. *Source*: Universal McCann data.

percentage of households or of target audience potentially exposed to a commercial, *gross rating points* are the sum of all the ratings figures. *Reach* is the percentage of households (or of target audience) exposed to a message at least once over a predetermined span. It is also called cume, which is short for cumulative audience. *Frequency* is simply the number of times an ad is used during a period of time. Thus, GRP is reach multiplied by frequency.

Advertisers generally assess the relative expense and efficiency of delivering a message via different media on the basis of cost per thousand households (CPM). Such data can be determined from a station's rate card or schedule, which, as posted with the Standard Rate and Data Service (SRDS), indicates how much half a minute will cost during a specific part of the day, day of the week, and season. Figure 7.2 illustrates CPM index trends for network television and newspapers since 1970. Over that span, CPM trends in network television have largely paralleled those for newspapers and magazines. However, whereas CPMs are normally used in sales of network time, advertisers evaluate local television stations on a similar calculation of cost per rating point (CPP), which is the cost of the advertising schedule purchased divided by gross rating points. CPPs provide comparisons of media efficiency *within* a broadcast medium.

Another measure, most often used in radio, is the *power ratio*, which is defined as a station's percentage of revenue in a market divided by its total audience percentage (of listeners over the age of 12). Ratios above 1.0 indicate that the station, or group of stations, is receiving a higher share of available market revenues than of available listening audience.[8]

As in any other business, discounts for purchases in quantity are normally available, but because unsold time is lost forever, prices become increasingly negotiable as the broadcast date approaches. Advertisers, stations, and program producers also sometimes engage in *barter*, a practice in which time is swapped for goods and services or, more commonly, for programming.

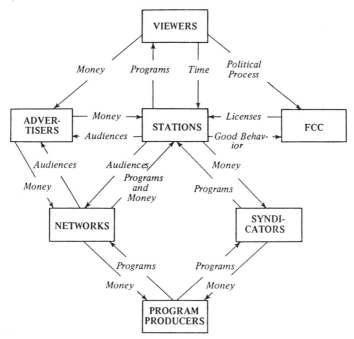

Figure 7.3. Organization of the television industry. *Source*: Owen *et al.* (1974). ©1974 Bruce M. Owen.

Barter-syndication deals, which amounted to more than $4 billion in 2005, provide advertisers with time that is generally at least 15% less expensive than on the networks.[9]

The microeconomic considerations in commercial advertising, broadcasting operations, and government regulation have been formally investigated in a wide range of studies, several of which will be noted in Section 7.2. The organization of the television industry is illustrated in Figure 7.3, and aggregate spending on various media since 1970 is presented in Table 7.1.

### Regulation

Broadcasting is one of the few entertainment sectors heavily regulated by the government. Such regulation was an outgrowth of the need, in the early years of this industry, to allocate scarce space in the broadcast frequency spectrum according to constraints imposed by technological factors and world political considerations.[10] Periodic meetings of the World Administrative Radio Conference (WARC) determine frequency allocations so that international frequency interference is minimized. Political and historical precedents have also been determinants as to which of several available television transmission systems a country has adopted.[11]

From the business-economics standpoint, knowledge of such issues is pertinent to strategic decisions that broadcasters and television equipment

Table 7.1. *Annual U.S. advertising expenditures, 1970–2005 (in $ billions)*

|                      | 1970   | 1980   | 1990    | 1995    | 2000    | 2005    |
|----------------------|--------|--------|---------|---------|---------|---------|
| Newspapers           | 5,704  | 14,794 | 32,281  | 36,317  | 49,050  | 47,335  |
| Magazines            | 1,292  | 3,149  | 6,803   | 8,580   | 12,370  | 12,847  |
| Farm publications    | 62     | 130    | 215     | 283     | NA[c]   | NA[c]   |
| Television, total    | 3,596  | 11,469 | 29,247  | 38,886  | 60,257  | 67,947  |
| Four networks[b]     | 1,658  | 5,130  | 9,863   | 11,600  | 15,888  | 16,128  |
| Cable networks       | —      | 45     | 2,000   | 4,500   | 11,765  | 18,296  |
| Syndication          | —      | 50     | 1,109   | 2,016   | 3,108   | 3,865   |
| Spot (national)      | 1,234  | 3,269  | 7,788   | 9,119   | 12,264  | 10,040  |
| Spot (local)         | 704    | 2,967  | 7,856   | 9,985   | 13,542  | 14,260  |
| Radio, total         | 1,308  | 3,702  | 8,726   | 11,338  | 19,295  | 19,640  |
| Network              | 56     | 183    | 482     | 480     | 780     | 814     |
| Spot (national)      | 371    | 779    | 1,635   | 1,959   | 3,668   | 3,469   |
| Spot (local)         | 881    | 2,740  | 6,609   | 8,899   | 14,847  | 15,357  |
| Yellow pages         | —      | 2,900  | 8,926   | 10,236  | 13,228  | 14,229  |
| Direct mail          | 2,766  | 7,596  | 23,370  | 32,866  | 44,591  | 55,218  |
| Business pubs        | 740    | 1,674  | 2,875   | 3,559   | 4,915   | 4,170   |
| Outdoor              | 234    | 578    | 1,084   | 1,263   | NA[c]   | NA[c]   |
| Internet             |        |        |         |         | 6,507   | 7,764   |
| Miscellaneous        | 3,848  | 7,558  | 16,237  | 22,102  | 32,083  | 35,692  |
| Total[a]             |        |        |         |         |         |         |
| National             | 11,350 | 29,815 | 73,380  | 96,933  | 151,664 | 172,797 |
| Local                | 8,200  | 23,735 | 56,210  | 68,214  | 95,808  | 98,277  |
| Grand total          | 19,550 | 53,550 | 129,590 | 165,147 | 247,472 | 271,074 |

[a] Total is sum of major categories.
[b] Three networks prior to 1990.
[c] Not available.
*Source*: Robert J. Coen, Universal McCann, Inc., New York.

manufacturers must make in response to changes in the regulatory environment. For example, government policies have guided the broadcast and equipment industries toward a timetable for adoption of digital high-definition television (HDTV) signals. Such HDTV sets, essentially computers compatible with other computers, provide picture resolution quality nearly as fine as on film and with aspect ratios approaching those of feature films (16:9).[12] But in the process of exchanging the old analog channel frequency allocations for the new digital ones, significant business uncertainties are created for both station owners and equipment manufacturers.[13]

## Organizational patterns and priorities

*Networks and affiliates*  In the United States, the most obvious manifestations of government regulation are the granting of licenses and the promulgation of rules concerning how many stations a single business organization is allowed to own. To prevent concentration of ownership in too few hands, prior to 1985 the FCC had permitted one corporation to own a maximum of seven AM and seven FM radio stations and a maximum of five VHF television stations (plus two UHFs). Since then, the limits have been lifted – originally to 12 stations each, so long as the total audience did not exceed 25% of the national television audience – and currently to at least 39%.[14]

Television networks – in effect, programming and audience-delivery wholesalers – were established in the late 1940s and early 1950s (and radio networks in the 1920s) by attracting independently owned affiliates to carry regularly scheduled programming produced by the network itself or by out-side contractors.[15] However, aside from news and sports programs, networks had not again until the 1990s been able to participate to any important degree in the ownership of productions. Networks in the United States now gener-ally fall into five main categories: English-language commercial (e,g., ABC, CBS, Fox, NBC, CW), Spanish-language commercial (e.g., Univision, Tele-mundo, TeleFutura), specialty (e.g., PBS, Bloomberg), shopping (e.g., HSN), and religious (TBN, CTN).

As of the late 1990s, the three original major national television corpo-rations (the networks) – Columbia Broadcasting (CBS), National Broad-casting (NBC), and American Broadcasting (ABC) – owned and operated (O&O) at least ten large-city television stations each, including local "flag-ships" in New York, Chicago, and Los Angeles. Meanwhile, Fox Broad-casting (FOX) has emerged as a full-fledged competitor to the three original majors.[16]

Nevertheless, each of the major webs, as they are often called in the trade press, has approximately 200 affiliates who normally still receive cash com-pensation to carry the scheduled national programming that is provided gratis by the network. Functioning as audience assemblers, networks thus actually operate by leasing the advertising time and signal distribution capabilities of their affiliates. Affiliate compensation in the period 6 to 11 p.m. might generally be 30% to 33% of the station's hourly rate and lower in other day-parts. But many factors, including area of coverage, number of competing UHFs and VHFs, and long-standing relationships, determine compensation rates.[17] Affiliates supplement network fare by buying reruns and talk shows and producing their own programs that include local news, normally the largest source of income.

Notably, it was not until the early 1970s that ABC became financially viable. An important catalyst for this change was government regulation that allowed local affiliates access to prime time (7 to 11 p.m. EST) through the *prime time access rule*. Such reversion of several hours per week (7 to 8 p.m.) to affiliates reduced the networks' inventories of evening time and drove prices up.[18]

In the mid-1980s, the trend toward economic deregulation gained momen-tum and led to a significant restructuring of the industry: Capital Cities Communications, a group station owner, acquired ABC (and is now owned by The Walt Disney Company); NBC was acquired by General Electric; CBS became a target of several takeover attempts (which ended in 2000 when Viacom acquired the network and then subsequently divested it in 2006); and Twentieth Century Fox and Metromedia merged most of their operations to form the core of a viable fourth network (FOX).

By the 1990s – with Time Warner (WB) and Viacom (UPN) also entering the field and with networks beginning to produce more of their prime-time productions and acquiring more O&Os – the traditional distinctions between affiliates and independent stations and between studios and networks had begun to blur. Broadcast networks have meanwhile faced increased competition from cable and have seen a need to integrate their operations more vertically by producing more shows in-house and sharing news-gathering and program development costs with other distribution outlets that often include cable and Internet partners.

Outside the United States, the organization and regulation of broadcasting varies substantially from country to country, but the most common arrangement is to have a mixture of public and private enterprises placed under the supervision of a government agency.[19] Yet it wasn't until the early 2000s that greater deregulation of government-controlled broadcasting began to be seen more frequently outside the United States. As privately owned, advertiser-supported networks become significant, they typically begin to assume many of the operating features that have characterized the American television system, with expenditures for programming tending to rise in line with total broadcast industry revenues.[20]

Key comparative data concerning television in 15 major countries are provided in Table 7.2. The growth of advertising in all media in the United States and around the world is illustrated in Figure 7.4.

*Ratings and audiences* By definition, the network with the most popular shows attracts the largest audience. The ratings leader can command prices at higher-than-average CPMs because advertising time (spots) on the most popular programs is normally in short supply relative to advertiser demand. Advertisers are interested in shows with high ratings and/or those that, regardless of overall ratings rankings, attract viewers with highly specific demographic characteristics (e.g., women ages 18 to 34) because such shows provide reach, consistency, and potential for creation of numerous merchandising opportunities.

In addition, the ratings leader garners higher prices because advertising-campaign managers who buy large quantities of time well in advance of use (i.e., "upfront" buyers) often bid aggressively to ensure that spots on programs attracting desired targeted audiences are obtained. Such large upfront buys, made by early summer, and just after new fall-season prime-time program schedules have been established, might command quantity discounts of 15% and provide advertisers with compensation (i.e., "make-goods") if a show delivers an audience that is smaller than expected.

Table 7.2. *Television outside the United States, selected countries, 2005*

|                | TV HH (millions) | TV ad exp.[a] (U.S. $ billions) | TV ad $s per HH |
|----------------|------------------|---------------------------------|-----------------|
| Australia      | 7.5              | 2.8                             | 373             |
| Canada         | 12.6             | 2.6                             | 206             |
| China          | 390.0            | 5.3                             | 14              |
| France         | 25.0             | 4.2                             | 168             |
| Germany        | 35.0             | 5.0                             | 143             |
| India          | 90.0             | 2.0                             | 22              |
| Italy          | 22.9             | 6.0                             | 262             |
| Japan          | 49.8             | 19.0                            | 382             |
| Mexico         | 21.0             | 2.7                             | 129             |
| Netherlands    | 7.0              | 1.2                             | 171             |
| Spain          | 16.0             | 3.8                             | 238             |
| Sweden         | 4.2              | 0.6                             | 143             |
| Switzerland    | 2.9              | 0.7                             | 231             |
| United Kingdom | 25.4             | 6.5                             | 256             |
| Total          | 709.3            | 62.4                            | 88              |
| Average        | —                | —                               | 188             |
| United States  | 111.5            | 55.1                            | 494             |

[a] For all forms of TV advertising including cable and satellite.
*Source*: Universal McCann, Zenith Optimedia, industry estimates.

Broadcast networks have traditionally sold upfront around 80% of the new season's inventory as compared with 65% for cable networks, though this is now changing rapidly as upfront becomes less important.[21] The remaining spots, available on a "scatter" basis, are then sold closer to broadcast time and may not provide advertisers with optimal frequency or reach (or minimum

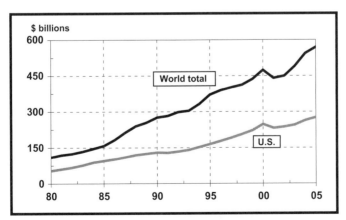

Figure 7.4. Total spending on advertising (all media) in the United States and around the world, 1980–2005. Based on data by Robert J. Coen, Universal McCann, Inc.

audience guarantees).[22] Although upfront prices historically correlate about 70% with scatter, pricing exceptions may occur with late-breaking campaigns or during periods of scarcity, when scatter prices can rise despite close proximity to the broadcast date.[23]

Yet except for programming-related outlays, which are the primary expense components, the costs of network operations remain relatively fixed regardless of ratings performance or numbers of affiliates.[24] Incremental revenues thus normally become almost pure operating profit for the ratings leader. Conversely, for the ratings laggard, weak ratings accentuate a decline in profitability. A greater proportion of total expenses is incurred in ordering new shows and in then extensively promoting them on introduction. Furthermore, as already noted, advertisers disappointed by poor ratings performance often must be compensated with additional "free" time through *make-goods* (more formally, they are audience-deficiency announcements). Such time compensation rapidly eats into profits and may offset strong earlier upfront sales while also reducing the inventory available for sale later in the year in the much more volatile scatter market.

In contrast to television, radio networks are much more varied and numerous, and they are more specifically targeted in terms of local-market demographic, ethnic, and other factors. But whether in television or in radio, significant leverage on profits accrues to the ratings leader. In network television, indeed, a prime-time ratings point won or lost may be worth at least $80 million in annual pretax profits.

The mechanics of all this might be sketched as follows:
Assume:

100 million households
price of a 30-second network spot = $125,000
eight spots per half-hour program
cost of programming = $600,000 per half-hour for *two* runs

Then:

Network gross profit per half-hour = $700,000.

As might be expected, the tremendous importance of ratings performance to the profitability of a broadcast enterprise has led to much research into the kinds of programs certain demographically targeted audiences prefer to view. A substantial body of research that investigates the behavioral characteristics of television audiences in general has also been developed. According to Barwise and Ehrenberg (1988), two important behavioral features have been observed: the *Duplication of Viewing Law* and the *Double Jeopardy Effect*.

In brief, the Duplication of Viewing Law states that "the percentage of the audience of program B which also watches program A simply varies with the rating of program A, with only small deviations."[25] The Double Jeopardy Effect, however, "occurs when people have to choose between broadly similar items that differ in popularity. The less popular items are not only chosen by

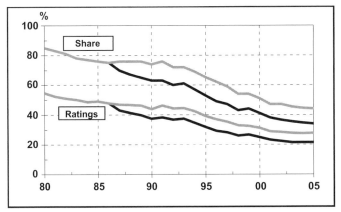

Figure 7.5. Combined ratings and shares for ABC, CBS, NBC, and FOX, 1980–2005.
*Source*: Nielsen Media Research.

fewer people, but are liked somewhat less by those who choose them."[26] In other words, viewers of programs with low ratings are less loyal than viewers of programs with high ratings.

The Double Jeopardy Effect has probably been felt most acutely at the networks, where ratings have been significantly eroded by the increasing competition from cable, independent stations, and home video (VCRs, DVDs, etc.). As Figure 7.5 illustrates, ratings and shares for the older three networks have been declining steadily. However, there comes a point at which a trade-off of profit for extra market share does not make economic sense.

*Inventories* Network prime-time inventories (of time allocated for commercial messages) prior to 1981 used to be limited to six minutes per hour (seven minutes during movies, sporting events, and specials) by voluntary adherence to unofficial guidelines of the National Association of Broadcasters (NAB). But after such adherence was found to be in violation of antitrust laws, the number of commercial minutes that a network sells during different times of day has been both varied and increased.[27] Of course, all other things being equal, an increase in the supply of time will cause prices to decline.

For network programs, of the usual 10 minutes per hour set aside for prime-time nonprogram material and 16 minutes per hour in all other dayparts, affiliates might normally retain 2.5 minutes (60 seconds at the start and end, 30 seconds in the middle), with 30 seconds of this used for network and station promos, teasers, identification, and program titles and credits. This compares with 4 to 12 minutes that affiliates retain (at least 7 minutes on weekends) in daytime.

Affiliates are, in turn, motivated to provide broadcast clearances for network shows because network programs are generally the most profitable for them to run; network programming, with its inherently high production value, tends to attract the largest audiences. Moreover, the shows are provided to affiliates without expenditure of cash and without the headaches of production financing and creation.[28]

*Independent and public broadcasting stations* Television stations not affiliated with a network are known as independents, and in recent years these stations have become serious competitors for network audiences. Independents try to counterprogram against network affiliates by offering news at times earlier or later than the networks, by providing viewers with more material of local interest, and by rerunning popular programs that were previously shown on networks. As such, these stations are the bulwark of the syndication market, into which shows canceled by the networks are sold if there are enough episodes to allow for *stripping*, which is continuous use of episodes over several days per week.

Although independent stations may purchase first-run programs, and to a limited extent self-produce programming, they normally rely on such syndicated products to fill prime-time schedules. Consequently, in cities with more than one independent station, there may be aggressive bidding to obtain rights to the most popular series coming off the networks. And because rights to a half-hour episode (the most efficient length) of a popular series may sell for upward of $75,000 in a major city, producers can often amass substantial sums from all markets (see Section 5.4). In recent years, though, stations have been increasingly inclined to conserve cash through the use of barter-syndication arrangements such as those noted in Chapter 5. Such arrangements have also been used to good effect by independents, known as *superstations*, that send their signals via satellite to cable systems around the country.[29]

Syndicated (usually first-run) radio programs also generally follow a unified theme (e.g., "The History of Rock 'n' Roll") or use a personality (e.g., Larry King). In payment for such programming, stations may make various arrangements, including combinations of cash, bartered goods and services, and time.

Considerably different in temper and means of funding, however, are the television and radio stations affiliated with the Public Broadcasting Service (PBS). PBS is actually a confederation of nonprofit, independently owned stations or station groups. The distinguishing feature here is that programs are not interrupted by commercial announcements but are instead usually "sponsored" (supported) by one or several corporate grants. Financing for public television programming is derived from viewers, from government subsidies, and from support of corporate contributors funneled through the nonprofit Corporation for Public Broadcasting, which was set up by an act of Congress in 1967. Programs distributed on PBS stations may be self-produced by affiliates or purchased from other sources.[30] Funding, identity, and purposing issues have also arisen with respect to the British Broadcasting Corp. (BBC), the world's oldest and most prominent public broadcaster.[31]

## 7.2 Economic characteristics

Macroeconomic relationships

Broadcasting industry growth inevitably traces a path similar to that of the U.S. economy. Although factors such as presidential elections and Olympic games (now every two years) noticeably affect supply and demand for the commercial-time inventory, macroeconomic trends are of overriding importance to the industry's secular financial performance.

In this respect, total corporate profits are perhaps the most important influence on how much companies will spend on advertising through newspapers, magazines, billboards, direct mail, and commercial broadcasting services. During periods of economic duress, companies may find that advertising budgets are tempting and expedient targets for cost cutting. But also, there are many firms, primarily those selling "soft" consumer products (e.g., soap, cosmetics, hamburgers), for which market-share and consumer-awareness considerations make it all but impossible to trim advertising spending significantly except under the most adverse circumstances. The variance of expenditures on advertising in relation to changes in corporate profits and the share trends of broadcast media versus newspapers are illustrated in Figure 7.6.[32]

Nevertheless, when the economy weakens, some firms must inevitably reduce advertising budgets, and a decline (unevenly apportioned) in overall demand for broadcasting services ensues. Large, nationally known brands continue to be advertised on network television with approximately the same degree of intensity regardless of conditions. But prices for network time soften to the extent that major, highly cyclical consumer-products companies cut back.

Smaller local businesses, however, normally feel a recession much more immediately and would thus more sharply curtail advertising expenditures on local independent stations. In other words, in an economic downturn, network and *national spot* (regional/local ads for national brands shown on local-station time) advertising may hold up much better than local advertising. The one mitigating factor for stations is that, as their spot rates decrease relative to those charged for network time, some ads normally going to networks might instead be placed locally.[33]

Since 1960, television revenues have, on the average, risen 14.1% in the contemporaneous presidential election/Olympics years and 7.1% in the others. Meanwhile, advertising as a percentage of personal-consumption expenditures has generally held to the range of 3.0% to 3.6%.

Microeconomic considerations

Broadcasting services, like national-defense services, are public goods: The cost of production is independent of the number of consumers who enjoy the benefits, and one person's consumption does not reduce the quantity available to others.[34] Moreover, broadcasting is a highly regulated industry

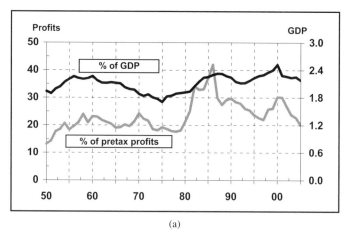

(a)

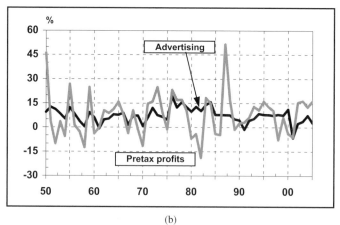

(b)

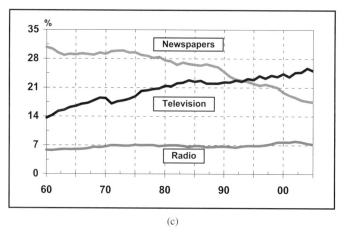

(c)

Figure 7.6. (a) Total U.S. advertising expenditures as a percentage of GDP and pretax corporate profits (excluding IVA adjustment, i.e., inventory valuation), 1949–2005. (b) Pretax corporate profits and spending for advertising, year-over-year percent changes, 1950–2005. (c) Percent shares of total advertising: television, radio, and newspapers, 1960–2005. *Source*: Based on data by Robert J. Coen, Universal McCann, Inc.

in which public-welfare and government-policy questions frequently arise. Economic theory has been helpful in analyzing the issues.

In fact, economic studies have been especially influential in setting the course of regulation in broadcasting and cable in the following areas: prime-time access rules, network financial-interest and programming-syndication activities, funding for public broadcasting, distant-signal-importation guidelines for cable systems, and proposals for low-power VHF "drop-ins" (small stations that do not interfere with standard stations on the same frequency in other communities). Yet because of the public-good characteristics of broadcasting services, and the requirement that service providers sometimes be granted monopoly powers, in most studies it has been difficult to evaluate the relative efficiencies of alternative market structures.

Against this background, several microeconomic analyses, including theories of program choice and models of network behavior, have appeared (Noll, Peck, and McGowan 1973). As Owen, Beebe, and Manning (1974, p. 101) noted, in many of these models,

competition under advertiser support tends to produce less diversity and more "wasteful duplication" than is socially optimal. This is a direct parallel to Hotelling's [1929] famous spatial competition example of "excessive sameness." Such duplication occurs because there is a tendency for a decentralized system of broadcasting, with limited channel capacity, to produce rivalry for large blocks of the audience with programs that are, if not identical, at least close substitutes.[35]

In all, the economic literature on issues pertaining to broadcasting and advertising has come to include many studies attempting to describe industry-organizational and program diversity developments in an environment that encompasses numerous advertiser and viewer-supported program choices.[36]

### 7.3 Financial-performance characteristics

Variable cost elements

Because operating costs are relatively fixed, growth in broadcast revenue is the key variable behind changes in industry profitability. If demand for commercial time is high, prices for spots rise but everything from the cost of powering the transmitter to the cost of programming does not vary much – at least over the short run. Conversely, a decline in demand for advertising will immediately and directly carve a chunk of profits out of the bottom line. None of this ought to suggest, however, that increases in operating costs may be ignored. In fact, long-run profitability will also be sensitive to changes in the general and administrative (G & A) and programming expense areas.

For networks, programming cost increases have been particularly steep, growing at a compound annual rate of 14.4% between 1971 and 1980 and at an estimated rate of 8% annually between 1980 and 2000. Although much of the more than $9 billion that the networks spend each year is for programs that are licensed from the television production divisions of movie studios, a considerable portion of their budgets is also allocated to self-produced programming in the form of news, sports, and daytime serials.

News, in fact, costs each of the first three major networks at least $500 million a year. But daytime drama serials (soap operas) can often be produced for about $150,000 per half-hour ($200,000 for an hour), and game shows for one-third to one-half as much (and talk shows for even less) because of relatively low performers' salaries, fixed studio locations, and greater use of videotape. These production costs are well below those for regular prime-time network series, in which the production cost per hour is now generally above $1.5 million ($2 million for dramas).[37] Reality programming is also relatively inexpensive to produce.[38]

For networks and some stations, daytime television is therefore the most profitable schedule segment, with NBC's long-running morning *Today* show, which in 2006 generated an estimated $250 million a year (on $500 million of revenues), the most profitable of all.[39] Daytime program costs are usually far lower, and there are more commercial slots than in prime time: twelve network minutes per hour in daytime versus six minutes per hour in prime time, with local stations having at least three minutes of "adjacencies" plus three minutes of promos in each period. The availability of more minutes thereby compensates for a smaller audience base. An hour-long soap, for example, will typically attract $1 million a day in revenue.

With such a significant portion of potential profits to be derived from daytime, networks have thus always had a strong incentive to increase, or to at least maintain, daytime ratings. In contrast, however, local news, accounting for 35% to 40% of the advertising base, provides the largest source of revenue for most affiliate stations.

Aggregate financial-performance numbers for television and radio stations as compiled by NAB annual surveys and by the FCC prior to 1980 show that G & A is the largest expense category for affiliated television stations. However, programming is the largest and probably most rapidly growing cost of operations for independents. Table 7.3 indicates revenue and expense category proportions for what might be a typical station.[40] Aggregate industry data are then presented in Table 7.4.

Financial-accounting practices

The timing of recognition of programming expense by a station and network is usually different from that for the producer–distributors discussed in Section 4.4. Stations or networks will not charge the expense when the product becomes "available" but rather when it is broadcast. Using accrual accounting, about two-thirds of the total program expense of a continuing (old) series will usually be recognized on first run and the remaining third on rerun. Cash payments, however, may vary in response to producer requirements and to relative bargaining strengths.

Table 7.3. *Typical television station revenues (total time sales) and expenses in percent by major categories*

| Total time sales (revenues) | % | Expenses | % |
|---|---|---|---|
| Network compensation | 7.5 | Engineering | 11.5 |
| National and regional | 47.5 | Program and production[a] | 25.5 |
| advertisements | | News | 13.5 |
| Local advertisements | 45.0 | Sales | 12.5 |
| | 100.0 | Advertisements and promotion | 4.0 |
| | | General and administrative | 33.0 |
| | | | 100.0 |

[a] The typical independent station spends a far greater percentage (perhaps up to 50% of all expenses) on program acquisition but much less (perhaps 6% of all expenses) on news. Because of such programming cost, the pretax margin of profit for independents is on average no more than one-half to two-thirds that of the typical affiliate.

As a percentage of operating costs at independent stations, amortization of syndicated television series cost has risen from 35% in the mid-1970s to over 45% to 50% in the 1990s. This compares with levels of about 25% for affiliates, which regularly receive about 65% of their programming from the networks.

Prior to 1975, accounting practices for program materials varied widely. Some broadcasters recorded neither program rights nor related obligations on their balance sheets. In that year, however, an AICPA position paper on this subject brought greater uniformity to the industry's procedures, which were finally formalized in 1982 by issuance of FASB Statement 63 (Table 7.5).

According to this statement, a broadcaster (licensee) will account for a license agreement for program material as a purchase of a right or group of rights. The licensee will then report an asset and a liability for the rights acquired and the obligations incurred when the license period begins and the following conditions have been met:

Table 7.4. *Radio and television broadcasting industry operating performances: composite of 24 companies, 2001–2005*

| | Revenues | Operating income | Operating margin[a] (%) | Assets | Operating cash flow |
|---|---|---|---|---|---|
| CAGR(%):[b] | 3.2 | 38.8 | NM[c] | 5.2 | −6.3 |

[a] Average margin, 2001–2005 = 19.4%.

[b] Compound annual growth rate.

[c] Not meaningful.

Table 7.5. *Recognition of acquired-program material assets, liabilities, and expenses: an illustration*

**Asset and liability recognition**[a]

| Film | License period | | Year of asset and liability recognition | | |
|------|------|------|------|------|------|
|      | From | To | 19X1 | 19X2 | 19X3 |
| A | 10/1/X1 | 9/30/X3 | $8,000,000 | | |
| B | 10/1/X1 | 9/30/X3 | 5,000,000 | | |
| C | 9/1/X2 | 8/31/X4 | | $3,750,000 | |
| D | 9/1/X3 | 8/31/X5 | | | $2,250,000 |

**Expense recognition**[a]

| Film | Year of expense recognition | | | | |
|------|------|------|------|------|------|
|      | 19X1 | 19X2 | 19X3 | 19X4 | 19X5 |
| A | | $4,800,000[b] | $3,200,000[c] | | |
| B | | 3,500,000[d] | 1,500,000[e] | | |
| C | | | 2,813,000[f] | $937,000[g] | |
| D | | | | 1,463,000[h] | $787,000[i] |
|   | | $8,300,000 | $7,513,000 | $2,400,000 | $787,000 |

[a] Under the gross approach, all costs under a license agreement are recorded as amortization of program cost.
[b] $8,000,000 × 60%.      [f] $3,750,000 × 75%.
[c] $8,000,000 × 40%.      [g] $3,750,000 × 25%.
[d] $5,000,000 × 70%.      [h] $2,250,000 × 65%.
[e] $5,000,000 × 30%.      [i] $2,250,000 × 35%.

*Source*: FASB Statement 63. © Financial Accounting Standards Board, High Ridge Park, Stamford, CT 06905, USA. Reprinted with permission. Copies of the complete document are available from the FASB.

1.  The cost of each program is known or is reasonably determinable.
2.  The program material has been accepted by the licensee in accordance with the agreement.
3.  The program is available for its first showing or telecast.

In addition, the asset will be segregated on the balance sheet between current and noncurrent based on estimated time of usage, and the liability segregation will be based on payment terms. The asset and liability are then reported either on a present-value basis in accordance with Accounting Principles Board (APB) Opinion 21 (which describes the general accounting treatment for discounting payables and receivables) or at the gross amount of the liability.

Capitalized costs of program-material rights are carried on the balance sheet at the lower of unamortized cost or estimated net realizable value on a program-by-program, series, package, or daypart basis, whereas network-affiliation agreements are presented as intangible assets.

Costs are then to be allocated to individual programs within a package on the basis of the relative value of each to the broadcaster. As determined earlier, capitalized costs are to be amortized on the basis of estimated number of future showings (or, when this is not possible, over the period of the agreement).

More specifically, feature programs are to be amortized on a program-by-program basis or approximation thereof for a package, whereas program series and other syndicated products are to be amortized as a series. Straight-line amortization may be used if all showings are expected to generate similar revenues (e.g., as might be the case with "evergreen" programs such as *The Honeymooners*).

In all, FASB Statement 63 provides broadcasters with considerable flexibility in terms of interest and program cost amortization alternatives. Such flexibility, however, makes it more difficult to directly compare the operating performance of companies using different accounting policies.[41]

## 7.4 Valuing broadcast properties

Although there are no absolute formulas for valuing broadcast properties, whose key assets are FCC licenses and network affiliation agreements, stations change hands often enough so that, at any given time, the going rate in the market can be readily determined.[42] Especially in radio, valuation analyses will likely begin with "stick" (i.e., broadcast license) value, the "assessed" worth of an *undeveloped* property in any given market and a concept akin to the value of a vacant lot in real estate.[43] In addition to current profitability, other important variables to consider include the following:

Interest rates

Regional location (fast-growing states are preferable to economically depressed areas)

Changes in regulatory stringency

Place on the channel selector/radio dial (in radio tuning, center is passed most frequently and is thus most desirable)

Allotted signal power and time of operation

Surrounding terrain (e.g., mountains and tall buildings may block signals)

Current program style and format relative to other local stations

Real estate value alternatives at transmitter and/or studio site

Amount of debt to be assumed

Short-term and intermediate-term potential effects of cable and other new local distribution services

The significance of interest rate levels is no different here than elsewhere. High real rates (i.e., as adjusted for the rate of inflation) not only undercut profits via macroeconomic effects on revenues, but they also reduce the

number of buyers who can obtain loans and service debt without strain. High
rates also diminish the alternative-use value of any real estate that is included
in a station transaction and, more noticeably, reduce the net present value of
future expected cash flows.[44]

In determining station values, however, the second most important consideration after taking interest rates into account is often whether or not a
significant improvement in profits can be effected through alterations in program content and style. In television this may entail changes in local news
and sports personalities or changes in prime-time access programs. In radio,
changing from "top 40" style to country and western, to all news or all talk,
to adult/contemporary (A/C), to middle-of-the-road (MOR), to current hits
(CHR), or to album-oriented rock (AOR) might be involved. Indeed, the rise
of FM versus AM properties was initiated by format alterations that appealed
to young, free-spending audiences.

All other things being equal, sales of stations with similar characteristics ought to then command about the same multiple of *operating cash flow*,
which is defined as operating income (earnings) before interest, taxes, depreciation, and amortization (EBITDA), or of *broadcast cash flow*, which is
EBITDA before corporate expenses.[45] Such cash flow definitions, though
now not as widely favored as in the past, are used because price and value
comparisons may be more accurately determined prior to consideration of
widely varying debt-financing arrangements and tax circumstances.[46]

In addition, comparisons using *net free cash flows* (i.e., net income plus
depreciation, amortization, and deferred taxes, less capital expenditures) are
often useful. A *cash flow margin*, that is, operating cash flow taken as a percentage of revenue, will also normally be calculated. For healthy properties,
margins generally average in the range of 25% to 45%, but the higher end of
the range is typically seen only at larger stations.

Leveraged buy-outs (LBOs) – in which money is borrowed against a station's assets (in reality, cash flow) – have also been used to help finance
purchases of broadcast properties.[47] But such leveraged transactions have
not always worked according to plan. In the mid-1980s, cash flow multiples
for some speculative properties rose to 14 or more in response to changes
(in 1984) in an FCC rule that permitted corporations to own as many as 12
television, 12 AM, and 12 FM outlets (but in markets collectively containing
no more than 25% of the nation's TV homes) instead of 7 each, the previous
limit.[48]

By the late 1980s, however, bank credit available for broadcast and
cable properties was severely circumscribed by the imposition of regulations against lending for highly leveraged transactions.[49] As a result, cash
flow multiples for media properties declined steeply. And many properties
bought earlier with relatively large amounts of debt as compared with equity
capital became practically insolvent (i.e., they were unable to cover their
operating and interest costs) once the economy turned down.[50]

We can approximate the value of a broadcast (and, similarly, as in Table 8.7, a cable) property in the following manner: Assign a multiple of cash flow, say in the range of eight to twelve times, a higher or lower figure depending on prevailing interest rates and similar recent transaction prices. Then subtract from the product of the assumed multiple times the cash flow an amount representing "net debt" (i.e., long-term debt minus net current assets). To then arrive at a per share estimate, divide the resulting difference by the number of shares outstanding:

value = (assigned multiple × projected cash flow)

− (long term debt − net current assets).

Such calculations focus attention on the difference in the value of media properties as measured by the going multiple of cash flow (i.e., the so-called private market value) and the value of the underlying publicly traded shares. A wide divergence will, of course, enhance takeover prospects.

Even so, however, it is not particularly easy to determine what a reasonable discount to private market value should be. Private market prices reflect the powers that derive from total control over an asset and, from the standpoint of a potential seller, the taxes that will have to be paid on liquidation of the asset (and that often loom large in the selling decision). In fact, because of normal uncertainties about the direction of interest rates and the course of economic growth, a significant speculative element is usually involved, and public-share discounts to private market values are often 30% or more.

## 7.5 Concluding remarks

The potential for broadcast industry profitability in any one year depends more directly on the overall condition of the economy than on anything else. But over the long run, growth will most likely be affected by several new developments that will challenge the preeminence of television and radio broadcasting as evolved since the late 1940s. Indeed, it is already quite evident that video content distribution is no longer limited to one means of transmission, a single time, or a particular playback device.

The major challenges have recently come from the growth of cable and satellite-related services, from the loss of audiences that are being diverted to use of other entertainment and information service platforms, and from new technology that increasingly enables viewers to skip through or altogether eliminate (i.e., zap) commercial ads and/or to email (distribute) video clips of programs on their own.[51] As a result, sweeps periods, upfront buying, the traditional 30-second spot, and pilots will likely become less important or disappear even as series are made available for round-the-clock viewing and television seasons are no longer crisply delineated.

Viewing on hand-held screens, including cellphones and video iPod-type devices, has accelerated these changes and will – in addition to larger retransmission consent cash payments from cable and satellite system operators – provide new sources of revenues.[52] And network television broadcasters will also use their programming to establish new Internet portals that circumvent Yahoo, MSN, and Google.[53] Yet none of this changes the fact that the traditional broadcast network model is in many respects already dysfunctional.

Cable has had the most important effect on broadcasting because new or upgraded systems are often able to distribute up to 500 channels without interference from tall buildings and hilly terrain and without constraint in transmission power. And cable has already significantly eroded network viewership from about 84% of homes in 1980 to an average share well under 50% in 2005. Network audience levels are being sustained only because of expansion in the number of television households to an estimated 112 million in 2007 from 79.9 million in 1980.

Cable has also grown to the point at which its inventories of time are large enough to mitigate broadcast spot pricing power. And although most cable channels normally will be devoted to video programming, data-transmission and pay and cable radio services with no advertising may begin to supplant commercial FM radio. Internet broadcasting, too, has already evolved (for radio) into an important distribution medium, and Web sites are in the early stages of coalescing into global radio and television networks.

All these elements have reduced the growth prospects for broadcasting profits. Even so, however, few businesses can regularly generate the high relative cash flows and pretax margins of over 20% that remain characteristic in broadcasting. And many advertisers will continue to be attracted to network television because of its great efficiency in reaching the mass of consumers at a relatively price-competitive cost per thousand. Especially at the local level, it will be difficult to replace the strong news and sports-programming capability of commercial stations.

In summary, broadcasting is a multifaceted, regulated industry now entering a period of maturity in which expansion will be slower and the challenges greater. It nevertheless remains a business in which profit margins are well above average and in which cash generation is unusually high. Broadcasters will, for the foreseeable future, continue to be a significant force in entertainment.

### Notes

**1.** McLuhan is saying that use of any communications media has an importance beyond just the content that the medium may convey. For instance, as Levinson (1999, p. 39) suggests, "the process of watching television has a more significant influence upon our lives than the specific program or content that we watch, or the art of talking on the phone has been more revolutionary in human affairs than most things said on the phone." McLuhan

(1964, 2001, p. 8) himself explained: "For the 'message' of any medium or technology is the change of scale or pace or pattern that it introduces into human affairs. The railway did not introduce movement or transportation or wheel or road into human society, but it accelerated and changed the scale of previous functions, creating totally new kinds of cities and new kinds of work and leisure. This happened whether the railway functioned in a tropical or a northern environment and is quite independent of the freight or content of the railway medium."

**2.** As Woolley (2004b) notes, however, digital subscription radio services like XM and Sirius have had to overcome significant regulatory challenges and barriers that have been erected as a result of National Association of Broadcasters (NAB) lobbying of the U.S. Congress on behalf of traditional analog broadcasters. See also Manly (2005b), McBride (2005b), and *BusinessWeek*, March 14, 2005. Ward (2004) discusses how advertisers have cooled to radio.

**3.** FM frequencies are between channels 6 and 7 on the VHF television spectrum; that is, channels 2 through 6 operate at 54 to 88 megahertz (MHz) and channels 7 through 13 operate at 174 to 216 MHz. Harmonic distortions prevent the use of channel 1 in VHF television transmissions. Also, to prevent interference, VHF-band stations are separated by one empty channel, while eight channels usually separate UHF stations.

**4.** Low-power VHF television (LPTV) stations were introduced in the late 1980s. LPTV can meet many strictly local programming needs at minimal cost and can be established, complete with satellite earth station and origination equipment, for about half a million dollars. With a 1-kilowatt (kW) transmitter and a high-gain antenna, a signal can then extend as much as 18 miles from the transmission point.

**5.** Starting in 2006, changes in the methods used by Nielsen Media Research rendered sweeps periods irrelevant for the ten largest markets, which represent around 30% of the national audience and around 50% of local advertising revenue. See Carter (2004b).

**6.** Despite technological improvements, measurement of audiences has become more difficult and subject to controversy as channels, networks, and sets have proliferated. Nielsen had long relied on "audimeters" (audience meters) in the largest markets (and diaries in the smaller ones), but sampling has been enlarged and has until recently depended on people meters that require viewers to log in their presence on a console attached to the television set. Gertner (2005) describes how Arbitron has developed portable people meters that automatically measure advertising exposure using subtle signal codes: Television shows are already viewed on computers, cellphones, iPods, and PlayStation Portables, for example. As audiences fragment and become technologically and demographically more diverse, the difficulty of measuring increases. Nielsen's largest global competitor is TNS, a European company. And ErinMedia specializes in providing precise viewing data from cable set-top boxes. Berry (1984) describes an earlier attempt by Britain's AGB Research to compete against Nielsen. See Couzens (1986), Jensen (1996), and Carter (2000), in which the potentially declining value of sweeps periods for ratings purposes is discussed, and also Barnes (2004a). The impact of Nielsen ratings for commercial breaks is discussed in Steinberg and Barnes (2006). The changeover from diaries to people meters is discussed in Clark (2006). Meters produce more accurate results because they reflect who is watching: Each household member is assigned a button on the meter.

Both Arbitron and The Birch Scarborough Research companies are perhaps better known for radio audience measurements.

**7.** As of the early 2000s, commissionable spot billings for the two leading national TV rep firms, Cox (Telerep, MMT, and HRP) and Chancellor (Blair/Petry/Katz), were over $8 billion. National sales average about 40% to 50% of a station's total revenue but are a larger part of the mix in major markets. At an average commission rate of 7% to 8%, estimated rep firm revenues were thus around $600 million. Rates are set as a percentage of *net* billings, defined as dollars paid for advertising minus ad agency commissions. Reps account for about 70% of TV, 15% of cable, and 55% of radio billings.

**8.**   Radio programmers also measure time spent listening (TSL). Average quarter-hour (AQH) ratings show the average percentage of an audience that tuned to a radio or television station within a specific quarter-hour period. TSL equals the number of average quarter-hours in the time period (e.g., there are 504 quarter-hours between 6 a.m. and midnight, Monday through Sunday) multiplied by the average quarter-hour audience and then divided by the cumulative audience (cume). Also, more than in television, radio stations tend to sell advertising against other stations in the same programming and demographic genre than against the larger media universe metrics.

**9.**   Barter syndication is discussed in Section 5.4. The growth of the business is shown in Table 5.13.

**10.**   In theory, allocation of scarce frequency space would normally be more efficient if free-market auction bidding, as in the 1994 example of the FCC's auctions of personal communication systems telephone frequencies, were permitted.

**11.**   Government regulation of all aspects of broadcasting is generally much more stringent in foreign countries. However, the United States was the first country to develop television into a mass medium and, as a result, to standardize the earliest (now technologically inferior) system, known as NTSC (National Television Systems Committee), with a 525-line scan. The same analog system was used in Canada, Mexico, Japan, and 23 other countries. But elsewhere around the world, there have been different standards with 625-line scans. The SECAM (sequential color and memory) system originated in France and was used in more than 20 nations, and the PAL (phase-alternation line) system was used in 37 others. Picture resolution with SECAM and PAL is superior to that with NTSC because of more scanning lines per frame, but their use of alternating current of 50 Hz (versus 60 Hz in the United States) leads to more flickering.

Also, in the old NTSC system, the electron beam produces 30 different pictures, or frames, per second, and each frame is made up of 525 scanning lines. By contrast, movies show 24 different frames a second interrupted by a shutter in the projector that reduces flicker by showing each frame twice.

To reduce flicker in the TV picture, however, each frame is separated in two and each half-frame (field) is shown separately, which means that each field composed of either odd or even scan lines is on the screen for one-sixtieth of a second. The process is known as interlacing.

**12.**   The total conversion from analog to digital in the United States is to be completed by February 17, 2009, while the changeover in the United Kingdom, France, and Japan will be completed in 2012, 2011, and 2011, respectively. In the United States, a fully digital HDTV standard was established in late 1996, although the basic elements were in place by 1993. The standard, similar to that used in computer monitors, includes a 1,080-line progressive-scan image. See Brinkley (1997, 1996), Andrews (1993), and *Broadcasting & Cable*, May 31, 1993. As with analog, however, the world is fragmented into different digital standards: Eurpean (DVB), North American (ATSC), and Japanese (ISDB). In the early 1990s, an HDTV (1,250-line, 60 Hz) system known as MUSE (Multiple Sub-Nyquist Sampling and Encoding) was just beginning to be implemented in Japan, even though which of several competing systems would prevail in the United States and Europe had not yet been determined. In Europe, the plans for HDTV had been to use 1,250-line 50-Hz signals based on a MAC (multiplexed analog component) signal standard for direct broadcast satellite distribution. As of 1998, HDTV has been defined as 720 lines or higher in progressive-scan and 1,080 lines in interlace format. The 720p format, used by ABC and FOX, sends a complete picture 60 times a second and is better at reproducing the fast movements of sports programming. See also Alpert (2005). Krantz (2005) discusses prospects for even higher resolutions (1,280 lines) in three-dimensional sets (HD3D), movie projectors, and games currently being developed.

**13.** Regulatory changes that had similarly broad effects on broadcast asset values occurred in the early 1960s, when Congress required the production of sets with UHF tuning capability, and in 1999, when the FCC relaxed television station (duopoly) ownership rules. The significant increase in viewers potentially able to receive UHF signals immediately increased the value of UHF station licenses, while the new duopoly rules – allowing a top-rated station in a market to merge with a lower-rated one as long as there remain at least eight independent commercial or noncommercial stations in that market – led to a station-buying spree by broadcasters eager to consolidate their industry positions. See *Electronic Media*, August 9, 1999.

**14.** Audience coverage rules were eased with the Telecom Act of 1996 and then again (up from 35% to at least 39%) by the FCC in 2003. Note that only half of UHF viewers are counted in determining audience percentage figures. Other significant rules pertain to cross-media ownership and foreign ownership. As of 2003, a broadcast company is permitted to own two TV stations in local markets in which there are five or more stations, and in radio a broadcaster can own up to eight stations if the market has at least 45 stations in total. Foreigners have long been limited to ownership positions of less than 25% of a holding company with broadcast licenses or 20% of a license directly. See Labaton (2003, 2004).

**15.** As Auletta (1991, p. 4) notes, "A network is an office building, where executives package programs they do not own and sell them to advertisers and local stations they do not control."

**16.** Fox's current collection of 25 O&O's was significantly enlarged through the $3 billion acquisition of the remaining 80% of New World Communications Group stations in 1996 that it did not yet control. The contrast is to the position as of 1989, when Fox operated a full schedule of prime-time programming on three nights of the week (Saturday, Sunday, and Monday) and owned and operated stations in the three major markets but, according to strictly interpreted FCC definitions, was intentionally not a network because it then provided less than fifteen hours a week of programming. By FCC definition, a network also has to provide interconnected program service to at least 25 affiliated licensees in ten or more states. At the time, this had significance with regard to the financial interest and syndication rules (discussed in Chapter 5) because, as a "nonnetwork," Fox had been permitted to have a financial interest in the programming that it developed and distributed.

**17.** By 1990, long-standing affiliate compensation relationships began to shift as the networks sought to lower their expense ratios in recognition of their diminished shares of audience. New affiliate compensation contracts appear to be evolving toward payments related to local market ratings performance. Compensation is still important for stations in smaller markets, where it might amount to 20% of revenues as compared with 4% of revenues for large-market station groups. Also, there have been instances in which stations have actually paid the networks for the privilege of affiliation. For example, in February 2000, Granite Broadcasting agreed to pay NBC $365 million over nine years. (See *Broadcasting & Cable*, February 21, 2000.) As of the early 1990s, annual compensation to affiliates by each of the networks was averaging approximately $125 million. By then, moreover, the greatly increased availability of first-run programming alternatives was making affiliate preemptions of network fare more frequent and was further pressuring the traditional network/affiliate "partnership" and compensation arrangements. See Flint (2000) for a discussion of reverse compensation and Carter (2002a) about the easing of ownership limitations and the potential to reduce affiliate compensation (a practice that began in the early days of radio) through purchase of more stations.

Another shift in compensation practices began in 1998, when CBS affiliates agreed to help fund about 10% of CBS's $4 billion purchase of NFL football rights with a complex system of advertising inventory exchanges and a decrease in network/affiliate compensation. And in 1999, Fox moved to reclaim 20 out of 90 weekly ad spots from affiliates. See Carter (1999) and also *Broadcasting*, August 8, 1983, and September 3, 1988; Cox (1989a); and *Electronic Media*, June 1, 1998.

**18.**    As it happens, ABC's ratings also began to improve, and by the late 1970s ABC finally ended the dominance CBS had held for over 20 years. There immediately ensued considerable switching of the affiliates of other networks to ABC. Another bout of affiliate switching involving FOX and CBS occurred in 1994.

**19.**    In Canada, for example, the Canadian Radio-Television and Telecommunications Commission (CRTC) is charged with the authority to license, regulate, and supervise all aspects of the Canadian broadcasting industry, which includes five major television networks. Two of the five are operated by the Canadian Broadcasting Corporation (a federal crown corporation with a budget of over C$1 billion) and provide basic national services in both English and French. The CTV Television Network Limited (CTV) operates a national, privately owned English-language network, and Les Télé-Diffuseurs Associes (TVA) and Quatre Saisons do the same in French-speaking areas.

In many countries, however, one significant difference from the American system is the use of programming quotas, which are not of regulatory concern in the United States. As of 1989, for example, the CRTC required that Canadian television stations devote 60% of their programming throughout the day and 50% of it in prime time to Canadian material. However, sports and news programming can be counted against these limits.

A major advertiser-supported network company outside the United States would, for example, be Grupo Televisa of Mexico.

**20.**    For instance, between 1980 and 1993, total television industry revenues, including broadcast and cable segments, rose by 160% (8% annually) in real terms while program expenditures rose by 165%. Throughout this period, the *expenditure/revenue ratio remained fairly constant* at around 32%. But for the networks, the share of total industry revenues (in 1993 prices) declined from 37% ($6.8 billion) in 1980 to 21.6% ($10.4 billion). And program expenditures as a proportion of network revenues rose from 52% in 1980 to 60% in 1993 as competition for audiences intensified.

**21.**    It is typical for around 5% of early summer upfront commitments, known as "holds," to be withdrawn by early September, when the "holds" must turn into firm orders for the fourth quarter. Advertisers thereafter also have options to give back a percentage of upfront buys for the first, second, and third quarters of the following year and often do not sign contracts until August or September. Yet because around 80% of new sitcoms and dramas fail, advertisers aren't obligated to buy time on replacement shows, which would usually command lower prices. Upfront figures normally exclude prime-time sports and specials. Changes in upfront sales also do not appear to correlate with total annual broadcast sales changes. See *Advertising Age*, August 26, 2002, and Steinberg (2004). A brief history of upfront selling, which began with ABC in 1962, and the reasons for its recent decline appear in Angwin and Vranica (2006). Advertiser dissatisfaction with the upfront buying process has as of 2007 led to experiments in which buyers participate in eBay-type auctions. See Vranica (2006).

**22.** Whatever time that remains after upfront and scatter have been sold (usually much less than 5% of time inventory) can be purchased by advertisers in what is known as "opportunistic buying" close to the broadcast date. Ads in the scatter market do not contain audience-delivery guarantees, but cable networks and syndicated programs make such guarantees for most of their commercials.

**23.** Pricing paradoxes also occur as the supply of network gross ratings points is reduced as a result of declining network ratings trends: Consumer products companies, trying to efficiently reach mass audiences that are not as dispersed as they are over so many assorted cable networks, are often willing to pay relatively high CPM prices for broadcast network ads even as the size of the total audience shrinks.

**24.** The network that leads the ratings has the potential to attract new affiliates. The addition of affiliates further boosts total network revenue because the percentage of the national population reached by an advertising message is thereby increased.

**25.** And "for pairs of programs on different days and different channels, the duplication of program B with A generally equals the rating of A." See Barwise and Ehrenberg (1988, p. 36).

**26.** Barwise and Ehrenberg (1988, p. 44) cite sociologist William McPhee as having recognized and named the Double Jeopardy Effect. In the same discussion, they also note that the percentage of audience in one week that watches another episode of the same show the following week is only about 40% in the United States and probably no more than 50% in Britain. Even among the most popular series, only a small percentage of the audience, perhaps under 2% or so, may see every episode of the season.

**27.** In 1982, a federal district court judge ruled that the NAB's code, which placed certain restrictions on the number of commercials and their scheduling, violated antitrust regulations. Shortly thereafter, ABC and CBS began to expand commercial availability, with ABC adding one minute per evening. Thus, all three older networks currently exceed the previous NAB nonprogram material standards of 10 minutes per hour in prime time and 16 minutes per hour in all other dayparts – not including promos for coming shows, public service ads, and other nonprogram material. At the behest of Congress, in 1991, limitations of 10.5 minutes per hour on weekends and 12.5 minutes on weekdays were placed on commercials in children's programming. See *Wall Street Journal* of March 30, 1992, and an *Advertising Age* survey of July 2, 1990. Nonprogram time per night at the four major broadcast networks averaged nearly 52.5 minutes in 2003.

By the late 1990s, prime-time commercial time per hour in many popular programs was estimated to have increased an additional 10%, offset in part by reduction of the number of spots used by the networks to promote their own programming schedules. And cable networks have in recent years generally averaged nearly 12 minutes of commercial time per hour. See press releases of American Association of Advertising Agencies and Association of National Advertisers for the latest data.

**28.** To wit: 2.5 minutes per hour on a popular network show will often generate substantially greater revenue for the affiliate than will a full 9 minutes accompanying a program that the local station has either self-produced or acquired elsewhere for cash or barter of time.

**29.** One of the best known of these had been Turner Broadcasting's Atlanta-based WTBS, which transmitted Atlanta Braves baseball games as far away as Alaska and which was transformed into a basic-cable channel as a result of the 1996 purchase by Time Warner. Reimposition of syndication exclusivity rules in the late 1980s limited the growth potential for superstations. And, by 1997, high fees charged to multisystem cable operators (MSOs) (e.g., 10 cents a month per sub, plus up to 12 cents a month per sub for distribution, plus no commercial time for local advertising) made MSOs reluctant to carry superstations. Most basic-cable networks set aside two minutes per hour for such advertising. As of 1997, Chicago's WGN is the last of the nationally distributed superstations. See *Broadcasting*, November 30, 1987, and *Variety*, January 6, 1997, for a complete discussion and history.

**30.** PBS television stations have from time to time considered the possibility of carrying a limited amount of commercial advertising to supplement their income. This idea was discussed in "PBS May Get a Few More Words from Its Sponsors," *BusinessWeek*, no. 2811 (October 10, 1983). Tucker (1982) also discusses the costs of operating public television. And *Broadcasting*, May 11, 1987, p. 60, provides a thorough review of the 20 years of Corporation for Public Broadcasting (CPB) history. As of 1990, the CPB had total income of $1.581 billion, of which federal appropriations accounted for 14.5% and total private contributions 53.1%.

**31.** The BBC was founded in 1922 by a group of radio manufacturers. It has historically been supported in part by license fees charged to television set owners. However, its role in a 400-channel commercial digital universe has, as also in the case of PBS in the United States, come to be questioned. See Champion *et al.* (2004).

**32.** The correlation between advertising expenditures and corporate profits for the post–World War period is approximately 0.97.

**33.** Picard (2001) found that advertising expenditures (in constant currency) declined an average of 5% when a 1% decline in GDP occurred. Also, print media are more affected by recessions than are broadcast media.

**34.** Movies and books have characteristics of both public and private goods: Content here is a public good, but delivery is in the manner of a private good in which consumption by one person makes the product or service unavailable for someone else (Owen *et al.* 1974, p. 15).

**35.** Hence, it shouldn't be surprising to see that even in a 500-channel universe, programs tend to look alike. Programs that are radically different are apt to fail. See also Rothenberg (1996).

**36.** A thorough review of such recent studies appears in Owen and Wildman (1992), where, for example, it is noted (p. 148) that biases "against programs that cater to minority-interest tastes, against expensive programs, and in favor of programs that produce large audiences ... are less pronounced for pay television [than for broadcast television] because the intensity of viewers' preferences is reflected in the prices they pay."

There are several other examples: Peterman and Carney (1978) found evidence that "larger buyers of network TV advertising do not purchase time at prices significantly below those charged smaller buyers." Fisher *et al.* (1980) studied the audience–revenue relationship for local television stations. Wyche and Wirth (1984) described a mathematical model that can be used to project future financial performance for a station. And Crandall (1972) analyzed the implications of FCC rules barring network investments in ancillary program rights.

Also, a most important article on the economics of advertising is by Stigler and Becker (1977). A follow-up on this, which suggests a net positive relationship between a firm's advertising and product output, is by Hochman and Luski (1988).

**37.** As suggested in Chapter 5, prime-time program producers may directly recover only 80% to 85% of the total production cost through the network license fees. Also, as noted, the proportion of self-produced versus licensed programming had been stable up to 1995 and since the 1970s, when antitrust cases against the three networks were settled by consent-decree agreements that had limited networks to producing no more than 2.5 hours per week of entertainment prime-time programming.

**38.** As of 2006, reality programs cost around $875,000 to $1 million per hour versus perhaps three times as much for a scripted hour and $1.2 million for a half-hour sitcom. Reality programming also has an additional advantage in that it appeals to younger viewers and, because it replaces scripted program content, it reduces demand for professionally performed and written dramas and comedies. As noted in Barnes (2006a), a program like NBC's *Deal or No Deal* costs $1.1 million per episode as compared to $2.7 million for the scripted drama *Heroes*, a first-year show with no name stars. See also "Reality TV, Ripening in the Heat of Summer," *New York Times*, May 29, 2006. As in movies, some of the ultimately most successful programming concepts often encounter initial resistance and are shopped around. This happened with ABC's *Desperate Housewives* (with the pilot script initially turned away by CBS, NBC, Fox, HBO, and Showtime) and, as described by Carter (2006), with Fox's *American Idol* (turned away by ABC and the other networks).

**39.** Late-night programming, as epitomized by NBC's *Tonight Show* with Jay Leno, can also be exceptionally profitable. As of 2004, costs for *Tonight* reportedly averaged around $1.5 million per week, while advertising brought in $3.5 million per week (at $60,000 for a 30-second spot), which translates into annual pretax profits of around $100 million or around 15% of the network's entire profit. And Carter (2004a) suggests that with the Leno and follow-up Conan O'Brien shows combined, NBC earned more than $200 million profit on $320 million of revenues – which is more than either ABC or Fox earned from their entire networks. CBS reportedly earned $100 million on revenue of $180 million from the competing Letterman show. By comparison, the final network episode of *Friends* in 2004 generated an estimated $2 million for a 30-second ad, which is close to Super Bowl prices and relatively high for an estimated 50 million viewers. The top-rated telecast of all time was the final (1983) episode of *M\*A\*S\*H* that attracted 105.4 million viewers at an inflation-adjusted price of $846,000 ($450,000 actual). See *Wall Street Journal*, April 27, 2004, and also Steinberg (2005).

**40.** As a percentage of operating costs at independent stations, film amortization of syndicated television series had risen from 35% in the mid-1970s to over 45% in the late 1980s. This compares with levels of about 25% for affiliates, which regularly receive about 65% of their programming from the networks.

**41.** Frankenfield (1994) notes, for example, that a licensee using the gross method of accounting for program costs would incur no interest expense; those using the net of imputed interest method would show an interest cost below the operating line, and thus a higher gross margin. Also, FASB Statement 63 provides considerable flexibility in selection of a program cost amortization schedule. Six methods prevail in the industry:

1. Income forecast
2. Arbitrary acceleration
3. Sum-of-the-runs digit
4. Sum-of-the-years digit
5. Straight-line-per-year
6. Straight-line-per-episode

In addition, FASB Statement 63 indicates that capitalized costs of program rights be recorded at the lower of unamortized cost or net realizable value using the following bases:

1. Program-by-program
2. Series
3. Package
4. Daypart

The daypart aspect is the most controversial because, arguably, write-downs might not be needed if a program can be shifted into a better daypart.

**42.** The FCC had a rule against "trafficking" that prevented turnover of a broadcast property more frequently than every three years. Under deregulation, this rule was abolished in November 1982, and the rate of station trading has increased. In 1995, there were $8.3 billion of radio and television station transactions ($7.9 billion in 2002) and over $6 billion of cable-system transactions (versus $3.5 billion and $1 billion, respectively, in 1988).

**43.** The concept of stick values, at one time believed to be nearly extinct, is still a part of industry jargon and is covered in *Broadcasting* of November 26, 1990.

**44.** Buyers may also sometimes pay 30% down and receive a loan from sellers for up to 70% of the station's value. The loan is usually repaid in ten annual installments. These terms appear to have evolved in response to capital-gains-tax treatments that were in effect during the 1960s and 1970s. In the late 1970s, with real interest rates low and credit readily available, the prices of television and FM radio properties rose steeply. As inflationary psychology took hold, transfer prices for television stations began to be affected by the assumption that there would be high inflation of both land and time prices well into the future.

**45.** The term *broadcast cash flow* is also used as a measure of operating performance, but it is defined as operating income before depreciation and amortization, write-down of franchise costs, and corporate expenses.

**46.** Depreciation and amortization policies may vary from one company to another, but treatments of these items tend toward uniformity. Also, an important aspect of station trading prior to the Tax Reform Act of 1986 was the ability of station owners to cash in on a station's increased market value at capital gains tax rates. The tax code had allowed owners to trade up to more expensive properties without paying any capital gains taxes at all through the use of tax-deferral certificates. The certificates had been granted for like-type exchanges or upgrades that produced the effect of deconcentrating local-media ownership. Such exchanges were very appealing to owners, who, after depreciation had been exhausted, faced the prospect of paying taxes on a rising stream of earnings.

Another important tax-related issue for the broadcasting and cable industries involves amortization of intangible assets. Amortizable intangible assets may include leasehold interests, broadcast rights, and program licenses. Nonamortizable intangibles may include FCC licenses and network affiliation agreements. This whole area is significant in considerations of a station's asset value but had been in a state of flux vis-à-vis the Internal Revenue Service. See also note 26 of Chapter 8 and *Broadcasting*, September 1, 1986, and August 7, 1989. As Smith and Parr (1994) note, under the Omnibus Budget Reconciliation Act of 1993, several classes of intangible assets, such as licenses, permits, or rights granted by the government, may be amortized over a 15-year period.

**47.** See "Limited Partnerships and Leveraged Buyouts: Growing Means to Broadcast Ownership," *Broadcasting*, November 14, 1983.

**48.** In an attempt to boost the prospects of the troubled radio industry, the FCC in 1992 voted to allow, by 1994, a licensee to own as many as 20 AM and 20 FM stations nationwide. However, the Telecommunications Act passed in early 1996 eliminates national ownership limits. In markets with 45 or more commercial radio stations, a broadcaster may own 8 stations, but no more than 5 of a kind (AM or FM) in markets with 30 to 44 stations. See *Broadcasting & Cable*, February 5, 1996.

**49.** Highly leveraged transactions, or HLTs, were officially defined as recapitalizations in excess of $20 million that (a) double liabilities and result in a leverage ratio above 50%; (b) result in total liabilities in excess of 75% of total assets; and (c) are so designated by a bank. The Federal Reserve Board in mid-1992 phased out such HLT restrictions. See *Cablevision*, May 7, 1990.

**50.** As an example, take a hypothetical property that was financed at ten times projected cash flow (c.f.) of $1 million. The total value is then $10 million, and in the late 1980s, banks would have typically financed 60% (or six times c.f.) of the total value. The remaining $4 million would have been funded through equity and subordinated debt. However, by the early 1990s, the same station might have been valued at eight times *trailing* cash flow of perhaps $800,000. Thus, with a value of $6.4 million (a loss of $3.6 million) the senior lender would be able to recoup the original $6 million in principal, but the remaining subdebt and equity positions would be worth only $400,000, or 10% of the original amount. Also, any new lenders would likely finance only $4 million, or about 60% of the station's new value. Under such conditions, the only way for a potential purchaser to finance the station might be for the seller to extend a loan to the buyer. See, for example, *Broadcasting*, July 9, 1990.

**51.** See Woolley (2003) for predictions that zapping of ads could seriously stunt the growth of ad-supported broadcast and cable networks and Woolley (2004a) about the potential impact of unbundling Internet-distributed programs. Manly and Markoff (2005) describe how television programs, like music, can now be downloaded and swapped (using BitTorrent) while commercials are skipped or deleted. The threat is to DVD sales of syndicated shows (and their typical 40% to 50% margins) as well as to conventional broadcast business models. The company YouTube, formed in 2005, is an example of self-distribution of video content. See *BusinessWeek*, April 10, 2006.

**52.** The economic implications are still evolving. For example, as noted in *BusinessWeek*, November 21, 2005, a *Desperate Housewives* download for video iPods sells for $1.99 an episode, of which Apple takes 79 cents and ABC earns $1.20. On the ABC network, the series generates an estimated $11.3 million in ad revenue per episode, which is equivalent to about 45 cents per viewer. Thus, even if 20% of the audience shifts from the network to iPods and ad revenues fall accordingly, ABC would still net $1.8 million more per episode than if such on-demand viewing were not available. In 2006 ABC was also first to announce that it will make much of its most popular programming available for free (ad-supported) viewing on the Internet at anytime. See Barnes (2006c).

**53.** See Gaither (2006).

## Selected additional reading

"A Survey of Television," *The Economist*, April 13, 2002.

Abrams, B. (1985). "TV 'Sweeps' May Not Say Much, but for Now That's All There Is," *Wall Street Journal*, February 28.

    (1984). "CBS Program Chief Picks Entertainment for 85 Million Viewers," *Wall Street Journal*, September 28.

Andrews, E. L., and Brinkley, J. (1995). "The Fight for Digital TV's Future," *New York Times*, January 25.

Barnes, B. (2005). "To Beat Up Rivals, TV Networks Do the Lineup Shuffle," *Wall Street Journal*, August 19.

Bary, A. (2003). "A Sound Idea: Satellite Radio Is Here, and XM Looks Like a Winner," *Barron's*, February 17.

Berman, S., and Flack, S. (1986). "Will the Network Take It out of Hollywood's Hide?," *Forbes*, 138(4)(August 25).

Besen, S. M., Krattenmaker, T. G., Metzger, R. A., Jr., and Woodbury, J. R. (1984). *Mis-regulating Television: Network Dominance and the FCC*. Chicago: University of Chicago Press.

Besen, S. M., and Soligo, R. (1973). "The Economics of the Network-Affiliate Relationship in the Television Broadcasting Industry," *American Economic Review*, June.

Block, A. B. (1990). *Out-Foxed: The Inside Story of America's Fourth Television Network*. New York: St. Martin's Press.

Botein, M., and Rice, D. M. (1980). *Network Television and the Public Interest*. Lexington, MA: Lexington Books, Heath.

Bylinsky, G. (1984). "High Tech Hits the TV Set," *Fortune*, 109(8)(April 16).

Carnegie Corporation (1979). *A Public Trust: The Landmark Reports of the Carnegie Commission on the Future of Public Broadcasting*. New York: Carnegie Corporation and Bantam Books.

Carter, B. (2003). "Reality TV Alters the Way TV Does Business," *New York Times*, January 25.

(2001a). "Can ABC Kick the Regis Habit?" *New York Times*, February 5.

(2001b). "The Thursday Night Fights," *New York Times*, January 18.

(1997a). "Could NBC Live without 'E.R.'?," *New York Times*, November 3.

(1997b). "Where Did the Reliable Old TV Season Go?," *New York Times*, April 20.

Chen, Y. C. (2001). "TiVo Is Smart TV," *Fortune*, 143(6)March 19.

Clemetson, L. (2004). "All Things Considered, NPR's Growing Clout Alarms Member Stations," *New York Times*, August 30.

Coase, R. H. (1966). "The Economics of Broadcasting and Government Policy," *American Economic Review*, 56(May).

Coffey, B. (2002). "Big Audio Dynamite," *Forbes*, 169(6)(March 18).

Colvin, G. (1984). "The Crowded New World of TV," *Fortune*, 110(6)(September 17).

David, G. (2004). "Hollywood Hitman," *Fortune*, 150(4)(August 24).

Day, J. (1996). *The Vanishing Vision: The Inside Story of Public Television*. Berkeley, CA: University of California Press.

Dee, J. (2002). "The Myth of '18 to 34'," *New York Times*, October 13.

Dejesus, E. X. (1996). "How the Internet Will Replace Broadcasting," *Byte*, February 1996.

Donlan, T. G. (1983). "Clear Signal: Deregulation Touches Off a Wave of Bids for TV Stations," *Barron's*, July 11.

Dreazen, Y. J. (2001). "Pittsburgh's KDKA Tells Story of How Radio Has Survived," *Wall Street Journal*, May 15.

Dupagne, M., and Seel, P. B. (1998). *High-Definition Television: A Global Perspective*. Ames: Iowa State University Press.

Eastman, S. T., and Ferguson, D. A. (1997). *Broadcast/Cable Programming: Strategies and Practices*, 5th ed. Belmont, CA: Wadsworth.

"Estimated U.S. Advertising Expenditures, 1935–1979," *Advertising Age*, April 30, 1980; September 14, 1981; May 30, 1983; May 6, 1985.

Fabrikant, G. (1987). "Not Ready for Prime Time?," *New York Times*, April 12.

Fatsis, S. (2003). "NBC Sports Maps a Future without the Big Leagues," *Wall Street Journal*, January 31.

Feder, B. J. (2003). "Satellite Radio Gains Ground with Right Mix of Partners," *New York Times*, April 21.

"Feeling for the Future: A Survey of Television," *The Economist*, February 12, 1994.

Flint, J. (2003). "As Cable Gains in Prime Time, Broadcasters' Cachet Is at Stake," *Wall Street Journal*, May 8.

(2002). "PBS Takes Tack of Commercial Peers: Think Young," *Wall Street Journal*, March 27.

(2000). "How NBC, Out of Sync with Viewers' Tastes, Lost Top Ratings Perch," *Wall Street Journal*, October 24.

Gitlin, T. (1985). *Inside Prime Time*. New York: Pantheon (Random House).

Goldenson, L., and Wolf, M. J. (1991). *Beating the Odds: The Untold Story behind the Rise of ABC*. New York: Charles Scribner's & Sons (Macmillan).

Goldsmith, C. (2002). "As BBC Flourishes, U.K. Is Shaking up the Rest of the Dial," *Wall Street Journal*, October 25.

Greenberg, E., and Barnett, H. (1971). "TV Program Diversity – New Evidence and Old Theories," *American Economic Review*, 61(2)(May).

Gunther, M. (2005). "Crime Pays," *Fortune*, 151(6)(March 21).

(2002a). "The Future of Television," *Fortune*, 145(7)(April 1).

(2002b). "Will Fox Ever Grow Up?," *Fortune*, 145(5)(March 4).

(1999). "The New Face of Network News," *Fortune*, 139(2)(February 1).

(1998). "What's Wrong with This Picture?," *Fortune*, 137(1)(January 12).

(1997). "How GE Made NBC No. 1," *Fortune*, 135(2)(February 3).

Hirschberg, L. (2005). "Give Them What They Want," *New York Times*, September 4.

Hoynes, W. (1994). *Public Television for Sale*. Boulder, CO: Westview Press.

Jensen, E. (1995a). "Why Did ABC Prosper While CBS Blinked? A Tale of 2 Strategies," *Wall Street Journal*, August 2.

(1995b). "CBS's Tisch Is Faulted by Insiders, Affiliates for Network's Struggle," *Wall Street Journal*, May 22.

(1994a). "Many TV Stations Switch Networks, Confusing Viewers," *Wall Street Journal*, October 7.

(1994b). "Major TV Networks, Dinosaurs No More, Tune In to New Deals," *Wall Street Journal*, March 17.

(1994c). "Public TV Prepares for Image Transplant to Justify Existence," *Wall Street Journal*, January 13.

Kagan, P. (1983). "Broadcasting Bonanza: TV Stations Are Fetching Record Prices," *Barron's*, October 17.

Kapner, S. (2002). "British Start Push to Open Media Sector," *New York Times*, May 9.

Kimmel, D. M. (2004). *The Fourth Network: How Fox Broke the Rules and Reinvented Television*. Chicago: Ivan R. Dee.

Kloss, I., ed. (2001). *Advertising Worldwide: Advertising Conditions in Selected Countries*. Berlin: Springer-Verlag.

Kneale, D. (1990a). "TV's Nielsen Ratings, Long Unquestioned, Face Tough Challenges," *Wall Street Journal*, July 19.

(1990b). "Duo at Capital Cities Scores a Hit but Can Network Be Part of It?," *Wall Street Journal*, February 2.

(1989a). "Seeking Ratings Gains, CBS Pays Huge Sums for Sports Contracts," *Wall Street Journal*, October 10.

(1989b). "CBS Frantically Woos Hollywood to Help It Win Back Viewers," *Wall Street Journal*, February 9.

Kupfer, A. (1991). "The U.S. Wins One in High-Tech TV," *Fortune*, 123(7)(April 8).

Labaton, S. (2002). "Appellate Court Eases Limitations for Media Giants," *New York Times*, February 20.

(2001). "Court Weighs Easing Limits on Big Media," *New York Times*, September 8.

La Franco, R. (1999). "Unions on the Ropes," *Forbes*, 163(8)(April 19).

Landro, L. (1984a). "TV Networks Are Again Producing Films for Release in Movie The-
    aters," *Wall Street Journal*, December 5.

    (1984b). "Independent TV Stations Assume Bigger Role in Broadcast Industry," *Wall
        Street Journal*, May 11.

Larson, E. (1992). "Watching Americans Watch TV," *The Atlantic Monthly*, (March).

Leinster, C. (1985). "NBC's Peacock Struts Again," *Fortune*, 112(3)(August 5).

Leonard, D. (2003). "The Unlikely Mogul," *Fortune*, 148(6)(September 29).

Levin, H. J. (1980). *Fact and Fancy in Television Regulation: An Economic Study of Policy
    Alternatives*. New York: Russell Sage Foundation.

Levine, J. (1990). "The Last Gasp of Mass Media?," *Forbes*, 146(6)(September 17).

Mahar, M. (1993). "Life after Cable," *Barron's*, May 10.

Manly, L. (2005a). "On Television, Brands Go from Props to Stars," *New York Times*,
    October 2.

"The Future of the 30-Second Spot," *New York Times*, March 27.

Mathews, A. W. (2002a). "In San Diego, Legal Quirks Help a Radio Empire," *Wall Street
    Journal*, October 4.

    (2000b). "Clear Channel Uses High-Tech Gear to Perfect the Art of Sounding Local,"
        *Wall Street Journal*, February 25.

Mathewson, G. F. (1972). "A Consumer Theory of Demand for the Media," *Journal of
    Business*, 45(2)(April).

Mayer, J. (1983). "Putting Ads on Public TV Angers Few," *Wall Street Journal*, March 24.

McBride, S. (2005). "Hit by iPod and Satellite, Radio Tries New Tune: Play More Songs,"
    *Wall Street Journal*, March 18.

McBride, S., and Wingfield, N. (2005). "As Podcasts Boom, Big Media Rushes to Stake a
    Claim," *Wall Street Journal*, October 10.

McChesney, R. W. (1993). *Telecommunications, Mass Media, and Democracy: The Battle
    for the Control of U.S. Broadcasting, 1928–1935*. New York and London: Oxford
    University Press.

McTague, J. (1996). "Couch-Potato War," *Barron's*, July 15.

Moore, T. (1986). "Culture Shock Rattles the TV Networks," *Fortune*, 113(8)(April 14).

Nelson, E., and Peers, M. (2003). "As Technology Scatters Viewers, Networks Go Looking
    for Them," *Wall Street Journal*, November 21.

Neuman, W. R. (1991). *The Future of the Mass Audience*. New York: Cambridge University
    Press.

Newcomb, P. (1989). "Negative Ratings," *Forbes*, 143(3)(February 6).

Noam, E. (1991). *Television in Europe*. New York and Oxford: Oxford University Press.

Peterman, J. L. (1979). "Differences between the Levels of Spot and Network Television
    Advertising Rates," *Journal of Business*, 52(4)(October).

Pfanner, E. (2004). "State-Aided Broadcasting Faces Scrutiny across Europe," *New York
    Times*, February 16.

Platt, C. (1997). "The Great HDTV Swindle," *Wired*, February.

Poltrack, D. F. (1983). *Television Marketing: Network/Local/Cable*. New York: McGraw-
    Hill.

Reitman, V. (1994). "Pittsburgh's WQED Failed to See Change in Public-TV Industry,"
    *Wall Street Journal*, January 17.

Rose, M., and Flint, J. (2003). "Behind Media-Ownership Fight, an Old Power Struggle
    Rages," *Wall Street Journal*, October 15.

Rothenberg, R. (1995). *Where the Suckers Moon: The Life and Death of an Advertising
    Campaign*. New York: Random House (Vintage).

Rublin, L. (1999). "Tuning Out," *Barron's*, November 8.

Rutherford, P. (1990). *When Television Was Young: Primetime Canada 1952–1967*. Toronto: University of Toronto.

Saddler, J. (1985). "Broadcast Takeovers Meet Less FCC Static, and Critics Are Upset," *Wall Street Journal*, June 11.

    (1984). "Push to Deregulate Broadcasting Delights Industry, Angers Others," *Wall Street Journal*, April 16.

Saporito, B. (1990). "TV's Toughest Year Is Just a Preview," *Fortune*, 122(13)(November 19).

Schatz, A., and Barnes, B. (2006). "To Blunt the Web's Impact, TV Tries Building Online Fences," *Wall Street Journal*, March 16.

Schmalensee, R. (1972). *The Economics of Advertising*. New York: North Holland Publishing Company (Elsevier).

Schmalensee, R., and Bojank, R. (1983). "The Impact of Scale and Media Mix on Advertising Agency Costs," *Journal of Business*, 56(4)(October).

Sellers, P. (1988). "Lessons from TV's New Bosses," *Fortune*, 117(6)(March 14).

Shames, L. (1989). "CBS Has Won the World Series. . . .Now It Could Lose Its Shirt," *New York Times Magazine*, July 23.

Shapiro, E. (1997). "A Wave of Buyouts Has Radio Industry Beaming with Success," *Wall Street Journal*," September 18.

Sharkey, B. (1994). "The Secret Rules of Ratings," *New York Times*, August 28.

Sherman, S. P. (1985). "Are Media Mergers Smart Business?," *Fortune*, 111(13).

Simon, C. (2000). "The Web Catches and Reshapes Radio," *New York Times*, January 16.

Simon, J. L. (1970). *Issues in the Economics of Advertising*. Urbana, IL: University of Illinois Press.

Smith, S. B. (1990). *In All His Glory: The Life of William S. Paley*. New York: Simon and Schuster.

Spence, A. M., and Owen, B. M. (1977). "Television Programming, Monopolistic Competition and Welfare," *Quarterly Journal of Economics*, 91.

Taub, E. A. (2001). "New Format for Radio: All Digital," *New York Times*, January 25.

"Television Ratings: The British Are Coming," *Fortune*, 111(7)(April 1, 1985).

"Television Turns 50," *Broadcasting*, May 1, 1989.

Telser, L. G. (1966). "Supply and Demand for Advertising Messages," *American Economic Review*, 56(May).

Tracey, M. (1998). *The Decline and Fall of Public Service Broadcasting*. New York and Oxford, U. K.: Oxford University Press.

Udelson, J. H. (1982). *The Great Television Race: A History of the American Television Industry, 1925–1941*. Tuscaloosa, AL: University of Alabama.

Weber, T. E. (1999). "Web Radio: No Antenna Required," *Wall Street Journal*, July 28.

Weisman, J. (1987). "Public TV in Crisis," *TV Guide*, (31, 32)(August 1, August 8).

Wirth, M. O., and Allen, B. T. (1980). "Crossmedia Ownership, Regulatory Scrutiny, and Pricing Behavior," *Journal of Economics and Business*, 33(1)(fall).

# 8
# Cable

*You cannot plan the future by the past.* – Edmund Burke, 1791

Though said some 200 years ago, this might well be a slogan for executives of fast-growing cable TV and other new video-media companies in which managements are in a never-ending scramble for franchises, funding, and subscribers. In this chapter, the historical and economic relationships among broadcasting, cable, and other new media are explored.

## 8.1 From faint signals

In the late 1940s, while the technological marvel of wireless broadcasting was still in an early phase of development, the first community-antenna television (CATV) systems were already being built in mountainous or rural regions where over-the-air television signals were difficult, if not impossible, to receive. CATV was an eminently logical idea, developed, according to legend, by television set retailers who wanted to sell more sets: With a good antenna atop a nearby mountain and a clear signal as retransmitted by wire (cable), a burgeoning number of new television households could be created.

Yet until the 1960s, with broadcasting expansively dominant, CATV remained a backwater of the video-communications business. Indeed, it took 15 years, from 1948 to 1963, to connect the first million subscribers. Broadcasters' aggressive lobbying against competition from cable was manifest in arcane FCC regulations limiting the number of distant signals that could be imported into large markets and in prohibiting (in 1970) pay cable systems from showing movies less than ten years old and sporting events that had been on commercial television during the previous five years.

In all, the history of the cable and related satellite television industry can be divided into three major periods. The first lasted from cable's inception as a small-town transmission service up to 1975, when the first satellites allowed nationwide signal distribution. The second lasted from 1975 to 1996, generally a time of greater regulatory freedom and expansion into big cities. The third, beginning with the Telecommunications Act of 1996, has already been a time of consolidation, system clustering, and adoption of digital distribution technologies.[1]

Pay services evolve

The dreams of pioneers notwithstanding, high and rising interest rates, inability to attract sufficient capital funding, and excessive rates of "churn" (i.e., household disconnects/total subscribers) plagued the industry well into the 1970s. By 1975, however, FCC restrictions on cable's distant signal–importation and programming options began to ease. "Superstations" that programmed for a national cable audience sprung up. And, more significantly, Time Inc., the giant magazine publishing company with interests in electronic communications, started a pay TV movie-distribution organization known as Home Box Office (HBO).[2] In contrast to over-the-air commercial-broadcast television services that provided viewers with ostensibly "free" signals, pay TV required that a subscribing household make monthly cash payments for programming.

Offering of a *premium pay cable* service as opposed to *basic cable* service (which simply brought a clearer signal from over-the-air broadcasts into the home) was not by itself revolutionary. What made the difference was that pay TV service could for the first time be nationally and simultaneously distributed to local franchises via earth-orbiting communications-satellite transponders. This technological advance made it possible to provide households simultaneously with several specially programmed movie and sports channels. Basic services thus became only the first of many pay "units" or tiers that the *multiple system operators* (MSOs) – companies that operated more than one cable system – could offer viewers. In addition, it then also became possible to sell movies or sports events such as boxing matches on an à la carte, or *pay-per-view* basis and to take advantage of channel bundling strategies. Economists have shown that such pricing strategies enhance profitability if buyers value a product or service differently but value the package similarly.[3]

Although it was largely unrecognized at the time (because of HBO's heavy start-up costs and losses), so was born not only a major new national television network but also the first serious threat to the movie industry's strong grip on distribution and pricing of its product. Five years elapsed before the filmed-entertainment companies fully understood what had happened and before a subsequently ill-fated attempt was made at launching Premiere, a pay-channel service owned by four leading studio-distributor companies.[4]

Proliferation of pay services was by then well in progress, and by the late 1970s there were several major national film and special entertainment–channel offerings in competition with HBO. The most important of these were Showtime, owned by the former Teleprompter and Viacom, and the Warner–Amex-sponsored The Movie Channel.[5] However, at least 50 other services catering to disparate groups of viewers had also been introduced.[6]

Nevertheless, the great eagerness with which new cable households embraced the plethora of pay-channel offerings misled many MSOs into bidding too aggressively for the then-unbuilt, large city franchises that had come up for proposal in the late 1970s and early 1980s. As a result, many financially overextended MSOs had to renege on their promises later as con-struction and operating cost estimates soared well beyond the points at which reasonable returns could be expected.

Also, despite enormous industry growth, many services during this time continued to experience substantial losses because revenues from subscrip-tions and other sources were insufficient to cover operating expenses, includ-ing those for program production and acquisition, for marketing to system operators and consumers, and for leasing of time on satellites.[7]

Passage of the Cable Communications Policy Act of 1984, allowing dereg-ulation (in 1987) of service pricing, clearly marked the industry's coming of age in terms of both political and economic power (Figure 8.1).[8] By the mid-1980s, with over half of all television homes subscribing to at least a minimal basic service, cable had become the dominant multichannel program-delivery system in the United States and Canada (Figure 8.2). And by 2003, cable's share of audience for the first time surpassed the combined viewership of the major broadcast networks.

Cable viewing currently accounts for more than 35% of total television viewing spread over more than 200 cable networks (Table 8.1), most of which are aimed at capturing specific audience-interest niches. Yet even with such niche-network proliferation, television programming, whether distributed via cable or broadcast networks, will likely remain geared largely to the taste preferences of mass audiences: The share of the prime-time audience taken by the top ten cable channels combined with the five major broadcast networks has remained fairly steady at around 90% since the early 1990s.

The future development and integration of video signal-compression methods along with the deployment of hybrid optical fiber and coax (HFC) network structures and Internet Protocol (IP) technologies are expected to enable the industry to compete vigorously in emerging

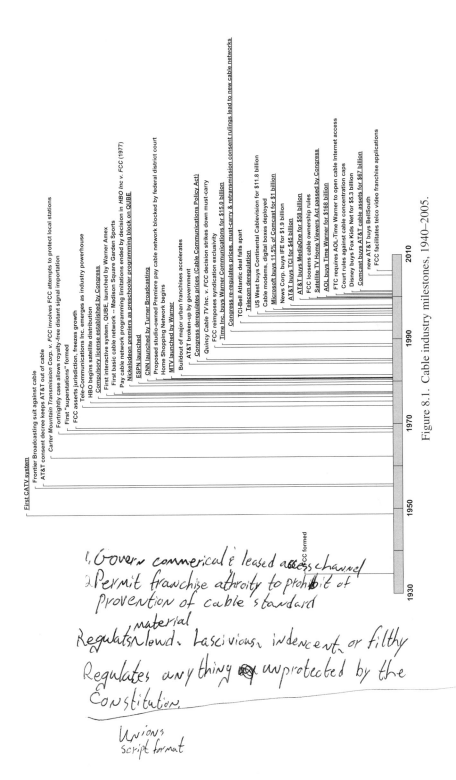

Figure 8.1. Cable industry milestones, 1940–2005.

1. Govern commercial & leased access channel
2. Permit franchise athroity to prohibit of
   provention of cable standard
                material
Regulatsn lewd. Lascivious, indencent, or filthy
Regulates anything unprotected by the
Constitution.

        Unions
        script format

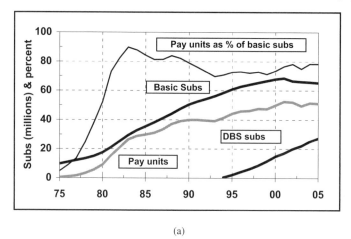

(a)

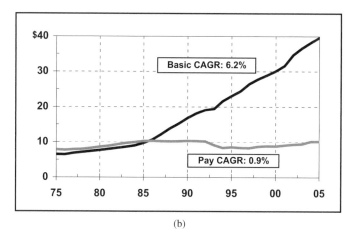

(b)

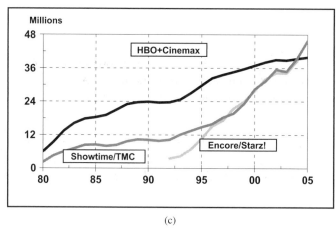

(c)

Figure 8.2. Cable industry trends, 1975–2005. (a) Number of basic cable and pay cable subscribers, and pay cable subscribers as a percentage of basic-cable subscribers. (b) Basic and pay cable estimated monthly rates. (c) Pay-channel service subscribers, major services, 1980–2005. *Source data*: Company reports and Paul Kagan & Associates, Inc., Carmel, California.

Table 8.1. *Top ten cable networks,[a] 2006*

| Rank | Cable network | Start-up date | Subscribers (millions) |
|------|---------------|---------------|------------------------|
| 1 | Discovery Channel | June 1985 | 92.3 |
| 2 | ESPN | September 1979 | 92.2 |
| 3[b] | CNN | June 1980 | 92.0 |
| 3[b] | USA Network | April 1980 | 92.0 |
| 5 | TNT (Turner Network Television) | October 1988 | 91.9 |
| 6 | Lifetime Television | April 1977 | 91.8 |
| 7[b] | Weather Channel | May 1982 | 91.7 |
| 7[b] | ESPN2 | October 1993 | 91.7 |
| 7[b] | Nickelodeon | February 1984 | 91.7 |
| 10 | A&E Networks | February 1985 | 91.6 |

[a] The subscriber number does not represent the actual viewing audience but rather the total universe that can receive the network in question.
[b] Tie.
*Source*: www.NCTA.com.

digital telecommunications markets. Meanwhile, cable-programming services will continue to evolve from the general to the particular.

## 8.2 Cable industry structure

### Operational aspects

Coaxial (and/or fiber optic) cable has the capability of bringing into each home over 100 interactive channels of entertainment and other services. But construction projects are very capital- and politics-intensive, and years may elapse from the point of conceptualization to the stage of operational profitability. Such delays provide the more rapidly deployed and less expensive noncable alternative programming services with opportunities for expansion.

In the days when the business was primarily a CATV service, and cable companies were essentially construction enterprises, not much more than a well-located large antenna, a couple of signal amplifiers, and a few miles of wire was needed for operations to begin. But proliferation of pay services, rapid growth in the number of urban-based customers, demands for upgrading or rebuilding of older one-way systems, and requirements for subscriber addressability have substantially increased the complexity of equipment and the size of capital investment required to operate efficiently.[9]

By the early 2000s, more than half of all U.S. cable subscribers were already being served by systems with 750 MHz of frequency bandwidth capacity (as compared with older systems with less than 300 MHz bandwidth). The newest fiber-optic systems now commonly have 1,000 MHz (1 gigahertz [GHz]) widths that can transmit more than 150 channels.

In the replacement of coaxial feeder and trunk line cables with fiber (fiber-to-the-curb [FTTC]), MSOs have also been changing system architectures from the traditional tree-and-branch arrangement to a hybrid-fiber-coax (HFC) arrangement that sends signals to a neighborhood hub (node). These nodes can serve several hundred homes and provide an upstream signal path for use with interactive programming.[10] But the key economic variable in such HFC systems is the ratio of nodes to subscribers.

Computers and transportation vehicles are two other major capital items. At the head-end facilities, from where signals are sent to subscribing households, computers monitor the system's wires and amplifiers for any failures that may occur and keep track of what each household is receiving. And computers are, of course, used to update records of connections, monthly billings, and program-guide shipments.

In addition, field-service personnel (whose salaries are a major operating expense) also require extensive fleets of trucks and other mobile equipment to connect and disconnect homes, install converters, and repair and maintain wires. Especially in large cities, where installation is complicated by the density of population and the need to construct underground conduits (instead of renting the use of telephone utility poles as in rural regions), the problems of maintenance, of customer service, and of signal piracy can be so severe as to reduce a system's profit potential noticeably. Table 8.2 shows a breakdown of U.S. cable systems by subscriber size and channel capacity, while Figure 8.3 illustrates the trend of concentration of cable system ownership. Such consolidation has enabled the largest MSOs to leverage more effectively against the stiff price demands (in terms of monthly fees per subscriber) of popular cable program networks and also to more forcefully counter challenges from direct-to-home digital satellite and telephone company service providers.

This is important because, in total, the typical system's largest cost category is for programming, which will often amount to approximately one-third of all costs. Personnel costs (salaries) are the second largest category, accounting for approximately 18% of the total operating budget (Table 8.3). As digital telephone and other Internet services are developed, however, the composition of revenue and cost categories is likely to change significantly from those of the early 2000s.

Franchising

Cable systems, by their very nature, operate in a way that is pretty close to what economists might define as being a natural monopoly: a market in which there is room for only one firm of efficient size (because its average cost continues to decline as its scale increases). They also bundle the provision of transmission services along with the provision of program services. It is therefore not surprising that government regulation – more a political

Table 8.2. *U.S. cable systems by estimated subscriber size and channel capacity, 2005*

| | Systems | % of total | Subscribers (millions) | % of total |
|---|---|---|---|---|
| *Size by subscribers* | | | | |
| 50,000 & over | 298 | 3.8 | 39.2 | 60.4 |
| 20,000–49,999 | 392 | 4.9 | 12.3 | 18.9 |
| 10,000–19,999 | 379 | 4.8 | 5.4 | 8.3 |
| 5,000–9,999 | 479 | 6.0 | 3.4 | 5.2 |
| 3,500–4,999 | 265 | 3.3 | 1.1 | 1.7 |
| 1,000–3,499 | 1,251 | 15.8 | 2.4 | 3.6 |
| 999 & under | 4,862 | 61.3 | 1.2 | 1.9 |
| Total | 7,926 | 100.0[a] | 64.9 | 100.0[a] |
| *Channel capacity* | | | | |
| 125 & over | 126 | 1.6 | 1.6 | 2.5 |
| 91–124 | 147 | 1.9 | 4.2 | 6.5 |
| 54–90 | 2,087 | 26.3 | 38.6 | 59.4 |
| 30–53 | 3,441 | 43.4 | 4.5 | 7.0 |
| Other | 2,125 | 26.8 | 16.0 | 24.6 |
| Total | 7,926 | 100.0[a] | 64.9 | 100.0[a] |

[a] Total not exact because of rounding.

*Source*: *Television & Cable Factbook*, No. 74. Washington, DC: Warren Publishing Inc., 2006.

process than an effective antidote to monopolistic conditions – has become a prominent part of the industry's economic landscape.[11] Despite considerable easing of federal regulation since the early 1970s, the FCC retains authority even (as the Supreme Court ruled in 1984) to preempt city and state controls.[12]

Nowhere, however, have the regulatory features been historically more visible than at the local community level from which franchises are originated and administered. Municipalities may receive up to 5% (normally 3% as a base) of system revenues and may negotiate strongly for other special benefits in return for granting a local monopoly.[13] Moreover, until recently, municipalities had governed increases on fees for basic services.[14]

Still, to bid successfully for a franchise that is yet to be constructed, cable companies must carefully forecast potential revenues and costs of operation over the typical 15-year franchise period. Franchise bidders also will often promise to contribute to the community fully equipped television studios, libraries, and "free" local-access channels.[15]

Construction proposals (so-called requests for proposals, or RFPs) obviously involve large expenditures of time and money without any assurance that a bid will be successful. Furthermore, in the event of a successful bid, several years will elapse between the time the franchise is awarded and the

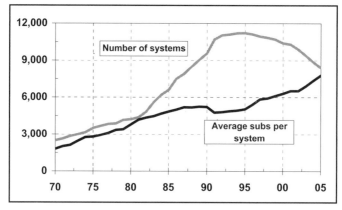

Figure 8.3. Cable system concentration trends, 1970–2005.

time the new system becomes fully operational (is "energized") and profitable. In the interim, financing and construction expenses may rise substantially over the original estimates, and the cream of the market may be skimmed by other technologies (discussed in Section 8.4) that can be potentially implemented more rapidly.

Revenue relationships

The introduction of pay cable services on a nationally distributed basis was crucial in launching the industry on a high-growth path, and the cable industry has indeed come to depend on subscription revenues for approximately 70% of total revenues (versus 30% from advertising). Basic-service channels (e.g., CNN, MTV) derive their revenues from commercial advertising and fixed monthly fees paid by the carriers as based on the available number of households reached. Premium services, however, operate with minimal or no advertising, but instead charge subscribers an additional monthly fee per channel or require payment for each view (pay-per-view).

In stark contrast to the broadcast model, where a mass-media network's revenues might approximate, say, $10 per *thousand* viewers every 15 minutes, a premium cable network can be more profitable with a smaller audience and a *monthly* revenue stream of only $5 per subscriber (i.e., $5,000 for every 1,000 subs). Given that the programming costs for such a network are typically around 65% of revenues, a pay network can thus be financially viable with audience ratings that are relatively miniscule as compared with those needed for broadcasters. The willingness of consumers to continue to subscribe to premium services at such prices, however, ultimately depends on the quantity and quality of the programming that is provided.

MSOs are, of course, perfectly capable of producing low-budget programs of local interest. But by and large, this is not what the pay customers want

Table 8.3. *Cable network and other program distribution services:*
*operating revenue and expenses for 2004*[a]

| Item | Total ($ millions) | Percent of total[c] |
|------|-------------------|----------------------|
| **Operating revenue**[b] | **104,690** | |
| Air time (advertising) | 16,548 | 15.8 |
| Specialty programming service | 18,090 | 17.3 |
| Basic programming service | 43,699 | 41.7 |
| Premium cable programming packages | 5,548 | 5.3 |
| Pay-per-view service | 2,661 | 2.5 |
| Program distribution equipment sales and rental | 2,205 | 2.1 |
| Internet access services | 8,582 | 8.2 |
| Telephony (local and l.d.) | 1,723 | 1.6 |
| Other | 5,634 | 5.4 |
| | | 100.0 |
| **Operating expenses** | **83,602** | |
| Annual payroll | 12,600 | 15.1 |
| Employer contributions to employee benefit plan | 2,515 | 3.0 |
| Contract labor | 1,550 | 1.9 |
| Total purchased services | 8,172 | 9.8 |
| Advertising and promotional services | 3,276 | 3.9 |
| Program and production costs | 32,247 | 38.6 |
| Depreciation | 15,341 | 18.4 |
| Other | 7,901 | 9.5 |
| | | 100.0 |

[a] Based on the North American Industry Classification System.
[b] Includes other amounts not shown separately.
[c] Total not exact because of rounding.
*Source*: U.S. Bureau of the Census, *Annual Survey of Communication Services.*

to see. It is far more convenient for the MSO to purchase, from wholesalers such as HBO or Showtime, the rights to play movies or to obtain special-interest programming by joining with other MSOs. In the case of movies or sports, there is then no need for each MSO to deal inefficiently with the large Hollywood studios on a picture-by-picture basis or with leagues for each game season. Thus have cable networks and their distribution counterparts at the MSOs become the two pillars on which the modern cable industry has been built.

For the filmed-entertainment premium programming wholesalers (HBO and Showtime, for example), relationships with the MSOs on one side and the program suppliers on the other are, nevertheless, complex. Because at least 500 titles a year (1,000 at HBO) are normally required to fill out a channel's schedule, wholesalers will commit to spending hundreds of millions of dollars to license in advance for a specified number of exhibitions a full (or nearly full) slate of a studio's output (sometimes exclusively) for a three- to five-year period.

Such arrangements provide studios with a solid base of production financing while assuring wholesalers a programming schedule that can retain the allegiance of their immediate customers, the MSOs. Nevertheless, license fees negotiated with the studios will typically be calibrated to the theatrical box-office performances of the films in these packages. If averaged over all new titles in a package, the fees might generally work out to an acquisition cost per film of under 20 cents a channel-subscriber, but possibly more as based on the popularity of the films included and the extent of exclusivity arrangements made.

In purchasing from the premium wholesaler, the MSO, in turn, abides by a rate card. This card sets a standard monthly minimum per household and also certain sliding-scale surcharges that are used by the wholesaler as an incentive for the MSO to sign up as many subscribers as possible.

A summary of a representative rate card prior to volume discounts, which can substantially lower the total cost to the MSO, might be as follows:

If the system charges over $12.00 a month, the wholesaler is to receive $6.25 + 50% of any amount over $12.00; systems at $11.00 to $12.00 pay $6.50 flat, and those under are scaled down $0.25 for each dollar until a floor rate of $5.00 flat is reached for systems charging under $6.50.

The wholesaler thus will normally receive a little over half of what the retailer (the MSO) charges the average household for the pay-channel service. Then, on average, about one-half of what the wholesaler receives (or around 25% of the retail price) is used to pay the program suppliers, be they movie studios or other production and/or distribution entities.[16]

Fortunately, the revenue-sharing relationships for basic networks are considerably simpler to describe. Although the types of arrangements between MSOs and such networks may vary considerably from one situation to another, it is common for each MSO to compensate a network for its programming on the basis of at least 5 or 10 cents, and sometimes, as in the case of ESPN or regional sports networks, much more than $1 a month per subscriber.[17] Thus basic networks now collectively derive at least one-half of their revenues from fees charged to MSOs, with less than half of total revenues garnered from the sale of national or regional advertising.[18] It remains an open question, though, as to how much advertising on cable viewers will tolerate as the price of basic services, as shown in Figure 8.2b, rises.[19]

A comparison of the growth of estimated advertising expenditures on cable services with expenditures on network television advertising of $16 billion in 2005 and national spot and local spending of approximately $11 billion and $14 billion, respectively, is illustrated in Figure 8.4. As may be inferred, commercial sponsorship of cable programming has indeed become increasingly attractive to advertisers as audiences for broadcast

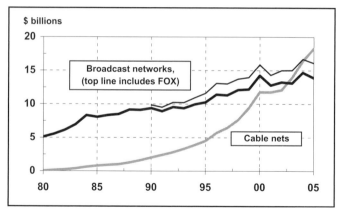

Figure 8.4. Cable network advertising revenues, 1980–2005. *Source data*: Robert Coen, Universal McCann, Inc.

network television have grown more slowly (if at all) and as demographic and income characteristics of cable audiences have improved.

Hence, unlike the situation for over-the-air broadcasters, financial support for cable programmers can come directly from viewers, from advertisers, from cable operators, or from a combination of all three sources. And, as compared with broadcast networks, cable networks are not for the most part burdened by affiliate relations, program development, and news division costs. Clearly, by the early 1990s, the cable industry, then with aggregate revenues of more than $22 billion and operating cash flows in excess of $7 billion, had reached and, in many respects, surpassed financial parity with the commercial broadcasting industry.

## 8.3 Financial characteristics

Capital concerns

The industry's tremendous thirst for capital to upgrade old systems and construct new ones ("new builds," in industry parlance) has led to concentration into fewer, but financially stronger, ownership entities. As can be seen from the data in Table 8.4, major publicly owned companies now control the largest subscriber groups.

Because capital costs for system expansions have been so large, it was not until the late 1980s that the industry could begin to show significant aggregate operating profits after deduction of interest expenses. Just as in broadcasting, however, the more relevant (and also conventional) measure of financial performance for cable industry companies is not operating profit but operating cash flow, defined as earnings before interest, taxes, and depreciation and amortization expense (EBITDA). As in broadcasting, this definition of cash flow is used to avoid comparative distortions that

Table 8.4. *Top five multiple-system cable operators, data in millions, 2006*

| Rank | System operator | Number of subscribers | Homes passed by cable |
|------|-----------------|-----------------------|-----------------------|
| 1 | Comcast Corporation | 24.1 | 42.0 |
| 2 | Time Warner Cable | 14.6 | 26.0 |
| 3 | Charter Communications | 6.2 | 12.5 |
| 4 | Cox Communications | 5.4 | 9.4 |
| 5 | Cablevision Systems | 3.1 | 4.8 |

*Source*: www.NCTA.com.

may arise as a result of financing and tax variations. (Nevertheless, the raw EBITDA metric has lost favor in recent years, and many analysts now prefer to arrive at an estimate that more closely approximates free cash flow, i.e., the cash that is available to the company for purposes other than new system construction.)

Cable operating margins, calculated by taking operating cash flows as a percentage of revenues, also provide a handy means of comparison among different operating systems. Such margins would normally fall into the range of 35% to 50% for most financially strong companies.[20]

For many analytical purposes, though, the most convenient way to understand the profitability and cash flow potential of a system is through use of population-density and penetration figures. Much of a system's operating cost is fixed and independent of subscriber numbers, and construction cost per mile may in some instances be essentially the same whether there is one subscriber or there are a thousand subscribers along that mile.[21] "Drop" charges (the cost of attaching a home to the main feeder cable) and the cost of installing converters (used to enable ordinary TV tuner circuits to display more signals) are the only major variable expenses related to subscriber density.[22]

A simple exercise, with the following assumptions, will illustrate:

A new 1,000-mile system costs an average of $15,000 per mile, or $15 million, to build.

Both basic and pay monthly service charges are $10.

Penetration of the 10,000 homes along the 1,000-mile route is 50%, and the ratio of pay to basic subscribers is also 50%.

The cable operating margin is 40%.

Thus, annual revenues from basic service would be $600,000 ($10/month × 12 months × 5,000 subscribers), pay-service revenues would be $300,000, and total revenues would then be $900,000. Applying a 40% operating margin, we obtain profits of $360,000, which is a 2.4% (360/15,000) annual return on total capital investment before accounting for depreciation, interest, and taxes.

The return on capital (ROC) in this example appears to be surprisingly inadequate for two reasons. First, the number of homes passed per mile of plant (i.e., the density) is far too low to support a new build. The density of ten homes per mile in this example compares with an average of about eighty homes per mile for all systems in the United States. Were this hypothetical system to contain the average homes per mile, and with all other things equal, the ROC would be 19.2%. (Also, in most instances, the returns to equity investors would be noticeably higher than in this example because most of the capital needed to build the system would be borrowed.)

In a modern system, moreover, the ratio of pay to basic subscribers would almost certainly be well over 50%. And any incremental pay revenues (as well as higher penetration levels) would significantly boost returns; once a system is in place, the cost of adding subscribers or tiers of service beyond the basic service is minimal.

Relating the total required investment per subscriber to the minimum average monthly charge that the system needs to stay in business over the long run reveals another interesting aspect. Assume, for example, that a 54-channel addressable system was to be built starting in 1995. Estimated investment per subscriber typical of the industry might then appear as in Table 8.5. If interest rates were around 10% per year and the system were depreciated over the usual 15-year franchise period at 6% per year, then, just to recover interest and depreciation, the minimum average monthly charge to each subscriber household would have to be $17.33 $[(0.10 + 0.06) \times \$1,300]/12$.

It has not been unusual for cable companies to be leveraged at six to seven times EBITDA and sometimes to have additional off–balance sheet debts tied to special purpose entities. As a result, total borrowing by the industry had grown by the early 2000s to around $80 billion, which implies an average of

Table 8.5. *Typical investment per subscriber, circa 2005*

| Fixed | |
| --- | --- |
| Plant (including labor) | $650 |
| Head end, vehicles, etc. | 125 |
| Origination, studios, and equipment | 75 |
| Other | 75 |
| Total fixed | 925 |
| *Variable* | |
| Converters (set-top boxes) | 300 |
| Drops | 75 |
| Total variable | 375 |
| Total per subscriber | $1,300 |

Table 8.6. *Cable system (video subscription service) operators, operating industry performance: composite of 24 companies, 2001–2005*

| | Revenues | Operating income | Operating margin[a] (%) | Assets | Operating cash flow |
|---|---|---|---|---|---|
| CAGR (%):[b] | 17.7 | NM[c] | NM[c] | 3.2 | 34.5 |

[a] Average margin, 2001–2005 = 3.5%.
[b] Compound annual growth rate.
[c] Not meaningful.

about $1,250 of debt per basic subscriber, backed by perhaps another $950 or so (per subscriber) in equity. With new builds costing at least $1,100 per subscriber, it is easy to see how billions of dollars more always have to be raised from bank loans and through issuance of shares and bonds and limited partnerships to maintain, upgrade, and expand systems into new fiber optic and digital-switching technologies. Recent industry operating data are shown in Table 8.6.

Accounting conventions

In the life-cycle development of a cable company, there are three distinct stages for which special accounting treatments have evolved and been codified – first by a March 1979 AICPA position paper and then by subsequent issuance in 1981 of FASB Statement 51. The three distinct stages are as follows:

1.  *Start-up*: the time between construction start and receipt of service by the first subscriber
2.  *Prematurity*: usually less than two years and coincident with construction completion; it is the time between first subscriber activation and maturation of the system
3.  *Maturity*: the system at maturity

Before the AICPA guidelines, major cable franchises generally capitalized all start-up expenses until the system was profitable. But under FASB Statement 51, construction, labor, interest, and other start-up expenses are normally capitalized only during the first phase. In effect, the prematurity period now bears a significant amount of cost, and installation-fee revenue accruals are not as high as they had been prior to implementation of FASB Statement 51. More specifically:

• In the second phase, most subscriber-related operating expenses are not capitalized, although plant costs may continue to be capitalized. Systemwide costs – such as for local programming, pole rentals, property taxes, and so forth – may be partially capitalized and partly expensed, the amounts depending on the ratio of the number of current subscribers to the expected number at the end of the prematurity phase. This formula is also used for depreciation and amortization, which must be over the same period and not longer than the life of the franchise.

- In addition, the amount of interest cost to be capitalized during prematurity is determined in accordance with FASB Statement 34, which indicates that the amount of interest cost capitalized shall not exceed the total amount of interest cost incurred by the system in that period.
- The initial costs of subscriber installations, however, are capitalized and depreciated over the period used for the whole system. Similarly, the costs of successful franchise application are capitalized and amortized according to standards for intangible assets as delineated in APB (Accounting Principles Board) Opinion 17.
- Except for installation fees (which can be accrued as revenues only to the extent offset by direct selling costs incurred), revenues from monthly subscriptions are recorded as income. If installation fees exceed marketing costs, the difference is capitalized and recorded as income over the expected average period during which the subscriber is expected to be active.

Within these guidelines, it is also important to make the distinction between operating cash flow (EBITDA) and cash flow from operations, a figure that appears on the cash flow statements filed with regulators. By capitalizing some or all out-of-pocket ongoing expenses pertaining to acquisition of customers, deployment of installation trucks, and purchases of set-top boxes, the all-important EBITDA numbers used for purposes of making investment comparisons might not be much affected, yet cash on the balance sheet will nonetheless still be depleted, and to the extent that it is depleted, financing risk rises.[23] In addition, accounting treatment differences that might distort EBITDA comparisons between companies have sometimes appeared in the areas of advertising revenue recognition practices, subscriber counts, and cable network fee amortization schedules.[24] Such distortions have become less numerous now that cable industry accounting definitions for revenue generating units (RGUs), customer relationships, and capital expenditures have been standardized (as of 2003).[25]

It should be further noted that, for cable systems that are being acquired, the excess price over book or fair value paid by the acquirer is now amortized over 15 years. Until the tax code was modified in 1993 under new Section 197, there had been uncertainties as to whether such amortizations of goodwill (the excess price over book value) and intangible franchise rights would be tax deductible.[26]

## 8.4 Development directions

Pay-per-view

Were it not for the introduction of pay movie and sports channels beginning in the 1970s, the cable industry today would be far smaller than it is. But clearly, the next step, along with the replacement of coaxial cable by optical fibers and the introduction of high-definition pictures, is the burgeoning of pay-per-view (PPV) services. Throughout most of the 1980s, an average of less than 15% of all cable converters were capable of being directly addressed from a system's head end, and subscription to pay *channels* rather than to specific program offerings was the only technologically practical means of sending several pay signals into the home.

But with the number of addressable households increasing rapidly and with the cost of computing power decreasing, such PPV services are slowly becoming a significant source of industry revenues. However, the degree to which such video-on-demand (VOD) offerings – including subscription VOD (SVOD), which provides multiple titles for a flat rate over a specified time – eventually cannibalize subscriptions to the more traditional pay-channel services (and also adversely affect video and DVD sales or rentals) is still an open question.[27]

Nevertheless, that PPV has the potential to be an extremely profitable service for cable operators to provide, even if half or more of the MSO's revenues are remitted to program originators or distributors, can be seen from the following simple example. Assume the following:

A universe of 25 million addressable homes
A response ("buy") rate of 4%, or 1 million households
A PPV price of $10
That the movie company or other program supplier retains 40% of the PPV price to the viewer
That a program wholesaler/distributor retains 10% in return for setting up marketing and distribution and the MSO retains 50%

Then, the program supplier will generate $4 million of revenue in one night, and the MSO $5 million.[28] For the movie company in this hypothetical situation, the amount could compare very favorably with what would ordinarily be obtained through licensing to a pay channel or through theatrical exhibition. And for the cable company, the potential exists for substantially enhanced profitability if the subscribing household makes more than one PPV selection a month or if the response rate is higher than 4%.[29]

Cable's competition

Cable has been, and will long continue to be, the major alternative distribution system to over-the-air broadcasts. Indeed, of all the broadcast-related media, cable's great advantage is that it is not at all constrained by electromagnetic spectrum availability. Cable, nonetheless, continues to be challenged by a veritable alphabet soup of competitors (or potential competitors) that include MMDS, SMATV, DBS, and a few smaller variants. Of these, DBS, using digital technology, has emerged as the most important.

*DBS/DTH* Direct broadcast satellites (DBS) can send pay and basic channel signals to small receiving dishes owned or leased by viewers and thus bypass the need for a cable system's transmission services. With advances in technology, DBS has evolved into what is known as direct-to-home (DTH) digital service that provides an economic advantage over other video distribution systems in that costs do not rapidly increase with the number of subscribers receiving the transmissions. DTH systems are also not burdened by local regulation of prices, services, or payments of franchise fees. DTH has become a significant competitor to cable in the United States and is already a strong challenger elsewhere.[30] Growth in the number of DBS subscribers in the United States is shown in Figure 8.2a.

*MMDS/LMDS* Multichannel multipoint distribution of signals (MMDS) via microwaves (sometimes also known as local multipoint distribution, or LMDS) has the tremendous advantage of not requiring streets to be dug up or telephone poles to be rented. The line-of-sight amplitude-modulated signals for such "wireless cable" systems can be distributed locally to apartment or office clusters equipped with special antennae.[31]

*SMATV* Satellite master antenna television (SMATV) is an extension of this concept, except that the master community antenna is actually a receiving dish that can pull pay-channel signals from satellite transponders and distribute them locally to homes and apartments located nearby. In densely populated areas, SMATV can often circumvent the extensive and expensive politicking that usually accompanies cable-franchise bidding and can skim some of the cable franchise's cream years before a cable system is built.

*STV* Subscription television (STV), using scrambled over-the-air UHF broadcast signals, was an early competitor to cable in the United States but could not provide the programming and visual quality to compete over the long run.[32]

Telephone companies

The telephone and cable industries have long been archenemies, and technological advances in the processing and distribution of digital signals have only intensified the competition. More computing power at ever-diminishing cost has made it financially feasible to send data, voice, and video signals

down the same types of electronic or optical pipes, thereby blurring the tech-
nilogical and even business strategy distinctions between the two industries.

Within the framework of regulatory changes such as those embodied in
the Telecommunications Act of 1996, convergence of the two industries
(e.g., the acquisition of TCI by AT&T in 1999 and the purchase of AT&T
cable assets completed by Comcast in 2002) follows naturally, although considerable differences remain. Cable system architecture, for instance, was
originally designed for one-way traffic, with one point (the head end) distributing only to other already specified points. The advent of IP telephony
operating through digital cable modems, however, has enabled cable companies to compete against the traditional telephone network's switched-circuit
systems.[33]

Cable companies also have audience-delivery expertise and well-
established agreements for access to programming that phone companies
lack. And cable already provides video signal quality standards that phone
companies cannot easily or inexpensively replicate on their own. As a
result, cable companies now often derive more than half of their total
revenues from digital Internet and telephony services, with the television
and movie programming businesses on which they were founded becoming almost a sideline. But coming from the other end, telephone companies (telcos) are beginning to provide content delivery through IP (IPTV)
services.[34]

As Figure 3.10 illustrated earlier (from a perspective centered on the major
movie distributors), the relationships that have evolved among cable, telephone, Internet, and content-provider companies are already quite complex.
Yet both telcos and cable companies will also end up competing with broadband over powerline (BPL) services that can deliver comparable products
via the electrical wiring that is present in all homes and offices.

## 8.5 Valuing cable-system properties

Although transfer prices are popularly and casually measured in terms of
price per subscriber (peaking at around $5,000 per sub around the year 2000
and later falling by 50%), this measure can be misleading. Some factors
that ought to be considered when making comparisons on the basis of per
subscriber averages are the following:

Long-term interest rates, which affect projected cash flows, construction
    costs, and perhaps consumers' willingness to take extra pay services
New-household formation expectancy and demographic and income mix,
    which depend on the location of the system
Franchise agreements, which may have widely differing terms
The quality and quantity of off-the-air signals, which influence the willing-
    ness of consumers to pay for television programming

The condition of a system's physical plant, which includes the number of
  miles of plant yet to be built, current channel capacity, and previous maintenance and repair policies
Prospects for changes in government regulation, especially with regard to
  subscriber pricing policies[35]
The probabilities that potential new competition from evolving technologies
  will slow subscriber growth and diminish pricing power

A potential buyer of a system would then weigh all the aforementioned
factors and decide upon an appropriate valuation multiple of the system's
EBITDA and asset base. Such a private market multiple would typically
range between eight and fifteen times the cash flow that is *projected* for the
next year (Table 8.7). The multiple would also be more precisely determined
by comparing it with cash flow multiples on similar, recently traded systems
and with estimates of the potential for generating new revenue streams –
economic value added (EVA) – on already invested capital. In such EVA
models, share valuations key off the difference between the weighted-average
cost of debt and equity capital (WACC) and the returns in excess of the
WACC:

$$\text{WACC} = \text{debt}/(\text{debt} + \text{equity}) \times r_d + \text{equity}/(\text{debt} + \text{equity}) \times r_e,$$

where $r_d$ is the cost of debt expressed as an interest rate and $r_e$ is the cost of
equity as estimated using risk premiums and risk adjustment factors (known
as betas).[36]
  In all instances, cash flow is the critical element that enables system maintenance and expansion, pay-down of debt, and diversification. Common measures of a cable company's financial strength would thus accordingly include
the calculation of a *coverage ratio* of cash flow to interest cost (EBITDA/net
interest) and of a *leverage ratio* of debt to cash flow ([long-term debt less
cash]/EBITDA). A coverage ratio of under 2:1 would normally be a sign
that a company runs a risk of default if business turns down, while a leverage
ratio of greater than 5:1 would suggest a relatively risky balance sheet profile.
Basic cable *networks* would also be compared using such ratios.[37]
  Just as with broadcasting properties, however, private market values, which
include an implicit control premium, are normally much higher than are seen
in public market trading of shares (see also Section 7.4).
  To estimate what the implied value per subscriber is for publicly traded
shares, the number of shares outstanding for a company should be multiplied
by the price of a share. Then the amount of debt should be added and the
result divided by the number of subscribers:[38]

$$\text{value per subscriber} = \frac{(\text{stock price} \times \text{shares outstanding}) + \text{debt}}{\text{number of subscribers}}.$$

Table 8.7. *Public and private market valuation
methods: examples*

| | |
|---|---:|
| **Public market values** | |
| Price per share | $11.50 |
| Shares outstanding | 60 |
| Total market value of equity[a] | 690 |
| plus | |
| Total long-term debt | 1,200 |
| Total less | 1,890 |
| Cash | 150 |
| Other off–balance sheet assets | 250 |
| Adjusted enterprise value (AEV) | 1,490 |
| EBITDA | 165 |
| Cash flow multiple (AEV/EBITDA) | 9.0 |
| **Private market values** | |
| EBITDA | 165 |
| times assumed multiple[b] | 10 |
| Unadjusted value | 1,650 |
| plus | |
| Cash | 150 |
| Other off–balance sheet assets | 250 |
| less | |
| Long-term debt | 1,200 |
| Net asset value | 850 |
| Shares outstanding | 60 |
| Net private market asset value per share | $14.17 |

[a] If preferred stock is in capitalization, its market value must
also be included.
[b] Derived by comparison with recent transfer-price multiples
for similar assets.

Using the same concepts, it is also possible to derive an estimate of the value
of whole cable (or broadcasting) industry segments.

## 8.6 Concluding remarks

Significant advances in signal distribution technology combined with generous applications of capital, and also several doses of deregulation, have
enabled the cable business to grow into a $70-billion-a-year giant in the
space of 50 years. Now that cable reaches into more than 65% of U.S. households, however, it is showing signs of maturity: The thirst for capital to
upgrade into fiber optics and to maintain plant is still present, but the growth

rate, as measured by the net addition of new subscribers and pay services, has slowed. Moreover, significant capital investments are still being made for the digital (i.e., IP) switches and other signal processing equipment that will be required to squeeze hundreds of new channels into presently available bandwidths and to grow Internet-related services – especially those relating to telephones.[39]

It is indeed the development of such broadband services that will drive industry cash flows to new heights.[40] Cable companies – originally only in the business of buying programming feeds wholesale and selling them retail – have become centers for distribution of digital communications services of all kinds and now derive less than half of their revenues from provision of video program services. With fiber optics and the appropriate digital switching devices, telephone and video services technologically resemble each other. And the old walls of regulatory and political considerations that had long prevented telcos from providing cable services and cable systems from providing telephone services have crumbled.[41]

Although legislative and regulatory turf battles between the telcos and the cable industry will likely extend into the future, it would appear that this epic political and economic power struggle is being resolved through technological developments that accelerate the blending of each industry's service capabilities into the other's.

Clearly, television sets are no longer passive devices. As Chapter 10 explains, they can even play games with you.

## Notes

**1.** A convenient brief history of cable is in Chapter 2 of Parsons and Frieden (1998).

**2.** A key decision that also helped launch HBO came in 1977, when the Washington D.C. Circuit Court of Appeals struck down the FCC's restrictions on pay television. See also Whiteside (1985).

**3.** By bundling channels various packages of channels into tiers instead of selling each channel separately (à la carte), MSOs astutely employed a pricing strategy that was first analyzed in relation to the block booking of movies by Stigler (1963). The enhanced profitability of bundling is the reason why MSOs have long been resistant to à la carte services. The economics is reviewed in Hoskins *et al.* (2004, pp. 230–234). Essentially, if two people have what's known as a *reservation price*, that is they are willing to pay $10 for one channel and $2 for another but their preferences are reversed, it is possible to charge both $12, or $24 total, which is more than the $20 total that they would pay without the bundling. Zimbalist (2003) provides additional background. The à la carte issue became serious in late-2005, when the FCC shifted its stand. If networks go à la carte, the fear of the cable companies is that both the monthly subscriber fees they charge MSOs and the amount of advertising based on viewership size would decline significantly, and that many smaller channels would not survive. See Siklos (2006), and Schatz *et al.* (2005).

**4.** This is also discussed in the notes to Section 3.4.

**5.** In 1983, The Movie Channel and Showtime were merged in order to compete with HBO, which in terms of subscribers (12 million) was substantially larger than the other two services combined.

**6.** The jointly owned Mattel/General Instruments Playcable channel, for example, provided properly equipped households with cable-interactive games and was one of the first unconventional experimental channels. The experiment was discontinued in 1984.

**7.** In fact, competitive and cost pressures were so great that CBS, for example, discontinued its advertiser-supported cable venture in 1982 with a write-down of about $30 million. A year later, RCA discontinued its Entertainment Channel at a cost of over $60 million.

**8.** The Cable Act of 1992, which re-regulated rates, showed that the industry had lost political influence – in part owing to arrogance and lack of focus on consumer satisfaction. As Crandall and Furchtgott-Roth (1996, p. 37) note, the act also addressed issues such as retransmission consent and consumer protection and service, and it placed restrictions on MSO ownership of other forms of video distribution. Rate relief (by 1999) for all but basic tier services was again, however, gained in the Telecommunications Act of 1996.

There are two types of arrangements by which broadcasters may, under federal law, seek cable-system carriage. "Must-carry" provisions can require that a local cable company carry a local broadcaster's signal. The typically smaller UHF or public television stations that use this provision are not paid for their programming, and no money changes hands. But under the alternative arrangement, the cable operator pays for the right to carry the signals (i.e., purchases retransmission consent through negotiations concerning price, channel placement, and other factors). Major networks and broadcasters usually have the upper hand here, yet if there is no agreement, a cable company is under no obligation to carry the signals.

**9.** The industry has spent billions of dollars just to replace previous-generation analog set-top converters (which adapt cable-frequency transmissions so that they can be seen on ordinary television receivers) with digital models.

**10.** In comparison, telephone networks use a star architecture in which each call signal is routed through a central office switch. All phone lines must pass through the switch.

**11.** A survey of regulation effects in a wide range of industries appears in Winston (1993). The specifics of cable regulation effects appear in Hazlett and Spitzer (1997), who found that deregulation following the Cable Act of 1984 led to price increases that were driven by quality upgrades in the cable packages offered to viewers. Reregulation of the industry in 1992 constrained prices but was also accompanied by a dramatic drop in viewer ratings for basic services, which suggests a loss of quality. See also note 34.

**12.** See *Broadcasting*, June 25, 1984.

**13.** In an important 1985 decision involving a suit by Preferred Communications, Inc., against Los Angeles, it was decided that a city may not create an artificial monopoly (Kelley 1985).

**14.** In 1983 and 1984, bills were proposed in Congress to limit cities' power. Passage of such legislation would have made it difficult for cities to refuse franchise renewals, would have allowed companies to modify onerous contracts under a significant change of circumstances, and would have limited municipal fees to 5% of gross annual revenues (Cohen 1983). In 1985, a compromise agreement included essentially all of these elements but, most significantly, terminated (by 1987) a municipality's right to regulate the price of basic cable services. As of 1985, cable systems also were no longer required to carry local broadcast signals, although legal battles on this issue had dragged on for several years.

**15.** In the early 1980s, the bidding procedure for a franchise was fraught with political considerations. That often meant that bidders would have to employ so-called rent-a-citizen schemes whereby local leaders would be offered shares of stock in the cable company at below market prices in return for supporting the company's bid. The issue, as seen from the perspective of the late 1980s, is discussed in *CableVision*, May 22, 1989.

**16.**   The 25% figure may be approximated by assuming that the average major-film rental is 25 cents per subscriber and that there is an average of ten such films per month, for a total of $2.50. This is around 25% of the total monthly retail charge.

**17.**   As of 2006, the average monthly charge to MSOs was $2.60 for ESPN, $1.00 for The Disney Channel, $0.90 for TNT, $0.76 for USA, $0.45 for Nickelodeon, and $0.50 for CNN. See Flint (2006, 2002a).

In an unusual twist News Corp. sought, in 1996, to rapidly build up to the required 15 million to 20 million subscribers for its fledgling 24-hour news channel by *offering* MSOs $10 a subscriber to carry the service. By 2006, however, Fox News Channel was *asking* for $1.00 per month per sub on renewals (up from around $0.30). A two-tier structure has evolved wherein the older major-brand cable networks such as CNN/Headline News can command 35 cents a subscriber (with volume discounts off the rate card), while newer networks must begin by providing programming for free or for a few cents per subscriber. Note also that an important dispute in the 2002 baseball season involved the Yankees Entertainment & Sports Network's (YES's) asking for $2.00 per month per subscriber from Cablevision Systems to be included in a basic tier. Cablevision, the largest MSO in the New York metropolitan area, wanted to make the 130 YES games only a premium-service package offering. As indicated in Grant (2004), an arbitration panel eventually supported the YES position. See *Forbes*, April 15, 2002, Sandomir (2002), and Solomon, J. D. (2002).

With the analog systems of the 1990s, 35 million cable homes and $150 million of investment were generally required for a start-up cable network to reach the threshold of profitability (i.e., to have a large enough base of viewers to attract large advertisers). But by recycling program content, the launch of a digital ad-supported network might only require $10 million and perhaps fewer than 4 million viewers. See *Broadcasting & Cable*, August 23, 1999. As recently as 2002, the most widely carried and developed networks were valued as much as $20 per subscriber, but those on digital tiers that reach only 40% of total subs have lower valuations. Established networks typically generate margins of 30–40%.

**18.**   The risk, of course, is that with commercial advertising beginning to appear more regularly, cable offerings are likely to more closely resemble those found on commercial television, where the theory of least objectionable programming (programs appealing to the largest mass audience) has held sway.

**19.**   Presumably, the higher the price of the service, the less advertising will be tolerated. In the limiting case of "free" over-the-air broadcasts, people would be expected to tolerate the most advertising.

Subscriber churn, discussed in Grant (2003), also continues to be a substantial problem, even in the digital age. The problem arises because "the average TV viewer who gets 41 to 50 channels watches 15 of them . . . for viewers with more than 121 channels, the number rises only to 18." Thus, not much has changed since a 1983 Benton & Bowles (ad agency) survey indicating that 17% of all current or previous cable subscribers canceled at least one pay service for reasons other than changing residence: 51% said shows were repeated too often; 42% said it was not worth the money. Only 10% of subscribers bought three pay channels at once, and 7% bought four or more (Landro 1983). It has been estimated that, on the average, pay tiers are discontinued (disconnected) by about 3.5% of system subscribers each month (sometimes rates are as high as 8%). This is at least double the rate for other utilities (telephone, gas, etc.) that are disconnected when households move.

**20.**   In terms of total operating costs, a typical system might have payroll accounting for about one-third of the total expenses and programming costs (for pay cable programs) about 40% of the same. Franchise fees may amount to around 4% of basic-service revenues but wouldn't necessarily include revenues from newer broadband Internet services.

**21.**   In practice, of course, it may cost at least $20,000 per mile to build a rural or suburban system and $175,000 per mile or more to build an urban franchise.

**22.**   In general, the early obsolete 12-channel systems might currently provide the highest margin of profit (up to 65% per subscriber) because they are not burdened by the costs of investment in modern equipment. However, the growth potential of such an old system is nil. On newer systems, most now with more than 55 channels, revenues per subscriber may be twice as high as on 12-channel systems. But because labor expenses for administration and maintenance rise sharply with an increase in the number of pay-programming options, margins on the newer systems may average 40% or less. See *Broadcasting*, December 19, 1983.

**23.**   See D. Solomon (2002).

**24.**   A notable example came to light in the fourth quarter 2002 earnings report of AOL Time Warner. As noted in Fabrikant and Thomas (2003), companies like Comcast and Cox Communications accounted for the fees received from new cable channels in a manner different from that of AOL Time Warner. When new networks are begun, they typically make minimum advertising commitments that are paid to the cable company. Time Warner booked most such revenue in the first year even though many other cable companies spread those fees out over the life of the contract, which usually extends over a five- to ten-year period. In contrast, Comcast had not given cable services such ad time and treated any such fees as an offset to expenses, booking them instead over the life of the contracts.

**25.**   Cable companies had widely varying definitions of revenue generating units (RGUs), customer relationships, and capital spending that hampered comparisons across different companies and led to abuses. In response, the National Cable Television Association (NCTA) standardized definitions. RGUs are the sum of total running analog, video, digital video, high-speed data, and telephony customers not counting additional outlets. Customer relationships are defined as the number of customers that received at least one level of service of some type. And capital expenditure categories are reported under customer premise equipment, commercial, infrastructure, line extensions, upgrade/rebuild, and support capital.

**26.**   Franchise rights are generally amortizable under Internal Revenue Code Section 1253, enacted by the Tax Reform Act of 1969. However, the Internal Revenue Service argued (in a 1978 cable system acquisition case involving Tele-Communications, Inc.) that a cable franchise is not covered by Section 1253. This was resolved in favor of the cable companies through a court decision in 1990 and by 1993 changes in the tax code (i.e., Section 197 intangibles). Thus, cable companies are now able to amortize franchise rights and goodwill. However, sports franchises are *not* considered to be Section 197 intangibles. See also note 46 of Chapter 7 and Smith and Parr (1994).

**27.**   For instance, a VOD unit might earn between 45% and 75% of a purchase price of $4, whereas the earnings on a DVD sale can easily be twice as high, thereby providing studios with an incentive to promote sales of DVDs instead of VOD services. In the model for analog PPV, the split of each sale is 45% for the studio, 45% for the cable operator, and 10% for the distributor. Also, as of 2001, studios got a guaranteed $1.90 per transaction for PPV on DirecTV.

**28.**   The first notable PPV movie experiment was done in early 1983. With about 2 million addressable converters in place, MCA offered its *Pirates of Penzance* first-run feature film to MSOs for a minimum of $6 per household. In charging viewers an average of $10 for the privilege of seeing the movie, MSOs are believed to have profited by about $4 million that night. But it wasn't until 1993 that Tele-Communications Inc., after investing $90 million in a nearly insolvent Carolco, indicated that it would attempt to release high-budget movies on

PPV prior to release in theaters. Warner Communications was the first company to attempt two-way cable service in late 1977 in Columbus, Ohio, under the trade name QUBE. QUBE later failed financially.

**29.** Response rates to PPV offerings have generally been in the 2% to 5% range of addressable homes with access to PPV services. Request Television (then co-owned by Reiss Media and Group W Satellite Communications) and Viewer's Choice (owned by eight MSOs, including Cox Cable, Viacom, Times Mirror, The Walt Disney Company, and Warner Brothers) became the leading PPV wholesaler/distributors with access to over 10 million addressable households as of 1992. Reiss began operations in November 1985 by effectively employing with each of its studio suppliers a "time-shared condominium" concept. The first Request Channel provided between two and four new movies each week augmented by special sporting and concert events. Request, however, was discontinued in 1998, leaving Viewer's Choice the dominant PPV service provider.

In comparison to Request, Viewer's Choice is an intermediary service that negotiates all deals with movie studios and event distributors to place their programs on MSOs. It thus takes a larger percentage of each transaction than did Request. See also *Variety*, July 22, 1991, and April 6, 1992, and *Broadcasting & Cable*, April 27, 1998.

**30.** DBS signals, transmitted via high-power satellites, are receivable from rooftop or window-mounted antenna dishes (or flat surfaces) that retail for at most $200. In Europe, Rupert Murdoch's Astra and British Satellite Broadcasting were two of the early entrants. In the United States, however, several major communications companies, including Comsat, RCA, and General Instruments, originally sponsored DBS service applications to the FCC in the early 1980s. After several false starts and substantial losses, most of the early entrants withdrew from this field.

It wasn't until 1994 that DBS finally made a start in the United States with the launch of a GM Hughes digital TV satellite. The satellite signal, with breakeven potential at fewer than 3 million subscribers, carries 175 channels of pay TV that are fed by two services, DirecTV and United States Satellite Broadcasting. PrimeStar, a service operated by a competing consortium of six cable company partners that include Tele-Communications Inc. (22%) and Time Warner, Inc., got off to a slower start in 1990 using analog signals. The services were originally thought to be most likely to prosper in rural areas where it would be uneconomical to provide regular cable. See *Broadcasting*, March 13, 1989, for a full historical discussion, *Broadcasting*, December 6, 1993, and *BusinessWeek*, March 13, 1995. DirecTV and Echo Star survive currently, with DirectTV bought by News Corp. in 2003 and then swapped to Liberty Media in 2006. As of 2006, cable retained the advantage of having high-definition, VOD, and Internet service capabilities, but the satellite service companies have nonetheless continued to expand to well beyond 20 million subscribers (20%+ share of households) in the United States. See Lashinsky 2004).

**31.** LMDS is a close cousin to MMDS. Instead of the 33-channel AM signal in MMDS, LMDS can carry 49 channels and uses an FM signal that can be received on a smaller dish antenna. For a description of "wireless cable," see *Broadcasting*, December 4, 1989, p. 86.

**32.** In Los Angeles in the early 1980s, ON-TV and SelecTV services were quite popular. Nationwide, STV subscribers numbered 2 million at the peak. STV has, however, fared better in France, where Canal Plus has, since 1984, signed up more than 4 million subscribers. Over the years, many other signal-distribution schemes have been either proposed or tested, but none of them has flourished. American Broadcasting, for example, initially implemented and then withdrew (in 1984) an addressable system in which a scrambled VHF signal was sent during unused network overnight hours to homes equipped with a descrambler and a VCR. Also, in the early 1990s, phone companies had sunk $500 million into Tele-TV, a failed interactive programming and VOD venture (history reviewed in *Variety*, October 27, 2003). More modern and successful distribution and storage hardware and software that enables time-shifted viewing is now marketed by TiVo, ReplayTV (acquired by D&M Holdings of Japan in 2003), UltimateTV from Microsoft, and Dish Network from EchoStar Communications. Disney's new MovieBeam service, described in Orwall (2003), is another service designed to store recent movies sent via broadcast airwaves to a hard drive. See also "In Embracing Digital Recorders, Cable Companies Take Big Risk," *Wall Street Journal*, April 26, 2004.

**33.** Around 2004 MSOs began to effectively compete against telcos and satellite companies by offering a "triple-play" package of services that, usually for $99 or so a month, includes cable, telephone, and Internet connections. Until recently, it had only been through Digital Subscriber Line (DSL) technology that phone companies had been able to use much of their copper-wire infrastructure, originally designed for two-way carriage of point-to-point messages, for delivery of relatively high-speed Internet services. Cable modems follow Data-Over-Cable Service Interface Specification (DOCSIS) standards. For a brief history of the competition between cable modems and DSL, see Young and Grant (2003).

**34.** As noted in Latour (2005), cable is regulatorily disadvantaged in video because telcos and satellite companies do not pay certain (franchise) fees to local governments ($2 billion in 2004) and telcos are not required to extend networks to all households. However, telcos are also disadvantaged because in phone service, cable companies do not incur taxes and fees levied on regular phone companies. See also Mehta (2005).

**35.** For example, in response to consumer complaints about pricing and service, Congress decided in the early 1990s to revise the previous 1984 Cable Communications Policy Act that had deregulated basic-cable service pricing if "effective competition" in a city was provided by the existence of at least three over-the-air broadcast signals. At the time, the specter of price regulation adversely affected valuations of MSO properties.

Reregulation in the form of the 1992 Cable Act also included a section requiring that, during 1993, broadcasters negotiate with MSOs in regard to payments for signal retransmission or elect to be carried by MSOs automatically. Many small broadcast stations, having no leverage with the MSOs, immediately opted for must-carry. However, important independent broadcasters and network affiliates opted to request signal retransmission payments from MSOs by arguing that, without such signals, the value of an MSO's service would be much diminished. In turn, the major MSOs, among them Tele-Communications Inc. and Time Warner, postured against the idea of paying anything.

The cable industry has historically fought legislative and regulatory battles with broadcasting interests. Moreover, the industry found must-carry rules to be cumbersome because of the limited channel capacity of many older systems and sought to have the rules changed (the Washington, DC, Court of Appeals repealed must-carry rules in 1985).

The political spotlight has also fallen on so-called compulsory license issues. In 1976, Congress passed a new copyright act that extended to cable television systems a compulsory license to retransmit broadcast signals and especially the right to carry all local broadcast signals without payment to owners of the programs being broadcast. Also see note 8.

Other FCC regulations, known as cable concentration caps, had restricted large MSOs to servicing 30% of subscribers and to provision of only up to 40% of programming from affiliated companies. A U.S. court ruled against this in 2001. See Labaton (2001).

**36.** The Stern Stewart consulting firm in New York City is known for its development of EVA and market-value-added (MVA) theory and practice. The cost of equity capital and methods involving estimation of the WACC and beta are described in standard finance texts.

**37.** Established cable networks generate a cash flow margin of at least 20%. Such networks might, without major affiliation agreements, be valued at only a few dollars per subscriber, whereas others with such affiliations might be worth $40 or more per subscriber. See also *Broadcasting*, August 12, 1991, and Boorstin (2003), in which high margins at The Disney Channel are described. For cable as well as other entertainment segments, the degree of riskiness at any point might be shown as:

Operating leverage elasticity indicator = change in operating profit (or EBITDA)/change

in sales.

**38.** See "Heard on the Street," *Wall Street Journal*, May 20, 1983.
**39.** By the end of 2006, more than half of 110 million households in the United States found cable company phone services to be available via Voice over Internet Protocol (VoIP) technology. See also Searcey (2005).
**40.** Broadband speeds are a function of bandwidth (the range of frequencies that a transmission pipe, wire, or cable is capable of carrying) and the signal-to-noise ratio of that medium. The maximum capacity was described in 1948 by the Shannon-Hartley theorem, which says that $C = B \times \log_2 (s/n + 1)$, where $C$ is capacity in bits per second, $B$ is the frequency bandwidth, and $s/n$ is the signal-to-noise ratio. See *Scientific American*, October 1999.
**41.** As of July 1992, for example, the Federal Communications Commission proceeded with plans to allow telephone companies to transmit a broad menu of television programming, including movie channels and home shopping, over their phone lines (i.e., to provide a "video dial tone"). However, the FCC stopped short of allowing telcos to produce programming, although a phone company would be permitted to acquire up to 5% of a programmer. Even more significant was the August 24, 1993, watershed ruling by a federal (Virginia) district court (in a Bell Atlantic suit) that struck down as unconstitutional the section of the 1984 Cable Act that restricts telcos from creating, owning, or packaging video programming distributed inside their telephone service regions. The Fourth Circuit Court of Appeals upheld the decision in November 1994. By late 1994, US West and Bell-South had won this right in the federal courts. And by March 1995, Judge Greene of the Federal District Court in Washington ruled that Bell Atlantic could compete directly with cable operators and broadcasters by transmitting programs anywhere in the country. See *New York Times*, March 18, 1995, and Grant (2005), in which it is noted that Comcast "was astonished at how complicated and risky the telephone business is compared with cable . . . Cable companies incur relatively little additional cost when customers don't pay their bills. When phone customers don't pay their bills they can leave behind hundreds of dollars in long-distance charges that the cable company may end up eating." See also Grant and Latour (2005).

# Selected additional reading

Angwin, J. (2004). "For Fox News, Ad-Sales Market Isn't Fair, Balanced," *Wall Street Journal*, May 20.

Angwin, J., and Pasztor, A. (2006). "Satellite TV Growth Is Losing Altitude as Cable Takes Off," *Wall Street Journal*, August 5.

Beatty, S. (2001). "What Are Space Aliens and Lingerie Doing on Learning Channel?," *Wall Street Journal*, March 27.

(2000). "Unconventional HBO Finds Its Own Success Is a Hard Act to Follow," *Wall Street Journal*, September 29.

Bibb, P. (1993). *It Ain't as Easy as It Looks: Ted Turner's Amazing Story*. New York: Crown.

Brauchli, M. W. (1993). "A Satellite TV System Is Quickly Moving Asia into the Global Village," *Wall Street Journal*, May 10.

Brown, K., and Latour, A. (2004). "Phone Industry Faces Upheaval as Ways of Calling Change Fast," *Wall Street Journal*, August 25.

Button, G. (1991). "Stan Hubbard's Giant Footprint," *Forbes*, 148(11)(November 11).

Cairncross, F. (1997). *The Death of Distance: How the Communications Revolution Will Change Our Lives*. Boston: Harvard Business School Press.

"Captain Comeback: Ted Turner Is Back from the Brink," *BusinessWeek*, no. 3115 (July 17, 1989).

Carnevale, M. L. (1993). "Telephone Service Seems on the Brink of Huge Innovations," *Wall Street Journal*, February 10.

Carvell, T. (1998). "Prime-Time Player (ESPN)," *Fortune*, 137(4)(March 2).

Cauley, L. (1995). "Phone Giants Discover the Interactive Path Is Full of Obstacles," *Wall Street Journal*, July 24.

Chippindale, P., and Franks, S. (1991). *Dished!: The Rise and Fall of British Satellite Broadcasting*. London: Simon & Schuster.

Cooney, J. (1983). "Cable TV's Costly Trip to the Big Cities," *Fortune*, 107(18) (April 18).

Crandall, R. W., and Waverman, L. (1995). *Talk Is Cheap: The Promise of Regulatory Reform in North American Telecommunications*. Washington, DC: The Brookings Institution.

Creswell, J. (2004). "Verizon Bets Big on Cable," *Fortune*, 149(11)(May 31).

Donlan, T. G. (1991). "Blurry Picture: Threat of Regulation, Competition Dims Outlook for Cable TV," *Barron's*, April 29.

Emshwiller, J. R. (1989). "Prying Open the Cable-TV Monopolies," *Wall Street Journal*, August 10.

Fabrikant, G., and Carter, B. (2003). "Cable's New Giant Flexes His Muscles," *New York Times*, October 20.

Flint, J. (2003). "ESPN's Risky New Game Plan," *Wall Street Journal*, October 24.

Gleick, J. (1993). "The Telephone Transformed – into Almost Everything," *New York Times*, May 16.

Grant, P., and Schatz, A. (2006). "For Cable Giants, AT&T Deal Is One More Reason to Worry," *Wall Street Journal*, March 7.

Gunther, M. (2004). "Comcast Wants to Change the World . . . But Can It Learn to Answer the Phone?," *Fortune*, 150(8)(October 18).

(2003). "Murdoch's Prime Time," *Fortune*, 147(3)(February 17).

(1999). "There's No Business Like Business Show Business," *Fortune*, 139(10) (May 24).

(1996). "The Cable Guys' Big Bet on the Net," *Fortune*, 134(10) (November 25).

Hazlett, T. W. (2000a). "TV Smackdown! (Cable vs. Broadcast)," *Wall Street Journal*, May 5.

(2000b). "Surprise, Surprise: Cable Rates Fall after Deregulation," *Barron's*, February 28.

(1993). "Why Your Cable Bill Is So High," *Wall Street Journal*, September 24.

"The HBO Story: 10 Years That Changed the World of Telecommunications," *Broadcasting*, November 15, 1982.

Keating, S. (1999). *Cutthroat: High Stakes and Killer Moves on the Electronic Frontier*. Boulder, CO: Johnson Books.

Kupfer, A. (1995). "Can Cable Win Its Phone Bet?," *Fortune*, 132(6)(September 18).

(1994a). "The Future of the Phone Companies," *Fortune*, 130(7)(October 3).

(1994b). "Set-Top Box Wars," *Fortune*, 130(4)(August 22).

(1994c). "The Baby Bells Butt Heads," *Fortune*, 129(6)(March 21).

(1993a). "Hughes Gambles on High-Tech TV," *Fortune*, 128(4)(August 23).

(1993b). "The No. 1 in Cable TV Has Big Plans," *Fortune*, 127(13)(June 28).

(1993c). "The Race to Rewire America," *Fortune*, 127(8)(April 19).

Labaton, S. (1999). "Ownership Rules in Cable Industry Loosened by F.C.C.," *New York Times*, October 9.

Laing, J. R. (2001). "King Cable: Why Cable Will Beat the Bells in the Race to Wire Your Home," *Barron's*, August 20.

Latour, A. (2005). "After a Year of Frenzied Deals, Two Telecom Giants Emerge," *Wall Street Journal*, February 15.

(2004). "Bells Join Race to Offer TV," *Wall Street Journal*, April 29.

Lee W. E. (1984). "A Regulatory Lock Box on Cable TV," *Wall Street Journal*, October 15.

Leonard, D. (2002). "The Most Valuable Square Foot in America," *Fortune*, 145(7) (April 1).

Lowenstein, R. (2004). "The Company They Kept," *New York Times*, February 1.

Mahar, M. (1988). "Captain Courageous and the Albatross," *Barron's*, July 11, and "The Baby Bells vs. the Big Gorilla?," *Barron's*, August 1.

Mahon, G. (1984). "Fine-Tuning Cable TV," *Barron's*, July 16.

Mehta, S. N. (2003). "King Comcast," *Fortune*, 148(2)(July 21).

Miller, I. R. (1997). "Models for Determining the Economic Value of Cable Television Systems," *Journal of Media Economics*, 10(2).

Mullen, M. (2003). *The Rise of Cable Programming in the United States*. Austin: University of Texas Press.

O'Connor, J. J. (1984). "Where's That Promised New World of Cable?," *New York Times*, November 24.

O'Donnell, T., and Gissen, J. (1982). "A Vaster Wasteland," *Forbes*, 129(11)(May 24).

O'Reilly, B. (1996). "First Blood in the Telecom Wars," *Fortune*, 133(4)(March 4).

Orwall, B., Solomon, D., and Beatty, S. (2001). "Why the Possible Sale of AT&T Broadband Spooks 'Content' Firms," *Wall Street Journal*, August 27.

Park, R. E. (1971). "The Growth of Cable TV and Its Probable Impact on Over-the-Air Broadcasting," *American Economic Review*, 61(May).

Pasztor, A., and Lippman, J. (2002). "How a Dream Deal in Satellite TV Ran into Static," *Wall Street Journal*, October 9.

Peers, M. (2003). "How Media Giants Are Reassembling the Old Oligopoly," *Wall Street Journal*, September 15.

Peers, M. and Grant, P. (2005). "Comcast, TV Program Owners Clash over Video-on-Demand," *Wall Street Journal*, January 27.

Richtel, M., and Belson, K. (2006). "Internet Calling Pressures Bells to Lower Rates," *New York Times*, July 3.

Roberts, J. L. (1992). "How Giant TCI Uses Self-Dealing, Hardball to Dominate Market," *Wall Street Journal*, January 27.

Robichaux, M. (2002). *Cable Cowboy: John Malone and the Rise of the Modern Cable Business*. Hoboken, NJ: John Wiley & Sons.

(1997). "Malone Says TCI Push into Phones, Internet Isn't Working for Now," *Wall Street Journal*, January 2.

(1996a). "Once a Laughingstock, Direct-Broadcast TV Gives Cable a Scare," *Wall Street Journal*, November 7.

(1996b). "As Satellite TV Soars, Big Firms Crowd the Skies," *Wall Street Journal*, March 11.

(1993). "How Cable-TV Firms Raised Rates in Wake of Law to Curb Them," *Wall Street Journal*, September 28.

(1992a). "Cable Firms Say They Welcome Competition but Behave Otherwise," *Wall Street Journal*, September 24.

(1992b). "Cable-TV Firms' Higher-Priced 'Tiers' Bring Cries of Outrage from Consumers," *Wall Street Journal*, January 15.

Robichaux, M., and Gruley, B. (1997). "Direct-Satellite TV Comes under Attack by Networks, Affiliates," *Wall Street Journal*, January 30.

Sandberg, J. (2000). "After 50 Years of Effort, Interactive TV May Be Here," *Wall Street Journal*, December 7.

Schiesel, S. (2004). "For Comcast, It's About Bundling Services," *New York Times*, February 16.

(2002). "Video on Demand Is Finally Taking Hold," *New York Times*, November 25.

(1999). "Local Signals May Be Costly for Satellite TV Providers," *Wall Street Journal*, December 13.

Sherman, S. (1994). "Will the Information Superhighway Be the Death of Retailing?" *Fortune*, 129(5)(April 18).

Sloan Commission (1971). *On the Cable: The Television of Abundance, Report of the Sloan Commission on Cable Communications*. New York: McGraw-Hill.

Smith, R. L. (1972). *The Wired Nation*. New York: Harper & Row.

Solomon, D., and Frank, R. (2001). "Comcast-AT&T Broadband Deal Cements Rise of Cable Oligopoly," *Wall Street Journal*, December 21.

"Subscription Television," *Broadcasting*, August 16, 1982.

U.S. Department of Commerce. (1988). *Video Program Distribution and Cable Television: Current Policy Issues and Recommendations*, NTIA Report 88–233, June.

Waldman, P. (1990). "New Fees Alter 'Basic' Idea of Cable TV," *Wall Street Journal*, January 23.

Whittemore, H. (1990). *CNN: The Inside Story*. Boston: Little, Brown.

Williams, M. J. (1984). "Slow Liftoff for Satellite-to-Home TV," *Fortune*, 109(5) (March 5).

Yoder, S. K., and Zachary, G. P. (1993). "Digital Media Business Takes Form as a Battle of Complex Alliances," *Wall Street Journal*, July 14.

# 9
# Publishing

*Publish or perish.*

That's the guiding premise for university professors. And, broadly speaking, so is it also for the major media and entertainment companies, which – in this digital age of bits and bytes – might accurately be said to *publish* movies, television programs, recorded music, and games much as they might publish books or magazines. Nowadays, all information, or content, is reducible, copyable, and transportable into the same raw material of bits and bytes, no matter what the original form.

## 9.1 Gutenberg's gift

First words

The first published work – one of great significance because of authorship, content, and form of delivery – was chiseled in stone and delivered from Mount Sinai by Moses. One might quip that, for the publishing industry, after delivery of the Ten Commandments, it's been downhill ever since.

   Still, from the drawings of early cavemen, to the hieroglyphs of the ancient Egyptians, and then on to the first printed book, it is evident that people

Table 9.1. *Publishing industry segments, 1980–2005*

|  | 1980 | % | 1990 | % | 2000 | % | 2005 | % |
|---|---|---|---|---|---|---|---|---|
| **Books & maps** | $6.5[a] | 17.7 | $16.2 | 21.1 | $33.7 | 25.9 | $42.2 | 28.8 |
| **Newspapers** | | | | | | | | |
| Personal consumption expenditures (PCEs) | 6.9 | 18.9 | 10.4 | 13.5 | 17.1 | 13.1 | 21.3 | 14.6 |
| Advertising & other[b] | 14.8 | 40.6 | 32.3 | 42.0 | 49.1 | 37.7 | 47.3 | 32.3 |
| **Magazines** | | | | | | | | |
| PCEs | 5.1 | 14.1 | 11.2 | 14.6 | 18.0 | 13.8 | 22.5 | 15.4 |
| Advertising & other | 3.1 | 8.6 | 6.8 | 8.8 | 12.4 | 9.5 | 12.8 | 8.7 |
| Total | $36.4 | 100.0 | $76.9 | 100.0 | $130.3 | 100.0 | $146.3 | 100.0 |

[a] Dollars in billions. All figures are rounded.
[b] Local ads.
*Source*: U.S. Department of Commerce, Universal McCann, Inc.

have always had a need to communicate with each other by publishing their thoughts, plans, and histories. Printing had already been developed in China in the sixth century A.D. But it wasn't until the year 1455 – when a German pioneer by the name of Johann Gutenberg and his partner, Johann Fust, set up a movable metal-type press to print a Latin bible – that the modern publishing era began. Today, world spending on books is estimated at $100 billion, of which approximately 35% is generated in the United States, where more than 150,000 titles a year (about the same as in the U.K.) are published.

   Table 9.1 provides a segment overview of the publishing business in the United States, and Figure 9.1 provides a timeline perspective. As the table illustrates, publishing industry revenues are now nearly $150 billion, or slightly over 1% of U.S. GDP. The largest component, around half, is derived from newspapers. The other half is split almost equally between magazines and books. However, it is also evident that books have taken, largely at the expense of newspapers, a rising share of total revenues.

Operating characteristics

Many of the operating characteristics seen in the broadcasting, cable, and other mass communications and software segments are also seen in publishing. As in these other segments, the cost of creating the content is sunk at the start and subsequent expenses of manufacturing and distribution are relatively small. The objective here, too, is to make demand more price-inelastic (as described in Chapter 1) and to stimulate unit volume sales since, on the margin, the contribution to profit of each additional unit sold is high.

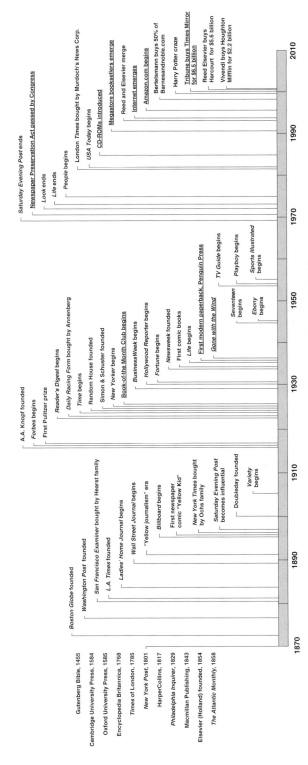

Figure 9.1. Milestones in publishing, 1455–2005.

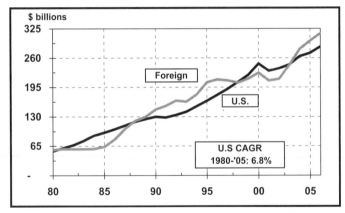

Figure 9.2. Total advertising expenditures, U.S. and foreign, 1980–2006. Based on data by Robert J. Coen, Universal McCann, Inc. See also Figure 7.4.

*Circulation* – which is the term used to describe unit demand for newspapers and magazines from sales on newsstands or through postal subscriptions – is normally (except for most books) supplemented by sales of advertising space that is strategically interspersed with content. In this way, broadcast services, newspapers, magazines, telephone directories, and Internet Web sites are all alike.

In fact, demand for advertising is central to the success of virtually all publishing enterprises. Profits are thus accordingly sensitive to changes in national and, sometimes, local economic conditions as reflected by changes in demand for advertising (Figure 9.2).[1] But raw material and distribution costs may also fluctuate cyclically and noticeably affect profitability, especially in the traditional publishing segments.

Still, it is the cost of creating the proprietary content to be published that is often the most difficult variable to predict and to control. As in other creative fields, the top people – the "star" writers of novels or magazine articles or syndicated newspaper columns or computer games – can all command

Table 9.2. *Publishing industry composite of 25 companies,[a] 2001–2005*

|  | Revenues | Operating income | Operating margin | Assets | Operating cash flow |
|---|---|---|---|---|---|
| CAGR (%)[b] |  |  |  |  |  |
| Books, total | 3.7% | 8.0% | 4.1% | 10.0% | 3.0% |
| Consumer magazines | 7.5 | NM[c] | NM[c] | NM[c] | 8.7 |
| Newspapers | 5.4 | 6.6 | 1.1 | −0.1 | 5.0 |

[a] Average margin, 2001–2005: books 10.1%, magazines 13.9%, newspapers 20.0%.
[b] Compound annual growth rate.
[c] Not meaningful.

considerable premiums for their services. Occasionally, the cost is greater than a publisher can bear. Table 9.2 furnishes the financial operating characteristics for a sample of the major publishing companies.

## 9.2 Segment specifics

Books

Book publishing, which accounts for about one-quarter of total publishing industry revenues, is composed of two major sectors: educational/professional and trade (otherwise known as general interest). Each sector has a distinct consumer demand and financial-economics profile. Revenue components by share are illustrated in Figure 9.3.

*Educational and professional* Relatively high operating margins and significant barriers to entry are characteristic features in the educational/professional segment.[2] In addition, revenues tend to be predictably tied to demographic trends, and content can often be easily repackaged for delivery by electronic media or through alternative distribution channels. This stands in contrast to trade/general publishing, which is hit-driven and thus inherently more volatile. On the educational side, sales to colleges amount to about half of revenues, while the elementary and high school components, the "ElHi" segment, make up the other half.

Demographic changes affecting school enrollments can, of course, be reliably predicted for as much as ten years into the future and can provide a solid base from which to forecast demand for educational books and related materials. But, also, about half of the states, mostly in the South and West, purchase

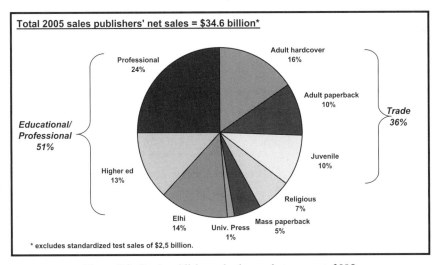

Figure 9.3. Book publisher sales by market segment, 2005.

educational materials at the state (rather than by district or school) level in a regular cycle of textbook adoption programs. In these procedures, state boards of education and adoption committees screen publishers' offerings and determine which books will be approved for purchase and which should be replaced.[3] Demand in ElHi is thus further affected by the school funding environment at state and local levels, with the amount allocated to education somewhat dependent on local economic conditions and, occasionally, on political considerations at the federal level.

In measuring demand for college textbook and professional materials, demographics are destiny, but the rate of change in technology and in subject emphasis modulates the demographic trends (i.e., the more rapid the change, the more sales are stimulated). Pricing, though, is generally not an important issue in ElHi, college, or professional segments because the cost of textbooks is typically small when compared with tuition and other education-related expenses.[4]

*anything*

*Trade* The consumer area, however, presents a much different economic profile of demand and cost than that seen on the educational/professional side. Given that the cost of manufacturing a hardcover trade book in quantity is seldom more than $2 to $3 a unit (and for paperbound, $1), profitability will generally rise disproportionally to increasing unit sales.[5] Also, as noted earlier, this segment is largely hit-driven and in that respect thus similar in character to the recorded music and video game businesses, in which it often makes sense to pay significant advances and royalty rates to the top content creators and to then spur demand by spending aggressively on promotion.[6] As with all such businesses, margins are, from year to year, apt to be volatile and to be affected by the cost of intense competition for top authors.

A financial model for a high-profile trade book deal might contain the following main features:[7]

Retail cover price of book = $26

Per unit revenue from book retailers is approximately one-half of retail price = $13

Royalty rate to author = 15% of cover price = $3.90 per unit

Advance to author (draw against future sales) = $7 million

Production and overhead expenses on 600,000 unit printing ($4 a copy) = $2.4 million

Sales of foreign rights to 20 countries and serial rights to major magazines = $3 million

Revenues on sold-out 600,000 unit printing at $13 a unit = $7.8 million

Total revenues = $7.8 million unit sales + $3 million ancillary rights sales = $10.8 million

Total cost = $7 million advance + $2.4 million printing cost = $9.4 million

Table 9.3. *How a typical $25 trade book cover price is allocated*

|  | Percent | Dollars |
|---|---|---|
| Manufacturing | 10.0 | $2.50 |
| Distribution | 8.0 | 2.00 |
| Marketing | 7.5 | 1.75 |
| Publisher's overhead | 8.0 | 2.00 |
| Author's share (average) | 10.0 | 2.50 |
| Retail store discount (average) | 47.0 | 11.75 |
| Cost of returns | 3.5 | 0.88 |
| **Available for publisher's profit** | **6.0%** | **$1.63** |

*Source*: Auletta (1997).

Publisher's pretax profit = $10.8 million − $9.4 million = $1.4 million.
Author earns out advance with 1.026 million unit sales at $3.90 + $3 million
  for rights = $7 million.

The influence of powerful retailers has also tended to reduce publishers' operating margins to the lower end of a range that had normally been, depending on category, between 8% and 17% of sales. The costs of marketing and of absorbing a rapidly increasing stock of slow-selling titles returned by retailers for credit – or through offerings of "shared" markdowns in which booksellers are paid a few dollars for each copy moved at a discount – have risen significantly in recent years (Table 9.3). And this has more recently led publishers to concentrate on the faster-growing third-party distribution side of the business. The pressure on publishers' margins has in part been a consequence of the relatively greater power of mass retailers, including Wal-Mart and Target as well as the large bookstore chains. These retailers account for at least 25% of adult-title sales (as compared to the online share of 15%), and are now able to demand a larger cut of the cover price even as a rising tide of returns (sometimes 35% or more of total shipments) gives credence to the industry adage of "Gone today, here tomorrow."[8]

The Internet, which already enables published content to be downloaded into an electronic book device, will gradually alter the traditional economic model and perhaps also eventually eliminate the returns problem. But for many more years to come, and until such e-books come to be widely used, the book business will likely remain under pressure.

Periodicals - Magazine, journals, comics

*Newspapers* Among the earliest versions of what we today call newspapers were the handwritten notices that ancient Romans posted in public areas. Other forerunners of modern papers appeared in Germany and other European countries in the sixteenth and seventeenth centuries and in colonial America by 1690. Today, in the United States, there are approximately 1,500 dailies with a combined circulation of 60 million readers and another 8,000 nondaily variants with combined circulation of over 5 million more. But only a dozen or so large companies dominate the business.[9]

Newspaper companies function as manufacturers and distributors of the editorial content that they create and also as service providers to advertisers seeking access to their readers. Like magazines, papers derive their revenues from a combination of advertising, subscriptions, and newsstand sales. However, approximately two-thirds of the content of the average paper in the United States is advertising, and some 80% of revenues (higher than in other countries) are derived from this source. Both newspaper and magazine revenues are thus normally sensitive to overall economic conditions, especially as affected by demand for local advertising in the case of papers or highly targeted advertising in the case of magazines.

Newspapers also differ from magazines because they are often monopolies in their markets and because frequency of publication is much greater (usually daily). With perishability of content and speed of delivery of utmost concern, the relative distribution and manufacturing costs rise above those that would be proportionately incurred by publications with less frequency of issuance.

On the average, the apportionment of revenues and costs in operating a newspaper as opposed to a magazine would be approximately as shown in Table 9.4. A salient feature of the newspaper business, though, is that advertising has consistently accounted for about 80% of revenues, with circulation accounting for the remaining 20%.

Of total newspaper advertising, which in the early 2000s was running at an annual rate of approximately $50 billion, the largest and most troubling component, accounting for half the total, is retailing-related advertising. In recent years, retailers have shifted their promotional spending away from print and into electronic media at the same time that retail industry consolidation has been occurring. This has made it difficult for publishers to raise advertising prices enough to keep pace with their own raw material and distribution-cost inflation.

In contrast, classified advertising, which accounts for about 37% of total newspaper advertising, has historically been by far the most profitable component of ad revenues. However, classified – which includes help-wanted, automotive, and real estate advertising – is also the most highly correlated to economic activity and to interest rates (inversely).

Publisher profits have thus tended to rise greatly when the economy is strong and to fall noticeably when the economy is weak. In this respect, national advertising, which is primarily related to the cyclically sensitive travel and financial service sectors and accounts for around 15% of total newspaper advertising, cannot normally provide an offset to declines in classified advertising.[10] Neither can such national advertising offset the

Table 9.4. *Newspapers versus magazines, estimated components of revenues and costs, 2005*

|                                              | Newspapers | Magazines |
| -------------------------------------------- | ---------- | --------- |
| Sources of revenue (%)                       |            |           |
| Advertising                                  |            |           |
| Retail                                       | 40         | 9         |
| Classified                                   | 32         | 12        |
| National                                     | 8          | 35        |
| Newsstand                                    | 17         | 10        |
| Subscription                                 | 3          | 34        |
| Total                                        | 100%       | 100%      |
| Costs as % of revenue                        |            |           |
| Advertising, selling, & promotion            | 12         | 13        |
| Editorial                                    | 14         | 12        |
| Production                                   | 20         | 21        |
| Distribution                                 | 13         | 6         |
| Postage                                      | 1          | 5         |
| Raw materials (e.g., paper, ink)             | 18         | 25        |
| Administrative & other                       | 9          | 9         |
| Total                                        | 87%        | 91%       |
| Operating profit margin (% of revenue)       | 13%        | 9%        |

accelerating loss of classifieds to Internet sites – though raw-material costs for newsprint and ink and for physical distribution will be reduced to the extent that readers desire to read the news on their screens rather than on paper.

The most important traditional determinants of newspaper profits are the costs of labor and newsprint (each component typically around 15% to 18% of all operating costs) and the demand for help-wanted advertising. As Figure 9.4 illustrates, labor cost appears to have been tamed in recent years through increased capital investment and productivity, but newsprint costs have continued to be volatile. Given that the industry produces approximately 20 billion units each year, even small changes in the cost of newsprint will significantly affect profitability. As for the longer term, gains in circulation and in classified advertising are likely to be increasingly difficult to achieve as households now derive an increasing share of their information from the electronic media.[11] Web logs (blogs) now turn mass media into media of and by the masses. And free morning newspapers, with greater comparative appeal to younger readers, have also gained traction in densely populated commuter markets and in Europe.[12] The result is that household penetration of daily newspapers in the United States has already fallen from around 100% in 1970 to under 55% today. Although, as Lewis (1995) notes, circulation is fairly price-inelastic, weekly paper circulation

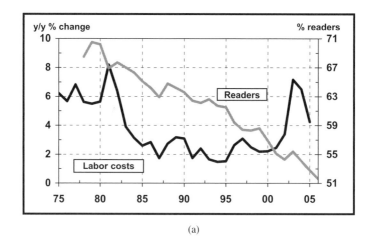

(a)

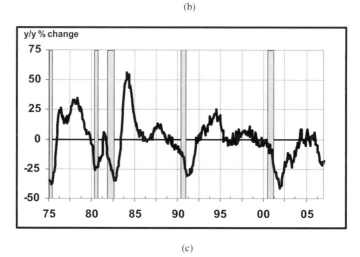

(b)

(c)

Figure 9.4. Newspaper profit determinants: (a) Average hourly wage changes in percent year-over-year, and average percent of adults as weekly readers. (b) Newsprint costs per ton (East Coast delivery), six-month moving average. (c) Year-over-year percent changes in help-wanted index (six-month moving average), 1975–2006. Bars indicate periods of recession.

has nonetheless been declining since the late 1980s, and for Sunday papers it has stalled (at around 62 million).[13]

Worse yet, the Internet has already siphoned off significant amounts of both classified advertising and consumers' time. As a result, publishers are applying their formidable information-gathering and cash flow resources to development of electronically delivered products and services.

*Magazines and other periodicals* The first magazines (named from the French *magasin*, or "storehouse") began to appear in Europe in the late 1600s. But it wasn't until the 1890s that mass market magazines, supported by the emergence of national advertisers, began to appear in the United States. Magazine publishing today is spread over more than 11,000 magazine and periodical titles and accounts for about one-fourth of all U.S. publishing revenues. Major categories include the following:

Consumer and general interest
Trade and technical
Farm
Noncommercial literary
Comics

Magazine operating characteristics are in many ways similar to those of newspapers. However, revenues for consumer magazines and periodicals are much more dependent on circulation, and total distribution costs are thus much more closely related to the costs of gaining such circulation and to the costs of postal delivery (Table 9.4).[14] The allocation of circulation revenues derived from newsstand and supermarket distribution for a typical popular weekly magazine (e.g., *Time*, *Newsweek*, *People*) is shown in Table 9.5.

As of 2005, about 55% of magazine revenues were being derived from ads versus 80% for newspapers. Magazines also derived 25% of revenues from subscriptions versus only 10% for newspapers. Magazine advertising revenues of approximately $13 billion (Table 9.1) amounted to only one-fourth the total ad spending in newspapers.

Although magazine publishers typically boast of the number of pages of advertising that are gained each year, appearances can be deceiving. In fact, it is impossible to gauge the financial health of a magazine without knowing how much is actually being charged for each page. More often than not, competition from a large and ever-proliferating number of magazines, targeting the same niche of readers, provides the advertiser with leverage to negotiate significant discounts to nominal rate card price schedules.[15] Given the prevalence of such discounting, net revenue realized per page is thus for most purposes of financial analysis a far better metric than total number of ad pages sold. But just as in other advertising-supported content distribution, it is the cost of reaching a thousand readers

Table 9.5. *Circulation revenue allocation and publisher's gross profit for a typical $3-per-copy weekly magazine cover price*

|                                               | Percent of cover price | Dollars    |
|-----------------------------------------------|------------------------|------------|
| Publisher                                     | 60                     | $1.80      |
| Distributor/wholesaler[a]                     | 15–20                  | 0.45–0.60  |
| Retailer                                      | 20–25                  | 0.60–0.75  |
| Total revenue                                 | 100%                   | $3.00      |
| Publisher costs for printing & transportation | 12                     | 0.36       |
| Assume 40% average sell-through per issue, 2 million copies printed |  |  |
| Total publisher circulation revenues per week (prior to advertising): $1.44 million |  |  |
| Publisher costs prior to content, racking costs, etc.: $720,000 |  |  |
| Gross profit = $720,000                       |                        |            |
| Gross profit margin = 50%                     |                        |            |

[a] Some distributors are national and may also be paid brokerage fees; thus the range varies. However, in recent years, leverage has generally shifted toward large-chain retailers.

(CPM) that is the industry's standard measure of comparison against other media.[16]

In the United States, few pure magazine and periodical publishers of size have remained independent, with part of the reason for this being that it usually takes at least five years for even successful titles to turn profitable. Most publishers have accordingly been absorbed by larger media and entertainment companies.[17] A comparable wave of consolidation has also occurred in the wholesale distribution end of the business, where margins have been narrowed.[18]

## Multimedia

Multimedia products – combining digitized text, sound, and pictorial data that are generally carried in the form of CD-ROMs, DVDs, or memory chips – are an outgrowth of the same technology that has made home computers, compact discs, and iPods/MP3 players common household items. And the economics of developing and distributing multimedia products has evolved as a hybrid of business practices seen in the filmed-entertainment, music, book publishing, and video game industries.

As in the music business, a small number of titles generate the bulk of the profit and cover the often-substantial losses on the majority of releases. Retailers also have full rights to return unsold units. However, most of the revenue stream, some 75% to 85% of the wholesale price, reverts to the publisher, who bears the risk of funding *both* development and marketing costs.

For developers, the costs of designing and externally funding a new title (to the gold master disc stage) will now generally range to over $1 million and be guided by work-made-for-hire publisher agreements.[19]

## 9.3 Accounting and valuation

Accounting

Accounting for publishing enterprises generally does not require unusual treatment and, indeed, the book industry in particular has many features that are also found in the music industry. A book company invests in printing plates, licenses rights from authors through royalty-related payments of advances and minimum guarantees, and provides return privileges. Accordingly, tax and accounting methods similar to those in music would apply.

For instance, FASB Statement 50 specifies that "such minimum guarantees shall be reported as an asset by the licensee and subsequently charged to expense in accordance with the terms of the licensing agreement. If all or a portion of the minimum guarantee subsequently appears not to be recoverable through future use of the rights obtained under the license, the nonrecoverable portion shall be charged to expense."

This principle applies to charging off the costs of printing plates and other such production elements and also to the treatment of royalties. Royalties earned by content creators are adjusted for returns (according to rules specified by FASB Statement 48) and are charged as an expense of the period in which sale of the item takes place.[20] Advance royalties paid are reported as an asset if the past performance and current popularity of the author suggest that the advance will be recoverable from expected future royalties. Otherwise, estimated unrecoverable royalties paid to the author would be charged as a period expense.

Sales of software products, however, are also governed by FASB Statement 86, which specifies that internally incurred costs in creating computer software are to be expensed as research and development until technological feasibility is established. Thereafter, all software production costs are to be capitalized and then amortized based on current and future revenue forecasts for each product, with an annual minimum equal to the straight-line amortization over the remaining estimated life of the product.

Valuation

Publishing companies, like those in other media-related industries, are valued primarily on comparisons of cash flow generation capabilities. As in broadcasting or cable, a multiple of projected cash flow – often described by financial analysts in terms of earnings before interest, taxes, depreciation, and amortization ( EBITDA ) – is determined by taking into consideration the multiples of similar recently traded properties and also the following basic elements:

Interest rates and stage of economic cycle
Demographic, technological, social, and cost trend changes
Degree of local monopoly/franchise power
Potential for raising the price of advertising
Potential for increasing circulation and subscriptions and for raising the prices of each
Opportunities to decrease cost and/or to raise standards of editorial inputs

The value that is thus derived would then (as described for cable in Chapter 8) be further adjusted for net debt and for the estimated worth of off–balance sheet items to arrive at the private market value of the property.[21] This is the price that a rational private investor might pay to take control of the property and its cash flows. In addition, this price estimate may also be used as a basis for measuring the relative investment attractiveness of publicly traded shares, which normally sell at a significant discount to the private market value estimate.[22] In book publishing, asset transfers are often assumed to be valued at approximately one times sales.

## 9.4 Concluding remarks

In a broad sense, everything that we see and hear in entertainment is, in one form or another, published. New digital production and distribution technologies, however, already enable almost anyone – at relatively little cost – to publish anywhere and potentially to reach everyone, wherever they may be. The effects on traditional publishing enterprises are thus likely to be as profound as they are disruptive.[23] With text, data, graphics, moving pictures, and sound now all being blended together into seamless webs of new "published" products and associated services, traditional publishing industry paradigms are being rapidly rendered obsolete.

## Notes

**1.** Critics note that much of today's advertising wastes money. For instance, competitors' expenditures cancel each other out if two companies producing similar soft drinks spend greatly to increase brand awareness and market share and neither gains.
**2.** As of 2004, it was estimated that educational publishers, after subtracting costs for author royalties, printing, distribution, and retail markup typically earned a profit of $15 to $20 from books selling at $100. See "College Books Move Online," *Wall Street Journal*, April 23, 2004.
**3.** In open states, local school districts decide how to spend their textbook money. But in adoption states, materials have to be "adopted" in order to qualify for state funding. When adoption cycles in major disciplines such as reading, math, or science coincide in several

populous states (especially Texas and California), profits of the winning publishers are, of course, significantly enhanced. See Stille (2002).

**4.** With prices relatively insensitive to changes in demand, an educational publisher's profits will be determined by how successfully a company competes for adoption programs. It might take three years and an investment of perhaps $30 million to create a new math program, and perhaps twice as much for reading. The barrier to entry is that these upfront costs must be carried for several years before any revenues are generated. Products generally stay in the market for five years, over which time capitalized development costs are amortized against revenues. The largest public textbook companies, in combination controlling approximately 62% market share as of 2002, include the U.K.-based Pearson, Canada's Thomson, and McGraw-Hill.

**5.** As Auletta (1997) notes, a $25 hardcover book costs $2.50 to manufacture, $2.00 to distribute, and $1.75 to market. Publishing company overhead is another $2.00 a copy, and the author might receive $2.50 a unit. However, the book is sold to stores at half the cover price, leaving $1.75 per copy as gross profit. Consequently, publisher net margins per book may be only 6%. However, profit margins on hardcovers that sell well are high. As noted in Trachtenberg (2004), 5 million copies is now considered a megaseller, and at this level, a publisher will generate around $50 million in revenues and $15 million in operating profit. Among the 5 million sellers have been the Harry Potter titles. As of 2004, the largest trade publishers (corporate parents in parentheses) were Random House (Bertelsmann), Penguin (Pearson), HarperCollins (News Corp.), and Simon & Schuster (CBS).

**6.** Large commercial publishers will often allocate $1 per book printed for marketing. To project the profit potential for a book, it is also necessary to (a) estimate the average unit costs of paper, printing, and binding (PPB); (b) provide an allowance for publishers' overhead, say, 25% of gross sales on a trade book; (c) account for the publisher's discount to booksellers and other distributors, usually 52%; and (d) deduct as cost the author's advance. See Stewart (1994) and Greco (1997, p. 160).

**7.** Similar deal elements are outlined in Trachtenberg (2003). An alternative to author royalties known as co-publishing is used occasionally and gives the author a much smaller advance but then a much higher share (up to 50%) of profits, however defined. For example, Wyatt (2006a) indicates that Stephen King signed a deal in 1997 with Simon & Schuster for *Bag of Bones* that paid the author a $2 million advance plus 50% of profit.

**8.** As Carvajal (1996) notes, "Returns are the most significant barometer of the financial success of a book, a measurement more critical than a ranking on a best-seller list because rejects cut directly into profits." Most returns (known as "rotting fruit") are shipped back within three to nine months. Independent stores generally sell 80% of the books ordered, superstores sell less than 70%, and discounters such as Wal-Mart sell about 60% – a situation that has led to a rising rate of returns and the Hollywood-style emphasis on obtaining wide distribution for a few, heavily promoted titles. See also Trachtenberg (2005). However, large wholesale distributors such as Ingram or Baker & Taylor act as buffers between publishers and retail outlets. To reduce the costs of return shipments, publishers often pay booksellers for keeping "remainders in place," which is another name for "shared" markdowns. See Kirkpatrick (2001). As of the early 2000s, the four largest chains – Barnes & Noble, Borders, Crown Books, and Books-A-Million – collectively accounted for more than 45% of the market. Retailers like these generally produce after-tax margins ranging from 2% to 3.5%. See also Wyatt (2006b).

**9.** The large public companies include Gannett, New York Times, and Dow Jones.

**10.** Ives (2005) discusses the importance of movie ads, which had increased from 8.2% of national ad revenue in 1995 to 14.2% in 2004. Also, as noted in Peterson (1997), the

*New York Times* has found that "national advertising is not only more profitable than classified or local advertising, it also spreads the sources of revenue across the country, better insulating the paper from local economic slumps." This paper's situation may, however, be unique in that it derives approximately 44% of total column inches in all editions from national advertising at premium prices. National ads thus account for 53% of all ad revenues. By contrast, in the *Los Angeles Times*, national ads only amounted to 15% of total column inches in 1996.

**11.**   This also makes traditional measures of growth of revenues per unit of circulation less relevant than previously.

**12.**   Bakker (2002) provides a history and analysis of the free newspapers.

**13.**   Sunday papers may account for up to half of a daily paper's revenues and earnings. See also *New York Times*, November 6, 2000.

**14.**   As described in Wolff (2000), there are significant additional costs of renting and manufacturing wire pockets at checkout counters. The cost to manufacture is $21, and the cost to rent at eye-level is $40 per year after an installation charge of $20 per counter. There are an estimated 300,000 such counters in the United States.

**15.**   Such discounts may be as much as 50% and may take the form of bonus pages, subsidies of various sales efforts, or a sharing of data bases. See Pogrebin (1996).

**16.**   CPMs  can also be more precisely defined on various criteria based on:

*Circulation*: advertising cost divided by thousands of circulation

*Impressions*: for a single publication, advertising cost divided by thousands of the average issue readership (AIR)

*Gross impressions*: the total advertising cost of a schedule divided by thousands of gross impressions delivered by that schedule

*Net coverage*: total advertising cost of a schedule divided by the thousands making up the net coverage (reach) of that schedule (where coverage/reach is the number of readers reached at least once)

**17.**   For instance, Time Warner is the largest magazine publisher in the world (e.g., *Time, Fortune, Sports Illustrated, Money*). Primedia, Bertelsmann, Meredith Publishing, Reader's Digest, and Hachette (France) are other majors. *TV Guide*, a magazine with the second-largest circulation in the United States, is partially owned by News Corp.

**18.**   As Knecht (1998) notes, until recently, "retailers paid wholesalers 80% of a magazine's cover price; now they typically pay just 70% to 75% . . . At the same time, wholesalers themselves have continued to pay publishers 60% of the cover price, so they have, in effect, shifted much of their margin to retailers." Subsequently, as noted in Rose (2001), supermarkets now push for discounts of 30% off the cover price, and when wholesalers bid against each other, cash signing bonuses of as much as $25,000 per store are sometimes paid. Note also the declining trend for newsstand sales; according to the Magazine Publishers of America, only 37.5% of magazines offered for sale in 2001 were sold as compared with 65% in 1973 and 48% in 1988 (the remainders are shredded and pulped).

**19.**   These are customarily structured with elements taken from the following basic models:

1.  The studio or publisher covers the direct costs of development of a gold master disc and an allocation of overhead, but it retains ownership of the copyright and most of the revenues. In return, the developer is assured a profit margin of 10% to 12%.

2.  The publisher provides the developer with an advance that is to be recouped against royalties and that may be scalable according to unit sales volume. Such royalties could

range from 7% to 25% of net wholesale revenues (i.e., revenues less reserves for returns) but will normally average no more than 12% to 15%.

Developers' choices for distribution would further include (a) selling all rights to a studio and/or publisher for a lump sum or, more commonly; (b) making an affiliate label deal in which the publisher arranges for manufacturing. In such deals, the affiliated company may receive up to 60% to 75% of the net wholesale price as a royalty but with the royalty range dependent on which party pays for the cost of goods sold. Otherwise, it may be assumed that a distributor will typically receive 20% to 30% of the wholesale price and that the publisher will retain the rest, on which amount 10% to 25% might then go to the developer.

Negotiations might also involve the deductibility of promotional units, exclusivity, coop advertising, the rights of portability to different hardware platforms and media carriers (including online), the rights to ancillary revenues, and the allocation of territorial distribution rights. The issues are, in fact, similar to those seen in the music business, in which reserves for returns, discounts, rebates, shipping charges, and stock-balancing costs are often adjustments that reduce earned royalties.

Normally, as a percent of net revenues, the cost of goods sold for a multimedia publisher of consumer-oriented software will amount to 30% to 40%; sales and marketing account for 15% to 30%, and product development entails about 15%. And in the case of distribution on cellphones, for example, a carrier such as Verizon would likely take 30% of sales. See also Schuyler (1995, p. 88).

**20.** As noted in Chapter 6, the key element of FASB Statement 48 is that the amount of future returns can be reasonably estimated. If so, then sales revenue and cost of sales reported in the income statement are reduced to reflect estimated returns.

**21.** As in other industries , enterprise value (EV) is determined by taking shares outstanding times price per share and then adding net debt and subtracting off–balance sheet assets. EV is then divided by EBITDA to obtain a multiple that allows value comparisons to be made.

**22.** Discounts to private value might be as much as 40%, and EBITDA multiples will, in publishing, typically range from six to ten times projections – with the long-run historical average ratio of total market value to EBITDA for newspaper publishers at approximately 8.2. Also, other corroborating valuation measures might include estimates of earnings-per-share growth and multiples of projected sales. Such measures are often more appropriate for young companies in new industries (e.g., Internet companies).

**23.** For example, print and broadcast media advertising availabilities, which are already largely standardized, will likely come to be traded in markets similar to those for stocks or bonds.

## Selected additional reading

Anderson, C. (1996). "The Software Industry," *The Economist*, May 25.

Angwin, J., and Hagan, J. (2006). "As Market Shifts, Newspapers Try to Lure New, Young Readers," *Wall Street Journal*, March 22.

Barringer, F. (2003). "Genteel Changes to Hardscrabble in Publishing," *New York Times*, January 18.

(2001). "Why Newspapers and Newsprint Makers Are at War," *New York Times*, May 14.

(2000). "Fissures in Sunday Papers' Pot of Gold," *New York Times*, November 6.

(1999). "As Data about Readers Grows, Newspapers Ask: Now What?," *New York Times*, December 20.

Blair, J. (2001). "The Dreams of Webzines Fizzle Out," *New York Times*, March 9.

Book Industry Study Group (1995). Book Industry Trends 1995. New York: Book Industry Study Group.

"Book Publishing," *The Economist*, April 7, 1990.

Callahan, P., and Helliker, K. (2001). "Knight Ridder Loses Readers but Charges More to Reach Them," *Wall Street Journal*, June 18.

Carvajal, D. (2006). "One Day Soon, Straphangers May Turn Pages with a Button," *New York Times*, April 24.

(1997). "Book Chains' New Role: Soothsayers for Publishers," *New York Times*, August 12.

Cose, E. (1989). *The Press: Inside America's Most Powerful Newspaper Empires*. New York: William Morrow.

Cuozzo, S. (1996). *It's Alive! How America's Oldest Newspaper Cheated Death and Why It Matters*. New York: Times Books.

Daly, C. P., Henry, P., and Ryder, E. (1997). *The Magazine Publishing Industry*. Boston: Allyn & Bacon.

Dealy, F. X., Jr. (1993). *The Power and the Money: Inside the Wall Street Journal*. Secaucus, NJ: Birch Lane (Carol Publishing).

Delaney, K. J., and Trachtenberg, J. A. (2005). "Publishers Challenge Google's Book-Scanning Efforts," *Wall Street Journal*, October 20.

Dessauer, J. P. (1996). *Book Publishing: The Basic Introduction*. New York: Continuum.

Diamond, E. (1994). *Behind the Times: Inside the New York Times*. New York: Villard.

Ellison, S. (2006). "Clash of Cultures Exacerbates Woes for Tribune Co.," *Wall Street Journal*, November 10.

Geiser, E., and Dolin, A., eds. (1985). *The Business of Book Publishing*. New York: Westview.

Glazer, S. (2005). "How to Be Your Own Publisher," *New York Times*, April 24.

Greco, A. N. (2000). "Market Concentration Levels in the U.S. Consumer Book Industry," *Journal of Cultural Economics*, 24(4)(November).

Hallinan, J. T. (2006). "Unlike Big Dailies, A Paper Prospers in Bismarck, N. D.," *Wall Street Journal*, February 8.

Heidenry, J. (1993). *Theirs Was the Kingdom: Lila and DeWitt Wallace and the Story of the Reader's Digest*. New York: W. W. Norton.

Kellner, T. (2004). "Who Needs a Muse?," *Forbes* 174(10)(November 15).

Kelly, K. (2006). "Scan This Book!," *New York Times*, May 14.

Kirkpatrick, D. D. (2003). "New 'Harry Potter' Book Sells 5 Million on First Day," *New York Times*, June 23.

(2001). "Book Returns Rise, Signaling a Downturn in the Market," *New York Times*, July 2.

(2000a). "Struggles over e-Books Abound," *New York Times*, November 27.

(2000b). "As Publishers Perish Libraries Feel the Pain," *New York Times*, November 3.

(2000c). "Quietly, Booksellers Are Putting an End to the Discount Era," *New York Times*, October 9.

Klebnikov, P. (1995). "The Twain Shall Meet," *Forbes*, 155(5)(February 27).

Knecht, G. B. (1997a). "Book Superstores Bring Hollywood-Like Risks to Publishing Business," *Wall Street Journal*, May 29.

(1997b). "Magazine Advertisers Demand Prior Notice of 'Offensive' Articles," *Wall Street Journal*, April 30.

(1996a). "Microsoft Puts Newspapers in Highanxiety.com," *Wall Street Journal*, July 15.

(1996b). "How Wall Street Whiz Found a Niche Selling Books on the Internet," *Wall Street Journal*, May 16.

Kuczynski, A. (2000a). "Consolidation Skews Field in Magazine Distribution," *New York Times*, October 23.

(2000b). "Strutting Her Stuff on Newsstands Coast to Coast," *New York Times*, October 2.

Lewin, T. (2003). "When Books Break the Bank," *New York Times*, September 16.

Munk, N. (1999). "Title Fight," *Fortune*, 139(12)(June 21).

Peterson, I. (1996). "At Times Mirror, What's the Plan?," *New York Times*, June 26.

Picard, R. G., and Brody, J. H. (1997). *The Newspaper Publishing Industry*. Needham Heights, MA: Allyn & Bacon.

Pogrebin, R. (1996). "A Magazine Only a Mother Could Love? Reader's Digest Seeks to Change," *New York Times*, July 22.

Reilly, P. M. (1996a). "Where Borders Group and Barnes & Noble Compete, It's a War," *Wall Street Journal*, September 3.

(1996b). "Guccione Sex Empire Falls from Penthouse into the Basement," *Wall Street Journal*, March 22.

(1996c). "Newspaper Company Faces Succession Fight Despite Family Control," *Wall Street Journal*, January 22.

Rose, M. (2003a). "In Fight for Ads, Publishers Often Overstate Their Sales," *Wall Street Journal*, August 6.

(2003b). "Times Co. Strikes a Tougher Stance in Business Deals," *Wall Street Journal*, February 4.

(2002). "Wedding 'Church' and 'State' Works at Time Inc. Unit," *Wall Street Journal*, October 1.

(2001). "Recession Transforms Once-Glamorous Job of Magazine Publisher," *Wall Street Journal*, December 4.

(2000). "Smaller Newspapers Are Now Getting Another Look," *Wall Street Journal*, March 14.

Rosse, J. N. (1967). "Daily Newspaper Monopoly, Competition, and Economies of Scale," *American Economic Review*, 57.

Seelye, K. Q. (2006). "What-Ifs of a Media Eclipse," *New York Times*, August 27.

(2005a). "At Newspapers, Some Clipping," *New York Times*, October 10.

(2005b). "Can Papers End the Free Ride?," *New York Times*, March 14.

Shawcross, W. (1992). *Murdoch*. New York: Simon & Schuster.

Steinberg, J., and Carr, D. (2004). "The Troubling Case of the Phantom Readers," *New York Times*, June 28.

Tebbel, J. W. (1987). *Between Covers: The Rise and Transformation of Book Publishing in America*. New York: Oxford University Press.

Tebbel, J. W., and Zuckerman, M. E. (1991). *The Magazine in America, 1741–1990*. New York: Oxford University Press.

Tedeschi, B. (2004). "Online Battle of Low-Cost Books," *New York Times*, July 12.

Trachtenberg, J. A (2004). "To Compete with Book Chains, Some Think Big," *Wall Street Journal*, August 24.

(2003). "Barnes & Noble Pushes Books from Ambitious Publisher: Itself," *Wall Street Journal*, June 18.

(2002). "Fresh Marketing Tactics Help Writer Push His Thrillers to Mass Audience," *Wall Street Journal*, May 14.

Wilke, J. R. (2000). "Tribune Co. Deal Puts Cross-Ownership Rule in the Cross Hairs," *Wall Street Journal*, March 14.

Wyatt, E. (2005). "Michael Crichton? He's Just the Author," *New York Times*, February 6.

# 10
# Toys and games

*It's not whether you win or lose, but how you play the game.*

In the age of computers, that statement takes on new meanings: Only a few people in the world can beat the best computerized chess-playing machines. And video games cannot ever really be defeated because, no matter how high the score, it is always the human who tires first or makes the fatal error.

This chapter, largely focusing on toys and computerized games, will show how microelectronic-chip technology has enabled game designers to conveniently and inexpensively transform plain television screens into playfields of extraordinary capability. And we shall see how, from a small kernel, there rapidly evolved a business that is currently of comparable global scale and more vibrant than either that of movies or music.

First, however, we gain important perspective by examining the traditional toy and game sectors.

## 10.1 Not just for kids

Throughout the ages, toys have always reflected the technological capabilities and the cultural traditions of the societies in which they have been developed. Early primitive toys, some found by archaeologists going back as far as 5,000 years, were made of clay or wood or cloth, for example. Hobbyhorses and toy pets were seen in early Greece. Children of medieval times played with miniatures of knights and cannons and dolls dressed as monks. Fashion dolls were favorites of French aristocracy in the Middle Ages, and doll cabinets decorated the homes of wealthy Dutch and German merchants in the 1700s. By the 1800s, introduction of sheet metal, porcelain, and rubber had eventually made a wider variety of toys available at more affordable prices.

Although Germany had by 1900 become the world's manufacturing center, American toymakers were beginning to gain ground, taking on a more modern cast when rapidly improving mass-production and distribution methods were combined with the introduction of new plastics materials. Later on, innovations in design, marketing, advertising, and distribution further strengthened the American presence even as manufacturing was shifted mostly to Asia.

Yet no matter where toys are made or marketed, it is clear that the types of toys that are popular change over time and reflect a society's cultural values and attitudes toward children. For example, as Cross (1997, p. 9) notes, in the early 1900s, middle-class Americans bought toys that trained their children for adult occupations, whereas modern toys "invite children into a fantasy world free of adults." Figure 10.1 provides a historical perspective.

Toys are the quintessential entertainment products. Indeed, it is the very potential for entertainment – play aspect, if you will – that makes something a toy instead of merely a nondescript object composed of plastic or wood or fiber or metal. The key additional ingredient, of course, is the imagination of the player. A toy, virtually by definition, alters a person's psychological state, diverting one's attention in the same way that (as noted in Chapter 1) all entertainment products and services do. Thus, the toy business is an integral part of the entertainment industry: It's not just for kids.

Financial flavors

In fact, the toy industry has evolved into a rather sizable business that in the United States annually generates over $20 billion of sales at wholesale and about $30 billion at retail as of the early 2000s. Moreover, the United States represents approximately 36% of total worldwide demand, with Western Europe, Asia, and Japan accounting (since the early 1990s) for approximately 28%, 13%, and 10%, respectively. As such, thousands of companies are involved in the global manufacture and distribution of toy and game products of all types.[1]

Although the toy manufacturing industry remains highly fragmented, among the largest companies, significant consolidation has already occurred and extends even to firms in mainland China and Hong Kong, where around 70% of the toys are made: Companies competing on a global basis require large amounts of capital and the advantages that derive from economies

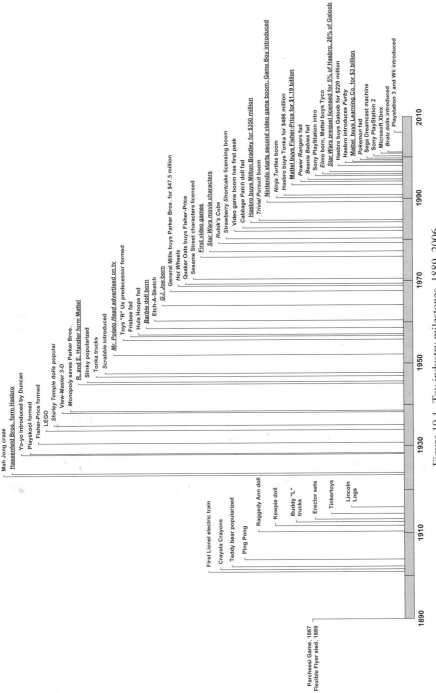

Figure 10.1. Toy industry milestones, 1889–2006.

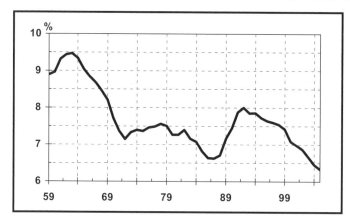

Figure 10.2. Toys (nondurable) as a percentage of total PCE on recreation, 1959–2005.

of scale in manufacturing, marketing, distribution, and advertising. In this regard, the toy industry is following the patterns established in other entertainment subsegments. Major entertainment companies will also often take an active interest in toy development through licensing and merchandising ventures that are expected to extend a film's (or television show's) franchise value. But the brand building occasionally works the other way around, with strong toy concepts boosting a film's revenue generating prospects.

By the late 1990s, the industry in the United States had come to be dominated by three major manufacturer/distributor organizations that accounted for an estimated half of total sales. Those companies include Mattel (Fisher-Price, Tyco, American Girl), Hasbro (Milton Bradley, Tonka, Kenner, Parker Bros., Galoob, Tiger Electronics, OddzOn), and Denmark's Lego. On the retail level, the business has come to be dominated by Wal-Mart (2005 share ~25%), Target, and other large discounters.[2] Even so, nondurable toys have accounted for a gradually declining share of total U.S. personal consumption expenditures on recreation (Figure 10.2).

Table 10.1. *Toy industry financial composite (eight companies),[a] 2001–2005*

|  | Revenues | Operating income | Operating margin (%) | Assets | Operating cash flow |
|---|---|---|---|---|---|
| CAGR (%):[b] | | | | | |
| 2001–2005 | 5.6 | 10.1 | 4.3 | 3.1 | 10.3 |

[a] Average margin, 2001–2005 = 12.3%.
[b] Compound annual growth rate.

Table 10.2. *Toy industry factory shipments of leading categories, estimated, 1985–2005*[a]

| Category | $ millions | |
| --- | --- | --- |
| | 1985 | 2005 |
| Infant/preschool | 824 | 3,200 |
| Dolls | 1,562 | 2,700 |
| Plush | 585 | 1,300 |
| Figures | 840 | 1,300 |
| Vehicles | 695 | 1,900 |
| Games and puzzles | 642 | 2,400 |
| Building/construction sets | 189 | 700 |
| Educational/scientific | 58 | 400 |
| Total[b] | 5,882 | 21,900 |

[a] Shipment figures are for first U.S. billing in dollars.
[b] Total excludes TV video games and other miscellaneous toy categories.
*Source*: Toy Manufacturers of America.

As can be seen from Table 10.1, toy manufacturers' revenues grew by 5.6% between 2001 and 2005. These averages, however, disguise the high variances of financial and operating performance that are a common and constant feature for both manufacturers and retailers. Such variance is somewhat more visible in Table 10.2 and in Figure 10.3, where the differing sales growth rates and dollar shipment volume changes of major product categories can be seen. The industry's volatility of demand and great seasonality,

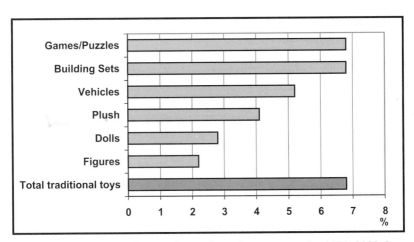

Figure 10.3. Comparative sales growth rates for major toy categories, 1983–2005. *Source data*: Toy Manufacturers Association.

with two-thirds of annual sales always coming in the last 12 weeks of the year, naturally add to the operational uncertainties and risks.


Building blocks

As noted by Owen (1986), the roots of the giant American toy companies are humble indeed. Even today, with all the sophisticated market research that these companies can so readily command, the reasons for the success or failure of particular toy lines are often not well understood. Sometimes a toy line such as the popular Strawberry Shortcake of the early 1980s or Pokémon of the late 1990s can be successfully created out of thin air. At other times, all the preplanning and advertising in the world cannot move a product – movie and television show tie-ins notwithstanding.[3] In all, experience suggests that a good story line and aspects of collectibility are the two essential ingredients in the creation of a long-lasting toy fad.[4]

So-called trademarked *staple* products, such as the board game Monopoly, Lego blocks, Mr. Potato Head, or the Barbie doll, then again, seem to have an almost timeless appeal. As might be expected, such products produce unusually high profit margins for the companies that make them. But although staples are to the toy industry what film libraries are to the studios, they are not normally a sufficient fuel for growth. For that, toy companies require luck, pluck, and lots of spending on product development and television marketing of an increasingly global nature. In this respect, the development process for new toys is similar to that in film and music. And, as in film and music, it is often the singularly profitable hit that pays for the many new product introductions that flop.

Nevertheless, the analogies between toys and other entertainment industries should not be stretched too far. The highly compressed seasonal pattern of retail demand combined with the enormous amount of physical inventory handling that is required to service this demand intensifies short-term delivery pressures on manufacturers and retailers.[5] More often than not, these pressures lead to inventory imbalances (of too many unsold products) that must be corrected before retailers are again "open-to-buy" (i.e., to order, in both a fiscal and physical sense) new toys for the next season.

Toy company valuation methods differ, too, since brand names, which are of little consequence in filmed entertainment, count for a lot here. Beyond the standard techniques of analysis used to project cash flows and cash flow multiples (as in the media industries), stock market and corporate borrowing-power valuations must, in addition, make allowance for intangible brand name assets.[6]

Moreover, although demographic arguments are frequently invoked to portray the industry's growth potential favorably, most such generalized arguments must be tempered. For instance, when forecasting changes in aggregate demand, it is usually more important to know the number of *first births* than it is to know the projected total number of children in the population. But, in

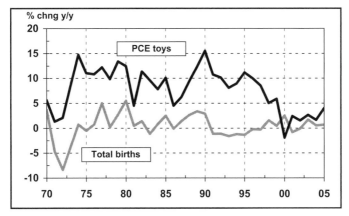

Figure 10.4. Annual percent change in total U.S. births versus annual percent change in PCE on toys, one year lagged, 1970–2005.

targeting a marketing campaign, it may be even more important to know the income level and demographic distribution of couples expecting a first child. Figure 10.4 illustrates the relationship between PCE spending and births and Figure 10.5 the typical per capita toy spending by age.[7]

## 10.2 Chips ahoy!

Toys may be differentiated from other entertainment industry segments, not so much because demand for them often tends to be so volatile and faddish as because a relatively high percentage of their cost components (value added) is tied up in the manufacture and movement of physically bulky inventory.

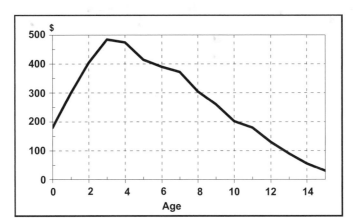

Figure 10.5. Approximate per capita spending on traditional toys by age category circa 2005. *Sources*: U.S. Department of Commerce, U.S. Census Bureau, National Center for Health Statistics, Mattel.

For most entertainment products and services, in contrast, the proportionally greatest amount of value added is to be found in the organized bits of information that we call programming, or software. Those bits are stored on optically scanned discs or other semiconductor materials and relayed via the Internet, cables, or over-the-air broadcast signals.

Because video games are again really no more than organized bits of information storable on inert media or capable of being electronically transmitted, they are indeed close technological cousins to many other entertainment-industry products. The only difference with video games, then, is that you need a computer to play them. As we shall see, both branches of the video game industry grow from the same roots and share a future governed by the rate of innovation in electronic-component and software design.[8]

Slots and pins

The history of coin-operated machines (coin-ops) can be traced to the late 1880s, when the first nickel-in-the-slot machines in the gambling halls of San Francisco were introduced. The checkered and colorful saga of their development and use in the United States, documented in Fey (1989), follows closely the development trend of the gaming industry, which is the topic of the next chapter. For now it is sufficient to note that, during the Great Depression of the 1930s, there began to emerge amusement-only machines – the forerunners of today's sophisticated pinball and video gadgets.

One of the most important early pin models was the *Ballyhoo*, introduced by a struggling Chicago-based company, Lion Manufacturing. Lion was predecessor to the Bally Manufacturing Company, which, along with several other Chicago companies, including Gottlieb, Williams, and Stern, had by the early 1970s become the leading worldwide producers of such machines.[9]

But there were two critical events in the mid-1970s: Bally replaced electromechanical pinball components with new electronic circuitry, and large cities such as Los Angeles, Chicago, and New York legalized placement of pins in general public locations. The effects were to catapult Bally to a position of industry leadership and to dramatically expand the demand for state-of-the-art electronic models with enhanced features. Thereafter, demand for pins declined until, by the year 2000, only one small privately held company remained.[10]

*Pong*: pre and après

As we now know, the market for coin-op machines was not limited to pinballs, and video games were already on the horizon by the end of the 1960s. In fact, their technological roots can be traced back to 1962, when an MIT graduate student demonstrated *Spacewar*, a science-fiction fantasy game played on a PDP-1 mainframe computer and a large-screen cathode-ray tube. That game attracted a wide cult following among computer buffs.

The next important step came in 1968, when a Sanders Associates engineer developed a console that could be used to display games on ordinary television sets. Sanders patented this idea and sold the rights to Magnavox, now a division of Philips, the large Dutch consumer electronics conglomerate.[11]

But it was not until the early 1970s that a young University of Utah engineering graduate, Nolan Bushnell, came to realize that the price of electronic computing power (integrated circuits) had declined to the point that adaptation of *Spacewar* from a large computer into coin-op form was becoming economically feasible. Bushnell and his associates began working on such a machine in a converted bedroom workshop. What they ultimately developed instead was a simple tennislike game that they named *Pong*.[12]

*Pong* took the industry by storm and quickly became the first coin-operated video game hit. And soon thereafter, commercial Pong-style home video games also appeared.[13] Yet despite early enthusiasm, consumer interest in this area proved much more fleeting and fickle than had been anticipated and, as price competition and losses mounted, most of the early manufacturers were forced to withdraw from the field.

Profits, moreover, proved to be just as elusive at Bushnell's company, Atari, where a rapidly growing market presence in coin-op and home video required greater infusions of capital and more professional management than the company could readily muster. By the end of 1976, the founders of Atari had sold their holdings to Warner Communications for about $28 million, a value approximating their sales in that year.[14]

At that point, coin-operated video games seemed just another passing fad. But introduction of *Space Invaders* – an arcade model produced by Japanese coin-op manufacturer Taito and sold through U.S. national distributor Bally–Midway – proved otherwise. With its more colorful graphics and quick-response shoot-'em-up play features, *Space Invaders* immediately captured the public's fancy, becoming the first popular machine to highlight the emerging capabilities of microelectronics and of software design.[15]

Quite logically, then, there soon followed a flurry of popular videos that employed the same or better hardware and even more imaginative software.[16] Of these, *Pac-Man* (in 1980) was especially significant in that it was the first to attract female video game players in large numbers.

By the late 1970s, the same software improvements and technological advances (faster microprocessors and larger memories) that permitted designers to produce spectacular aural and visual effects for coin-op machines were also being applied to home video units. It was thus only a short while before the programmable consoles that had been languishing for lack of software suddenly began to sell in large numbers: Consumers had finally discovered that they could play a reasonable facsimile of their favorite arcade games at home. The impact on Atari was astounding. Unprofitable for the first three years under the aegis of parent Warner Communications, Atari had, by the end of 1979, hit its stride. By either self-designing or licensing

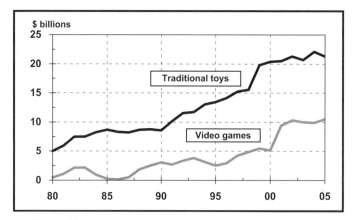

Figure 10.6. Home video game and toy sales, U.S. manufacturers' shipments in dollars, 1980–2005. *Source data*: Nintendo of America, Inc., and TMA.

the most popular arcade concepts for cartridge format, the company had captured some 80% of the worldwide market for home video games.[17]

Industry sales of consoles and cartridges rose from practically zero in 1977 to over $2 billion at wholesale ($3 billion at retail) in 1982.[18] By then, as Figure 10.6 shows, video game hardware and software sales accounted for nearly one-third of total U.S. toy manufacturers' shipments.

*Pong* had indeed pinged.

## 10.3 Structural statements

Home video games

All of this, however, was too good to last. By late 1982, the public's fascination with arcade games had begun to wane, and fewer hit concepts were becoming available for conversion to cartridges. At the same time, the market was flooded with imitative software of all types.[19] Thus it was not until the late 1980s that the industry's previously amorphous structure, at least on the software side, had stabilized and become, in many respects, rationalized along the lines of the recorded-music and book-publishing businesses.

Until 1986, when Japan-based Nintendo (in Japanese, "leave it to heaven") introduced a more technologically sophisticated and user-friendly game console, the hardware side was also in disarray.[20] But with tight control of software development and marketing, Nintendo was able to revive and to then capture up to 80% of a once-again booming market in which no significant competition appeared until the early 1990s.[21] At that point, the annual operating profits of Nintendo had already grown to over $1 billion – an amount exceeding the 1991 profits of all the major Hollywood studios *combined*.

By the late 1990s, sales of game hardware and software, led by Sony's PlayStation, had grown to be comparable in size (around $7 billion) to U.S.

domestic box-office revenues. Thereafter, worldwide sales of consoles, games, and accessories, stimulated by intense competition between Sony's PlayStation 2, Nintendo's GameCube, and Microsoft's Xbox, quickly grew to exceed $20 billion. In fact, over the six years from introduction of PlayStation in 1995, Sony alone sold more than 110 million consoles and 880 million games. By 2007, modern game consoles (including the latest PlayStation3, Xbox, and Nintendo's Wii models) were in more than half of U.S. households.

With change the only constant, the game industry has moved (on an apparent five-year upgrade cycle beginning with Atari around 1980) toward standards that utilize ever more powerful Internet-accessible computer platforms and that allow enjoyment of massively multiplayer online games (MMOGs; e.g., *World of Warcraft*, *EverQuest*, *Second Life*, and *Ultima Online*). Players of such online games are now able to create and even to monetize in the real world entire virtual universes and lives.[22] With the low-cost processing power that is already available, games too are, in effect, turned into interactive movies.[23] The major difference, though, between traditional films and these is that the players become actors in their own uniquely unfolding stories with multiple twists and turns. Small wonder, then, that movie studios, typically earning 10% to 20% of a licensed game publisher's profits, have found the licensing of concepts and characters to game developers to be lucrative.[24]

Coin-op

Coin-op has had a far more rigid industry structure than that seen in home video games. But fluctuations in demand have nevertheless been quite large (Figure 10.7), and the industry's dominant companies have, in response,

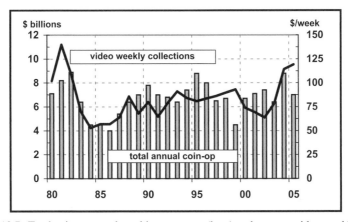

Figure 10.7. Total coin-operated machine revenues (bars) and average video weekly gross collections (right scale), 1980–2005.

become vertically integrated in performance of the four functions that define a presence in the coin-op business. Those functions include the following:

*Game design*, wherein designs may often cost more than $2 million per model.

*Manufacturing and assembly*, in which component producers of monitors, printed circuit boards, and memory and microprocessor chips participate. Both coin-op and home segments consume a significant portion of world-wide electronic-component production.[25]

*Distribution*, through which machines of various manufacturers are whole-saled, serviced, and sometimes exchanged. Distributors supply credit to smaller operators to finance purchase of machines and generally support new-model demand by accepting trade-ins of used equipment. Conversion kits, primarily new circuit boards that enable existing cabinets and monitors to be adapted for new games, may also be provided.

*Operation or ownership of locations*, either of arcades or of a string of smaller locations in which the machines are placed. Operators and location owners will normally split revenues on a 50:50 percentage or some similar ratio after a certain minimum payment or guarantee to the route operator has been assured.[26]

Profit dynamics

For the manufacturer, a hit game, like a hit movie or record, can generate extraordinary returns, particularly in home versions, for which the profitability can far exceed that of the coin-ops.[27] Indeed, by the late 1990s, games such as Nintendo's *GoldenEye* or *Legend of Zelda* had generated domestic gross revenues of more than $200 million even though the cost of production and development had been no more than $6 million for each game.[28] Such revenue-to-cost ratios are far more impressive than, say, in movies, where the production cost for most projects able to generate in excess of $200 million in revenues would be typically several times higher. MMOGs such as *World of Warcraft* have even greater profit-generating potential if only because monthly subscription fees provide repetitive cash flows that go beyond merely the initial sale of software.[29] And games on cellphones now provide another new source of revenues.

Although most games will not be nearly as profitable as these (or, e.g., collectively all versions of *The Sims*), substantial benefits yet accrue to console manufacturers such as Sony or Nintendo through the license fees/royalties of between $5 and $10 a unit that they normally impose on outside game developers. As in other entertainment segments, however, it takes only a few big winners to handsomely offset the more modest returns or losses on the majority of titles released.[30] The only essential precondition for this to happen is that there must already exist a large installed base of compatible consoles or computers.[31]

Still, it is this kind of potential profitability (especially as ultimately projected on a global scale) that continues to attract consumer electronics companies and software developers to a business that thrives on technological improvements of game-playing multimedia machines for the home and for arcades and indoor theme park attractions.[32]

## 10.4 Concluding remarks

This chapter has told of boom and bust, of delight in transforming a television screen into a magnificent fantasyland, and of despair in discovering that losses can sometimes come more easily than gains. Demand for a specific toy or game line, like that for a specific movie, is often volatile, faddish, and unpredictable. But consolidation of companies into global giants in manufacturing, marketing, and distribution has – along with the resulting assemblage of diversified portfolios (libraries) of branded toy concepts – led to industry earnings trends that are now generally less dependent than previously on the success of just a few promotional items. Technology is also now advancing so rapidly that it is becoming ever more difficult to distinguish between a toy and the living thing that it is designed to impersonate.

As of the early 2000s, domestic consumer spending on game software alone (i.e., not counting hardware) is again of the same order of magnitude as that spent on either movies or music. In fact, the technological sophistication of game software has already reached the stage at which development processes, story lines, visual presentation qualities, and impacts on emotions are comparable to those in filmed entertainment. Movies and games, two highly collaborative art forms, are becoming increasingly integrated, and it is now often difficult to distinguish where one ends and the other begins. The same applies to online games, in which the edges between real and virtual lives are blurring.[33]

Moreover, recent advances in telecommunications make it likely that the structure of both the home video and coin-op segments will be changed significantly. With fiber optic and wireless linkages to the Internet, highly compressed digital signal transmission capabilities, and substantially greater computing power available at relatively low cost, video games of both varieties will be deliverable to consoles with lightning speed and efficiency. No longer will coin-op require the frequent physical movement of bulky cabinets and circuit boards. And no longer will the home player be limited in selection of titles or of playing partners.

In addition, computerized games will increasingly incorporate artificial intelligence and so-called virtual-reality capabilities and will evolve away from those requiring only simple hand–eye coordination skills to those in which thinking strategies and abstract reasoning are helpful factors. Thus will be provided challenging interactive role-playing "experiences" that are likely to progressively divert time and spending away from the more traditional media sectors.[34]

No matter what the technology or the format, however, the essence of a successful game will always be the same: It is simple to understand and to play on an elementary level, but it is addictive and maddeningly difficult – and forever impossible – to fully master.[35] Be it a game or a toy, the essential element will always be the product's ability to engage the player's fantasies. Toys and games are, in the end, merely the means through which stories are stimulated, amplified, and conveyed.

Surely, we will continue to be charmed in ways we can only begin to imagine, for as Frude (1983) has noted with regard to the eventual development of personal robots, another form of computerized entertainment:

the scene is set for entirely new dimensions of human simulation. And the preposterous notion that a future "personal friend" might be purchased off the shelf now has to be seriously considered . . . [But still,] getting a machine to laugh is easy. Getting it to laugh at a joke is very, very difficult.

## Notes

**1.** According to Toy Manufacturers of America (TMA) data, the U.S. toy industry in 1998 shipped 3.37 billion toys, constituting an estimated 125,000 to 150,000 individual products (i.e., stock keeping units, or SKUs).

**2.** Relationships between toy manufacturers and retailers, like those between movie distributors and exhibitors, are sometimes strained. Yet it is a rare toy manufacturer who will refuse to help an important retailer out of an inventory problem. The manufacturer will usually provide the costly incentives (i.e., markdown money), sometimes in the form of rebates or price cuts, that are required to clear the shelves. Such incentives may range as high as 3% of the product line's sales. Toy industry investors would thus do well to regard manufacturers' receivables more as inventories held in storage by the retailer than as final sales in the strictest sense of financial accounting. As has been proven time and again, harsh post-Christmas earnings surprises may await investors who are unaware that receivables from retailers are not solid until the toys actually sell-through to consumers.

**3.** See, for example, Watkins (1986) and especially Stern and Schoenhaus (1990) for discussions of the toy development process.

**4.** As Lyman (1999) notes, "Power Rangers had the story line without the collecting and Beanie Babies had the collecting without the story line. Pokémon has both."

**5.** For example, it is usually easy enough to make more prints so that a popular movie can be shown in more theaters; it is next to impossible to make and deliver more copies of a popular toy the week before Christmas.

**6.** In determining the value of a brand name, most methods would take total brand sales and then subtract cost of goods sold, selling, general and administrative expenses, and depreciation in order to arrive at an operating profits figure. From this, an amount equal to what could be earned on a basic or generic version of the product is deducted. A tax rate is then applied to this adjusted amount to estimate what net brand profit might be. Finally, a multiple, depending on how strong the brand is in terms of consumer recognition, stability, leadership, internationality, support, and protection, would be used to make a final assessment of the brand's value. In the *Financial World* analysis of July 8, 1996, the Barbie and Fisher-Price values had grown to $2.5 billion and $1.1 billion, respectively. For more recent data, see "The Best Global Brands," *BusinessWeek*, August 6, 2001. Brand assets are extensively covered in Aaker (1991).

**7.**   Parents tend to buy more toys for a first child than for any other.

**8.**   Software is the instruction set that controls a machine's functions.

**9.**   By that time, the worldwide market had become fairly mature and predictable, with Gottlieb (eventually renamed Mylstar) later discontinued by its owner (Coca-Cola) and Williams holding dominant market positions. In the late 1980s, Bally sold its pin and video business to a successor company of Williams, WMS Industries.

**10.**   Stern Pinball of Melrose Park, Illinois, is the remaining company that sells about 10,000 machines a year, down from 100,000 global industry sales at the peak in 1992. See *The Economist*, March 11, 2000.

**11.**   The Sanders engineer was Ralph Baer, and the Sanders patents were eventually licensed to all major home video game manufacturers. The name of the aforementioned MIT graduate student is Steve Russell.

**12.**   Bushnell and his associates produced a version of *Spacewar* called *Computer Space*. But with sales of only 1,500 units, *Computer Space* was not a commercial success and the rights to it were sold to Nutting Associates, the small firm that had originally agreed to produce it.

Still, following this, Bushnell wanted his design company, Syzygy, to develop a driving game. However, for a tiny outfit with limited resources and experience, that was a rather ambitious goal. To gain the necessary skills, Bushnell had the company start by building a prototype that could simulate the simplest game he could think of: tennis. Much to the surprise of its designers, the game was fun to play. But because manufacturers were not interested in producing it, Syzygy had no choice but to assemble the product itself. *Pong*, as it was known, became an instant rage in bars and restaurants where pinball was popular.

In all, Syzygy – by early 1973 renamed Atari after a term (meaning prepare to be engulfed) from the Japanese game of go – sold about 10,000 units, and 90,000 or so copies or adaptations from other manufacturers flooded the market. Bushnell subsequently bought controlling interest in the company from his associates and then sold the renamed Syzygy (Atari) to Warner Communications. See also Owen (1983), Kubey (1982), and Markoff (2002).

**13.**   Consoles dedicated to playing only a few variations of one or two games were introduced in 1972 under the Magnavox Odyssey label. And several other companies at once joined Magnavox. Besides Atari, the other manufacturers included Coleco, Fairchild Instrument, National Semiconductor, and RCA.

**14.**   Losses at Fairchild and at Warner's new Atari division continued into 1977, when both companies introduced new cartridge-loaded programmable consoles that they hoped would turn the tide. Although these models were a distinct improvement over the previous generation of dedicated machines, they did little to excite the average consumer. Game-design capabilities were at a primitive stage, and the semiconductor chips used in consoles and cartridges had small and relatively expensive memories. There was no software.

Around this time, Bally Manufacturing and RCA also made major efforts to enter the programmable market, but both companies soon found their participation unrewarding. Bally sold its loss-plagued division to Astrocade, a private company that eventually folded, and RCA discontinued its line. Long-suffering Fairchild also gave up on the business.

**15.**   *Space Invaders* was also instrumental in raising coin-op-industry unit-volume expectations well beyond the 20,000 or so that was considered exceptional in the heyday of pinball. Taito again began selling the arcade console in 2003.

**16.**   The hit parade included *Asteroids* and *Missile Command*, developed by Atari, *Defender* from Williams Electronics, and the ubiquitous *Pac-Man* and its variants, designed by the private Japanese company Namco and distributed in coin-op version by Bally and in cartridges by Atari.

**17.**   Atari's revenues, which had been $28 million in 1976, expanded to over $2 billion in 1982, while annual operating income went from a loss of several million dollars to profits of more than $320 million.

By 1980, the industry's potential looked good enough for Mattel, then the largest toy company in the United States, to introduce its Intellivision brand of consoles. Intellivision's key selling point was pictorial resolution (graphics) superior to that of Atari's 1977-vintage Video Computer System (VCS) and to the older Odyssey line. In short order, Mattel garnered about a 16% share of market – second only to Atari's.

Nevertheless, Intellivision was vulnerable in two areas: Its price was relatively high compared with that of the VCS (at retail over $200 versus about $150 for Atari), and it was largely dependent on a software library of generic sports-related games instead of arcade hits. This provided Coleco, a late (1982) entrant, with the opportunity to surpass Mattel's unit volume with ColecoVision, a lower-priced product that successfully combined high-resolution graphics with top-licensed arcade titles.

Although Atari and Mattel initially had complete control of titles for their own cartridge formats, by late 1981, growth of console shipments had attracted several other plug-compatible software designers and manufacturers, including Activision, Parker Bros. (a division of General Mills), Coleco, CBS, and Imagic.

**18.**   Unit sales in that year climaxed at an estimated 8.3 million consoles and 77 million cartridges.

**19.**   The first inexpensive home computers then also began to come to market. These home computers included the Texas Instruments (TI) model 99/4A and the Commodore model VIC-20. Both machines were marketed with the promise of combining education and game entertainment.

**20.**   During this time, as saturation became more evident to all participants, price cutting and wholesale dumping of excess hardware and software inventories accelerated, thereby producing aggregate industry losses that amounted to an astounding $1.5 billion in 1983 alone. The largest losses were at Atari ($539 million), Mattel ($361 million), and Texas Instruments ($660 million).

**21.**   Nintendo was joined in this revival by a much shrunken Atari and by another Japanese company, Sega Enterprises Ltd. However, Nintendo's software, particularly titles such as *Super Mario Bros. 2* and *The Legend of Zelda*, which each sold over 3 million copies, were especially important in maintaining the company's leading share of market. (*Super Mario Bros.*, introduced in 1987, had sold 9.1 million units and, by 2002, had grossed $7 billion.) In fact, the company delivered 7 million hardware units and 32.5 million software units in 1988, and nearly 9 million game sets and 60 million software units were sold in 1990 (with *Super Mario Bros. 3* selling 8 million units).

From the fall of 1986 through year-end 1989, the company estimated that 19 million Nintendo hardware units and 101.5 million Nintendo and Nintendo-licensed software units had been sold. Industry totals for the same period were estimated at 24.5 million hardware units and 125 million software units. Although NEC, a large Japanese electronics company, also launched another potentially serious challenge to Nintendo's primacy in 1990, Sega ultimately proved to be the more important competitor. See also Pollack (1986) and especially Sheff (1993) for a detailed history.

By 1999, the largest installed base was Nintendo's portable 8-bit Game Boy with 80 million units sold since its introduction in 1989. The 8-bit Nintendo Entertainment System, introduced in 1985, had sold 35 million units, the 16-bit Sega Genesis and Super Nintendo systems introduced in the early 1990s each had sold about 20 million units, and the 64-bit Sony PlayStation of 1995 had sold an estimated 23 million units.

As recounted in Wingfield (2006b), games like *The Sims*, the bestselling computer video game of all time, first appeared in the late 1980s and have sold more than 60 million copies ($1 billion) since then. A newer game like *Spore* (circa 2006) reportedly cost more than $20 million to develop. See also Seabrook (2006) and Chaplin and Ruby (2005).

**22.**   See Hof (2006).

**23.**   Marriott (2003) discusses one of the earliest examples of significant and expensive film and game integration for *Enter the Matrix*, and Marriott (2004) discusses the increasingly blurry distinction between movies and games. Clark (2004) shows how new video chip technology accelerates this process. Fritz and Graser (2004) show how game development and marketing costs are beginning to resemble those in films. Schiesel (2004) notes, however, that popular movie titles often do not translate well into popular game concepts. As M. Wallace (2005) describes, massively multiplayer game (MMPG) platforms have also become worlds in which virtual assets can be swapped for real cash on specialized Web sites (e.g., www.gamingopenmarket.com or www.ige.com) or on eBay. Thompson (2005) relates how game playing experts have begun to make short films, called "machinima," directly using the scenes and characters generated by the game itself.

**24.**   Development costs for such games had generally ranged between $3 million to $5 million as of the early 2000s but could go much higher as per note 27. Only about 5% of all game titles reach sales of 1 million units, the point at which they are regarded as being a notable success or "hit" in the same way as a movie grossing $100 million at the box office. Video game companies pay movie studios upfront licensing fees for the rights to create, develop, and produce the games, and studios will also earn royalties after the game company recoups the costs of making the game. Additional payments may be further scaled to box-office performance of the related film. Levine (2005) notes that games tied to films can require 18 to 24 months and $10 million for development, with publishers' advances against future royalties of 15%. A typical deal appears to be for a studio to receive $3 million to $5 million up front against 9% of the revenues for licensing a title to a game maker. See also *Variety*, December 18, 2000.

**25.**   At the peak in 1982, for example, it is estimated that video games absorbed about 25% of all 16K ROMs (read-only memories) and up to 50% of all 32K ROMs produced. Rarely would there be a demand for more than 30,000 units.

**26.**   On locations, receipts per square foot are important. At the height of the *Pac-Man* or *Asteroids* frenzy of the early 1980s, for example, some locations were taking in $400 or more per week on a machine that cost $2,400. However, under more normal conditions, collections will average significantly below $100 a week on machines that have been out for a while. Servicing is the responsibility of the operator, who is often indirectly supported for parts, labor, and financing by local wholesaler/distributor branches. Operators and location owners exercise control over the pricing and frequency of play, and they may have obvious opportunities to divert cash if strict accounting is not enforced. All estimates as to the annual coin-drop are thus approximations based on number of units in use and average play per machine. Street operators will try to extend the useful life of a machine by "rotating" it to a different location. Arcade operators will also use variable pricing on tokens to enable higher collections during times of peak demand and to encourage greater use at slower times of the day. But the income per week and resale value for a typical machine usually decline rapidly in the first year. And once a machine's drawing power begins to decline, the owner has to make a financial decision based on projected cash flows, taxes, and salvage values. To provide perspective, according to a 1982 survey by *Play Meter*, a video machine required an average of $117 per week over a 10.5-month period to break even after considering operating costs for rent, taxes, and license fees.

**27.**   The *Madden* NFL Football game series is an example of a blockbuster hit equivalent to *Titanic* in the movies. By 2005, the 1989 title had sold more than 43 million units for a total of well over $1.1 billion and had become the top-selling video game of all time. Electronic Arts, the game's developer, spends between $5 million and $10 million a year for upgrades. Also, more than 10 million copies of Take-Two's *Grand Theft Auto III* have been sold since 2001. Nintendo's huge late-1980s success, *Super Mario Brothers 2*, provides another example of potential profitability. If at least one-third of Nintendo's 15 million console owners bought a copy, direct gross profit can be estimated to have amounted to more than $45 million according to the following assumptions: Actual manufacturing and shipping costs were probably well under $5 a unit; the basic development and/or licensing cost was $1 million; advertising and promotion were $4 million; and the average wholesale price was about $15.

**28.**   But by the early 2000s, games for the PlayStation 2, Xbox, or GameCube had become so complex that development of a new game title could require two years of effort and cost $10 million, with marketing and translation to different formats adding another $40 million of expense. Moreover, as noted in Tran (2002), Sony and Microsoft adopted differing strategies, with Microsoft going with a "closed" system network in which it manages the game servers and controls everything from billing to matching players and Sony going with an open system in which developers manage their own games online and decide whether and how much to charge users. Fritz and Graser (2004) illustrate how the game business has begun to financially resemble the film business, with major game production costs reaching $15 million and marketing adding another $10 million. As of 2006, the complexities of game development had pushed the price for a major title up to $40 million, which implies that publishers need to sell at least half a million copies to earn significant profits. Schiesel (2005a) notes that Rockstar's *The Warriors* required efforts of 50 people from programmers to costume directors over four years. See also the *Financial Times*, August 7, 2002, and *BusinessWeek*, February 26, 2005, and January 8, 2007, about PS2 sales longevity.

**29.**   As Schiesel (2005c) notes, the subscription fee to *World of Warcraft* is $14.99 a month in addition to $49.99 for software. In its first year (after November 2004), the game generated at least $200 million in subscription revenue and another $50 million in retail sales. And by 2007, *World of Warcraft*, made by Blizzard Entertainment, had signed up more than 7 million subscribers around the world and was generating an annual revenue stream of more than $1 billion as based on the $30 to $50 price of the game software and another $15 monthly subscription fee. As noted by Schiesel (2006), it "has become the first truly global video-game hit since Pac-Man." See Schiesel (2005b) and Wingfield (2006c) about the popularity of MMOG *RuneScape*.

**30.**   A typical deal for an independent game studio developer selling marketing and distribution rights to a big publisher might, as of 2007, be for a $5 million advance against 15% royalties. This means that even sales of a million units at a wholesale price of $30 do not trigger additional payments, and it is worth noting that few games are likely to do so well as to compare with hits like *Tomb Raider* or *Splinter Cell*. The three top-selling computer games of the last half of the 1990s were *Myst* and its sequel *Riven*, with sales of $203 million (5.6 million copies), *Doom* and its sequels, with sales of $109 million (4.3 million units), and *MS Flight Sim* games, with sales of $174 million (4 million units). However, few of the games with budgets of $5 million or more for design, programming, production, and marketing are likely to sell the more than 150,000 units that would be required to reach breakeven on the assumption of a wholesale price of around $30 a unit. See *Forbes*, October 18, 1999, and December 27, 1999, p. 288.

**31.** In the early 1980s, the Atari VCS had an installed base of over 10 million, and hits such as *Asteroids, Space Invaders*, and *Pac-Man* were bought by at least 50% and perhaps up to 75% of console owners.

**32.** The profit dynamics of games are obviously quite similar to those of other entertainment industry segments. On a game cartridge that sells for $40, the wholesale price would normally be about $24 as of the 1990s. A software manufacturer's sales rep would also receive a commission of about 5% for marketing services provided to toy stores. Royalties might amount to $1 or $2 per unit and manufacturing costs up to $10, depending on the media material used. Also, software royalties paid by publishers to game developers might normally range between $1.00 and $1.50 a unit. Developers might also receive advances against royalties, just as in the music business. Chace (1983) discusses such arrangements as they appeared in the early 1980s.

Software development deals in Silicon Valley are structured differently from those in Hollywood, where about 65% of a project's revenues (total revenues minus the standard 35% distribution fees) would generally be available for recoupment of costs and potential payouts to participants. In game development, a typically lower percentage (perhaps 15%) is available for such cost recoupments and participant payouts that are, by definition, related to sales rather than profitability (the Hollywood model).

**33.** As *Warcraft* has demonstrated, the most successful mainstream games for the general public are easily accessible and allow for many different things to be done in a *community* of players.

**34.** Lewis (2003) provides an apt comparison of time spent by gamers as contrasted against time spent in viewing television. For the Electronic Arts game, *Madden 2004*, it may well be that 4 million people play the game for 100 hours, or a total of 400 million person-hours. However, one of the most popular television shows, *The Sopranos*, might draw 11 million viewers for all 13 one-hour episodes for a total of 143 person-hours. On average, it is estimated that Americans devoted 75 hours a year to playing games in 2003.

**35.** When a new arcade game is introduced, players' skills specific to that game obviously are not well honed and many coins per unit time are dropped. But as familiarity with the machine's features increases, players are able to endure longer on a single coin, thereby reducing the operator's return. In recognition of this, operators sometimes use "speed-up" kits that make the game more challenging to skilled players.

## Selected additional reading

Asakura, R. (2000). *Revolutionaries at Sony: The Making of the Sony PlayStation and the Visionaries Who Conquered the World of Video Games*. New York: McGraw-Hill Professional Publishing.

Bannon, L. (2001). "Taking Cues from GE, Mattel's CEO Wants Toy Maker to Grow Up," *Wall Street Journal*, November 14.

(1999). "Mattel Tries to Adjust as 'Holiday Barbie' Leaves under a Cloud," *Wall Street Journal*, June 7.

Bannon, L., and Vitzhum, C. (2003). "One-Toy-Fits All: How Industry Learned to Love the Global Kid," *Wall Street Journal*, April 29.

Barnes, J. E. (2001). "Dragons and Flying Brooms," *New York Times*, March 1.

Belson, K. (2002). "Rival to Pokémon Keeps Market Hot," *New York Times*, October 6.

Brooker, K. (1999). "Toys Were Us," *Fortune*, 140(6)(September 27).

Bylinsky, G. (1991). "The Marvels of 'Virtual Reality'," *Fortune*, 123(11)(June 3).

Canedy, D. (1999). "Takeovers Are Part of the Game," *New York Times*, February 9.

Carlton, J. (1995). "Nintendo, Gambling with Its Technology, Faces a Crucial Delay," *Wall Street Journal*, May 5.

Carlton, J., and Hamilton, D. P. (1999). "Can a New Machine Called the Dreamcast End Sega's Nightmare?," *Wall Street Journal*, September 7.

Chua-Eoan, H., and Larimer, T. (1999). "Beware of the Pokemania," *Time*, November 22.

Churbuck, D. (1990). "The Ultimate Computer Game," *Forbes,* 145(3)(February 5).

Clark, D. (1995). "Multimedia's Hype Hides Virtual Reality: An Industry Shakeout," *Wall Street Journal*, March 1.

Cohen, S. (1984). *Zap: The Rise and Fall of Atari*. New York: McGraw-Hill.

Dee, J. (2003). "Playing Mogul," *New York Times*, December 21.

Delaney, K. J. (2004). "Ads in Videogames Pose a New Threat to Media Industry," *Wall Street Journal*, July 28.

Deutsch, C. H. (1989). "A Toy Company Finds Life after Pictionary," *New York Times*, July 9.

Diamond, D. (1987). "Is the Toy Business Taking Over Kids' TV?," *TV Guide*, 35(14) (June 13).

Flax, S. (1983). "The Christmas Zing in Zapless Toys," *Fortune*, 108(13)(December 26).

Fowler, G. A. (2003). "Copies 'R' Us," *Wall Street* Journal, January 31.

Gaither, C. (2001a). "Video Game Field Becomes Crowded and Highly Profitable," *New York Times*, December 17.

  (2001b). "Microsoft Explores a New Territory: Fun," *New York Times*, November 4.

Gunther, M. (1999). "The Newest Addiction," *Fortune*, 140(3)(August 2).

Guth, R. A. (2003). "Videogame Giant Links with Sony, Snubbing Microsoft," *Wall Street Journal*, May 12.

Guth, R. A., and Khanh, T. I. (2002). "Microsoft Must Woo Game Makers from Japan If Its Xbox Is to Thrive," *Wall Street Journal*, March 26.

Hays, C. L. (2000). "The Road to Toyland Is Paved with Chips," *New York Times*, February 17.

Hector, G. (1984). "The Big Shrink Is on at Atari," *Fortune*, 110(1)(July 9).

Herz, J. C. (1997). *Joystick Nation*. Boston: Little, Brown.

Hubner, J., and Kistner, W. F., Jr. (1983). "What Went Wrong at Atari," *InfoWorld*, November 28 and December 5.

Hutsko, J. (2000). "88 Million and Counting: Nintendo Remains King of the Handheld Game Players," *New York Times*, March 25.

Kent, S. L. (2000). *The First Quarter: A 25-year History of Video Games*. Marietta, OH: BWD Press.

King, S. R. (1999). "Mania for 'Pocket Monsters' Yields Billions for Nintendo," *New York Times*, April 26.

Losee, S. (1994). "Watch Out for the CD-ROM Hype," *Fortune*, 130(6)(September 19).

Markoff, J. (1994). "For 3DO, a Make-or-Break Season," *New York Times*, December 11.

McLean, B. (2005). "Sex, Lies, and VideoGames," *Fortune*, 152(4)(August 22).

Miller, G. W. (1997). *Toy Wars: The Epic Struggle between G.I. Joe, Barbie, and the Companies That Make Them*. New York: Times Books.

Moffat, S. (1990). "Can Nintendo Keep Winning?," *Fortune*, 122(12)(November 5).

Morris, B. (1996). "The Brand's the Thing," *Fortune*, 133(4)(March 4).

Nocera, J. (1984). "Death of a Computer: How Texas Instruments Botched the 99/4A," *InfoWorld*, June 4 and June 11; see also *Texas Monthly*, April.

Nulty, P. (1982). "Why the Craze Won't Quit," *Fortune*, 106(10)(November 15).

Orbanes, P. E. (2004). *The Game Makers: The Story of Parker Brothers.* Boston: Harvard Business School.

Palmer, J. (1989). "'Joy Toy' Nintendo's Future Not All Fun and Games," *Barron's*, June 26.

Patrick, A. O. (2006). "In Tots' TV Shows, a Booming Market, Toys Get Top Billing," *Wall Street Journal*, January 27.

Pereira, J. (1996a). "If You Can't Locate That Special Plaything, Call, or Blame, a Scalper," *Wall Street Journal*, June 24.

(1996b). "Toy Business Focuses More on Marketing and Less on New Ideas," *Wall Street Journal*, February 29.

(1994). "The Toy Industry, Too, Is Merging Like Crazy to Win Selling Power," *Wall Street Journal*, October 28.

(1993). "Toy Industry Finds It's Harder and Harder to Pick the Winners," *Wall Street Journal*, December 21.

(1991). "Nintendo Is Counting on New Super Game to Rescue U.S. Sales," *Wall Street Journal*, May 10.

(1989). "As Ghosts of Yules Past Haunt the Toy Shelves, 'Gottahaves' Are Gone," *Wall Street Journal*, December 12.

Pereira, J., and Bannon, L. (1995). "Toy Makers' Addiction to Hollywood Figures Reshapes Kids' Play," *Wall Street Journal*, July 13.

Pereira, J., and Bulkeley, W. M. (1998). "Toy-Buying Patterns Are Changing and That Is Shaking the Industry," *Wall Street Journal*, June 16.

Pereira, J., and Rohwedder, C. (1998). "Block by Block, Lego Is Building a Strategy for the Interactive Age," *Wall Street Journal*, February 9.

Pham, A. (2005). "Cellphone Industry Is Poised to Ring Up Big Sales," *Los Angeles Times*, May 30.

Pollack, A. (1995). "'Morphing' into the Toy World's Top Ranks," *New York Times*, March 12.

(1993). "Sega Takes Aim at Disney's World," *New York Times*, July 4.

Ressner, J. (1982). "Atari Celebrates First Decade of Record-Breaking Growth," *Cash Box*, November 20.

Rheingold, H. (1991). *Virtual Reality: The Revolutionary Technology of Computer-Generated Artificial Worlds.* New York: Summit Books (Simon & Schuster).

Richtel, M. (2005). "At This Restaurant, the Video Games Come with the Meal," *New York Times*, May 30.

Schiesel, S. (2006). "The Video Game Goes Minimalist: Nintendo Comes Full Circle," *New York Times*, June 4.

"Sega!," *BusinessWeek*, no. 3359 (February 21, 1994).

Sella, M. (1994). "Will a Flying Doll . . . Fly?," *New York Times*, December 25.

Sheff, D. (2005). "New Babes in Toyland: Trollz," *New York Times*, January 4.

Spiers, J. (1992). "The Baby Boomlet Is for Real," *Fortune*, 125(3)(February 10).

Tagliabue, J. (2001). "Lego Tinkered with Success, and Is Now Paying a Price," *New York Times*, December 25.

Takahashi, D. (2002). *Opening the X-Box: Inside Microsoft's Plan to Unleash an Entertainment Revolution.* Sacramento, CA: Prima (Random House).

Tanzer, A. (1991). "Heroes in a Half Shell," *Forbes*, 148(10)(October 23).

Taub, E. (2004). "In Video Games, Sequels Are Winners," *New York Times*, September 20.

Thompson, C. (2006). "Saving the World, One Video Game at a Time," *New York Times*, July 23.

Tkacik, M. (2003a). "To Lure Older Girls, Mattel Brings In a Hip-Hop Crowd," *Wall Street Journal*, July 18.

   (2003b). "Care Bears' Second Act," *Wall Street Journal*, June 11.

Trachtenberg, J. A. (1996). "How Philips Flubbed Its U.S. Introduction of Electronic Product," *Wall Street Journal*, June 28.

Turner, R. (1993) "Video-Game Innovator Lures Corporate Giants to 'Interactive' Media," *Wall Street Journal*, January 7.

U.S. International Trade Commission (1984). *A Competitive Assessment of the U.S. Video Game Industry*. Washington, DC: USITC Publication 1501.

Wojahn, E. (1988). *Playing by Different Rules: The General Mills/Parker Brothers Merger*. New York: American Management Association.

Zachary, G. P. (1990). "Computer Simulations One Day May Provide Surreal Experiences," *Wall Street Journal*, January 23.

# Part III
## Live entertainment

# 11
# Gaming and wagering

*It's better to be born lucky than to be born rich.*

Perhaps nowhere is the preceding sentiment more appropriately expressed than in gaming and wagering, where kings and queens play amidst snake eyes and wild jokers and horses run for the roses. This chapter explores the essential economic features of this fascinating business, for whose services consumers spend more in the aggregate than for any other form of entertainment.

## 11.1 From ancient history

At first

Interest in betting on the uncertain outcome of an event is not a recently acquired human trait. As noted by Berger and Bruning (1979, p. 10), "archaeologists believe that cave men not only beat their wives, they wagered them as well." Evidence of mankind's strong and continuing interest in gambling is found in the following historical examples:

In biblical times, the selection of Saul to govern the Hebrew kingdom was determined by lot.

An ivory gaming board was found in the tomb of Egyptian pharaoh
Tutankhamen.

Palamedes, according to Greek mythology, invented dice and taught soldiers
how to play with them during the siege of Troy. Ancient Greek worshippers
played dice games and bet on horse races.

The Romans invented the lottery, and they wagered on the outcomes of
chariot races. The emperor Nero was said to be addicted to such racing.

The earliest playing cards were of Chinese origin and were derived from
Korean playing sticks. Cards similar to those of today were used by the
French in the fourteenth century and are descended from tarot decks used
for fortune telling. France's Louis XV had a deck made of silver, and
England's Henry VIII was a notorious gambler.

The sailing of the *Mayflower* to plant a colony in the New World was financed
by a lottery. So were some great educational institutions, including Harvard, Yale, and Dartmouth. So was the colonial army that helped create
the United States.

## Gaming in America

*Preliminaries* Wagering already had a long and colorful history thousands
of years before the United States came into being. But, as Findlay (1986)
describes, in the process of its development, the United States added a few
exciting chapters of its own – the often ambivalent American public attitudes
toward legalization of such activities notwithstanding.

Even in colonial times, there appears to have been some pretty fast action:
Consider that four years after the *Mayflower* landed, the Virginia Assembly
passed a law against gambling, and legislation passed in Boston in 1630
also decreed that "all persons whatsoever that have cards, dice, or tables in
their houses shall make away with them before the next court under pain of
punishment."[1]

Then there was the country's first lavish casino, referred to as a "rug joint,"
which opened in New Orleans for round-the-clock operation in 1827. By
1832, a similar place (no doubt frequented by many of the fledgling nation's
politicians) had been opened in Washington, DC, on Pennsylvania Avenue.

The year 1850 saw San Francisco, with its gold-rush mentality and 1,000
assorted establishments, become the gambling capital of the West. The cowboy's Midwestern equivalent was meanwhile to be found in Dodge City,
Kansas. But all kinds of wagering and card playing were also prevalent on
Mississippi riverboats, in the terminal port city of New Orleans, and in New
York and Chicago. New York, for instance, had an estimated 6,000 gambling
locations in the 1850s, and by the 1920s, Miami had become an important
hub luring serious bettors.

Although gambling is certainly not unique to the American character,
this country has contributed to the development of games such as poker
and craps and toward rationalizing the marketing and operating procedures

Table 11.1. *Gross handle, revenues, and margins in the United States,*
*1985–2005*

| Year | Total legal gross wager (handle), $ billions | Gross revenues (win), $ billions | Gross margin (retention rate or win rate), % |
|---|---|---|---|
| 2005 | 1,058.30 | 84.64 | 8.0 |
| 2004 | 949.80 | 78.82 | 8.3 |
| 2003 | 894.30 | 73.02 | 8.2 |
| 2002 | 901.79 | 69.04 | 7.7 |
| 2001 | 861.15 | 65.06 | 7.6 |
| 2000 | 832.47 | 62.15 | 7.5 |
| 1999 | 768.95 | 58.38 | 7.6 |
| 1998 | 681.57 | 54.10 | 7.9 |
| 1997 | 638.85 | 50.97 | 8.0 |
| 1996 | 587.37 | 47.90 | 8.2 |
| 1995 | 557.48 | 44.39 | 8.0 |
| 1994 | 482.10 | 39.79 | 8.3 |
| 1993 | 394.11 | 34.70 | 8.8 |
| 1992 | 336.66 | 30.39 | 9.0 |
| 1991 | 304.30 | 26.68 | 8.8 |
| 1990 | 303.09 | 26.20 | 8.6 |
| 1989 | 251.20 | 23.52 | 9.4 |
| 1988 | 231.60 | 21.36 | 9.2 |
| 1987 | 185.85 | 18.38 | 9.9 |
| 1986 | 166.47 | 16.92 | 10.2 |
| 1985 | 159.16 | 15.34 | 9.6 |
| CAGR:[a] | | | |
| 1985–2002 | 9.9 | 8.9 | |

[a] Compound annual growth rate, 1982–2005 (%).
*Source*: Adapted from E. M. Christiansen data (Christiansen Capital Advisors, New York)
originally published in *Gaming Business* (April, May, June, and August 1984) and *Gaming*
*& Wagering Business* (July and August) 1985–2000. See Table 11.3.

used in modern casinos and lotteries. Indeed, with gross industry revenues
exceeding $80 billion (Table 11.1) as of 2005, gaming and wagering activities
have become a regular part of life for all income classes and ethnic groups.

*The Nevada experience* Nevada's history as a center for betting goes back to
the mid-1800s. There, as in San Francisco, a boom in precious metals mining attracted many rough-and-ready customers for gambling and affiliated
services, including liquor sales and prostitution. Nevertheless, the territory's
attitude toward legalization of gaming fluctuated – depending on the perceived degree of corruption and cheating – for over half a century before
the state of Nevada finally legalized, in 1931, what could not in practice be
stopped.

Curiously, before World War II, gaming activity in Reno was far more developed than in Las Vegas. "Founded" in 1905 by the sale of some Union Pacific railway junction property to private interests, and incorporated in 1911, Las Vegas did not actually begin to come into its own until the 1930s. The catalyst for change was construction of Hoover (alias Boulder) Dam, a major Bureau of Reclamation project located in Boulder City, about 30 miles away. Completion of the dam brought water and electric power to the region and stimulated commercial growth. Also, many itinerant construction workers, who had bought their supplies and had spent their free time gambling in Las Vegas, eventually settled there permanently.

Las Vegas, however, only began to emerge as a world-famous entertainment capital just after the Second World War. The city's proximity to the burgeoning population of Los Angeles and the increasing availability of low-cost air travel contributed significantly to its success. In addition, there was Benjamin "Bugsy" Siegel. As Skolnick (1978, p. 111) indicates,

it had been Siegel's ambition to build a luxurious complex that would offer gambling, recreation, entertainment, and other services catering to the area's increasing tourist trade . . . Siegel had persuaded the crime syndicate that he could transform Las Vegas into a legal gambling oasis for organized crime, and he received their backing in 1943. With their support, he started to work on his initial venture – really the first of the major Strip hotels – the Flamingo.[2]

Nevada's decision (in 1946–1947) to establish and to fund – through taxes on gross casino winnings – regulation and enforcement agencies that would ensure fair and honest conduct of the games and of casino operations was of further importance.[3] The irony, of course, was that, at the start of legalized modern gaming in Nevada, often the only operators with enough expertise to run the games fairly were people previously affiliated with illegal organizations.

As might be expected, the "connections" of some of those operators created law-enforcement problems that surfaced most noticeably in the 1950s as attempts at state licensing and gaming-control functions came into conflict with formidable mob interests in what was already a lucrative and rapidly growing business. Indeed, it was not until the mid-to-late 1960s that organized crime's grip on the industry's finances began to be loosened as a result of pressure from the Justice Department and other federal government investigative agencies and as a result of large-scale investments by billionaire Howard Hughes.

This process was further accelerated by passage in 1969 of the Corporate Gaming Act, which allowed companies with publicly traded shares to own and operate casinos in the state of Nevada. Ownership by large corporations provided an important means of financing casino-hotel expansions, of attracting middle-class and convention-related customers, and of developing an untainted corps of professional managers. The foundation was thus already long in place for Las Vegas, in particular, to evolve into the world-class destination resort that it became once the first of the large-scale (3,000-room) properties, such as the Mirage Hotel, were opened beginning in the late 1980s.

*Enter New Jersey* New Jersey's involvement in casino gaming began much differently than Nevada's. New Jersey's Atlantic City had been a popular ocean resort in the early 1900s. Gradually, however, because of neglect and because of the increasing availability of low-cost air travel, it decayed into an economically depressed slum-by-the-sea. It was always clear, though, that with its proximity to dense population centers in Philadelphia and New York, the town would make an especially attractive location for casinos. And so – with the promise of stimulating urban renewal and providing extra funding for senior citizens' programs – began the efforts of developers to legalize gambling. Voters rejected the first referendum for statewide gambling in 1974, but in 1976 they approved a second one limiting casinos to Atlantic City.

Public reaction to New Jersey's legalization was awesome. Immediately on opening the first Atlantic City casino in 1978, Resorts International was overwhelmed by enormous crowds betting huge stakes. And over the years immediately following, the early momentum continued. Despite having only one-tenth as many first-class hotel rooms (5,000 as of 1984) as its Nevada counterpart, Atlantic City had begun to compete effectively with Las Vegas as a major center for entertainment and gaming (Figure 11.1 and Table 11.2). By 1984, for example, table-game and slot revenues in New Jersey had come to within 3% of the Las Vegas total of around $2 billion, and annual visitor arrivals in Atlantic City had reached 28.5 million as compared with 12.8 million in Las Vegas.[4]

Still, there remain considerable differences in the way the casino gaming business operates in Nevada as compared with Atlantic City. In Nevada,

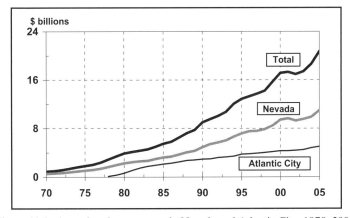

Figure 11.1. Annual casino revenues in Nevada and Atlantic City, 1970–2005.

Table 11.2. *Gaming win in Atlantic City and Nevada, 1975–2005*

| Year | Atlantic City and Nevada casino revenues ($ billions) | Nevada total June fiscal year taxable gaming revenues ($ billions) | Las Vegas (Clark County) | | Atlantic City | |
|---|---|---|---|---|---|---|
| | | | Gross winnings ($ billions) | Visitors (millions) | Gross winnings ($ billions) | Visitors (millions) |
| 1975 | 1.066 | 1.066 | 0.770 | 9.2 | | |
| 1976 | 1.188 | 1.188 | 0.846 | 9.8 | | |
| 1977 | 1.380 | 1.380 | 1.015 | 10.1 | | |
| 1978 | 1.805 | 1.671 | 1.236 | 11.2 | 0.134 | 7.0 |
| 1979 | 2.306 | 1.980 | 1.424 | 11.7 | 0.325 | 9.5 |
| 1980 | 2.917 | 2.274 | 1.617 | 11.9 | 0.643 | 13.8 |
| 1981 | 3.563 | 2.463 | 1.676 | 11.8 | 1.100 | 19.1 |
| 1982 | 4.093 | 2.600 | 1.751 | 11.6 | 1.493 | 23.0 |
| 1983 | 4.454 | 2.683 | 1.887 | 12.3 | 1.771 | 26.4 |
| 1984 | 4.943 | 2.991 | 2.008 | 12.8 | 1.952 | 28.5 |
| 1985 | 5.367 | 3.228 | 2.233 | 14.2 | 2.139 | 29.3 |
| 1986 | 5.647 | 3.366 | 2.393 | 15.2 | 2.281 | 29.9 |
| 1987 | 6.205 | 3.710 | 2.738 | 16.2 | 2.496 | 31.8 |
| 1988 | 6.809 | 4.074 | 3.003 | 17.2 | 2.735 | 33.1 |
| 1989 | 7.119 | 4.312 | 3.290 | 18.1 | 2.807 | 32.0 |
| 1990 | 7.864 | 4.912 | 3.870 | 21.0 | 2.952 | 31.8 |
| 1991 | 8.403 | 5.411 | 4.152 | 21.3 | 2.992 | 30.8 |
| 1992 | 8.913 | 5.697 | 4.378 | 21.9 | 3.216 | 30.7 |
| 1993 | 9.319 | 6.018 | 4.727 | 23.5 | 3.301 | 30.2 |
| 1994 | 10.069 | 6.647 | 5.431 | 28.2 | 3.423 | 31.3 |
| 1995 | 10.901 | 7.153 | 5.718 | 29.0 | 3.748 | 33.3 |
| 1996 | 11.340 | 7.522 | 5.784 | 29.6 | 3.814 | 34.0 |
| 1997 | 11.479 | 7.573 | 6.152 | 30.5 | 3.906 | 34.1 |
| 1998 | 11.907 | 7.874 | 6.347 | 30.6 | 4.033 | 34.3 |
| 1999 | 12.663 | 8.498 | 7.211 | 33.8 | 4.164 | 33.7 |
| 2000 | 13.756 | 9.456 | 7.671 | 35.8 | 4.301 | 33.2 |
| 2001 | 13.968 | 9.665 | 7.637 | 35.0 | 4.303 | 33.4 |
| 2002 | 13.682 | 9.300 | 7.631 | 35.1 | 4.382 | 33.2 |
| 2003 | 14.052 | 9.564 | 7.831 | 35.5 | 4.488 | 32.2 |
| 2004 | 14.730 | 9.923 | 8.711 | 37.4 | 4.807 | 33.3 |
| 2005 | 16.024 | 11.006 | 9.717 | 38.6 | 5.018 | 34.9 |
| CAGR:[a] | | | | | | |
| 1970–2005 | 10.1 | 8.9 | 9.8 | 5.1 | — | — |
| 1980–2005 | 7.1 | 6.5 | 7.4 | 4.8 | 8.6 | 3.8 |
| 1990–2005 | 4.9 | 5.5 | 5.9 | 4.2 | 3.8 | 0.6 |

[a] Compound annual growth rate (%).

*Sources*: Las Vegas Convention/Visitors Authority and Atlantic City Casino Association.

hundreds of locations scattered throughout the state are licensed to provide a wide variety of casino gaming services (from simple banks of slot machines to race and sports books), and the 60 largest casinos, according to 2005 *Nevada Gaming Abstract* data, account for over 80% of total gross revenues. In contrast, as of the early 2000s, there were only 13 large casino-hotels in operation in Atlantic City, all of them located within five miles of each other. Because of earlier New Jersey regulations and the constraints imposed by regulation and real estate, however, the older casinos are much less varied in the size and in the scope of their offerings than are their Nevada counterparts.[5] Atlantic City operators also depend on gambling for around 90% of revenues as compared with Nevada, where the percentage derived from noncasino sources such as rooms, food, and entertainment is (as of 2005) around 50% and rising.[6]

Thus, while Las Vegas truly became a global entertainment capital – a citywide theme park in itself – Atlantic City casinos remain largely a collection of slot-machine malls attracting primarily day-trip visitors. To at least in part remedy this situation, Las Vegas–style properties (e.g., the Borgata) have begun to be built in Atlantic City.

Moreover, the employment and tax revenue generating potential of such casinos has, despite many often-heard objections based on social welfare and other considerations, inevitably inspired other run-down urban and aging seashore sites to attempt replication. The most notable of these in the United States is in Detroit, where a limited number of casinos began to operate in the late 1990s. New government recommendations and regulations will allow similar large casinos to sprout in sea resorts such as Blackpool, the English equivalent of Atlantic City, Macau, on the south coast of China, and also in Singapore.[7]

*Horse racing* Horse racing has also had a particularly interesting history, with direct antecedents of the American experience traceable to England, where a public racecourse was opened in Smithfield, London, in 1174. By the eighteenth century, racing had developed into an important English sport (governed by the Jockey Club, formed in 1750), and records of breeding and race results had begun to be published (in the *Racing Calendar*).

The first American racetrack with regularly scheduled meetings was founded in Hempstead (Long Island), New York, in 1665, and tracks soon appeared in several other colonies. It was not until 1821, however, that the first Thoroughbred racecourse was built. And it was only after the Civil War that the sport began to achieve wide popularity because of the development of pari-mutuel ("between ourselves") betting. Prior to that time, betting had been handled by bookmakers who had posted arbitrary odds: With a pari-mutuel system, bets could be pooled and the odds determined by the opinions of bettors as measured by the amounts wagered on each horse.

Although the racing segment, as Table 11.3 indicates, generates annual gross revenues of approximately $3 billion and has been boosted by interstate broadcasting of races (i.e., "simulcasting"), this total is now considerably

Table 11.3. *Gross handle and revenues in the United States (in $ billions), 1985–2005[a]*

| | | | | Total legal gambling | | | | | | | | | | | | | |
|---|---|---|---|---|---|---|---|---|---|---|---|---|---|---|---|---|---|
| | | Casinos, slots Nev/NJ | Table games | State lotteries (regular) | State lotteries (video) | Total horses | Dog racing | Jai alai | Legal book-making total | Card rooms (except Nevada) | Bingo | Charitable gambling[c] (except bingo) | Indian reservation | Non-casino gaming devices | Cruise ships | River-boats | Com-mercial, other |
| Year | Total | | | | | | | | | | | | | | | | |
| **Gross wager (handle)** | | | | | | | | | | | | | | | | | |
| 2005[b] | 1,058.30 | | | | | | | | | | | | | | | | |
| 2004 | 949.80 | | | | | | | | | | | | | | | | |
| 2003 | 894.30 | | | | | | | | | | | | | | | | |
| 2002 | 901.79 | 155.79 | 194.18 | 39.38 | 29.05 | 16.48 | 1.92 | 0.16 | 1.98 | 13.87 | 4.10 | 5.63 | 195.62 | 15.65 | 9.57 | 181.65 | 36.76 |
| 2001 | 859.15 | 154.14 | 201.36 | 36.36 | 25.07 | 15.99 | 1.94 | 0.18 | 2.10 | 14.03 | 4.02 | 5.61 | 166.59 | 14.76 | 9.14 | 176.18 | 33.71 |
| 2000 | 832.47 | 156.44 | 211.99 | 35.40 | 21.42 | 16.04 | 1.99 | 0.19 | 2.39 | 13.62 | 4.27 | 5.63 | 143.13 | 15.77 | 8.73 | 167.95 | 27.50 |
| 1999 | 768.95 | 147.16 | 202.80 | 34.13 | 17.41 | 15.85 | 2.13 | 0.20 | 2.55 | 13.19 | 4.29 | 5.49 | 124.76 | 18.12 | 8.34 | 157.38 | 15.15 |
| 1998 | 681.57 | 137.52 | 181.76 | 35.06 | 13.93 | 16.04 | 2.19 | 0.15 | 2.41 | 11.01 | 3.97 | 6.65 | 102.28 | 17.09 | 7.58 | 135.51 | 8.45 |
| 1997 | 638.85 | 133.90 | 189.25 | 34.24 | 11.86 | 15.34 | 2.25 | 0.21 | 2.57 | 10.42 | 3.91 | 6.03 | 81.93 | 16.19 | 6.53 | 115.82 | 8.38 |
| 1996 | 587.37 | 126.84 | 178.72 | 33.84 | 9.10 | 14.88 | 2.43 | 0.27 | 2.61 | 9.93 | 3.96 | 5.67 | 66.00 | 14.44 | 6.11 | 104.42 | 8.15 |
| 1995 | 557.48 | 121.30 | 185.58 | 32.52 | 6.36 | 14.77 | 2.73 | 0.30 | 2.60 | 9.44 | 4.13 | 5.65 | 57.67 | 12.86 | 5.757 | 88.08 | 7.74 |
| 1994 | 482.10 | 113.03 | 170.83 | 30.02 | 4.45 | 14.16 | 2.94 | 0.32 | 2.66 | 9.31 | 4.25 | 5.05 | 41.06 | 8.91 | 5.10 | 63.80 | 6.19 |
| 1993 | 394.11 | 102.56 | 150.91 | 26.94 | 3.88 | 13.72 | 3.24 | 0.38 | 2.26 | 8.35 | 4.23 | 4.89 | 28.96 | 7.41 | 4.49 | 27.12 | 4.78 |
| 1992 | 336.66 | 94.56 | 143.62 | 25.55 | | 14.08 | 3.31 | 0.43 | 2.11 | 8.43 | 4.18 | 4.70 | 16.73 | 3.84 | 4.28 | 7.42 | 3.44 |
| 1991 | 304.30 | 84.40 | 149.74 | 20.99 | | 13.93 | 3.50 | 0.49 | 2.26 | 8.40 | 4.23 | 4.61 | 5.44 | 0.36 | 4.08 | 1.10 | 0.77 |
| 1990 | 303.09 | 76.17 | 161.64 | 21.02 | | 14.14 | 3.47 | 0.56 | 2.16 | 8.38 | 4.07 | 4.47 | 2.64 | 0.31 | 3.71 | | 0.38 |
| 1989 | 251.20 | 65.79 | 127.77 | 19.49 | | 13.93 | 3.21 | 0.55 | 1.84 | 7.56 | 3.79 | 4.22 | 1.00 | 0.25 | 1.76 | | 0.02 |
| 1988 | 231.60 | 57.67 | 126.30 | 17.05 | | 13.67 | 3.26 | 0.64 | 1.73 | 3.45 | 3.67 | 3.58 | 0.35 | 0.23 | | | |
| 1987 | 185.83 | 32.79 | 112.04 | 13.14 | | 13.14 | 3.20 | 0.71 | 1.38 | 3.13 | 3.98 | 2.00 | 0.31 | | | | |
| 1986 | 166.47 | 28.50 | 101.44 | 12.48 | | 12.38 | 3.02 | 0.67 | 1.19 | 1.12 | 3.60 | 1.79 | 0.29 | | | | |
| 1985 | 159.16 | 26.18 | 99.56 | 10.21 | | 12.24 | 2.70 | 0.66 | 1.13 | 1.10 | 3.44 | 1.68 | 0.25 | | | | |
| CAGR[d] (%): 1985–2005 | 9.9 | | | | | | | | | | | | | | | | |

**Gross revenues (win)**

| Year | | | | | | | | | | | | | | | | | |
|---|---|---|---|---|---|---|---|---|---|---|---|---|---|---|---|---|---|
| 2005 | 84.64 | | | | | | | | | | | | | | | | |
| 2004 | 78.82 | | | | | | | | | | | | | | | | |
| 2003 | 73.02 | | | | | | | | | | | | | | | | |
| 2002 | 69.04 | 9.54 | 4.10 | 16.50 | 2.30 | 3.52 | 0.43 | 0.04 | 0.12 | 0.88 | 1.12 | 1.51 | 14.48 | 1.32 | 0.68 | 10.44 | 2.07 |
| 2001 | 65.06 | 9.34 | 4.22 | 15.51 | 1.97 | 3.42 | 0.43 | 0.04 | 0.13 | 0.97 | 1.12 | 1.47 | 12.74 | 1.23 | 0.65 | 9.97 | 1.86 |
| 2000 | 62.15 | 9.29 | 4.41 | 15.56 | 1.71 | 3.44 | 0.45 | 0.04 | 0.13 | 0.95 | 1.03 | 1.43 | 10.94 | 1.56 | 0.62 | 9.01 | 1.57 |
| 1999 | 58.38 | 8.74 | 4.24 | 15.10 | 1.42 | 3.38 | 0.49 | 0.04 | 0.12 | 0.91 | 1.04 | 1.38 | 9.61 | 2.00 | 0.59 | 8.34 | 0.97 |
| 1998 | 54.10 | 8.09 | 3.83 | 15.37 | 1.26 | 3.36 | 0.48 | 0.03 | 0.07 | 0.74 | 0.97 | 1.64 | 7.89 | 1.83 | 0.54 | 7.29 | 0.69 |
| 1997 | 50.97 | 7.61 | 3.91 | 15.39 | 1.10 | 3.25 | 0.51 | 0.05 | 0.10 | 0.70 | 0.96 | 1.56 | 6.83 | 1.74 | 0.46 | 6.17 | 0.63 |
| 1996 | 47.90 | 7.29 | 3.78 | 15.31 | 0.89 | 3.18 | 3.18 | 0.06 | 0.09 | 0.68 | 0.96 | 1.47 | 5.61 | 1.48 | 0.43 | 5.54 | 0.62 |
| 1995 | 44.39 | 7.09 | 3.86 | 14.62 | 0.62 | 3.07 | 0.61 | 0.06 | 0.10 | 0.76 | 0.98 | 1.51 | 4.04 | 1.41 | 0.41 | 4.65 | 0.60 |
| 1994 | 39.79 | 6.61 | 3.57 | 13.67 | 0.46 | 2.90 | 0.63 | 0.07 | 0.16 | 0.73 | 0.99 | 1.39 | 3.42 | 1.08 | 0.36 | 3.26 | 0.49 |
| 1993 | 34.70 | 6.16 | 3.23 | 12.82 | | 2.86 | 0.70 | 0.08 | 0.12 | 0.66 | 1.04 | 1.29 | 2.59 | 0.92 | 0.32 | 1.46 | 0.45 |
| 1992 | 30.39 | 5.83 | 3.12 | 11.43 | | 2.93 | 0.69 | 0.08 | 0.10 | 0.66 | 1.03 | 1.24 | 1.63 | 0.57 | 0.31 | 0.42 | 0.35 |
| 1991 | 26.68 | 5.24 | 3.20 | 10.23 | | 2.84 | 0.70 | 0.10 | 0.11 | 0.66 | 1.05 | 1.23 | 0.72 | 0.16 | 0.29 | 0.08 | 0.06 |
| 1990 | 26.20 | 4.89 | 3.41 | 10.29 | | 2.90 | 0.69 | 0.11 | 0.13 | 0.66 | 1.02 | 1.19 | 0.49 | 0.13 | 0.26 | | 0.03 |
| 1989 | 23.52 | 4.35 | 3.10 | 9.63 | | 2.82 | 0.63 | 0.11 | 0.11 | 0.30 | 0.91 | 1.12 | 0.12 | 0.12 | 0.20 | | 0.00 |
| 1988 | 21.36 | 4.01 | 3.05 | 8.42 | | 2.76 | 0.63 | 0.12 | 0.10 | 0.28 | 1.06 | 0.71 | 0.12 | 0.10 | | | |
| 1987 | 18.38 | 3.59 | 2.81 | 6.58 | | 2.66 | 0.62 | 0.14 | 0.09 | 0.25 | 0.92 | 0.62 | 0.11 | | | | |
| 1986 | 16.92 | 3.15 | 2.59 | 6.33 | | 2.43 | 0.59 | 0.13 | 0.08 | 0.06 | 0.92 | 0.54 | 0.10 | | | | |
| 1985 | 15.34 | 2.91 | 2.54 | 5.21 | | 2.39 | 0.53 | 0.13 | 0.06 | 0.05 | 0.91 | 0.53 | 0.09 | | | | |
| CAGR[d] (%): | | | | | | | | | | | | | | | | | |
| 1985–2005 | 8.9 | 7.1 | 3.7 | 6.8 | NM | 1.7 | −2.2 | −18.5 | 3.9 | 16.3 | −0.5 | 5.4 | NM[e] | NM | NM | NM | NM |

[a] Some figures may not be precise because of rounding.

[b] Gross wager data by segment after 2002 not available.

[c] The previous 1985 estimate of $582 million in gross revenues for charitable games has been subsequently reduced to $525 million.

[d] Compound annual growth rate.

[e] Not meaningful.

*Source:* Adapted from E. M. Christiansen data originally published in *Gaming Business* (April, May, June, and August 1984), and *Gaming & Wagering Business* (July and August) 1985–2000. See Table 11.1.

below revenues derived from casino table games. Nevertheless, even with minimal growth of interest in recent years, horse racing (including Thoroughbred, quarter horse, and harness varieties) has remained legal in more than 40 states.[8]

*Lotteries*  In contrast to racing, growth of interest in lotteries has been explosive. Lotteries, which began in Rome more than 2,000 years ago, have been common throughout the history of the United States. According to Scarne (1974, pp. 150–152), there were half a dozen of them operating in each of the 13 colonies before the American Revolution, and by 1831 there was an average of one major drawing per week in New York City alone. However, with many of the lotteries of that time privately owned and subject to little or no control, abuses and irregularities began to appear, and public opinion gradually turned against them. An act of Congress in 1890 finally forbade the sending of lottery tickets through the mails, and by 1894, the Louisiana Legislature had phased out the last of the legal lotteries of the nineteenth century.

  Some 70 years would elapse before the state of New Hampshire (in 1964) revived the lottery as a fund-raising mechanism. The popularity of this approach to balancing state budgets was such that by 1995 lotteries had been legalized in 37 jurisdictions (and also in all Canadian provinces) and gross ticket sales had exceeded $25 billion, or almost $100 per capita (Figure 11.2).[9] By 1994, similar financing considerations led even England to reinstate its national lottery, which had been banned by Parliament since 1826.

*Indian reservations, riverboats, and other wagering areas*  The most significant developments of the early 1990s, however, came from the expansion of casino gaming activities onto Indian reservations and riverboats. The

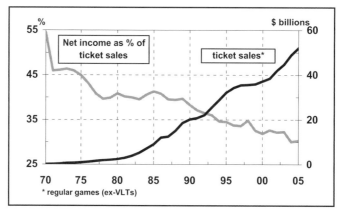

Figure 11.2. Lottery ticket sales and net government revenues as a percent of sales in the United States, 1970–2005. *Source data*: *Gaming and Wagering Business* and *La Fleur World Lottery Almanacs*.

Table 11.4. *Estimated U.S. casino gaming square footage by category, 2006*

|  | Square feet (in thousands) |
|---|---|
| Atlantic City | 1,300 |
| Nevada |  |
|    Las Vegas strip | 3,000 |
|    Laughlin | 525 |
|    Reno/Sparks | 925 |
|    Other | 3,750 |
|      Total Nevada | 8,200 |
| Riverboats | 1,600 |
| Indian tribal lands | 2,000 |
| Total | 11,800 |

*Sources*: *Nevada Gaming Abstract*, 2006, New Jersey Casino Control Commission Annual Report, and industry estimates.

federal government's Indian Gaming Regulatory Act (IGRA) of 1988 opened the floodgates by allowing Indian tribes to operate on their reservations, and without restrictions, all forms of gambling previously approved by a state.[10]

Many such state–tribal compacts have, in fact, often been negotiated under conditions of great controversy because the states (themselves hard pressed to find sources of tax revenues) have looked more seriously at gaming as a potential new source of income. In 1989, South Dakota used low-stakes casino gaming to revitalize tourism.[11] In 1991, Colorado did the same in the tourist towns of Black Hawk, Central City, and Cripple Creek. Iowa and Illinois also launched their first riverboat casinos in 1991. And by the mid-1990s, several state legislatures, including those of Mississippi (1992), Louisiana (1993), Missouri (1994), and Indiana (1996), had already moved toward legalization of riverboat or other casino-type operations. Although most such riverboats are fairly small by comparison with Las Vegas casino standards, they are collectively large enough to affect the growth of gaming in Nevada and Atlantic City (Table 11.4). Indeed, as of the early 2000s, more than 750 commercial and Indian casinos operated in 33 states.

Travel is generally a part of the gaming casino experience, although with so many competing nearby alternatives, the distance traveled does not necessarily have to be far from home. For instance, video lottery terminals (VLTs) – in effect, slot machines tied into a lottery – were widely legalized in the early 1990s. VLTs compete for revenues against established amusement video machines and online ticket lottery systems by essentially turning local restaurants and taverns (and also racetracks) into minicasinos.

Bingo, too, has developed into an important legalized casino activity that generates gross wagering of about $1 billion in the 46 states where it is played.[12] Indeed, bingo attracts some 40 million participants and is the most widespread of all legalized wagering games. And public poker clubs, which have long been legal in certain populous California counties, are still expanding rapidly even as the game is becoming a new source of revenues for charities.

Gaming on the Internet, however, has already become a major source of activity, even though its legal status in the United States remains ambiguous. If and when federal and state laws are changed, the major casino operators will become more deeply involved. In this regard, the U.S. Interstate Wire Act (Statute 18 U.S.C. §1084), which prohibits the taking of bets over a network that crosses state or international borders, is a prominent and controversial feature of the current landscape. Already, more than $12 billion (in 2007) of Internet-based, primarily sports-related revenue after paying out winnings is being collected by offshore Web sites every year.[13]

The significance of Web-based gaming, however, also extends to changes in the way bets are placed and odds are determined. Instead of bettors wagering against the house, they may now, especially in sports, bet directly against each other using peer-to-peer betting services. Such services, which operate similarly to file-sharing programs in music, allow individuals to easily and efficiently set the terms of their own wagers, thereby diminishing the role of casinos.[14]

From all this it would thus appear that the gaming and wagering pie, while continuing to grow at above-average rates in comparison with the overall economy, will continue to be divided into more specialized slices. Similar patterns are also appearing outside the United States, especially in Canada, Western Europe, and Australia.[15] Major events in the industry's U.S. history are depicted in Figure 11.3.

## 11.2 Money talks

The $84.6 billion sum of gaming and wagering activity in the United States listed in Table 11.1 represents the total revenue (before expenses) that legal gaming operators have retained, or, in other words, won. Conversely, it also represents the *net* amount that players have *lost*. Of this total, lotteries (at around $23 billion) and casinos ($38 billion) have been the most important if not fastest-growing major components (Figure 11.4).[16] By comparison, domestic movie ticket sales in 2005 were only around $9 billion and recorded music sales about $11 billion.[17] Globally, the amount spent on gaming and wagering is estimated to be a multiple of at least four to five times that risked in the United States.

Macroeconomic matters

The rate of growth of legalized gambling has been well above that of the aggregate economy for the entire post–World War II period. There is, moreover,

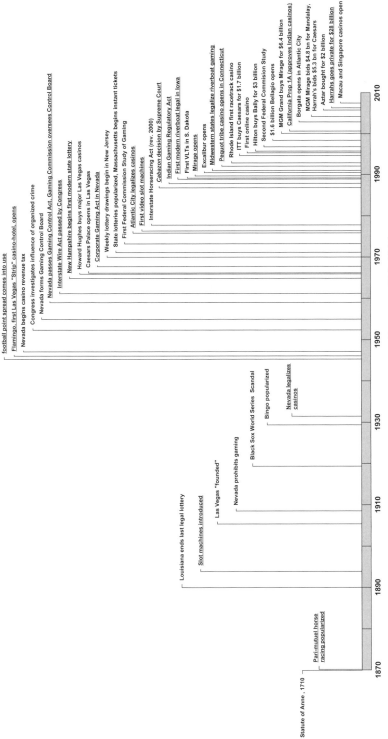

Figure 11.3. Gaming industry milestones, 1710–2006.

Statute of Anne, 1710

Pari-mutuel horse racing popularized

Louisiana ends last legal lottery

Slot machines introduced

Las Vegas "founded"

Nevada prohibits gaming

Black Sox World Series Scandal

Bingo popularized

Nevada legalizes casinos

football point spread comes into use

Flamingo, first Las Vegas "Strip" casino-hotel, opens

Congress investigates influence of organized crime

Nevada begins casino revenue tax

Nevada forms Gaming Control Board

Nevada passes Gaming Control Act, Gaming Commission oversees Control Board

Interstate Wire Act passed by Congress

New Hampshire begins first modern state lottery

Howard Hughes begins buys major Las Vegas casinos

Caesars Palace opens in Las Vegas

Corporate Gaming Act in Nevada

Weekly lottery drawings begin in New Jersey

State lotteries popularized, Massachusetts begins instant tickets

First Federal Commission Study of Gaming

Atlantic City legalizes casinos

First video slot machines

Interstate Horseracing Act (rev. 2000)

Cabazon decision by Supreme Court

Indian Gaming Regulatory Act

First modern riverboat legal in Iowa

First VLTs in S. Dakota

Mirage opens

Excalibur opens

Midwestern states legalize riverboat gaming

Pequot tribe casino opens in Connecticut

Rhode Island first racetrack casino

ITT buys Caesars for $1.7 billion

First online casino

Hilton buys Bally for $3 billion

Second Federal Commission Study

$1.6 billion Bellagio opens

MGM Grand buys Mirage for $6.4 billion

California Prop 1A (approves Indian casinos)

Borgata opens in Atlantic City

MGM Mirage bids $4.8 bn for Mandalay, Harrah's bids $5.3 bn for Caesars

Aztar bought for $2 billion

Harrahs goes private for $28 billion

Macau and Singapore casinos open

1870    1890    1910    1930    1950    1970    1990    2010

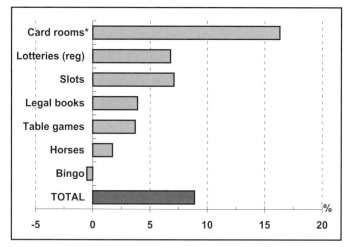

Figure 11.4. Compound annual growth rate comparisons of U.S. gaming revenues by category, 1985–2005.
*Ex-Nevada.
*Source data*: *Gaming and Wagering Business.*

reason to believe that the growth rate for *illegal* gambling, which probably amounts to at least an additional 15% of the legal total (there is no way to easily measure it) has also probably kept pace. In part, gaming's compound annual growth rate, averaging above 10% during much of the last third of the century, has been a function of simply making the services more widely available and convenient for players to access. However, none of this could have happened if the public's perceptions of gaming and entertainment–spending preferences had not shifted. In 1960, net public spending (losses to operators of casinos, pari-mutuels, and bingo) on gaming and wagering accounted for around 0.2% of disposable income, whereas the current share has by now approximately quadrupled (Figure 1.14c).

Still, with game operators often leveraged financially and operationally, the industry's sensitivity to adverse business cycle fluctuations is potentially high. Indeed, spending patterns during the recessions of the early 1980s, 1990s, and in 2001 suggest that gaming revenues may be somewhat sensitive to both regional and national economic conditions.[18] In an economic downturn, for example, convention-trade travel to Atlantic City and Nevada would normally be curtailed as businesses attempt to pare expenses; as a result, average spending per visitor might be reduced (Figure 11.5).

Many other factors may also decisively affect revenue growth trends in a region. Among the most important are the following:

Airfares and the cost and availability of gasoline
Recent number of room and square footage additions as a percentage of total
   industry capacity

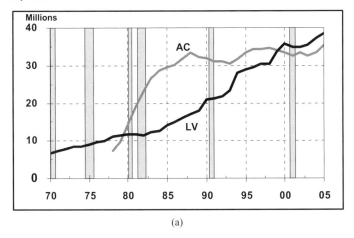

(a)

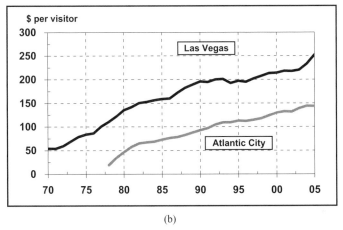

(b)

Figure 11.5. Las Vegas versus Atlantic City, 1970–2005: (a) number of visitors and (b) spending per visitor.

Dollar-exchange rates against major Asian and European currencies
Percentage of players coming from outside the region
Projected rates of inflation and employment

Funding functions

In the early 2000s, municipalities and states collected more than $22 billion from taxes and license fees imposed on gaming and wagering, which in the United States is regulated by a hodgepodge of state and local laws that reflect the ambivalence of the population toward the conduct of these activities. Most jurisdictions have few if any qualms about permitting church or social bingo – a game that, as Cook (1979) notes, has a high cost to the player. Nor do people seem to object to lotteries – a game with even higher costs to the player than bingo. Yet people often rise up in moral indignation against casinos and racetracks, where the operators' percentage is much lower. As Rose (1986) discusses, other anomalies often appear: In communities such as those near Los Angeles, only card games of a precisely defined type are allowed to be played. And in Nevada, the acknowledged sports- and race-book and gaming capital of the world, a state lottery is *illegal*.

The logic concerning when and where gaming establishments may adver-tise has also been peculiar. The FCC, for example, follows a set of antilottery laws passed before 1900. However, state-sponsored lotteries, charity events, and Indian-run casinos are exempted from the rules. Until the late 1990s, pri-vately owned casinos thus could advertise only on cable: On broadcast televi-sion they had only been allowed to mention their noncasino attractions, such as golf courses and restaurants, even while competing casinos operated by Indian tribes had been exempted from such restrictions as far back as 1988.[19]

It is not surprising, then, that all this ambivalence and confusion spills over into the politics of regulation and legalization. Legalization in a state or city is always easier to achieve if, by reason of history and culture, the dominant population groups favor such activities. But what usually precipitates a move toward legal sanction is a need for more social-welfare funding than can be comfortably raised via direct taxation.

Unfortunately, the public may thus sometimes be fooled into thinking that legalization is a costless way to raise net additional revenues. But several studies – including those of Goodman (1994, 1995), Abt *et al.* (1985), Skol-nick (1978, 1979), and Mahon (1980) – indicate that legalization of gaming is not a taxpayers' panacea. As Grinols (2004) has shown, the total costs often outweigh the benefits. Gaming may, for instance, divert revenues needed to support other local retail business establishments. The net revenues raised from its legalization are often relatively small compared with budget gaps – especially if the additional costs of law enforcement and regulation and treat-ments for new player addictions are also taken into account. Moreover, as Sternlieb and Hughes (1983) and Goodman (1995, p. xi) have suggested, such legalizations tend to spawn huge, politically powerful bureaucracies that may ultimately operate against the public interest and that shift the role of government from being a watchdog of gambling to becoming its leading promoter. Indeed, some states have, in effect, already become as addicted as are problem gamblers.[20]

### Regulation

Government regulation is more visible in gaming than in any other entertainment-industry segment. It has developed from historical experience with a cash business that has often nourished the coffers of organized crime, deprived government of tax revenues, and plainly cheated ordinary players.

Regulative power usually rests in the state legislatures, which formally legalize gaming activities such as lotteries, tracks, and casinos. Legislators also establish agencies to oversee that all such activities are conducted honestly and competently and with full accounting of tax revenues to the state. To achieve those ends, regulatory enforcement, investigative, and licensing agencies work in conjunction with local-community interests to promulgate specific standards and rules of conduct.

In racing, for example, there is the New York State Racing and Wagering Board, which institutes measures to safeguard the integrity of racing and compiles statistical and other information concerning New York Racing Association tracks and off-track betting (OTB) parlors. More widely known, however, are the Nevada and New Jersey gaming commissions, which oversee licensing and regulation of casino gaming and slot-machine operations in those states. New Jersey's regulatory bodies are to a great extent patterned on those earlier developed in Nevada, where there is a two-tier structure: The Gaming Control Board works at the staff level on investigation and audit, and the Gaming Commission acts as a quasi-judicial body that deliberates on licensing, revocations, and other related matters.

Agents and investigators representing the Federal Bureau of Investigation (FBI) and the Internal Revenue Service (IRS) have generally played a role ancillary to that of the state commissions. But should any of the state bodies prove ineffectual, it is likely that the federal government would immediately become more actively and visibly involved in industry affairs. The most direct influence would then probably be felt through augmentation of tax-reporting requirements.[21]

The difficulty of designing regulation that balances the needs of the business with what is perceived to best serve the public's interest can be seen in the case of New Jersey, where, in its zeal to ensure that casinos would be impervious to influence by organized crime, the legislature in that state incorporated particularly detailed instructions in bills to legalize Atlantic City gaming. All employees – initially including restaurant busboys, hotel bellhops, and parking attendants far removed from gaming-transactions areas – had to be licensed.[22]

As Atlantic City gaming matured, many of these early regulations proved to be unnecessarily stringent, if not actually detrimental to industry growth and profitability. Those standards were then somewhat relaxed as the commission and its enforcement division began to concentrate on licensing of top executives and of people who directly oversee gaming activities and grant credit (dealers, pit bosses, shift managers, and cage personnel). Licensing of slot machines and of companies supplying the industry with goods and services (linen, liquor, food, etc.) also took priority.

Without close scrutiny at the financial-accounting and operational levels, there is a natural tendency for illegal activities to arise. Frauds and tax evasions are still occasionally discovered in lotteries (e.g., irregular printing of tickets), in horse racing (e.g., substitution by "ringers," use of illegal drugs on animals, and fixing of races), and in casinos (e.g., skimming money before reporting to the state). The presence of a strong regulative mandate and

Table 11.5. *U.S. gaming company financial operating performance: composite of 22 companies, 2001–2005*

|  | Revenues | Operating income | Operating margin (%)[a] | Assets | Operating cash flow |
|---|---|---|---|---|---|
| CAGR (%)[b] | 3.4 | 7.4 | 3.9 | 10.6 | 5.0 |

[a] Average margin, 2001–2005 = 16.3%.
[b] Compound annual growth rate.

ample funding for enforcement and licensing personnel can largely mitigate these problems, providing assurance to the public that games are being fairly conducted and that governments are properly receiving all revenues due.

Regulation is initiated and designed to support the commonweal. Segments of the legalized-gaming industry – even when not directly owned or operated by a state – will thus normally have a close and lasting relationship with regulatory bodies that have been established and are controlled by elected officials. Accordingly, as Skolnick (1978) suggests, there is always the potential for gaming interests to become so politically powerful that they circumvent the spirit if not the actual letter of the law. The policy dilemma is that the stricter the regulation, the greater are the incentives for subversion and corruption of the regulators.

### Financial performance and valuation

The variety of companies that derive some or all of their income from the operation of legalized gaming and wagering activities is surprisingly broad.[23] In addition to the relatively well-known casino-hotel companies, there are manufacturers of computer components and designers of software used in lottery systems management. There are producers of sophisticated slot and poker machines. Plastics and paper companies make dice and playing cards. And breeding and real estate firms are involved in racing. However, of all these categories, the most readily definable and investable grouping is that of the casino-hotel operators.

Although casino returns on investment (ROI) have varied greatly from company to company, the casino industry has generally prospered in recent decades.[24] Moreover, as shown in Table 11.5, growth rates of revenues, assets, and operating income have mostly remained in balance, thereby enabling the industry to borrow heavily against a relatively small equity base.

Most investors or lenders would thus value a gaming enterprise by analyzing its potential in terms of earnings before taxes, interest, depreciation, and amortization (EBITDA). The multiple that would then be applied to such a projected cash flow figure would be a function of interest rates, local market growth and competitive considerations, the worth of underlying real estate for alternative uses, and general economic conditions.[25]

Similarly, enterprise value (EV) could be estimated as follows:

EV = (number of shares × price) + net debt − off–balance sheet assets,

wherein

net debt is defined as long-term debt − cash.

These concepts and methodologies – and the existence of normally deep public market discounts to estimated private market values – are similar to those used in valuations of media properties (Sections 7.4 and 8.5).

## 11.3 Underlying profit principles and terminology

There are uncountable variations on the thousands of card, dice, and numbers games that have been invented over the millennia. But of these, only a few have been standardized for use in today's legalized-gaming environment. This section presents a framework for understanding how games generate profits on the transactions level.

Principles

It is easy to arrive at an impression that a casino's profits come only out of the collective hides of the losing bettors. But, surprisingly, a governing principle behind the conduct of every profit-making betting activity is to *pay less than true odds* to the winners. Indeed, it is the payment of less than true odds to winners (out of the losers' pool) that provides the casino with its "edge" (Table 11.6), the racetrack with its "take," and the lottery with its "cut." In other words, losers' money is used to compensate winners, but not as adequately as game mathematics would require. Hence, profits are, in a sense,

Table 11.6. *Characteristics of casino games*

| Games | Edge[a] (%) | Frequency of play (min.) |
|---|---|---|
| American roulette | 2.7 | 0.75 |
| French roulette | 1.4–2.7 | 1.5–2 |
| Blackjack | At least 0.6 | 2–3 |
| Punto banco | 1.25 | 2–3 |
| Craps | 1.4–5.6 | 1.5–2 |
| Baccarat banque | 0.9–1.5 | 2–3 |

[a] In a rational world it might be expected that the edge would be inversely proportional to the frequency with which the game is played, but this is clearly not so in the actual casino world. In any case, many players are under the illusion that the more often they can play, the more likely they are to win.

*Source*: Royal Commission on Gambling (1978, p. 451). Final Report, London, July 1978, Vol. 2, p. 451.

derived from both losers and winners. Pari-mutuel betting, in which various taxes, track fees, and "breakage" charges (see Appendix B) are deducted from the pool of funds contributed by winners and losers, provides another example of this.

With a statistical advantage established, operating profitability is then affected by the number of decisions or completed betting events per unit time. A second governing principle is thus found in the steady pressure to raise or to maintain the rate of decision as high as possible so that statistical advantages are compounded as much as possible over time. If winners are shortchanged of true odds by even a small percentage often enough, then the aggregate amount kept by the game operator (the "house") can be substantial.[26]

A third governing principle in the operation of games of chance is applied when betting limits (the maximum amount permitted to be wagered on each decision) are imposed. Murphy (1976) notes that in a game with 50:50 odds (e.g., tossing pennies or betting double or nothing), the usual assumption is that over a long period of time the outcome will be even. This, however, is untrue if one player has limited capital and the other has infinite capital: The expected outcome for the player with limited capital is total loss. The imposition of a betting limit (which, in effect, artificially constrains the player's capital relative to that of the game operator) itself practically guarantees that over an extended period the operator will win all, even without benefit of a house edge.[27] In such cases, it is thus not the edge, but the limit, that defeats the gambler.

In practice, rather than dividing their stake into many smaller units and rebetting, players have the highest probability of winning if they make just one large bet; the house's edge here has minimal opportunity to grind down the player's capital. However, because most people would not enjoy going to a casino or track and making only one bet, people instead trade off the probability of winning for entertainment value derived through extended playing time: Duration of playing time is the great equalizer for the casino. An excerpt from *Gambling Times* illustrates:[28]

In playing red or black on roulette with one $100 bet, the house edge is 5.26% (there are 18 reds, 18 blacks, and 2 greens – so odds are 20 to 18 against) and a bet may be expected to be won 47.37% of the time – almost an even chance. Now suppose $5 units are bet until $100 are either won or lost. Out of 1,000 trials, on average 873 times there would be a loss of $100, and only 127 times a win of $100. The average amount to bet to obtain a decision would be $1,451 compared to $100 with one large bet.

As for sports betting, an important principle noted by Moore (1996, p. 5) is that "it is the collective public perception that controls the odds." A bookmaker's proposed odds payoff schedule, his "line," thus does not express an opinion on how the two teams will fare. It instead represents the linemaker's expert opinion on what numbers will induce half the public to bet on the underdog and the other half to bet on the favorite.

Terminology and performance standards

A positive expected return to the game operator is realized over many betting events, be they dice rolls, card flips, slot-machine pulls, races run, or lottery tickets sold. The total amount bet is called the *handle*, and the amount that remains for the game organizer after the betting-event result has been determined is the *win*.

In casino table games, cash or cash equivalents, such as credit slips called *markers*, are collected (dropped) into sealed boxes under the tables. The dollar-equivalent aggregates in the boxes have thus become known as the *drop* – a term that also applies to the coins (and/or tokens) fed into slot machines.[29] The *win rate*, expressed as a percentage, is then the total win (over time) divided by the total drop. This percentage is usually referred to as the *hold*.[30] In contrast, at tracks, states charge a fixed percentage of the handle as a "fee" for participation.

Although the operator's positive-expected-return percentage produced by trials over many betting events is generally small – ranging from almost nil at some points in a blackjack game to over 15% for some bets in craps, at the Big Six Wheel, in lotteries, in bingo, and at the track – win rates normally range between 10% and 25% of the drop in casinos, 17% or more of the handle in racing, and approximately 50% of the handle in lotteries. In effect, then, the win percentage may be viewed as the average proportion of the bankroll of all players taken collectively that typically would be retained by the game operator. Note here, however, that the casino's "edge" (its expected value per unit bet, or, in casino jargon, the house p.c.) in table games is expressed as a percentage of the handle and not as a percentage of the drop (even though these might sometimes be the same).

Moreover, the similarity of conversion of cash at the track into tickets and the converting of cash at the casino into chips does not mean that the handle at tracks and lotteries can be compared with the drop in a casino. In casinos, handle is typically not the drop and may turn out to be a multiple of the drop because (a) it is unusual for all chips (cheques) purchased and counted in the drop to be immediately "invested" in the game and (b) "reinvestment" of chips won or retained in the course of play may increase the handle without correspondingly increasing the drop through additional chip purchases. Such, though, is not the case with pari-mutuel tickets, in which there is no fractional retention of the ticket's value. The full face amount of the ticket is bet in each race.

Assume a one-roll-decision dice game in which the casino edge is 2%. The following numerical example should help clarify the terminology. Say there are five bettors, each betting $10 on a throw of the dice. The handle is then $50. Assume further that the players are not using cash but instead chips issued by the casino and bought at the table for cash. The drop will then also be $50 at the start of the game. Theoretically, for each decision, the casino ought to expect to win 2%, or $1, of the total amount bet. Of course, this may or may not happen over the short run, but it will, on average, occur over the long run (i.e., over many betting decisions).

Now assume for a moment that on the first roll, the players collectively come out even and that they then bet the second roll identically to the first. The handle at that table has now risen to $100, while the drop has remained $50; no player had to buy more chips.[31]

Another hypothetical situation can be examined to illustrate how the hold is over 10% even when the house's edge may be 1%. Suppose that a player beginning with a $100 stake, and buying $100 worth of chips, on each decision happens to experience the long-run average loss specific to that game of 1% per decision. On the first deal of the cards, the casino wins $1, and the player has $99 left over. On the second deal, the casino wins $0.99, and the player has $98.01 remaining. If we extrapolate, after 11 decisions the player has less than $90, and the casino has more than $10; at this stage, the win as percentage of the drop (the hold) is over 10% (with the handle over $1,000).

Most games have win rates that over time are characteristic and thus can be used as statistical-norm benchmarks against which the performance of a specific table (or of a casino with many tables) may be measured. Nevada's characteristic win-rate averages, for example, are shown in Figure 11.6 and in Table 11.7. From the figure, we can see that baccarat is the most volatile (i.e., has the highest variance) of all games in terms of gross win fluctuations. Indeed, the variance is so great that casinos occasionally encounter losing months at their baccarat pits.[32]

Analysis of casino game performances may also be extended well beyond the rudiments just presented. Detailed knowledge of the probability for each betting-decision result (and of the average number of events per final decision) is required to calculate cost as a percentage of money bet. Such knowledge may then be used to determine the true cost to the casino of player junkets and comps (which, in the case of baccarat, often absorb a comparatively high 30% to 40% of the baccarat win). An interesting rule-of-thumb mentioned by Kilby (1985), for example, is that a casino has earnings potential of around one average bet per hour. That is, if the average bet is $25, then the casino can expect on average to win that amount in each hour of play.[33]

With slots often accounting for over two-thirds of a casino's revenues and floor space, managers are also motivated to compare ROI performances of various machines. A model that can be used for such purposes is described by Johnson (1984, p. 62). As illustrated in the following, it includes variables for coin denomination, hold, average coins played, and cycle time.

Johnson's model uses three equations:

1.  denomination $\times$ hold $\times$ average coins played $=$ win per game
2.  average daily drop $\div$ win per game $=$ games played
3.  games played $\times$ cycle time $\div$ hours operated daily $=$ utilization rate

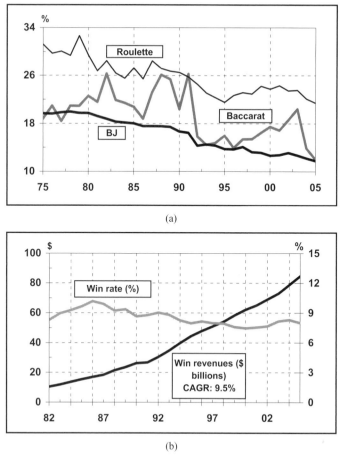

(a)

(b)

Figure 11.6. Win rate characteristics in Nevada, 1975–2005: (a) by game and (b) U.S. average for all games.

A sample calculation is then:

1.  0.05 (denomination) × 0.15 (percentage hold) × 2.2 (average coins played) = $0.0165.
2.  To win $25, this machine must be played 1,515 ($25/$0.0165) times.
3.  If an average cycle time of ten seconds is assumed, it will take 15,152 seconds (4.21 hours) or a 17.5% utilization rate over 24 hours to reach these earnings.

Although ROI comparisons are made on a win-per-unit basis, the coin-in or handle (i.e., the total number of coins and bills) that a machine attracts is another frequently analyzed aspect because it is an indicator of the relative popularity of a particular game.[34] New technology now also makes it easy

Table 11.7. *Hold (% win to drop) for Nevada, 1975–2005*[a]

|                               | Major table games | | | | |
|-------------------------------|-----------|-------|----------|----------|-------|
|                               | Blackjack | Craps | Roulette | Baccarat | Total |
| Nevada (% total win by source)[b] | | | | | |
| Mean                          | 18.4      | 9.3   | 2.6      | 5.9      | 36.2  |
| Hold (% win to drop)          | | | | | |
|   Mean              | 16.1      | 16.0  | 25.8     | 19.2     | 19.3  |
|   Variance          | 7.7       | 5.1   | 8.8      | 15.0     | 7.3   |

[a] Fiscal years ended June 30 beginning in 1984.
[b] Including slots.
*Source*: Nevada Gaming Control Board data.

for managers to maximize returns by quickly altering a machine's themes and payouts according to time of day and anticipated player preferences.[35]

## 11.4 Casino management and accounting policies

Marketing matters

One way to understand the business of a casino (or that of any other wagering establishment) is to visualize it as a retailer, ostensibly of betting opportunities but, in actuality, of experiences that are stimulating, exciting, and *entertaining*. That such experiences have an inherent value to customers is proven time and again by the fact that – although on balance they receive nothing tangible in return for the money they spend – the customers tend to come back for another visit. Also, players are, for the most part, insensitive to price. The marketing challenge is to get customers into the store through advertising, marketing, and publicity and then to keep them shopping for as long as possible under conditions in which "the customer sets the price . . . decides when the show begins and how long it will last."[36]

Casinos in particular have found it necessary to create marketing images that most appeal to the core of players they are likeliest to attract. The largest chains then make further marketing refinements on the basis of statistical experiments that determine which incentives are the most profitable to implement for each category of player. For example, many of Harrah's casino-hotels have long and very profitably catered to low- and midbudget players who do not require extensive credit-granting facilities or lavish meal and entertainment services. In contrast, Mirage Resorts (a property of MGM Mirage) has – without sacrificing the important and vastly broader upper-middle-income player group – profitably exploited the so-called high-roller niche in which practically any whim of the free-spending gamer is

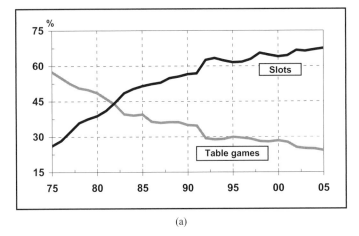

(a)

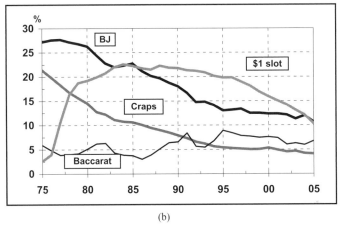

(b)

Figure 11.7. Nevada dollar volume market shares for table games versus slots, (a) general categories and (b) by game, 1975–2005. *Source*: Nevada Gaming Control Board.

indulged.[37] In addition, some casinos still attract players by developing tour and travel discount packages and junkets.[38]

Even with all this, however, market shares for individual companies do not remain static, and it is crucial for managements to accommodate the shifting demands of players by altering the mix of their games over time. In recent years, for instance, technological advances in the design of electronic slot machines (including video poker and blackjack) have made them so popular that they have come to account, at the expense of table games, for a steadily rising share of overall industry revenues (Figure 11.7).

But the optimal mix of slots to table games may also, as Greenlees (1988, p. 12) has noted, vary considerably from one region to another. As has already been shown in Figure 11.5, the average amounts of money and time spent by visitors to Las Vegas differ greatly from those spent by visitors to Atlantic City. This is because expenditures per visit and number of visits per year are economically sensitive to the distance of the casino from the customer's home. Frequency of visits and expenditure per year are inversely related to distance while expenditure per visit is directly related to distance.[39]

Cash and credit

Large casinos will often have millions of dollars in cash and equivalents either in play or ready for play at the tables and slot machines. To attract and to retain business, most casinos also will often extend credit and *comps* (free goods and services) to their better customers. The short-run management problem, then, is to oversee and control the flow of cash, credit, and comps, preventing the abuses by employees and by customers that can naturally be anticipated when there is regular and close contact with sizable amounts of money.

Achievement of such control requires implementation of highly detailed and regimented rules of conduct. But enforcement of the rules must also be accompanied by a strong commitment from upper management to subject any deviations and irregularities to close scrutiny. In practice, this means that operating procedures are broken into many small and well-defined steps: Many people must watch many people as credits and comps are granted and as the cash moves from the pockets of the players into the tables and slots, into the counting rooms, and then finally into bank vaults. The same applies with regard to chips, cash, and credits that are recycled back to tables and cashiers' windows as seed money to conduct the games.

Of all such activities, however, it is in the granting of credit that the casino establishes what is probably the most sensitive and important of relationships with its customers. Credit that is extended and then promptly repaid normally generates very profitable activity because the casino's edge is applied to a bigger volume of play than it would otherwise receive.[40]

But credit also has another, darker side. As Friedman (1974, 1982) has noted, casinos must win their money twice, first having to beat credit players at the tables and then having to collect the amounts they are owed. If a customer receives more credit than can be recycled in full over a reasonable time after play, casino margins will suffer from bad-debt write-offs. Accordingly, strict credit-granting procedures have been developed in both Nevada and New Jersey.[41] Using bank references and other information, managers can, for instance, certify with Central Credit Inc. in Nevada that the customer is in good standing at banks and at other hotel-casinos.

Credit policies also usually reflect casino marketing strategies, the effects of which can generally be seen on the balance sheet through bad-debt allowances as a percentage of accounts receivable. The Circus Circus hotel-casino in Las Vegas, for example, has a largely cash clientele and therefore virtually no need for bad-debt reserves. Conversely, Caesars Palace has largely positioned itself as a high-roller's shrine, and its allowances have been relatively large as measured in absolute dollars or as a percentage of receivables. Important deviations from prior reserve-percentage norms often signal changes in marketing policies – or in accounting procedures that may significantly influence reported earnings.

Moreover, rapid growth of receivables net of reserves as compared with the growth of gross win is often an early-warning indicator that current-period performance is perhaps being unsustainably boosted by "borrowing" from performance in future periods. In effect, players are being granted more credit than they can repay over a reasonably short time, and the likelihood is that they are being tapped out (or "burned" out).[42]

Procedural paradigms

Fill slips record the value of the bills, coins, and chips that the cashier's cage issues to the gaming tables, and credit slips record the value of these items returned to the cage. Nevada Gaming Commission Regulations [number 6.040(5)] specify the method that must be used to transfer cash and equivalents between tables and the cage.[43]

According to the regulations (and following Friedman's [1974, 1982] presentation), "all fill slips and credit slips shall be serially numbered in forms prescribed by the board," and the serial numbers must include letters of the alphabet "so that no gaming establishment may ever utilize the same number and series. . . . All series numbers that are received by the establishment must be accounted for. All void slips shall be marked 'VOID' and shall require the signatures of the 2 persons voiding the slip."

In addition, there are several detailed regulations as to how drop boxes are unlocked with two different keys – one issued by the cage and the other by the accounting department at the time the count is scheduled. Once the drop box is opened, regulations specify that the contents of each box or bag be counted and verified by three counting employees and that all agree on the count, credit, and fill slips taken from the box.

The count team notes shift win, shift currency drop, shift fill and credits, and shift IOUs to the cage, and the team typically sorts a box's contents into (a) currency, (b) chips, (c) fill slips, (d) chip credit slips, and (e) name credit slips. A table shift's records – its *stiff sheets* – will then include the table's opening chip bank (inventory) as a fill slip and the shift's closing chip bank as a chip credit. Calculations by shift can then be made as follows:

currency + chips + name credits + chip credits + closing bank

   = table income

opening bank + fills = table fills

table income − table fills = table win

More specifically, the win or loss at each table in each shift may, as illustrated in AICPA (1984, p. 7), be computed as in the following example:

| | | |
|---|---:|---:|
| Cash in the drop box | | $6,000 |
| Credit issued and outstanding | | 3,000 |
| Total *drop* | | 9,000 |
| Beginning table inventory | $14,000 | |
| Chip transfers | | |
|     Fills | 5,000 | |
|     Credits | (1,000) | |
| | 18,000 | |
| Less: ending table inventory | 11,000 | 7,000 |
| Win | | $2,000 |

Of course, all accounts, including cash, hold IOUs (a customer's check that a casino agrees not to process until some time in the future), and others are verified and balanced according to standard journal-entry procedures. In addition, table-game and slot results are regularly analyzed by shift, using statistical tests to signal possible significant deviations in win and drop figures from previously established averages. In this way, casino managers can detect where there might be any fraud by employees or customers.

When aggregated over longer periods, perhaps a week or a month, these statistics may be analyzed to indicate trends in win per square foot. Such data permit relative-efficiency comparisons to be made with experiences in prior periods and with the performances of other casinos and are similar to sales-per-square-foot calculations used in the retailing industry. Table 11.8, for example, shows Nevada revenues and average-win-per-square-foot data by game category.

## 11.5 Gambling and economics

The psychological roots of the desire to gamble are complex and not completely understood. And some psychologists (e.g., Halliday and Fuller 1974) indeed view gambling as a neurosis rather than a form of entertainment. Economists, however, deal with the demand for gaming services through utility-function models. In such models, consumers express their preferences by making purchases according to the utility they expect to derive from the goods or services bought.

To see how this line of thinking evolved, we have to go back over 200 years. At that time, some mathematicians were concerned about resolving the so-called St. Petersburg paradox, which was presented in the form of a

Table 11.8. *Nevada gaming revenue analysis, fiscal year 2006*

| Category | Statewide | Las Vegas Strip |
|---|---|---|
| **Revenue per square foot**[a] | | |
| Pit[b] | $2,498 | $4,422 |
| Coin-operated devices[c] | 1,279 | 1,549 |
| Poker and pan | 903 | 1,188 |
| Race and sports | 569 | 687 |
| Total casino | $1,442 | $2,056 |
| **Casino department % of revenues from:** | | |
| Pit[b] | 29.3% | 42.8% |
| Coin-operated devices[c] | 67.2 | 53.3 |
| Poker and pan | 1.4 | 1.7 |
| Race book | 1.0 | 1.0 |
| Sports pool | 1.1 | 1.2 |
| Total revenue | 100.0% | 100.0% |

[a] Statewide includes 274 locations, Las Vegas Strip 40 locations.
[b] Includes keno and bingo.
[c] Primarily slot machines.
*Source*: Nevada Gaming Abstract, State Gaming Control Board.

coin-tossing game. In theory, because the expected value (payoff, or return) of the game was infinite, players should have been willing to pay an infinite amount to participate. Yet no one was willing to do so.

Mathematicians Daniel Bernoulli and Gabriel Cramer solved the mystery by rejecting the principle of maximum expected return and by substituting instead the concept of expected utility. By recognizing the diminishing marginal utility of money (the additional utility derived from additional units decreases as the money value of the prize increases), they could explain the paradox: Participants would determine the amount they were willing to play in a St. Petersburg type of game according to the game's expected utility and *not* its expected monetary returns.

Significant further work on the nature of utility functions was done in the 1930s, when it was demonstrated that, unless the function is bounded, new paradoxes can be constructed. It then remained for von Neumann and Morgenstern (1944) to show, in their classic 1940s work on game theory, how the expected-utility hypothesis leads to optimal decisions under conditions of uncertainty.

Friedman and Savage (1948) then published an important study discussing the application of the expected-utility concept to choices made by individuals. Why, they asked, would many people purchase insurance (pay a premium to avoid risk) and also gamble (undertake risk)? To answer, they postulated

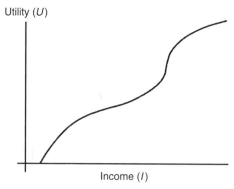

Figure 11.8. An individual's utility function. *Source*: Friedman and Savage (1948).

(as shown in Figure 11.8) that, over some range, the marginal utility of wealth increases, which means that the utility functions of individuals contain both concave (risk-aversion curves graphically represented as outward-bending from the origin) and convex (risk-affinitive) segments. Also, as Yaari (1965) has suggested, players often substitute, for the objective or true probabilities of a game, their own subjective beliefs about those probabilities.

In contrast to the theoreticians just cited, however, other economists have examined the gaming industry through a variety of standard econometric modeling approaches. Eadington (1976), for example, estimated for the Nevada economy the coefficients in a production function of the form $Q = f(K, L, M)$, where $Q$ represents volume of finished product, $K$ is capital equipment, $L$ is labor, and $M$ is quantity of raw materials. From this he was able to draw conclusions concerning economies of scale and the optimal mix and marginal productivities of various games and devices. Still others (e.g., Asch *et al.* 1984) have, moreover, suggested that there are certain betting situations in which behavior in the securities markets is comparable to that in casinos and that market-efficiency theories may therefore be applicable.

Economic analysis is also important in determining whether introduction of casinos into a previously casino-free region produces a net benefit to the people of that region. To justify such development, a region must demonstrate that the revenues generated by attracting visitors from outside the community (and the attendant economic multiplier effects) are large enough to cover the increased social and government operating costs (of regulation, police, health care, etc.) that the community will surely incur once the casinos are opened.

In all, the academic literature on gambling and economics has developed rapidly because gaming and wagering activities have so many quantifiable aspects and because economic analysis can be readily applied to everything from game playing to the determination of optimal casino comp and credit policies.[44]

## 11.6 Concluding remarks

In total, more is spent on gaming and wagering activities than on movies and recorded music combined. This remarkable situation has, in part, since the early 1950s, reflected changes in American lifestyles as well as advances in lottery, racing, communications, and slot-machine technologies.[45] However, the industry's growth potential depends on an unusually broad assortment of social, political, and economic factors.

As economists Ignatin and Smith (1976) have noted, the one constant throughout is that gambling possesses both consumption and investment characteristics; it provides direct utility with the hope of financial gain. In other words, people do not gamble only for money; they also gamble because it is entertaining.

## Notes

**1.** Berger and Bruning (1979, p. 17).

**2.** The Flamingo Hotel was designed by Siegel to attract the rich and famous to the middle of the desert. The hotel started a building boom that was not to slow until the early 1980s, when more than 50,000 hotel rooms were available to host some of the largest business conventions in the world. Also see Puzo (1976).

**3.** Taxes are currently at a rate of 6.75% (raised from 6.25% in 2003) of gross winnings in Nevada and 8% in New Jersey, where a surcharge of 1.25% of gross revenues to be invested in urban development over 25 years also exists. In Detroit, the 18% tax on gross income is divided 55% to Detroit and 45% to Michigan. Taxes in Missouri, Iowa, and Louisiana are in the range of 20% to 22%, but Illinois is a bit higher. As noted in Sanders (2005), once gaming is established, states tend to raise tax rates.

**4.** However, the average length of stay of Atlantic City visitors is probably a little less than a day, and for many visitors just a few hours. In Las Vegas, the average length of stay is about 3.8 days.

**5.** Regulations vary widely by jurisdiction and change over time. See Braunlich *et al.* (1999), Cabot (1995), and the Web site www.CasinoLaw.com.

**6.** See Sorkin (2004) and Schwartz (2003).

**7.** For example, Alvarez (2004) discusses Blackpool. New infrastructure improvements connecting Hong Kong to Macau along with the arrival of modern American casinos have already made Macau, with revenues estimated to reach $12 billion by 2010, the major gaming destination of Asia. Singapore should by then also generate at least $3 billion. By 2006, Macau had surpassed the Las Vegas strip with revenues of $6.95 billion. See Sanders and Stanley (2006).

**8.** According to *Gaming Business*, in 1983 there were 92 Thoroughbred racing associations, which attracted 51.1 million patrons and handled about $7.2 billion, and 62 standardbred (harness) racing associations that reported a total annual handle of $2.81 billion and a total attendance of 23.3 million. In more recent years, these figures have not changed appreciably. But many tracks have tried to hold onto or enlarge their customer bases, successfully adding slot machines and video lottery terminals to their facilities and simulcasting races to out-of-state tracks (for "signal" fees of approximately 3% of the handle). Guth and Shagan (2001) argue that the heavy state regulation seen in this industry ought to be significantly eased. See also McLean (2001).

Thoroughbred horses can trace their lineage back at least a century, and there are three types of races: claiming, allowance, and stakes. The commercial market for Thoroughbreds is governed by supply and demand factors relating to the expected returns on investment, first through racing and then through breeding. Yearling sales, which are sales of horses in their second year of life, are an important indicator of the industry's economic vibrancy. Such sales rise and fall in long-term cycles that can be readily obtained from *The Jockey Club Online Fact Book* and the National Thoroughbred Racing Association.

**9.** Net revenues retained by the states would normally be about half as much. The rest, after deduction of administrative and selling expenses, is returned to the public as prizes.

**10.** As Harden and Swardson (1996) note, Indian gaming began in 1975, when the Oneidas of New York began to use bingo as a fund-raising mechanism to pay for a fire department. The Oneidas argued that because they are an Indian nation, their sovereignty entitled them to run their own game. The Seminoles of Florida quickly began their own high-stakes bingo game and were challenged in *Seminole Tribe v Butterworth*, a landmark 1981 case.

The Indian Gaming Regulatory Act (IGRA) of 1988 had its roots in two U.S. Supreme Court decisions. In *McClanahan v Arizona Tax Commission* (1973), the Court pronounced that Indian tribes "have a right to make their own laws and be governed by them," which essentially recognized certain tribes as sovereign nations. And in *Bryan v Itasca County, Minnesota* (1976), the Court said that states lack civil regulatory jurisdiction over Indian tribes and members on their reservations or trust lands.

In a later decision, *California v Cabazon Band of Mission Indians* (1987), the Court decided that, if a state didn't have a public policy against gaming activities and allowed various forms of gambling, the state could neither prohibit nor regulate gaming activities on tribal lands. Congress, then recognizing the sovereignty of Indian tribes, passed the IGRA. This act established an independent federal regulatory body (the National Indian Gaming Commission) and federal standards governing the operation of gaming on reservations.

Three categories of gaming activities have been defined:

Class I: Traditional social gaming activities for prizes of minimal value, the regulation of which is the responsibility of the tribal government.

Class II: Primarily bingo, but also lotto, pull-tabs, and card games. The National Indian Gaming Commission (NIGC) regulates such games.

Class III: All other games not otherwise classified – which means casino-type gaming. Such games must be approved by tribal ordinance and be conducted in conformity with a tribal–state compact entered into by the tribes and the states. The compact must be approved by the NIGC.

As of 2005, 200 Native American tribes had established 350 casinos in 30 states and were generating more than $22 billion a year. Goodman (1995, pp. 111–113) describes background for the *Cabazon* decision in more detail. Barlett and Steele (2002) discuss serious loopholes and defects that have led to widespread misallocations of resources and corruption, and other similar problems are discussed in Emshwiller and Binkley (2004). See also Butterfield (2005a), Sanders and Emshwiller (2005), and Bordewich (2006).

**11.** In North Dakota, where low-stakes charity games are legal, the state receives 5%, the charity 65%, and the location owner 30% of the casino's gross win. Similar charity-designated games are also conducted in Canadian provinces. In Alberta, for instance, charities split 10% of their gaming profits with the provincial government, and the operator is entitled to 40%. See also note 12.

**12.** From surveys, Scarne (1974) estimated a bingo handle of about $3 billion. However, Abt *et al.* (1985) estimated that same handle for 1982; also see Christiansen (1989) and Cook (1979).

**13.** However, as the U.S. Congress (1999) National Gambling Impact Study suggests, the Interstate Wire Act, the history of which is covered in Schwartz (2005), is fraught with ambiguity. For example, does the phrase "wire communications" include the Internet? What types of wagering and gambling are allowed? And where does jurisdictional authority reside? Some argue that because the Internet didn't exist at the time of the statute's formulation, the intent of the law applies only to telephone communications. Complications also arise from interpretations of the U.S. Penal Code. For instance, Section 47.05 says that "(a) A person commits an offense if, with the intent to further gambling, he knowingly communicates information as to bets, betting odds, or changes in betting odds or he knowingly provides, installs, or maintains equipment for the transmission or receipt of such information." Section 47.06 says, in regard to possession of gambling devices, equipment, or paraphernalia, that

> A person commits an offense if, with the intent to further gambling, he knowingly owns, manufactures, transfers, or possesses any gambling device that he knows is designed for gambling purposes or any equipment that he knows is designed as a subassembly or essential part of a gambling device.

As noted by the *National Gambling Impact Study Commission Report* (1999), the countries with laws in place to extend Internet gambling licenses include Australia, Antigua, Austria, Belgium, Costa Rica, Curaçao, Dominican Republic, Finland, Germany, Honduras, the United Kingdom, and Venezuela. Updated licensing information is available at www.igamingnews.com. Also see Cukier (2000). As of 2004, there were approximately 1,800 Internet gambling sites worldwide, with about half the dollar amount of bets originating in the United States.

**14.** Betting service companies such as Betbug allow anyone downloading its software to propose a wager and the scan the Web to find a bettor to take the other side. Betbug takes a 5% fee from the winning amount. Betfair take bets from more than 80 countries, with 80% from Britain. Betfair lists hundreds of sporting events and, depending on the size of the bet, takes 2% to 5% from the winner's take. See Richtel (2004).

**15.** In Canada, for example, casino gaming has been legal since 1969, when the Canadian federal government's criminal code allowed provinces or charities to establish casinos using the games of roulette or blackjack. More recently, video lottery terminals and slot machines have been approved. Casino licenses are held either by provincial governments or by nonprofit organizations. Also, just as in the United States, Indian tribes (or bands, in Canada) have been in the process of developing a special legalistic framework for the provision of gaming services on their reservations. See also *Gaming & Wagering Business*, April 1993. One of Canada's largest casinos opened in Windsor, Ontario, in May 1994.

**16.** These numbers are also not to be confused with the gross amounts bet, or the handle. See also Scarne (1978) and Christiansen (1998).

**17.** There is evidence to suggest that the majority of players consider gaming to be a form of entertainment. In a survey by the U.S. Congress (1976), 81% of respondents said that one of the reasons they bet at a casino is to have a good time. See Supplementary Table S.11.1.

**18.**   Historically, the industry has experienced only two important setbacks in the postwar period – in 1981 and in 1991 – and both episodes coincided with an economic recession. It seems likely, however, that new competition will heighten the industry's future sensitivity to changes in the overall economy. The slowdown in 2001 was, in part, related to the terrorist attacks of September 11.

**19.**   In September 1997, the Ninth Circuit Court of Appeals ruled unconstitutional a federal law banning the broadcast of gaming ads. This ultimately led to a June 1999 Supreme Court decision that struck down a federal law that had banned casino gambling ads on television and radio. See also Greenhouse (1999) and Ritter (1999).

**20.**   As of 1985, for example, cash transactions above $10,000 have had to be reported to the Treasury Department.

**21.**   See especially Butterfield (2005b), who shows that many states now derive substantial percentages of revenues from gambling. In all, Nevada, Oregon, Louisiana, Rhode Island, and South Dakota generate more than 10% of total revenues from taxes on casinos, slots at racetracks, and lotteries. For example, in Rhode Island, gambling revenue had by 2004 become the third-largest source of income.

**22.**   Acting on the wishes of the legislature, the commission specified the following:

* Minimum size of table bets
* Numbers of tables and slots of different denominations and types allowed in each casino
* Hours of operation
* Number of square feet of public space relative to number of rooms
* Numbers of security guards required
* Number of days per week that live entertainment had to be provided (in the first off-peak seasons, there were days when there were more performers on stage than people in the audience)
* Various other aspects of hotel-casino operations, including limitations on marketing that are normally considered in the province of management

**23.**   Major public casino companies as of 2007 include Harrah's Entertainment (owning the former Caesars and Bally), MGM Mirage (owning the former Mandalay and Circus Circus), and Boyd. Racing companies include Hollywood Park and Santa Anita Consolidated. Gtech is prominent in lotteries, and the dominant slot machine manufacturer is International Game Technology.

**24.**   There are, however, exceptions: In May 1989, the Atlantis (originally Playboy) hotel-casino next to the Atlantic City convention center went bankrupt. It failed for a number of reasons, but mostly because it was never able to overcome its initial design handicap of having the casino spread over three floors.

**25.**   Multiples have generally ranged between five and nine in recent years. Also, in evaluating individual casino properties for the purposes of merger or acquisition, "casino" cash flow, which is EBITDA before corporate expenses, might be considered a more appropriate measure against which to apply a multiple than against EBITDA itself.

**26.**   For this reason, when a management attempts to assess the profitability of, for example, "junkets" (in which travel, hotel, and other expenses are paid by the casino-hotel in return for a promise to gamble a certain minimum over a few days' time), it should use a formula including an estimate of the house edge, the average number of decisions per hour, and the average size of betting units. Similar criteria should be used in determining whether or not a bettor qualifies for "comps" (complimentaries), which may include any, or all, of free drinks and meals, shows, rooms, and transportation.

**27.**   However, Binion's Horseshoe in downtown Las Vegas has had a unique policy whereby the player's limit is as high as his first bet. Also, a group of very high-stakes players can "pool" their play.

**28.**   See also the "Gambler's Ruin" formula.

**29.**   For slot machines, the coins-in, or slot handle, is obviously a known quantity and is reasonably well correlated with the slot drop (i.e., what falls into a slot machine's bucket after winners have been paid out). However, as explained later in the text, in table games, the handle is, under actual playing conditions, difficult to calculate and may be quite different from the drop. According to Nevada Gaming Control Board regulations, the statistical drop is defined as cash plus foreign chips and tokens plus pit credit issues and less pit credit payments in cash.

**30.**   Definitions of hold percentage are somewhat different in Nevada and in New Jersey. New Jersey's definition includes all cash and markers, but Nevada's definition does not include markers that may be redeemed at the table where the credit slip originated. All other things being equal, New Jersey hold figures are normally lower by 3% to 4% than those of Nevada. The hold percentage, or the hold p.c., as it is also known, of course should not be confused with percentages used to express casino advantages (expected values) for table games. Such casino advantages are stated as percentages of handle and not as percentages of drop.

**31.**   If, however, as is more likely, players initially buy many more chips than they bet on each decision (some lose and some tend to walk away from a table without betting all the chips initially bought), then the ratio of handle to drop does not grow as rapidly as in this example.

**32.**   Win rates, of course, also depend on game rules, which may vary (especially in Nevada) according to the discretion of management.

**33.**   Consider another illustration: In craps, on the "pass line," the average cost per roll as a percentage of money bet is 0.42%. This is determined by taking the house advantage of 1.41% and dividing by the average number of rolls per decision, which is 3.38. The average cost per roll of the dice to the player, or conversely win per roll for the casino, can then be used to determine how long on the average it would take for the casino to generate a certain amount of revenue, or what minimum average pass bet at the table might be required to win a certain amount. If in one hour of play, for example, there is an average of 60 rolls, then 60 rolls per hour times 0.0042 cost per roll equals 0.252. For the casino to win $500 in that hour from just the pass line bets, the average pass line bet for the whole table would have to be $500/0.252 or $1,984.13.

**34.**   Rivlin (2004) notes that, on modern machines, a typical cycle time between games is around six seconds, which implies that in an hour, the $2 per game player will place bets worth $1,200. As of 2004, total slot wagering in the United States (i.e., the handle) thus easily totaled $1 billion per *day*.

**35.**   Note that use of coins and bills in slot machines is an anachronism. In modern machines, credit cards and printed tickets obviate the need for physical processing of heavy coins and tokens and allow the player to choose the value of each credit wagered. This helps reduce operating costs and enhances marketing opportunities. See also Richtel (2006).

**36.**   Provost (1994, p. 59). However, as noted in Binkley (2004), casino marketing tactics and applied technologies can influence the customer's behavior.

**37.**   It is estimated that perhaps 20% of players may account for 80% of the upper-end business. See also Binkley (2000), who describes Harrah's statistics-based marketing.

**38.**   Junkets, in which rooms, meals, and travel costs may be picked up (i.e., "comped") by the casino, have diminished in popularity because the casinos have found that junkets are not as profitable as they had been thought to be. For instance, a casino wanting to earn at least $100 should know that if it costs $400 to bring a junket player in the door, it must – on the assumption of a 20% hold (win/drop) – realize a minimum drop that averages $2,500. As noted in Stefanelli and Nazarechuk (1996, p. 135), a casino is generally "willing to comp guests up to one half of the amount it expects to win from them." Players are rated by (a) buy-in amount to the game, (b) average bet, (c) largest bet, and (d) duration of play. However, an average *bet-to–buy-in ratio* often serves as a simple proxy for a bettor's intensity of play and thus the level of comps warranted by such play. A low bet-to–buy-in ratio will artificially inflate the drop and thereby depress the hold percentage.

For table games, the comps rating , equal to the player's theoretical loss times percentage return, would be a function of

(average bet) × (hours played) × (speed of game) × (casino advantage).

Generally, the number of decisions per hour would fall into the following ranges:

| | |
|---|---|
| Baccarat | 50 to 110 |
| Blackjack | 60 to 100 |
| Craps | 75 to 145 |
| Roulette | 25 to 35 |

**39.**   Indications are that demand falls by 30% to 35% when distance is doubled.

**40.**   The volume increase is a direct function of the credit extension itself and may also be indirectly affected by the exciting atmosphere that surrounds high-stakes tables, where smaller noncredit bettors may feel that they should become less conservative with their funds.

**41.**   Credit play is, however, much less significant on most riverboat and Indian reservation casinos. Also note that prior to June 1983, gaming debts were not legally enforceable in Nevada. See Rose (1986).

**42.**   For instance, in 1983, receivables in Atlantic City casinos rose at about twice the rate of win and foreshadowed the potential for a noticeably slower growth of revenues (win) in 1984. See also AICPA (1984).

**43.**   The cage, as noted in Eade (1996, p. 157), is the casino's operational nerve center, which is responsible for the custodianship of, and accountability for, the casino's bankroll, provides a vital link to the casino pit areas, deals with customer transactions, interfaces with every casino department, and is responsible for the preparation and maintenance of internal control forms.

**44.**   For example, see Williams (2003) and Walker (2007).

**45.**   Internet wagering would already probably be much larger if not for the Interstate Wire Act of 1956. An analysis of the Internet Gambling Enforcement Act of 2006 appears in Rose (2006).

## Selected additional reading

Alchian, A. A. (1953). "The Meaning of Utility Measurement," *American Economic Review*, March.

"All Bets Are On," *The Economist*, September 30, 2004.

Auerbach, A. H. (1994). *Wild Ride: The Rise and Tragic Fall of Calumet Farm Inc., America's Premier Racing Dynasty*. New York: Henry Holt.

Barron, J. (1989a). "Has the Growth of Legal Gambling Made Society the Loser in the Long Run?," *New York Times*, May 31.

(1989b). "States Sell Chances for Gold as a Rush Turns to a Stampede," *New York Times*, May 28.

Bary, A. (2003). "Rolling the Dice: Will Borgata Rejuvenate Atlantic City?," *Barron's*, July 21.

Bass, T. A. (1985). *The Eudaemonic Pie*. Boston: Houghton Mifflin.

Bassett, G. W., Jr. (1981). "Point Spreads versus Odds," *Journal of Political Economy*, 89(4).

Berenson, A. (2003). "The States Bet More on Betting," *New York Times*, May 18.

Binkley, C. (2003). "As Casinos Face a Slowdown, Steve Wynn Plots a Comeback," *Wall Street Journal*, January 22.

(2001a). "Las Vegas Casinos Take a Big Gamble on Highest Rollers," *Wall Street Journal*, September 7.

(2001b). "In Drive to Unionize, Casino Dealers Defy a Las Vegas Tradition," *Wall Street Journal*, March 6.

(2000a). "MGM's Mirage Deal May Close a Chapter in Gambling Business," *Wall Street Journal*, March 7.

(2000b). "'The Finest Casino That Could Be Built,' That Was the Goal," *Wall Street Journal*, February 2.

Blum, H., and Gerth, J. (1978). "The Mob Gambles on Atlantic City," *New York Times*, February 5.

Brenner, R., and Brenner, G. A. (1990). *Gambling and Speculation: A Theory, a History, and a Future of Human Decisions*. New York: Cambridge University Press.

Brisman, A. (1999). *American Mensa Guide to Casino Gambling*. New York: Sterling.

Bulkeley, W. M. (1995). "Electronics Is Bringing Gambling into Homes, Restaurants and Planes," *Wall Street Journal*, August 16.

Bulkeley, W. M., and Stecklow, S. (1996). "Long a Winner, Gtech Faces Resistance Based on Ethical Concerns," *Wall Street Journal*, January 16.

Cabot, A. N., and Balestra, M., eds. (2006). *Internet Gambling Report IX*. Newton, MA: Casino City Press.

Calonius, E. (1991). "The Big Payoff from Lotteries," *Fortune*, 123(6)(March 25).

Camerer, C. (1989). "Does the Basketball Market Believe in the Hot Hand?," *American Economic Review*, (December) 79; and comment by Brown, W. O., and Sauer, R. D. (1993). *American Economic Review*, 83(December).

Charlier, M. (1992). "Casino Gambling Saves Three Colorado Towns but the Price Is High," *Wall Street Journal*, September 23.

Clark, K. (2005). "Against the Odds," *U.S. News & World Report*, May 23.

Clark, T. L. (1987). *The Dictionary of Gambling and Gaming*. Cold Spring, NY: Lexik House.

Clotfelter, C. T., and Cook, P. J. (1989). *Selling Hope: State Lotteries in America*. Boston: Harvard University Press.

Cook, J. (1980). "The Most Abused, Misused Pension Fund in America," *Forbes*, 126(10) (November 10).

Cook, J., and Carmichael, J. (1980). "Casino Gambling: Changing Character or Changing Fronts," *Forbes*, 126(9)(October 27).

Cordtz, D. (1990). "Betting the Country," *Financial World*, 159(4)(February 20).

Crist, S. (1989). "Race Tracks Step Lively to Keep Up with Bettors," *New York Times*, May 29.

Curry, B. (1984). "State Lotteries: Roses and Thorns," *State Legislatures*, March.

Demaris, O. (1986). *The Boardwalk Jungle*. New York: Bantam.

Dombrink, J., and Thompson, W. N. (1990). *The Last Resort: Success and Failure in Campaigns for Casinos*. Reno and Las Vegas: University of Nevada Press.

Durso, J. (1991). "On Horse Farms, a Season of Distress Lingers," *New York Times*, April 23.

Eadington, W. R. (1999). "The Economics of Casino Gambling," *Journal of Economic Perspectives*," 13(3)(Summer).

Earley, P. (2000). *Super Casino: Inside the "New" Las Vegas*. New York: Bantam.

Eisler, K. I. (2001). *Revenge of the Pequots: How a Small Native American Tribe Created the World's Most Profitable Casino*. New York: Simon & Schuster.

Elkind, P. (1997). "The Big Easy's Bad Bet," *Fortune*, 136(11) (December 8).

     (1996). "The Number Crunchers," *Fortune*, 134(9)(November 11).

Emshwiller, J. R. (1992). "California Card Casinos Are Suspected as Fronts for Rising Asian Mafia," *Wall Street Journal*, June 1.

Epstein, R. A. (1967). *The Theory of Gambling and Statistical Logic*. New York: Academic Press.

Evans, R. L., and Hance, M. (1998). *Legalized Gambling: For and Against*. Chicago: Carus Publishing.

Friess, S. (2003). "A Whopper Joins Las Vegas's Convention Lineup," *New York Times*, January 5.

Gaylord, B. (2001). "Australia Balks at New Online Casinos," *New York Times*, January 9.

Hamer, T. P. (1982). "The Casino Industry in Atlantic City: What Has It Done for the Local Economy?," *Business Review*, Federal Reserve Bank of Philadelphia, January/February.

Harris, R. J., Jr. (1984). "Circus Circus Succeeds in Pitching Las Vegas to People on Budgets," *Wall Street Journal*, July 31.

Hirshey, G. (1994). "Gambling: America's Real National Pastime," *New York Times Magazine,* July 17.

Horwitz, T. (1997). "In a Bible Belt State, Video Poker Mutates into an Unholy Mess," *Wall Street Journal*, December 2.

Johnston, D. (1992). *Temples of Chance: How America Inc. Bought Out Murder Inc. to Win Control of the Casino Business*. New York: Doubleday.

Kilby, J., and Fox, J. (1998). *Casino Operations Management*. New York: Wiley.

Klein, F. C. (1983). "Horse Racing Gives Bush-League Owner Thrills, Little Profit," *Wall Street Journal*, August 31.

Lancaster, H. (1985). "Investing in Horses Is a Lot Like Betting: Some Luck, Some Skill, Maybe a Payoff," *Wall Street Journal*, March 15.

     (1980). "Casino 'Hosts' Pamper High-Rolling Bettors to Keep Them Rolling," *Wall Street Journal*, September 3.

Lehne, R. (1986). *Casino Policy*. New Brunswick, NJ: Rutgers University Press.

Levine, L. (1995). "Requiem for a Thoroughbred?," *Forbes*, 156(14)(December 18).

Liebau, J. (1983). "Tearing Up the Turf," *Barron's*, August 8.

Longstreet, S. (1977). *Win or Lose: A Social History of Gambling in America*. Indianapolis: Bobbs-Merrill.

Mason, J. L., and Nelson, M. (2001). *Governing Gambling*. New York: Century Foundation.

Meier, B. (1994). "Behind the Glow of Jackpots, Scrutiny for a Lottery Giant," *New York Times*, December 19.

Messick, H., and Goldblatt, B. (1976). *The Only Game in Town: An Illustrated History of Gambling*. New York: Crowell.

Millman, J. (2002). "Burgeoning Indian Casinos Get Ahead in Part by Dodging Labor Regulations," *Wall Street Journal*, May 7.

Morehead, A. H., and Mott-Smith, G., eds. (1963). *Hoyle's Rules of Games*. New York: Signet Books, New American Library.

Morrison, M. (2001). "Casino Royale: The Foxwoods Story," *Wall Street Journal*, August 21.

Myerson, A. R. (1996). "A Big Casino Wager That Hasn't Paid Off," *New York Times*, June 2.

O'Brien, T. L. (1998). *Bad Bet: The Inside Story of the Glamour, Glitz, and Danger of America's Gambling Industry*. New York: Times Books.

O'Donnell, J. R., and Rutherford, J. (1991). *Trumped! The Inside Story of the Real Donald Trump*. New York: Simon & Schuster.

Orwall, B. (1996a). "The Federal Regulator of Indian Gambling Is Also Part Advocate," *Wall Street Journal*, July 22.

(1996b). "Gambling Industry Hopes to Hit Jackpot through Consolidation," *Wall Street Journal*, June 10.

(1995). "Casinos Aren't for Kids, Many Gambling Firms in Las Vegas Now Say," *Wall Street Journal*, December 7.

Orwall, B., Rundle, R. L., and Rose, F. (1997). "Hilton and ITT Took Two Different Paths to This Confrontation," *Wall Street Journal*, January 29.

Paher, S., ed. (1976). *Nevada Official Bicentennial Book*. Las Vegas: Nevada Publications.

Painton, P. (1989). "Boardwalk of Broken Dreams," *Time*, 134(13)(September 25).

Passell, P. (1994a). "Foxwoods, a Casino Success Story," *New York Times*, August 8.

(1994b). "The False Promise of Development by Casino," *New York Times*, June 12.

Peterson, I. (1995). "After 20 Years, Atlantic City Starts to Reap Casinos' Benefits," *New York Times*, December 26.

Pileggi, N. (1995). *Casino: Love and Honor in Las Vegas*. New York: Simon and Schuster.

Pollack, A. (2000). "Las Vegas Glitz Is Set to Go West," *New York Times*, March 10.

Pollock, M. (1987). *Hostage to Fortune: Atlantic City and Casino Gambling*. Princeton, NJ: Center for Analysis of Public Issues.

Pulley, B. (1999). "Living Off the Daily Dream of Winning a Lottery Prize," *New York Times*, May 22.

(1998a). "Regulators Find Easy Path to Gambling Industry Jobs," *New York Times*, October 28.

(1998b). "Casino Changes the Fortune of a Hard-Luck Illinois City," *New York Times*, July 21.

(1998c). "Casinos Paying Top Dollar to Coddle Elite Gamblers," *New York Times*, January 12.

Reinhold, R. (1989). "Las Vegas Transformation: From Sin City to Family City," *New York Times*, May 30.

Richtel, M. (2006). "No More Cheap Shrimp Cocktail," *New York Times*, May 6.

   (2002). "A Credit Crisis for Web Casinos," *New York Times*, January 21.

Roemer, W. F., Jr. (1994). *The Enforcer: The Chicago Mob's Man over Las Vegas*. New York: Ivy Books (Ballantine).

   (1990). *War of the Godfathers: The Bloody Confrontation between the Chicago and New York Families for Control of Las Vegas*. New York: Donald I. Fine.

Rose, I. N. (2006). "Casinos on Cruise Ships, Why Not on Airplanes?," *Gaming Law Review*, 10(6)(December).

Ross, I. (1984). "Corporate Winners in the Lottery Boom," *Fortune*, 110(5)(September 3).

Rudoren, J. (2006). "Seeking New Sources of Money, Charities Get In on Poker Craze," *New York Times*, February 6.

Sack, K. (1995). "Gambling Owners Spend Lavishly to Gain a Voice in Many States," *New York Times*, December 18.

Sanders, P. (2006). "Casinos Emerge as Winners in Wake of Hurricane Katrina," *Wall Street Journal*, August 3.

Scheibla, S. H. (1984). "Good Horse Sense?," *Barron's*, December 31.

Schwartz, D. G. (2006). *Roll the Bones: The History of Gambling*. New York: Gotham Books.

   (2005). *Cutting the Wire: Gambling Prohibition and the Internet*. Reno, NV: University of Nevada Press.

Schwartz, E. I. (1995). "Wanna Bet?," *Wired*, October.

Seligman, D. (1987). "Turmoil Time in the Casino Business," *Fortune*, 115(5)(March 2).

   (1975). "A Thinking Man's Guide to Losing at the Track," *Fortune*, XCII(3) (September).

Sheehan, J., ed. (1997). *The Players: The Men Who Made Las Vegas*. Reno: University of Nevada Press.

Simon, B. (2004). *Boardwalk of Dreams: Atlantic City and the Fate of Urban America*. New York: Oxford University Press.

Spanier, D. (1992). *Welcome to the Pleasuredome: Inside Las Vegas*. Reno: University of Nevada Press.

Swartz, S. (1985). "New Jersey Casino Commission Stirs Controversy with Rulings," *Wall Street Journal*, March 11.

Thalheimer, R., and Muktar, M. A. (1995). "The Demand for Parimutuel Horse Race Wagering and Attendance," *Management Science*, 41(1)(January).

Thompson, W. N. (2001). *Gambling in America: An Encyclopedia of History, Issues, and Society*. Santa Barbara, CA: ABC-CLIO.

Thorp, E. O. (1962). *Beat the Dealer*. New York: Random House (Vintage Books paperback, 1966).

Treaster, J. B. (1982). "Mob Alliance to Share Casino Riches Reported," *New York Times*, September 1.

Turnstall, J., and Turnstall, C. (1985). "Mare's Nest: The Market in Thoroughbreds Is a Mess," *Barron's*, July 15.

Useem, J. (2000). "The Big Gamble: Have American Indians Found Their New Buffalo?," *Fortune*, 142(7)(October 2).

Vinson, B. (1986). *Las Vegas behind the Tables!* Grand Rapids, MI: Gollehon.

Wartzman, P. (1995). "Gambling Is Proving to Be a Poor Wager for State of Louisiana," *Wall Street Journal*, September 11.

Wells, K. (1988). "Philip Anderson Has a Feeling He Knows What's in the Cards," *Wall Street Journal*, January 13.

Wilgoren, J. (2002). "Midwest Towns Feel Gambling Is a Sure Thing," *New York Times*, May 20.

Wong, A. (2001). "Perfectas by Personal Computer," *Wall Street Journal*, August 27.

Yoshihashi, P. (1990). "More States Like Odds on Sports Betting Despite Fierce Opposition to Legalization," *Wall Street Journal*, February 1.

Ziemba, W. T., and Hausch, D. B. (1984). *Beat the Racetrack*. New York: Harcourt Brace Jovanovich.

# 12
# Sports

*It ain't over 'til it's over.* – Yogi Berra

In sports today, chances are the game's not over 'til there's another television commercial.

This chapter concentrates on sports, which is as much an entertainment business as any thus far discussed. The exposition underscores the importance of links to broadcasting, cable, and wagering segments and illustrates how tax-law considerations are at the core of many sports business decisions. But it also indicates why professional sports may be the only business "where the owners want regulation, and labor – the players – want the free market."[1]

## 12.1 Spice is nice

Early innings

Trivia buffs might delight in learning that the first recorded Olympic running event occurred in Olympia, Greece, in 776 B.C.[2] Yet sporting activities had by then already been developing for thousands of years – from the earliest

420

days of history and from a time when spears and clubs and bows and arrows were used in the provision of food and shelter.

It has indeed been a long journey from those early, primitive times to today's organized professional leagues, whose games are instantly televised to a global audience. But actually, it was not until the middle of the nineteenth century that the modern organizations first evolved. The catalyst was the Industrial Revolution, which expanded the middle class and, accordingly, the "leisure time" available. As roads and automobiles and other modern forms of communication and travel were invented and then perfected, rates of growth accelerated. Even so, the underlying principles of the games themselves have not been changed very much. Basketball dates from at least 1891. Predecessor concepts for baseball go back as far as 1744. And notions for games resembling football and hockey can be traced, respectively, to 1609 A.D. and to 2000 B.C.

Since 1929, when the relevant economic data series were first defined, personal consumption expenditures on spectator sports have varied widely. As Figure 1.14 illustrates, spending in this area naturally declined during both World War II and the Korean War. And a peak of spending relative to PCE on recreation services (at nearly 8%) then appeared in 1968. However, the sports-spending time series does not suggest any discernible sensitivity to routine business-cycle fluctuations.

Trends in *admissions* to major professional sports contests also appear to have little correlation to the overall economic cycle. As indicated by Table 12.1, attendance at football (National Football League [NFL]), Major League Baseball (National League [NL] and American League [AL]), basketball (National Basketball Association [NBA]), and hockey (National Hockey League [NHL]) games expanded at an average annual rate of approximately 2.3% from 1980 to 2005. Over this span, basketball has had the highest compound annual growth rate (3.1%) and football the lowest (1.0%). But since 1990, attendance gains for baseball and hockey games have been greater than for the other sports.

None of this has in any important way affected the values of team franchises, which are essentially local monopolies created and controlled by the owners' associations. These franchises benefit from tax-deductible amortizations of personal service contracts that are not available to other industries and from de facto municipal subsidies that often appear in stadium-financing agreements. As such, not even normal short-run competitive pressures have an effect: Franchises can report operating losses year after year and still maintain a high or rising valuation upon transfer.[3]

Nevertheless, there is an underlying sensitivity of franchise values to changes in player contract standards, to changes in tax and antitrust laws and, perhaps most importantly, to changes in the demand for broadcast and cable rights. Such rights values have also been influenced by the events shown in Figure 12.1.

Table 12.1. *Attendance at professional sports exhibitions, 1960–2005[a]*

| | Attendance (millions) | | | | |
|---|---|---|---|---|---|
| Year | Baseball | Basketball | Football[b] | Hockey[c] | Total |
| 2005 | 74.9 | 21.3 | 17.0 | 20.2 | 133.4 |
| 2000 | 71.4 | 20.1 | 16.4 | 20.3 | 128.2 |
| 1995 | 51.3 | 19.9 | 15.8 | 17.1 | 104.1 |
| 1990 | 55.5 | 18.6 | 17.7 | 13.7 | 105.4 |
| 1985 | 47.7 | 11.5 | 14.1 | 12.8 | 86.1 |
| 1980 | 43.7 | 10.7 | 14.1 | 12.8 | 81.3 |
| 1970 | 29.2 | 7.1 | 10.0 | 6.5 | 52.8 |
| 1960 | 20.3 | 2.0 | 4.2 | 2.6 | 29.0 |
| CAGR[d] | | | | | |
| 1980–2005 | 2.2 | 3.1 | 1.0 | 2.6 | 2.2 |

[a] Includes regular season, playoff, and championship attendance. The numbers of teams in 2005 were 30 in baseball, 30 in basketball, 32 in football, and 30 in hockey. Two new teams were added to basketball in 1988 and two more in 1989. In 1961, there were 16 baseball, 9 basketball, 14 football, and 6 hockey teams.
[b] National Football League.
[c] National Hockey League.
[d] Compound annual growth rate (%).
*Source*: Statistical Abstract of the United States, U.S. Department of Commerce Bureau of the Census.

## Media connections

The most striking feature of the modern sports business is how dependent it has become on broadcasting and cable industry revenue growth. Indeed, in the absence of this electronic-media coverage and the fees so generated, many fewer professional teams and probably many fewer fans would have been created: In 1960, there were 42 professional sports franchises, mostly in the northeastern United States. But by 2000, more than 110 franchises had been spread into all regions of the country. Moreover, since 1980, the annual number of hours of sports programming aired by the major broadcast networks and cable systems has more than doubled to approximately 10,000.

All this growth began with, and has been largely governed by, the Sports Broadcasting Act, which Congress passed in 1961. This legislation gave sports leagues the right to act as a cartel (i.e., free of any antitrust sanction) in bargaining with television networks and had a most beneficial effect on development of interest in all professional sports.

Although sales of transmission rights for sporting events are still heavily weighted toward over-the-air broadcasters, as the cable subscriber base has grown to two-thirds of television homes, cable has become much more important as a source of team revenues: By the mid-1980s, major boxing

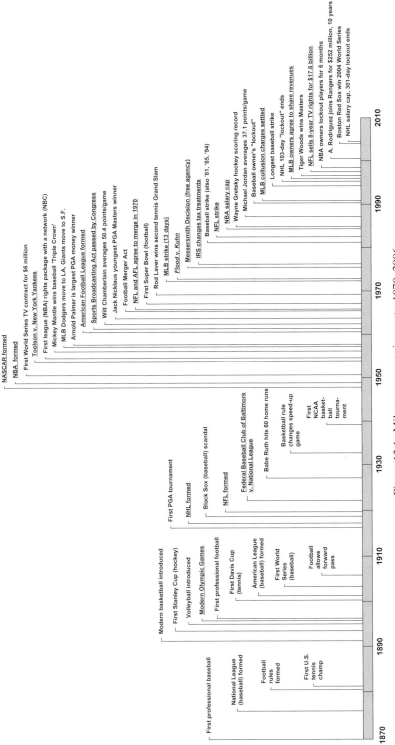

Figure 12.1. Milestone events in sports, 1870–2006.

Table 12.2. *Hours of broadcast network and cable network sports events,*
*2005*

| Sport | Broadcast hours | % of total | Hours cable | % of total |
|---|---|---|---|---|
| Motor sports | 182 | 9 | 5,429 | 18 |
| Baseball (MLB) | 118 | 6 | 1,416 | 5 |
| Basketball (NBA, NCAA, etc.) | 278 | 14 | 2,346 | 8 |
| Football (NFL, NCAA, etc.) | 612 | 32 | 3,074 | 10 |
| Golf | 386 | 20 | 819 | 3 |
| Hockey (NHL) | – | 0 | 211 | 1 |
| Tennis | 101 | 5 | 745 | 2 |
| Other | 241 | 13 | 15,918 | 53 |
| TOTAL | 1,918 | 100[a] | 29,958 | 100[a] |

[a] Total not exact due to rounding.
*Source*: Nielsen Media Research.

events had already become the province of pay-per-view cable and other
sports offerings had become the mainstay for primarily advertiser-supported
cable networks. It thus seems that cable could eventually become a foremost
licensee of rights to major sporting events such as the World Series and the
Super Bowl.[4]

To a large degree, then, it is the expectation of steadily increasing aggregate
broadcast and cable rights prices in local, national, and international markets
that has made investments in professional sports so attractive for major media
and entertainment companies or for wealthy private investors able to take
advantage of favorable tax treatments.[5] In contrast, the appreciation potential
of broadcast rights for collegiate and other amateur sports events appears to
be more limited.[6]

Of course, other media, including most daily newspapers and many specialized magazines and Web sites, have also benefited from the spread of
sports. The costs of producing fresh stories and articles in this area are relatively low, and the stories also attract readers that many advertisers want to
reach. Such articles, in turn, fortify reader interest in, and spending for, local
team events.

Table 12.2 illustrates the number of network hours allocated to sports
events.

The wagering connection

Wagering has always been an integral part of sports because a contest is
always more exciting when spectators are personally involved in the outcome.
As such, betting on almost any type of match, from baseball through boxing,
is legal and well developed in Nevada (and also in England). Everywhere
else in the United States, however, legal sports betting is largely limited

to racetracks (horses and dogs). Still, the absence of legal sanction has not stopped people from risking tens of billions of dollars each year on the results of football, baseball, basketball, hockey, boxing, and automobile racing.[7]

The spice that wagering adds to spectator sports is, moreover, also immediately reflected in increased demand for coverage by electronic and print media. The potential for high ratings leads sponsors to pay high prices for commercial time and leads stations, networks, and cable systems to then bid aggressively for rights to distribute the programs. Because revenues generated from sales of these rights are essential to the operation of spectator-sports enterprises, wagering indirectly provides important financial underpinnings by creating demand for information that would otherwise be of limited value and interest.

## 12.2 Operating characteristics

Revenue sources and divisions

As Scully (1995, p. 19) notes, "all professional sports leagues restrict entry, assign exclusive franchise territory, and collude on a revenue-sharing formula." And although each professional sport or team may have its own special problems and circumstances, each shares concerns over (a) the potential for tax-shelter, stadium-lease, and transfer pricing benefits for franchise owners; (b) the prices received for broadcast and cable rights; and (c) the cost of player salaries. Nevertheless, each of the three major sports (football, baseball, and basketball) has evolved differently with regard to these fundamentally common concerns.

Football, for example, has always been highly dependent on network-television money, which is a fact that became especially evident in the early 1980s, when the NFL signed a $2 billion, five-year contract with the national broadcast networks that was for the first time sufficiently large to provide each club with a profit before gate receipts were counted (and that by the late 1990s had grown to $18 billion).[8] A financial cushion on this order of magnitude readily permits revenues to be shared among all teams – with each team receiving an equal share of media and licensing revenues and 40% of gate receipts at away games even though revenues from suites and stadium sponsorships, which have recently become a larger fraction of total revenues, are not shared. The cushion furthermore insulates owners from the normal adverse financial consequences of prolonged mismanagement, incompetence, or competition.[9] As a result – despite considerable disparity in on-field performances – the richest NFL team has usually generated only about 20% more gross revenue than the poorest (because, unlike in baseball, there are no local TV contracts in football).

Moreover, until recently, football's allocation arrangements – which contained elements of immunity or exemption from antitrust laws also seen in baseball – tended to reduce aggressive bidding for star athletes and to

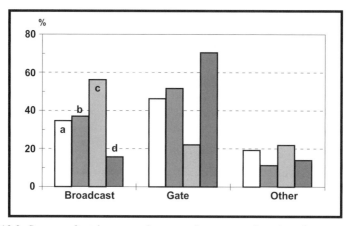

Figure 12.2. Sources of total revenues in percent by category for selected sports and teams: (a) baseball, New York Mets, 1986; (b) basketball, Boston Celtics, 1998; (c) football, Green Bay Packers, 2000; (d) hockey, Florida Panthers, 1996. *Sources*: Durso (1986) and Celtics and Panthers.

diminish the general usefulness of free-agency status for players (because every team must abide by a dollar limit on player salaries).[10] This is in contrast to the traditional situation in baseball and basketball, where free-agency status has long been effective and has led to the signing of many multimillion-dollar-per-year contracts.[11]

The operating structures of baseball and basketball have also differed markedly from that of football because a lesser percentage of total revenues in baseball and basketball has been shared by the teams, and local market size and gate receipts have historically been much more important determinants of profitability.[12] In the NFL, only eight games a year are played at home as compared with Major League Baseball (MLB) in which 81 games are played at home and season ticket inventories tally into the millions.

In both baseball and basketball, as Figure 12.2 illustrates, ticket sales have typically accounted for approximately 40% of total revenues, with concession income from parking fees, advertising, and food and drink sales contributing additional attendance-related income.[13] By contrast, in football's socialistic revenue-sharing structure, it is much less important for a team to fill the stadium every Sunday: Approximately one-third of the league's ticket sales (22% of $6.0 billion in revenues in 2004) are put into a visitors' pool and split evenly by the teams.[14]

Even so, however, as of the late 1990s, salary-cost pressures and slower growth of media-rights prices began to gradually push revenue-sharing and salary-cap agreements of all the major sports into closer conformity.[15] Collective bargaining agreements in the NFL and NBA already tie labor costs to revenues, thus enabling greater profitability to be spread over more teams than in MLB, where such links have not been negotiated.

Labor issues

Player salary costs in professional sports have, in recent years, often accounted for as much as 60% of total team operating expenses. And it is therefore not surprising to find that many conflicts between players and owners have involved player-compensation issues.

The stormy and well-publicized labor relationships that characterize modern professional sports can probably be best understood in the context of several landmark legal decisions, the most significant of which was *Federal Baseball Club of Baltimore v National League*, which was argued in the U.S. Supreme Court in 1922. At the time, big league baseball was essentially operated as a cartel in which teams agreed not to hire away each other's players. This case nevertheless provided baseball clubs with continued immunity from antitrust laws and thus with the ability to hold on to young players as team property for the duration of their playing careers. Under these conditions, players had no choice but to accept whatever salaries the team owners decided was fair.

*Toolson v New York Yankees* in 1953 presented the court with yet another opportunity to correct the obvious economic imbalances, but again the justices decided that baseball was entitled to a special status, and they passed the responsibility for any changes on to a reluctant Congress, which, until recently, was satisfied with the status quo.[16]

Legal challenges by players against the owners, however, finally began to succeed in the 1970s. Although the MLB reserve clause (that originated in 1887) held up under appeal in 1972 in the case of Curt Flood (*Curt Flood v Bowie Kuhn* [1971]), free agency was approved in late 1975 in what came to be known as the Messersmith Decision.[17]

Prior to this decision, a team would sign a contract with a player for a brief period, usually one season, and, under the so-called reserve system, could then hold on to the player for much longer by exercising options to extend contract terms. The system effectively eliminated competition and suppressed player salaries. It also created a valuable property right for the club owners. But after the Messersmith Decision, baseball players could, under much less restrictive conditions, become free agents and bargain with other clubs once their contracts expired.

Although football and basketball were never granted the special antitrust immunity of baseball, as Michener (1976, p. 482) has noted, both sports often acted as if they were immune.[18] Indeed, in both sports, although an athlete could in theory become a free agent after "playing out his option" on a reduced salary, an indemnity system (wherein the player's new team had to compensate his previous team) effectively reduced the player's value to a prospective new owner of his contract.[19]

The court decisions of the 1970s gave athletes the right to negotiate for higher compensation with teams other than their own, and contract terms are no longer necessarily extended beyond an initial period. As a result, in all

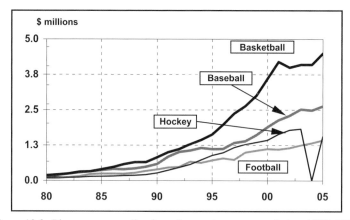

Figure 12.3. Player compensation in major sports, average salaries, 1980–2005.

major sports, but especially in baseball, the implementation of free-agency has significantly raised the level of player compensation (Figure 12.3) while also bolstering player-representation unions.[20] None of this has, however, happened without considerable labor strife (Table 12.3).

Although soccer has yet to attain the status of a major sport in the United States, it is *the* major sport for the rest of the world. As might be expected, rapid growth of global private broadcast interests has led to a media, marketing, and player-compensation structure for professional soccer that is beginning to resemble that of the other major sports.[21]

## 12.3 Tax accounting and valuation

Tax issues

From an economic point of view, the tax loopholes that provide benefits to professional team owners make little sense. As Zimbalist (1992, p. 35) has noted:

(a) The overwhelming share of the value of a franchise is derived not from players' contracts but from the monopoly rent that is generated from belonging to a league that confers exclusive territorial rights. The value of these territorial rights does not diminish over time.
(b) The value of players does not depreciate over time. Most players reach peak performance beyond the midpoint of their careers.

Despite such economic advantages, however, in many cases it would be difficult for high-income owners to justify investments in professional sports franchises if it were not for the tax benefits that might also accrue. It is thus worthwhile to at least outline the major tax concepts.[22]

*Historical development*  Prior to 1954, there was a uniform practice of signing players to one-year contracts and of then expensing the acquisition costs of such player contracts during the year of play. In 1954, however, the IRS

Table 12.3. *History of significant management-labor disputes in sports,*
*1969–2006*

| League | Year | Setting |
|--------|------|---------|
| MLB | 1969 | Lockout of spring training by owners to the end of February |
|  | 1972 | Players walk out through the first half of April. Complete regular season schedule play. |
|  | 1976 | Lockout by owners, end of February to mid-March |
|  | 1981 | Player strike, mid-June to first week of August. Owners had strike insurance. Split-season format used to determine league champions. |
|  | 1985 | Player strike, 2 days |
|  | 1990 | Lockout by owners from mid-February to mid-March (32 days) |
|  | 1994 | Player strike beginning early August. Strike wiped out 52 days of the 1994 season playoffs, and World Series, as well as 25 days of the 1995 season. Strike lasted 232 days. |
|  | 2002 | Player strike concerning issues of team revenue-sharing averted at last minute |
| NBA | 1995 | League locks out players in off-season |
|  | 1998 | Lockout by owners for 191 days, resulting in partial cancellation of regular season |
| NFL | 1982 | Player strike from September until the end of November. Reduced regular season schedule, with expanded playoffs. |
|  | 1987 | Player strike from end of September to end of October. Replacement players used for three games; schedule reduced by one game. |
|  | 2001 | NFL locks out referees in preseason |
| NHL | 1992 | Player walkout on April 1 |
|  | 1994 | Lockout by owners for 103 days of regular NHL season |
|  | 2004 | Lockout by owners, whole season. Salary cap issues. |

*Sources*: Quirk and Fort (1999, p. 69), *New York Times*, ESPN.

made a distinction between purchase of a single player's contract and purchase of substantially the entire roster of a baseball club's contracts acquired at one time. In the former case, expensing the cost over one year would remain appropriate; in the latter, the aggregate amount assignable to players' contracts was to be capitalized and then expensed over the useful life of the assets.

These rulings remained in effect until 1967, when the IRS reconsidered treatment of individual player contracts in light of baseball's reserve clause, which effectively tied a player to a team for his entire career despite the one-year term of his contract. A team's effective long-term control over its athletes implied, according to the IRS, that the cost of individual players' contracts ought also to be capitalized and then expensed over the useful life of the asset.

Then, in the early 1970s, guidelines pertaining to professional-football expansion agreements provided favorable tax treatment to franchise owners. Of a greatest importance was the IRS allowance that payments from new teams to established teams could be allocated between the franchise cost and the cost of player contracts for the veterans picked in the expansion draft. Because proceeds allocated to franchise cost were to be treated as capital gains, while proceeds allocable to player contracts were subject to recapture (of tax benefits by the IRS), owners were naturally provided with incentive to allocate as much as possible to franchise costs.[23]

Because most clubs were (and still are) owned by private individuals or by a small number of partners, owners' income from other sources could then be sheltered as long as the franchise was held as a sole proprietorship, partnership, or so-called subchapter S corporation (or subsidiary of a profitable, privately held corporation). All that needed to be done was to buy a franchise and to then allocate a large percentage (say 80% to 90%) of the purchase price to player contracts. The resulting large write-downs and reported losses would provide substantial tax savings, and after a few years, the franchise could be sold at a gain (Horvitz and Hoffman, 1976, p. 178).

In effect, prior to the mid-1970s, player-contract depreciation deductions would be converted into capital gains because sellers would allocate most of the purchase price to the franchise asset and very little to player contracts, and buyers would allocate a large portion of the purchase price to depreciable player contracts.

*Current treatments* By 1976, concern about potential abuses of professional-franchise ownership had risen to the point at which Congress felt it necessary to take corrective action against overstating the basis for depreciation, claiming large tax losses despite positive cash flows, and avoiding depreciation recapture on players who had retired or were otherwise eliminated from the roster. The new law specified that franchise buyers and sellers would have to agree on an allocation formula that no more than 50% of the purchase price of a franchise would be allocable to player contracts and that there would be special recapture provisions designed to prevent the stocking of a team with new players possessing substantially undepreciated contracts just before sale of a franchise.

Since 1976, several important court decisions have further defined the tax and accounting ramifications in this area, but issues involving the tax deductibility of television and cable rights amortizations have not been settled until recently.[24] As of 2004, Congress passed a bill allowing franchise owners to write off the full value of their franchises over 15 years, whereas previous laws had generally limited teams to writing off only the value of player contracts over three to five years. The biggest items subject to the expanded write-offs are television and radio contracts.[25]

## Asset valuation factors

The cash flow valuation methods applied to media properties described in Chapters 7 and 8 would also provide the basis for measuring asset values here.

But at a minimum, the estimated worth of a professional sports franchise would further require detailed knowledge of the following:

Demographic composition and potential size of the local market

Degree of competing professional sports activity as a determinant of ticket pricing and local-broadcast/cable-revenue potential

Stadium ownership arrangements and real estate development potential, if any

Player-contract status and union-contract stipulations

Potential for network broadcast, regional cable, and international revenues

IRS treatments of deductions for player contracts and broadcast/cable rights

Current and forecasted interest rates

Cash flow volatility (the lower the volatility, the higher the value)[26]

Of these elements, stadium ownership arrangements have recently taken on greater significance in view of the need for team owners faced with rapidly rising costs to capture and control as much of the ancillary revenue streams as possible.[27] In this regard, local and national political considerations have also become important.[28] Meanwhile, as Garrity (2000) suggests, rapidly rising franchise values and player salaries have significantly increased the industry's reliance on access to large amounts of capital that are structured primarily in the form of debt financings. Table 12.4 provides a selected sample of recent professional team transactions.

## 12.4 Sports economics

Two economic features are central to the business of professional sports: the cartel structure of the leagues and the monopsonistic (single-buyer or -employer) position of the teams vis-à-vis their players. Over time, monopsony power (which derives from the immobility of newly drafted players and the limited applicability elsewhere of the specialized skills that such players possess) has been somewhat weakened by free-agency. But the cartel structure has remained largely unchanged.[29]

Franchise owners have argued that their cartel agreements to block competition are needed to uphold franchise values. Although such arguments stand on weak legal ground, they make economic sense in that restriction on the number of clubs and maintenance of territorial exclusivity tends to support the relative and absolute quality of play. That is, professional sports contests would attract fewer fans if the quality of play were low and the uncertainty of the game results were to be reduced.

An interesting early mathematical model of a professional league that is useful for illustrative purposes was presented in Quirk and Hodiri (1974).[30] This model employed concepts such as a team's inventory of playing skills and cost per unit of playing skills acquired. Starting with the assumption that a league is in steady-state equilibrium (the stock of playing skills of each

Table 12.4. *Selected sample of recent professional team transactions*

| League | Team | Price ($ millions) | Year | Buyer |
|--------|------|--------------------|------|-------|
| MLB | Baltimore Orioles | 174 | 1993 | |
| | L.A. Dodgers | 311 | 1998 | News Corp. |
| | Florida Marlins | 150 | 1999 | |
| | Cleveland Indians | 323 | 2000 | |
| | Boston Red Sox + Fenway Park + 80% NE Sports Net | 660 | 2001 | New York Times + private individuals |
| | Anaheim Angels | 180 | 2003 | |
| | L.A. Dodgers | 375 | 2003 | |
| | Milwaukee Brewers | 220 | 2005 | |
| | Atlanta Braves | 460 | 2006 | Liberty Media |
| NFL | Philadelphia Eagles | 185 | 1995 | |
| | Cleveland Browns | 530 | 1998 | |
| | Washington Redskins + new stadium | 800 | 1998 | |
| | New York Jets | 635 | 1998 | |
| | Minnesota Vikings | 600 | 2005 | |
| | Atlanta Falcons | 545 | 2002 | |
| NBA | New Jersey Nets | 300 | 2004 | |
| | Boston Celtics | 360 | 2002 | |
| | Denver Nuggets + Colorado Avalanche + Pepsi Center | 400 | 2000 | |
| | Philadelphia '76ers + Flyers | 430 | 1996 | Comcast |
| NHL | L.A. Kings | 100 | 1995 | |

team remains fixed over time) and that franchise owners are motivated solely by profits from operations, the model showed the following:

(a) Franchises located in areas with high drawing potential have stronger teams than franchises in low–drawing potential areas.
(b) On balance, franchises in low–drawing potential areas sell players to franchises in high–drawing potential areas.
(c) If local television revenues are ignored, the distribution of playing strengths among teams is independent of the gate-sharing arrangements.
(d) The higher the share of television and radio revenues accruing to the home team, the higher are the costs of players, and the smaller is the chance of survival for low–drawing potential franchises.[31]

Another important early study of sports economics is one by Rottenberg (1956), who argued that free-agency in the labor market would not necessarily

used in those sectors can be readily applied in the study of sports economics. The major trends currently include the following:

More sharing of network-broadcast and cable revenues by professional baseball, basketball, and hockey teams[39]

Emergence of large local and regional cable networks that support collegiate and individual athletic events

Greater emphasis on player mobility and player rights as reserve-clause control by owners is weakened

Significantly increased bargaining power of pay cable networks and pay-per-view promoters relative to broadcast networks in obtaining distribution rights to major sporting events

## Notes

1.  See Ozanian and Taub (1992).
2.  See Durant (1969).
3.  Indeed, Quirk and Fort (1992, p. 62) indicate that "on average, over their league histories, baseball franchise prices have been increasing at a rate of about 8% per year, NBA basketball franchises at about 16% per year, and NFL franchises at about 20% per year. . . . There is insufficient information about prices of NHL franchises." Estimates in Sheehan (1996, p. 45) are even higher for Major League Baseball (MLB).
4.  An indication of the migration from broadcast to cable was renewal of the NBA contract in 2002. The NBA's six-year $4.6 billion deal with Time Warner and Walt Disney Co. left few games on free television (and follows the previous four-year $2.46 billion deal with NBC and Turner Broadcasting). As noted in Fatsis (2002b), broadcast networks have instead come increasingly to prefer sports programming known as "time buys" in which the networks sell airtime to independent production companies at a rate of perhaps $250,000 an hour. The outside producer then finds advertisers and pays all production costs, with the network supplying on-air talent and coordination. Under these conditions, the network does not have to guarantee an audience to advertisers, ratings become secondary, and the network gets to present sports events without expense. Examples include Ladies Professional Golf Association (LPGA) Championships, Grand Prix auto racing, and Tour de France cycling.
5.  For instance, as La Pointe (1989) indicated, a sports bidding war erupted in 1989 among the cable and broadcast networks. CBS paid $1.1 billion for four years of MLB, and NBC paid $600 million for four years of NBA games. Yet even with such hefty aggregate payments, in the average year perhaps one-third of league teams may report losses. However, without more details concerning the methods of accounting, it is difficult for outsiders to know how much credence to place in such profit and loss statements. Deferred player salaries, an important potential liability for professional teams, might, for example, be an area of differences in accounting treatments. Also, owners may often benefit by paying themselves large salaries, writing contracts with other businesses that they own, and saving on taxes from the depreciation tax shield. However, as noted in Walker (2002), it has become more difficult of late to sell smaller market teams at ever-higher prices.
6.  Whereas a degree of immunity from application of antitrust laws exists for professional teams, a 1984 Supreme Court decision found that the National Collegiate Athletic Association's (NCAA's) exclusive agreements with three television networks violated federal antitrust statutes. That decision left NCAA colleges free to negotiate individual contracts

lead to a concentration of the best players in the richest teams. The
is that a reserve clause is not necessary to ensure competitive l
that the main effect of the reserve clause is that players rece
that are below their value to the team that employs them. Rott
among the first to propose reserve-clause alternatives such as rever
and the capping of salaries.[32] Neale (1964) then showed how p
sports teams are natural monopolies with peculiar operating and
characteristics.[33] For instance, there is no precise or unambiguous
of output in the professional sports market: Is it total points scor
won percentage, total tickets sold, or something else?

Last but not least was Scully's (1974) work, which was the first
cally demonstrate how the amount that teams pay for baseball play
to the marginal revenue products (MRPs) of those players. The tw
ing equations were based on the idea that winning percentage is a fu
team productivity [ $pctwin = f(productivity)$] and that revenue is a
of winning percentage [$revenue = g(pctwin)$].

Economic analysis also proves useful in analyses of competitive
of teams in the same league, effectiveness of league-imposed salary
"luxury" taxes, revenue-sharing, reverse order entry drafts, and ot
schemes and notions that have become common to all professional
In this regard, the *Coase Theorem* is broadly applicable to many areas
sports, where rights and obligations are contractually bound.[35] The
suggests that it does not make a difference if a player is a free agent ow
rights to his or her services, or if a team owner has the right to hold the
contract (i.e., as in reserve clauses). In either case, the player should, in
end up playing for the team that places the highest value on the servi

In all, the extensive literature produced since these early studies
suggests the following:

A strong positive correlation between economic and athletic perfor
exists.

Restrictive labor market practices such as reserve clauses have been u
clubs to extract monopsony rents from player services.[36]

Under free-agency, player compensation rates generally reflect margina
enue production expectations.

The earnings distribution in individual sports is more skewed than in
sports.

Athletes and teams respond to incentives as predicted by general econ
theory.[37]

## 12.5 Concluding remarks

A professional sports franchise is "a private enterprise that customers –
fans – treat like a public institution."[38] Sports will continue to be a highly
ible and important entertainment segment tightly linked to the broadcast
cable, and wagering industries. As such, the tools and methods of anal

with commercial broadcast and cable networks and nullified the NCAA's traditional role as sole exclusive negotiator for broadcast rights to college football games. Fatsis (2003) discusses antitrust in college football.

Although the Supreme Court decision increases opportunities for cable and regional sports networks and independent broadcasters to bid for licenses to show games of local interest, the amounts being paid by these new bidders had for a while in the aggregate proved to be below the amounts that had regularly been obtained in contracts negotiated by the NCAA. In 1994, however, CBS extended its coverage of NCAA games through 2002 in a $1.73 billion rights package (which averages out to $216 million a year, or a 50% gain over the $143 million CBS paid for annual rights in the previous deal negotiated in 1989). In 1999, CBS further extended its contract by 11 years, bidding $6.2 billion. See *Wall Street Journal*, November 19, 1999.

**7.** According to Christiansen (1989), for instance, the illegal gross handle for such activities in 1988 was probably greater than $26 billion, with the largest portion wagered on football. Peer-to-peer betting services are increasingly important for sports-related Internet betting.

**8.** Gate receipts are shared 65:35 between home and visiting teams. In 1980, the net profit margin for NFL teams was 5.2%, and net income was $694,000. This compares with total television payments of only $926,000 for the NFL title game in 1963 (Michener 1976, p. 360). Under the 1982 television contract, teams derived an average of $14.2 million per year from television. Siklos (2007) estimates that in 2007, NFL operating profit was around $1 billion.

**9.** See, for example, the discussion by Frank (1984) of the United States Football League.

**10.** As Moldea (1989, p. 82) notes, the U.S. Supreme Court ruled in 1957 that, "unlike major league baseball, the NFL was subject to federal antitrust laws." But relaxation of antitrust-law restraints has enabled leagues to bargain with networks as a unit. In this respect, the sports business has an advantage not available to other entertainment segments. Also see Rivkin (1974).

**11.** Fisher and Ozanian (1999) note that by the late 1990s, football's revenue-sharing arrangements had begun to change. The NFL revenue-sharing rule requires league network television and league-wide licensing to be shared equally among all teams. Revenues from general seating (amounting to $750 million in 1998) are split 66:34 between home and visiting teams.

Also, the NFL salary cap rule limited player salaries to 48% of total league revenues, but this limit began to be circumvented with a loophole that allows player-signing bonuses to be amortized over the life of a player's contract. This gives teams that play in high-revenue stadiums (e.g., Cowboys or Redskins) a substantial advantage in signing the best players. The rich-market teams take in additional revenues from luxury suites, corporate sponsorships, and concessions that do not have to be shared and that can be applied to such signing bonuses. As Fatsis (2004, 2005) explains, the long-run socialistic revenue-sharing arrangements of the NFL are beginning to malfunction as teams develop unshared local revenue sources and as teams spend more than the salary cap by amortizing the costs of signing bonuses so that less of the bonuses count against the cap. Brown (2006) notes that the salary cap was raised to $109 million in 2007 and that players are entitled to 59.5% of total revenues.

**12.** As shown in Lowry (2003), with $4.8 billion of revenues in 2002, the NFL teams shared equally 63% as compared with 20% of $3.5 billion for MLB (34% in 2003), 35% of $3.0 billion for the NBA, and 9% of $2.0 billion for the NHL. Indeed, in baseball and basketball, the size of the local market and the degree of competence demonstrated are much more highly correlated to the total amount of television, cable, and stadium-admission revenues that can be attracted than is the case in football. In the NBA and NHL, gate receipts are not shared with the visiting team; the home team takes 100%. In baseball, there is limited sharing of gate (ticket and concession) receipts, but not nearly to the extent of that in the NFL. Helyar (1995) notes that "The economic underpinning of the league has long been its generous revenue-sharing arrangements: equal sharing of network television money and a 60–40 home-visitor gate split." See also Waggoner (1982).

Major League Soccer (MLS), covered by Lubove (1995), uses a co-op organizational model in which approximately half of all revenues from ticket sales, local television, and sponsorships are shared equally among all teams. All national television rights and commercial tie-ins are also split evenly.

**13.**   Local broadcast/cable license fees, which have averaged 25% of a team's total revenues, may become proportionally more important as a source of income if national network payments grow less rapidly. The team income disparities that might then arise could put more pressure on baseball and basketball owners to share more of the locally generated revenues than they now do. In fact, large-market teams already take in far more from sale of local rights than do their small-market counterparts. For example, in 1990, the New York Yankees received $55.6 million from local broadcast revenues, while the Seattle Mariners took in only $3 million. Cable and pay TV revenues are split 75% home club, 25% visitors.

Of course, license fees from sales of network television rights, which *are* shared, remain significant. As of the mid-1980s, baseball franchises began splitting the income from network broadcasts, with each major league team deriving about $7 million annually (before other possible deductions) from this source. By 1990, this amount had doubled to $14 million per team. For historical perspective it might be noted that radio, television, and cable-rights fees paid to baseball's major league teams rose from a mere $44.5 million in 1975 to almost $268 million in 1984.

As for hockey, the NHL agreed (in 1994) to have a number of its games televised by Fox Sports and ESPN. In this five-year deal ending in the 1998 to 1999 season, the NHL was guaranteed to receive about $150 million in either advertising sales or rights fees. The 1999 NHL deal was for $600 million over five years. But after a 20% decline of ratings, ABC dropped hockey in 2004. See McCafferty (2004) for details on a proposed luxury tax and salary cap.

**14.**   NFL teams typically spend around 10% of game receipts for stadium rent. There is also a salary cap at 65% of revenues and, in 2004, $2.6 billion of television fees were evenly split by 32 teams.

**15.**   As of 1993, for instance, the NBA and the NBC network announced a new four-year $750 million rights deal. The parties here agreed to share advertising revenues once NBC reached a certain sales level (about $1.06 billion) over the four years. Annual payments were escalated in the first three years of the deal. A later NBA deal won by NBC/Turner was for $2.64 billion for four years. However, as Sandomir (2001a) notes, beginning with the 2002 season, power for the subsequent NBA contract shifted to cable, with ESPN and ABC Sports paying $1.6 billion for four years, and TNT, which is owned by Time Warner, paying from $800 million to $1 billion.

Under baseball's 1993 agreement, MLB would receive no rights fee for its games but instead would retain 87.5% of the revenues derived from the deal, with the ABC and NBC networks splitting the rest until the joint venture investment is recovered. After that, the split goes to 80:10:10. See *Broadcasting & Cable*, May 31, 1993.

Also, in 1995, MLB made a $1.7 billion contract to air games between 1996 and 2000 on a combination of Fox, NBC, ESPN, and the Fox Sports/Liberty cable networks. See *Daily Variety*, November 7, 1995.

In 1998, the NFL negotiated rights fees for the years 1998 to 2005 of $17.6 billion. The NFL's previous rights deals (in $ billions) were as follows: 1994 to 1997, $4.39; 1990 to 1993, $3.65; 1987 to 1989, $1.43; and 1982 to 1986, $2.07. For 2003 to 2007 the contract with DirecTV is for $2 billion as compared with that of 1998 to 2002, which was for $1 billion. On the next round of six-year contract extensions (for 2006 through 2011) at the end of 2004, the NFL then received $700 million a year from DirecTV for exclusive rights to out-of-market Sunday games, while Fox paid $713 million a year for National Football Conference Sunday games and CBS paid $621 million for American Football Conference contests. By April 2005, NBC had paid $600 million annually for Sunday night games and two Super Bowls, and ESPN had paid $1.1 billion for *Monday Night Football*. The combined CBS and Fox deals amount to $8 billion, an increase of more than 25%. See *Wall Street Journal*, April 19, 2005; *New York Times*, January 14, 1998; and Sandomir (1998, 2001b). At the end of 1993, the Fox network won the rights to four years of National Football Conference games with a bid of $1.58 billion. NBC also paid $880 million for other NFL games, including two Super Bowls, while ABC retained its package of Monday night games plus one Super Bowl for $950 million. Rights fees for regular network broadcasts for 1994 to 1997 thus totaled $3.41 billion. By way of comparison, the National Association for Stock Car Auto Racing's (NASCAR's) 1999 deal with Fox/NBC/TBS was for six years and $2.4 billion. On NASCAR, see O'Keefe and Schlosser (2005).

In 1990, CBS wrote off $115 million of its $1.06 billion baseball contract because of a World Series sweep and the effects of a spring lockout, and it wrote off $282 million more a year later. Fox, in 1995, took a $350 million write-off to reflect future losses on its $1.58 billion NFL contract and in February 2002 wrote down $909 million of contracts ($387 million NFL, $297 million NASCAR, and $225 million MLB). All this continues to suggest that the bidding for such rights has reached unsustainable levels.

**16.** As Bradsher (1994) notes, "The antitrust exemption – which no other major league sport shares – allows baseball owners to impose industry-wide salary limits, while remaining partially shielded from any lawsuits that the players may file. The exemption also allows a majority of the owners to block other owners who may want to move their franchises to new cities, and to reserve players' freedom to move up to a certain level of service." As of early 1997, the owners committed to negotiate a partial end to antitrust exemption.

**17.** The case of *Flood v Kuhn* served to advance some of the issues that ultimately led to free-agency, wherein veteran players became eligible free agents after six seasons, and those with three seasons of experience could seek arbitration. The original reserve system was secretly adopted in 1879 and first implemented by the National League in 1880. It was designed to minimize players' bargaining power and to prevent a few wealthy owners from destroying a league's competitive balance by buying all the best talent. See also Demmert (1973), who, from the perspective of the early 1970s, argues that competitive balance has generally not been attainable: The richest teams in the most lucrative markets, regardless of new-talent draft policies, have over the long term tended to field clubs with the highest overall athletic quality. McCartney (2004), however, explains how richer teams now subsidize the poorer through enhanced revenue-sharing that finances player salaries and is designed to make teams from small markets become competitive. Player contracts of briefer duration also permit greater circulation of free agents.

Prior to free-agency, baseball's so-called waiver rules had restricted the sale of a player's contract to a team outside the league, and an owner wishing to make such a sale had to first secure agreement from each team owner in the league to relinquish the right to purchase the player's contract at a fixed price. Union contracts still generally require a player testing free-agency to give his old club an opportunity to match a new team's offer. Teams losing valuable players may be entitled to receive some compensation. These issues are discussed in Miller (1991). Charges of collusion by MLB owners against players were settled in December 1990 at a total cost to the league of $280 million. See also note 19 and Korr (2002).

**18.**   Several times during the 1960s and 1970s, the NFL attempted to obtain immunity from the Sherman Antitrust Act of 1890, which declared "every contract, combination . . . or conspiracy in restraint of trade or commerce to be illegal." One of the key cases was *John Mackey et al. v National Football League*, which was filed in 1972 by the players' union to fight against the so-called Rozelle Rule. As Harris (1986, p. 71) notes, this rule, named after the league's commissioner, suggested that "any franchise whose contract with a player expired had the right to compensation from the player's new employer should that player subsequently work for another franchise. The compensation was to be a player of equal caliber, selected by the commissioner." The effect of this, Mackey argued, was to suppress player salaries by reducing competition between franchises. Mackey won the original case, but an appeals court decision in October 1976 said, in effect, that the labor issues should be settled by collective bargaining. Both sides agreed on a contract in February 1977. The Supreme Court's *Radovich* decision of 1957 established that the NFL's reserve clause, almost identical to baseball's, was in violation of the Sherman Act. Baseball was and still is the only sport exempt from antitrust laws. As of the early 2000s, the NFL is seen as having the most favorable and peaceful labor relations of any of the major pro sports leagues. In a contract lasting through 2007, NFL players had agreed to a cap on salaries but at the same time negotiated that about 65% to 70% of all shared revenues goes to players. Public-policy implications deriving from baseball's immunity to antitrust laws and the previously severe restrictions on the economic mobility of players enmeshed in the reserve system are extensively reviewed in Markham and Teplitz (1981). Note that in 1998 Congress lifted MLB's immunity with respect to collective bargaining. Leeds and von Allmen (2004, Chapter 4) contains a concise but thorough summary of sports antitrust history and issues.

**19.**   In the NBA, owners and players in 1988 settled on free-agency after four years' experience. In the NFL, a free-agency agreement for players with five years' experience and with expired contracts was reached in 1993. However, under the so-called Rooney Rule, the top clubs are not allowed to go into the free-agent market unless they have lost a free agent. Also, should salary costs reach 67% of designated NFL revenues, eligibility for free-agency drops to four years. See Scully (1995, pp. 37–40).

**20.**   As Abrams (2000, p. 39) shows, however, *median* salaries in baseball have not risen at nearly the rate of average salaries. Also, the effectiveness of free-agency was challenged in 1987 as team owners apparently stopped aggressively bidding against each other (i.e., colluded). See, for example, Spitz (1987) and Miller (1991). However, as evidenced by the enormous contract commitments made to players in each sport, competitive bidding had soon resumed, with the highest-paid athletes in 2000 being as follows:

| Sport | Player | Team | Total contract in $ millions | Number of years |
| --- | --- | --- | --- | --- |
| MLB | Alex Rodriguez | Rangers | $252.0 | 10 |
| NBA | Kevin Garnett | Timberwolves | 126.0 | 6 |
| NFL | Troy Aikman | Cowboys | 85.5 | 9 |
| NHL | Jaromir Jagr | Penguins | 48.0 | 6 |

*Source*: Chass (2000).

Still, as noted by Fatsis (2002a), bidding was again tempered by 2002 as a result of new restrictions on MLB team debt, a tax on top club payrolls that exceed $117 million, and a surge of expenses such as player insurance. As an offset and as noted in Morell (2003), teams have begun to test price elasticities of demand by charging higher prices for major matchups.

As shown in Table 12.3, there have been numerous strikes or threats of strikes and lockouts in professional sports. Baseball players went on strike in 1972 (13 days), 1981 (50 days), 1985 (2 days), and 1994 (34 days), and football players walked out in 1982 and 1987. Baseball team owners' lockouts occurred in 1976 and 1990 (during spring training). The NBA owners' lockout beginning in 1998 lasted 191 days. And hockey players struck for 10 days in the 1992 postseason playoffs, didn't work for half of the 1994 to 1995 season, and were locked out of the whole 2004 to 2005 season (La Pointe, 2005). In baseball, *final offer arbitration* (FOA) was a "concession" to the players in 1972 that arguably (Leeds and von Allmen [2004, p. 270]) may have had at least as large an effect on salaries as did movement toward free-agency.

The 1982 National Football League Players Association strike was based on an attempt to gear compensation to a fixed percentage of gross revenues and to create a salary scale based on seniority and performance. The players did not achieve their initial primary objective of sharing a percentage of gross revenues from network television and therefore did not significantly alter the balance of power of owners over athletes. But their collective salary pool totaling $1.6 billion over five years amounted to just under 50% of gross revenues, as compared with 35% to 44% before the strike. In addition, a modest salary scale was established as was the right to bargain for income above minimums that started at $30,000 per year for rookies and went up to $200,000 per year for veterans.

A Minneapolis jury reached an important decision in September 1992. In a suit challenging the NFL's system of limited free-agency, the jury ruled that the NFL's Plan B free-agency system (introduced in 1989) violated the federal antitrust laws. Still, professional baseball and basketball, as of 1992, had more liberal free-agency than football. See, for example, *New York Times*, September 12, 1992. The outcome in football, however, is similar to the situation in the 1981 Major League Baseball Players Association strike, in which the primary issue was compensation to clubs losing players through free-agency transfers. The complicated settlement delineates rules for player rankings and performances under which such transfers are conducted.

The Basketball Players Association in the NBA and the National Hockey League Players Association negotiated with team owners on issues similar to those in football and baseball. But a new revenue-sharing agreement was developed in the NBA in 1983. The agreement was designed to prevent richer franchises from dominating the game, to create more consistent competition between teams, and to stop cost escalation caused by free-agency. Beginning in the 1984 to 1985 season, the NBA guaranteed players 53% of the league's gross revenue, which included money from rapidly growing sales of regional pay cable rights. The 53% was distributed among 23 teams, with a "cap" for the richest teams and a "floating minimum" for the poorest. See "The NBA's Ingenious Move to Cap Players' Salaries," *BusinessWeek*, October 31, 1983, and Barra (1995), who illustrates how the NFL's 49ers were able to circumvent salary caps.

Reluctant MLB owners also approved an agreement with the players in November 1996 that applied for at least five years beginning in 1996. The agreement called for a "luxury" tax of 35% to be put on the proportion of 1997 payroll over $51 million, and it forced the 13 clubs with the highest revenues to contribute to a pool to be divided by the 13 teams with the lowest revenues. See *New York Times*, November 27, 1996. Also, in the MLB contract agreement of 2002, teams place 34% of their net local revenue in a pool and divide it equally among all teams. Additional money is taken from baseball's central fund and distributed to the bottom tier of teams as ranked by revenues. See *New York Times*, August 31, 2002; Staudohar (2002); and Fatsis (2006b).

**21.**   Until a 1995 landmark ruling in the European Court of Justice broke the cartel arrangements, teams could field only three nonlocal players. European Union players, however, are now no longer counted as foreigners; at the end of a contract, a player becomes a free agent. Soccer clubs used to be able to block player trades or insist on big fees for allowing them. In the United States, MLS is the professional organization that now controls the sport. The North American Soccer League (1967 to 1985) was its predecessor. Since its founding in 1996 through 2004 the league has lost an estimated $350 million. See also Lubove (1995), Freedman (2004), Gage (2005), and *BusinessWeek*, September 23, 1996; *BusinessWeek*, March 23, 1998; "Can Soccer Be Saved?," *BusinessWeek*, July 19, 2004; and *Business-Week*, November 22, 2004, which describes how owners share equally in losses and the league controls player allocation to the teams. Fatsis (2006a) provides a recent overview.

**22.**   In recent years, tax-law revisions and court interpretations have made this an exceedingly complicated subject, the discussion of which lies largely beyond the scope of this book. More detail is presented in Horvitz and Hoffman (1976), Raabe (1977), Ambrose (1981), and Harmelink and Vignes (1981).

**23.**   Other IRS rulings further indicated that the "option clause" in football-player contracts would be regarded as similar to baseball's "reserve clause," that television revenue did not constitute "passive investment income" (and would therefore not adversely affect election of subchapter S treatments), and that franchise proceeds received in return for relinquishment of exclusive territorial rights would be granted favorable capital-gains treatment.

In 1974, two additional regulations concerning amortization of intangibles and the distinction between nonamortizable goodwill and amortizable intangibles also helped set the stage for employing sports-franchise ownership as a tax shelter.

**24.**   Important cases included *Laird v United States*; *First Northwest Industries of America, Inc., Houston Chronicle Publishing Co. v United States*; and *KFOX Inc. v United States*. However, tax deductibility of intangible asset amortizations would now, in most instances, follow the 1993 tax code revisions, which provide a write-down period of 15 years for so-called Section 197 intangible assets. Professional sports franchises, however, are specifically excluded from this category. See also Smith and Parr (1994).

Scully (1995, p. 137) notes that sports team owners, unlike those holding franchises in other industries, cannot amortize the goodwill of the business. Also, "broadcast rights (*Laird; McCarthy v. United States* [1986]), exclusive territorial rights, and parking and concessions are considered part of the franchise value and are not depreciable." This implies that, as the value of broadcast rights rises, the depreciable component of the franchise price at the time of sale declines.

**25.**   See Wilson (2004) for a full explanation of positive impact on franchise values.

**26.**   Professional team valuations as of 1991 appear in Baldo (1991). Roughly, the multiples are 2.5 times revenues for football and basketball teams, 2 times revenues for baseball, and 1.8 times revenues for hockey. Baseball's multiple is lower than football's because the revenue stream, more dependent on gate receipts, is less predictable. Hockey's multiple is even lower because hockey, without a national TV contract, is most dependent on gate receipts. The most valuable team in this study was the New York Yankees, estimated at that time to be worth $225 million. The average NFL team was estimated to be worth $132 million, while the average MLB team was worth $121 million and teams in the NBA and NHL were worth $70 million and $44 million, respectively. This study had been extended in

Ozanian and Taub (1992, 1993) and now appears annually in *Forbes* magazine surveys, e.g., Burke (2006). Sports franchise valuation using discounted cash flow methods is illustrated in Damodaran (1996, pp. 488–493). Major recent transactions are shown in Table 12.5, with additional details in note 24, Chapter 12, of the previous edition (6th) of this book. See also Sandomir (1999).

**27.** Baade (1994) analyzed 48 U.S. cities between 1958 and 1987, including cities that hosted professional teams, and found that professional sports stadiums and teams generally have no significant impact on a region's economic growth: "...sports spending simply substitutes for other forms of leisure spending." See also Forsyth (1995), Coates and Humphreys (2000), Siegfried and Zimbalist (2000), Frangos (2004), *BusinessWeek*, November 20, 2000, and *New York Times*, January 10, 2002.

**28.** For example, see Wayne (1996) and Laing (1996), who notes that, in the 1990s, 30 professional sports facilities have been built in the United States at a total cost of $4 billion.

**29.** A cartel is characterized by its ability to

- Prevent new competitors from entering the market and to integrate new competitors into the cartel
- Produce outputs that are substitutes for the outputs produced by other firms (i.e., are homogeneous)
- Divide the market into territories controlled by members and establish production quotas
- Enforce structural rules and defeat incentives to "cheat"

**30.** This is also more recently explored in Quirk and Fort (1992) and in Scully (1989).

**31.** Another early inquiry by Noll (1974) concerned demand for sports contests. Among the factors that, a priori, can be expected to influence demand are ratios of skillful to unskillful players, a winning as opposed to a losing home team, population size and characteristics of the city in which a game is played, amount of competing entertainment available, and ticket prices (e.g., average price per seat). Noll's regression results for baseball attendance in the 1970 and 1971 seasons, for example, indicated that

(a) A negative correlation between attendance and income gives the impression that baseball is a working-class sport.
(b) There is a strong positive effect on attendance from winning a pennant.
(c) The drawing power of baseball is substantially enhanced if a team has star players.
(d) The demand for baseball appears relatively price-inelastic, which means that teams could raise ticket prices without significant loss of paid attendance.

**32.** Fort (2005, p. 348) considers Rottenberg the father of sports economics.

**33.** Neale (1964, p. 3) also notes that a season of games is a "peculiar mixture: it comes in divisible parts, each of which can be sold separately, but it is also a joint and multiple yet divisible product." This also appears in Leeds and von Allmen (2004, p. 105).

**34.** Typical measures of competitive balance are expressed in terms of standard deviations and the Herfindahl–Hirschman Index discussed in Chapter 1, note 26. Standard deviations are based on the mean number of wins for, say, a league division, which can then be compared to standard deviations of other divisions, that of the whole league, or that of other leagues. The mean for the average winning percentage of all teams in a league or division in any year is 0.500, so that the standard deviation is found by squaring all the team win percentages minus 0.500, dividing by N, the number of teams, and then taking the square root of the entire result. As Leeds and von Allmen (2004, Chapter 5) further explain, two additional ways to measure competitive balance also include calculations of what are known in statistics as Lorenz curves and Markov chains.

**35.** Named after Nobel Laureate winner Ronald Coase.

**36.** As Demmert (1973, p. 96) has noted, "institutional restrictions on the economic mobility of professional athletes … serve as a rent transfer mechanism, assuring the economic viability of the league at the expense of the players." And as Scully (1989, p. 191) has noted, "equalization of playing strengths within a league occurs only through the equalization of revenue among the clubs, or, lacking that development, through a system of player reservation, reverse order drafting, and a ban on the cash sale of player contracts."

**37.** Comprehensive surveys and updates of the literature appear in Dobson and Goddard (2002) and in Downward and Dawson (2000).

**38.** The quote is attributable to Helyar (2003).

**39.** Despite this, publicly traded shares of professional sports teams have generally not proven to be good investments because opportunities to expand are usually minimal and there is considerable upward pressure on wages, frequent labor strife, and dependence on the performance of a few key employees. Shares of the Boston Celtics and the Florida Panthers had been publicly traded, as were the Cleveland Cavaliers, the Milwaukee Bucks, the New England Patriots, and the Baltimore Orioles in the 1970s. The Cleveland Indians were briefly public in the late 1990s. As of 2006, the NFL has barred corporate ownerships, but in MLB the Tribune Co. owns the Chicago Cubs, Rogers Communications owns the Toronto Blue Jays, and Nintendo owns the Seattle Mariners.

## Selected additional reading

Abrams, B. (1984). "How Networks Vied in Grueling Bidding for '88 Winter Games," *Wall Street Journal*, February 22.

Abrams, R. I. (2000). *The Money Pitch: Baseball Free Agency and Salary Arbitration*. Philadelphia: Temple University Press.

Alster, N. (1991). "Major League Socialism," *Forbes*, 147(11)(May 27).

(1990). "Hoops Go Global," *Forbes*, 146(8)(October 15).

"A Survey of Football (Soccer)," *The Economist*, June 1, 2002.

Badenhausen, K. (2004). "LeBron James: The NBA's $2 Billion Man," *Forbes*, 173(3) (February 16).

Badenhausen, K., and Kump, L. (2001). "Cashing In," *Forbes*, 168(7)(September 17).

Badenhausen, K., and Sicheri, W. (1999). "Baseball Games," *Forbes*, 163(11)(May 31).

"Baseball Strike Issues," *New York Times*, August 1, 1981.

Bates, J. (2002). "The Dodgers' Team Color Is Now a Deep Shade of Red," *Los Angeles Times*, August 19.

Behar, R. (1987). "Spreading the Wealth," *Forbes*, 140(3)(August 10).

Blustein, P. (1983). "Are Baltimore Orioles Best Team in Baseball, or Just the Best Run?," *Wall Street Journal*, October 5.

Bulkeley, W. M. (1985). "Sports Agents Help Athletes Win – And Keep Those Super Salaries," *Wall Street Journal*, March 25.

Burck, C. G. (1977). "Why the Sports Business Ain't What It Used to Be," *Fortune*, XCV(5)(May).

Byrne, J. (1986). *The $1 League: The Rise and Fall of the USFL*. New York: Prentice-Hall.

Chass, M. (2002). "Baseball Negotiators Shift Their Sights to Next Off-Season," *New York Times*, March 27.

(2001). "Back to Business: Baseball Votes to Drop 2 Teams," *New York Times*, November 7.

(1996). "Reluctant Baseball Owners Approve Pact with Players," *New York Times*, November 27.

(1988). "7 in Baseball Collusion Case Win Free Agency," *New York Times*, January 23.

(1985). "Baseball Strike Is Settled; Games to Resume Today," *New York Times*, August 8.

Comte, E., and Chakravarty, S. N. (1993). "How High Can David Stern Jump?," *Forbes*, 151(12)(June 7).

Crist, S. (1998). "All Bets Are Off," *Sports Illustrated*, January 26.

El-Bashir, T. (1999). "NHL Seeks Aid to Keep Canada's Sport in Canada," *New York Times*, September 25.

Euchner, C. C. (1993). *Playing the Field*. Baltimore: Johns Hopkins University Press.

Fabrikant, G. (1999). "Remote Control of Cable Sports," *New York Times*, April 1.

Fatsis, S. (2004). "It's Time for Money, Uh, March Madness," *Wall Street Journal*, March 15.

(2003a). "Sports Teams for Sale," *Wall Street Journal*, February 13.

(2003b). "NBC Sports Maps a Future without the Big Leagues," *Wall Street Journal*, January 31.

(2003c). "What Price Touchdowns?," *New York Times*, January 3.

Fatsis, S., and Flint, J. (2001). "How the XFL Became One of the Biggest Flops in Television History," *Wall Street Journal*, April 23.

Fatsis, S., and Orwall, B. (2002). "For Disney, Owning Teams Conflicts with Bottom Line," *Wall Street Journal*, August 29.

Ferguson, D. G., Stewart, K. G., Jones, J. C. H., and Le Dressay, A. (1991). "The Pricing of Sports Events: Do Teams Maximize Profit?" *Journal of Industrial Economics*, 3(March).

Fishof, D., and Shapiro, E. (1983). *Putting It on the Line: The Negotiating Secrets, Tactics & Techniques of a Top Sports and Entertainment Agent*. New York: William Morrow.

Fort, R. D. (2006). *Sports Economics,* 2nd ed. Upper Saddle River, NJ: Prentice-Hall.

Friedman, R. (1985a). "They Get Little Ink. But 15 Other People Also Own Yankees," *Wall Street Journal*, April 16.

(1985b). "Playing Basketball in the Minors Offers Only Minor Rewards," *Wall Street Journal*, February 26.

(1984). "Holmes-Coetzee Bout, a Promoter's Dream, Becomes a Nightmare," *Wall Street Journal*, May 22.

Galarza, P. (1995). "The Mighty Bucks: Companies Are Learning How to Make Money with the Sports Teams They Own," *Financial World*, 164(25)(December 5).

Goff, B. L., and Tollison, R. D., eds. (1990). *Sportometrics*. College Station, TX: Texas A & M University Press.

Gorman, J., and Calhoun, K. (with Rozin, S.). (1994). *The Name of the Game: The Business of Sports*. New York: Wiley.

Gorn, E. J., and Goldstein, W. (1993). *A Brief History of American Sports*. New York: Farrar, Straus & Giroux (Hill and Wang).

Grant, P. (2003). "Yankees' Push for TV Profits Sparks Clash of Heavy Hitters," *Wall Street Journal*, June 12.

Gratton, C. and Solberg, H. A. (2006). *The Economics of Sports Broadcasting*. New York: Routledge.

Gunther, M. (1997). "They All Want to Be Like Mike," *Fortune*, 136(2)(July 21).

Hamburger, T., and Binkley, C. (2001). "Bid to Outlaw Betting on College Sports Faces Very Long Odds," *Wall Street Journal*, April 3.

Harris, D. (1986). "New Troubles in the N.F.L.," *New York Times Magazine*, September 7.

Hart-Nibbrig, N., and Cottingham, C. (1986). *The Political Economy of College Sports*. Lexington, MA: Heath.

Harwood, S. J. (1983). "Valuation of Player Contracts When Acquiring a Professional Baseball Team – An Analysis of Selig v. United States," *Taxes*, 61(10).

Hausman, J. A., and Leonard, G. K. (1997). "Superstars in the National Basketball Association: Economic Value and Policy," *Journal of Labor Economics*, 15(4).

Helyar, J. (2001). "A Team of Their Own," *Fortune*, 143(10)(May 14).

(1997). "Free Agency Proves to Be the Cat's Meow for Jags and Panthers," *Wall Street Journal*, January 10.

(1996a). "How Atlanta Went from Baseball Clowns to Kings of Diamond," *Wall Street Journal*, October 1.

(1996b). "A City's Self-Image Confronts Tax Revolt in Battle on Stadiums," *Wall Street Journal*, March 19.

(1995a). "How Nashville Seeks, at High Cost, to Win Oilers from Houston," *Wall Street Journal*, November 21.

(1995b). "Baseball Players' Agent Offers Bargains on Stars in a Buyer's Market," *Wall Street Journal*, April 14.

(1994a). "Canadian Clubs Appear to Skate on Thin Ice amid Hockey Lockout," *Wall Street Journal*, November 15.

(1994b). "How Fear and Loathing in Baseball Standoff Wrecked the Season," *Wall Street Journal*, September 15.

(1994c). "NFL Story: New Man Takes Over the Eagles That Laid Golden Eggs," *Wall Street Journal*, August 18.

(1994d). "Baseball's Journeymen Face a New Challenge: The Low-Ball Salary," *Wall Street Journal*, April 4.

(1994e). "The Inflated Riches of NBA Are Pulling at the League's Seams," *Wall Street Journal*, February 11.

(1991a). "How Peter Ueberroth Led the Major Leagues in the 'Collusion Era,'" *Wall Street Journal*, May 20.

(1991b). "Play Ball! The Price Fans Pay Is Going, Going, Gone Up," *Wall Street Journal*, April 8.

(1991c). "Game? What Game? Arenas Emphasize Ambiance and Amenities to Entice Fans," *Wall Street Journal*, March 20.

(1990a). "Baseball's Expansion Is a High-Stakes Game of Money and Politics," *Wall Street Journal*, December 21.

(1990b). "Lure of TV Loot Loosens Old College Ties," *Wall Street Journal*, November 14.

(1984a). "Green Bay Packers Are Threatened by Football's Changing Economics," *Wall Street Journal*, December 14.

(1984b). "More Cities Plan Domed Stadiums, but Returns May Prove to Be Small," *Wall Street Journal*, May 17.

Hofmeister, S. (2002). "Baseball Owners, Players Balk at a Level Playing Field," *Los Angeles Times*, August 16.

Jennings, K. M. (1990). *Balls & Strikes: The Money Game in Professional Baseball*. New York: Praeger.

Johnson, R. S. (1999a). "How One College Program Runs the Business: Inside Longhorn Inc.," *Fortune*, 140(12)(December 20).

(1999b). "Speed," *Fortune*, 139(7)(April 12).

(1998). "The Jordan Effect," *Fortune*, 137(12)(June 22).

(1997a). "Take Me Out to the Boardroom," *Fortune*, 136(2)(July 21).

(1997b). "Tiger! Now the Sky's the Limit for Golf – the Game and the Business," *Fortune*, 135(9)(May 12).

Jordan, P. (1994). "Buddy's Boys and Their $100 Million Toys," *New York Times*, September 18.

Kirkpatrick, D. D., and Fabrikant, G. (2003). "A Cable Network of Their Own," *New York Times*, November 2.

Klatell, D. A., and Marcus, N. (1988). *Sports for Sale: Television, Money, and the Fans*. New York: Oxford University Press.

Klein, F. C. (1985). "Sports Teams Are Losing Their Bet That Fans Will Pay for TV Events," *Wall Street Journal*, February 19.

Krise, S. A. (1975). "Certain Tax Implications of Professional Sports," *CPA Journal*, April.

La Franco, R. (1997). "Profits on Ice," *Forbes*, 159(9)(May 5).

Laing, J. R. (2003). "Golf Glut," *Barron's*, July 26.

Lancaster, H. (1988). "Baseball Owners Found in Collusion in Free-Agent Case," *Wall Street Journal*, September 1.

(1987). "Timeout: Despite Success of Celtics Sale, Doubts Remain about Sports Offerings," *Wall Street Journal*, May 8.

(1985). "USFL Facing a Fourth-and-Long as It Staggers into Third Season," *Wall Street Journal*, February 26.

Lane, R. (1995). "Pugilism's Lopsided Economics," *Forbes*, 156(14)(December 18).

Leifer, E. (1996). *Making the Majors: The Transformation of Team Sports in America*. Cambridge, MA: Harvard.

Leonhardt, D. (2001). "How to Re-energize Baseball and Win New Fans," *New York Times*, August 12.

Lewis, M. (2003). "The Trading Desk," *New York Times,* March 30, and *Moneyball: The Art of Winning an Unfair Game*. New York: W. W. Norton & Co.

Linden, D. W. (1991). "Bases Loaded, Nobody Out," *Forbes*, 147(7)(April 1).

Lineberry, W. P., ed. (1973). *The Business of Sports*. New York: H. W. Wilson.

Lueck, T. J. (1987). "Baseball Entrepreneurs Score in Bush Leagues," *New York Times*, August 24.

MacCambridge, M. (2004). *America's Game: The Epic Story of How Pro Football Captured a Nation*. New York: Random House.

Mallios, W. S. (2000). *The Analysis of Sports Forecasting: Modeling Parallels between Sports Gambling and Financial Markets*. Dordrecht, The Netherlands, and Norwell, MA: Kluwer Academic Publishers.

McCartney, S. (2000). "Why a Baseball Superstar's Megacontract Can Be Less Than It Seems," *Wall Street Journal,* December 27.

Merwin, J. (1984). "It's Show Time," *Forbes*, 133(4)(February 13).

(1983). "Big League Baseball's New Cash Lineup," *Forbes*, 131(7)(March 28).

(1982). "The Most Valuable Executive in Either League," *Forbes*, 129(8)(April 12).

Miller, J. E. (1990). *The Baseball Business: Pursuing Pennants and Profits in Baltimore*. Chapel Hill, NC: University of North Carolina Press.

Moore, T. (1986). "It's 4th & 10 – The NFL Needs the Long Bomb," *Fortune*, 114(3)(August 4).

(1985). "Baseball's New Game Plan," *Fortune*, 111(8)(April 15).

Moores, J. (2002). "Damn Yankees," *Wall Street Journal*, May 14.

(1999). "Bring Competition Back to Baseball," *Wall Street Journal*, April 5.

Morgenson, G. (1992). "Where the Fans Still Come First," *Forbes*, 149(10)(April 27).

Nocera, J., and Useem, J. (2004). "How the Curse Was *Really* Reversed," *Fortune*, 150(10)(November 15).

Noll, R. G. (1999). "The Business of College Sports," *Milken Institute Review*, Third Quarter.

Noll, R. G., and Zimbalist, A., eds. (1997). *Sports, Jobs & Taxes: The Economic Impact of Sports Teams and Stadiums*. Washington, DC: Brookings Institution Press.

Norton, E. (1993). "Football at Any Cost: One City's Mad Chase for an NFL Franchise," *Wall Street Journal*, October 13.

Ozanian, M. K. (2004). "Ice Capades," *Forbes*, 174(11)(November 29).

(2000). "Too Much to Lose," *Forbes*, 165(14)(June 12).

(1998). "Selective Accounting," *Forbes*, 162(13)(December 14).

(1997). "Fields of Debt," *Forbes*, 160(13)(December 15).

Phillips, M. M. (1997). "Top Sports Pros Find a New Way to Score: Getting Equity Stakes," *Wall Street Journal*, April 18.

Postrel, V. (2002). "Strategies on Fourth Down, from a Mathematical Point of View," *New York Times*, September 12.

"Professor Hardball," *BusinessWeek*, no. 3098, April 3, 1989.

Pulley, B. (2006). "The King and His Sport, at Twilight," *Forbes*, 177(9)(April 24).

(2004). "The $1 Billion Football Team," *Forbes*, 174(5)(September 20).

Queenan, J. (1991). "Squeeze Play: Plutocrat Players, Balky Payers May End Baseball's Big Boom," *Barron's*, April 29.

Rader, B. G. (1984). *In Its Own Image: How Television Has Transformed Sports*. New York: The Free Press.

Rhoden, W. C. (1999). "A Lockout, Not Love-In for Players," *New York Times*, January 7.

Robichaux, M. (1990). "If Baseball Hurls Shutout, Many Will Be Losers," *Wall Street Journal*, January 23.

(1989). "Dallas Cowboys Face Financial Predicament Spreading in the NFL," *Wall Street Journal*, October 23.

Robinson, E. (1997). "It's Where You Play That Counts," *Fortune*, 136(2)(July 21).

Rosen, S. (1981). "Economics of Superstars," *American Economic Review*, 71(5)(December).

Rosentraub, M. S. (1997). *Major League Losers*. New York: Basic Books.

Roth, D. (2000). "The NBA's Next Shot," *Fortune*, 141(4)(February 21).

Rottenberg, S. (1956). "The Baseball Players' Labor Market," *Journal of Political Economy*, 64(June).

Sandomir, R. (1996). "America's Small-Town Team," *New York Times*, January 13.

Saporito, B. (1991). "The Owners' New Game Is Managing," *Fortune*, 124(1)(July 1).

(1987). "The Life of a $725,000 Scab," *Fortune*, 116(9)(October 26).

Schaaf, P. (2004). *Sports, Inc.: 100 Years of Sports Business*. Amherst, NY: Prometheus Books.

Sharp, A. M., Register, C. A., and Grimes, P. W., (1999). "The Economics of Professional Sports," in *Economics of Social Issues*, 14th ed. Burr Ridge, IL: Irwin.

Shropshire, K. L. (1995). *The Sports Franchise Game*. Philadelphia: University of Pennsylvania Press.

(1990). *Agents of Opportunity: Sports Agents and Corruption in Collegiate Sports*. Philadelphia: University of Pennsylvania Press.

Shropshire, K. L., and Davis, T. (2002). *The Business of Sports Agents*. Philadelphia: University of Pennsylvania Press.

Sims, C. (1993) "It's Not Just How Well You Play the Game . . . ," *New York Times*, January 31.

Smith, T. K. (1992). "Players Charge NFL with Trying End Run on Disability Benefits," *Wall Street Journal*, December 7.

Smith, T. K., and Norton, E. (1993). "One Baseball Statistic Remains a Mystery: The Real Bottom Line," *Wall Street Journal*, April 2.

Spiers, J. (1996). "Are Pro Sports Teams Worth It?," *Fortune*, 133(1)(January 15).

Staudohar, P. D. (2005). "The Hockey Lockout of 2004–05," *Monthly Labor Review* (December), U.S. Department of Labor.

(2002). "Baseball Negotiations: A New Agreement," *Monthly Labor Review* (December), U.S. Department of Labor.

(1999). "Labor Relations in Basketball: The Lockout of 1998–99," *Monthly Labor Review* (April), U.S. Department of Labor.

(1997). "The Baseball Strike of 1994–95," *Monthly Labor Review* (March), U.S. Department of Labor.

(1996). *Playing for Dollars: Labor Relations and the Sports Business*. Ithaca, NY: Cornell University Press.

(1990). "The Baseball Strike of 1990," *Monthly Labor Review*, 113(10)(October), U.S. Department of Labor.

(1988). "The Football Strike of 1987: The Question of Free Agency," *Monthly Labor Review* (August), U.S. Department of Labor.

Stevenson, R. (1990). "Pony Up $95 Million? Sure, for a Baseball Team." *New York Times*, September 23.

Stewart, B. (2007). *Sport Finance and Finding*. Oxford, UK: Elsevier.

Sullivan, N. J. (1992). *The Diamond Revolution: The Prospects for Baseball after the Collapse of Its Ruling Class*. New York: St. Martin's.

Symonds, W. C. (2004). "Breaking the Curse," *BusinessWeek*, no. 3880 (April 26).

Tagliabue, J. (2000). "Hoop Dreams, Fiscal Realities," *New York Times*, March 4.

Thurow, R. (1997). "Women's NBA Pins Hopes on Clean Play and Hard Marketing," *Wall Street Journal*, June 12.

Thurow, R., and Helyar, J. (1995). "Jerry Jones Thinks NFL Revenue Sharing Is a Bit Socialistic," *Wall Street Journal*, September 28.

Vardi, N. (2004). "Hardball," *Forbes*, 173(9)(April 26).

Walker, S. (2002). "How *Not* to Fix Baseball," *Wall Street Journal*, August 23.

(1999a). "Full Count and Empty Seats," *Wall Street Journal*, October 12.

(1999b). "Why Softer Ratings Could Mean the NFL Is Fumbling Away Its Fun," *Wall Street Journal*, January 29.

Weber, B. (1986). "The Man Who Built the Mets," *New York Times Magazine*, August 3.

Wermiel, S. (1984). "NCAA Pacts to Televise College Football Violate Antitrust Law, High Court Rules," *Wall Street Journal*, June 28.

White, G. E. (1996). *Creating the National Pastime: Baseball Transforms Itself, 1903–1953*. Princeton, NJ: Princeton University Press.

"Who Says Baseball Is Like Ballet?," *Forbes*, 107(7)(April 1, 1971).

Wise, M. (1999). "With Little Time on Clock, N.B.A. and Players Settle," *New York Times*, January 7.

Wise, M., and Roberts, S. (1999). "N.B.A., Once a Dream Team, Is Torn by Fight for Control," *New York Times*, January 10.

Zimbalist, A. (2001). "Competitive Balance in Major League Baseball," *Milken Institute Review*, First Quarter.

(1999). *Unpaid Professionals: Commercialism and Conflict in Big-Time College Sports.* Princeton, NJ: Princeton University Press.

# 13
# Performing arts and culture

The performing arts traditionally generate more psychic than pecuniary income, and they operate under somewhat different economic assumptions than the other entertainment industries thus far discussed. In fact, many organizations in this segment are nonprofit, requiring for their very existence substantial subsidization from government and private-foundation grants and from contributions by individuals.

Although the fundamental creative processes in the performing arts have remained essentially unchanged for centuries, technological developments have been important in mitigating the pernicious effects of inexorably rising costs. Fortunately, it still doesn't cost anything to wish performers well by telling them to "break a leg."

## 13.1 Audiences and offerings

The potential widespread appeals of live performances notwithstanding, there are severe time and financial constraints that limit audience size and scope. This was already apparent even as far back as the eighteenth century, when a theater ticket cost more than a full day's wage. As Baumol and Bowen

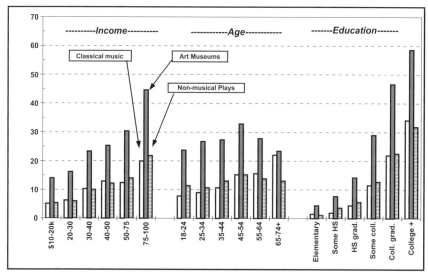

Figure 13.1. Characteristics of the culture audience by income distribution, educational attainment, and age in selected performance categories. Bars show the percentage of survey respondents participating. *Source*: U.S. NEA survey (2002).

(1968) indicated in their seminal study, the audience for high culture is dominated by highly educated individuals in high-income brackets, which is an observation supported by the more recent data presented in Figure 13.1.

Although education appears to have a somewhat stronger effect than income, another hypothesis as to why the audience for live performances seems to become ever more exclusive was offered by Linder (1970), who noted that as economic growth increases our incomes and the available array of consumption goods, there is a tendency toward more "goods intensity" at the expense of time spent on cultural activities. Time to consume goods does not increase commensurately with the number of goods available. Attendance at live performances, of course, normally requires a relatively large allocation of time and often entails substantial expenditures on tickets and on incidentals (Figure 13.2).

Trends in demand for the major performing arts categories may be inferred from the selected data of Table 13.1, and a timeline representation of significant events is presented in Figure 13.3.

## Commercial theater

*On and off Broadway* Professional drama became an important entertainment medium during colonial times, although it was not until the nineteenth century that theater organized into a stock system of local resident companies permanently engaged at a particular location. However, not long thereafter,

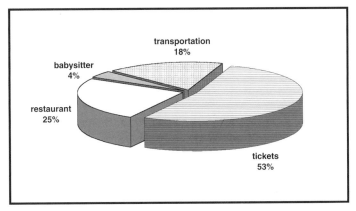

Figure 13.2. Cost of going out: ticket expense and associated costs of attendance at live performances for New York City (percentage distribution of total expenses by type). *Source*: William J. Baumol and William G. Bowen, *Performing Arts: The Economic Dilemma*. A Twentieth Century Fund Study, ©1966, Twentieth Century Fund, New York.

accomplished performers began to form touring companies, which, by the late 1800s, had mostly replaced resident stock companies.

By the early 1900s, syndicates owning chains of theaters and controlling bookings and fees had become dominant. The famous Shubert chain, for example, was formed in this period. But this was largely a transition phase as commercial theater further evolved into the current structure wherein producers select a play, raise funds, and hire a director and cast, while theater owners generally handle box-office personnel and stagehands, advertising and sales functions, and sometimes musicians. As Poggi (1968, p. xv) has noted:

Like so many of our social and economic institutions, the commercial theater has become highly centralized . . . At the beginning of the century there were usually 250 to 300 productions touring the country at the height of each season; now there are about 20. In the late 1920s there were usually more than 250 productions opening on Broadway in a single season; now there would seldom be more than 60.

Still, however, it is Broadway – essentially the theater district in New York City – that attracts a significant portion of commercial theater receipts in the United States, that defines an industry, and that is of greatest historical significance.[1] Broadway attendance (an estimated 45% to 50% coming from tourists) and ticket-price trends are illustrated in Figure 13.4a, from which it can be seen that the number of tickets sold (demand) only recently rose above the peak of the 1970s.[2] The lines in Figure 13.4b representing the number of play-weeks (plays times weeks of run) in each season meanwhile provide an approximation of the supply of performances available.

In addition, it can be seen from Figure 13.4c that gross receipts from commercial theater presentations on the road have at times overshadowed gross

Table 13.1. *Selected data for U.S. legitimate theater, opera companies, and symphony orchestras, 1980–2005 (receipts and expenditures in millions of dollars; for season ending in year shown, except as indicated)*

| Item | 1980 | 1990 | 2000 | 2005 |
|---|---|---|---|---|
| *Legitimate theater[a]* | | | | |
| Broadway shows | | | | |
|   New productions | 67 | 35 | 37 | 29 |
|   Playing weeks[b,c] | 1,541 | 1,070 | 1,484 | 1,500 |
|   Number of tickets sold (thousands) | 9,380 | 8,039 | 11,938 | 12,003 |
|   Gross box-office receipts | 143 | 283 | 666 | 862 |
| Road shows | | | | |
|   Playing weeks[c] | 1,351 | 944 | 964 | 597 |
|   Gross box-office receipts | 181 | 367 | 616 | 532 |
| *Opera companies[d]* | | | | |
| Number of companies | 79 | 98 | 98 | 108 |
|   Expenses[e] | 122.4 | 321.2 | 636.7 | 795.4 |
| Performances[f] | 1,312 | 2,336 | 2,153 | 2,100 |
| Total attendance (millions)[g,h] | 5.5 | 7.5 | 6.7 | (NA) |
| Main season attendance (millions)[f,h] | (NA)[j] | 4.1 | 4.3 | 3.6 |
| *Symphony orchestras[i]* | | | | |
| Concerts | (NA) | 18,931 | 33,154 | 37,196 |
| Attendance (millions) | (NA) | 24.7 | 31.7 | 26.5 |
| Gross revenue | (NA) | 377.5 | 734.0 | 1,437.3 |

[a] *Source*: *Variety*, New York, NY, various June issues, copyright.
[b] All shows (new productions and holdovers from previous seasons).
[c] Eight performances constitute one playing week.
[d] *Source*: OPERA America, Washington, DC.
[e] U.S. companies.
[f] Prior to 1993, U.S. and Canadian companies; beginning 1993, U.S. companies only.
[g] Includes educational performances, outreach, etc.
[h] For paid performances.
[i] *Source*: American Symphony Orchestra League, Inc., Washington, DC. For years ending Aug. 31. Data represent all U.S. orchestras, excluding college/university and youth orchestras.
[j] NA = not available.

receipts on Broadway. This shift in economic balance has also led to the development of publicly owned companies that specialize in the production and staging of off-Broadway performances. As shown in Table 13.2, returns on investment in a major musical production can be relatively high and long-lasting even in comparison with potential returns on popular films.[3] Table 13.3 presents Broadway's top ten longest running shows.

In recent years, musical reproductions (touring versions of current or recent Broadway hits) or restorations (adaptations of past Broadway hits) have

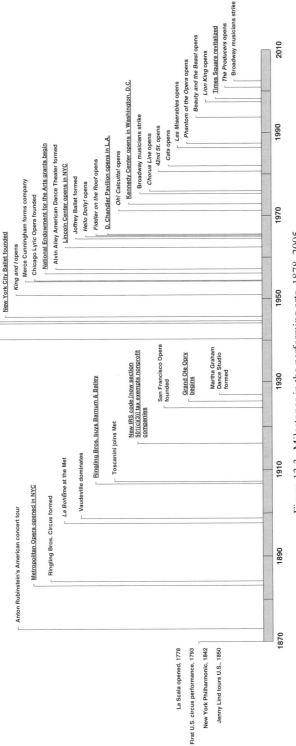

Figure 13.3. Milestones in the performing arts, 1878–2005.

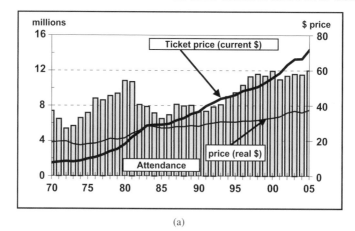

(a)

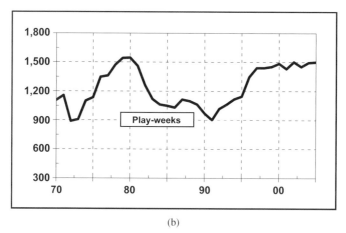

(b)

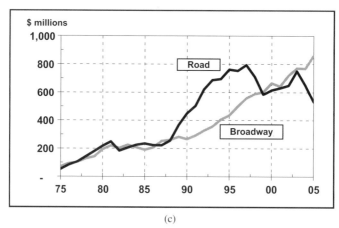

(c)

Figure 13.4. Broadway theater trends: (a) prices and ticket sales, (b) play-weeks, and
(c) gross sales on Broadway versus the road, 1970–2005 seasons. *Source data*: *Variety* and
League of American Theatres and Producers.

Table 13.2. *Characteristics of a major hit musical versus a major hit movie*

|  | **Musical:** *Phantom of the Opera* | **Motion picture:** *Jurassic Park* |
|---|---|---|
| Global box office | $2 billion | $913 million |
| Average production & premarketing cost | $9 million | $70 million |
| Length of run | 10+ years | 20 weeks |

accounted for more than 80% of total commercial theater ticket sales. And many successful Broadway shows have also set up for long runs in Las Vegas – thereby significantly changing the economics of Broadway production financing and touring.[4]

The commercial theater segment also competes with, as well as benefits from, the existence of permanent nonprofit theaters (sometimes called regional or repertory theaters), which are resident in communities around the country. These resident theaters, supported by a combination of subscription fees, foundation grants, individual contributions, and ticket and merchandise sales, present a variety of plays (including the classics and those of Broadway and off-Broadway) and have sometimes been the source of new productions that later move on to commercial success and/or are adapted by Hollywood filmmakers. Such theaters attempt to preserve, develop, and extend the availability of performing arts productions and have become substantial enterprises.[5]

Table 13.3. *Top ten Broadway long runs, 2006*

| Show | Designation | Opening season | No. performances |
|---|---|---|---|
| *Phantom of the Opera*[a] | Musical | 1987–88 | 7,645 |
| *Cats* | Musical | 1982–83 | 7,485 |
| *Les Misérables* | Musical | 1986–87 | 6,680 |
| *A Chorus Line* | Musical | 1975–76 | 6,137 |
| *Oh, Calcutta!* | Revival | 1976–77 | 5,959 |
| *Beauty and the Beast*[a] | Musical | 1993–94 | 4,972 |
| *Rent*[a] | Musical | 1995–96 | 4,193 |
| *Miss Saigon* | Musical | 1990–91 | 4,097 |
| *Chicago*[a] | Music-Rev. | 1996–97 | 3,971 |
| *The Lion King*[a] | Musical | 1997–98 | 3,563 |

[a] Still running.

*Source*: League of American Theatres and Producers, LiveBroadway.com

*Circus* According to Murray (1956, p. 26), elements of the circus that included performances by equilibrists and prestidigitators had already begun to emerge in Egypt as early as 2500 B.C. And circus has subsequently flourished in many different times and places, beginning the modern era in the circus ring of a horseback-trick rider in England in 1768 and America in 1785 (Culhane 1990, p. 2). At first, small traveling shows, including fiddlers, jugglers, and acrobats, moved from city to city in covered wagon caravans. Later, circuses staged permanently based performances, which led eventually to the American development of huge multiring spectacles.

Today, however, circus is generally considered to be one of the major performing arts in Europe, but not in the United States – where companies are not government subsidized and are instead operated by private for-profit organizations. As such, circus companies seem to be best categorized as a permanent traveling form of commercial theater operating with a blend of the economic features seen in both theater and theme-park operations.

Of the approximately ten major domestic circuses, few are believed to be more than marginally profitable even though annual American attendance at circus performances exceeded 20 million in the early 2000s. The problem in circus, as in several of the other performing arts, is that cost efficiencies are difficult to attain given the size and structure of the spectacle that must be assembled and then disassembled every few days or weeks.[6]

### Orchestras

The history of orchestras also extends back to colonial times, but it was not until the founding of the New York Philharmonic in 1842 that formal organizations proliferated. In the early years, orchestras relied on a few wealthy patrons for support: J. P. Morgan, Andrew Carnegie, and Joseph Pulitzer were important contributors to the New York Philharmonic; Henry Higginson was guarantor of the Boston Symphony.

Today, the approximately 1,600 orchestras in the United States are categorized by the American Symphony Orchestra League according to the size of their budgets. Such major orchestras as those in Boston, Chicago, Cleveland, Los Angeles, New York, and Philadelphia would naturally attract the bulk of expenditures at concerts staged by professional groups.

### Opera

Opera is drama set to music, and the development of opera has closely followed that of drama. The roots of opera can be traced to ancient Greek theater presentations and to the religious plays of the Middle Ages that illustrated biblical stories with action and music. However, it was not until the 1600s that opera evolved into a distinctive form using complicated plots and more varied orchestral arrangements. This form flourished in Europe over the next 200 years.

In the United States, opera seemingly came of age in 1883 with the organization in New York City of what was to become known as the Metropolitan

Opera Company. However, as a reflection of the complexity and cost of staging grand opera, there are currently four major opera companies in the country: the Metropolitan (2005 budget of $211 million), the San Francisco Opera (2004 budget of $57 million), the Chicago Lyric Opera (2004 budget of $63 million), and the New York City Opera (2004 budget of $39 million). Also, companies in Los Angeles and Houston have recently become more prominent.

The economic problem inherent in opera is that when all lead and supporting singers, chorus, dancers, orchestra, conductor, and extras are included, there are 200 or more professionals on a payroll sustained by, at most, 4,000 seats per performance. It is thus understandable that even some fairly large cities do not have permanent grand-opera companies.

Dance

Little of professional ballet, a European art form, was seen in the United States before World War II. And not until the 1960s did significant philanthropic grants begin to support it. Major professional dance companies now include the New York City Ballet, the San Francisco Ballet, and the American Ballet Theatre.

Modern dance, in contrast, has an essentially American flavor. There are now at least half a dozen important modern dance groups, most of which are dependent on a single choreographer and small groups of financial benefactors.

## 13.2 Funding sources and the economic dilemma

The core of the economic dilemma, as originally outlined by Baumol and Bowen (1968), is that it is virtually impossible to raise the productivity of live performances substantially. It takes as long to play a Brahms concerto today as it did 100 years ago, and a scene by Shakespeare requires the same acting time it did 350 years ago. Meanwhile, over the long run, productivity (output per person-hour) has steadily grown in nearly every other segment of the economy. As it happens, a live performance is unique in that it is itself an end product and is consumed at the point of production.

This economic dilemma – the productivity lag in the arts – becomes ever more pronounced as productivity in other sectors increases, as real-income growth makes society more goods-intensive, as operating costs rise in line with overall inflation, and as ticket prices rise relatively rapidly in an attempt to cover "income gaps."[7] Such gaps, of course, tend also to narrow the financially feasible range of artistic presentations, favoring those plays, operas, ballets, and concerts that require fewer performers and/or that require less rehearsal time.

Empirical studies indeed suggest that ticket prices for live performances have risen at rates consistently higher than the consumer price index. And studies such as Baumol and Bowen's confirm that higher ticket prices reduce demand, especially from less well-to-do and younger segments of the

Table 13.4. *Financial support for the arts from the NEA, 1970–2005 ($ millions)*[a]

| Type of fund and program | 1970 | 1980 | 1990 | 2000 | 2005 |
|---|---|---|---|---|---|
| Funds available[b] | 15.7 | 188.1 | 170.8 | 85.2 | 108.8 |
| Program appropriation | 6.3 | 97.0 | 124.3 | 66.0 | 99.5 |
| Grants awarded (number) | 556 | 5,505 | 4,475 | 1,882 | 1,949 |
| Funds obligated | 12.9 | 166.4 | 157.6 | 83.5 | 104.4 |

[a] For years ending June 30 in 1970 and 1995; other fiscal years ending September 30.

[b] Includes other funds, not shown separately. Excludes administrative funds. Gifts are included through 1980 and excluded thereafter.

*Source*: NEA, www.arts.endow.gov.

population. Moreover, in periods of economic recession, even upper-income consumers may reduce spending in this area.

Nonetheless, there can be few educated people who would argue that live performing arts should be allowed to wither. From a purely practical viewpoint, traditional theater, opera, and dance forums provide a training ground for performers in the mass-entertainment media. Also, these training grounds undeniably enrich the surrounding society, making it more interesting, more spiritually invigorating, and more "human." Still, in a world chronically mired in a crisis of budgets, a significant problem in the funding of a broadly diversified range of cultural activities remains. The solution to the problem, both in the United States and abroad, has been to fund through philanthropy and subsidy.[8] But, over a long period, the amount of total operating income derived from government sources in the United States is generally no more than 10% to 15%, while ticket income ranges from 30% to 50%.

As would be expected, the likelihood of regular contributions to the arts rises substantially with income, and contributions by individuals and estates are estimated to be the largest single source of voluntary funding; combined contributions from corporations and foundations account for only 10% or so of all private philanthropic support. Major orchestras and operas meanwhile appear to receive proportionately more regular contributions than theater or dance.[9]

Performing and visual arts are further subsidized by government funding through state and local arts councils and through federal participation in matching-grant programs of the National Endowment for the Arts (Table 13.4). And the federal tax exemption for nonprofit organizations under Internal Revenue Service code section 501(c)(3) also helps. Yet, national-government support has a much longer and deeper tradition in Europe than in the United States, where emphasis has often been on construction of cultural centers tied to urban-renewal projects rather than on reduction of operating deficits. It is thus evident that the arts require support from a diverse set of benefactors.

Although it can be argued that, on purely economic grounds, taxpayers' financial support for money-losing arts programs enjoyed by an elite few is a waste of resources better spent elsewhere, justification of some government subsidy is usually made under the following assumptions:

Support for the arts opens opportunities for development of talented individuals from nonaffluent backgrounds.

Such support has educational benefit, exposing young people to cultural activities that they might not otherwise encounter.

Support encourages artistic innovation, which is a source of economic growth.

Arts are public goods that, when provided to individuals, automatically become available to, and are of collective benefit to, other members of the community.

In this respect, arts are thus goods with both public and private characteristics and, like education, most economists believe that they can justifiably be supported by a combination of public and private contributions.[10]

But there is more. For private corporations, support of cultural activities often stimulates local commercial activity and provides new business opportunities that have positive feedback effects on prospects for employment and for profits. For individuals, especially in North America, purely aesthetic pleasures are often further complemented by substantial tax benefits. And for the society as a whole, there are, as noted by Frey and Pommerehne (1989, p. 19), the following positive externalities:

- An *option value* to having a supply of culture even if an individual does not currently use the supply
- A *bequest value* for future generations unable to express preferences on currently existing markets
- An *existence value* such as for historic landmark buildings, which, once destroyed, cannot be rebuilt
- A *prestige value* even for those who are not at all interested in art[11]

## 13.3 The play's the thing

Production financing and participations

Financial support for the arts, whether from public or private sources, is normally dedicated to the development of specific facilities or to the patronage of fixed dance, orchestral, and opera groups: Usually, no direct financial return on investment is expected. But when it comes to funding of theater, the motives for sponsorship are often much more speculative and entrepreneurial than in any of the other arts. In fact, the financing and development process for new commercial-theater productions most closely resembles that used for films.

To start, a producer normally acquires, through the signing of an option contract, the rights to a play or other literary property that is to be adapted for stage.[12] Such contracts will usually provide for an advance against future royalties and will apply to the interim period in which all the artistic and financial elements ultimately needed to mount a stage production are to be assembled.[13]

Once an option is acquired, a producer then sometimes seeks financing by approaching prospective individual investors known as *angels*. Angels must indeed love theater because tax sheltering is much more effective in oil, real estate, and professional sports franchises than on Broadway, where opportunities for depreciation are limited.[14] As such, then, an angel must also have enough income to afford a tax loss (write-off) because, historically, the odds against ever seeing a return on investment are well over two to one.[15] An estimated 80% of shows never fully recover their costs.

Indeed, given the high costs of today's productions, a run on Broadway is increasingly likely to be funded by a large entertainment company rather than by a group of individual investors contributing relatively small amounts to the total. The large companies can more readily afford the risk and will often use the Broadway run as a means of establishing a project for possible use in other media, or in other locations, without requiring that a show turn an immediate profit.[16]

Although financing is occasionally in the form of sale of stock in a corporation organized for production of a play, it may further be in the form of a large development investment that is granted by film studios in return for eventual, and perhaps strategically valuable, movie rights. Broadway's major theater owners (essentially the Shubert Organization, the Nederlander Organization, and Jujamcyn Theaters) might also take a piece of the action and function as producers.[17] More typically, though, an offering prospectus describing anticipated running and start-up costs of a show is circulated to interested individual investors. Such investors are offered, in return for their capital, a share of potential profits (usually half of any profits earned by the production) through a limited partnership or, since 1994, a limited liability company (LLC) arrangement.[18]

Other investors might include the play's director, leading performer or performers, and individual theater owners (Table 13.5). Directors and lead performers will usually receive a small percentage (e.g., 5%) of the play's earnings in addition to a salary or fee, whereas theater owners may (depending on season, theater quality, and the producer's reputation) receive 20% to 30% of the box-office gross. However, as noted by Baumol and Bowen,

the locus of control of a production is sharply divided between the producer and the owner of the theater in which the play is performed.

While the producer selects his play, controls the artistic standards of the production, raises the funds invested in it, hires the director and the cast, sets wages and decides on outlays on costumes and scenery, there are other matters which he normally does not control

Table 13.5. *Typical financial participations
in theater productions*

| | |
|---|---|
| *Gross participation (%)* | |
| Playwright | 10 |
| Lead performer | 5 |
| Director | 2 |
| Theater manager | 25 |
| *Profit participation (%)* | |
| Playwright | 5–10 |
| Director | 5 |
| Lead performer | 5–10 |
| Other performers and show manager | 10 |
| Producer | 15 |
| Investors | 50–60 |

completely. A powerful producer can obtain a contract giving him a substantial voice in what may be termed the marketing of a play, but usually this is left largely in the hands of the theater owner, who often supplies, in addition to box office personnel and ushers, several stagehands and, where appropriate, several musicians. He bears part of the cost of advertising, consults in the setting of ticket prices, and supplies tickets to brokerage agencies. He has complete control of the box office, into which a producer may even be refused admittance . . . .

The theater owner normally receives a percentage of the weekly gross of a play so that, aside from the advantages of length of run, it is in his interest to house a successful play. Since the contract usually provides that he can eject a play from his theater when the weekly gross falls below a prespecified figure, it is alleged that box-office personnel have sometimes been instructed to refuse to sell tickets to potential patrons, stating that all the seats were already sold. (Baumol and Bowen 1968, pp. 20–21)

As in movie deals, variations from fairly standardized percentages are based on the relative bargaining power of the participants. A major star in a small play can receive weekly guarantees plus increasing percentages of gross after receipts reach certain levels. Directors may receive fairly large upfront fees and smaller percentages of weekly grosses. Playwrights normally earn at least a minimum author's royalty of 10% weekly (but 5% of weekly receipts for nonmusical productions off-Broadway).[19] And the show's general manager will receive a fee plus weekly salary and perhaps a small percentage of net profits, if any.[20]

Operational characteristics

A private placement memorandum will estimate the weekly breakeven and weekly net profit at capacity for a show that is up and running. But even relatively modest productions require extensively detailed budgets and

Table 13.6. *Budget estimates for a $1 million*
*Broadway stage production: an example, circa 2000*[a]

| | |
|---|---:|
| Scenery | $60,000 |
| Props | 17,000 |
| Costumes | 30,000 |
| Electric and sound | 40,000 |
| Fees | 100,000 |
| Rehearsals | 80,000 |
| Advertising | 260,000 |
| Other costs | 100,000 |
| Total production costs | $687,000 |
| Pre-New York (rehearsals, hauling) | $108,000 |
| Bonds (AEA, IATSE, ATPAM, theater) | 70,000 |
| Reserve for contingency and preview losses | 135,000 |
| Total capitalization | $1,000,000 |

[a] In the early 1980s, the cost of a similar production was approximately one-fourth the cost in 2000.

forecasts because of the many small items that will always collectively add up to significant amounts.

The estimates in Table 13.6 illustrate how each million dollars of investment in a Broadway production might typically be apportioned, excluding any of the percentage of gross that might nowadays be paid for star performers.[21] As can be seen, advertising expenses constitute a major component of total running costs. In this example, the weekly breakeven, including all royalties, is approximately $250,000 per week and, at capacity, weekly receipts and net profits were estimated at $320,000 and $70,000, respectively.

The high fixed costs of operation naturally create a large leveraged effect on profits and, also, a tendency to have either a bona fide hit with substantial profit potential or an outright failure: Usually, there is little likelihood of anything in between the extremes.

Figure 13.5 illustrates the sensitivity of profits to changes in box-office receipts for a play with running costs of $100,000 per week, average ticket prices of $30, and seating of 500. Here it is assumed that the production does not garner additional revenues from cable television or movie-rights sales, or from any other such ancillary sources, and that royalties and other payments are not scaled (usually they are). If there are eight performances per week, then, under these conditions, breakeven requires an average capacity utilization of 83.3% (417 seats); figures consistently below that level will cause losses to mount rapidly.[22] Yet levels of 70% or less are not unusual.[23]

Moreover, in budgeting for a show, prospective investors should have a solid grasp of labor union contract stipulations. Relationships with the

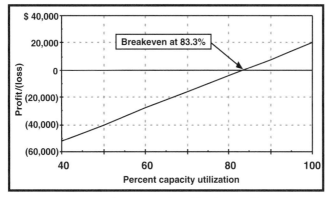

Figure 13.5. Breakeven capacity utilization: an illustration.

Actors' Equity Association, the Dramatists' Guild (playwrights), the Society of Stage Directors and Choreographers, and the International Alliance of Theatrical Stage Employees may have important financial ramifications on performing-arts productions.[24]

In all, theatrical producer Sol Hurok perhaps summed it up best when he said, "If I would be in this business for *business*, I wouldn't be in this business."[25]

## 13.4 Economist echoes

Studies of the economics of the performing arts are relatively recent, and the basic literature is still in development.[26] Work on the theoretical statistical behavior of the film business, described in Section 4.5, also fits nicely here, where an overall economic perspective may be gained through consideration of a few important concepts that involve organizational features, elasticities, price discrimination, and externalities.

Organizational features

As Caves (2000, p. 2) indicates, several "bedrock properties" are commonly seen in the types of contracts and business structures that have evolved in the production, distribution, and marketing of entertainment and culture-related goods and services. The basic economic properties (with Caves's designation in italics) of creative activities are as follows:

- Demand is highly uncertain in the sense that no one knows in advance how consumers will value new products and services (*nobody knows*).
- Creative workers, unlike those in jobs that are primarily functional and standardized, care greatly about what they produce (*art for art's sake*).
- Many creative ventures (e.g., Broadway musicals or films) require diverse skills and specialized workers with unpredictable vertically differentiated skills (*motley crew*).

- Creative products (and also artists) are usually differentiated both vertically (product A is better than product B) and horizontally (product A and product B are similar in character and quality but not identical) (*A list/B list*).
- Most creative products (e.g., paintings) can differ in many ways through small differences (*infinite variety*).
- With time being of the essence in the creation of many properties (e.g., movies and concerts), close temporal coordination by all contributing elements is required (*time flies*).
- Royalties and rent payments are often collected in small lump-sum payments stretched over long periods of time (*ars longa*).

These common aspects help explain, for example, why the few large movie studios have a need for the services of so many small, independent creative companies and why cultural and performing arts segments use the types of contracts and ownership structures that they do. Indeed, option contract forms prevail in creative industries because many of the costs often incurred are fixed but also sunk (irrecoverable) at various well-defined stages of production.[27]

The concept of cultural capital, introduced by Throsby (2001, p. 46), provides further perspective from which to view the organizational features of creative industries. Such capital exists in both tangible (e.g., buildings, paintings, sculptures) and intangible forms (e.g., ideas, beliefs, practices, values) that give rise to a flow of cultural services.[28]

Elasticities

As Heilbrun and Gray (2001, p. 102) have noted, "most studies have shown the demand for attendance at the live performing arts to be price-inelastic." What this means is that consumers of such services are not especially sensitive to changes in price: A rise in price does not cause a proportionate decline in demand as might be measured by number of tickets sold per unit time.[29]

But empirical studies suggest that *income* elasticities with regard to the demand for performing arts cluster around 1.0.[30] It seems that, as incomes rise, the greater opportunity cost of time spent on cultural activities may offset the pure positive income effect that derives from higher purchasing power. Over the longer term, this further implies that overall demand for the performing arts and for cultural events will probably grow at about the same rate as that of the domestic economy.

Price discrimination

Nevertheless, existing differences in elasticity of demand among potential members of an audience might still be exploited by a discriminating monopolist – which would be an economist's way of describing the producer of a specific performance or event. In such instances, a price-discrimination

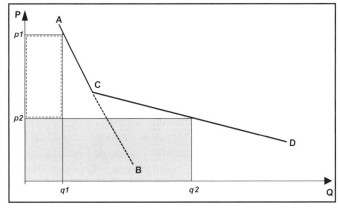

Figure 13.6. Price discrimination and the consumer surplus.

strategy, wherein different parts of the audience can be charged different prices (see Chapter 1), might be implemented so as to maximize the monopolist's income.[31] The producer would then thereby extract what is known as the consumer surplus: The price difference between what consumers actually pay and what they would be willing to pay.

This is illustrated in Figure 13.6 (and in Figure 1.8c), where the quantities of theater seats sold to business guests is $q_1$ and to tourists with discount tickets is $q_2$. The theater's total revenue is $p_2q_2 + (p_1 - p_2)q_1$. Selling all seats at the lower price of $p_2$ would provide revenues of $p_2q_2$, and all at $p_1$ would make $p_1q_1$. But price discrimination raises the total above what would likely be received by setting a single selling price.[32]

## Externalities

According to economic theory, and as noted by Hendon *et al.* (1980, p. 21), "art goods themselves are not public goods. . . . [A] necessary but not sufficient condition for a pure public good is that it can be jointly consumed perfectly. The exclusion principle says that a product, though jointly consumed, can be provided in separable units to various consumers. Because admission to an artistic event (or right to use) can be provided in separable units, the exclusion principle is operable in the arts." But, in addition, "the more definitive externalities generated by the arts usually flow to special-interest groups."[33]

## 13.5 Concluding remarks

Performing arts organizations seem always to live at the edge of a financial precipice. This condition is, of course, a function of live-audience size limitations, the great expense of coordinating an effective production, and the perpetually high cost of money for risky ventures. Live performances are also economically inefficient because, unlike manufactured goods, performances are "consumed" at the point of production.

From an economist's view, however, the most important and ineluctable element is that productivity cannot be raised significantly in the performing arts: On the programming-cost side, an hour of performance still takes an hour, whether it is done before a camera for distribution on television or cable or in front of a live audience.[34]

Revenues derived from the new media are becoming significant considerations in financing of the arts. The flow of story lines often goes from Broadway (and/or the London stage) to Hollywood and back again, each being reinforced and reinvigorated by the other.[35] Backers of commercial-theater productions may also look increasingly to cable television license fees or home video presentation formats to enhance profits and to reduce the risk of loss. And it seems likely that the convenience and relatively low cost of home-viewing options will encourage more frequent sampling by people who would not otherwise have an interest in seeing such events. Through technological advances more people are able to enjoy more performances than ever before.

Cultural achievements reflect the discipline, devotion, and intelligence of individuals and also the most basic values of the society. That is why, for example, the free expression inherent in two distinctly American art forms, jazz and modern dance, could not have developed or thrived in an authoritarian environment.

Still, no matter what the politics, the economic dilemma for performing arts cannot be circumvented. In a free society, some manner of subsidy – usually a combination of government support and tax incentives for private individuals and corporations – is normally required to sustain or to expand high-culture activities.

## Notes

**1.**  As Figure 13.4c shows, until 1989, stage productions garnered most of their dollars on Broadway – legally defined as a production in the Broadway District of New York City in a theater seating more than 499 persons. In contrast, "off-Broadway" is defined as a New York City production in a theater seating no more than 499 and no fewer than 99. However, as Pogrebin (1999) suggests, Broadway is no longer the domain of the stage play.

**2.**  In looking at this, Baumol and Baumol (1984) noted that, over the 50 years following the Great Depression, top Broadway prices rose about 14-fold, while movie-ticket prices rose 35-fold. Admission trends for less expensive off-Broadway performances are probably quite similar, but data on this are not reliable. See also Disch (1991).

**3.**  Hughes (2005a) notes that the cost of launching a Broadway musical was about $8 million to $9 million in 2005 and that Broadway now uses road shows as a way to recoup costs in the same way that the movie industry uses DVD revenues. However, as noted by Leonhardt (2006a), road shows have encountered their own set of problems.

**4.**  As recounted in Green (2005), Las Vegas profit numbers are substantially above Broadway's. An 1,800-seat Vegas showroom playing ten shows a week for 48 weeks at 85%

capacity and $100 a ticket takes in $73 million, which is several multiples of what a 300-seat Broadway theater can generate.

**5.** The following table profiles the not-for-profit theater segment:

U.S. nonprofit theater survey universe, 2004

| Number of theaters | 1,477 |
|---|---|
| Attendance | 32.1 million |
| Subscribers | 1.8 million |
| Performances | 169,000 |
| Productions | 11,000 |
| Revenues (earned income) | $856.2 million |
| Contributions | $714.6 million |
| Total income | $1,570.8 million |
| Expenses | $1,464.4 million |
| Earned dollars as % of total income | 55% |
| Contributed dollars as % of total income | 45% |

*Source*: Theatre Communications Group, *Theatre Facts 2004*
(www.tcg.org).

Note also that musical rights for community theaters are mostly controlled by four companies: Music Theatre International, Rodgers & Hammerstein Theatre Library, Tams-Witmark Music Library Inc., and Samuel French Inc. These firms, which already own more than 500 scripts and scores, purchase licensing rights to Broadway shows, typically offer authors guarantees and advances against royalties (ranging between $25,000 and $2 million), and charge local theaters up to 15% of their box-office take. See *Wall Street Journal*, June 5, 1998, and Reich (1996).

**6.** According to Hirsch (1987), Ringling played, in 1987, before 11 million people in 89 cities at ticket prices ranging from $6.00 to $11.50. Revenues in 1987 were $250 million, but according to Gilpin (1993) revenues were probably twice as much by 1993. Labor costs are 50% of budget; ads and promotion consume another 25%; and train costs, arena rentals, props, and equipment and insurance expenses absorb the remainder of the budget. Even when owned by Mattel, which purchased the company for $47 million in December 1970, the huge Ringling Bros. and Barnum & Bailey (RB&BB) units (Red and Blue, each with 350 employees) were not financially impressive.

Most circuses cover their costs at the gate and make profits with concessions. RB&BB's yearly advertising and promotion budget was between $10 million and $12 million, with half this total going to TV and 25% to newspapers, according to *Advertising Age*, December 12, 1983. A review of the RB&BB history at age 100 appears in *Variety*, January 11, 1984, with a follow-up appearing in *Variety*, July 24, 1995. See also *Time*, May 4, 1970, and *Amusement Business*, August 15, 1970. Other recent touring groups include The Big Apple Circus, The Carson & Barnes Circus, the Clyde Beatty–Cole Bros. Circus, the Pickle Family Circus, the Culpepper & Merriweather Great Combined Circus, the Royal Hanneford Circus, and the Canadian Cirque du Soleil. Cirque, along with its permanent venues (e.g., Las Vegas), is now the other major company generating nearly on par with Ringling more than $500 million of revenues (compared to Ringling's estimated $600 million) as of 2005. See Collins, G. (2005).

**7.**  However, as Heilbrun and Gray (2001, 1993, p. 133) note, the rising real incomes that are derived from rising productivity in the overall economy make higher ticket prices more affordable for more people, thus mitigating some of the adverse productivity-lag effects. Also, Cowen (1998, p. 21) views technological progress as having had an important positive effect on productivity in the arts (e.g., French impressionists benefited from new paints made possible by advances in chemistry).

**8.**  Characteristics of various funding sources appear in Balfe (1993).

**9.**  However, some private-institution grants (from foundations, corporations, and labor unions) are regularly directed toward specific support of other organizations and projects, including those in museums, music, architecture, and literature. Note also that, in recent years, symphony orchestras and theater, opera, and dance companies have steadily derived approximately 55% to 60% of total revenues from earned income, while private support and public funding have accounted for roughly 35% to 40% and 5% to 10%, respectively, of revenues.

**10.**  These and several additional assumptions used to argue for support of the arts have been challenged by Grampp (1989, pp. 233–269), who believes that art should support itself.

**11.**  Throsby (2001, p. 28) follows a similar line in noting that there are aesthetic, spiritual, social, historic, symbolic, and authenticity values for works of art as well as buildings and tourist attractions. Throsby also introduces contingent valuation methods (CVMs), which attempt to elicit information concerning the minimal level of compensation required by an individual to forgo consumption of a public good or the maximum amount an individual would be willing to pay to obtain a nonmarket amenity. In this regard, see also Van Kooten and Bulte (2000, p. 113).

**12.**  In practice, copyright considerations are often illegally ignored in small off-off-Broadway or regional productions. Copyrights would, of course, be enforced in any important commercial production.

**13.**  In acquiring rights to a play, the producer adheres to Dramatists' Guild option-contract stipulations that provide the playwright with a nonrefundable deposit to be forfeited if the play is not produced within a year or some shorter period. In addition, the dramatist is entitled to royalties on a sliding scale, between 5% and 10% of the box-office gross, and to the bulk of receipts from ancillary rights, including film, cable television, and foreign productions.

A prominent example is the Rodgers & Hammerstein musical *Oklahoma!*. The fees for rights for a major performance of this show are customarily in the area of 8% of box-office gross, with an advance against royalties of $18,000 or more. See *Variety*, March 29, 1993.

**14.**  Yet, as Frey and Pommerehne (1989, p. 35) have noted, theatrical productions *can* be profitable if the audience size is large, the fixed costs are small, there is price discrimination (e.g., seats with a better view are priced higher), and there are subsidiary sources of income (e.g., video, films).

**15.**  The New York State Attorney General's office had at one time compiled statistics on offering prospectuses for Broadway and off-Broadway shows. Over the 11 seasons between 1972 to 1973 and 1982 to 1983, for example, some 948 shows in this sample (which included shows that never opened but excluded some very prominently successful shows in which funding was privately raised) lost a grand total of $66.6 million on capitalizations of $267.5 million. There was not a single season in which these shows, in the aggregate, generated profits.

Rosenberg and Harburg (1993, p. 14) illustrate that the percentage of Broadway musicals (including revivals) that failed to return investors' funds, the "flops," consistently averaged 76% of the projects launched between 1945 and 1990. The figure is close to the flop average between 1925 and 1935. Rothstein (1988) also notes that in the 17 months after *Starlight Express* opened (in March 1987), this show took in $35 million and was seen by more than 925,000 people – and it had not yet recouped its investment. As of 1995, one of the most expensive nonmusical flops had been *On the Waterfront*, which lost its entire $2.6 million capitalization after eight performances. But in early 2003, *Dance of the Vampires* closed after a loss of $12 million (56 performances), giving it, along with *Capeman* and *Carrie*, the distinction of being among the costliest flops in Broadway history. Other recent musical flops as listed in Berfield (2005) include *The Mambo Kings* in 2005; *Bombay Dreams*, with 284 performances in 2004; and *Seussical*, with 198 performances in 2000. See also McKinley (2003) and Mandelbaum (1991).

Given the high likelihood of loss and the need for more capital, producers have more recently structured deals in which investors are able to recoup investments more rapidly. In the traditional approach, the creative team, cast, and theater owner are paid first out of the weekly box office, after which theater expenses and other costs are deducted. Only then, as Hughes (2006) notes, do investors receive a return. In another variation of this, a profit or royalty pool is set up, but the show has to be profitable before investors are paid. The newer formulas, especially used for the more expensive musical productions, tack on a weekly amount to a show's operating budget – in effect, an amortization allowance. In the case of *The Wedding Singer*, capitalized at $11.75 million in 2006, investors receive around 2% of the capitalization per week until they have recouped 110% of their investment.

**16.** Despite the odds against success, angels, as well as large entertainment companies, continue to be attracted to Broadway: Every so often a show (e.g., *The Producers*, first staged in 2001) will provide spectacular returns on investment, especially when eventual revenues from sales of cable television, movie, recording, and other rights, as well as profits from road-show productions, are included. See also Blumenthal (2001).

That is because when shows are successful, they are incredibly so. According to *Variety* of February 15, 1989, *Cats* had become the most profitable (in absolute dollars) theatrical production to date, earning net profit in North America (United States and Canada) of approximately $44 million (and another $14.5 million from the London and other foreign editions). The base investment made by the Shubert Organization, ABC Entertainment, Metromedia Corp., and Geffen Records in 1982 was $3.9 million, and the Andrew Lloyd Webber production thus returned over 11 times the investment in North America alone. Because Webber, as author, and the other royalty participants receive about 25% as a license fee plus royalties, the actual gross profit was $58 million. As of June 1997, when it became the longest-running show in Broadway history, *Cats* was still grossing more than $350,000 a week and had generated revenues of more than $329 million on Broadway and $2.2 billion worldwide. However, *Phantom of the Opera* had by early 1998 actually grossed more, with $335 million in Broadway revenues and $2.6 billion in worldwide ticket sales. By 2003, *Phantom* had become the third–longest running show after *Les Misérables*, which opened in 1987 for a cost of $4.5 million and closed in 2003 (as second-longest runner) after grossing more than $390 million in 6,612 performances on Broadway ($1.8 billion worldwide). As McKinley (2004) reports, *Wicked* was also one of the quickest returns of capital, recouping its $14 million capitalization in 14 months, whereas *Avenue Q* required 10 months to recoup $3.5 million. See Grimes (1997); *Variety*, January 26, 1998; and *New York Times*, October 3, 2002.

Other big winners have included *Hello, Dolly*, which netted $9 million on a $420,000 investment (a 21-to-1 return, with investors splitting the profit equally with the producer, David Merrick). *Fiddler on the Roof* earned $12.4 million on a $375,000 investment. And Disney's *Beauty and the Beast*, with an initial investment believed to be $11.9 million, was also a huge success despite its cost. See Witchel (1994) and Lyman (1997). Disney's *Lion King* is believed to be the most expensive, costing $20 million (*New York Times*, November 29, 2003). As noted in Barnes (2005a), by 2005 it had taken in over $2 billion from all sources.

Reibstein (1986) suggests that, to succeed, straight plays should generally have weekly production costs that are half or less of the theater's box-office capacity, although musicals will usually range higher. Weber (1993) suggests that a musical should now be able to pay back within a year. Also see Passell (1989) and Adler (2004).

**17.**   Rosenberg and Harburg (1993, p. 8) note that as of 1991, the Shubert Organization owned or operated seventeen theaters, the Nederlander ten, and Jujamcyn five, with the proportion of the Broadway gross taken by each organization split approximately 53%, 28%, and 19%, respectively. Analysis of the increasingly integrated role of nonprofit producers and theater owners (who benefit from tax exemptions) with the major theater owners is given in Rockwell (2002).

**18.**   The New York Limited Liability Company Law became effective in October 1994 and has stirred debate as to whether an LLC structure offers significant advantages over traditional limited partnerships. See Farber (1995) and Wasser (1995).

As in films, financing can be exempt from full SEC registration and fall under Regulation A or Regulation D if the number of investors is relatively few and the capital raised is under $5 million. See Farber (1997).

Also, until 1990, New York State theatrical law did not permit a pool of capital to be raised for the financing of more than one show. Andrew Lloyd Webber's Really Useful Group (RUG) was the first company to attempt, in 1990, to solicit investment capital for more than one show and for shows that are not specifically identified. RUG had hoped to raise $20 million from a private placement offering to finance *Aspects of Love* and a touring company of *Phantom of the Opera*. However, the offering was not as large as had been planned. See *Variety*, October 1, 1990.

**19.**   For off-Broadway productions, Farber (1993, p. 6) notes that if the author is not well known, the usual royalty payment is a rate of 5% of the gross weekly box office for nonmusicals and a rate of 6% for musicals. But the rate for famous authors would scale up to 10%. Off-Broadway producers' fees are usually between 1% and 2% of gross weekly box-office receipts, with the higher amount sometimes only after recoupment of costs. Also, investors in a show's limited liability partnership would normally receive 50% of the producing company's profits.

**20.**   Box-office cash flows may also be diverted from the production or be collected in ways that are disadvantageous for the producer. For example, as Collins (1992) notes, ticket brokers sometimes offer box-office workers payments, known as "ice," for a block of seats to a hit show. The brokers then resell the tickets at a premium. The practice reduces the number of good seats available to the public and potentially caps the producer's total receipts at a point below which they would otherwise be.

**21.**   See Hughes (2005b).

**22.**   If $X$ = utilization percentage, then the formula is $X = \$100,000/(500 \text{ seats} \times \$30$ ticket price $\times 8$ performances).

**23.**   See Lawson (1983).

**24.**   Although all Broadway productions follow contract-specified minimum-scale guidelines, the percentage of unemployed members of performing-arts unions is chronically high, and for smaller productions, union specifications are often ignored or waived. For instance, in order to encourage low-budget productions (e.g., off-Broadway) that will provide good experience for new performers, Equity waives many of its minimums in theaters with seating of fewer than 100. Still, as noted in McKinley (2005), off-Broadway productions have recently been faced with financial problems as the average production cost ranges above $500,000. This article illustrates the commercial off-Broadway costs for the musical *Little Ham*, which opened in 2002, as:

| | |
|---|---|
| Physical production (scenery, props, costumes, etc.) | $69,500 |
| Fees (for set design, choreography, makeup, and managers) | 71,834 |
| Rehearsal salaries (actors, understudies, etc.) | 79,400 |
| Rehearsal expenses (hall rentals, audition pianists, etc.) | 5,000 |
| Advertising and publicity | 86,000 |
| General and administrative (fees, insurance, payroll taxes, etc.) | 78,548 |
| Cost of developmental production | 150,000 |
| Total production cost | $540,282 |

**25.** *New York Times*, August 28, 1970.

**26.** Several important works, including those of Baumol and Bowen (1968), Blaug (1976), Netzer (1978), and Throsby and Withers (1979), can be cited. Topics of potential interest to economists, all treated in the volume edited by Hendon *et al.* (1980), include a mathematical model for support of the arts (Seaman 1980), an analysis of artistic innovation using information theory (Owen and Owen 1980), development of a composer supply function (Felton 1980), and estimation of a demand function for Broadway theater tickets (Kelejian and Lawrence 1980). In addition, Moore (1968) developed a model of demand for theater as a function of income, the supply of shows, and the real price of tickets. The *Journal of Cultural Economics* is also an important source for the most recent studies in this field.

**27.** Following a similar line of analysis, Throsby (2001, p. 107) presents a model of artistic production (creativity) that, among other things, includes variables for the level of cultural value produced, the level of economic value produced, arts labor time, earned income, and several other factors.

**28.** More broadly, the economics of culture industries is being increasingly analyzed within the context of political, sociological, and psychological impacts in books such as those by Hesmondhalgh (2002) and Steinert (2003).

**29.** Such price elasticity estimates appear to range from 0.4 to 0.9. See also Gapinski (1986).

**30.** The empirical work is compared in Heilbrun and Gray (2001, p. 99).

**31.** Economists classify price discrimination into three categories. In the most common third-degree form, monopolists exploit the differences in elasticities of demand in two different markets in order to increase total revenue by the highest amount possible. In second-degree discrimination, higher prices are first charged for smaller amounts demanded than for larger amounts even if the costs of providing the differently sized units are the same. In first-degree discrimination, the seller charges the buyer the highest price the buyer is willing to pay for that unit, and the seller charges a different price for each unit, thereby totally eliminating the consumers' surplus. Frank (2006) also argues that price discrimination enables consumers "to enjoy both lower prices and higher quality than would be possible if sellers charged the same price to everyone."

**32.** Another form of price discrimination appears when tickets to major events are "scalped," that is, resold by third parties at prices that are usually much higher than at the box office. The issue is explored in Happel and Jennings (1995).

**33.** Frey and Pommerehne (1989, p. 46) note that "theaters, operas, ballet and orchestras behave differently with respect to output, inputs and the production process depending on whether they are co-operatively run, profit-oriented and private, or nonprofit-oriented and public." And in this vein, Hansmann (1981) explores the reasons for the preponderance of nonprofit-institution involvement in the high-culture performing arts and notes that high fixed production costs relative to marginal costs and overall demand force performing-arts groups to engage in price discrimination if they are to survive without subsidy. But because opportunities for effective ticket-price discrimination are limited, the nonprofit-organization structure seems best suited for encouraging voluntary donations. Also, in examining the nonprofit aspects, DiMaggio (1984, p. 57) suggests that, "because nonprofit organizations need not maximize net income, public policy assumes that they will maximize something else . . . a combination of services and aesthetic quality."

**34.** In reference to the network television business, for example, it has been noted by Baumol and Baumol (1984, p. 36) that there will be

> an initial period of decline in total costs (in constant dollars) followed by a period in which . . . costs begin to behave in a manner more and more similar to the live performing arts. The reason is that the cost of the highly technological component (transmission cost) will decline, or at least not rise as fast as the economy's inflation rate. At the same time, the cost of programming increases at a rate surpassing the rate of inflation.
>
> If each year transmission costs decrease and over-the-line or programming expenses increase, eventually programming cost will begin to dominate the overall budget. . . . One of the major networks reports . . . that while over-the-line costs comprised 30% to 35% of a dramatic presentation 10 years ago, they now constitute 50% of the budget.

A consequence is that financially strapped performing arts companies are increasingly being merged. See Russell (2006).

**35.** See, for example, Isenberg (2005).

## Selected additional reading

Albrecht, E. (1995). *The New American Circus*. Gainesville, FL: University Press of Florida.

Andresky, J. (1983). "So You Want to Be an Angel?," *Forbes*, 131(3)(January 31).

Atkinson, B. (1990). *Broadway*, rev. ed. New York: Limelight Editions (reprint) and (1974) Macmillan.

Barnes, B. (2005). "To Push Musicals, Producer Shakes Up Broadway Tactics," *Wall Street Journal*, March 10.

Baumol, H., and Baumol, W. J., eds. (1984). *Inflation and the Performing Arts*. New York: New York University Press.

Benedict, S., ed. (1991). *Public Money and the Muse: Essays on Government Funding for the Arts*. New York: The American Assembly (Columbia University).

Bianco, A. (2004). *Ghosts of 42nd Street*. New York: HarperCollins (William Morrow).

Biddle, L. (1988). *Our Government and the Arts: A Perspective from the Inside*. New York: American Council for the Arts.

Blackmon, D. A. (1998). "Forget the Stereotype: America Is Becoming a Nation of Culture," *Wall Street Journal*, September 17.

Blau, J. R. (1989). *The Shape of Culture: A Study of Contemporary Cultural Patterns in the United States*. New York: Cambridge University Press.

Blumenthal, R. (1997). "On Broadway, Serious Plays Are Headed for Serious Trouble," *New York Times*, January 9.

Brockett, O. G. (1979). *The Theater: An Introduction*, 4th ed. New York: Holt, Rinehart and Winston.

Cherbo, J. M., and Wyszomirski, M. J., eds. (2000). *The Public Life of the Arts in America*. New Brunswick, NJ: Rutgers University Press.

Cherbo, J. M., Wyszomirski, M. J., and Stewart, R. A., eds. (2007). *Understanding the Arts and Creative Sector in America*. New Brunswick, NJ: Rutgers University Press.

Clark, L. H., Jr. (1985). "Why Can't the Arts Be More Businesslike?," *Wall Street Journal*, June 11.

Collins, G. (2000). "Three Circuses, a Ring at a Time," *New York Times*, December 26.

Cornes, R., and Sandler, T. (1996). *The Theory of Externalities, Public Goods and Club Goods*, 2nd ed. New York: Cambridge University Press.

Cowen, T. (2006). *Good & Plenty: The Creative Successes of American Arts Funding*. Princeton, NJ: Princeton University Press.

Cox, M. (1984). "Orchestra Thrives by Playing the Music People Didn't Want," *Wall Street Journal*, July 19.

Croft-Cooke, R., and Cotes, P. (1976). *Circus: A World History*. New York: Macmillan.

Dunning, J. (1986). "Dance as Big Business May Pose a Threat to Dance as Art," *New York Times*, March 30.

Feld, A., O'Hare, J., and Schuster, J. M. D. (1983). *Patrons Despite Themselves. Taxpayers and Arts Policy. A Twentieth Century Fund Report*. New York: New York University Press.

Frey, B. (2003). *Arts & Economics: Analysis & Cultural Policy*, 2nd ed. Berlin: Springer Verlag.

Gapinsky, J. H. (1984). "The Economics of Performing Shakespeare," *American Economic Review*, 74(3)(June).

Godley, W. (1977). "The Economics of the Arts," *Economic Journal*, 87(September).

Goldstein, M. (1995). "Re-Inventing Broadway," *New York*, May 29.

Goodman, W. (1984). "Scholars Debate Need to Aid Arts," *New York Times*, May 2.

Greenhouse, S. (2003). "The Sound of Disharmony in Theater World," *New York Times*, March 9.

Gunther, M. (1999). "The Greatest Business on Earth," *Fortune*, 140(9)(November 8).

Haithman, D. (1997). "Opera to Die For," *Los Angeles Times*, February 2.

Hoelterhoff, M. (1987). "New York City (Opera) on $112,452 a Day," *Wall Street Journal*, August 18.

Hoge, W. (2000). "A Major New Role as Theater Mogul for Lloyd Webber," *New York Times*, January 10.

Holland, B. (2003). "How to Kill Orchestras," *New York Times*, June 29.

(1999). "The Metropolitan Opera: Where Opera, for Good or Ill, Is Grand," *New York Times*, May 2.

Honan, W. H. (1989). "Arts Dollars: Pinched as Never Before," *New York Times*, May 28.

Hughes, R. J. (2002). "As Funds Fade, Symphonies Cut Their Programs," *Wall Street Journal*, October 9.

Hummler, R. (1990). "Expenses Take Off for Off-Broadway Shows," *Variety*, September 24.

Kinzer, S. (2003). "As Funds Disappear, So Do Orchestras," *New York Times*, May 14.

(2002). "An Orchestra That Won't Give Up," *New York Times*, March 20.

Kleinfield, N. R. (1994). "How Shubert Fund Produces and Directs," *New York Times*, July 10.

Kozinn, A. (2006). "Check the Numbers: Rumors of Classical Music's Demise Are Dead Wrong," *New York Times*, May 28.

(1993). "City Opera Turns 50, but Who's Counting?," *New York Times*, July 25.

Kroeger, B. (1987). "Raising a Million for 'Les Mis,'" *New York Times*, July 19.

La Franco, R. (1996). "Popera," *Forbes*, 158(1)(July 1).

Langley, S. (1990). *Theatre Management and Production in America*. New York: Drama Book Publishers.

Larson, G. O. (1983). *The Reluctant Patron*. Philadelphia: University of Pennsylvania Press.

Leslie, P. (2004). "Price Discrimination in Broadway Theatre," *RAND Journal of Economics*, 35(3).

Lowry, W. M., ed. (1978). *The Performing Arts and American Society*. New York: The American Assembly (Columbia University).

Lyman, R. (1997). "Two Powerhouses of the Theater Meld Broadway and the Road," *New York Times*, June 9.

Lynes, R. (1985). *The Lively Audience: A Social History of the Visual and Performing Arts in America, 1890–1950*. New York: Harper & Row.

Malitz, N. (1995). "A Hardy Survivor Rides the Wave of the Future," *New York Times*, March 19.

Marks, P. (2002a). "If It's a Musical, It Was Probably a Movie," *New York Times*, April 14.

(2002b), "For Little Musical That Could, a 42-year Run," *New York Times*, January 9.

(1996). "Broadway's Producers: A Struggling, Changing, Breed," *New York Times*, April 7.

Marsh, B. (1992). "Bunting & Red Tape: The Modern Circus Walks a High Wire," *Wall Street Journal*, August 31.

Martin, F. (1994). "Determining the Size of Museum Subsidies," *Journal of Cultural Economics*, 18.

Mayer, M. (1983). "The Big Business of Grand Opera," *Fortune*, 108(8)(October 17).

McCarthy, K. F., Brooks, A., Lowell, J., and Zakaras, L. (2001). *The Performing Arts in a New Era*. Santa Monica, CA: Rand Institution and Pew Charitable Trusts.

McCarthy, K. F., Ondaatje, E. H., and Zakaras, L. (2004). *Gifts of the Muse: Reframing the Debate about the Benefits of the Arts*. Santa Monica, CA: Rand Corporation.

McElroy, S. (2006). "Now, for the Accounting of the Opera," *New York Times*, January 8.

McKinley, J. (2005). "Drawn to Broadway from Near and, Mostly, Far," *New York Times*, January 13.

(2004). "Close Call on Broadway Had Its Roots on the Road," *New York Times*, July 15.

(2003a). "The Case of the Incredible Shrinking Blockbuster," *New York Times*, November 2.

(2003b). "Heavy Losses Expected as Theaters Go Dark," *New York Times*, March 8.

(2003c). "Rising Costs Alter Rules for Shows on Tour," *New York Times*, February 10.

(2001). "For the Asking, a $480 Seat," *New York Times*, October 26.

Miller, J. (1996). "As Patrons Age, Future of Arts Is Uncertain," *New York Times*, February 12.

Moore, T. G. (1966). "The Demand for Broadway Theatre Tickets," *Review of Economics and Statistics*, 48(1)(February).

Mulcahy, K. V., and Swain, C. R., eds. (1982). *Public Policy and the Arts*. Boulder, CO: Westview Press.

Murray, M. (1956). *Circus!* New York: Appleton-Century-Crofts.

National Endowment for the Arts (1997). *American Canvas*. Washington, DC: NEA.

(1981). *Conditions and Needs of the Professional American Theater*. Washington, DC: NEA.

O'Connell, V. (1997). "Why the 'Angels' Invest in Broadway," *Wall Street Journal*, October 17.

Oestreich, J. R. (1997). "Opera Enjoys Its Charmed Life," *New York Times*, April 28.

Olson, E. (2000). "Keeping the Show Going in a Circus-Saturated Land," *New York Times*, December 28.

Osborne, C. L. (1991). "Opera's Fabulous Vanishing Act," *New York Times*, February 17.

Peacock, A., and Rizzo, I., eds. (1994). *Cultural Economics and Cultural Policies*. Dordrecht and Boston: Kluwer Academic Publishers.

Pedersen, L. (1996). "The Risks of Buying into Broadway," *New York Times*, December 8.

Pogrebin, R. (2004). "Deficit Threatens Dance Troupe in Harlem," *New York Times*, May 26.

(2001). "Along the Hudson, at Tent of Dreams," *New York Times*, April 6.

Pope, K., and King, T. R. (1995). "Andrew Lloyd Webber Is Planning an Empire Built on His Musicals," *Wall Street Journal*, May 4.

Revzin, P., and Patner, A. (1989). "Conductor Barenboim Survives Tough World of Orchestral Music," *Wall Street Journal*, May 2.

Robertson, C. (2006). "Nielsen Brings a New Marketing Strategy to Broadway," *New York Times*, August 1.

Rose-Ackerman, S., ed. (1986). *The Economics of Nonprofit Institutions*. New York: Oxford University Press.

Rosen, S. (1981). "The Economics of Superstars," *American Economic Review*, 71(5) (December).

Rosen, S., and Rosenfield, A. (1997). "Ticket Pricing," *Journal of Law & Economics*, XL(2)(October).

Ross, A. (1994). "Easy Does It: The Met Edges into the Future," *New York Times*, May 15.

Russell, J. H. (2005). "The Great Green Way," *Wall Street Journal*, October 22.

Shapiro, E. (1998). "From the Hinterlands, an Upstart Producer Barrels up Broadway," *Wall Street Journal*, April 28.

Silk, L. (1978). "The Metropolitan Opera – The High Price of Being Best: The Books Reveal the Cost Squeeze," *New York Times*, February 12.

Smith, P. J. (1998). "A New Birth for American Opera," *New York Times*, September 27.

Snyder, L. (1977). "How to Lose Less on Broadway," *Fortune*, XCV(5)(May).

Taylor, F., and Barresi, A. L. (1984). *The Arts at a New Frontier: The National Endowment for the Arts*. New York: Plenum.

Throsby, D. (1994). "The Production and Consumption of the Arts: A View of Cultural Economics," *Journal of Economic Literature*, 23(1).

Tindall, B. (2004). "The Plight of the White-Tie Worker," *New York Times*, July 4.

Tommasini, A. (2003). "Fewer Nights for San Francisco Opera," *New York Times*, January 30.

(1998). "A Crowd of Old Musicals Squeezes the New," *New York Times*, August 16.

Towse, R., ed. (2003). *A Handbook of Cultural Economics*. Cheltenham, U.K.: Edward Elgar.

(1997). *Cultural Economics: The Arts, the Heritage and the Media Industry*. Cheltenham, U.K.: Edward Elgar.

Trachtenberg, J. A. (1996). "How to Turn $4,000 into Many Millions: The Story of 'Rent'," *Wall Street Journal*, May 23.

Vogel, H. L. (2007). "Arts Economics," in *Understanding the Arts and Creative Sector in America*, edited by J. M. Cherbo, M. J. Wyszomirski, and R. A. Stewart. New Brunswick, NJ: Rutgers University Press.

Wakin, D. J. (2006). "In Cities Across the United States, It's Raining Concert Halls," *New York Times*, September 3.

(2004). "American Ballet Theater Trims Costs, Trying to Keep the Cuts Offstage," *New York Times*, October 27.

Weber, B. (2003). "Theater's Promise? Look Off Broadway," *New York Times*, July 2.

(1999). "Making a New Opera Fly Financially," *New York Times*, August 11.

(1998). "Gambling on a Trip from 'Ragtime' to Riches," *New York Times*, February 19.

Wickham, G. (1985). *A History of the Theatre*. New York and Cambridge: Cambridge University Press.

Yee, B., and Inverne, J. (2005). "Give My Regards to Shanghai," *Wall Street Journal*, April 29.

# 14
# Amusement/theme parks

*Mickey is the mouse that roared.*

The American themed amusement park industry – begun in July 1955 by Mickey Mouse, the famous Disney character – has evolved into a multi-billion-dollar entertainment segment that draws visitors from around the world and has spawned many imitations. In this chapter, the economic outlines of amusement/theme park operations are sketched.

## 14.1 Flower power

Gardens and groves

The roots of this business extend back to medieval church-sponsored fairs and to seventeenth-century France, whose concept of pleasure gardens with fountains and flowers gradually spread throughout Europe. London's Vauxhall Gardens, for example, were established in 1661.[1] By the eighteenth century, as Kyriazi (1976) has noted, entertainment and circus acts, including trapeze and tightrope scenes, ascension balloons, and music, were added. In England, meanwhile, affiliations with nearby taverns or inns also became common.

It was not until the 1873 Vienna World's Fair, held at The Prater, though, that mechanical rides and fun houses were introduced. As Mangels (1952, p. 4) describes it,

> for more than three hundred years, elaborate outdoor amusement centers have existed in several European countries. Known usually as "pleasure gardens" they were remarkably similar to those of today in their general layout and variety of entertainment. Some of the larger parks provided events and devices which thrilled their visitors as keenly as present-day attractions. Queens of the slack wire and daredevils of the flying rings brought gasps of fascinated terror, much as they do beneath the Big Top today . . . free balloon ascensions, and parachute jumps held crowds spellbound as far back as the seventeen-nineties.

In the United States, however, amusement areas did not begin to appear until the late 1800s, when streetcar companies began to build picnic groves to attract weekend riders. But still, as Adams (1991, p. 19) notes, it was the World's Columbian Exposition, held in Chicago in 1893, that "introduced most of the essential elements of American amusement parks." Soon there-after, food and rides came to be emphasized, and major facilities such as New York's Coney Island sprang into national prominence.[2] Although, by the 1920s, some 1,500 such parks existed in the United States, the Great Depression, the development of movies, television, and automobiles, and the decay of inner cities eventually led to the demise of most.

Modern times

Walt Disney, at first a struggling cartoonist and later a successful filmmaker, liked spending time with his children. Unfortunately, there were few bright, clean parks where all members of the family could have fun. So being an extraordinarily imaginative and entrepreneurial fellow, he envisioned cre-ation of such a park modeled in part after the famous Tivoli Gardens (founded in 1843) that he had seen in Copenhagen.[3]

As the legend goes, Disney brought his plans for an amusement park con-taining themed areas before a rather skeptical and reluctant group of bankers. However, with perseverance, bank loans supplemented by borrowing on his life insurance policies, and the sale of concession rights and a 34% equity stake to the young American Broadcasting Company, he nevertheless man-aged in 1955 to open Disneyland amidst the Anaheim, California, orange groves.[4] The rest, as they say, is history.

Disneyland's immediate success led to numerous expansions. But it was not until the late 1960s that other large public companies began to invest heavily in this business.[5] And the Disney company itself did not until 1971 extend into the swamps of Florida to construct, for an estimated $300 million, the core of Disney World.[6]

As of the early 2000s, theme parks in the United States, which num-ber about 30 majors and a host of smaller ones, generated over $15 billion a year from more than 150 million visitors (Table 14.1).[7] And, as of 2005,

Table 14.1. *Estimated attendance (millions) at major theme park facilities in the United States, 1984–2005*[a]

| Year | Admissions | Year | Admissions |
|------|------------|------|------------|
| 2005 | 149.7 | 1994 | 120.3 |
| 2004 | 144.5 | 1993 | 122.2 |
| 2003 | 142.9 | 1992 | 120.7 |
| 2002 | 130.5 | 1991 | 110.9 |
| 2001 | 135.6 | 1990 | 113.1 |
| 2000 | 147.9 | 1989 | 110.3 |
| 1999 | 139.4 | 1988 | 104.0 |
| 1998 | 137.0 | 1987 | 102.3 |
| 1997 | 136.9 | 1986 | 95.3 |
| 1996 | 133.5 | 1985 | 83.3 |
| 1995 | 129.0 | 1984 | 78.3 |
| CAGR[b] | | | |
| 1980–2005 | 2.6 | | |
| 1990–2005 | 1.9 | | |
| 1995–2005 | 1.5 | | |

[a] Fiscal years.
[b] Compound annual growth rate (%).

it is estimated that, on a global basis, the industry generated approximately $21 billion in revenues from attendance of around 550 million people.[8]

In fact, the concept of *location-based entertainment* (LBE) has come to be used as a broader way to more accurately describe technologically sophisticated away-from-home attractions, the largest examples of which are the major theme parks.[9] It is thus not surprising – in view of advances in technology, design, and marketing – that American-style LBE concepts of the late twentieth century are being exported back to Europe and elsewhere around the globe.[10] A compilation of such major theme parks and annual visitor estimates appears in Table 14.2, and a history of developments is displayed in Figure 14.1.

## 14.2 Financial operating characteristics

Operating a theme park is very much like operating a small city: The streets should be frequently swept clean and occasionally repaved; sewer and sanitation systems should be efficient yet invisible; and police, fire, and health departments should be trained and available at a moment's notice. Those elements alone are difficult for most cities to handle well. But, in addition, a park also issues its own currency in the form of ticket books, and it provides visitor-transportation systems, live-entertainment services, and sometimes extensive shopping, hotel, and car-care facilities.

Table 14.2. *Selected major theme park facilities*

| Facility | Year opened | Approximate number of annual visitors, 2005 (millions) |
|---|---|---|
| *North America* | | |
| Disney World, Florida[a] | 1971 | 43.0 |
| Disneyland, California[b] | 1955 | 20.4 |
| Universal Studios, Florida[c] | 1990 | 10.4 |
| Universal Studios Tour, California | 1964 | 4.6 |
| Sea World, Florida | 1973 | 5.6 |
| Busch Gardens, Florida | 1959 | 4.3 |
| Sea World, California | 1963 | 4.1 |
| Knotts Berry Farm, California | 1940 | 3.5 |
| Six Flags Great Adventure, New Jersey | 1973 | 3.0 |
| Kings Island, Ohio | 1972 | 3.3 |
| Cedar Point, Ohio | 1870 | 3.1 |
| Six Flags/Magic Mountain | 1971 | 2.8 |
| Six Flags/Great America, Illinois | 1976 | 2.9 |
| Canada's Wonderland, Toronto | 1981 | 3.7 |
| Six Flags/Texas | 1961 | 2.3 |
| Six Flags/Georgia | 1967 | 2.1 |
| Hersheypark, Pennsylvania | 1907 | 2.7 |
| Busch Gardens, Virginia | 1975 | 2.6 |
| Kings Dominion, Virginia | 1975 | 2.2 |
| *Europe* | | |
| Disneyland, Paris | 1992 | 10.2 |
| Tivoli Gardens, Denmark | 1843 | 3.3 |
| De Efteling, Netherlands | 1951 | 3.7 |
| Port Aventura, Spain | 1995 | 3.0 |
| Alton Towers, U.K. | 1924 | 2.5 |
| Europa Park, Germany | 1975 | 3.5 |
| Liseberg Park, Sweden | 1923 | 2.7 |
| Asterix, France | 1989 | 1.3 |
| Thorpe Park, U.K. | 1979 | 1.3 |
| Duinrell, Netherlands | 1935 | 1.2 |
| Grona Lund, Sweden | 1883 | 1.1 |
| *Other* | | |
| Tokyo Disneyland, Japan[d] | 1983 | 25.4 |
| Universal Studios, Osaka | 2001 | 8.8 |
| Lotte World, S. Korea | 1989 | 8.5 |

[a] Includes Magic Kingdom, Disney–MGM Studios, EPCOT, and Animal Kingdom.
[b] Includes Disneyland and Disneyland's California Adventure.
[c] Includes Universal Studios and Islands of Adventure.
[d] Includes Tokyo-Disneyland and Disney Sea.
*Source*: *Amusement Business.*

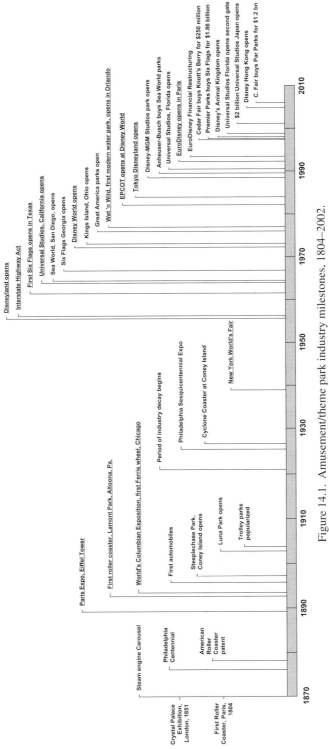

Figure 14.1. Amusement/theme park industry milestones, 1804–2002.

Table 14.3. *U.S. theme park industry operating performance: composite of seven companies, 2001–2005*

| | Revenues | Operating income | Operating margin (%)[a] | Assets | Operating cash flow |
|---|---|---|---|---|---|
| CAGR (%)[b] | 5.7 | NM[c] | NM[c] | 4.0 | −0.3 |

[a] Average margin, 2001–2005 = 16.4%.
[b] Compound annual growth rate.
[c] Not meaningful.

Furthermore, parks – subject as they are to seasonal and circadian rhythms of attendance and to rapidly changing weather patterns – usually depend on a largely unskilled seasonal workforce that turns over at inherently high rates. In all, it is not easy to juggle these elements and to further generate a stream of consistently rising profits (Table 14.3). For a specific park, operating-margin performance may thus be uneven and volatile: One year the problem may be high fuel prices; the next it may be abnormally hot summer temperatures, rainy spring weekends, or competition from other events.

No matter what the uncertainties, however, operating leverage, also familiar in the airline and hotel businesses (and described in *Travel Industry Economics: A Guide for Financial Analysis*) is a constant feature. The costs of labor, electricity, insurance, and so forth remain relatively fixed, and once the breakeven point is reached, every additional admission ticket sold produces a high marginal profit.[11]

Such is the case until the park becomes crowded. At that point, long lines at popular attractions reduce opportunities for impulse spending, crimp the initial good mood of the visitors, and entail additional labor and materials costs. Most parks will find that, in analyzing daily results, marginal-profit curves as a function of attendance would probably be similar to the one shown in Figure 14.2.

Table 14.4 furthermore demonstrates how sensitive operating profits are to changes in two key variables: visitor-days (attendance equivalent to the number of separate visitors times the number of days of operation) and average per capita spending. In this example, it is assumed that, because of climatic factors, a park has an effective operating season of 100 days per year, that on an average day there are 25,000 visitors, and that average per capita spending on admissions, rides, foods, beverages, and trinkets is $20. With a relatively stable operating expense of $30 million, operating earnings, as shown in column A, will be $20 million.

If we assume, however, that the number of visitors increases by 20% to 30,000 per day, while expenses remain largely unchanged, then operating profit will increase by 50% to $30 million (column B). And the same 50% increase in operating profit will naturally appear if attendance holds constant

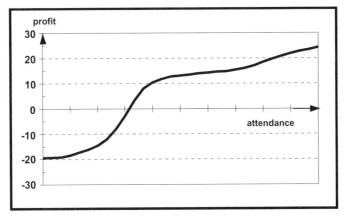

Figure 14.2. Profit as a function of attendance: an illustration.

and per capita spending rises by 20% (column C). But finally, assume that per capita spending *and* attendance each rise by 20% (column D). Then operating profit will increase to $42 million – a gain of 110% over that shown in column A.

In the real world, though, operating expenses will rise along with attendance, per capita spending will tend to decrease as attendance rises to near capacity (if only because the crowds are immobilized), and the gains in profit will not be as large as indicated in this simplistic example. But substantial operating leverage, both up and down, will nonetheless still be visible in actual results.

Because the compounding of changes in both attendance and spending has such a great impact on profits, park managers devote much of their time to figuring how each input factor can be increased without adversely affecting any of the others. Toward this end, many fancy mathematical modeling techniques (e.g., linear programming, production-function, and queuing-system estimators) can be used to improve the efficiency of park operations. Norms for average daily attendance conditioned on weather, queuing times, and price elasticities may then be established and tested much as though parks were production-line factories.

Table 14.4. *Theme park operating leverage: an example*

|  | A | B | C | D |
|---|---|---|---|---|
| Visitors, avg./day | 25,000 | 30,000 | 25,000 | 30,000 |
| Visitor-days (attend.) | 2,500,000 | 3,000,000 | 2,500,000 | 3,000,000 |
| Per cap. spending ($) | 20.00 | 20.00 | 24.00 | 24.00 |
| Total annual rev. ($) | 50,000,000 | 60,000,000 | 60,000,000 | 72,000,000 |
| Operating expenses | 30,000,000 | 30,000,000 | 30,000,000 | 30,000,000 |
| Operating profits ($) | 20,000,000 | 30,000,000 | 30,000,000 | 42,000,000 |

Table 14.5. *Financial ratio averages for major theme parks, foreign and domestic, 2003[a]*

|                                                        | U.S. & Canada | Europe |
| ------------------------------------------------------ | ------------- | ------ |
| **Mean operating days per year**                       | 203.0         | 181.0  |
| **Mean number of visits per persons per season[b]**    | 2.9           | 1.5    |
| **Mean percentage of total revenue[b]**                |               |        |
| Admissions                                             | 51.5          | 50.2   |
| Food                                                   | 16.9          | 23.9   |
| Merchandise                                            | 10.4          | 6.2    |
| Games                                                  | 6.3           | 9.5    |
| **Mean operating expenses as a% of total revenues**    |               |        |
| Employee wages and benefits                            | 29.3          | 19.3   |
| Repair and maintenance                                 | 5.3           | 5.6    |
| Advertising                                            | 5.2           | 5.3    |
| ROA[c]                                                 | 3.8           | 5.1    |
| **Operating Margin**                                   | 12.7          | 23.6   |

[a] Selected non-Disney parks with >0.5 million admissions.
[b] Parks open >201 days a year.
[c] Return on assets.
*Source*: International Association of Amusement Parks & Attractions, 2003 Season Survey.

Theme park operating performance depends on region, weather patterns, number of season days, local demographic and income characteristics, and the amount of capital recently invested. Consequently, it is difficult to establish a representative statistical composite for a typical park. Each facility must develop its own set of standards. Table 14.5 provides some recent industry sample ratios.

### 14.3 Economic sensitivities

A sense of how this industry's operating performance compares with those of other economic segments is not easily derived. But evidence from the North American Industry Classification System (NAICS) and the U.S. *Census of Selected Service Industries*, which provides data on employment and payrolls (Table 14.6), suggests that parks in the aggregate have been able to gradually reduce the inherent labor intensity of operations (i.e., payroll as a percent of receipts).

Unfortunately, there are also difficulties in correlating overall theme park admissions trends with important economic time series such as those for GDP or real disposable income. Although an economic recession could be expected to affect admissions growth trends adversely at high-profile themed resort parks, other parks more dependent on day-trip and regional visitors ought to fare relatively better in such an environment.

Table 14.6. *Service industry census comparisons for amusement parks in the United States, 1977–2002*

| | Receipts ($1,000) | Payroll (annual) ($1,000) | Employees (paid) | Receipts per employee ($) | Payroll as % of receipts |
|---|---|---|---|---|---|
| 2002 | 8,310,328 | 1,779,737 | 95,059 | 87,423 | 21.4 |
| 1997 | 6,828,719 | 1,611,090 | 106,794 | 63,943 | 23.6 |
| 1992 | 5,311,781 | 1,297,545 | 80,875 | 65,679 | 24.4 |
| 1987 | 3,469,836 | 818,881 | 60,414 | 57,434 | 23.6 |
| 1982 | 1,823,728 | 603,654 | 46,464 | 39,250 | 33.1 |
| 1977 | 1,172,419 | 352,898 | 37,014 | 31,675 | 30.1 |

*Source*: *U.S. Census of Selected Service Industries, Economic Census.*

As might be anticipated, however, aggregate theme park admissions do seem to be positively correlated with respect to consumer credit as a percent of personal income and negatively correlated with respect to the unemployment rate. But the lags, as suggested by Figure 14.3, are not well defined. Some additional variables to consider would include changes in real admission-ticket and fuel prices, changes in airline fares and foreign exchange rates, and demographic shifts over time.

As is the case for performing arts, it is likely that the demand for theme park services is more sensitive to the total cost of travel relative to incomes than to anything else. The price of oil has thus become a key variable given that it directly affects the ability of consumers to afford travel and that it also feeds immediately into the operating costs and pricing of theme park, hotel,

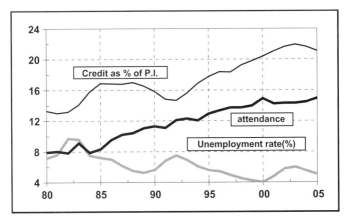

Figure 14.3. Theme park attendance (including Disney's), selected sample in the United States in tens of millions versus the unemployment rate (%) and consumer credit as a percentage of personal income, 1977–2005.

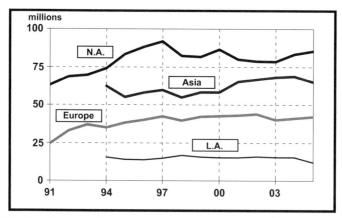

Figure 14.4. Attendance total for top ten parks in North America, Latin America, Asia, and Europe, 1991–2005. *Source*: *Amusement Business* data.

car rental, and airline services. Worldwide park attendance trends are shown in Figure 14.4.

## 14.4 Valuing theme park properties

Real estate – the key asset of any park – normally has the potential to provide the long-term returns on investment that, in the end, may surpass the average annual returns obtainable from day-to-day operations. However, for this to occur, the real estate usually needs to be developed for additional uses (housing, offices, studios, etc.) that are compatible with the park's operations. It also helps, as a hedge against future inflation, if the park happens to lie in the path of ongoing population expansion (e.g., Disneyland, just south of Los Angeles), or if the park, through its own qualities, is able to congeal what would otherwise be haphazard population growth around itself (e.g., Disney World near Orlando).[12]

Given the long-term operating nature of all major parks, the usual established methods for valuing other entertainment properties may also be applied here. As in the broadcasting and cable (or airline and hotel) industries, for example, theme park asset values are taken as a multiple of projected operating earnings before taxes, interest, and depreciation and amortization (EBITDA). Such multiples would normally be expected to vary inversely to interest rates. Other factors affecting the multiple applied to this definition of cash flow would include the following:

Age and condition of the park's rides and attractions
Demographic and income trends in the surrounding region
Potential for expanding ride and admissions capacity
Potential for raising prices and/or per capita spending
Prospects for development of nearby transportation facilities
Proximity of other similar attractions

Again, as in other entertainment segments, public market valuations are often considerably below what private market valuations, based on a multiple of cash flow, might be. Well-situated theme parks with proven operating characteristics are thus often attractive candidates for leveraged buy-outs in which large institutions will lend a major percentage of the required funding for the buy-out based on the security of the park's cash flow.[13]

## 14.5 Concluding remarks

Admissions growth trends for the major facilities in the United States have, over long periods, held consistently above the growth trend of real GDP. More recently, though, there have been signs of slowing. Large theme parks are no longer a novelty, and they compete for time and attention with many other entertainment alternatives.

The amount of capital investment and technological sophistication required to maintain a leadership position has also grown enormously. New motion simulator rides and other computer-controlled "experiences," such as those developed in the framework of "virtual reality" and interactive video games, are the new frontiers in the evolution of theme park concepts. It is no wonder then that major media companies still view theme park tie-ins as a natural fit.

The industry seems to be rather mature in North America, where it has developed into an entertainment form dominated by those few large firms having the marketing expertise and capital to continuously upgrade and expand their facilities. Now, faster growth is more likely to be seen in other parts of the world. Regardless of location, though, the degree of success will have as much to do with intangible elements – quality of design, efficiency of service, and public fancy – as with anything else.

## Notes

**1.** Actually, the oldest amusement park is Bakken, just north of Copenhagen, which began attracting visitors in 1583. See *Amusement Business*, March 3, 1996.

**2.** Indeed, the first true amusement park was Steeplechase Park at Coney Island, which was opened in 1897 by George Tilyou. Also, as Nasaw (1993, p. 85) notes, Luna Park, in competition with Steeplechase and Dreamland, in 1904 attracted 4 million people – a remarkable number for that time.

**3.** See Thomas (1976, Chapter 20). Also, as Adams (1991, p. 435) notes, the underlying concepts had been proven in Tilyou's Steeplechase Park.

**4.** The 160-acre site for Disneyland was selected by the Stanford Research Institute.

**5.** In attempts to emulate Disney's concepts on a smaller scale, the Marriott Corporation, Taft Broadcasting, Six Flags, and others began a construction boom that lasted throughout most of the 1970s. A total of at least $500 million was spent in the construction of parks such as Busch Gardens Old Country, Great Adventure, Kings Dominion, Great America, and Canada's Wonderland. As of 1997, the largest corporate park operators after Disney in terms of total admissions were Anheuser–Busch (Sea World, Busch Gardens Tampa,

FL, and Williamsburg, VA), Six Flags (partly owned by Time Warner), Paramount (Kings Island, Kings Dominion, Canada's Wonderland), and Seagram (Universal Studios, Orlando and Los Angeles). In 2004, Universal parks were owned by NBC Universal. As of 2007, Time Warner and Paramount were no longer directly involved in the industry.

**6.** That was, of course, followed by another initial investment of $1.1 billion to open the EPCOT Center in 1981 as well as $500 million for the Studio Tour that opened in 1989.

**7.** A subset of the themed amusement business involves regularly scheduled state fairs and regional expositions. These fairs are, in essence, movable, impermanent theme parks that have operating characteristics similar to those of permanent facilities. According to compilations by *Amusement Business*, the industry trade journal, in 1999 the top 50 fairs attracted combined attendance of 45.5 million. But because only about 60% of all admissions are paid, the industry generates less than $200 million at the gate. Several times this amount, however, is derived from activities conducted within the fairs.

Water parks, another subset, have also become popular in recent years. In 1999, an estimated 63 million people visited the nation's approximately 100 water parks, according to *Amusement Business* estimates. See also Lyon (1987).

**8.** A study by consulting firm Economics Research Associates indicates that in the year 2000, 340 parks worldwide generated a combined attendance of 545 million and revenues of $13.5 billion, with North America accounting for 49% of all revenues. The data include North American parks with attendance above 500,000 and "significant" parks elsewhere. In the 1990s, the number of parks and revenues approximately doubled and attendance grew by 80%. See *Amusement Business*, January 10, 2000.

**9.** Location-based entertainment is a recent nomenclature that has been generally used to describe ride-simulator theaters and advanced video-game arcades built in urban or suburban shopping centers. However, LBE is a term that could as well be used to describe theme parks, movie theaters, themed restaurants, sports stadiums, or casinos. LBE companies generate revenues by selling and/or leasing systems and production equipment, by licensing film software to operators, or by owning and operating attractions.

**10.** A number of major European parks date to the early 1900s. As shown in Brown and Church (1987), Alton Towers in the United Kingdom was opened in 1924 and Kantoor (Duinrell) in the Netherlands in 1935.

Also, Asian parks are becoming important, especially in Japan, Indonesia, and Korea. Disney, for example, has a park project in Hong Kong.

**11.** Both traditional carnival-type games and electronic video games also generate high marginal profits.

**12.** Particularly in the case of smaller parks, it is conceivable, though not likely, that operation of the park turns out to be merely an interim holding action in anticipation of the maturation of higher-value alternative uses. In such instances, the park would be worth more dead than alive.

**13.** In 1983, Taft Broadcasting Company sold to Kings Entertainment Company theme parks that included Kings Island, Kings Dominion, Carowinds, and Hanna Barbera Land for $167.5 million. In 1984, Marriott sold its 195-acre Santa Clara property to the city of Santa Clara for $101 million and the 325-acre Gurnee, Illinois, park to Bally Mfg. for about $114.5 million. Also, in 1982, Six Flags parks (six facilities with 1982 attendance of approximately 12.6 million) were bought by Bally Mfg. for $147 million plus assumption of about $100 million in debt. Six Flags was subsequently again transferred to Wesray Capital Corp. by Bally Mfg. in 1987 for approximately $350 million plus assumption of $250 million of debt. Then, in 1994, Time Warner Inc. sold the properties to an investment consortium at a value of approximately $1.1 billion. The Six Flags facilities were ultimately bought by Premier Parks in April 1998 for $965 million. Also, in 2000, Rank Group Plc agreed to sell its 50% interest in Universal Studios Escape to Blackstone Group Partners for $275 million.

## Selected additional reading

Bannon, L. (1996). "Universal Studios' Plan to Expand in Florida Moves Disney to Battle," *Wall Street Journal*, October 2.

Belson, K. (2003). "A Japanese Theme Park Company Fails," *New York Times*, February 27.

Berck, J. (1994) "When Broadway Meets the Midway, It's Big Business," *New York Times*, August 28.

Braithwaite, D. (1967). *Fairground Architecture: The World of Amusement Parks, Carnivals, & Fairs*. New York: Praeger.

Eisner, M. D. (1998). *Work in Progress*. New York: Random House.

Eliot, M. (1993). *Walt Disney, Hollywood's Dark Prince: A Biography*. New York: Carol Publishing (Birch Lane).

Faison, S. (1999). "Even If You Build Them . . . ," *New York Times*, August 3.

Finch, C. (1975). *The Art of Walt Disney: From Mickey Mouse to the Magic Kingdoms*. New York: Harry N. Abrams.

Flower, J. (1991). *Prince of the Magic Kingdom: Michael Eisner and the Re-Making of Disney*. New York: Wiley.

Fowler, G. A., and Marr, M. (2005). "Disney's China Play," *Wall Street Journal*, June 16.

Gabler, N. (2006). *Walt Disney: The Triumph of the American Imagination*. New York: Knopf.

Grover, R. (1997). *The Disney Touch*, rev. ed. Chicago: Irwin.

Gubernick, L. (1999). "How Safe Is That Theme Park?," *Wall Street Journal*, July 23.

Gumbel, P., and Turner, R. (1994). "Fans Like Euro Disney but Its Parent's Goofs Weigh the Park Down," *Wall Street Journal*, March 10.

Hannon, K. (1987). "All Aboard!," *Forbes*, 140(3)(August 10).

Jackson, C., and Gamerman, E. (2006). "Rethinking the Thrill Factor," *Wall Street Journal*, April 15.

Lainsbury, A. (2000). *Once upon an American Dream: The Story of Euro Disneyland*. Lawrence, KS: University Press of Kansas.

Marr, M., and Cutler, K-M. (2005) "Fine Line on Wild Rides," *Wall Street Journal*, July 1.

McDowell, E. (1998). "The New Monster of the Midway," *New York Times*, June 21.

Mosley, L. (1987). *Disney's World: A Biography*. Briarcliff Manor, NY: Stein and Day.

Mrowca, M. (1983). "Amusement Park in Ohio Has Its Ups and Downs but Continues to Draw Crowds after 114 Years," *Wall Street Journal*, July 8.

Ono, Y. (1990). "Theme Parks Boom in Japan as Investors and Consumers Rush to Get on the Ride," *Wall Street Journal*, August 8.

Prada, P. (2001). "*Ja, Ja*, Americana's *Fabulosa*," *Wall Street Journal*, June 21.

Rayl, A. J. S. (1990). "Making Fun: Theme Parks of the Future," *Omni* 13(2)(November).

Ross, I. (1982). "Disney Gambles on Tomorrow," *Fortune*, 106(October 4).

Schickel, R. (1968). *The Disney Version: The Life, Times, Art and Commerce of Walt Disney*. New York: Simon & Schuster.

Schweizer, P., and Schweizer, R. (1998). *Disney: The Mouse Betrayed*. Washington, DC: Regnery Publishing.

Setoodeh, R. (2004). "Step Right Up!," *Wall Street Journal*, July 12.

Spindle, B. (2001). "Cowboys and Samurai: The Japanizing of Universal," *Wall Street Journal*, March 22.

Tagliabue, J. (2000). "Giving Theme Parks a Whirl: Europeans Warm to an American Experience," *New York Times*, September 2.

(1995). "Step Right Up, Monsieur!: Growing Disneyfication of Europe's Theme Parks," *New York Times*, August 23.

Tanikawa, M. (2001). "Japanese Theme Parks Facing Rough Times," *New York Times*, March 2.

Welsh, J. (1999). "Premier Parks Intends to Grow Big by Thinking Small," *Wall Street Journal*, May 12.

Wrighton, J., and Orwall, B. (2005). "Despite Losses and Bailouts, France Stays Devoted to Disney," *Wall Street Journal*, January 26.

# Part IV
Roundup

# 15
# Performance and policy

*Time flies when you're having fun.*

Entertainment is a big and rapidly changing international business, and the study of its economic characteristics is still at an early stage. As a platform for such studies, this book has attempted to convey a sense of the industry's dynamics in relation to the financial and economic features that enduringly characterize entertainment enterprises. This closing chapter provides a review and summary of those features and also discusses the choices and implications for making public policy decisions.

## 15.1 Common elements

As seen in Chapter 1, leisure time – broadly defined as time not spent at work – has been expanding slowly, if at all, in recent years. And over the long run, the potential to expand leisure time depends notably on the rate of gain in economic productivity, which is in turn affected by the rate of technological development.

If we deduct life-sustenance activities from nonwork time, we have what is known in the vernacular as free time. But time is never really free in an economic sense because there are always alternative-opportunity costs.

Entertainment, defined as that which has the effect of pleasurably diverting the psyche, thus competes for – and is ultimately limited by – the amount of free time available.

Beyond these generalities are several frequently observed industry characteristics.

***Many are called, but few are chosen:*** Perhaps the most noticeable tendency of entertainment businesses is that in the steady-state growth phase (i.e., after a segment has attained a size at which long-run domination by several large companies has been established), *profits from a very few highly popular products are generally required to offset losses from many mediocrities.* This is evident in movies, television productions, toys and video games, and recorded music – segments in which revenues from new product introductions often appear to be statistically distributed according to power laws (i.e., by distributions that have unstable means and infinite variances). In the performing arts category, however, rarely do even a few occasional huge hits counterbalance chronic operating deficits.

***Marketing expenditures per unit are proportionally large:*** Many entertainment products or services have unique features that must continuously be brought to the attention of potential consumers. In addition, the life cycle of an entertainment product may be very brief. Therefore, be it casinos in Las Vegas, theme parks in Florida, or a new video game, *per unit marketing expenditures tend to be large relative to total unit costs of operation or production.* For instance, it may be recalled that marketing typically adds at least 50% to the cost of the average major feature film release. In economic terms, such spending on marketing attempts to shift the demand schedule to the right and to make demand less sensitive to price (i.e., more price-inelastic).

***Ancillary markets provide disproportionately large returns:*** Indeed, as a result of *sunk-cost characteristics* – wherein almost every dollar of revenue goes first toward recoupment of direct costs – *entertainment products often derive a large proportion of their returns from ancillary or secondary markets.* This also means that *price-discrimination opportunities between classes of consumers having different demand elasticities can be exploited.* Films, for instance, on the average now derive over half their revenues from exposures on cable and home video rather than from initial theatrical release. And spin-offs of character licenses into popular TV series or movie sequels and novelizations may often be sources of significant additional income. Price-discrimination effects are readily observed in the pricing of tickets to cultural events and in the sequencing of a movie through various exhibition windows.

***Capital costs are relatively high; oligopolist tendencies are prevalent:*** As happens in many other industries, once beyond the very early stages of a segment's development, *the cost of capital and the amount of it required for operations becomes a formidable barrier to entry by new competitors.* Most entertainment industry segments thus come to be ruled by large companies with relatively easy access to large pools of capital. Such oligopolistic tendencies can, for example, be seen in distribution of recorded music and movies, and in the gaming, theme park, cable, video game, and broadcasting industries.

***Public-good characteristics are often present:*** With pure public goods, the cost of production is independent of the number of consumers; that is, consumption by one person does not reduce the amount available for consumption by another. Although delivered to consumers in the form of private goods, *many entertainment products and services, including movies, records, television programs, and sports contests, have public-good characteristics.*

***Many products and services are not standardized (which is good for entrepreneurs and bad for relative-productivity gains):*** There are four important consequences of such nonstandardization:

1.  Despite the oligopolistic framework, *there is considerable freedom for the entrepreneurial spirit to thrive.* That is, operas, plays, movies, ballets, songs, and video games are uniquely produced and are normally originated by individuals working alone or in small groups and not by giant corporate committees. One can become rich and famous as a direct result of one's own creative efforts.
2.  *The entrepreneurial spirit and thus the importance of the individual to the productive process is accommodated by means of widely varying, and uniquely tailored, financing arrangements.* This is especially evident in movies, recorded music, and sports. Option contracts are central.
3.  *Where the production is the product itself* (e.g., live performance of music or dance), *it is difficult to enhance productivity.* To some extent, this aspect also appears in areas as diverse as filmmaking, sports, and casino gaming.
4.  Under the aforementioned conditions, *the costs of creating and marketing entertainment products such as movies and television programs tend to rise at above-average rates.*

***Technological advances provide the saving grace:*** Fortunately, ongoing *technological development makes it ever easier and less expensive to manufacture, distribute, and receive entertainment products and services.* Over the long run, this leads to more varied and more affordable mass-market entertainment. But at the same time, technology also enables entertainment products and services to be customized once creation, production, and distribution become enmeshed by the network economy.

***New entertainment media tend not to render older ones extinct:*** New ways to deliver entertainment products and services are constantly evolving. Although *introduction of new entertainment media may diminish the importance of existing forms, the older forms are rarely rendered extinct.* Introduction of broadcast television or of home videos has not stopped people from wanting to see movies in theaters or from going to Broadway shows or from listening to radio. Broadcast coexists with cable. And even in the age of the Internet, people still buy plenty of newspapers, books, and magazines.

*Entertainment products and services have universal appeal: Demand for
entertainment cuts across all cultural and national boundaries,* and many
cravings (for laughter, for music, or for gambling) have deep-seated psychological roots. This means that many entertainment products have worldwide
market appeal and that incremental revenues from international sources can
have an important effect on profitability.

## 15.2 Public policy issues

Entertainment and media businesses always gravitate toward and indeed normally thrive in a free-market environment. Yet major sectors of the entertainment and media businesses have been surrounded, contained, and intertwined
by government regulations and sporadic interventions. Broadcasting, cable,
and gaming come immediately to mind, but antitrust has been an issue for
film exhibitors and distributors from the start and antitrust exemption is a
feature of professional sports.

   The balances between regulation and intervention and support and subsidy are as much questions answered by political, cultural, and sociological
considerations as by those of economics and technology. Whether in the
United States or elsewhere, though, the basic concerns are always expressed
in terms of:

* degree of regulatory oversight and stringency
* free market (laissez-faire) versus intervention
* concentration of ownership versus diversity
* subsidies and tax breaks
* operating efficiencies and industry structures

All these issues can and often will be mixed together in the political arenas and, sometimes, the public policy that emerges will weigh on corporate
profits, the effectiveness of management or the growth prospects for the
industry notwithstanding. At other times, subsidies of various kinds promote
politically inspired agendas that help one industry at the expense of another
without noticeable benefit to the public at large. Yet trade-offs and opportunity costs of best alternatives forgone are always present and should never
be ignored in the process of making policy decisions.

   For films, tax credits or tax-related subsidies appear in many different
guises. Quotas, such as the one that requires at least half of all programming transmitted in the European Union to be of European origin, are also
common. Similarly, in most countries, including the United States, ownership of broadcasting companies by foreign interests is either not allowed
or limited to minority percentages. In cable and phones, government policy
affects competitor access to distribution systems. Such policies often diminish the gatekeeper power and the potential profitability of the companies that
own the distribution lines. Restrictions on cross-ownership of newspapers,

cable, and broadcast assets in the same market have the same effect and are motivated as much by concern over concentration of economic power as for interest in maintaining diversity of political opinion.

Cultural or nonprofit situations are also greatly influenced by policy decisions. Why, for example, do we decide to spend public money or provide tax breaks in support of cultural centers where rich people go to the theater and the opera or to subsidize sports stadiums instead of using the same money to fight poverty and provide more health care and education? How does a society train and sustain its art and culture if it doesn't provide such subsidies? Should countries provide tax credits for filmmaking instead of for construction of schools and power plants? Or should the government encourage and legitimize gaming and wagering, perhaps at the expense of other nearby enterprises?

Free-ridership occurs when the marginal cost of supplying a service like broadcasting to one additional, nonexcludable viewer is zero. In music and video, the technological worry is about "piracy," but this terminology is often misleading: When most people download content from the Web without paying and for their own (noncommercial) use only, they are usually behaving more like free-riders than pirates. In these areas and many others in media and entertainment, public policy decisions affect the rate of technological change and the profits that may ultimately be earned from such change. If the policy favors software (content) over hardware, or vice versa, does the public benefit more or less over the long haul? How are the content creators and artists compensated?

In each situation, the public policy that emerges has a great and often lasting affect on the profits and growth prospects. But there are no easy answers.

## 15.3 Guidelines for evaluating entertainment securities

The preceding chapters provide a background for analysis of entertainment industry investments. However, many factors not explicitly treated here (Federal Reserve monetary policy, overall economic trends, and investor psychology) also influence investment performance (Figure 15.1).

Happily, it is not necessary to delve into those subjects to extract a few basic investment-decision guidelines.

### Cash flows and private market values

Most entertainment and media companies are first analyzed in terms of what a private buyer or acquiring public corporation might be willing to pay for the right to obtain access to the cash flow (often represented by EBITDA) of the enterprise. Public market valuations are often in the range of one-half to three-quarters of private values, which are estimated from going-rate multiples of projected cash flow (minus debt) that have been paid in recent private transactions.

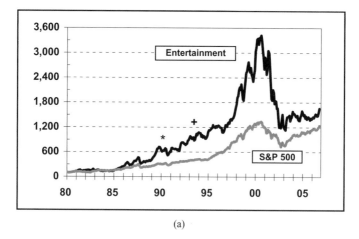

(a)

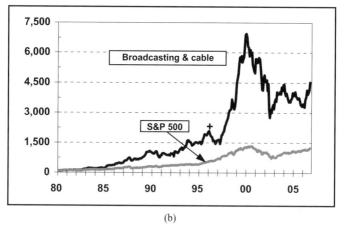

(b)

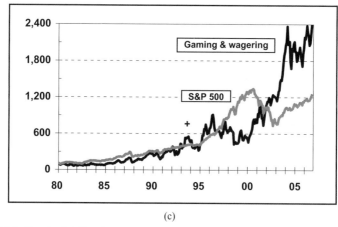

(c)

Figure 15.1. Standard & Poor's stock price indices for (a) entertainment, (b) broadcasting, (c) gaming and wagering, (d) toys, and (e) publishing versus the S&P 500 stock composite index, 1980–2006, based on month-end prices. + indicates major takeover events.

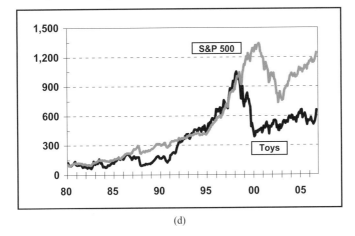

(d)

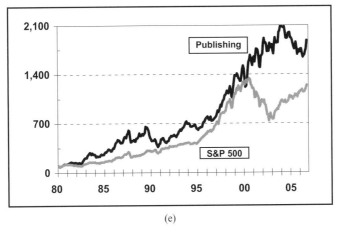

(e)

Figure 15.1. (*cont.*)

### Debt/equity ratios

The ability to service debt varies widely among entertainment companies, but it is always a function of the volatility of projected cash flows. The less volatile the cash flow, the higher the debt level relative to equity that can be comfortably accommodated on the balance sheet. Casino-industry companies, for instance, would generally be expected to experience far less cash flow volatility than companies in the toy and game industries. And, by and large, the major movie and record companies, relying on libraries and catalogs as they do, would usually fall somewhere in the middle of the volatility range.

### Price/earnings ratios

For entertainment stocks, the price/earnings ratio seems to have lost a great deal of its usefulness as a tool in comparative investment analysis. In movies and television, for example, earnings trends can be easily distorted because of accounting conventions that require management forecasts of anticipated revenues and recognition of syndication earnings when a series is made available. If price/earnings ratios are nevertheless used to compare entertainment stocks with alternative investments, then adjustments for such differences in the accounting practices must obviously be made.

### Price/sales ratios

Because price-to-sales ratios do not suffer from the accounting distortions that are frequently present in the calculation of earnings, such ratios have become increasingly popular in the evaluation of common stocks. For entertainment securities, however, the price/sales ratio (price per share divided by revenues per share) is perhaps most useful as a "reality check" – especially if adjustments that smooth or normalize sales over several periods are made to take into account any evidence that current period sales may be far above or below trend. Sales may be temporarily boosted far above trend, for example, with release of an unusually popular movie, toy, or recording, or may be temporarily depressed far below trend because of an economic recession. Price/sales ratios generally will correlate with the size of profit margins.

### Enterprise values

The total value of an enterprise is found by multiplying the number of shares outstanding and then adding net debt (i.e., total debt minus cash) and adjusting for off–balance sheet assets. Enterprise value (EV) is then often compared with earnings before interest and taxes (EBIT), EBITDA, or any other preferred measure of cash flow. When applied to similar companies in the same industry, such ratios enable firms with different capital structures to be compared on the same basis. EV ratios are thus somewhat more reliable than P/E ratios in deciding how expensive a stock is relative to its industry group.

### Book value

Book value – the amount of stockholders' equity on the balance sheet – is a traditional yardstick for financial analysis. But it normally has little relevance in the evaluation of entertainment company stock prices because the key earnings power may reside – as in the case of film libraries or song catalogs – in assets that have already been largely or completely written down. Moreover, in the case of real estate assets (studio backlots, theme park facilities, transmission tower sites), the historical cost basis is usually far below what a property might currently be worth. And brand names and other intangible assets (e.g., intellectual property) may have considerable value and yet not be reflected in the stated book numbers.

## 15.4 Final remarks

Entertainment has proven to be one of life's essentials, ranking perhaps just behind food, shelter, and clothing in its importance to many people. Indeed, once a society develops to the point at which there is what economists call discretionary income, a substantial portion of this income is likely to be spent on entertainment products and services.

Technological development has been the driving force behind the growth of the entertainment industries. And, as such, it leads indirectly to an increase in leisure time availability through economic productivity enhancements and leads directly to qualitative improvements and cost reductions in manufacturing and distribution.

Trends into the early 2000s still generally suggest that the entertainment industries will in the aggregate continue to develop at faster-than-average rates and that they will continue in the process of integrating vertically and globally. Yet the industries are already quite mature in the United States, and expansion will increasingly be linked to the rate of growth of middle-class populations outside North America.

Nevertheless, the one thing that we can be certain of is that no matter what the growth rate or how large the corporate entities become, entertainment industries will always remain dependent on the vitality and creativity of individuals. In this respect, they will not have changed at all.

# Appendix A
# Sources of information

The most convenient sources of macroeconomic data for use in entertainment-industry studies include the following regular U.S. Department of Commerce publications:

- *Survey of Current Business*, containing personal-consumption expenditure figures for the preceding four years
- *Business Conditions Digest*, especially for detailed industrial price data
- Labor Department, *Monthly Review* and *Handbook of Labor Statistics*, for articles and data on labor and employment issues
- *Census of Manufactures* and, especially, *Census of Selected Services*, which contains regional data on revenues, employment, and productivity
- *Statistical Abstract* for historical series
- *Industrial Outlook*, published every year with forecasts for the next five years

Information on specific entertainment-business topics is also widely available in the following regularly published non–government sponsored magazines, newspapers, and journals:

*Advertising Age*
*Billboard*
*Broadcasting & Cable*
*CableVision*
*Cable World*
*Cash Box*
*Editor & Publisher*
*Gaming & Wagering Business*
*Multichannel News*
*The Hollywood Reporter*

*Play Meter*
*Publisher's Weekly*
*Replay*
*Street & Smith's SportsBusiness Journal*
*The Journal of Cultural Economics*
*The Journal of Media Economics*
*The Journal of Sports Economics*
*Television Digest*
*Television Week*
*Variety* (daily and weekly)

# Appendix B
# Major games of chance

In studying the financial economics of gaming, it is essential to have at least a cursory knowledge of game characteristics. This appendix is designed to provide such knowledge, but it is by no means intended as a complete guide. Many other widely available books contain far greater detail concerning the finer points of play strategy and money management (i.e., the number of units wagered at each betting decision).[1] Tax consequences may also have some relevance.[2]

## Blackjack

In blackjack, alternatively known as twenty-one or vingt-et-un, the player's goal is to receive cards totaling more than those of the dealer, but not exceeding 21 – and to do this before the dealer has to show his or her hand. An ace card can be counted as either 1 or 11, other numbers count as their actual values, and picture cards count as 10. Suits do not matter. The payoff to a winning player is equivalent to the amount bet, that is, even money – except in the case of "blackjack" (a "natural" 21 on the first two cards), when the payoff is three units to two.

The game operator's advantage in blackjack is difficult to compute at any point of play. However, from the top of a deck, blackjack ordinarily provides the house with an edge of a little over 2%.[3] As the game progresses, however, the house edge (which depends importantly on the fact that the dealer turns over his or her cards *after* the player has gone bust) may disappear, and a skilled card counter can take advantage of such moments by increasing the size of the bet at that time. Blackjack is thus the only casino game that can be beaten by players, and it is this well-advertised fact that has made it the most popular of casino table games.

To win consistently, however, skills in card counting, in play strategy, and in money management must be employed simultaneously in the typical high-speed, pressurized casino environment.[4] But because attainment of such skills requires innate ability in mathematics and extensive study and practice (the patience for which is not apt to be found in most players), the threat to casino profits from self-proclaimed card counters is usually more imagined than real.

The presence of card counters has nonetheless tended to unnerve managements, and rather than simply foiling recognized counters by setting low betting limits, casinos have devised a multitude of card-cutting and multideck variations.

## Craps

Craps has long been a favorite in American casinos and, along with poker, is a quintessential American game. It evolved from the English game, hazard, and was adopted and refined by American blacks in New Orleans in the early 1800s. Thereafter it spread to immigrant neighborhoods on the East Coast. In contrast to 21, in which probability calculations are especially complicated, the house edge in bank craps as regularly conducted in casinos can be readily computed.

Two cubes (dice) – each die's surfaces marked one through six with embedded dots – are thrown by the player ("shooter") against a backboard on the opposite side of the table. Betting decisions are dependent on the sum of dots on the top surfaces of the dice after they come to rest.

There are 36 possible outcomes (6 × 6), and the probabilities of a number being thrown are measured against those outcomes. With two cubes, there are more ways (six) to make a 7 (i.e., 1:6, 2:5, 3:4, 4:3, 5:2, 6:1) than to make any other number (Table B.1), and craps uses this as a central theme for decision making.

So-called front-line bets in craps generate a house edge of 1.41%, calculated by the following method:

Assume a perfect dice shooter on each new comeout roll throws each of the 11 numbers exactly as often as predicted for the long run by probability theory.

Table B.1. *(a) Number of ways to throw a given number with two dice and (b) point numbers and odds that 7 appears first*

| (a) | | (b) | |
|---|---|---|---|
| Roll | Ways | Number | Odds |
| 2 | 1 | 4 | 2 to 1 |
| 3 | 2 | 5 | 3 to 2 |
| 4 | 3 | 6 | 6 to 5 |
| 5 | 4 | 8 | 6 to 5 |
| 6 | 5 | 9 | 3 to 2 |
| 7 | 6 | 10 | 2 to 1 |
| 8 | 5 | | |
| 9 | 4 | | |
| 10 | 3 | | |
| 11 | 2 | | |
| 12 | 1 | | |
| Total | 36 | | |

To avoid complicated arithmetic with fractions and to derive a lowest common multiple, multiply 36 possible outcomes by 55, which is 1,980.

Then, out of 1,980 throws, a 7 will appear 6/36 of the time (i.e., 330 times). Similarly, a 4 will be made 3/36 of the time (or 165 times), and so forth.

After adding all the winning figures as shown in Table B.2, we can see that there will be 976 winning rolls and 1,004 losing rolls; the house edge is thus the difference of 28 rolls out of 1,980, or 1.41%.

Table B.2. *Front-line bets in craps*

| Number | Times thrown | Winning rolls |
|---|---|---|
| Natural 7 | 330 | 330 |
| Natural 11 | 110 | 110 |
| Craps 2, 3, 12 | 220 | — |
| Point 4 | 165 | 55 |
| Point 10 | 165 | 55 |
| Point 5 | 220 | 88 |
| Point 9 | 220 | 88 |
| Point 6 | 275 | 125 |
| Point 8 | 275 | 125 |
| Totals | 1,980 | 976 |

*Source*: *Scarne's Guide to Casino Gambling*. Copyright © 1978 by John Scarne Games, Inc. Reprinted by permission of Simon and Schuster, Inc.

## Roulette

Historians disagree on the origin of roulette. Some say it was invented by the French mathematician Blaise Pascal in 1655; others support more arcane theories. In any event, the game has evolved into European and American versions; the European wheel has a single zero, whereas the American one has zero and double zero.

Mixed in standardized format around the roulette wheel are the numbers 1 through 36 and, in addition, depending on the version, either zero or both zero and double zero. The numbers on the wheel have adjacent background colors that alternate red and black and are arranged so that alternate low and high, odd and even, and red and black numbers are as mathematically balanced as possible. A perfect balance cannot be achieved because the sum of the numbers 1 through 36 is 666; the odd numbers sum to 324, and the even numbers sum to 342.

By placing one or more chips on a number, color, or odd or even, the player is betting that a ball spinning near the rim of the wheel will stop on that number, color, or number type. Payoffs on winning odd-even or black-red bets are 1:1, but for a specific number the payoff is 35:1. With an American double-zero wheel, a total of 38 positions are possible, and so the correct odds are 37:1. Thus, the casino keeps 2/38 (5.26%) in the American game or 1/37 (2.70%) in the European game.

Other betting variations that are often offered by casinos normally do not significantly affect the casino's percentages. For instance, the *en prison* option reduces the house advantage by half on even-money bets (i.e., color, high-low number, or odd-even). On such bets, when zero or double zero is the outcome of the last spin of the wheel, players may settle for half the original wager or let the original amount ride (imprison the wager). If the choice is to let it ride and the following spin is a winner, the original bet is returned intact.

## Baccarat

Baccarat and its close cousins, Punto Banco, Chemin de Fer, and Baccarat en Banque, are popular high-stakes games in casinos all over the world. All current versions are derived from the Italian *baccara*, first introduced into France circa 1490 and later adopted as a favorite game of the nobility. But it was not until the late 1950s that modern baccarat was taken seriously by Las Vegas casinos.

The earlier Chemin de Fer is played the same way as baccarat, except that in Chemin, the casino takes no risk because players bet against each other – the house merely acts as a "cutter" for a standard 5% charge taken from the player-banker's winning bet (coup).

In American baccarat, eight standard 52-card decks are shuffled and placed in a "shoe." There may be as many as 12 people seated at the table, and each makes a bet by placing chips for the *Player*, for the *Banker*, or for a tie hand. Winning bets (subject to commissions, as discussed below) are paid even money, and ties usually are paid at 8 to 1.

A bettor and the dealer are each dealt two cards, with picture cards and 10 counting as zero and number cards counting their actual face values. Should the two-card sum be in double digits (i.e., 10 or more), then the right-hand digit is considered the card count. A two-card sum of 14 would thus be counted as 4.

Normally, the gamer's goal is for the side he or she is betting on – either Player or Banker – to have a two-card count of 9. However, if either side has less than 8 or 9 (a "natural"), there are fairly standardized rules that specify when additional cards may be drawn. A count of zero is "baccarat."

Through complicated arithmetic it has been determined, according to Scarne (1978, p. 266), that the chance of the Player's side winning is about 49.33% and for the Banker's side, 50.67%. The Player's disadvantage, or cost to participate, is thus about 1.34%. However, to even out the sides (and save time on making change), the casino retains a 5% "commission" out of the Banker's winnings (it actually recaptures 5% of excess payoff). (Because the Banker's side, on average, wins 50.67% of the hands dealt, the actual charge is 2.53% [0.5067 times 5%].) In so reducing the aforementioned Banker's advantage of 1.34% by 2.53%, the Banker's cost of play after commission then nets to about 1.19% (1.34 minus 2.53). Thus, the casino's edge is somewhere between 1.19% and 1.34%.[5] But on bets that Banker and Player have tie hands, casinos usually pay 8 to 1 and have an edge of 14.36%. Consequently, although bets on ties may typically account for only 3% of the total money wagered, they represent perhaps 10% of the total won by the house.

Because most of the play, at a rate of about 70 hands an hour, is concentrated on Player or Banker – where the margins are thin – the casino win results for baccarat are generally far more volatile than for any of the other games.

## Slots

Slot machines have steadily evolved since first introduced in San Francisco in 1887 and, for most casinos, they now draw over 40% of revenues and an even larger share of profits.

In recent years, the performance of slots has been greatly enhanced by the development of sophisticated electronic microprocessors. Nonetheless, the basic concept of slot play remains the same as always: to line up certain randomly generated symbols on a window or video screen. In return for so doing, players are rewarded with various levels of monetary prizes determined proportionally by the probability of occurrence.

For example, in a mechanical three-reel model with 20 different symbols per reel, and with each reel spinning independently, the probability of three of the same figures lining up is 1/20 × 1/20 × 1/20, or 0.000125, which is 1 in 8,000. Of course, as in other games, the casino will profit by setting the actual payout to be less than 7,999 to 1. Yet in new microprocessor-controlled machines, "virtual" reels, wherein each reel may represent 256 different numbers, can be created with a much wider range of payouts and probabilities. In New Jersey, by law, slot machines cannot pay out less than 83% of the drop, but there is no such rule in Nevada.

Slot machines today come in many different versions, including "progressives" (which are linked to the coin-drop in other machines), color-action (nonreel) videos, and multiline-payoff models. But whatever the type, the chief advantages to casinos are the low operating costs and relatively high hold percentages of slots as compared with table games: A modern machine bought at a cost of $10,000 can readily generate $200 or more per day and up to $100,000 a year. Indeed, because of the low operating costs, casinos have also emphasized coin-operated machine adaptations of blackjack and poker.[6]

### Other casino games

Poker

America's all-time favorite private card game, poker, is believed to have evolved from an ancient Persian card game, *As-Nas*. Variations of the game eventually appeared in Europe, and by the early 1800s it had been brought to Louisiana by French settlers. *Poque*, as it was initially known, was refined by active use on the Mississippi riverboats of the 1800s and then spread rapidly through the North after the Civil War.

The principal concept in the game's many variations is to arrange the dealt cards in sequence of value and in suits and to determine the relative ranking of each player's final hand to establish a winner of the money pool (pot) generated during the course of play. Players bet according to the actual and perceived strengths of the various hands, with bluffing a normal part of strategy.

Despite poker's popularity in private settings, it has not been an important contributor to the earnings of publicly owned bricks-and-mortar casino companies: The impact has instead been greatest for the newer online game operators. Most licensed poker clubs (in California and Nevada) that host the games charge an hourly fee for playing based on the minimum-size bet. Other operators will more generally charge a commission, or so-called rake-off, that equals 5% of the pot. As noted in Bary (2005), a table with eight or nine players generates an average of $60 to $70 per hour of rake (i.e., revenues for the house), and perhaps $1,000 a day. This compares with a slot machine, which takes up much less space and can typically average $350 a day.

Online poker and electronic video-poker machines, for which management usually sets payout percentages, have become increasingly popular in recent years. Poker has also been popularized through televised tournaments and online availability of games. See O'Brien (2006).

## Keno

Keno, which is normally a more important profit maker for Nevada casinos than is poker, also benefits from conversion to electronic video units. Keno is played by marking several numbers (spots) out of a total of 80 with a crayon (in the manual version) or with a light pen (in the electronic version). Winning spots are then determined by a random-number generator, and payoffs are made to winners in proportion to how many spots match the preselected choices of the bettor. According to calculations by Scarne (1974, p. 499), the house percentage on a keno ticket varies between approximately 20% and 25% and depends on the number of spots on the ticket.

## Big Six Wheel

The Big Six Wheel is fairly popular in Atlantic City, and it has been a staple in Nevada for a long time. In older versions, the wheel's rim is divided into 54 spaces, in each of which are representations of the faces of three dice bearing different combinations of the numbers 1 through 6. The Big Six operator normally has a favorable advantage ranging to over 22%, which makes this game one of the most profitable for casinos. As can be seen from Atlantic City monthly statistics, casino hold percentages often approach 50% on the Big Six.

## Bingo

Bingo, an offspring of the Italian lotto game, has been historically prominent in the development of Indian gaming ventures. It emerged after World War I and spread rapidly during the Great Depression years as a backroom attraction at vaudeville shows and carnivals. It remains one of the most popular and widely legalized of wagering activites and is normally very profitable for operators.

The traditional game is played to fill a card's row, column, or diagonal containing numbers between 1 and 75 under the word "bingo." A random-number selector or caller picks the numbers that qualify to fill the card, and the first card so filled is declared prize winner. The house edge for bingo is calculated to be around 22%.

## Pai Gow, Fan Tan, and Sic Bo

Players from the Orient have a long history of interest in gambling, and this is reflected in marketing studies of Nevada and Atlantic City casinos indicating that such players are among the most avid. To accommodate these good customers, Nevada casinos have introduced three favorite Chinese games, Pai Gow, Fan Tan, and Sic Bo, the first of which is the most important.

Originated in ancient China, *Pai Gow* is played with 32 specially designed dominoes that are scrambled and then placed in eight stacks of four. The dealer and as many as seven players are each dealt one stack of four specially marked dominoes (or cards), with the player to receive the first stack determined by rolling three dice. The house retains a 5% commission on all winning bets.

*Fan Tan*, in contrast, is basically a game of guessing the number of beans in a cup. (A card game has taken the same name, but it is not similar.) A pile of beans is "cut" with a long, thin wand, four at a time, until 4, 3, 2, or 1 is the winning number or section. The house retains 5% of all winning bets as commission.

*Sic Bo* was first brought into the United States by migrant Chinese in the mid-1800s. Three dice are placed in a sealed shaker, and bettors select individual numbers or combinations of numbers that will appear on the dice after shaking. Winning payoffs are made according to the game layouts.

## Pan

Pan, short for *panguingue*, is sometimes found in Nevada casinos or is played in commercial clubs. It is a card game related to rummy. The standard 52-card deck is modified by eliminating all eights, nines, and tens. The sevens are in sequence with jacks, and aces rank low, below deuces. Eight decks are generally used, and to each hand, ten cards are dealt, five at a time.

By discarding and drawing, a meld or grouping of three cards of the same rank, or a sequence of three in the same suit, is composed. Several rules govern the game, in which the object is to be the first to meld exactly 11 cards.

As in poker or the Chinese games, the house will normally take a percentage of the pot (5%) for conducting the game.

## Trente-et-quarante (Rouge et Noir)

This card game is rarely found in U.S. casinos but is quite popular in Europe. In *trente-et-quarante* (literally, thirty-and-forty), a dealer and croupier cut and shuffle a six-deck shoe in which cards are dealt face up in two rows: The first and farthest away is the black row, and the nearest is the red row. Dealing continues until the sum of points on the cards exceeds 30 but never 40.

The black row is dealt until the critical value of 40 or less is reached; then the red row is similarly presented. Suits have no value; face cards count 10, aces 1, and others their pip value.

Players can bet on four even-money propositions: red versus black and color versus inverse. The color row whose total is closer to 30 is the winner. When the color of the first card dealt in the black row is the same as the color of the winning row, then color wins; otherwise inverse wins. The bank makes its money when – on an average of once every 47 hands – the total for each row is 31 (called the *refait* or *un après*). The bank then collects half of each player's stake, which provides an advantage of 1.25%.[7] All other ties are disregarded, and as in roulette, an *en prison* option may be available.

Mathematical studies of this game have indicated that, as in blackjack, there may be times during the course of play in which the house may have little or no edge. However, it is not clear that effective card-counting strategies exist.

## Lotteries

Lotteries have been around a long time and have been used for many purposes. For instance, the concept appeared in classical Greek mythology, and Roman emperors entertained dinner guests with door-prize drawings. But the first recorded money lottery designed to raise funds for government appeared in Italy in 1530. A British defense lottery was also held in 1566. Yet it was the Virginia Company, which colonized Virginia, that provided the prototype for other early American colonial lottery financings. Indeed, founding fathers Benjamin Franklin and George Washington both sponsored lotteries. And many public-works programs and educational institutions, including Harvard, Yale, Columbia, and Princeton, were, in part, financed through this means.

Although lottery drawings were very popular in the early 1800s, several large swindles cooled the fervor and, by midcentury, most states had banned sales of lottery tickets. Illegal lottery sales then flourished, and these became especially common in the 1920s and 1930s.

It was not until 1964, when the state of New Hampshire introduced a sweepstakes game, that lotteries were legally renewed, and by the end of the 1980s, a majority of the states, the District of Columbia, and all Canadian provinces had legalized lotteries as a means of raising funds for welfare and public-works grants.

As a percentage of sales, states typically net about 36% to 38%: Administrative expenses absorb up to 6%, system operators and designers receive 2% to 3%, retail vendors receive a commission of 5%, and winning players receive an average of about 50%. However, payouts of 50% to players appear to be relatively generous only until comparison is made against casino-game payouts, which exceed 85%. Moreover, states may pick up extra income from interest earned on funds escrowed in the time between prize drawings and payments to winners (out of annuities).

Modern lotteries have evolved in several distinct stages. The original New Hampshire–style lotteries employed a sweepstakes concept that had limited appeal because of relatively small payoffs and a long time between ticket purchase and event decision. However, that was remedied in a second stage of development in which many more "instant-winner" scratch-off-type tickets and online three-digit daily number games were introduced, with significant increases in sizes of cash prizes and in numbers of retail outlets handling sales.

By the late 1970s, a third phase of expansion was initiated as greater sophistication of online computer systems made it possible to introduce games of the so-called lotto variety. These games select winners on almost a daily basis and allow for buildup of substantial prize money over several drawings: If the major prize is not won, the money spills over into the pool used for subsequent drawings.

However, as of the mid-1980s, the industry entered a fourth phase featuring the placement of microprocessor-controlled lottery machines – video lottery terminals (VLTs) – that may use bingo, keno, or other similar random-number generator–based concepts. Such machines are essentially hybrid slot and video game units. Starting in 1992, Rhode Island first allowed such VLTs to be used at racetracks, which are known as "racinos" and which have spread to many other states. See Bulkely (2006).

## Tracks

Horse races were popular during the reign of England's Henry II (1154–1189), and New York's first English governor regularly scheduled them in 1665. To this day, horse and dog racing is where direct government participation in legalized betting is greatest.

Many betting variations are now allowed at tracks specializing in thoroughbred racing, harness racing, or greyhound racing. In addition to standard wagering on *win* (bettor collects if the selection bet to win finishes first), *place* (collects on first or second finish), and *show* (collects on first, second, or third finish), more exotic bets such as the quinella, exacta, and daily-double have been designed to heighten public interest.

The variations, however, have not changed the operational economics whereby the state may take up to 20% of pari-mutuel sales, and so-called breakage (actually a rounding of winners' payout to the last nickel or dime) further adds to the state's advantage.

The player's disadvantage at the track generally ranges upward of 17% and depends on the betting variations used and the aggressiveness with which winners reinvest their gains in other races. Another disadvantage as compared with sports-book betting is that the price of the bet is not fixed but changes right up to the moment before the race begins. Astute sports bettors, however, can often use time to their benefit. See also Scarne (1974, p. 51).

## Sports book

Wagering on sports events is probably the most common type of gaming, and it is certainly among the most widespread of illegal activities in the United States. Legal sports betting based on the same principles used by neighborhood bookies is sanctioned and available only in Nevada gaming establishments or at betting shops in England.

Beginning in the late 1930s, the concept most frequently used in both the legal and illegal variety is that of a *point spread*, which, in theory, mathematically compensates for the different abilities of competing teams. As calculated by expert handicappers, the spread is how many points the winning team's score must exceed the losing team's score in order for wagers on the winning team to be paid. For example, if team $A$ is favored to beat team $B$ by 4 points, and it does so by only 3 points, wagers on the underdog win.

Sports-book operators generally attempt to equalize the total *amounts* bet on both sides of the book and to avoid a "push" (making the exact point spread) by adjusting the spread, or *line*, that is offered to bettors. In football and basketball, for example, wagers (based on a point spread) are normally made at odds of 11:10, which means that whether betting favorite or underdog, in effect you wager $11 to win $10. The bookie thus retains a $1 commission known in the vernacular as vigorish or "vig."

In practice, however, this implies a return to the bookmaker of 4.5% because the bookmaker receives $11 from each side (a total of $22) and, no matter which team wins, retains $1 out of the $22 in total wagered. The bookmaker will obviously attempt to move the point spread (or line) so that an equal number of dollars are wagered on both teams. But if the line has been moved, as it often is, so that the numbers of dollars on each side are uneven, then the operator might make more or less than the theoretical 4.5% or might actually lose. As Moore (1996, p. 100) shows, the *theoretical keep percentage* equals (true odds minus payoff odds)/true odds. Yet, in fact, for all of Nevada, the sports-book hold percentage in recent years has averaged around 2.8% compared with an average race-book hold of approximately 15%.

As Gollehon (1986) explains, baseball betting differs in that it uses a "money-line" rather than a point-spread system. This is because baseball teams are rated in terms of probability of winning rather than of team point scoring potential. However, unlike most other wagering situations, where odds of winning are quoted, in baseball it is the odds *against* winning that are quoted. Thus, in baseball, odds on a favored team may be quoted at 7 to 5, for example, with the first number representing the number of times (out of 12 contests) that a team will typically be expected *not* to win.

The next step is to convert these odds figures into dollar amounts bet. To convert to the bookmaker's $100 betting units requires, for instance, that odds of 7 to 5 be converted to wagers of $140 and $100, respectively. Accordingly, the money-line quoted says −140, with the minus sign in front of the quote to indicate that the team is favored to win. To go with the favored team, a bettor must then put up $1.40 to win each $1.00 and, using the same line, put up $1.00 to win $1.30 on the underdog (which would be quoted as +130). In this case, known as a "dime-line," there is a 10-cent difference between what the favorite takes from the bettor and what the underdog gives. All of this is analogous to the situation in craps, where the bettor who prefers the favored team "lays" the odds, and the bettor who prefers the underdog "takes" the odds.

Theoretically, then, the bookmaker breaks even when the favored team wins and wins when the underdog wins. This works out to about a 2% return to the operator as compared to around 6% in football: Of the total of $240 bet on a −140 and +130 line, the operator keeps $10 of the $240 it holds if the underdog wins, which should be half the time if the line is correct. The larger the difference (e.g., there are 20-cent lines), the more profit potential there is for the operator.

Because of the nature of the games and the different ways in which they are bet, football especially attracts far more action (about 40% of all Nevada sports wagering according to Manteris and Talley [1991]) than baseball. (Of a total $1.9 billion in Nevada sports betting in 2004, 44% involved football and 20% baseball.) However, the spread of sophisticated electronic terminals and computers, which are able to equalize the book automatically and instantaneously by adjusting the spread, will eventually make sports betting technically, if not legally, playable almost anywhere.

## Notes

**1.** Economists familiar with the efficient-market hypothesis will recognize many of the concepts (a martingale, for instance) that are involved in money management. A martingale is any system of trying to make up losses in previous bets by doubling or otherwise increasing the amount bet. The pyramid or D'Alembert system is also popular.

**2.** Players should also be aware that the IRS requires bingo and slot-machine winners of over $1,200, and keno winners of over $1,500, to file form W-2G. In the case of lotteries and racetrack winners, withholding of 20% for federal taxes may begin at $1,000.

**3.** Estimates are approximate and assume application of basic strategy.

**4.** Mezrich (2002) describes how sophisticated card counting works in practice.

**5.** Silberstang (1980, p. 388) has slightly different figures of −1.36% for Player and −1.17% for Banker. Also see Thorp (1984).

**6.** For revenue participation games, in which the units are placed on the casino floor at no cost to the operator, arrangements are for the operator to pay the equipment manufacturer a fixed daily fee, a share of revenues, or a combination of both. Typically, in revenue-sharing, the win per unit per day is split between the operator and the machine manufacturer on an 80/20 basis, whereas the daily fee is approximately $75 per day. Details of revenue-sharing arrangements, in effect, leasing of machines, is provided in Rivlin (2003).

**7.** Numbers are from Barnhart (1983) and differ from those of Scarne (1978).

# Appendix C
# Supplementary data

Entertainment industry data of interest to economists and investors are voluminous, and the material most significant to the flow of discussion has been placed in the text. The following additional data of historical interest have been organized according to chapter topics.

Table S1.1. *Aggregate economic statistics relating to spending on recreational goods and services, 1970–2005 ($ billions)*

| Year | Disposable income | Personal consumption expenditures | PCE on recreation | Recreation as % of disp. income | PCE on total recreation services | Recreation services as % of rec. PCE |
|---|---|---|---|---|---|---|
| 1970 | 735.7 | 648.465 | 43.104 | 5.86 | 15.058 | 34.93 |
| 1971 | 801.8 | 701.868 | 46.028 | 5.74 | 16.329 | 35.48 |
| 1972 | 869.1 | 770.602 | 51.478 | 5.92 | 17.606 | 34.20 |
| 1973 | 978.3 | 852.417 | 57.589 | 5.89 | 19.728 | 34.26 |
| 1974 | 1071.6 | 933.427 | 63.402 | 5.92 | 22.513 | 35.51 |
| 1975 | 1187.4 | 1034.394 | 70.541 | 5.94 | 25.388 | 35.99 |
| 1976 | 1302.5 | 1151.913 | 78.155 | 6.00 | 28.358 | 36.28 |
| 1977 | 1435.7 | 1278.609 | 85.535 | 5.96 | 31.428 | 36.74 |
| 1978 | 1608.3 | 1428.535 | 96.097 | 5.98 | 34.732 | 36.14 |
| 1979 | 1793.5 | 1592.215 | 108.858 | 6.07 | 38.777 | 35.62 |
| 1980 | 2009.0 | 1757.133 | 117.481 | 5.85 | 43.602 | 37.11 |
| 1981 | 2246.1 | 1941.060 | 130.840 | 5.83 | 50.610 | 38.68 |
| 1982 | 2421.2 | 2077.268 | 140.898 | 5.82 | 56.842 | 40.34 |
| 1983 | 2608.4 | 2290.557 | 156.923 | 6.02 | 63.638 | 40.55 |
| 1984 | 2912.0 | 2503.286 | 174.764 | 6.00 | 69.734 | 39.90 |
| 1985 | 3109.3 | 2720.305 | 189.717 | 6.10 | 77.709 | 40.96 |
| 1986 | 3285.1 | 2899.724 | 206.941 | 6.30 | 83.677 | 40.44 |
| 1987 | 3458.3 | 3100.234 | 226.812 | 6.56 | 89.963 | 39.66 |
| 1988 | 3748.7 | 3353.616 | 251.662 | 6.71 | 102.126 | 40.58 |
| 1989 | 4021.7 | 3598.496 | 272.410 | 6.77 | 114.257 | 41.94 |
| 1990 | 4285.8 | 3839.937 | 290.166 | 6.77 | 125.907 | 43.39 |

| | | | | | |
|---|---|---|---|---|---|
| 1991 | 4464.3 | 3986.066 | 301.980 | 6.76 | 132.907 | 44.01 |
| 1992 | 4751.4 | 4235.265 | 321.319 | 6.76 | 146.596 | 45.62 |
| 1993 | 4911.9 | 4477.887 | 351.014 | 7.15 | 160.372 | 45.69 |
| 1994 | 5151.8 | 4743.286 | 383.372 | 7.44 | 171.389 | 44.71 |
| 1995 | 5408.2 | 4975.787 | 418.151 | 7.73 | 187.921 | 44.94 |
| 1996 | 5688.5 | 5256.832 | 448.367 | 7.88 | 202.471 | 45.16 |
| 1997 | 5988.8 | 5547.400 | 474.475 | 7.92 | 215.065 | 45.33 |
| 1998 | 6395.9 | 5879.483 | 505.798 | 7.91 | 229.269 | 45.33 |
| 1999 | 6695.0 | 6282.474 | 546.067 | 8.16 | 248.593 | 45.52 |
| 2000 | 7194.0 | 6739.378 | 585.712 | 8.14 | 268.265 | 45.80 |
| 2001 | 7486.8 | 7055.038 | 604.024 | 8.07 | 284.137 | 47.04 |
| 2002 | 7830.1 | 7350.721 | 629.877 | 8.04 | 299.056 | 47.48 |
| 2003 | 8169.2 | 7703.630 | 659.897 | 8.08 | 317.706 | 48.14 |
| 2004 | 8664.2 | 8211.504 | 708.374 | 8.18 | 341.552 | 48.22 |
| 2005 | 9031.3 | 8742.351 | 756.303 | 8.37 | 360.632 | 47.68 |
| CAGR (%)[a] | | | | | | |
| 1929–2005 | 6.4 | 6.4 | 7.0 | 0.6 | 7.3 | 0.3 |
| 1959–2005 | 7.3 | 7.5 | 8.5 | 1.1 | 9.2 | 0.6 |
| 1970–2005 | 9.6 | 9.8 | 11.2 | 1.5 | 11.9 | 0.7 |
| 1980–2005 | 6.2 | 6.6 | 7.7 | 1.5 | 8.8 | 1.0 |

[a] Compound annual growth rate.

*Source:* Department of Commerce.

Table S1.1. (cont.)

| Year | Movies | Casinos | Pari-mutuel | Lotteries | Spectator sports | Cable | Comm. theater |
|------|--------|---------|-------------|-----------|------------------|-------|---------------|
| 1970 | 1.629 | 0.510 | 1.096 | 0.061 | 1.136 | 0.295 | 0.531 |
| 1971 | 1.733 | 0.570 | 1.195 | 0.104 | 1.222 | 0.340 | 0.530 |
| 1972 | 1.744 | 0.691 | 1.263 | 0.223 | 1.198 | 0.410 | 0.571 |
| 1973 | 1.647 | 0.854 | 1.449 | 0.351 | 1.207 | 0.512 | 0.622 |
| 1974 | 2.022 | 1.050 | 1.559 | 0.428 | 1.249 | 0.643 | 0.697 |
| 1975 | 2.197 | 1.254 | 1.662 | 0.531 | 1.333 | 0.783 | 0.780 |
| 1976 | 2.074 | 1.494 | 1.802 | 0.634 | 1.423 | 0.951 | 0.933 |
| 1977 | 2.368 | 1.725 | 1.883 | 0.803 | 1.582 | 1.237 | 1.071 |
| 1978 | 2.752 | 2.227 | 1.988 | 0.967 | 1.842 | 1.554 | 1.313 |
| 1979 | 2.823 | 2.640 | 2.121 | 1.104 | 2.070 | 1.878 | 1.512 |
| 1980 | 2.578 | 3.171 | 2.291 | 1.240 | 2.292 | 2.458 | 1.773 |
| 1981 | 2.721 | 4.454 | 2.508 | 1.465 | 2.361 | 3.596 | 2.035 |
| 1982 | 3.134 | 5.124 | 2.590 | 1.964 | 2.692 | 4.655 | 2.131 |
| 1983 | 3.188 | 5.766 | 2.639 | 2.648 | 3.062 | 6.070 | 2.439 |
| 1984 | 3.421 | 6.268 | 2.834 | 3.462 | 3.472 | 7.279 | 2.804 |
| 1985 | 3.244 | 6.801 | 2.844 | 4.608 | 3.279 | 8.292 | 3.188 |
| 1986 | 3.338 | 7.186 | 2.927 | 5.403 | 3.283 | 9.433 | 3.895 |
| 1987 | 3.443 | 7.931 | 3.000 | 6.007 | 3.365 | 10.711 | 4.039 |
| 1988 | 3.884 | 8.988 | 3.424 | 7.274 | 3.738 | 12.497 | 4.391 |
| 1989 | 4.572 | 9.587 | 3.345 | 8.323 | 4.504 | 14.591 | 4.430 |
| 1990 | 5.136 | 11.461 | 3.477 | 8.722 | 4.808 | 16.676 | 5.204 |

| | | | | | | |
|---|---|---|---|---|---|---|
| 1991 | 5.231 | 12.310 | 3.411 | 8.943 | 5.293 | 17.925 | 5.442 |
| 1992 | 4.939 | 14.931 | 3.366 | 9.783 | 5.633 | 19.883 | 6.042 |
| 1993 | 5.056 | 19.095 | 3.350 | 10.833 | 6.357 | 21.810 | 7.083 |
| 1994 | 5.308 | 24.076 | 3.519 | 12.013 | 6.790 | 21.372 | 7.565 |
| 1995 | 5.612 | 28.528 | 3.702 | 13.188 | 7.433 | 23.862 | 8.054 |
| 1996 | 6.099 | 32.454 | 3.857 | 13.980 | 8.851 | 27.174 | 8.555 |
| 1997 | 6.608 | 36.248 | 4.018 | 14.247 | 9.201 | 30.131 | 9.175 |
| 1998 | 7.220 | 38.812 | 4.412 | 14.428 | 9.774 | 33.139 | 9.236 |
| 1999 | 7.931 | 43.142 | 4.853 | 14.614 | 10.598 | 37.234 | 9.901 |
| 2000 | 8.587 | 49.046 | 4.986 | 14.625 | 11.477 | 40.424 | 10.337 |
| 2001 | 8.991 | 52.328 | 5.085 | 15.196 | 12.382 | 44.033 | 10.859 |
| 2002 | 9.597 | 56.357 | 5.312 | 16.328 | 13.501 | 46.506 | 11.679 |
| 2003 | 9.873 | 62.887 | 5.236 | 17.364 | 14.259 | 49.935 | 11.900 |
| 2004 | 9.857 | 70.779 | 5.644 | 18.631 | 15.144 | 56.171 | 12.391 |
| 2005 | 9.721 | 76.328 | 6.180 | 19.932 | 15.856 | 62.977 | 12.747 |
| CAGR (%)[a] | | | | | | | |
| 1929–2005 | 3.5 | — | 9.1 | | 7.5 | | 6.3 |
| 1959–2005 | 5.0 | 14.7 | 5.6 | 24.0 | 8.9 | 21.2 | 8.3 |
| 1970–2005 | 6.6 | 19.3 | 7.2 | 32.7 | 11.4 | 25.9 | 10.8 |
| 1980–2005 | 5.5 | 13.6 | 4.0 | 11.7 | 8.0 | 13.9 | 8.2 |

[a] Compound annual growth rate.

Table S1.2. *Average hours and earnings for production or nonsupervisory workers, selected industry categories, 1965–2005*

| Year | Total private[a] | | | Manufacturing | | | Services | | |
|---|---|---|---|---|---|---|---|---|---|
| | Weekly hours | Hourly earnings | Weekly earnings | Weekly hours | Hourly earnings | Weekly earnings | Weekly hours | Hourly earnings | Weekly earnings |
| 1965 | 38.8 | $2.46 | $95.45 | 41.2 | $2.61 | $107.53 | 35.9 | $2.05 | $73.60 |
| 1970 | 37.1 | 3.23 | 119.83 | 39.8 | 3.35 | 133.33 | 34.4 | 2.81 | 96.66 |
| 1975 | 36.1 | 4.53 | 163.53 | 39.5 | 4.83 | 190.79 | 33.5 | 4.02 | 134.67 |
| 1980 | 35.3 | 6.66 | 235.10 | 39.7 | 7.27 | 288.62 | 32.6 | 5.85 | 190.71 |
| 1985 | 34.9 | 8.57 | 299.09 | 40.5 | 9.54 | 386.37 | 32.5 | 7.90 | 256.75 |
| 1990 | 34.5 | 10.01 | 345.35 | 40.8 | 10.83 | 441.86 | 32.5 | 9.83 | 319.48 |
| 1991 | 34.3 | 10.32 | 353.98 | 40.7 | 11.18 | 455.03 | 32.4 | 10.23 | 331.45 |
| 1992 | 34.4 | 10.57 | 363.61 | 41.0 | 11.46 | 469.86 | 32.5 | 10.54 | 342.55 |
| 1993 | 34.5 | 10.83 | 373.64 | 41.4 | 11.74 | 486.04 | 32.5 | 10.78 | 350.35 |
| 1994 | 34.7 | 11.12 | 385.86 | 42.0 | 12.07 | 506.94 | 32.5 | 11.04 | 358.80 |
| 1995 | 34.5 | 11.43 | 394.34 | 41.6 | 12.37 | 514.59 | 32.4 | 11.39 | 369.04 |
| 1996 | 34.3 | 12.03 | 412.74 | 41.3 | 12.75 | 526.55 | 32.6 | 11.57 | 376.72 |
| 1997 | 34.5 | 12.49 | 431.25 | 41.7 | 13.14 | 548.22 | 32.8 | 12.05 | 394.77 |
| 1998 | 34.5 | 13.00 | 448.04 | 41.4 | 13.45 | 557.12 | 32.8 | 12.59 | 412.78 |
| 1999 | 34.3 | 13.47 | 462.49 | 41.4 | 13.85 | 573.17 | 32.7 | 13.07 | 427.30 |
| 2000 | 34.3 | 14.00 | 480.41 | 41.3 | 14.32 | 590.65 | 32.7 | 13.60 | 445.00 |
| 2001 | 34.0 | 14.53 | 493.20 | 40.3 | 14.76 | 595.19 | 32.5 | 14.16 | 460.32 |
| 2002 | 33.9 | 14.95 | 506.07 | 40.5 | 15.29 | 618.75 | 32.5 | 14.56 | 472.88 |
| 2003 | 33.7 | 15.35 | 517.30 | 40.4 | 15.74 | 635.99 | 32.4 | 14.96 | 483.89 |
| 2004 | 33.7 | 15.67 | 528.36 | 40.8 | 16.15 | 658.59 | 32.3 | 15.26 | 493.30 |
| 2005 | 33.8 | 16.11 | 543.65 | 40.7 | 16.56 | 673.61 | 32.4 | 15.71 | 508.66 |

[a] Data relate to production workers in mining and manufacturing, construction workers in construction, and nonsupervisory workers in transportation and public utilities, wholesale and retail trade, finance, insurance, real estate, and services.

Source: *Employment and Earnings*, U.S. Department of Labor, Bureau of Labor Statistics, www.bls.gov.

Table S3.1. *Percent of total yearly movie admissions by age category, 1985–2005*

| Age group | 12–15 | 16–20 | 21–24 | 25–29 | 30–39 | 40–49 | 50–59 | 60+ |
|---|---|---|---|---|---|---|---|---|
| 1985 | 14 | 21 | 18 | 14 | 18 | 7 | 4 | 4 |
| 1986 | 14 | 21 | 17 | 14 | 20 | 8 | 3 | 3 |
| 1987 | 11 | 21 | 15 | 15 | 18 | 10 | 5 | 5 |
| 1988 | 12 | 20 | 12 | 13 | 20 | 11 | 5 | 7 |
| 1989 | 11 | 19 | 14 | 16 | 18 | 12 | 4 | 7 |
| 1990 | 11 | 20 | 11 | 14 | 20 | 12 | 5 | 7 |
| 1991 | 12 | 19 | 12 | 12 | 19 | 13 | 5 | 8 |
| 1992 | 13 | 16 | 11 | 11 | 19 | 15 | 7 | 8 |
| 1993 | 9 | 17 | 10 | 13 | 19 | 15 | 7 | 11 |
| 1994 | 10 | 14 | 11 | 10 | 18 | 16 | 8 | 12 |
| 1995 | 9 | 16 | 11 | 12 | 20 | 16 | 7 | 10 |
| 1996 | 11 | 16 | 11 | 11 | 18 | 16 | 8 | 8 |
| 1997 | 9 | 17 | 11 | 12 | 19 | 15 | 9 | 9 |
| 1998 | 10 | 18 | 9 | 10 | 17 | 16 | 11 | 9 |
| 1999 | 11 | 20 | 10 | 12 | 18 | 14 | 7 | 8 |
| 2000 | 10 | 17 | 11 | 12 | 18 | 14 | 10 | 8 |
| 2001 | 12 | 16 | 10 | 9 | 19 | 17 | 9 | 8 |
| 2002 | 10 | 17 | 12 | 11 | 17 | 15 | 8 | 9 |
| 2003 | 11 | 16 | 12 | 9 | 19 | 14 | 11 | 8 |
| 2004 | 11 | 17 | 10 | 9 | 18 | 16 | 10 | 9 |
| 2005 | 12 | 16 | 10 | 11 | 17 | 15 | 10 | 10 |

**Frequency of attendance (%)**

| Frequency | Total public (ages 12+) | | Adult public (ages 18+) | | Teenagers (ages 12–17) | |
|---|---|---|---|---|---|---|
| | 2005 | 1981 | 2005 | 1981 | 2005 | 1981 |
| Frequent[a] | 24 | 25 | 21 | 22 | 47 | 50 |
| Occasional[b] | 34 | 29 | 33 | 30 | 41 | 32 |
| Infrequent[c] | 13 | 10 | 14 | 10 | 8 | 5 |

[a] Attend movies at least once a month.

[b] Attend movies once in 2–6 months.

[c] Attend movies less than once in 6 months.

*Source*: MPAA study conducted by Opinion Research Corp.

Table S3.2. *United Artists' revenues and operating income by division,*
*1972–1979*

| Year | Revenues ($ thousands) | | Operating income ($ millions) | | Margin (%) | |
|---|---|---|---|---|---|---|
| | Theatrical | Television | Theatrical | Television | Theatrical | Television |
| 1979 | 380,997 | 57,000 | 23.2 | 18.9 | 6.1 | 33.2 |
| 1978 | 294,490 | 76,010 | 31.8 | 19.1 | 10.8 | 25.1 |
| 1977 | 318,483 | 59,691 | 38.7 | 16.8 | 12.1 | 28.1 |
| 1976 | 229,482 | 55,543 | 16.6 | 10.9 | 7.2 | 19.6 |
| 1975 | 187,399 | 29,626 | 14.2 | 4.8 | 7.6 | 16.2 |
| 1974 | 142,667 | 40,606 | 8.0 | 8.7 | 5.6 | 21.4 |
| 1973 | 163,843 | 51,725 | 14.8 | 14.1 | 9.0 | 23.3 |
| 1972 | 152,749 | 50,620 | 9.1 | 11.0 | 6.0 | 21.7 |

*Source*: UA-Transamerica corporate reports.

Table S3.3. *Average price of a movie ticket in America, 1933–1962*[a]

| Year | Admission price (¢) | Year | Admission price (¢) |
|---|---|---|---|
| 1933 | 23 | 1948 | 40.1 |
| 1934 | 23 | 1949 | 46 |
| 1935 | 24 | 1950 | 52.8 |
| 1936 | 25 | 1951 | 52.8 |
| 1937 | 23 | 1952 | 60 |
| 1938 | 23 | 1953 | 60 |
| 1939 | 23 | 1954 | 44.7 |
| 1940 | 24.1 | 1955 | 49.8 |
| 1941 | 25.2 | 1956 | 49.7 |
| 1942 | 27.3 | 1957 | 50.5 |
| 1943 | 29.4 | 1958 | 50.5 |
| 1944 | 31.7 | 1959 | 51 |
| 1945 | 35.2 | 1960 | 69 |
| 1946 | 40.3 | 1961 | 69 |
| 1947 | 40.4 | 1962 | 70 |

[a] Between 1942 and 1953, there was an amusement tax on movie tickets. In 1942 the tax
was 2.7 cents; in 1953, 10 cents. The figures given for those years include the tax.
*Source*: *Real Facts.* © Random House, Inc. Through 1962, these statistics were compiled
by *Film Daily Yearbook*. The Research Department of the Motion Picture Association of
America is the source for data beginning in 1963.

Table S3.4. *Major-distributor North American theatrical rental market shares in percent, 1970–2006*[a]

| Year | Sony/Columbia[b] | Disney | Fox | MGM/UA[c] | Orion[d] | Paramount | Tri-Star[b] | Warner[e] | Universal |
|---|---|---|---|---|---|---|---|---|---|
| 2006 | 19 | 16 | 15 | 2 | | 10 | | 12 | 9 |
| 2005 | 10 | 11 | 15 | 2 | | 9 | | 16 | 11 |
| 2004 | 14 | 13 | 10 | 2 | | 7 | | 13 | 10 |
| 2003 | 13 | 17 | 9 | 4 | | 8 | | 13 | 12 |
| 2002 | 17 | 13 | 10 | 4 | | 8 | | 12 | 9 |
| 2001 | 9 | 11 | 11 | 6 | | 11 | | 15 | 12 |
| 2000 | 9 | 15 | 10 | 1 | | 11 | | 12 | 15 |
| 1999 | 9 | 17 | 11 | 4 | | 12 | | 14 | 13 |
| 1998 | 11 | 16 | 11 | 3 | | 16 | | 11 | 6 |
| 1997 | 20 | 14 | 11 | 3 | | 12 | | 11 | 10 |
| 1996 | 10 | 21 | 13 | 5 | 1 | 13 | — | 16 | 8 |
| 1995 | 13 | 19 | 8 | 6 | 0 | 10 | — | 17 | 13 |
| 1994 | 5 | 20 | 9 | 3 | 0 | 14 | 5 | 16 | 13 |
| 1993 | 11 | 17 | 11 | 2 | 1 | 10 | 7 | 19 | 14 |
| 1992 | 13 | 19 | 14 | 1 | — | 10 | 7 | 20 | 12 |
| 1991 | 9 | 14 | 12 | 2 | 9 | 12 | 11 | 14 | 11 |
| 1990 | 5 | 16 | 13 | 3 | 6 | 15 | 9 | 13 | 13 |
| 1989 | 8 | 14 | 6 | 6 | 4 | 14 | 7 | 19 | 17 |
| 1988 | 3 | 20 | 11 | 10 | 7 | 16 | 6 | 11 | 10 |
| 1987 | 4 | 14 | 9 | 4 | 10 | 20 | 5 | 13 | 8 |
| 1986 | 9 | 10 | 8 | 4 | 7 | 22 | 7 | 12 | 9 |
| 1985[f] | 10 | 3 | 11 | 9 | 5 | 10 | 10 | 18 | 16 |
| 1984 | 16 | 4 | 10 | 7 | 5 | 21 | 5 | 19 | 8 |
| 1983 | 14 | 3 | 21 | 10 | 4 | 14 | — | 17 | 13 |
| 1982 | 10 | 4 | 14 | 11 | 3 | 14 | — | 10 | 30 |
| 1981 | 13 | 3 | 13 | 9 | 1 | 15 | — | 18 | 14 |
| 1980 | 14 | 4 | 16 | 7 | 2 | 16 | — | 14 | 20 |
| 1979 | 11 | 4 | 9 | 15 | 5 | 15 | — | 20 | 15 |
| 1978 | 11 | 5 | 13 | 11 | 4 | 24 | — | 13 | 17 |
| 1977 | 12 | 6 | 20 | 18 | 4 | 10 | — | 14 | 12 |

(*cont.*)

Table S3.4. (cont.)

| Year | Sony/Columbia[b] | Disney | Fox | MGM/UA[c] | Orion[d] | Paramount | Tri-Star[b] | Warner[e] | Universal |
|---|---|---|---|---|---|---|---|---|---|
| 1976 | 8 | 7 | 13 | 16 | 5 | 10 | — | 18 | 13 |
| 1975 | 18 | 6 | 14 | 11 | 5 | 11 | — | 9 | 25 |
| 1974[g] | 7 | 7 | 11 | 9 | 4 | 10 | — | 23 | 19 |
| 1973[h,i] | 7 | 5 | 19 | 11 | 3 | 9 | — | 16 | 10 |
| 1972 | 9 | 5 | 9 | 15 | 3 | 22 | — | 18 | 5 |
| 1971 | 10 | 8 | 12 | 7 | 3 | 17 | — | 9 | 5 |
| 1970 | 14 | 9 | 19 | 9 | 3 | 12 | — | 5 | 13 |
| Mean | 10 | 10 | 13 | 8 | 4 | 14 | 7 | 15 | 13 |

[a] Feature film rentals from U.S. and Canadian theaters, expressed in percentages of total industry rentals (including those of minor distributors) except after 1993, when figures are based on box-office estimates (which track rentals closely). Percentages do not add to 100% in any year; the residual amount is accounted for by smaller and/or defunct distributors.

[b] Tri-Star Pictures began operations in April 1984 and was absorbed by Columbia Pictures late 1987; corporate name was changed to Columbia Pictures Entertainment. Columbia and Tri-Star retain separate marketing controls, but certain administrative functions are performed by Triumph Releasing, an entity that has no operational significance. Metro-Goldwyn-Mayer, Inc. acquired Orion in 1997.

[c] MGM/UA means the present distribution company as well as the "old" UA, which took over domestic distribution of MGM product late in 1973.

[d] Includes old American International Pictures (1970–1979) and Filmways Pictures (1980–1981). Name changed to Orion in 1981.

[e] Allied Artists Pictures had a 4% market share in 1974 (insignificant in other years). Lorimar acquired assets in 1981. Lorimar began domestic distribution operations in August 1987. Warner Bros. acquired Lorimar in late 1988.

[f] Embassy Pictures market shares were as follows: 3% in 1980, 5% in 1981, 1% in 1983 and 1985, nil in 1984, insignificant in other years. Company bought by Columbia Pictures in 1985. Dino De Laurentiis acquired Embassy's theatrical production-distribution operations from Columbia later in 1985. Name changed to De Laurentiis Entertainment Group; distribution operations resumed June 1986. Market share for 1986 just over 2%; for 1987, just over 1%.

[g] Pre-1974, the "old" MGM market shares were as follows: 4% in 1970, 9% in 1971, 6% in 1972, and 5% in 1973. Company exited distribution late in 1973.

[h] National General Pictures (most of its release schedule being CBS-Cinema Center Films) market shares were as follows: 7% in 1970, 8% in 1971, 3% in 1972, and 8% in 1973. NGP also released First Artists product under a commitment transferred to Warner Bros. in 1974 when NGP folded.

[i] Cinerama Releasing Corp. (most of its releases being ABC Pictures product) market shares were as follows: 3% over 1970–1973 period. CRC folded thereafter.

Source: Variety, January 18, 1989. © A. D. Murphy and The Hollywood Reporter.

Table S3.5. *Approximate movie theater admissions[a] in seven major developed countries, 1970–2005*

| Year | England | France | Germany | Italy | Japan | Netherlands | Spain |
|------|---------|--------|---------|-------|-------|-------------|-------|
| 2005 | 164.6 | 175.7 | 125.3 | 90.5 | 160.5 | 20.4 | 126.0 |
| 2004 | 171.3 | 195.3 | 156.7 | 97.9 | 170.1 | 22.3 | 143.9 |
| 2003 | 167.3 | 174.1 | 149.0 | 87.5 | 162.3 | 24.7 | 137.4 |
| 2002 | 175.9 | 183.0 | 163.9 | 111.4 | 160.8 | 24.1 | 139.0 |
| 2001 | 157.0 | 184.4 | 177.9 | 110.4 | 163.3 | 23.9 | 146.8 |
| 2000 | 143.6 | 166.0 | 152.5 | 106.5 | 135.4 | 21.5 | 135.4 |
| 1999 | 140.3 | 153.6 | 149.0 | 105.0 | 144.8 | 18.6 | 131.4 |
| 1998 | 136.5 | 170.1 | 148.9 | 118.4 | 153.1 | 20.1 | 112.1 |
| 1997 | 140.4 | 148.1 | 143.1 | 100.4 | 140.7 | 18.9 | 105.0 |
| 1996 | 125.1 | 136.6 | 132.9 | 95.9 | 119.6 | 16.8 | 104.3 |
| 1995 | 116.1 | 130.2 | 124.5 | 90.7 | 127.0 | 17.2 | 94.0 |
| 1994 | 125.1 | 124.4 | 132.8 | 98.2 | 123.0 | 16.0 | 89.1 |
| 1993 | 114.4 | 132.7 | 130.5 | 92.2 | 130.7 | 15.9 | 87.7 |
| 1992 | 102.5 | 116.7 | 105.9 | 83.6 | 125.6 | 13.7 | 83.3 |
| 1991 | 101.5 | 117.5 | 119.9 | 88.6 | 138.3 | 14.9 | 79.1 |
| 1990 | 96.4 | 121.9 | 102.5 | 90.7 | 145.5 | 14.6 | 78.5 |
| 1989 | 91.6 | 120.9 | 101.0 | 94.8 | 143.6 | 15.6 | 78.1 |
| 1988 | 83.5 | 124.8 | 108.9 | 93.1 | 144.8 | 14.8 | 69.6 |
| 1987 | 78.4 | 136.7 | 108.1 | 108.8 | 143.9 | 15.5 | 85.7 |
| 1986 | 74.0 | 167.8 | 105.2 | 124.9 | 160.8 | 14.9 | 87.3 |
| 1985 | 70.2 | 175.0 | 104.2 | 123.1 | 155.1 | 15.3 | 101.1 |
| 1984 | 53.8 | 190.8 | 112.1 | 131.6 | 150.5 | 16.5 | 118.6 |
| 1983 | 65.7 | 198.8 | 125.3 | 162.0 | 170.4 | 20.2 | 141.0 |
| 1982 | 64.0 | 201.9 | 124.5 | 195.4 | 155.2 | 22.0 | 155.9 |
| 1981 | 86.0 | 189.2 | 141.3 | 215.2 | 149.5 | 26.7 | 173.0 |
| 1980 | 101.0 | 174.8 | 143.8 | 241.9 | 164.4 | 27.9 | 176.0 |
| 1979 | 111.9 | 178.1 | 142.0 | 276.3 | 165.1 | 28.4 | 200.5 |
| 1978 | 126.1 | 178.5 | 135.5 | 318.6 | 166.0 | 30.5 | 220.1 |
| 1977 | 103.5 | 170.3 | 124.2 | 373.9 | 165.2 | 26.3 | 244.9 |
| 1976 | 103.9 | 177.3 | 115.1 | 454.5 | 171.0 | 26.5 | 249.3 |
| 1975 | 116.3 | 181.7 | 128.1 | 513.7 | 174.0 | 28.3 | 255.8 |
| 1974 | 138.5 | 179.4 | 136.2 | 544.4 | 185.7 | 28.1 | 262.9 |
| 1973 | 134.2 | 176.0 | 144.3 | 544.8 | 185.3 | 26.5 | 278.3 |
| 1972 | 156.6 | 184.4 | 149.8 | 553.7 | 187.4 | 25.0 | 295.2 |
| 1971 | 176.0 | 177.0 | 161.4 | 535.7 | 216.8 | 28.7 | 295.3 |
| 1970 | 193.0 | 184.4 | 167.4 | 525.0 | 254.8 | 24.1 | 330.9 |

[a] In millions.

*Source*: Annual country statistical abstracts, trade publications, and *Screen Digest*.

Table S6.1. *Music industry physical and digital shipments in millions of units and dollars, 1980–2005*

| Years | LPs/EPs | Cassettes | CDs | Total (ex-DVD) | Digital |
|---|---|---|---|---|---|
| *Units shipped* (*net after returns*) | | | | | |
| 2005 | 1 | 3 | 705 | 749 | 380 |
| 2004 | 1 | 5 | 767 | 814 | 144 |
| 2003 | 2 | 17 | 746 | 798 | |
| 2002 | 2 | 31 | 803 | 860 | |
| 2001 | 2 | 45 | 882 | 969 | |
| 2000 | 2 | 76 | 943 | 1,079 | |
| 1999[a] | 3 | 124 | 939 | 1,161 | |
| 1998[a] | 3 | 159 | 847 | 1,124 | |
| 1997 | 3 | 173 | 753 | 1,063 | |
| 1996 | 3 | 225 | 779 | 1,137 | |
| 1995 | 2 | 273 | 723 | 1,113 | |
| 1994 | 2 | 345 | 662 | 1,123 | |
| 1993 | 1 | 340 | 495 | 956 | |
| 1992 | 2 | 366 | 408 | 896 | |
| 1991 | 5 | 360 | 333 | 801 | |
| 1990 | 12 | 442 | 287 | 866 | |
| 1989 | 35 | 446 | 207 | 807 | |
| 1988 | 72 | 450 | 150 | 762 | |
| 1987 | 107 | 410 | 102 | 707 | |
| 1986 | 125 | 345 | 53 | 618 | |
| 1985 | 167 | 339 | 23 | 653 | |
| 1984 | 205 | 332 | 6 | 680 | |
| 1983 | 210 | 237 | 1 | 578 | |
| 1982 | 244 | 182 | | 578 | |
| 1981 | 295 | 137 | | 635 | |
| 1980 | 323 | 110 | | 684 | |
| *Dollar value* | | | | | |
| 2005 | 14 | 13 | 10,520 | 11,195 | 499 |
| 2004 | 19 | 24 | 11,447 | 12,155 | 184 |
| 2003 | 22 | 108 | 11,233 | 11,854 | |
| 2002 | 21 | 210 | 12,044 | 12,614 | |
| 2001 | 27 | 363 | 12,909 | 13,741 | |
| 2000 | 28 | 626 | 13,215 | 14,324 | |
| 1999[a] | 32 | 1,062 | 12,816 | 14,585 | |
| 1998[a] | 34 | 1,420 | 11,416 | 13,723 | |
| 1997 | 33 | 1,523 | 9,915 | 12,237 | |
| 1996 | 37 | 1,905 | 9,935 | 12,534 | |
| 1995 | 25 | 2,304 | 9,377 | 12,320 | |
| 1994 | 18 | 2,976 | 8,465 | 12,068 | |
| 1993 | 11 | 2,916 | 6,511 | 10,047 | |
| 1992 | 14 | 3,116 | 5,327 | 9,024 | |
| 1991 | 29 | 3,020 | 4,338 | 7,834 | |
| 1990 | 87 | 3,472 | 3,452 | 7,541 | |
| 1989 | 220 | 3,346 | 2,588 | 6,580 | |
| 1988 | 532 | 3,385 | 2,090 | 6,255 | |
| 1987 | 793 | 2,960 | 1,594 | 5,568 | |
| 1986 | 983 | 2,500 | 930 | 4,651 | |
| 1985 | 1,281 | 2,412 | 390 | 4,388 | |
| 1984 | 1,549 | 2,384 | 103 | 4,370 | |
| 1983 | 1,689 | 1,811 | 17 | 3,814 | |
| 1982 | 1,925 | 1,385 | | 3,642 | |
| 1981 | 2,342 | 1,063 | | 3,970 | |
| 1980 | 2,290 | 776 | | 3,862 | |

[a] Includes DVDs in totals.

*Source*: Recording Industry Association of America. www.RIAA.org.

## Table S11.1. *Reasons for gambling*

| Reasons for betting[a] | % | Reasons for not betting[a] | % |
|---|---|---|---|
| To have a good time | 81 | Not available | 48 |
| For excitement | 47 | Don't know about it | 27 |
| Challenge | 35 | Not interested | 26 |
| To make money | 35 | Other things to do | 23 |
| To pass the time | 23 | Don't think about it | 22 |
| Something to look forward to | 21 | Odds against you | 22 |
| Chance to get rich | 11 | Don't want to lose money | 16 |
| Net activity reasons | 94 | Don't have the money | 16 |
| Net money reasons | 43 | Waste of money | 14 |
| | | Illegal | 10 |
| | | Not lucky | 8 |
| | | Net money reasons | 53 |
| | | Net activity reasons | 55 |
| | | Net moral reasons | 8 |
| | | Net legal reasons | 12 |

[a] Respondents chose one, two, or three reasons from a list of eleven provided for betting and eighteen provided for not betting.

*Source*: U.S. Congress (1976).

Table S11.2. *Nevada and New Jersey casino industry statistics, 1970–2005*

| | Las Vegas | | | Atlantic City | |
|---|---|---|---|---|---|
| | Total hotel/ motel rooms | Hotel occ. rate (%) | Casino sq. ft. | Total hotel rooms | Casino sq. ft. (000s)[b] |
| 1970 | 25,430 | 70.0 | | | |
| 1971 | 26,044 | 82.5 | | | |
| 1972 | 26,619 | 86.5 | | | |
| 1973 | 20,198 | 88.3 | | | |
| 1974 | 32,826 | 86.0 | | | |
| 1975 | 35,190 | 84.2 | | | |
| 1976 | 36,245 | 85.9 | | | |
| 1977 | 39,350 | 85.3 | | | |
| 1978 | 42,620 | 86.9 | | 724 | 55.0 |
| 1979 | 45,035 | 86.8 | | 1,572 | 115.0 |
| 1980 | 45,815 | 82.8 | | 3,257 | 270.0 |
| 1981 | 49,614 | 80.5 | | 4,781 | 412.1 |
| 1982 | 50,270 | 76.1 | | 4,770 | 425.8 |
| 1983 | 52,529 | 77.4 | | 4,779 | 422.7 |
| 1984 | 54,129 | 78.1 | | 5,494 | 510.1 |
| 1985 | 53,067 | 84.7 | | 6,342 | 577.7 |
| 1986 | 56,494 | 86.3 | | 6,351 | 593.6 |
| 1987 | 56,474 | 87.0 | | 6,835 | 664.5 |
| 1988 | 61,394 | 89.3 | 1,206.6 | 7,314 | 696.2 |
| 1989 | 67,391 | 89.8 | 1,261.8 | 7,584 | 648.6 |
| 1990 | 73,730 | 89.1 | 1,557.9 | 8,828 | 770.5 |
| 1991 | 76,879 | 85.2 | 1,570.2 | 9,419 | 775.2 |
| 1992 | 76,523 | 88.8 | 1,584.5 | 8,961 | 777.7 |
| 1993 | 86,053 | 92.6 | 1,539.0 | 8,946 | 797.2 |
| 1994 | 88,560 | 92.6 | 1,954.0 | 9,227 | 839.9 |
| 1995 | 90,046 | 91.4 | 2,013.3 | 9,398 | 875.2 |
| 1996 | 99,072 | 93.4 | 2,203.0 | 10,531 | 987.3 |
| 1997 | 105,347 | 90.3 | 2,302.8 | 11,894 | 1,040.6 |
| 1998 | 109,365 | 90.3 | 2,386.0 | 11,880 | 1,075.5 |
| 1999 | 120,294 | 92.1 | 2,576.8 | 11,361 | 1,043.2 |
| 2000 | 124,270 | 92.5 | 2,656.5 | 11,361 | 1,047.5 |
| 2001 | 126,610 | 88.9 | 2,737.3 | 11,431 | 1,067.5 |
| 2002 | 126,787 | 88.8 | 2,824.9 | 11,711 | 1,105.3 |
| 2003 | 130,482 | 89.6 | 2,824.5 | 14,253 | 1,239.8 |
| 2004 | 131,503 | 92.0 | 2,862.0 | 15,134 | 1,264.3 |
| 2005 | 133,186 | 91.8 | NA[c] | 15,124 | 1,298.7 |
| CAGR[a] 1970–2005 (%) | 4.8 | | | | |

[a] Compound annual growth rate.
[b] Excludes simulcasting.
[c] Not available.
*Sources*: Nevada Gaming Abstract, New Jersey Casino Control Commission, and www.gaming.unlv.edu.

Table S11.3. *Selected financial data for major Las Vegas Strip hotel-casinos, fiscal 2006 (amounts represent 40 locations)*

**Casino department**

| Revenue (in millions) | Dollars | % |
|---|---|---|
| Pit revenue (includes keno and bingo) | 2,586 | 42.8 |
| Coin-operated devices | 3,223 | 53.3 |
| Poker and pan | 102 | 1.7 |
| Race book | 58 | 1.0 |
| Sports pool | 73 | 1.2 |
| Total revenue | 6,041 | 100.0 |

**Rooms department**

| Revenue | Dollars | % |
|---|---|---|
| Room sales | 3,279 | 85.2 |
| Complimentary rooms | 570 | 14.8 |
| Total revenue | 3,849 | 100.0% |

**Ratios**

| | |
|---|---|
| Total current assets to total current liabilities | 87.9% |
| Total capital to total liabilities | 111.9 |
| Total complimentary expense to gaming revenue | 23.8 |
| Total revenue to average total assets | 49.4 |
| Return on invested capital[a] | 9.3 |
| Return on average assets[b] | 8.3 |

**Statistical averages**

| | | | |
|---|---|---|---|
| Average pit revenue per room per day | $92.06 | Average beverage sales per room per day | $29.29 |
| Average slot revenue per room per day | $114.74 | Average rooms department payroll per room per day | $30.55 |
| Average food sales per room per day | $76.39 | Average room rate per day | $137.05 |

**Gaming revenue per square foot of floor space**

| Area | No. of casinos operationg | Average area in square feet | Gaming revenue per square foot |
|---|---|---|---|
| Pit (includes bingo and keno) | 38 | 15,389 | 4,422 |
| Coin-operated devices | 40 | 52,020 | 1,549 |
| Poker and pan | 28 | 3,077 | 1,186 |
| Race and sports | 32 | 5,826 | 687 |
| Total casino | 40 | 73,455 | 2,056 |

[a] Equals total of net income (before federal income taxes and extraordinary items) and interest expense divided by the total of average total assets less average current liabilities.
[b] Equals total of net income (before federal income taxes and extraordinary items) and interest expense divided by the average total assets.

*Source*: Nevada Gaming Control Board.

Table S13.1. *Broadway theater statistics, 1970–2005*

| Season beginning | Show attendance (millions) | Average price per ticket ($) | Play-weeks | Plays New | Plays Revivals | Musicals New | Musicals Revivals | Grosses ($ million) B'way | Grosses ($ million) Road |
|---|---|---|---|---|---|---|---|---|---|
| 1970 | 7.4 | 7 | 1,107 | | | | | | |
| 1975 | 7.182 | 10 | 1,136 | 18 | 21 | 16 | 5 | 70.8 | 52.6 |
| 1976 | 8.815 | 11 | 1,348 | 24 | 9 | 10 | 8 | 93.4 | 82.6 |
| 1977 | 8.621 | 12 | 1,360 | 20 | 7 | 7 | 5 | 103.8 | 106.0 |
| 1978 | 9.116 | 14 | 1,472 | 22 | 5 | 17 | 3 | 128.1 | 143.9 |
| 1979 | 3.381 | 15 | 1,541 | 29 | 7 | 20 | 5 | 143.4 | 181.2 |
| 1980 | 10.822 | 18 | 1,545 | 25 | 7 | 19 | 7 | 194.5 | 218.9 |
| 1981 | 10.694 | 22 | 1,461 | 24 | 4 | 12 | 4 | 221.2 | 249.5 |
| 1982 | 8.102 | 25 | 1,259 | 24 | 9 | 13 | 4 | 203.1 | 184.3 |
| 1983 | 7.899 | 29 | 1,119 | 14 | 7 | 11 | 4 | 226.5 | 206.2 |
| 1984 | 7.157 | 29 | 1,062 | 14 | 9 | 5 | 2 | 208.0 | 226.0 |
| 1985 | 6.527 | 29 | 1,049 | 12 | 9 | 11 | 1 | 190.6 | 235.6 |
| 1986 | 6.968 | 30 | 1,031 | 15 | 11 | 11 | 2 | 207.2 | 224.3 |
| 1987 | 8.143 | 32 | 1,114 | 11 | 3 | 14 | 3 | 253.5 | 223.0 |
| 1988 | 7.968 | 33 | 1,097 | 13 | 7 | 7 | 1 | 262.1 | 255.5 |
| 1989 | 8.039 | 35 | 1,062 | 15 | 5 | 9 | 5 | 283.4 | 367.1 |
| 1990 | 7.314 | 37 | 970 | 14 | 1 | 9 | 3 | 267.2 | 450.2 |
| 1991 | 7.366 | 40 | 901 | 15 | 10 | 7 | 3 | 292.4 | 502.7 |
| 1992 | 7.857 | 42 | 1,018 | 8 | 10 | 9 | 0 | 327.7 | 620.6 |
| 1993 | 8.116 | 44 | 1,062 | 12 | 10 | 6 | 7 | 356.0 | 687.7 |
| 1994 | 9.045 | 45 | 1,117 | 8 | 11 | 2 | 3 | 406.3 | 694.6 |
| 1995 | 9.468 | 46 | 1,146 | 8 | 13 | 7 | 4 | 436.1 | 762.3 |
| 1996 | 10.318 | 48 | 1,440 | 10 | 11 | 7 | 4 | 499.4 | 752.9 |
| 1997 | 11.283 | 49 | 1,440 | 10 | 9 | 9 | 3 | 557.3 | 794.1 |
| 1998 | 11.605 | 51 | 1,440 | 11 | 7 | 11 | 5 | 588.1 | 711.4 |
| 1999 | 11.365 | 53 | 1,452 | 11 | 6 | 10 | 3 | 602.6 | 584.5 |
| 2000 | 11.938 | 56 | 1,485 | 9 | 7 | 6 | 4 | 665.6 | 615.6 |
| 2001 | 10.958 | 59 | 1,430 | 10 | 11 | 6 | 3 | 642.5 | 630.1 |
| 2002 | 11.389 | 63 | 1,501 | 8 | 10 | 7 | 6 | 720.6 | 648.2 |
| 2003 | 11.605 | 66 | 1,452 | 12 | 10 | 8 | 5 | 771.0 | 751.3 |
| 2004 | 11.527 | 67 | 1,495 | 11 | 12 | 11 | 3 | 768.6 | 649.5 |
| 2005 | 12.003 | 72 | 1,500 | 16 | 5 | 13 | 3 | 861.6 | 531.9 |

*Sources: Variety* June 2006 and League of American Theatres and Producers.

# Glossary

This abbreviated glossary has been mainly compiled with help (and permission) from two sources: *Dictionary of Marketing and Related Terms in the Motion Picture Industry*, by Donn Delson, Bradson Press, Thousand Oaks, California, 1979 (a lexicon of motion picture terminology), and *The McGraw-Hill Dictionary of Economics*, McGraw-Hill, New York, 1974. The *Dictionary of Economic and Statistical Terms*, U.S. Department of Commerce, was supplementary. Additional references include Oakey (1983), Konigsberg (1987), and Cones (1992).

**Above-the-line costs:** Those production-period costs related to acquiring the story rights and screenplay and signing the producer, director, and major members of the cast.

**ADI (area of dominant influence):** An Arbitron (ARB) audience-market classification designating a certain market area in which local stations have partial or complete signal dominance over stations from other market areas. Commonly referred to as a television broadcast area. Similar to Nielsen DMA (designated market area).

**Advance:** Monies paid by an exhibitor to a distributor prior to the opening of a film in a market as an "advance" against film rentals due. Advances, unlike guarantees, are refundable if the film does not generate enough box-office revenue at the exhibitor's theater to justify the advance film-rental monies paid out. The portion not earned by the distributor in film rental will be returned to the exhibitor.

**Affiliate:** Generally, an independently owned broadcast station that contracts with a network to show that network's programming in certain time periods. Each of the three older major U.S. networks (ABC, NBC, and CBS) has approximately 200 affiliated stations. Fox now also has over 160 affiliates.

**Aggregate:** The familiar type of summary series shown in most statistical reports. Generally, it is a total, such as the gross national product or retail sales, but sometimes it is an average, such as the index of industrial production or the index of wholesale prices.

**AM (amplitude modulation):** Technically, the variation of the amplitude of a radio wave in accordance with the sound being broadcast. AM radio broadcasting is from 535 to 1,705 kilohertz. Signal reception occurs in two ways: either via ground waves that follow the curvature of the Earth or via bounced sky waves that are reflected off the ionosphere back to Earth. AM signals are subject to atmospheric or local interference but generally are unimpeded by topographic or physical obstructions.

**Amortization of debt:** A gradual reduction of a debt through periodic payments covering the interest and part of the principal. Generally, amortization is used when the credit period is longer than a year. Common examples of amortization of debt are mortgage payments on homes, which extend over a period of 20 years or more.

**Amortization of negative costs:** Accounting procedure by which negative cost is charged against film revenue.

**Answer print:** A positive print made from the original negative that is balanced for color and sound. "Answers" the question affirmatively that a viable working negative exists from which prints can be made for commercial presentation.

**ARB (American Research Bureau):** One of the major companies involved in national research for television and radio. ARB publishes numerous audience-market surveys throughout the year, rating the comparative audience viewing and listening habits for each medium both locally and nationally.

**Aspect ratio:** The ratio of the horizontal to the vertical dimensions of a movie or television screen.

**Asset:** A physical property or intangible right, owned by a business or an individual, that has a value. An asset is useful to its owner either because it is a source of future services or because it can be used to secure future benefits. Business assets are usually divided into two categories: current and fixed.

**Asset values:** The implied price buyers might be willing to pay to obtain control of an asset's profit- and/or cash-generating potential. Asset values fluctuate according to changes in general economic conditions, interest rates, and expected returns.

**Audience, primary or target:** A particular audience composition or demographic to which a message is believed to have the most appeal and is therefore primarily directed.

**Availability:** 1. The date when a motion picture is able to be shown commercially in a market as offered by the distributor to the exhibitor. 2. Commercial-broadcast time periods available for purchase, including radio time periods (e.g., Drive Time, Housewife Time) and television programming.

**Bandwidth:** A measure of the capacity of a communications channel in terms of the range of frequencies that can be contained or transmitted within defined upper and lower limits. A television channel, for example, normally occupies a bandwidth of approximately 6 MHz (6 million cycles per second).

**Basic service:** Initial cable television service that usually consists of 12 to 20 channels available off the air and satellite channels supported by advertising.

**Below-the-line costs:** All costs, charges, and expenses incurred in the production of a motion picture other than the above-the-line costs, including items such as extras, art and set costs, camera, electrical, wardrobe, transportation, raw film stock, and so forth.

**Bicycling (print):** The use of one print in two theaters for staggered showings. Originated with the transporting by bicycle of consecutive reels of film from one theater to another and back again.

**Bid:** A written notification from a theater-exhibition company in response to a bid solicitation from a distribution company competing for the right to license a motion picture for showing in a given market beginning on or about a specific date. This notification usually includes commitments, if applicable, for minimum playing time, clearances, guarantees, advance, film-rental terms, and advertising terms.

**Bid request:** A written notification from a distributor to all motion-picture exhibitors who own or operate theaters in a market area, informing them that a specific motion picture is available for showing in that area on or about a certain date and inviting them to submit a bid to license that picture. This request may contain suggestions such as length of playing time, guarantees, advances, film-rental terms, advertising terms, deadlines for submission, and so forth. Such a bid request usually specifies that bid offers must be received by a certain time and date, usually no later than ten days subsequent to its issuance.

**Blind bidding:** The practice by which film-distribution companies, through a bid-request letter and without having previously screened the film, request that interested exhibition companies submit bids to license a motion picture for showing in a market.

**Block booking:** Governed by the Paramount consent decree of 1948, major distributors were forbidden to employ the practice of tying together one or more motion pictures for licensing within a market. The basic premise of this decree is that motion pictures must be licensed picture by picture, theater by theater, so as to give all exhibitors equal opportunities to show a given film.

**Bond:** 1. A written promise to pay a specified sum of money (principal) at a certain date in the future or periodically over the course of a loan, during which time interest is paid at a fixed rate on specified dates. Bonds are issued by corporations, states, localities (municipal bonds), foreign governments, and the U.S. government, usually for long terms (more than ten years), although any security issued by the U.S. government for more than five years is defined as a bond. 2. In movies, *completion bonds* are insurance policies that assure distributors and/or financiers that their investments in the movie will not be lost because of incompletion.

**Booker:** The person responsible for all aspects of monitoring and trafficking the actual motion-picture prints throughout the markets over which the branch office has jurisdiction.

**Book value:** The value of a corporation according to its accounting records. It is computed by subtracting all debts from assets; the remainder represents total book value. Total book value is also referred to as net assets. If a corporation has assets of $300,000 and debts of $100,000, its total book value is $200,000. In reports of corporations, the book value is usually represented on a per share basis. This is done by dividing the total book value by the number of shares. In the example given above, if the corporation had 10,000 shares outstanding, its book value would be $20 per share. The book value differs from the par value of the shares and also from the market value.

**Box-office receipts:** The money that has been paid by the public for admission (tickets) to see a specific motion picture.

**Branch:** The office located in a given city that is staffed by employees of a film-distribution company and is responsible for bidding out (licensing) the film company's products, servicing prints to legitimate customers, and collecting on film rentals due. Business is generally conducted with exhibitors within certain geographic regional boundaries of relative proximity to the branch. The major distribution companies will have individual branches in 20 to 30 major U.S. cities. Branch staffs consist of the branch manager, sales representatives, bookers, cashiers, and clerical personnel.

**Break:** 1. Each stage of the release of a motion picture within a market (first-run break, second-run break, etc.) consisting of a distinct array of theaters playing a motion picture in a given "availability." 2. The commercial time available for sale either within a particular show or between two shows on television or radio.

**Breakeven point:** The specific volume of sales at which a firm neither makes nor loses money. Above this point, a firm begins to show a profit; below it, the firm suffers a loss. Breakeven-point analysis is used to compute the approximate profit or loss that will be experienced at various levels of production. In carrying out this analysis, each expense item is classified as either fixed (constant at any reasonable level of output) or variable (increasing as output increases and decreasing as output declines).

**Business cycle:** Alternate expansion and contraction in overall business activity evidenced by fluctuations in measures of aggregate economic activity such as the gross national product, the index of industrial production, and employment and income. A business cycle may be divided into four phases: expansion, during which business activity is successively reaching new high points; leveling out, during which business activity reaches a high point and remains at that level for a short period of time; contraction, during which business volume recedes from the peak level for a sustained period until the bottom is reached; and recovery, during which business activity resumes after the low point has been reached and continues to rise to the previous high mark.

**Cable TV:** Transmission of a television signal for home viewing by wire (cable) as opposed to airwave broadcast. A fee or monthly subscription charge is assessed. Often used in remote or isolated viewing areas, many cable systems offer subscribers an opportunity to see movies, sporting events, and other special programming not available on free TV.

**Capitalized value:** The term applied to a technique used to determine the present value of an asset that promises to produce income in the future. To calculate the present value, the total future income expected must be discounted, that is, offset against the cost (as measured by the current interest rate) of carrying the asset until the income has actually been realized. If the asset promises a stream of income, its capitalized value is calculated by adding together the present discounted value of the income in each year. The general formula for this calculation is $I/(1+r)^t$, where $I$ is the annual income, $r$ is the current rate of interest, and $t$ is the number of years involved. In this manner, an investor confronted with a choice of properties can determine which alternative is the most remunerative, though the formula tells nothing about the relative risks involved.

**Cash flow:** The sum of profits and depreciation allowances. (Instead of profits, many economists use retained earnings, which are profits after taxes and after deductions for dividend payments.) Gross cash flow is composed of total profits plus depreciation; net cash flow is composed of retained earnings plus depreciation. Thus, cash flow represents the total funds that corporations generate internally for investment in modernization and expansion of plants and equipment and for working capital. The growth of depreciation allowances over the years has made them a much more important part of cash flow than retained earnings. To facilitate comparisons of property values, however, entertainment businesses often take cash flow to be profits prior to deductions of interest, depreciation and amortization, and taxes.

**Clearance:** The relative exclusivity a theater specifies as a condition to licensing a motion picture within a market. A theater may request an exclusive run within an entire market or may request exclusivity for exhibition of a motion picture only over those theaters that are in geographic proximity and may be considered competitive.

**Commercial:** An advertisement broadcast on a television or radio station for which the station receives some form of compensation (also called spot announcement).

**Common stock:** The capital stock of a corporation that gives the holder an unlimited interest in the corporation's earnings and assets after prior claims have been met. Common stock represents the holder's equity or ownership in the corporation. Holders of common stock have certain fundamental legal rights, including the following: preemptive rights; the right, in most cases, to vote for the board of directors, who actually manage the company; the right to transfer any or all shares of stock owned; and the right to receive dividends when they are declared by the board of directors.

**Competition:** The condition prevailing in a market in which rival sellers try to increase their profits at one another's expense. In economic theory, the varieties of competition range from perfect competition, in which numerous firms produce or sell identical goods or services, to oligopoly, in which a few large sellers with substantial influence in the market vie with one another for the available business. Early economists envisioned perfect competition as the most effective assurance that consumers would be provided with goods and services at the lowest possible prices.

**Complementary goods:** Goods that must be accompanied by another good to be useful (e.g., perfect complements would be a left shoe and a right shoe). Contrariwise, close substitutes would be margarine and butter.

**Compulsory license:** A rule, legislated by the U.S. Congress, that permits cable systems to carry all TV station signals in their geographic area without having to pay any money for the rights.

**Contract:** The mutually binding licensing agreement between a distribution company and an exhibition company for the showing of a motion picture at a particular theater on or about a given date. Included are the terms for computing payment for film rental, playing time, clearance, advertising sharing, and so forth.

**Convertible debenture:** A certificate issued by a corporation as evidence of debt that can be converted at the option of the holder into other securities (usually common stock, but sometimes preferred stock) of the same corporation. Each debenture can be converted into a specified number of shares of stock at a stipulated price for a certain period.

**Correlation:** The statistical technique that relates a dependent economic variable to one or more independent variables over a period of time to determine the closeness of the relationship between the variables. This technique can be used for business forecasting. When more than one independent variable is used, the relationship is called a multiple correlation.

**Cost per thousand (CPM):** Determined by dividing the cost of a print or broadcast advertisement or of a total advertising campaign by the total estimated audience, computing the total audience on a base of thousands.

**Cost recovery:** Accounting method of amortization in which all costs are charged against earned revenue and no profit is recognized until cumulative revenue equals cumulative costs. This method is not acceptable for financial-statement reporting under generally accepted accounting principles.

**Cross-collateralization:** The practice in film and music distribution of off-setting profits in one territory or nation or category of earnings by losses in others. It is a practice that obviously favors the distributors.

**Current assets:** Cash or other items that will normally be turned into cash within one year and assets that will be used up in the operation of a firm within one year. Current assets include cash on hand and in the bank, accounts receivable, materials, supplies, inventories, marketable securities, and pre-paid expenses.

**Current liabilities:** Amounts owed that will ordinarily be paid by a firm within one year. The most common types of current liabilities are accounts payable, wages payable, taxes payable, and interest and dividends payable.

**Day and date release:** Simultaneous (same day, same date) release of a motion picture in two or more theaters in a given market. Also used to indicate simultaneous opening in two or more markets (e.g., "L.A. and New York, day and date openings").

**Debenture:** A bond that is not protected by a specific lien or mortgage on property. Debentures (debts), which are issued by corporations, are promises to pay a specific amount of money (principal) at a specified date or periodically over the course of the loan, during which time interest is paid at a fixed rate on specified dates.

**Demand:** The desire, ability, and willingness of an individual to purchase a good or service. Desire by itself is not equivalent to demand: The consumer must also have the funds or the ability to obtain funds to convert the desire into demand. The demand of a buyer for a certain good is a schedule of the quantities of that good that the individual would buy at possible alternative prices at a given moment in time. The demand schedule, or the listing of quantities that would be bought at different prices, can be shown graphically by means of the demand curve. The term *demand* refers to the entire schedule of possibilities, not only to one point on the schedule. It is an instantaneous concept expressing the relationship of price and the quantity that is desired to be bought, with all other factors being constant.

**Depreciation:** A reduction in the value of fixed assets. The most important causes of depreciation are wear and tear (loss of value caused by the use of an asset), the effects of the elements (i.e., decay or corrosion), and gradual obsolescence, which makes it unprofitable to continue using some assets until they have been fully exhausted. The annual amount of depreciation of an asset depends on its original purchase price, its estimated useful life, and its estimated salvage value. A number of different methods of figuring the amount of depreciation have been developed. Using the simple straight-line method, which considers depreciation a function of time, the annual depreciation cost is calculated by dividing the cost of the asset (original minus salvage cost) equally over its entire life.

**Designated market area:** Nielsen audience-market classification that designates a certain market area in which local stations have partial or complete dominance over stations from other market areas. Similar to Arbitron ADI.

**Direct-distribution expense:** Expense incurred in relation to the distribution of a specific picture: The two largest items relating to the release of any picture are prints and advertising and publicity costs. Other direct expenses include such things as checking costs, freight, guild payments, trade-association fees and assessments, market research, and certain taxes.

**Discount rate:** 1. Interest rate charged member banks by the Federal Reserve for the opportunity to borrow added reserves. 2. Percentage by which a bank will discount the financing value of a filmmaker's distribution contract.

**Discounted–cash flow method:** A method of measuring the return on capital invested. The value of a project is expressed as an interest rate at which the project's total future earnings, discounted from the time that they accrue to the present, equal the original investment. It is more precise than most of the other methods used to measure return on capital invested because it recognizes the effect of the time value of money. It can be used to determine whether a given project is acceptable or unacceptable by comparing each project's rate of return with the company's standard.

**Discretionary spending:** A measure, developed by the National Industrial Conference Board, that reflects the extent of consumer spending as the result of a decision relatively free of prior commitment, pressure of necessity, or force of habit. It includes all personal expenditures not accounted for specifically or in equivalent form in imputed income, fixed commitments, or essential outlays. The series measures the growth and ability of American consumers to exercise some degree of discretion over the direction and manner of their spending and saving.

**Distribution fee:** Contractual rate assessed by a distributor on the gross film revenue. Used in computation of contingent compensation (i.e., profit participation).

**Drop:** A term used in the gaming industry to indicate the total monetary-equivalent value of cash, IOUs ("markers"), and other items that are physically deposited or dropped into a cash box of a gaming table or slot machine.

**EBITDA:** Earnings before deduction of interest, taxes, and depreciation and amortization. Often used as a convenient representation of the cash flow of media and travel-related businesses. In recent years, however, EBITDA has lost analytical favor because it doesn't include the cash flow required to service debts (interest payments) and to purchase or construct new projects, services, or equipment. In times of rapid technological or business change, such purchases will normally require cash outlays that exceed depreciation and amortization.

**Econometrics:** The branch of economics that expresses economic theories in mathematical terms in order to verify them by statistical methods. It is concerned with empirical measurements of economic relations that are expressible in mathematical form. Econometrics seeks to measure the impact of one economic variable on another to enable the prediction of future events or provide advice on economic-policy choices to produce desired results. Economic theory can supply qualitative information concerning an economic problem, but it is the task of econometrics to provide the quantitative content for these qualitative statements.

**Economic growth:** An increase in a nation's or an area's capacity to produce goods and services coupled with an increase in production of these goods and services. Usually, economic growth is measured by the annual rate of increase in a nation's gross national product (GNP) as adjusted for price changes.

**Economic model:** A mathematical statement of economic theory. Use of an economic model is a method of analysis that presents an oversimplified picture of the real world.

**Economics:** The social study of production, distribution, and consumption of wealth.

**Elastic demand:** The percentage change induced in one factor of demand divided by a given percentage change in the factor that caused the change. For example, if the price of a commodity is raised, purchasers tend to reduce their buying rate. The relationship between price and purchasing rate, which is known as the elasticity of demand, expresses the percentage change in the buying rate divided by the percentage change in price.

**Elasticity:** The relative response of one variable to a small percentage change in another variable.

**Equilibrium:** The state of an economic system in which all forces for change are balanced so that the net tendency to change is zero. An economic system is considered to be in equilibrium when all the significant variables show no change over a period of time.

**Equity:** 1. Amount of capital invested in an enterprise. It represents a participative share of ownership, and in an accounting sense it is calculated by subtracting the liabilities (obligations) of an enterprise from its assets. 2. The shorthand name for the Actors' Equity Association, the actors' labor union.

**Excess reserves:** The surplus of cash and deposits owned by commercial member banks of the Federal Reserve System over what they are legally required to hold at Reserve Banks or in their own vaults. The excess-reserve position of a bank is an indication of its ability to invest in government bonds or to make loans to customers. Therefore, if the Federal Reserve System is trying to stimulate business in periods of economic sluggishness, it buys government bonds from private sellers, thus increasing bank reserves, and vice versa.

**Film rental:** The monies paid by the exhibitor to the distributor as rental fees for the right to license a film for public showing. The amount is generally computed weekly on a consecutive seven-day basis (Wednesday through Tuesday or Friday through Thursday, depending on the day on which the film first opens in the market). Film rental may be determined by several different methods, including a 90:10 basis, sliding scale, fixed percentage, minimums (floors) that relate specifically to the gross box-office receipts, or a flat-fee basis that is a predetermined, unchanging amount. The film rental earned usually changes from week to week, with the distributor's relative share generally decreasing and the exhibitor's share increasing from the first through subsequent weeks.

**FM (frequency modulation):** Technically, the variation of the frequency of a radio wave in accordance with the sound being broadcast. Radio (audio) transmission from 88 to 108 megahertz. The signal is unaffected by atmospheric interference, but it is a high-fidelity, line-of-sight beam impeded by topographic or physical obstructions.

**Foreign exchange:** All monetary instruments that give residents of one country a financial claim on another country. The use of foreign exchange is a country's principal means of settling its transactions with other countries.

**Four-wall:** A technique used by some distribution companies in which theaters are offered a flat weekly rental fee that is guaranteed to the exhibitor regardless of the film's revenue intake at the box office. The distributor pays all advertising expenses and usually hires personnel to be at each theater for supervision and nightly collection of all monies taken in at the box office. The exhibitor faces almost no risk in that rental income is guaranteed. The distributor incurs a greater risk but is also in the position, should the film be successful, of reaping the benefits of 100% of the monies taken in at the box office, less advertising, administrative, and rental costs.

**Franchise:** 1. A contractual agreement between a cable operator and a government body that defines the rights and responsibilities of each party in the construction and operation of a cable system within a specified geographic area. 2. A territorial agreement between a league and team owners.

**Free reserves:** The margin by which excess reserves exceed borrowings at Federal Reserve Banks. Free reserves are a better indicator of the banking system's ability to expand loans and investments than excess reserves. Manipulation of the net free-reserve position of member banks is an indication of the monetary policy that the Federal Reserve wishes to pursue.

**Gross domestic product (GDP):** The measure of the value of all goods and services produced in a country no matter whether that output belongs to natives or foreigners. It is different from GNP, which measures output belonging to U.S. citizens and corporations wherever that output is created. In the United States the differences between the values of the two series have been slight. *See* Gross national product.

**Gross national product (GNP):** The most comprehensive measure of a nation's total output of goods and services. In the United States, the GNP represents the dollar value at current prices of all goods and services produced for sale plus the estimated value of certain imputed outputs, that is, goods and services that are neither bought nor sold. The rental value of owner-occupied dwellings and the value of farm products consumed on the farm are the most important imputed outputs included; the services of housewives are among the most important nonmarket values included. The GNP includes only final goods and services; for example, a pair of shoes that costs the manufacturer $2.50, the retailer $4.50, and the consumer $6.00 adds to the GNP only $6.00, the amount of the final sale, not $13.00, the sum of all the transactions. The GNP can be calculated by adding either all expenditures on currently produced goods and services or all incomes earned in producing these goods and services.

**GRP (gross rating point):** A rating basis for determining the estimated percentage of households or target audience exposed to a broadcast commercial or magazine advertisement (newspaper GRP data generally are not readily available). GRPs are the sums of all rating points and an indication of potential exposure. One rating point is equal to 1% of the population of the total universe in which the advertising campaign is being run. However, this does not mean that 100 GRPs provide advertising exposure to 100% of the population, for this measurement does not eliminate audience duplication from its number totals. GRPs can be computed on the basis of reach multiplied by average frequency.

**Gross rentals:** The total of the distributor's share of the money taken in at the box office computed on the basis of negotiated agreements between the distributor and the exhibitor (also called gross proceeds).

**Gross win:** The casino equivalent of revenues or sales in other businesses. It is from the gross win that operating expenses must be deducted.

**Handle:** A term used in the gaming industry to indicate the total dollar amount bet on the outcome of an event.

**Head end:** The electronic-origination center of a cable system and the site of signal-processing equipment.

**Hold:** A term used in the gaming industry to indicate how much of the drop is retained (won) by the game operator through the course of play. Hold can be expressed as a percentage of the drop, in which case it is known as the hold percentage, often in a shorthand way called "win."

**Holdover figure:** A minimum weekly dollar figure for monies taken in at the theater box office that a film must reach to be held over for another week. This figure is mutually agreed on by the exhibitor and distributor when the terms under which the film will be played are originally established. It is an objective means by which either the exhibitor or the distributor may insist that the picture continue if the figure was achieved or, if not, cease to be shown in a specific theater.

**Homes passed:** The number of households in a market that a cable system has the ability to serve. This does not mean that these homes have elected to utilize the cable system.

**Homes using television:** The estimated percentage of the homes in which people are viewing television at any given time. The result of extrapolations made on the basis of audience-measurement techniques.

**Income effect:** A term used in demand analysis to indicate the increase or decrease in the amount of a good that is purchased because of a price-induced change in the purchasing power of a fixed income. When the price of a commodity declines, the income effect enables a person to buy more of this or other commodities with a given income. The opposite occurs when the price rises. By using indifference curves, it is possible to separate the income effect from the so-called substitution effect, in which the demand for a price-reduced good rises as it is substituted for other goods whose prices have remained constant.

**Indifference curve:** A graphic curve that represents the various combinations of two goods that will yield the consumer the same total satisfaction. For example, a household may receive the same satisfaction from consuming four pounds of steak or one pound of chicken. By assuming that the two commodities can be substituted for each other, it is possible to draw an indifference schedule that contains all of the possible combinations of the commodities that will yield the same satisfaction. When the schedule is plotted on a graph, with one commodity along the vertical axis and another along the horizontal axis, the curve that connects the points is called an indifference curve.

**Inelastic demand (inelasticity):** A term used to describe a proportionally smaller change in the purchase rate of a good than the proportional change in price that caused the change in amount bought. When the demand for a product is inelastic, a relatively large price change is necessary to cause a relatively small increase in purchase. To calculate the elasticity of demand, the percentage change in buying rate (the quantity bought per period of time) is divided by the percentage change in price.

**Inflation:** A persistent upward movement in the general price level. It results in a decline in purchasing power.

**Interest:** The price paid for the use of money over a period of time. Individuals, businesses, and governments buy the use of money. Businesses pay interest for the use of money to purchase capital goods because they can increase production and productivity through the introduction of new plants and new machines.

**Inventory:** The supply of various goods kept on hand by a firm to meet needs promptly as they arise and thus assure uninterrupted operation of the business. In manufacturing, for example, inventory includes not only finished products awaiting shipment to selling outlets but also raw materials and countless other items required for the production and distribution of the product.

**Labor force:** According to the concept of the U.S. Department of Labor and the U.S. Bureau of the Census, the noninstitutionalized population, 16 years of age or older, who either are employed or are looking for work.

**Legs:** In the movie business the term indicates a film that attracts strong audience interest and that will therefore run (play) in theaters for a relatively long time.

**Liabilities:** The debts or amounts of money owed by an individual, partnership, or corporation to others. Considered from another point of view, liabilities are the claims or rights, expressed in monetary terms, of an individual's or a corporation's creditors. In accounting, liabilities are classified as either short-term or long-term liabilities or as secured or unsecured liabilities. Short-term liabilities are those that will be satisfied, or paid, within one year.

**Local Marketing Agreement (LMA):** In the broadcasting industry, an LMA is a time-brokerage arrangement between two separately owned stations in the same geographic area that allows one station to exchange programming for the right to sell advertising time on the other station. LMAs are designed so as to save costs by combining the marketing efforts of at least two local broadcast stations.

**Macroeconomics:** Modern economic analysis concerned with data in aggregate as opposed to individual form. It concerns itself with an overall view of economic life considering the total size, shape, and functioning of economic experience rather than the workings of individual parts. More specifically, macroeconomics involves the analysis of the general price level rather than the prices of individual commodities, national output or income rather than the income of the individual firm, and total employment rather than employment in an individual firm.

**Make-good:** An offer by a medium to rerun, at no additional charge, an advertisement or commercial. Generally of equal or greater value than the original placement and used to compensate advertisers for unanticipated ratings shortfalls.

**Marginal cost:** The additional cost that a producer incurs by making one additional unit of output. If, for example, total costs were $13,000 when a firm was producing two machine tools per day and $18,000 when it was producing three machine tools per day, the marginal cost of producing one machine tool was $5,000. The marginal cost may be the same or higher or lower in moving from three to four machine tools. The concept of marginal cost plays a key role in determining the quantity of goods that a firm chooses to produce. The purely competitive firm, which faces a given price set in the market, increases its output until marginal cost equals price. That point is the firm's best-profit output point. The imperfectly competitive firm equates marginal cost to marginal revenue (additional revenue) to obtain the highest profits. For most firms, marginal costs decline for a while and then begin to rise.

**Marginal revenue:** The additional revenue that a seller receives from putting one more unit of output on the market.

**Margins:** *See* Profit margin.

**Market share:** The ratio of a company's sales, in units or dollars, to total industry sales, in units or dollars, on either an actual basis or a potential basis for a specific time period.

**Mechanical rights (royalties):** The rights to reproduce and to distribute to the public copyrighted materials. Mechanical royalties, usually on a per copy basis, are paid to obtain such rights.

**Microeconomics:** Modern economic analysis concerned with data in individual form as opposed to aggregate form. It is concerned with the study of the individual firm rather than aggregates of firms, the individual consuming unit rather than the total population, and the individual commodity rather than total output. Microeconomics deals with the division of total output among industries, products, and firms and the allocation of resources among competing uses. It is concerned with the relative prices of particular goods and the problem of income distribution.

**Model:** The expression of a theory by means of mathematical symbols or diagrams.

**Modern portfolio theory:** A theory that enables investment managers to classify, estimate, and control the sources of investment risk and return.

**Monopoly:** A market structure with only one seller of a commodity. In pure monopoly, the single seller exercises absolute control over the market price because there is no competitive supply of goods on the market. The seller can choose the most profitable price and does so by raising the price and restricting the output below what would be achieved if there were competition.

**Monopsony:** A market structure with a single buyer of a commodity. Pure monopsony, or buyer's monopoly, is characterized by the ability of the single buyer to set the buying price. In the case of a monopsonist who maximizes profits, both the buying price and the quantity bought are lower than they would be in a competitive situation.

**MPEG (Motion Picture Experts Group):** Pertains to two video standards that had been developed as of the early 1990s. MPEG-1, which provides VCR-quality video, was originally developed for CD-ROM systems and operates at 1.5 Mbps (million bits per second) with resolution of $352 \times 240$ pixels at 30 frames per second, whereas MPEG-2 was first initiated by broadcasters for live video services that can be transmitted at 6 Mbps with $720 \times 480$ or $1,270 \times 720$ pixels at 60 frames per second. It is used for encoding movies on DVDs. MPEG-4 is the latest version that incorporates Apple's Quicktime in highly compressed files used in broadband distribution.

**MSO (multiple-system operator):** A company that owns and operates more than one cable television system.

**Multimedia:** A term broadly used to describe the convergence of digitalized computer, telephone, and cable technologies in the development of new entertainment software applications that mix text, audio, and video.

**National income:** The total compensation of the elements used in production (land, labor, capital, and entrepreneurship) that comes from the current production of goods and services by the national economy. It is the income earned (but not necessarily received) by all persons in the country in a specified period.

**Negative cost:** All the various costs, charges, and expenses incurred in the acquisition and production of a motion picture. These include such items as facilities (sound stage, film lab, editing room, etc.) and raw material (set construction, raw film stock, etc.). It is typically segregated as above-the-line production-period costs and post-production-period costs.

**Negotiated deal:** If the film-distribution company rejects all bid offers submitted by exhibitors for the right to license a film for exhibition within a market, the branch office will in turn either rebid the picture, suggesting different terms, or send out a notice to all exhibitors by which it offers to negotiate openly in an effort to award the film to the theater that offers the most attractive deal.

**Net profits (contractual):** Generally, the amount of gross receipts remaining after deducting distribution fees, distribution expenses, negative cost (including interest), certain deferments, and gross participations.

**Nielsen station index (NSI):** A service provided by the A. C. Nielsen Company for rating television viewing habits, audience profiles, and other factors on a local basis or within a given broadcast area.

**Nonborrowed reserves:** A reserve aggregate consisting of total bank reserves (deposits of the Federal Reserve and vault cash) minus borrowings by member banks from the Federal Reserve.

**Oligopoly:** A type of market structure in which a small number of firms supply the major portion of an industry's output. The best-known example in the U.S. economy is the automobile industry, in which three firms account for 65% of the output of passenger cars. Although oligopolies are most likely to develop in industries whose production methods require large capital investments, they also cover such diverse items as cigarettes, light bulbs, chewing gum, detergents, and razor blades. In economic theory, the term *oligopoly* means a mixture of competition and monopoly. The benefit or harm to the economy at large by oligopolies remains in dispute.

**Operating income:** Earnings before interest, other income, and taxes.

**Opportunity costs:** The value of the productive resources used in producing one good, such as an automobile, instead of another good, such as a machine tool. With relatively fixed supplies of labor and capital at any given time, the economy cannot produce all it wants of everything.

**Output Deal:** Agreements with distributors (e.g., foreign theatrical, pay TV) in which the distributor agrees to pay a specific amount for the distribution rights for a specific number of films, with the price sometimes adjusted for box-office performance and production costs.

**Outstandings:** A term used by film exhibitors and distributors to indicate the amount of money one might owe the other for film rentals and/or advertising expenses.

**Overage:** In movies and music, generally any dollar amount beyond which advances and guarantees have been earned or, in industry parlance, have been recouped. The term is also applied to extensions of payments for work rendered beyond that stipulated in original contracts.

**Paretian optimum:** A situation that exists when no one (say person *A*) in a society can move into a position that *A* prefers without causing someone else (person *B*) to move into a position that *B* prefers less. In other words, a situation is not a Paretian or social optimum if it is possible, by changing the way in which commodities are produced or exchanged, to make one person better off without making another person (or persons) worse off. *See* Second-best theory.

**Partnership:** A type of business organization in which two or more persons agree on the amounts of their contribution (capital and effort) and on the distribution of profits, if any. Partnerships are common in retail trade, accounting, and law.

**Pay-per-view:** A cable service that makes available to a subscriber an individual movie, sporting event, or concert on payment of a fee for that single event.

**Pay TV:** A generic term used to indicate subscriber-paid-for television presented in an uncut and uncensored format.

**Periodic-table computation method:** An accounting method of amortization in which cost is related to gross revenue recorded during a period; may be based on an average table established from experience with previously released films.

**Personal-consumption expenditures:** Expenditures that reflect the market value of goods and services purchased by individuals and nonprofit institutions or acquired by them as income in kind. The rental value of owner-occupied dwellings is included, but not the purchases of dwellings. Purchases are recorded at cost to consumers, including excise or sales taxes, and in full at the time of purchase whether made with cash or on credit.

**Personal income:** According to the concept of the U.S. Department of Commerce, the amount of current income received by persons from all sources, including transfer payments from government and business, but excluding transfer payments from other sources. Personal income also includes the net incomes of unincorporated businesses and nonprofit institutions and non-monetary income such as the estimated value of food consumed on farms and the estimated rental value of homes occupied by their owners.

**Price/earnings ratio:** The current market price per share of a company's stock expressed as a multiple of the company's per share earnings.

**Print:** 1. A copy made from the master for the purpose of motion-picture presentation. For all intents and purposes, the print is the specific motion-picture release because the master is preserved for additional duplication. A distribution company may make only a few copies or more than 1,500 prints on the basis of expected or experienced success with a particular motion picture. 2. Advertising placed in newspapers as part of an advertising campaign.

**Production function:** The various combinations of land, labor, materials, and equipment that are needed to produce a given quantity of output. The production function expresses the maximum possible output that can be produced with any specified quantities of the various necessary inputs. Every production function assumes a given level of technology; once technological innovations have been introduced, the production function changes.

**Production overhead:** Those costs and expenses incurred for the production of motion pictures in general that cannot be directly charged to specific pictures. They include such things as salaries of production-department executives and their related expenses, story-abandonment costs, certain studio-facility costs, and general and administrative costs relating to the production area.

**Productivity:** The goods and services produced per unit of labor or capital or both; for example, the output of automobiles per person-hour. The ratio of output to all labor and capital is a total productivity measure; the ratio of output to either labor or capital is a partial measure. Anything that raises output in relation to labor and capital leads to an increase in productivity.

**Profit margin:** Net profit from operations divided by net sales and expressed as a percentage. This percentage measures the efficiency of a company or an industry. Nevertheless, profit margins vary widely among industries and among companies within a given industry. *See* Returns.

**Profits:** The amount left over after a business enterprise has paid all its bills.

**Public good:** A good for which the costs of production are independent of the number of people who consume it. National defense is an example, for one person's consumption does not diminish the quantity available to others. TV programs are almost pure public goods because the program, no matter how it is recorded, remains unchanged regardless of how many people view it. In contrast, pure *private goods*, once consumed by an individual, are no longer available for someone else. For private goods, say a slice of bread, the costs of production *are* related to the number of people who consume it.

**Reach:** The number of households or the target audience exposed to an advertising message at least one time over a predetermined period of time (also called *cume*).

**Reach and frequency:** Criteria for evaluating the level of cumulative audience exposure for an advertising campaign on the basis of a percentage of all persons or households who are exposed to the advertising (reach) and the average number of exposures (frequency) over a given period of time: reach × frequency = gross rating points.

**Regression line:** A statistical term that indicates a relationship between two or more variables. The regression line was first used by Sir Francis Galton to indicate certain relationships in his theory of heredity, but it is now employed to describe many functional relationships. A regression, or least-squares, line is derived from a mathematical equation relating one economic variable to another. The use of regression lines is important in determining the effect of one variable on another.

**Required reserves:** The percentages of their deposits that U.S. commercial banks are required to set aside as reserves at their regional Federal Reserve

Bank or as cash in their vaults. Reserve requirements vary according to the category of the bank.

**Returns:** 1. The earnings or profit compensations received for owning assets or equity positions. Also, returns on sales are equivalent to profit margins. 2. The term used in the record business in regard to goods sent back to the manufacturer or distributor for credit.

**Risk:** The exposure of an investor to the possibility of gain or loss of money. Profit is the investor's reward for assuming the risk of economic uncertainty, such as changes in consumer tastes or changes in technology. The financial risk is based on natural, human, and economic uncertainties.

**Scatter market:** In network television, the remnants of unsold commercial time that remain after preseason upfront buying has been completed.

**Second-best theory:** A theory that analyzes alternative suboptimal positions to determine the second best when some constraint prevents an economy from reaching a Paretian optimum. *See* Paretian optimum.

**Secular trend:** A statistical term denoting the regular, long-term movement of a series of economic data. The secular trend of most economic series is positive, or upward, indicating growth, the angle of the trend depending on how fast or how slow the growth rate is.

**Share of audience:** The percentage of total households or population (either local or national depending on survey criteria) that are using television or radio during a specific time and that are also tuned into a particular program.

**Sherman Antitrust Act:** A U.S. federal statute, enacted in 1890, that forbids all contracts in restraint of trade and all attempts at monopolization. The main purposes of the act were to prevent the exercise and growth of monopoly and to restore free enterprise and price competition.

**Spot TV:** Local TV commercial time purchased on a given TV station within a specific market through a local salesperson within that market or through a national representative of the station.

**Stripping:** Generally applied to the use of off-network syndicated series episodes several times a week, as in a continuous strip.

**Superstation:** Independent TV stations (in Atlanta, Boston, Chicago, Dallas, Los Angeles, and New York) that broadcast their programming nationally via satellite to cable systems. The systems pay for copyrights and also several cents a subscriber every month to the satellite companies (common carriers) that distribute the signals.

**Supply:** The ability and willingness of a firm to sell a good or service. The firm's supply of a good or service is a schedule of the quantities of that good or service that the firm would offer for sale at alternative prices at a given moment in time. The supply schedule, or the listing of quantities that would be sold at different prices, can be shown graphically by means of a supply curve. The term *supply* refers to the entire schedule of possibilities, not to one point on the schedule. It is an instantaneous concept expressing the relationship of price and the quantity that would be willingly sold with all other factors being constant.

**Syndication:** A term usually applied to the process whereby previously exhibited or recorded material is reused by (licensed to) a collection of buyers such as independent television and radio stations.

**Tax credit:** A legal provision permitting U.S. taxpayers to deduct specified sums from their tax liabilities.

**Tax deduction:** A legal provision permitting U.S. taxpayers to deduct specified expenditures from their taxable income.

**Terms:** The conditions under which the distributor agrees to allow the exhibitor to show its product in a given theater and the exhibitor agrees to show the product. Relates to items such as the basis on which film rental will be paid (as a percentage of weekly gross box-office receipts or flat fee), the playing time (number of weeks), choice of theater, dollar participation in cooperative advertising expenditure, and clearance over other theaters.

**Time buys:** Broadcast airtime that is sold to outside producers as a substitute for self-produced or bought programming and usually contains off-beat sporting events such as bull-riding, skateboarding, and curling.

**Time series:** A set of ordered observations of a particular economic variable, such as prices, production, investment, and consumption, taken at different points in time. Most economic series consist of monthly, quarterly, or annual observations. Monthly and quarterly economic series are used in short-term business forecasting.

**UHF (ultra-high frequency):** Television signals in the range of 300 to 3,000 megahertz. Television channels 14 through 83.

**Underwriter:** Any person, group, or firm that assumes a risk in return for a fee; usually called a premium or commission.

**Unemployment rate:** The number of jobless persons expressed as a percentage of the total labor force. The United States counts as unemployed anyone 16 years of age or over who is out of work and would like a job (even if that person is doing little about finding one).

**Unique (Web site) visitors:** The total number of users who visited the Web site or online property at least once in a given month. All unique visitors are counted only once.

**Upfront buying:** In network television, the preseason purchasing of commercial time in selected program blocks.

**Utility:** The ability of a good or a service to satisfy human wants. It is the property possessed by a particular good or service that affords an individual pleasure or prevents pain during the time of its consumption or the period of anticipation of its consumption. The degree of utility of a good varies constantly. Thus, utility is not proportional to the quantity or type of the good or service consumed.

**VHF (very high frequency):** Television signals in the range of 30 to 300 megahertz. Television channels 2 through 13.

**Warrant:** An option that gives the holder the privilege of purchasing a certain amount of stock at a specified price for a stipulated period.

**Win:** *See* Gross win.

**Window:** In films and television, the period of time during which contracts permit exclusive exhibition of a product. For example, a home video market release window would normally follow a film's initial domestic theatrical window, three to six months later. This would be followed by the opening of pay television, syndication, and other windows.

**Working capital, net:** The excess of current assets over current liabilities. These excess current assets are available to carry on business operations. As demand increases in prosperous times, a large volume of working capital is needed to expand production.

**Workweek:** The number of weekly hours per factory worker for which pay has been received, including paid holidays, vacations, and sick leaves. In the United States, workweek figures cover full-time and part-time production and related workers who receive payment for any part of the pay period ending nearest the fifteenth of the month. Because of increasing amounts of paid holidays, vacations, and sick leave, the paid workweek exceeds the number of hours actually worked per week. The average-workweek series compiled from payroll data by the U.S. Bureau of Labor Statistics differs from the series of weekly hours actually worked that is compiled from household surveys by the U.S. Bureau of the Census. It also differs from the standard or scheduled workweek because of such factors as absenteeism, part-time work, and stoppages.

**Write-off:** The act of removing an asset from the books of a company. The term *write-off* is related to *write-down*, but the latter is more closely associated with partial reduction of the book value of the asset rather than with removing the asset from the books entirely.

**Yield:** The percentage that is derived from dividing the annual return from any investment by the amount of the investment.

# References

Aaker, D. A. (1991). *Managing Brand Equity*. New York: Free Press.

Abcarian, R., and Horn, J. (2006). "Underwhelmed by It All," *Los Angeles Times*, August 7.

Abrams, R. I. (2000). *The Money Pitch: Baseball Free Agency and Salary Arbitration*. Philadelphia: Temple University Press.

Abt, V., Smith, J. F., and Christiansen, E. M. (1985). *The Business of Risk: Commercial Gambling in Mainstream America*. Lawrence: University of Kansas Press.

Acheson, K., and Maule, C. J. (2005). "Understanding Hollywood's Organization and Continuing Success," in *An Economic History of Film*, edited by J. Sedgwick and M. Pokorny. London: Routledge.

Adams, J. A. (1991). *The American Amusement Park Industry: A History of Technology and Thrills*. Boston: Twayne Publishers (G. K. Hall & Co.).

Adler, M. (1985) "Stardom and Talent," *American Economic Review*, 75 (March).

Adler, S. (2004). *On Broadway: Art and Commerce on the Great White Way*. Carbondale, IL: Southern Illinois University Press.

Aguiar, M., and Hurst, E. (2006). "Measuring Trends in Leisure: The Allocation of Time over Five Decades," Working Paper, No. 06-2. Boston: Federal Reserve Bank of Boston.

AICPA (1984). *Audits of Casinos*. New York: American Institute of Certified Public Accountants.

Akst, D., and Landro, L. (1988). "In Hollywood's Jungle the Predators Are Out and Feasting on Stars," *Wall Street Journal*, June 20.

Albert, S. (1998). "Movie Stars and the Distribution of Financially Successful Films in the Motion-Picture Industry," *Journal of Cultural Economics*, 22, and in Sedgwick and Pokorny (2005), eds., *An Economic History of Film*. London: Routledge.

Alpert, B. (2005). "HDTV: Who Wins, Who Loses," *Barron's*, May 23.

Alvarez, L. (2004). "A Struggling Resort Dreams of a Date with Lady Luck," *New York Times*, May 17.

Ambrose, J. F. (1981). "Recent Tax Developments Regarding Purchases of Sports Franchises – The Game Isn't Over Yet," *Taxes*, 59(11)(November). Chicago: Commerce Clearing House.

Amdur, M. (2003). "Sharing Pix Is Risky Business," *Variety*, November 17.

Anderson, C. (2006). *The Long Tail: Why the Future of Business Is Selling Less of More*. New York: Hyperion.

(2004). "The Long Tail," *Wired*, 12.10 (October).

Andrews, E. L. (1993). "Top Rivals Agree on Unified System for Advanced TV," *New York Times*, May 25.

Angeli, M. (1991). "My Name Is Bond. Completion Bond," *New York Times*, August 11.

Angwin, J. (2002). "Web Radio Showdown," *Wall Street Journal*, May 15.

Angwin, J., and Vranica, S. (2006). "Marketer's Tactic Signals Big Shift in a TV Ad Ritual," *Wall Street Journal*, January 4.

Appleton, D., and Yankelevits, D. (2002). *Hollywood Dealmaking: Negotiating Talent Agreements*. New York: Allworth Press.

Asch, P., Malkiel, B. G., and Quandt, R. E. (1984). "Market Efficiency in Racetrack Betting," *Journal of Business*, 57(2)(April).

Auletta, K. (1997). "The Impossible Business," *The New Yorker,* October 6.

(1991). *Three Blind Mice: How the TV Networks Lost Their Way*. New York: Random House.

Avalon, M. (2002). *Confessions of a Record Producer.* San Francisco: Backbeat Books.

Baade, R. A. (1994). "Stadiums, Professional Sports, and Economic Development: Assessing the Reality," *Heartland Policy Study No. 62* (April 4). Detroit: The Heartland Institute.

Bagamery, A. (1984). "We Sell Space, Not Fantasy," *Forbes*, 133(3)(January 30).

Bagwell, K. (2001, 2005). *The Economics of Advertising*. Northampton, MA: Edward Elgar Publishing. See also *The Economic Analysis of Advertising*, 2005, www.columbia.edu/cu/economics/discpapr/DP0506-01.pdf.

Bakker, G. (2005). "America's Master," in *An Economic History of Film*, edited by J. Sedgwick and M. Pokorny. London: Routledge.

Bakker, P. (2002). "Free Daily Newspapers – Business Models and Strategies," *International Journal on Media Management*, 4(3) and http://users.fmg.uva.nl/pbakker/freedailies/.

Baldo, A. (1991). "Secrets of the Front Office," *Financial World,* 160(14)(July 9).

Balfe, J. H., ed. (1993). *Paying the Piper: Causes and Consequences of Arts Patronage*. Champaign, IL: University of Illinois Press.

Balio, T., ed. (1976). *The American Film Industry*. Madison: University of Wisconsin Press, rev. ed. 1985.

Banks, J. (1996). *Monopoly Television: MTV's Quest to Control the Music*. Boulder, CO: Westview Press.

Bannon, L., and Lippman, J. (2000). "Mattel and Hasbro Get Licenses for Harry Potter," *Wall Street Journal*, February 11.

Bardeen, W. T., and Shaw, C. (2004). "Tax-Motivated German Financing of the U.S. Film Industry," www.gsb.columbia.edu/chazenjournal.

Barlett, D. L., and Steele, J. B. (2002). "Wheel of Misfortune: Look Who's Cashing in at Indian Casinos," *Time*, December 16.

Barnes, B. (2006a). "NBC Universal to Slash Costs in News, Prime-Time Programs," *Wall Street Journal*, October 19.

(2006b). "Local Stations Struggle to Adapt as Web Grabs Viewers, Revenue," *Wall Street Journal*, June 12.

(2006c). "Disney Will Offer Many TV Shows Free on the Web," *Wall Street Journal*, April 10.

(2005a). "How 'Wicked' Cast Its Spell," *Wall Street Journal*, October 22.

(2005b). "New Hope on TV's 'Bubble'," *Wall Street Journal*, February 21.

(2004a). "For Nielsen, Fixing Old Ratings System Causes New Static," *Wall Street Journal*, September 16.

(2004b). "Trusting Gut Instincts, WB Network Stops Testing TV Pilots," *Wall Street Journal*, May 3.

Barnhart, R. T. (1983). "Can Trente-et-Quarante Be Beaten?," *Gambling Times*, 3(8)(December).

Barnouw, E. (1990). *Tube of Plenty: The Evolution of American Television*, rev. 2nd ed. New York: Oxford University Press.

Barra, A. (1995). "How the 49ers Beat the Salary Cap," *New York Times*, January 8.

Barrett, N. S. (1974). *The Theory of Microeconomics Policy*. Lexington, MA: Heath.

Barrionuevo, A. (2004). "Joining Film Fight, Hungary Tries to Go Hollywood," *Wall Street Journal*, August 26.

Bart, P., and Guber, P. (2002). *Shoot Out: Surviving Fame and (Mis)Fortune in Hollywood*. New York: Penguin (Berkley).

Barwise, P., and Ehrenberg, A. (1988). *Television and Its Audience*. London: Sage.

Bary, A. (2005). "Hold 'em!," *Barron's*, February 21.

Baskerville, D. (1982). *Music Business Handbook*, 3rd ed. Denver, CO: Sherwood.

Baumgarten P. A., Farber, D. C., and Fleischer, M. (1992). *Producing, Financing, and Distributing Film*, 2nd ed. New York: Limelight Editions. (First edition by Drama Book Specialists, New York, in 1973.)

Baumol, W., and Baumol, H. (1984). "In Culture, the Cost Disease Is Contagious," *New York Times*, June 3.

Baumol, W. J., and Bowen, W. G. (1968). *Performing Arts – The Economic Dilemma*. New York: Twentieth Century Fund; Cambridge, MA: MIT Press.

Becker, G. S. (1965). "A Theory of the Allocation of Time," *Economic Journal*, LXXV(299)(September).

Becker, G. S., and Murphy, K. M. (1993). "A Simple Theory of Advertising as Good or Bad," *Quarterly Journal of Economics*, November.

Bell, L. A., and Freeman, R. B. (2000). "The Incentive for Working Hard: Explaining Hours Worked Differences in the U.S. and Germany," NBER Working Paper 8051 (December). New York: National Bureau of Economic Research (www.nber.org).

Belson, K. (2006a). "As DVD Sales Slow, Hollywood Hunts for a New Cash Cow," *New York Times*, June 13.

(2006b). "In Sony's Stumble, the Ghost of Betamax," *New York Times*, February 26.

(2003). "Heavyweights Are Choosing Sides in Battle over Next DVD Format," *New York Times*, December 29.

Berfield, S. (2005). "The Making of *The Color Purple*," *BusinessWeek*, November 21.

Berger, A. J., and Bruning, N. (1979). *Lady Luck's Companion*. New York: Harper & Row.

Berney, R. (2004). "Independent Distribution," in *The Movie Business Book*, edited by J. E. Squire. New York: Simon & Schuster (Fireside).

Bernstein, C. (1990). "The Leisure Empire," *Time*, 136(27)(December 24).

Berry, E. J. (1984). "Nielsen May Face U.K. Rival in Researching TV Audiences," *Wall Street Journal*, February 2.

Biederman, D., and Phillips, L. (1980). "Negotiating the Recording Agreement," in *Counseling Clients in the Entertainment Industry*, edited by M. Silfen. New York: Practising Law Institute.

Bikhchandani, S., Hirshleifer, D., and Welch, I. (1992). "A Theory of Fads, Fashion, Custom, and Cultural Change as Informational Cascades," *Journal of Political Economy*, 100(5).

Binkley, C. (2004). "Taking Retailers' Cues, Harrah's Taps into Science of Gambling," *Wall Street Journal,* November 22.

    (2000). "Casino Chain Mines Data on Its Gamblers, and Strikes Pay Dirt," *Wall Street Journal*, May 4.

Blaug, M., ed. (1976). *The Economics of the Arts*. Boulder, CO: Westview Press, London: Martin Robertson.

Bluem, A. W., and Squire, J. E., eds. (1972). *The Movie Business: American Film Industry Practice*. New York: Hastings House.

Blumenthal, H. J., and Goodenough, O. R. (2006). *This Business of Television*, 3rd ed. New York: Billboard/Watson-Guptill.

Blumenthal, R. (2002). "Charges of Payola over Radio Music," *New York Times*, May 25.

Blumenthal, R. G. (2001). "Bialystock, Bloom, & You," *Barron's*, June 18.

Boorstin, J. (2003). "Disney's 'tween Machine," *Fortune*, 148(6)(September 29).

Bordewich, F. M. (2006). "The Least Transparent Industry in America," *Wall Street Journal*, January 5.

Boucher, F. C. (1986). "Performing Music Licensing Procedures," *Billboard*, November 24.

Boucher, G. (2005). "Up, Up . . . and Away," *Los Angeles Times*, December 31.

Boyer, P. J. (1988). "Sony and CBS Records: What a Romance," *New York Times Magazine,* September 18.

Bradsher, K. (1994). "Congressmen Pledge to Revoke Baseball's Antitrust Exemption," *New York Times*, December 24.

Braunlich, C., Cabot, A., Thompson, W., and Tottenham, A. (1999). *International Casino Law*, 3rd ed. Reno, NV: Institute for the Study of Gambling and Commercial Gaming, University of Nevada.

Breglio, J. F., and Schwartz, S. (1980). "Introduction to Motion Picture Production and Distribution and Motion Picture Financing," in *Counseling Clients in the Entertainment Industry*, edited by M. Silfen. New York: Practising Law Institute.

Breimer, S. F. (1995). *Clause by Clause: The Screenwriter's Legal Guide*. New York: Dell Trade Paperback.

Brinkley, J. (1999). "Disk vs. Disk: The Fight for the Ears of America," *New York Times*, August 8.

    (1997). *Defining Vision: The Battle for the Future of Television*. New York: Harcourt Brace & Co.

    (1996). "Defining TVs and Computers for a Future of High Definition," *New York Times*, December 2.

Brown, A. C. (1984). "Europe Braces for Free-Market TV," *Fortune*, 109(4)(February 20).

Brown, C. (2006). "Owners in N.F.L. Accept Labor Deal," *New York Times*, March 9.

(2002). "Hollywood May Be Saying auf Wiedersehen to Funds," *Los Angeles Times*, June 17.

(1991). "Who Lost the Turtles?," *Premiere*, 4(6)(February).

Brown, J., and Church, A. (1987). "Theme Parks in Europe," *Travel & Tourism Analyst*, London: The Economist, February.

Bulkeley, W. M. (2006). "To Boost Revenues, State Lotteries Wager on Slots," *Wall Street Journal*, March 30.

Bunn, A. (2002). "The Wasteland," *New York Times*, June 23.

Burke, M. (2006). "A New Test for an Old Raider," *Forbes*, 178(5)(September 18).

Burton, J. S., and Toth, J. R. (1974). "Forecasting Long-Term Interest Rates," *Financial Analysts Journal*, 30(5)(September/October).

Butterfield, F. (2005a) "Indians' Wish List: Big City Sites for Casinos," *New York Times*, April 8.

(2005b). "As Gambling Grows, States Depend on Their Cut to Bolster Revenues," *New York Times*, March 31.

Cabot, A. N., ed. (1995). *Nevada Gaming Law*, 2nd ed. Las Vegas: Lionel Sawyer & Collins.

Carlson, M. B. (1984). "Where MGM, the NCAA, and Jerry Falwell Fight for Cash," *Fortune*, 109(2)(January 23).

Carr, D. (2005). "Smartest Guys Well Outside of Hollywood," *New York Times*, May 23.

Carter, B. (2006). *Desperate Networks*. New York: Doubleday, and "How a Hit Almost Failed Its Own Audition," *New York Times*, April 30.

(2004a). "News Analysis: Why Make Leno a Lame Duck?," *New York Times*, September 29.

(2004b). "Shorten TV Season? Rules Shifting at Networks," *New York Times*, February 8.

(2002a). "New Life for Networks," *New York Times*, February 21.

(2002b). "*Friends* Deal Will Pay Each of Its 6 Stars $22 Million," *New York Times*, February 12.

(2001a). "HBO Bets Pentagon-Style Budget on a World War II Saga," *New York Times*, September 3.

(2001b). "It's Decision Time at Networks on 'Frasier' and 'Dharma'," *New York Times*, February 26.

(2000). "Who Needs the Sweeps?," *New York Times*, April 24.

(1999). "Broadcast Network Executives Struggle to Reinvigorate Their Business," *New York Times*, January 4.

Carter, B., and Rutenberg, J. (2003). "Shows' Creators Say Television Will Suffer in New Climate," *New York Times*, June 3.

Carvajal, D. (1996). "Many, Many Unhappy Returns," *New York Times*, August 1.

Caves, R. E. (2000). *Creative Industries: Contracts between Art and Commerce*. Cambridge, MA: Harvard University Press.

Chace, S. (1983). "Computer Game: Key Software Writers Double as Media Stars in a Promotional Push," *Wall Street Journal*, December 12.

Champion, M., Nelson, E., and Goldsmith, C. (2004). "To BBC's Rivals, 'Auntie' Is Too Big for Its Britches," *Wall Street Journal*, September 28.

Chaplin, H., and Ruby, A. (2005). *Smartbomb: The Quest for Art, Entertainment, and Big Bucks in the Videogame Revolution*. Chapel Hill, NC: Algonquin Books.

Chass, M. (2000). "Alex Rodriguez Strikes It Rich in Texas," *New York Times*, December 12.

Christiansen, E. M. (1998). "1997 U.S. Gross Annual Wager," *Gaming and Wagering Business*, July and August issues.

(1989). "1988 U.S. Gross Annual Wager," *Gaming and Wagering Business*, 10(7)(July) and 10(8)(August).

Clark, D. (2004). "Videogames Get Real," *Wall Street Journal*, April 14.

Clark, M. M. (2006). "Nielsen's 'People Meters' Go to Top 10," *Wall Street Journal*, June 30.

Coates, D. C., and Humphreys, B. R. (2000). "The Stadium Gambit and Local Economic Development," *Regulation*, 23(2).

Cobb, C., Halstead, T., and Rowe, J. (1995). "If the GDP Is Up, Why Is America Down?," *The Atlantic Monthly*, 276(4)(October).

Cohen, L. (1983). "Cable-Television Firms and Cities Haggle over Franchises That Trail Expectations," *Wall Street Journal*, December 28.

Colker, D. (2006). "All-You-Can-Eat Movies Can Leave You Hungry," *Los Angeles Times*, February 5.

Collins, G. (2005). "In a Daring Leap, Ringling Loses Its Three Rings," *New York Times*, December 31.

(1992). "The Daunting Task of Preventing Theft at Theater Box Offices," *New York Times*, March 25.

Collins, S. (2005). "Some Television Reruns Hit Their Prime on DVD," *Los Angeles Times*, November 13.

Columbia Pictures Industries. (1982). *Columbia Pictures Industries Financial Factbook, 1981*. New York: Columbia Pictures Industries.

Colvin, G. (1983). "The Battle for TV's Rerun Dollars," *Fortune*, 107(7)(May 2).

Cones, J. W. (1998). *43 Ways to Finance Your Feature Film: A Comprehensive Analysis of Film Finance*, updated edition. Carbondale, IL: Southern Illinois University Press.

(1997). *The Feature Film Distribution Deal: A Critical Analysis*. Carbondale, IL: Southern Illinois University Press.

(1992). *Film Finance & Distribution: A Dictionary of Terms*. Los Angeles: Silman-James.

Cook, J. (1979). "Bingo!," *Forbes*, 124(3)(August 6).

Couzens, M. (1986). "Invasion of the People Meters," *Channels*, June.

Cowen, T. (2002). *Creative Destruction: How Globalization Is Changing the World's Cultures*. Princeton, NJ: Princeton University Press.

(1998). *In Praise of Commercial Culture*. Cambridge MA: Harvard University Press.

Cox, M. (1989a). "Networks Overhaul Payouts for Affiliates," *Wall Street Journal*, May 31.

(1989b). "The 'Toxic Avenger' May Not Win Any Prizes, but Fans Don't Care," *Wall Street Journal*, August 18.

Crandall, R. W. (1972). "FCC Regulation, Monopsony, and Network Television Program Costs," *Bell Journal of Economics*, 3(2)(autumn).

Crandall, R. W., and Furchtgott-Roth, H. (1996). *Cable TV: Regulation or Competition*. Washington, DC: The Brookings Institution.

Crockett, R. O. (2005). "iPod Killers?," *BusinessWeek*, April 25.

Cross, G. (1997). *Kids' Stuff: Toys and the Changing World of American Childhood*. Boston: Harvard University Press.

Cukier, K. N. (2000). "The Big Gamble," *Red Herring*, April.

Culhane, J. (1990). *The American Circus: An Illustrated History.* New York: Henry Holt and Company.

Curran, T. (1986). *Financing Your Film: A Guide for Independent Filmmakers and Producers.* New York: Praeger.

Damodaran, A. (1996). *Investment Valuation.* New York: John Wiley & Sons.

Daniels, B., Leedy, D., and Sills, S. D. (1998, 2006). *Movie Money: Understanding Hollywood's (Creative) Accounting Practices.* Los Angeles: Silman-James.

Dannen, F. (1990). *Hit Men: Power Brokers and Fast Money Inside the Music Business.* New York: Times Books/Random House.

Davis, L. J. (1989). "Hollywood's Most Secret Agent," *New York Times Magazine,* July 9.

Davis, M. D. (1973). *Game Theory: A Nontechnical Approach.* New York: Basic Books.

De Grazia, S. (1962). *Of Time, Work and Leisure.* New York: Twentieth Century Fund.

Deidda, L. G., and Cerina, F. (2002). "Do We Need More Time for Leisure?," Working Paper CRENoS (Centre for North South Economic Research, University of Cagliari and Sassari, Sardinia).

Dekom, P. J. (1984). "Transition in the Motion Picture Industry – Financing and Distribution, 1984," in *Counseling Clients in the Entertainment Industry,* edited by M. Silfen, pp. 189–203. New York: Practising Law Institute.

Delaney, K. J. (2004). "After IPO, Can Ads Keep Fueling Google?," *Wall Street Journal,* April 29.

Dellarocas, C., Awad, N. F., and Zhang, X. M. (2004). "Exploring the Value of Online Reviews to Organizations: Implications for Revenue Forecasting and Planning," Working Paper, MIT and University of Michigan, http://ccs.mit.edu/dell/papers/movieratings.pdf.

Demmert, H. G. (1973). *The Economics of Professional Team Sports.* Lexington, MA: Heath.

Desai, M. A., Veblen, M. F., and Loeb, G. J. (2002a). "The Strategy and Sources of Motion Picture Finance," *Harvard Business School Case* 9-203-007. Cambridge, MA: Harvard.

  (2002b). "Tax-Motivated Film Financing at Rexford Studios," *Harvard Business School Case* 9-203-005. Cambridge, MA: Harvard.

DeSerpa, A. C. (1971). "A Theory of the Economics of Time," *Economic Journal,* December.

De Silva, I. (1998). "Consumer Selection of Motion Pictures," in *The Motion Picture Mega-Industry,* edited by B. R. Litman. Needham Heights, MA: Allyn & Bacon.

De Vany, A. S. (2004a). *Hollywood Economics: How Extreme Uncertainty Shapes the Film Industry.* New York: Routledge.

  (2004b). "Motion Picture Directors: Luck, Talent and Rewards," in *Economics of Art and Culture,* edited by V. A. Ginsburgh. Amsterdam: Elsevier.

De Vany, A., and Walls, W. D. (1997). "The Market for Motion Pictures: Rank, Revenue, and Survival," *Economic Inquiry,* 4(35), October 1997.

  (1996). "Bose-Einstein Dynamics and Adaptive Contracting in the Motion Picture Industry," *The Economic Journal,* November.

DiMaggio, P. J. (1984). "The Nonprofit Instrument and the Influence of the Marketplace on Policies in the Arts," in *The Arts and Public Policy in the United States,* edited by W. M. Lowry. New York: The American Assembly (Columbia University).

DiOrio, C., and McNary, D. (2002). "Hollywood's Runaway Train," *Variety,* February 4.

Disch, T. M. (1991). "The Death of Broadway," *The Atlantic Monthly,* 267(3)(March).

Dobson, S., and Goddard, J. (2002). *The Economics of Football (English)*. New York: Cambridge University Press.

Doman, M. (2001). "Regal Tiff Slows 'Rush 2' a Bit," *The Hollywood Reporter*, August 13.

Donahue, S. M. (1987). *American Film Distribution: The Changing Marketplace*. Ann Arbor, MI: UMI Research Press.

Donnelly, W. J. (1986). *The Confetti Generation*. New York: Henry Holt.

Dorfman, R., and Steiner, P. O. (1954). "Optimal Advertising and Optimal Quality," *American Economic Review*, 44(5)(December).

Downward, P., and Dawson, A. (2000). *The Economics of Professional Team Sports*. New York: Routledge.

Duhigg, C. (2005). "Indies, Major Labels Tune In to a New Act," *Los Angeles Times*, August 14.

Durant, J. (1969). *Highlights of the Olympics: From Ancient Times to the Present*, 3rd ed. New York: Hastings House.

Durso, J. (1986). "Mets a Baseball 'Jewel' in Attendance, Revenue," *New York Times*, August 22.

Eade, R. H. (1996). "Casino Cage Operations," in *The Gaming Industry: Introduction and Perspectives*. Las Vegas: University of Nevada; New York: John Wiley & Sons.

Eadington, W. R., ed. (1976). *Gambling and Society*. Springfield, IL: Thomas.

Eberts, J., and Ilott, T. (1990). *My Indecision Is Final: The Rise and Fall of Goldcrest Films*. London: Faber and Faber (paperback 1992).

Eisbruck, J. H. (2005). "Blockbuster or Flop? The History and Evolution of Film Receivables Securitization, 1995–2005," *Journal of Structured Finance*, fall.

Elberse, A. (2006). "The Power of Stars in Creative Industries: Do Stars Drive the Success of Movies?," Cambridge, MA: Harvard Business School Working Paper Series, No. 06–002.

Eliashberg, J., Elberse, A., and Leenders, M. A. (2006). "The Motion Picture Industry: Critical Issues in Practice, Current Research, and New Research Directions," *Marketing Science*, 25(6), and Cambridge, MA: Harvard Business School Working Paper Series, No. 05–059.

Eliashberg, J., and Shugan, S. M. (1997). "Film Critics: Influencers or Predictors?," *Journal of Marketing*, 61(2)(April).

Eliot, M. (1989). *Rockonomics: The Money behind the Music*. New York: Franklin Watts.

Eller, C. (2002). "Jilters Regret Missing 'Wedding'," *Los Angeles Times*, September 14.

Elton, E. J., Gruber, M. J., Brown, S. J., and Goetzmann, W. N. (2003). *Modern Portfolio Theory and Investment Analysis*. Hoboken, NJ: John Wiley & Sons.

Emshwiller, J. R., and Binkley, C. (2004). "As Indian Casinos Grow, Regulation Raises Concerns," *Wall Street Journal*, August 23.

Epstein, E. J. (2006). "Gross Hysteria: Do the Studios Really Overpay Top Talent Like Peter Jackson?," *Slate*, January 23.

(2005). *The Big Picture: The New Logic of Money and Power in Hollywood*. New York: Random House.

Fabrikant, G., and Thomas, L., Jr. (2003). "One-Two Punch for Investors: AOL and Cable Unit," *New York Times*, January 31.

Farber, D. C. (1997). *Producing Theatre: A Comprehensive Legal and Business Guide*, 2nd rev. ed. New York: Limelight Edition.

(1995). "Theater Lawyers Seem to Be Avoiding LLCs," *New York Law Journal*, January 20.

(1993). *From Option to Opening: A Guide to Producing Plays Off-Broadway*, 4th rev. ed. New York: Limelight Editions.

Fatsis, S. (2006a). "A Longtime Loser, Pro Soccer Begins to Score in the U.S.," *Wall Street Journal*, June 17.

(2006b). "Playing Hardball," *Wall Street Journal*, April 28.

(2005). "The Battle for the NFL's Future," *Wall Street Journal*, August 29.

(2004). "Can Socialism Survive?," *Wall Street Journal*, September 20.

(2003). "In College Football, Also-Rans Fight for Bigger Share of the Pot," *Wall Street Journal*, November 25.

(2002a). "Baseball Stars Discover Owners Now Have the Upper Hand," *Wall Street Journal*, December 23.

(2002b). "The New Game in TV Sports," *Wall Street Journal*, January 21.

Felton, M. (1980). "Policy Implications of a Composer Labor Supply," in *Economic Policy for the Arts*, edited by W. S. Hendon, J. L. Shanahan, and A. J. MacDonald, pp. 186–198. Cambridge, MA: Abt Books.

Fey, M. (1989). *Slot Machines*. Reno, NV: Liberty Belle Books.

Fielding, R., ed. (1967). *A Technological History of Motion Pictures and Television: An Anthology from the Journal of the Society of Motion Picture and Television Engineers*. Los Angeles: University of California Press.

*Final Report* (1978). London: Royal Commission on Gambling, July, Vol. 2.

Findlay, J. M. (1986). *People of Chance: Gambling in American Society from Jamestown to Las Vegas*. New York: Oxford University Press.

Fisher, D., and Ozanian, M. K. (1999). "Cowboy Capitalism," *Forbes*, 164(7)(September 20).

Fisher, F. M., McGowan, J. J., and Evans, D. S. (1980). "The Audience-Revenue Relationship for Local Television Stations," *Bell Journal of Economics*, 11(2)(autumn).

Fleming, M. (2006). "CAA: Super-Size Me," *Variety*, August 21.

Flick, R. (1988). "ASCAP's Out of Tune with Composers," *Wall Street Journal*, May 27.

Flint, J. (2006). "Fox News Wants $1 per Customer Anniversary Gift," *Wall Street Journal*, April 25.

(2004). "Dearth of Network Sitcoms Hurts Stations Seeking Reruns," *Wall Street Journal*, January 21.

(2002a). "TNT Upsets Cable Operators with a New Bill," *Wall Street Journal*, October 14.

(2002b). "NBC Reaps Profits by Shooting for Viewers with More Money," *Wall Street Journal*, May 20.

(2001). "NBC and Viacom Unit Sign 'Frasier' Deal," *Wall Street Journal*, March 7.

(2000). "How the Top Networks Are Turning the Tables on Their Affiliates," *Wall Street Journal*, June 14.

Forsyth, R. W. (1995). "Stadiums Built with Taxpayer Funds Don't Pay Their Way," *Barron's*, November 13.

Fort, R. (2005). "The Golden Anniversary of 'The Baseball Players' Labor Market'," *Journal of Sports Economics*, 6(November).

Fowler, G. A. (2006). "Estimates of Copyright Piracy Losses Vary Widely," *Wall Street Journal*, June 2.

Frangos, A. (2004). "Bigger and Better," *Wall Street Journal*, September 20.

Frank, A. D. (1984). "The USFL Meets the Sophomore Jinx," *Forbes*, 133(4)(February 13).

Frank, R. H. (2006). "How Much Is that Laptop?," *New York Times*, July 6.

Frank, R. H., and Cook, P. J. (1995). *The Winner-Take-All Society*. New York: The Free Press (Simon & Schuster).

Frankenfield, W. C. (1994). "What Are the Generally Accepted Accounting Principles in the Broadcasting Industry?," *Broadcast Cable Financial Journal*, June–July.

Frascogna, X. M., and Hetherington, H. L. (1978). *Successful Artist Management*. New York: Billboard/Watson-Guptill.

Freedman, M. (2004). "Madness of Crowds," *Forbes*, 173(7)(April 12).

Frey, B. S., and Pommerehne, W. W. (1989). *Muses & Markets: Explorations in the Economics of the Arts*. London: Basil Blackwell.

Friedman, B. (1974, 1982). *Casino Management*, rev. and enlarged edition. Secaucus, NJ: Lyle Stuart.

Friedman, M., and Savage, L. J. (1948). "The Utility Analysis of Choices Involving Risk," *Journal of Political Economy*, 56(4)(August).

Fritz, B., and Graser, M. (2004). "Is the Game Getting Lame?," *Variety*, May 10.

Fritz, B., and Snyder, G. (2006). "Hollywood Seeking the Missing Link," *Variety*, April 10.

Frude, N. (1983). *The Intimate Machine: Close Encounters with Computers and Robots*. New York: New American Library.

Gage, J. (2005). "Russian Roulette," *Forbes*, 175(8)(April 18).

Gaither, C. (2006). "TV's Path to Web Remains Unclear," *Los Angeles Times*, April 23.

Gapinski, J. H. (1986). "The Lively Arts as Substitutes for the Lively Arts," *American Economic Review*, 76(2)(May).

Garey, N. H. (1983). "Elements of Feature Financing," in *The Movie Business Book*, edited by J. E. Squire. New York: Simon & Schuster (Fireside).

Garrity, B. (2000). "Coming Up Short," *Investment Dealers' Digest*, June 5.

Gelatt, R. (1977). *The Fabulous Phonograph, 1877–1977*, 2nd rev. ed. New York: Macmillan.

Gerse, S. (2004). "Overseas Tax Incentives and Government Subsidies," in *The Movie Business Book*, edited by J. E. Squire. New York: Simon & Schuster (Fireside).

Gertner, J. (2005). "Our Ratings, Ourselves," *New York Times*, April 10.

Ghez, G. R., and Becker, G. S. (1975). *The Allocation of Time and Goods over the Life Cycle*. New York: National Bureau of Economic Research.

Gibbs, N. (1989). "How America Has Run Out of Time," *Time*, 133(17)(April 24).

Gilder, G. (2000). *Telecosm: How Infinite Bandwidth Will Revolutionize our World*. New York: The Free Press (Simon & Schuster) and www.forbes.com.

Gilpin, K. (1993). "The Circus Is Just One of His Acts," *New York Times*, March 24.

Ginsburgh, V. A. (2004), ed. *Economics of Art and Culture*. Amsterdam: Elsevier.

Gladwell, M. (2006). "The Risk Pool," *The New Yorker*, August 28.

Goettler, R. L., and Leslie, P. (2003). "Cofinancing to Manage Risk in the Motion Picture Industry," working paper, Stanford University and Carnegie Mellon University, www.stanford.edu/p̄leslie/cofinancing.pdf and www.gsia.cmu.edu/amdrew/goettler/public/papers/movies.

Goldberg, M. (1988). "Inside the Payola Scandal," *Rolling Stone*, January 14.

Goldman, K. (1992). "The One-Hour Drama Stages a Comeback on TV after Being Preempted by Sitcoms," *Wall Street Journal*, September 1.

Goldsmith, J. (2004). "Hollywood Plexed by Plex Success," *Variety*, May 17.

Goldstein, P. (2006a). "Too Much of a Good Thing," *Los Angeles Times*, October 24.

    (2006b). "Make Way for Studio Outsiders on the Red Carpet," *Los Angeles Times*, February 1.

    (2005). "This Year, the Safe Bets Are Off," *Los Angeles Times*, January 26.

Gollehon, J. (1986). *All about Sports Betting*. Grand Rapids, MI: Gollehon.

Gomes, L. (2006). "It May Be a Long Time Before the Long Tail is Wagging the Web," *Wall Street Journal*, July 26.

Goodell, G. (1998). *Independent Feature Film Production: A Complete Guide from Concept through Distribution*. New York: St. Martin's Griffin.

Goodell, J. (1999). "World War MP3," *Rolling Stone*, July 8.

Goodman, R. (1995). *The Luck Business: The Devastating Consequences and Broken Promises of America's Gambling Explosion*. New York: The Free Press (Simon & Schuster).

(1994). *Legalized Gambling as a Strategy for Economic Development*. Northampton, MA: Broadside Books.

Gorham, J. (2002). "Teutonic Tinsel," *Forbes*, 169(3)(February 4).

Gottman, J. M. (1981). *Time Series Analysis: A Comprehensive Introduction for Social Scientists*. New York: Cambridge University Press.

Graham, M. B. W. (1986). *RCA and the VideoDisc: The Business of Research*. New York: Cambridge University Press.

Grampp, W. D. (1989). *Pricing the Priceless: Art, Artists, and Economics*. New York: Basic Books.

Grant, P. (2006). "Online Video Goes Mainstream, Sparking an Industry Land Grab," *Wall Street Journal*, February 21.

(2005). "Comcast Plans Major Rollout of Phone Service over Cable," *Wall Street Journal*, January 10.

(2004). "It's Yankees 1, Cablevision 0, in TV-Fee Fight," *Wall Street Journal*, March 25.

(2003). "Digital World Churns as Cable Homes Ignore Many Channels," *Wall Street Journal*, September 24.

Grant, P., and Latour, A. (2005). "In Risky Move, a New AT&T Bets on Internet Technology," *Wall Street Journal*, November 21.

Grant, P., and Orwall, B. (2003). "After Web Blow-up Shift to Broadband Quietly Went On," *Wall Street Journal*, January 8.

Greco, A. N. (1997). *The Book Publishing Industry*. Boston: Allyn and Bacon.

Green, J. (2005). "Live on the Strip: Broadway's Second City," *New York Times*, October 2.

Greenhouse, L. (1999). "Justices Strike Down Ban on Casino Gambling Ads," *New York Times*, June 15.

Greenlees, E. M. (1988). *Casino Accounting and Financial Management*. Reno and Las Vegas: University of Nevada Press.

Greenwald, B. C. N., Kahn, J., Sonkin, P. D., and van Biema, M. (2001). *Value Investing: From Graham to Buffett and Beyond*, paperback ed. New York: John Wiley & Sons.

Grimes, W. (1997). "With 6,138 Lives, 'Cats' Sets Broadway Mark," *New York Times*, June 19.

Grinols, E. L. (2004). *Gambling in America: Costs and Benefits*. New York: Cambridge University Press.

Gross, D. (2004). "Does a Free Download Equal a Lost Sale?," *New York Times*, November 21.

Grover, R., and Green, H. (2003). "Hollywood Heist: Will Tinseltown Let Techies Steal the Show?," *BusinessWeek*, no. 3841, July 14.

Gubernick, L. (1999). "A Night at the Previews," *Wall Street Journal*, October 1.

(1989a). "Last Laugh," *Forbes*, 143(4)(May 15).

(1989b). "Living Off the Past," *Forbes*, 143(12)(June 12).

Guth, L. A., and Shagan, M. D. (2001). "Revisiting Regulation: Why the Reins Should Be Loosened on Thoroughbred Horse Racing," *Milken Institute Review*, Third Quarter.

Halliday, J., and Fuller, P., eds. (1974). *The Psychology of Gambling*. New York: Harper & Row.

Hamilton, J. D. (1994). *Time Series Analysis*. Princeton, NJ: Princeton University Press.

Hamlen, W. A., Jr. (1991). "Superstardom in Popular Music: Empirical Evidence," *Review of Economics and Statistics*, LXXIII(4)(November).

Hansell, S. (2004). "Selling 'Nemo' Online, Trying to Repel Pirates," *New York Times*, June 14.

(2003). "E-Music Sites Settle on Prices: It's a Start," *New York Times*, March 3.

Hansmann, H. (1981). "Nonprofit Enterprise in the Performing Arts," *Bell Journal of Economics*, 12(2)(autumn).

Hanssen, F. A. (2005). "Revenue Sharing and the Coming of Sound," in *An Economic History of Film*, edited by J. Sedgwick and M. Pokorny. London: Routledge.

Happel, S. M., and Jennings, M. M. (1995). "The Folly of Anti-Scalping Laws," *The Cato Journal*, 15(1)(spring/summer).

Harden, B., and Swardson, A. (1996). "America's Gamble," *Washington Post*, March 3–6.

Harmelink, P. J., and Vignes, D. W. (1981). "Tax Aspects of Baseball Player Contracts and Planning Opportunities," *Taxes*, 59(8)(August). Chicago: Commerce Clearing House.

Harmon, A. (2003). "Studios Using Digital Armor," *New York Times*, January 4.

(2002a). "Copyright Hurdles Confront Selling of Music on the Internet," *New York Times*, September 23.

(2002b). "Grudgingly, Music Labels Sell Their Songs Online," *New York Times*, July 1.

(2002c). "CD Technology Stops Copies, but It Starts a Controversy," *New York Times*, March 1.

(2000). "Potent Software Escalates Music Industry's Jitters," *New York Times*, March 7.

Harris, D. (1986). *The League: The Rise and Decline of the NFL*. New York: Bantam.

Harris, L. (1995). *The Harris Poll 1995, 68*. New York: Louis Harris & Associates, Inc.

Harris, W. (1981). "Someday They'll Build a Town Here, Kate," *Forbes*, 128(October 26).

Hazelton, J. (1998). "Goodwill Hunting," *Screen International*, March 13.

Hazlett, T. W., and Spitzer, M. L. (1997). *Public Policy toward Cable Television: The Economics of Rate Controls*. Cambridge, MA: The MIT Press; Washington, DC: The AEI Press.

Healey, J., and Phillips, C. (2005). "Piracy Spins a Global Web," *Los Angles Times*, October 9.

Hedges, J. N., and Taylor, D. E. (1980). "Recent Trends in Worktime: Hours Edge Downward," *Monthly Labor Review*, U.S. Department of Labor, 103(3)(March).

Heilbrun, J., and Gray, C. M. (2001). *The Economics of Art and Culture*, 2nd ed. New York: Cambridge University Press.

Helyar, J. (2003). "Ride 'em Cowboy," *Fortune*, 148(6)(September 29).

(1995). "Losers on the Field, L.A. Rams Win Big in Move to Missouri," *Wall Street Journal*," January 27.

Henderson, J. M., and Quandt, R. E. (1971). *Microeconomic Theory: A Mathematical Approach*, 2nd ed. New York: McGraw-Hill.

Hendon, W. S., Shanahan, J. L., and MacDonald, A. J., eds. (1980). *Economic Policy for the Arts*. Cambridge, MA: Abt Books.

Hennessee, J. A. (1978). "Gross Behavior: How to Get Your Percentage Back," *Action* (Directors Guild), January/February.

Hesmondhalgh (2002). *The Cultural Industries*. London: Sage.

Hirsch, J. (1987). "Big Business under the Big Top," *New York Times*, October 4.

Hirschberg, L. (2004). "What Is an American Movie Now?," *New York Times*, November 14.

Hochman, O., and Luski, I. (1988). "Advertising and Economic Welfare: Comment," *American Economic Review*, 78(1)(March).

Hof, R. D. (2006). "My Virtual Life," *BusinessWeek*, May 1.

Hoffman, C. (2006a). "Talent Agents Get Into Film Fundraising," *Los Angeles Times*, November 3.

(2006b). "Talent Firms May Merge to Keep Pace," *Los Angeles Times*, March 13.

Hofmeister, S. (1994). "Appeal of 'Direct-to-Video' Grows among Film Studios," *New York Times*, November 8.

Holland, B. (2002). "Copyright Arbitration Royal Panel Takes Middle Ground on Digital Licensing Rates," *Billboard*, March 2.

Holloway, L. (2002). "BMG Plans to Simplify Royalty Deductions," *New York Times*, November 21.

Holson, L. M. (2006a). "Hollywood Puts the Squeeze on Talent," *New York Times*, November 6.

(2006b). "Wall St. Woos Film Producers, Skirting Studios," *New York Times*, October 14.

(2005a). "Before You Buy a Ticket, Why Not Buy the DVD?," *New York Times*, December 19.

(2005b). "Can Hollywood Avoid the Death Eaters?," *New York Times*, November 6.

(2002). "Big Hollywood Hits Don't Ensure Big Profits," *New York Times*, September 2.

Horn, J. (2006a). "Far Removed From the Multiplex," *Los Angeles Times*, August 8.

(2006b). "Investors Hope to Cruise but Sometimes Sink," *Los Angeles Times*, May 16.

(2006c). "Hollywood Studios Rewriting Pay System for Their Talent," *Los Angeles Times*, January 13.

(2005a). "Agency's Talent Pool Is Fast Becoming an Ocean," *Los Angeles Times*, October 14.

(2005b). "DVD Sales Figures Turn Every Movie Into a Mystery," *Los Angeles Times*, April 17.

(2005c). "How the Moguls Came to Love Retail," *Los Angeles Times*, April 17.

Horvitz, J. S., and Hoffman, T. E. (1976). "New Tax Developments in the Syndication of Sports Franchises," *Taxes*, 54(3)(March). Chicago: Commerce Clearing House.

Hoskins, C., McFadyen, S., and Finn, A. (2004). *Media Economics*. Thousand Oaks, CA: Sage.

(1997). *Global Television and Film*. Oxford, U.K.: Oxford University Press.

Hoskins, C., and Mirus, R. (1988). "Reasons for the U.S. Dominance of the International Trade in Television Programmes," *Media, Culture and Society*, 10.

Hotelling, H. (1929). "Stability in Competition," *Economic Journal*, March.

Huberman, B. A. (2001). *The Laws of the Web: Patterns in the Ecology of Information*. Cambridge, MA: MIT Press.

Hughes, R. J. (2006). "Les Biz: Broadway's New Investors," *Wall Street Journal*, January 20.

(2005a). "Give Me Discards from Broadway," *Wall Street Journal*, June 17.

(2005b). "Broadway's New Deal," *Wall Street Journal*, March 11.

Huizinga, J. (1955). *Homo Ludens: A Study of the Play-Element in Culture*. Boston: Beacon Press.

Hull, J. B. (1984). "Music Charts Move against False 'Hits'," *Wall Street Journal*, February 16.

Ignatin, G., and Smith, R. (1976). "The Economics of Gambling," in *Gambling and Society*, edited by W. R. Eadington, pp. 69–91. Springfield, IL: Thomas.

Ip, G. (1999). "Analyst Discovers Order in the Chaos of Huge Valuations for Internet Stocks," *Wall Street Journal*, December 27.

Isenberg, B. (2005). "Doing the Broadway Shuffle," *Los Angeles Times*, April 24.

Ives, N. (2005). "Will Box-Office Blues Put Newspapers in Red?," *New York Times*, May 16.

Jacobs, J. A., and Gerson, K. (1998). "Who Are the Overworked Americans?," *Review of Social Economy*, LVI LVI (4)(Winter).

Jayakar, K. P., and Waterman, D. (2000). "The Economics of American Theatrical Movie Exports: An Empirical Analysis," *Journal of Media Economics*, 13(3).

Jensen, E. (1996). "Networks Blast Nielsen, Blame Faulty Ratings for Drop in Viewership," *Wall Street Journal*, November 22.

Johnson, R. (2005a). "The Lawsuit of the Rings," *New York Times*, June 27.

(2005b). "Good News in Hollywood. Shhh," *New York Times*, January 31.

(1984). "Applying the Utilization Theory to Slot Decisions," *Gaming Business*, April.

Johnson, W. (1985). "The Economics of Copying," *Journal of Political Economy*, 93(11).

Juster, F. T., and Stafford, F. P. (1991). "The Allocation of Time: Empirical Findings, Behavioral Models, and Problems of Measurement," *Journal of Economic Literature*, 29 (June).

Kafka, P. (2003). "The Road to Riches," *Forbes*, 172(1)(July 7).

Kagan, P. (1995). *Motion Picture Investor*, no. 145 (January).

Kahn, J. (2000). "Presto Chango! Sales Are Huge!," *Fortune*, 141(6)(March 20).

Kapner, S. (2003). "U.S. TV Shows Losing Potency around World," *New York Times*, January 2.

Kelejian, H., and Lawrence, W. (1980). "Estimating the Demand for Broadway Theater: A Preliminary Inquiry," in *Economic Policy for the Arts*, edited by W. S. Hendon, J. L. Shanahan, and A. J. MacDonald. Cambridge, MA: Abt Books.

Kelley, D. (1985). "Cable Television Unshackled? The Courts Have Just Struck a Blow for Freedom of Speech," *Barron's,* April 22.

Kelly, K. (2006a). "Defecting Staff and Stars, Doldrums in Hollywood Spur Changes at ICM," *Wall Street Journal*, October 25.

(2006b). "Defying the Odds: Hedge Funds Bet Billions on Movies," *Wall Street Journal*, April 29.

(2005). "Can New Ownership and Capital Infusion Fuel ICM Comeback?," *Wall Street Journal*, November 2.

(2002). "Where Music Will Be Coming From," *New York Times*, March 17.

(1998). *New Rules for the New Economy*. London and New York: Penguin Books.

Kelly, K., and Marr, M. (2006). "Sweetheart Star Deals Go Sour," *Wall Street Journal*, January 13.

Kiger, P. J. (2004). "Chew. Spit. Repeat." and "Great Moments in Mogul Handling," *Los Angeles Times*, February 29.

Kilby, J. (1985). "Estimating Revenue through Bet Criteria," *Gaming and Wagering Business*, 6(3)(March).

Kindem, G., ed. (1982). *The American Movie Industry: The Business of Motion Pictures.* Carbondale: Southern Illinois University Press.

King, T. (2002). "The 'Gosford Park' Goof," *Wall Street Journal*, March 1.

Kirkland, K. (2000). "On the Decline in Average Weekly Hours Worked," *Monthly Labor Review*, July.

Kirkpatrick, D. D. (2003). "Action-Hungry DVD Fans Sway Hollywood," *New York Times*, August 17.

——— (2001). "Slow Sales Add Pressure to Cut Prices of Books," *New York Times*, January 1.

Kneale, D. (1988). "How Wouk Epic Became a Sure Loser," *Wall Street Journal*, November 11.

Kneale, D., and Carnevale, M. L. (1991). "In TV Rerun Ruling, Hollywood Interests Prove Special Indeed," *Wall Street Journal*, April 10.

Knecht, G. B. (1998). "How Magazines Arrive on Shelves, and Why Some Soon May Not," *Wall Street Journal*, February 26.

Knight, A. (1978). *The Liveliest Art: A Panoramic History of the Movies.* New York: Macmillan.

Knoedelseder, W. (1993). *Stiffed: A True Story of MCA, The Music Business, and the Mafia.* New York: HarperCollins.

Konigsberg, I. (1987). *The Complete Film Dictionary.* New York: New American Library.

Koopmans, L. H. (1974). *The Spectral Analysis of Time Series.* New York: Academic Press.

Korr, C. P. (2002). *The End of Baseball as We Knew It: The Players Union, 1960–81.* Champaign, IL: University of Illinois Press.

Krantz, M. (2005). "Television that Leaps off the Screen," *New York Times*, July 3.

Krasilovsky, M. W., and Shemel, S. (1994). *More about This Business of Music.* New York: Billboard (Watson-Guptill).

Kraus, R. (1978). *Recreation and Leisure in Modern Society*, 2nd ed. Santa Monica, CA: Goodyear Publishing.

Kronemyer, D. E., and Sidak, J. G. (1986). "The Structure and Performance of the U.S. Record Industry," *1986 Entertainment and the Arts Handbook*. New York: Clark Boardman.

Kronholz, J. (1984). "Pop and Rock Tours Like Michael Jackson's Grow More Complex," *Wall Street Journal*, July 9.

Kubey, C. (1982). *The Winners' Book of Video Games.* New York: Warner Books.

Kyriazi, G. (1976). *The Great American Amusement Parks: A Pictorial History.* Secaucus, NJ: Citadel Press.

Labaton, S. (2004). "Court Orders Rethinking of Rules Allowing Large Media to Expand," *New York Times*, June 25.

——— (2003). "Regulators Ease Rules Governing Media Ownership," *New York Times*, June 3.

——— (2001). "U.S. Court Ruling Lets Cable Giants Widen Their Reach," *New York Times*, March 3.

Laing, J. R. (1996). "Foul Play?," *Barron's*, August 19.

Lake, M. (2002). "Cram Session: The Evolution of an Ever Deeper Disc," *New York Times*, January 31.

Landler, M. (2004). "Europe Reluctantly Deciding It Has Less Time for Time Off," *New York Times*, July 7.

Landro, L. (1990). "Warner Bros.' Success at Box Office Feeds Its Global Ambitions," *Wall Street Journal*, June 1.

   (1983). "Pay-TV Industry Facing Problems after Misjudging Market Demand," *Wall Street Journal*, June 29.

Landro, L., and Saddler, J. (1983). "Network, Film Moguls Blitz Capital in Battle for TV Rerun Profits," *Wall Street Journal*, November 8.

Lane, F. S. (2001). *Obscene Profits: Entrepreneurs of Pornography in the Cyber Age*. New York: Routledge.

Lane, R. (1994). "I Want Gross," *Forbes*, 154(7)(September 26).

La Pointe, J. (2005). "N.H.L. Cancels Hockey Season in Labor Battle," *New York Times*, February 17.

   (1989). "Television Lavishes Money on Sports, But Does It Pay?," *New York Times*, December 3.

Lardner, J. (1987). *Fast Forward: Hollywood, the Japanese, and the VCR Wars*. New York: W. W. Norton.

Lashinsky, A. (2004). "Murdoch's Air War," *Fortune*, 150(12)(December 13).

Latour, A. (2005). "To Meet the Threat from Cable, SBC Rushes to Offer TV Service," *Wall Street Journal*, February 16.

Lawson, C. (1983). "Broadway Is in Its Worst Slump in a Decade," *New York Times*, January 3.

Leeds, J. (2006). "Squeezing Money from the Music." *New York Times*, December 14.

   (2005). "Wipe Egg off Face, Try Again," *New York Times*, April 17.

   (2004). "Music Industry Is Trying Out New Releases as Digital Only," *New York Times*, November 22.

   (2002). "Radio Industry's Discomfort Grows over Payola-Like Practice," *Los Angeles Times*, October 21.

Leeds, M. A., and von Allmen, P. (2004). *The Economics of Sports*, 2nd ed. Boston: Addison Wesley.

Leedy, D. J. (1980). *Motion Picture Distribution: An Accountant's Perspective*. Los Angeles: David Leedy, C.P.A., P.O. Box 27845.

Leipzig, A. (2005). "The Sundance Odds Get Even Longer," *New York Times*, January 16.

Leonard, D. (2003). "Songs in the Key of Steve," *Fortune* 147(9)(May 12).

Leonhardt, D. (2006a). "Broadway's Touring Shows Find Tickets Harder to Sell," *New York Times*, August 20.

   (2006b). "Changes Ahead for a Theater Near You," *New York Times*, February 15.

Lessing, L. (1971). "Stand By for the Cartridge TV Explosion," *Fortune*, April, LXXXIII(4).

Lev, B. (2001). *Intangibles: Management, Measurement and Reporting*. Washington, DC: Brookings Institute.

   (2000a). "The New Math," *Barron's*, November 20.

   (2000b). "New Math for a New Economy," *Fast Company*, January–February.

Levine, R. (2005). "Story Line Is Changing for Game Makers and Their Movie Deals," *New York Times*, February 21.

Levinson, P. (1999). *Digital McLuhan: A Guide to the Information Millennium*. New York: Routledge.

Levy, H., and Sarnat, M. (1972). *Investment and Portfolio Analysis*. New York: Wiley.

Lewis, P. (2003). "The Biggest Game in Town," *Fortune*, 148(5)(September 15).

Lewis, R. (1995). "Relation between Newspaper Subscription Price and Circulation, 1971–1992," *Journal of Media Economics*, 8(1).

Lieberman, D. (2005). "TVs Turn into Vending Machines for Programs," *USA Today*, November 30.

Linder, S. B. (1970). *The Harried Leisure Class*. New York: Columbia University Press.

Linfield, S. (1987). "The Color of Money," *American Film*, 12(4).

Lipman, J. (1990) "Movie Merchandising Takes Off, Bat-Style," *Wall Street Journal*, January 5.

Lippman, J. (2005). "The Rights Stuff," *Wall Street Journal*, July 15.

(2004). "Thinking Outside the Box Office," *Wall Street Journal*, May 21.

(2002a). "Record Debut for 'Spider-Man' Signals Hollywood's New Rules," *Wall Street Journal*, May 6.

(2002b). "TV, Movie Actors Reject SAG Plan for Investments," *Wall Street Journal*, April 22.

(1999). "Stop Action," *Wall Street Journal*, March 22.

(1995). "Talent Agents Now Often Share Billing," *Wall Street Journal*, August 17.

Litman, B. R. (1998). *The Motion Picture Mega-Industry*. Needham Heights, MA: Allyn & Bacon.

Lowe, P. M. (1983). "Refreshment Sales and Theater Profits," in *The Movie Business Book*, edited by J. E. Squire, pp. 344–349. New York: Simon & Schuster/Fireside.

Lowry, T. (2003). "The NFL Machine," *BusinessWeek*, no. 3817, January 27.

Lubove, S. (2004). "Shootout in Hollywood," *Forbes*, 173(12)(June 7).

(1999). "Conspiracy Theory," *Forbes*, 164(13)(November 29).

(1995). "Major League Soccer: Can It Work?," *Forbes*, 156(14)(December 18).

Lyman, R. (2002). "Summer of the Spinoff," *New York Times*, April 17.

(2001). "Even Blockbusters Find Fame Fleeting in a Multiplex Age," *New York Times*, August 13.

(1999). "Pokémon Is Catching, and Keeping, Them," *New York Times*, November 13.

(1997). "An Endangered Species: The Angels of Broadway," *New York Times*, May 27.

Lyon, R. (1987). "Theme Parks in the USA," *Travel & Tourism Analyst*, London: The Economist Publications, January.

MacDonald, G. (1988). "The Economics of Rising Stars," *American Economic Review*, 78(March).

Mahon, G. (1980). *The Company That Bought the Boardwalk*. New York: Random House.

Mair, G. (1988). *Inside HBO: The Billion Dollar War between HBO, Hollywood and the Home Video Revolution*. New York: Dodd, Mead.

Mandelbaum, K. (1991). *Not Since Carrie: Forty Years of Broadway Musical Flops*. New York: St. Martin's Griffin.

Mangels, W. F. (1952). *The Outdoor Amusement Industry: From Earliest Times to the Present*. New York: Vantage Press.

Manly, L. (2005a). "Networks and the Outside Producer: Can They Co-Exist?," *New York Times*, June 20.

(2005b). "Satellite Radio Takes Off, Altering the Airwaves," *New York Times*, April 5.

Manly, L., and Markoff, J. (2005). "Steal This Show," *New York Times*, January 30.

Manteris, A., and Talley, R. (1991). *SuperBookie: Inside Las Vegas Sports Gambling*. Chicago: Contemporary Books.

Margolies, J., and Gwathmey, E. (1991). *Tickets to Paradise: American Movie Theaters and How We Had Fun*. Boston: Little, Brown and Company (Bulfinch Press).

Marich, R. (2005). *Marketing to Moviegoers*. Oxford, U.K.: Elsevier (Focal Press).

Markham, J. W., and Teplitz, P. V. (1981). *Baseball Economics and Public Policy*. Lexington, MA: Heath.

Markoff, J. (2004). "Internet Use Said to Cut into TV Viewing and Socializing," *New York Times*, December 30.

(2002). "A Long Time Ago, in a Lab Far Away. . . .," *New York Times*, February 28.

(2000). "A Newer, Lonelier Crowd Emerges in Internet Study," *New York Times*, February 16.

Marks, P. (2002). "If It's a Musical, It Was Probably a Movie," *New York Times*, April 14.

Marr, M. (2005). "How DreamWorks Misjudged DVD Sales of Its Monster Hit," *Wall Street Journal*, May 31.

(2004). "Screenwriters Press for Bigger DVD Payday," *Wall Street Journal*, April 5.

Marr, M., and Kelly, K. (2006). "With Special Effects the Star, Hollywood Faces New Reality," *Wall Street Journal*, May 12.

Marr, M., and Peers, M. (2004). "To See Why MGM Is in Play, Just Take a Look in Its Vault," *Wall Street Journal*, July 7.

Marriott, M. (2004). "Movie or Game: The Joystick Is a Tipoff," *New York Times*, March 25.

(2003). "A Thin Line between Films and Joysticks," *New York Times*, February 20.

Martin, D. (2004). "Cablers' Bland Ambition," *Variety*, January 19.

Marx, S. (1975). *Mayer and Thalberg: The Make-Believe Saints*. New York: Random House; Los Angeles: Samuel French (1988).

Masters, K. (1999). "Star Wars," *Vanity Fair*, (464) (April).

Mathews, A. W., and Ordonez, J. (2002). "Music Labels Say It Costs Too Much to Get Songs on Radio," *Wall Street Journal*, June 10.

Mathews, A. W., Peers, M., and Wingfield, N. (2002). "Music Industry Is Finally Online, but There Aren't Many Listeners," *Wall Street Journal*, May 7.

McBride, S. (2006a). "Until Recently Full of Promise, Satellite Radio Runs Into Static," *Wall Street Journal*, August 15.

(2006b). "Movie Debut: Films for Sale by Download," *Wall Street Journal*, April 3.

(2005a). "Hollywood's Digital Delay," *Wall Street Journal*, October 27.

(2005b). "Two Upstarts Vie for Dominance in Satellite Radio," *Wall Street Journal*, March 30.

McBride, S., and Fowler, G. A. (2006). "Studios See Big Rise in Estimates of Losses to Movie Piracy," *Wall Street Journal*, May 3.

McCafferty, J. (2004). "Hockey Fight," *CFO*, September.

McCartney, S. (2004). "Leveling the Field," *Wall Street Journal*, October 18.

McDougal, D. (1998). *The Last Mogul*. New York: Crown.

(1991). "A Blockbuster Deficit; 'Batman' Accounts Show a $35.8-Million Deficit: The Film May Never Show Profit," *Los Angeles Times*, March 21.

McKinley, J. (2005). "Off Broadway, Success Grows Costly and Rare," *New York Times*, February 1.

(2004). "'Wicked' Reaches Financial Nirvana," *New York Times*, December 21.

(2003). "'Dance of the Vampires', a $12 million Broadway Failure, Is Closing," *New York Times*, January 16.

McLean, B. (2001). "Billion-Dollar Horse Play," *Fortune*, 144(8)(October 29).

McLuhan, M. (1964, 2001). *Understanding Media: The Extension of Man*. New York: McGraw-Hill; Cambridge, MA: MIT Press (1994); and New York: Routledge Classics.

McLuhan, M., and McLuhan, E. (1988). *Laws of Media: The New Science*. Toronto: University of Toronto Press.

McNamara, M. (2006). "When the 'Yes' Becomes a 'No'," *Los Angeles Times*, July 9.

McNary, D. (2006). "Production Pacts Get Dicey," *Variety*, August 7.

(2003). "Return of the Runaways," *Variety*, February 17.

McTague, J. (2005). "Going Underground," *Barron's*, January 3.

Mehta, S. N. (2006). "Money Men," *Fortune*, 153(10)(May 29).

(2005). "One Big Baby Bell," *Fortune*, 151(6)(March 21).

Meza, A. (2005). "Hollywood's Bankers," *Variety*, February 7.

Mezrich, B. (2002). *Bringing Down the House: The Inside Story of Six M.I.T. Students Who Took Vegas for Millions*. New York: Simon & Schuster (Free Press).

Michener, J. A. (1976). *Sports in America*. New York: Random House; paperback, Fawcett Crest/Ballantine Books (1983).

Miller, M. (1991). *A Whole Different Ball Game: The Sport and Business of Baseball*. New York: Birch Lane Press (Carol Publishing Co.); paperback (Fireside), Simon & Schuster (1992).

Mlodinow, L. (2006). "Meet Hollywood's Latest Genius," *Los Angeles Times*, July 2.

Moldea, D. E. (1989). *Interference: How Organized Crime Influences Professional Football*. New York: Morrow.

Moore, J. (1996). *The Complete Book of Sports Betting*. New York: Carol Publishing (Lyle Stuart).

Moore, S. M. (2002). *The Biz: The Basic Business, Legal and Financial Aspects of the Film Industry*, 2nd ed. Los Angeles: Silman-James.

Moore, T. G. (1968). *The Economics of the American Theater*. Durham, NC: Duke University Press.

Moran, A., ed. (1996). *Film Policy: International, National and Regional Perspectives*. London: Routledge.

Morell, J. (2003). "How Much for Tickets? You Need a Scorecard," *New York Times*, June 8.

Mortimer, J. H. (2000). "*The Effects of Revenue-Sharing Contracts on Welfare in Vertically-Separated Markets: Evidence from the Video Rental Industry*." Los Angeles: UCLA Department of Economics, hollandj@ucla.edu.

Moul, C., ed. (2005). *A Concise Handbook of Movie Industry Economics*. New York: Cambridge University Press.

Mullaney, T. J., and Grover, R. (2003). "The Web Mogul," *BusinessWeek*, October 13.

Muller, P. (1991). *Show Business Law: Motion Pictures, Television, Video*. Westport, CT: Quorum.

Munoz, L. (2006). "For Lions Gate, Cable Has Become a Reliable Profit-Making Machine," *Los Angeles Times*, July 9.

(2004). "Coming Soon: A Hard Sell," *Los Angeles Times*, November 24.

Murphy, A. D. (1983). "Distribution and Exhibition: An Overview," in *The Movie Business Book*, edited by J. E. Squire. New York: Simon & Schuster/Fireside.

(1982). "21 Fundamental Aspects of U.S. Theatrical Film Biz," *Daily Variety*, October 26.

Murphy, J. M. (1976). "Why You Can't Win," *Journal of Portfolio Management*, fall.

Murray, M. (1956). *Circus! From Rome to Ringling*. New York: Appleton-Century-Crofts.

Naggar, D., and Brandstetter, J. D. (1997). *The Music Business (Explained in Plain English)*. San Francisco: DaJé Publishing.

Nardone, J. M. (1982). "Is the Movie Industry Contracyclical," *Cycles*, 33(3)(April).

Nasaw, D. (1993). *Going Out: The Rise and Fall of Public Amusements*. New York: Harper-Collins (Basic Books).

Nash, C., and Oakey, V. (1974). *The Screenwriter's Handbook*. New York: Barnes & Noble (Harper & Row).

*National Gambling Impact Study Commission Report* (1999). Washington, DC: U.S. Government Printing Office and www.ngisc.gov.

Neale, W. C. (1964). "The Peculiar Economics of Professional Sports," *Quarterly Journal of Economics*, 78(February).

Nelson, E., and Flint, J. (2002). "Deal for 'Friends' Offers NBC Time to Seek New Hit," *Wall Street Journal*, December 23.

Netzer, D. (1978). *The Subsidized Muse: Public Support for the Arts in the United States*. New York: Cambridge University Press.

Neulinger, J. (1981). *To Leisure: An Introduction*. Boston: Allyn and Bacon.

Newcomb, P. (1989). "Welcome Back, Grace Slick," *Forbes*, 143(10)(May 15).

Nochimson, D., and Brachman, L. (2003). "Contingent Compensation for Theatrical Motion Pictures," *UCLA 27th Annual Entertainment Law Symposium*. Los Angeles: UCLA School of Law.

Noll, R., ed. (1974). *Government and the Sports Business*. Washington DC: Brookings Institution.

Noll, R. G., Peck, M. J., and McGowan, J. J. (1973). *Economic Aspects of Television Regulation*. Washington, DC: Brookings Institution.

Nussenbaum, E. (2003). "Coming Soon to a Theater Near You: The Moviemercial," *New York Times*, September 21.

Oakey, V. (1983). *Dictionary of Film and Television Terms*. New York: Barnes & Noble.

O'Brien, T. L. (2006). "Is Poker Losing Its First Flush?," *New York Times*, April 16.

O'Donnell, P., and McDougal, D. (1992). *Fatal Subtraction: The Inside Story of Buchwald v. Paramount*. New York: Doubleday.

Oh, J. (2001). "International Trade in Film and the Self-Sufficiency Ratio," *Journal of Media Economics*, 14(1).

O'Keefe, B., and Schlosser, J. (2005). "America's Fastest Growing Sport," *Fortune* 152(5)(September 5).

Ordonez, J. (2002). "Pop Singer Fails to Strike a Chord Despite the Millions Spent by MCA," *Wall Street Journal*, February 26.

Orwall, B. (2003). "No Late Fees: Disney Will 'Beam' Rental Movies Directly into Homes," *Wall Street Journal*, September 29.

Orwall, B., and Peers, M. (2002). "The Message of Media Mergers: So Far, They Haven't Been Hits," *Wall Street Journal*, May 10.

Orwall, B., Peers, M., and Zimmerman, A. (2002). "DVD Gains on Tape, but Economics Have Hollywood in a Tizzy," *Wall Street Journal*, February 5.

Ovadia, A. (2004). "Consumer Products," in *The Movie Business Book*, edited by J. E. Squire. New York: Simon & Schuster (Fireside).

Owen, B. M., Beebe, J. H., and Manning, W. G., Jr. (1974). *Television Economics*. Lexington, MA: Heath.

Owen, B. M., and Wildman, S. S. (1992). *Video Economics*. Cambridge, MA: Harvard University Press.

Owen, D. (1986). "Where Toys Come From," *The Atlantic Monthly*, October.

——— (1983). "The Second Coming of Nolan Bushnell," *Playboy*, 30(6)(June).

Owen, J. D. (1988). "Work-Time Reduction in the U.S. and Western Europe," *Monthly Labor Review*, 111(12)(December).

(1976). "Workweeks and Leisure: An Analysis of Trends, 1948–75," *Monthly Labor Review*, U.S. Department of Labor, 99(8)(August).

(1970). *The Price of Leisure*. Montreal: McGill–Queen's University Press.

Owen, V., and Owen, P. (1980). "An Economic Approach to Art Innovations," in *Economic Policy for the Arts*, edited by W. S. Hendon, J. L. Shanahan, and A. J. MacDonald. Cambridge, MA: Abt Books.

Ozanian, M. K., and Taub, S. (1993). "Foul Ball," *Financial World*, 162(11)(May 25).

(1992). "Big Leagues, Bad Business," *Financial World*, 161(14)(July 7).

Paris, E. (1984). "Ronald Reagan Is Not the Only Actor Who Made Good," *Forbes*, 133(5)(February 27).

Parsons, P. R., and Frieden, R. M. (1998). *The Cable and Satellite Television Industries*. Needham Heights, MA: Allyn and Bacon.

Passell, P. (1989). "Broadway and the Bottom Line," *New York Times*, December 10.

Passman, D. S. (2000). *All You Need to Know about the Music Business*, rev. ed. New York: Prentice-Hall.

Peers, M. (2005). "Stock Gambit Strains Relations between Two Media Titans," *Wall Street Journal*, March 3.

(2003). "After Living on Rented Time, Blockbuster Plunges into Sales," *Wall Street Journal*, February 13.

Peterman, J. L., and Carney, M. (1978). "A Comment on Television Network Price Discrimination," *Journal of Business*, 51(2)(April).

Peterson, I. (1997). "Times Expanding Nationwide Distribution," *New York Times*, January 22.

Philips, C. (2002). "BMG to Roll Out Royalty Plan," *Los Angeles Times*, November 20.

(2001). "Music Data Being Altered, Some Say," *Los Angeles Times*, July 13.

Picard, R. G. (2001). "Effects of Recessions on Advertising Expenditures: An Exploratory Study of Economic Downturns in Nine Developed Nations," *Journal of Media Economics*, 14(1).

Pierce, J. R. (1980). *An Introduction to Information Theory: Symbols, Signals and Noise*, 2nd rev. ed. New York: Dover.

Poggi, J. (1968). *Theater in America: The Impact of Economic Forces, 1870–1967*. Ithaca, NY: Cornell University Press.

Pogrebin, R. (1999). "Nary a Drama on Broadway," *New York Times*, December 28.

(1996). "The Number of Ad Pages Does Not Make the Magazine," *New York Times*, August 26.

Pogue, D. (2006). "Renting Movies with a Box and a Beam," *New York Times*, June 1.

Pokorny, M. (2005). "Hollywood and the Risk Environment of Movie Production in the 1990s," in *An Economic History of Film*, edited by J. Sedgwick and M. Pokorny. London: Routledge.

Pollack, A. (1986). "Video Games, Once Zapped, in Comeback," *New York Times*, September 27.

Porter, M. E. (2001). "Strategy and the Internet," *Harvard Business Review*, March.

Postrel, V. (2000). "The Golden Formula for Hollywood Success," *New York Times*, March 23.

Prag, J., and Cassavant, J. (1994). "An Empirical Study of Determinants of Revenues and Marketing Expenditures in the Motion Picture Industry," *Journal of Cultural Economics*, 18(3).

Provost, G. (1994). *High Stakes: Inside the New Las Vegas*. New York: Dutton (Truman Talley).

Putnam, David (1997). *The Undeclared War: The Struggle for Control of the World's Film Industry*. London: HarperCollins. (U.S. title [1998], *Movies and Money*. New York: Knopf.)

Puzo, M. (1976). *Inside Las Vegas*. New York: Grosset & Dunlap.

Quirk, J., and Fort, R. (1999). *Hard Ball: The Uses and Abuses of Market Power in Professional Sports*. Princeton, NJ: Princeton University Press.

(1992). *Pay Dirt: The Business of Professional Team Sports*. Princeton, NJ: Princeton University Press.

Quirk, J., and Hodiri, M. (1974). "The Economic Theory of a Professional Sports League," in *Government and the Sports Business*, edited by R. Noll, pp. 33–80. Washington, DC: Brookings Institution.

Raabe, W. (1977). "Professional Sports Franchises and the Treatment of League Expansion Proceeds," *Taxes*, July. Chicago: Commerce Clearing House.

Ramstad, E. (1999). "Circuit City Pulls the Plug on Its DIVX Videodisk Venture," *Wall Street Journal*, June 17.

Ravid, S. A. (1999). "Information, Blockbusters and Stars: A Study of the Film Industry," *Journal of Business*, 72(4)(October).

Read, O., and Welch, W. L. (1976). *From Tin Foil to Stereo: Evolution of the Phonograph*. Indianapolis: Bobbs-Merrill and Howard W. Sams.

Reibstein, L. (1986). "Broadway 'Angels' Often Settle for Glitz, but the Prospects for Profit Are Improving," *Wall Street Journal*, January 28.

Reich, H. (1996). "Why Can't the Arts Survive on their Own?," *Chicago Tribune*, August 26.

Rhodes, J. (2006). "'Scrubs': To Find an Audience, Let It All Hang Out," *New York Times*, April 9.

Rich, F. (2001). "Naked Capitalists," *New York Times*, May 20.

Richtel, M. (2006). "From the Back Office, a Casino Can Change the Slot Machine in Seconds," *New York Times*, April 12.

(2004). "Gambling Sites Offering Ways to Let Any User Be the Bookie," *New York Times*, July 6.

(2003). "Entertainment Industry Loses in Web Case," *New York Times*, April 26.

Riding, A. (2003). "Filmmakers Seek Protection from U.S. Dominance," *New York Times*, February 5.

Ritter, S. (1999). "Supreme Court to Review Ban on Casino Ads," *Wall Street Journal*, January 18.

Rivkin, S. (1974). "Sports Leagues and the Federal Antitrust Laws," in *Government and the Sports Business*, edited by R. Noll. Washington, DC: Brookings Institution.

Rivlin, G. (2004). "The Tug of the Newfangled Slot Machines," *New York Times*, May 9.

(2003). "I Dream of Royalties," *New York Times*, September 28.

Robb, D. (1992). "Net Profits No Myth, but Hard to Get Hands On," *The Hollywood Reporter*, August 17, August 24, and August 31.

(1990a). "Paramount Says 'America' $17–18 Mil Below Break-Even," *Daily Variety*, March 21.

(1990b). "Buchwald, Par Experts Wrestle in Profits Bout," *Variety*, June 27.

Roberts, K., and Rupert, P. (1995). "The Myth of the Overworked American," *Economic Commentary*. Cleveland: Federal Reserve Bank of Cleveland, January 15.

Roberts, P. (1995). "The Art of Goofing Off," *Psychology Today*, 28(4)(July/August).

Robinson, J. P. (1989). "Time's Up," *American Demographics*, 11(7)(July).

Robinson, J. P., and Godbey, G. (1997). *Time for Life: The Surprising Ways Americans Use Their Time*. University Park, PA: Penn State Press.

Rockwell, J. (2002). "Profit or Not, It's All Showbiz," *New York Times*, September 22.

Rones, P.L., Ilg, R. E., and Gardner, J. M. (1997). "Trends in Hours of Work since the Mid-1970s," *Monthly Labor Review*, BLS, U.S. Department of Labor, April.

Root, W. (1979). *Writing the Script: A Practical Guide for Films and Television*. New York: Holt, Rinehart & Winston.

Rose, I. N. (2006). "The Unlawful Internet Enforcement Act of 2006 Analyzed," *Gambling Law Review,* 10(6)(December).

(1986). *Gambling and the Law*. Los Angeles: Gambling Times.

Rose, M. (2001). "Magazine Wholesaler Pressures Publishers, Adding to Their Woes," *Wall Street Journal*, March 5.

Rosen, D., and Hamilton, P. (1987). *Off-Hollywood: The Making and Marketing of American Specialty Films*. New York and Colorado: The Independent Feature Project and The Sundance Institute.

Rosen, S. (1981) "The Economics of Superstars," *American Economic Review*, 71(December).

Rosenberg, B., and Harburg, E. (1993). *The Broadway Musical: Collaboration in Commerce and Art*. New York: New York University Press.

Rothenberg, R. (1996). "Planet of the Apers," *Esquire*, 126 (1)(July).

Rothman, W. (2003). "Beyond the CD: A Bid to Burnish Records' Sheen," *New York Times*, March 13.

Rothstein, M. (1988). "'Starlight Express' Out of the Tunnel?," *New York Times*, August 20.

Rottenberg, S. (1956). "The Baseball Players' Labor Market," *Journal of Political Economy*, 64.

Roud, R. (1983). *A Passion for Films*. New York: Viking Press.

Rudman, N. G., and Ephraim, L. A. (2004). "The Finishing Touch: The Completion Guarantee," in *The Movie Business Book*, edited by J. E. Squire. New York: Simon & Schuster (Fireside).

Rusco, F. A., and Walls, W. D. (2004). "Independent Film Finance, Pre-Sale Agreements, and the Distribution of Film Earnings," in *Economics of Art and Culture,* edited by V. A. Ginsburgh. Amsterdam: Elsevier.

Russell, J. H. (2006). "Music's Merger Mania," *Wall Street Journal*, May 6.

Rybczynski, W. (1991). "Waiting for the Weekend," *The Atlantic Monthly*, 268(2)(August), and *Waiting for the Weekend* (1991), New York: Viking.

Salamon, J. (1984). "Blue Dots: Selling U.S. Films Abroad," *Wall Street Journal*, May 22.

Salemson, H. J., and Zolotow, M. (1978). "It Didn't Begin with Begelman: A Concise History of Film Business Finagling," *Action*, 11(7)(July/August). Los Angeles: Directors Guild of America.

Sanders, P. (2005). "Across Crawfish Country, Casino Operators Fear State's Bid for Taxes," *Wall Street Journal*, March 21.

Sanders, P., and Emshwiller, J. R. (2005). "At Indian Casinos, Odds Grow Longer for Some Tribes," *Wall Street Journal*, September 27.

Sanders, P., and Stanley, B. (2006). "Casino Giants Take Their Vegas Battle to Tables of Macau," *Wall Street Journal*, September 6.

Sandomir, R. (2002). "YES-Cablevision Feud Has No End in Sight," *New York Times*, April 16.

(2001a). "Cable Said to Muscle Out NBC for N.B.A. Rights," *New York Times*, December 15.

(2001b). "Networks May Seek Relief from N.F.L.," *New York Times*, October 19.

(1999). "How Green Is Your Gridiron?," *New York Times*, March 13.

(1998). "How One Network's Urgency Spelled Riches for the N.F.L.," *New York Times*, January 17.

Sansweet, S. (1983). "As New Studio Starts Work, It Seeks Credibility," *Wall Street Journal*, May 23.

Scarne, J. (1978). *Scarne's Complete Guide to Gambling*. New York: Simon & Schuster.

(1974). *Scarne's New Complete Guide to Gambling*. New York: Simon & Schuster.

Schatz, A., Grant, P., and Karnitschnig, M. (2005). "Cable Companies See New Threat in FCC Shift on a la Carte Service," *Wall Street Journal*, November 30.

Schiesel, S. (2006). "Online Game, Made in U.S., Seizes the Globe," *New York Times*, September 5.

(2005a). "Gangs of New York," *New York Times*, October 16.

(2005b). "Conqueror in a War of Virtual Worlds," *New York Times*, September 6.

(2005c). "World of Warcraft Keeps Growing, Even as Players Test Its Limits," *New York Times*, February 10.

(2004). "Aiming for Hit Games, Films Come up Short," *New York Times*, May 27.

Scholl, J. (1992). "Lights! Camera! Money! Hollywood's Bonding Companies Are Feeling the Pinch," *Barron's*, June 8.

(1989a). "No Rockford Trials," *Barron's*, April 3.

(1989b). "The Rockford File," *Barron's*, February 6.

Schor, J. B. (1991). *The Overworked American: The Unexpected Decline of Leisure*. New York: Basic Books.

Schumer, F. R. (1982). "More Than Merely Colossal," *Barron's*, June 21.

Schuyler, N. (1995). *The Business of Multimedia*. New York: Allworth Press.

Schwartz, D. G. (2005). *Cutting the Wire: Gambling Prohibition and the Internet.* Reno, NV: University of Nevada Press.

(2003). *Suburban Xanadu: The Casino Resort on the Las Vegas Strip and Beyond*. New York: Routledge.

Scott, A. O. (2004). "What Is a Foreign Movie Now?," *New York Times*, November 14.

Scully, G. W. (1995). *The Market Structure of Sports*. Chicago: University of Chicago Press.

(1989). *The Business of Major League Baseball*. Chicago: University of Chicago Press.

(1974). "Pay and Performance in Major League Baseball," *American Economic Review*, 64 (December).

Seabrook, J. (2006). "Game Master," *The New Yorker*, November 6.

Seaman, B. (1980). "Economic Models and Support for the Arts," in *Economic Policy for the Arts*, edited by W. S. Hendon, J. L. Shanahan, and A. J. MacDonald, pp. 80–95, Cambridge, MA: Abt Books.

Searcey, D. (2005). "As Verizon Enters Cable Business, It Faces Local Static," *Wall Street Journal*, October 28.

Sedgwick, J., and Pokorny, M., eds. (2005). *An Economic History of Film*. London: Routledge.

Seligman, D. (1982). "Who Needs Unions?," *Fortune*, 106(1)(July 12).

Shannon, C. E., and Weaver, W. (1949). *Mathematical Theory of Communications*. Urbana-Champaign, IL: University of Illinois Press.

Sharp, C. H. (1981). *The Economics of Time*. Oxford: Martin Robertson.

Sheehan, R. G. (1996). *Keeping Score: The Economics of Big-Time Sports*. South Bend, IN: Diamond Communications.

Sheff, D. (1993). *Game Over: How Nintendo Zapped an American Industry*. New York: Random House.

Shelley, K. J. (2005). "Developing the American Time Use Survey Activity Classification System," *Monthly Labor Review*, (June), U.S. Department of Labor.

Shemel, S., and Krasilovsky, M. W. (1985). *This Business of Music* (5th rev. ed., 1988). New York: Billboard.

Shone, T. (2004). *Blockbuster: How Hollywood Learned to Stop Worrying and Love the Summer*. New York: Free Press.

Shy, O. (2001). *The Economics of Network Industries*. New York: Cambridge University Press.

Siegfried, J., and Zimbalist, A. (2000). "The Economics of Sports Facilities and Their Communities," *Journal of Economic Perspectives*, summer.

Siklos, R. (2007). "Beyond the X's and O's, a Lesson in How to Be Big," *New York Times*, February 4.

   (2006). "Why Can't I Just Have the Cable Channels I Want?," *New York Times*, April 16.

Silberstang, E. (1980). *Playboy's Guide to Casino Gambling*. New York: Playboy Press.

Sisario, B. (2004). "Old Songs Generate New Cash for Artists," *New York Times*, December 28.

Skolnick, J. H. (1979). "The Social Risks of Casino Gambling," *Psychology Today*, 13(2)(July).

   (1978). *House of Cards*. Boston: Little, Brown.

Smith, E. (2006). "Music You Can See: Warner Plans to Sell Albums on DVDs," *Wall Street Journal*, August 4.

   (2004a). "Music Industry Struggles to Get Cellphone's Number," *Wall Street Journal*, September 13.

   (2004b). "Why a Grand Plan to Cut CD Prices Went off the Track," *Wall Street Journal*, June 4.

Smith, G. V., and Parr, R. L. (1994). *Valuation of Intellectual Property and Intangible Assets*, 2nd ed. New York: John Wiley.

Smith, S. J. (1986). "The Growing Diversity of Work Schedules," *Monthly Labor Review*, U.S. Department of Commerce, BLS, November, 109(11).

Snyder, G. (2006). "Other People's Money," *Variety*, January 23.

   (2005). "Hollywood Gets Grossed Out," *Variety*, June 13.

Sochay, S. (1994). "Predicting the Performance of Motion Pictures," *Journal of Media Economics*, 7(4).

Solomon, D. (2002). "Investors' Faith in Cable Industry Declines," *Wall Street Journal*, April 11.

Solomon, J. D. (2002). "The Sports Market Is Looking Soggy," *New York Times*, April 21.

Sorkin, A. R. (2004). "Is There Life after Blackjack? Ask MGM," *New York Times*, December 26

   (1997). "Soundscan Makes Business of Counting Hits," *New York Times*, August 11.

Spitz, B. (1987). "Is Collusion the Name of the Game?," *New York Times Magazine*, July 12.

Sporich, B. (2003). "Laser-Sharp Profit: Television to DVD," *The Hollywood Reporter*, June 12.

Spring, J. (1993). "Seven Days of Play," *American Demographics*, 15(3) March.

Squire, J. E., ed. (1983; 2nd ed., 1992, 3rd ed. 2004). *The Movie Business Book*. New York: Simon & Schuster/Fireside.

Stanley, R. (1978). *The Celluloid Empire: A History of the American Motion Picture Industry*. New York: Hastings House.

Staudohar, P. D. (2002). "Baseball Negotiations: A New Agreement," *Monthly Labor Review*, 126(12)(December). Washington, DC: Bureau of Labor Statistics.

Stefanelli, J. M., and Nazarechuk, A. (1996). "Hotel/Casino Food and Beverage Operations," in *The Gaming Industry: Introduction and Perspectives*, New York: John Wiley & Sons.

Steinberg, B. (2004). "TV Networks May Not Be 'Upfront'," *Wall Street Journal*, June 18.

Steinberg, B., and Barnes, B. (2006). "Nielsen Plans to Track Viewership of TV Commercials for First Time," *Wall Street Journal*, July 11.

Steinberg, J. (2006). "Digital Media Brings Profits (and Tensions) to TV Studios," *New York Times*, May 14.

(2005). "A TV Duel at Sunrise," *New York Times*, May 30.

Steinert, H. (2003). *Culture Industry*. London: Polity Press (Blackwell).

Stern, S., and Schoenhaus, T. (1990). *Toyland: The High-Stakes Game of the Toy Industry*. Chicago: Contemporary Books.

Sternlieb, G., and Hughes, J. W. (1983). *The Atlantic City Gamble*. New York: Twentieth Century Fund; Cambridge, MA: Harvard University Press.

Stevenson, R. W. (1990). "The Magic of Hollywood's Math," *New York Times*, April 13.

Stewart, J. B. (1994). "Moby Dick in Manhattan," *The New Yorker*, June 27 and July 4.

Stigler, G. J. (1963). "*United States v. Loew's Inc.*: A Note on Block-Booking," in *The Supreme Court Review*, edited by P. Kurland. Chicago: University of Chicago Press.

Stigler, G. J., and Becker, G. S. (1977). "De Gustibus non est disputandum," *American Economic Review*, 67(March).

Stille, A. (2002). "Textbook Publishers Learn: Avoid Messing with Texas," *New York Times*, June 29.

Strauss, N. (2002). "Record Labels' Answer to Napster Still Has Artists Feeling Bypassed," *New York Times*, February 18.

Sweeting, P. (2004). "The Video Retailer" in *The Movie Business Book*, edited by J. E. Squire. New York: Simon & Schuster (Fireside).

Swertlow, F. (1982). "How Hollywood Studios Flimflam Their Stars," *TV Guide*, 30(18)(May 1).

Taub, E. A. (2003). "DVDs Meant for Buying but Not for Keeping," *New York Times*, July 21.

Thaler, R. H. (1992). *The Winner's Curse: Paradoxes and Anomalies of Economic Life*. Princeton, NJ: Princeton University Press.

Thomas, B. (1976). *Walt Disney: An American Original*. New York: Simon & Schuster. (Pocket Books, 1980.)

Thompson, C. (2005). "The Xbox Auteurs," *New York Times*, August 7.

Thorp, E. O. (1984). *The Mathematics of Gambling*. Secaucus, NJ: Lyle Stuart.

Throsby, D. (2001). *Economics and Culture*. New York: Cambridge University Press.

Throsby, D., and Withers, G. A. (1979). *The Economics of the Performing Arts*. New York: St. Martin's Press.

Thurm, S., and Delaney, K. J. (2004). "Yahoo, Google and Internet Math," *Wall Street Journal*, May 10.

Torkildsen, G. (1999). *Leisure and Recreation Management*, 4th ed. London: SPON Press and Routledge.

Trachtenberg, J. A. (2005). "Quest for Best Seller Creates a Pileup of Returned Books," *Wall Street Journal*, June 3.

——— (2004). "To Publishers, Megahits Mean Very Big Numbers," *Wall Street Journal*, November 2.

——— (2003). "Out Just a Week, Clinton's Book Is in the Black," *Wall Street Journal*, June 16.

——— (1984). "Low Budget," *Forbes*, 133(7)(March 26).

Tran, K. T. L. (2002). "Sony, Microsoft: The Online Games Begin," *Wall Street Journal*, April 10.

Trost, C. (1986). "All Work and No Play? New Study Shows How Americans View Jobs," *Wall Street Journal*, December 30.

Trumpbour, J. (2002). *Selling Hollywood to the World: U.S. and European Struggles for Mastery of the Global Film Industry, 1920–1950*. New York: Cambridge University Press.

Tucker, W. (1982). "Public Radio Comes to Market," *Fortune*, 106(8)(October 18).

Tunick, B. (2002). "Due for a Facelift," *Investment Dealers' Digest*, November 11.

Uichitelle, L. (2006). "Seizing Intangibles for the G.D.P.," *New York Times*, April 9.

U.S. Congress (1999). National Gambling Impact Study Commission Report.

U.S. Congress (1989). *Survey of Home Taping and Copying*. Washington, DC: Office of Technology Assessment.

U.S. Congress (1976). *Gambling in America*. Washington, DC: Commission on the Review of the National Policy toward Gambling.

U.S. Department of Commerce (1993). *Globalization of the Mass Media*. Washington, DC: National Telecommunications and Information Administration, NTIA Special Publication 93–290.

U.S. National Endowment for the Arts (1997). *Survey of Public Participation in the Arts*.

Van Kooten, G. C., and Bulte, E. H. (2000). *The Economics of Nature: Managing Biological Assets*. Oxford, U.K.: Blackwell.

Varian, H. R. (2000). "The Internet Carries Profound Implications for Providers of Information," *New York Times*, July 27.

Veblen, T. (1899). *The Theory of the Leisure Class*. New York: Macmillan. (Paperback, New American Library, 1953.)

Verrier, R. (2006a). "Cinema Chains Seek Investors to Finance Digital Projectors," *Los Angeles Times*, July 9.

——— (2006b). "Hollywood Unions Reach Contracts for Cellphone Shows," *Los Angeles Times*, April 25.

Vogel, H. L. (2005). "Movie Accounting," in *A Brief Handbook of Movie Economics*, edited by C. Moul. New York: Cambridge University Press.

von Neumann, J., and Morgenstern, O. (1944). *Theory of Games and Economic Behavior*. New York: Wiley.

Vranica, S. (2006). "Advertisers Turn to eBay to Buy TV Time," *Wall Street Journal*, August 4.

Wadhams, W. (1990). *Sound Advice: The Musician's Guide to the Recording Industry*. New York: Schirmer Books (Macmillan).

Waggoner, G. (1982). "Money Games," *Esquire*, 97(6)(June).

Walker, D. M. (2007). *The Economics of Casino Gambling*. Berlin: Springer-Verlag.

Walker, S. (2002). "As Strike Looms, Few New Baseball Buyers Step Up to Plate," *Wall Street Journal*, August 29.

Wallace, B. (2005). "Crouching U.S. Studios, Hidden Chinese Market," *Los Angeles Times*, December 30.

Wallace, M. (2005). "The Game Is Virtual. The Profit Is Real," *New York Times*, May 29.

Ward, S. (2004). "Losing the Signal," *Barron's*, August 30.

Warner, M. (2004). "How a Meek Comic Book Company Became a Hollywood Superpower," *New York Times*, July 19.

Wasser, D. M. (1995). "Theater: Limited Partnerships Preferred over LLC," *New York Law Journal*, September 8.

Wasser, F. (2002). *Veni, Vidi, Video: The Hollywood Empire and the VCR*. Austin, TX: University of Texas.

Watkins, L. M. (1986). "A Look at Hasbro's 'Moondreamer' Dolls Shows Creating a Toy Isn't Child's Play," *Wall Street Journal*, December 29.

Waxman, S. (2003). "'Rings' Shows Trend toward Global Premieres," *New York Times*, December 22.

Wayne, L. (1996). "Picking Up the Tab for Fields of Dreams," *New York Times*, July 27.

Weber, B. (1993). "Make Money on Broadway? Break a Leg," *New York Times*, June 3.

Wechsler, D. (1990). "Profits? What Profits?," *Forbes*, 145(4)(February 19).

  (1989). "Every Trick in the Books," *Forbes*, 143(11)(May 29).

Weinberg, C. B. (2005). "Profits out of the Picture," in *A Concise Handbook of Movie Industry Economics*, edited by C. Moul. New York: Cambridge University Press.

Weinraub, B., and Carter, B. (2002). "TV Networks Favor Pilots They've Made," *New York Times*, April 1.

Weinstein, M. (1998). "Profit Sharing Contracts in Hollywood: Evolution and Analysis." *Journal of Legal Studies*, January, and abridged version (2005), "Movie Contracts: Is 'Net' 'Gross'?", in *An Economic History of Film*, edited by J. Sedgwick and M. Pokorny. London: Routledge.

Welch, W. L., and Burt, L. B. S. (1994). *From Tinfoil to Stereo: The Acoustic Years of the Recording Industry, 1877–1929*. Gainesville, FL: University Press of Florida.

Welles, C. (1983). "How Accountants Helped Orion Pictures Launch Its Financial Comeback," *Los Angeles Times*, May 15.

Werner, R. A. (2005). *New Paradigm in Macroeconomics: Solving the Riddle of Japanese Macroeconomic Performance*. Houndmills, U.K.: Palgrave Macmillan.

Whitaker, B. (2002). "Screen Actors Guild Agrees to New Rules for Talent Agencies," *New York Times*, February 26.

White, A., ed. (1988). *Inside the Recording Industry: An Introduction to America's Music Business*. Washington, DC: Recording Industry Association of America.

Whiteside, T. (1985). "Onward and Upward with the Arts, Cable Television," *The New Yorker*, 61(13)(May 20):45–87; 61(14)(May 27):43–73; 61(15)(June 3).

Wildman, S. S., and Siwek, S. E. (1988). *International Trade in Films and Television Programs*. Cambridge, MA: Ballinger.

Williams, L. V., ed. (2003). *The Economics of Gambling*. London: Routledge.

Wilson, D. (2004). "Bill Would Raise Franchise Value of Sports Teams," *New York Times*, August 2.

Wingfield, N. (2006a). "The Knights of Networking," *Wall Street Journal*, October 5.

  (2006b). "Master of the Universe," *Wall Street Journal*, May 27.

  (2006c). "The Power Players," *Wall Street Journal*, February 18.

  (1999). "The Tricky Task of Tracking Web Users," *Wall Street Journal*, November 22.

Wingfield, N., and Smith, E. (2003). "With the Web Shaking Up Music, A Free-for-All in Online Songs," *Wall Street Journal*, November 19.

Winston, C. (1993). "Economic Deregulation: Days of Reckoning for Microeconomists," *Journal of Economic Literature*, September.

Witchel, A. (1994). "Is Disney the Newest Broadway Baby?," *New York Times*, April 17.

Wolff, M. (2000). "Checkout Clout," *New York*, March 27.

Woolley, S. (2004a). "The Television Will Be Revolutionized," *Forbes*, 174(11)(November 29).

(2004b). "Broadcast Bullies," *Forbes*, 174(4)(September 6).

(2003). "Zapped to Death?," *Forbes*, 172(6)(September 29).

Wyatt, E. (2006a). "Religious Broadcaster Gets Rich Contract for Next Book," *New York Times*, March 15.

(2006b). "Publishers Find Growth in Comics," *New York Times*, February 13.

Wyche, M. C., and Wirth, M. O. (1984). "How Economic and Competitive Factors Affect Station Results," *Television/Radio Age*, January 9.

Yaari, M. E. (1965). "Convexity in the Theory of Choice under Risk," *Quarterly Journal of Economics*, May.

Young, S., and Grant, P. (2003). "How Phone Firms Lost to Cable in Consumer Broadband Battle," *Wall Street Journal*, March 13.

Zeisel, J. S. (1958). "The Workweek in American Industry 1850–1956," in *Mass Leisure*, edited by E. Larrabee and R. Meyerson. Glencoe, IL: The Free Press.

Ziegler, B. (1996). "Slow Crawl on the Internet," *Wall Street Journal*, August 23.

Zimbalist, A. (2003). "Sports and Cable Television," *Milken Institute Review*, December.

(1992). *Baseball and Billions*. New York: Basic Books.

Zollo, P. (1989). "The Per-Program License: Broadcaster's New Cost-Cutting Initiative," *The Hollywood Reporter*, August 29.

# Index